ENGLISH LITERATURE

1660-1800

A Bibliography of Modern Studies

ENGLISH LITERATURE
1660-1800

A Bibliography of Modern Studies

COMPILED FOR

Philological Quarterly

By Ronald S. Crane, Louis I. Bredvold,
Richmond P. Bond, Arthur Friedman,
and Louis A. Landa

VOLUME I · 1926-1938

FOREWORD BY

Louis A. Landa

PRINCETON
PRINCETON UNIVERSITY PRESS
1950

LONDON : GEOFFREY CUMBERLEGE
OXFORD UNIVERSITY PRESS

PRINTED IN THE UNITED STATES OF AMERICA

CONTENTS

FOREWORD

"The eighteenth century," declared Augustine Birrell in 1887, "has been well abused by the nineteenth." "So far as I can gather," he added, "it is the settled practice of every century to speak evil of her immediate predecessor." He professed to see, as the nineteenth century was drawing to its close, a kindlier attitude, a "desire to die at peace with all centuries." To a degree he was right. After Frederic Harrison had issued his spirited and sympathetic *A Few Words About The Eighteenth Century* in 1883, such Carlylian and Arnoldian pejoratives as "Age of Cant," "arid of air," and "touched with frost," were repeated with less confidence. Nevertheless, vestiges of the old attitude remained, to become a heritage for the present century; and Saintsbury, as late as 1916, felt constrained to raise that impertinent question—Is Pope a poet? Although he answered with a resounding affirmative, the mere fact that he considered the point at all is a commentary on the vitality, the will-to-survive, inherent in bizarre attitudes.

A decade later, when the *Philological Quarterly* annual eighteenth-century bibliography made its first appearance (1926), the corrective process was well under way. A generation of scholars had appeared who were engaged in a vigorous and tolerant evaluation of eighteenth-century literature, of its authors, and of the cultural background from which they emerged. As the years passed, the number of scholars attracted to the period steadily increased; the annual flow of books and articles became more and more formidable. Today anyone who begins a study of the eighteenth century has a heritage of scholarship of which the twentieth century may reasonably be proud. For twenty-five years the *Philological Quarterly* bibliography has listed this annual increment of scholarship and, to a considerable degree, given it critical appraisal. To Professor Ronald S. Crane belongs the credit for originating the bibliography and giving to it the character it has steadily maintained. His able successors, Professors Louis I. Bredvold and Richmond P. Bond, continued the early policies; and the present editors, Professor Arthur Friedman and I, have changed only to the extent of enlarging the number of scholars who annually contribute reviews.

At the Modern Language Association of America in 1946 the two discussion groups devoted to eighteenth-century English literature approved a resolution calling for reproduction of the *Philological Quarterly* bibliographies in convenient form. Since then the need has become greater because single issues for the first fifteen years are no longer available; and few scholars possess the entire series. It is proposed now, in pursuance of that resolution, to issue the series from 1926 to the present by photolithography.

Herewith is Volume I. For the benefit of those not familiar with the *Philological Quarterly* bibliography it should be mentioned that each annual issue contains the scholarship of the preceding year. Thus the issue for 1926 is actually a bibliography of studies for the year 1925. In this reprint the original pagination of each annual issue has been preserved at the top of the page, to permit quick reference to the subdivisions and use of cross references in the original issues. At the bottom of the pages continuous pagination has been inserted. An index to Volumes I and II is included in Volume II, its references being to the continuous pagination. To simplify the search for a particular author or scholarly study, the Index lists both eighteenth-century authors and modern scholars. Although the series might have been rearranged with a certain advantage, that advantage has been foregone, not lightly but with good reason: the economical method adopted has made it possible to retain the special character of the annual issues with their numerous signed and unsigned reviews, the many brief evaluations and descriptive comments, and the listing of reviews from other journals. If these two volumes prove to be as useful as the compilers hope, the design conceivably could be enlarged to include future supplements at appropriate intervals, to carry the bibliography of eighteenth-century studies beyond the chronological limit of the present project, 1950. This thought suggests another, a long-recognized desideratum—a bibliography of eighteenth-century studies for the years 1900 to 1924, a project, indeed, already in progress.

In the twenty-five years of its existence, the editors of the annual bibliography have had aid from many scholars, as will be apparent from the credits in each issue. A few, however, who have assisted with the compilation and in other ways should be mentioned here.

Particularly Professor Moody E. Prior should be singled out for his collaboration with Professor Crane in 1932.

Professor Crane also received aid on occasions from the late William Knox Chandler and from Charles Kerby-Miller. Professor Bredvold acknowledged aid in 1935 from Kathleen E. Murphy. Professor Bond acknowledged aid during his tenure from Marjorie N. Bond, Allen T. Hazen, H. T. Swedenberg, Jr., and W. K. Wimsatt, Jr. Professor Friedman and I have had valuable aid from John Loftis, Assistant Editor since 1949, and from James L. Clifford. And I personally wish to acknowledge constant assistance from my wife, who has perennially, uncomplainingly, accepted the tasks I set for her, many of them perilously near to drudgery.

To Dean Harvey H. Davis of the State University of Iowa Graduate College grateful thanks are due for permission to reprint from the pages of *Philological Quarterly*. And finally a very special case. The compilers, and eighteenth-century scholars generally, owe a great debt of gratitude to Professor Baldwin Maxwell, the editor of *Philological Quarterly*. Year after year he has given generously of his pages for the annual bibliography, and the obligation to him is now deepened by his willingness to permit this reprint.

LOUIS A. LANDA

Princeton University

1926

ENGLISH LITERATURE OF THE RESTORATION AND EIGHTEENTH CENTURY: A CURRENT BIBLIOGRAPHY

By RONALD S. CRANE
University of Chicago

This bibliography attempts to list the more significant books and articles published during the year 1925, together with a few books bearing a 1924 imprint the inclusion of which seemed to be warranted by special circumstances. Owing to limitations of space, the list makes no pretence to completeness in any of its parts; I have, in fact, deliberately excluded a large number of publications which, in my judgment, contribute nothing new in the way either of fact or of interpretation. I shall be grateful to anyone who will inform me of important omissions, or call my attention to privately printed or otherwise not easily accessible publications which should be included in subsequent installments of the bibliography.[1] Professors G. R. Havens, H. M. Jones, and A. D. McKillop have kindly furnished me with the notes signed with their respective initials.

LIST OF ABBREVIATIONS

AHR=American historical review.
Archiv=Archiv für das Studium der neueren Sprachen und Literaturen.
Beiblatt=Beiblatt zur Anglia.
EHR=English historical review.
ES=Englische Studien.
GRM=Germanisch-romanische Monatsschrift.
JEGP=Journal of English and Germanic philology.
MLN=Modern language notes.
MLR=Modern language review.
MP=Modern philology.
N&Q=Notes and queries.
PMLA=Publications of the Modern Language Association of America.
PQ=Philological quarterly.
RAA=Revue anglo-américaine.
RCC=Revue des cours et conférences.
RELV=Revue de l'enseignement des langues vivantes.
RES=Review of English studies.
RH=Revue historique.
RHL=Revue d'histoire littéraire de la France.
RLC = Revue de littérature comparée.

[1] It is expected that hereafter these will appear annually in the April issue of the *Philological Quarterly.*

RSH=*Revue de synthèse historique.*
SP=*Studies in philology.*
TLS=*Times* [London] *literary supplement.*
SRL=*Saturday review of literature.*

I. BIBLIOGRAPHICAL AIDS

Annual bibliography of English language and literature. Volume V, 1924. Edited for the Modern Humanities Research Association by A. C. Paues. Cambridge: Bowes & Bowes, 1925.

The Ashley library: a catalogue of printed books, manuscripts and autograph letters collected by Thomas James Wise. Volume VI [and VII]. London: Printed for private circulation only, 1925.

The following eighteenth-century writers are represented in these two volumes: Sterne (mainly in Vol. V; important), Swift (important), Nahum Tate, Thomson, Sir Samuel Tuke, Vanbrugh, Waller (important), and Mary Wollstonecraft.

Autograph letters, historical documents and author's original manuscripts. London: Maggs Bros., 1925. Catalogue No. 459.

Unusually rich in eighteenth-century manuscripts, many of which are printed in full or in part.

Baugh, A. C. "American bibliography for 1924. I. English language and literature." *PMLA,* XL (1925), 1-20.

See especially pp. 12-15.

Chapman, R. W. "A technical use of *book.*" *Library,* 4th series, VI (1925), 278-79.

English literature and printing from the 15th to the 18th century. London: Maggs Bros., 1925. Catalogues 461 and 462.

An important catalogue, with a great many eighteenth-century titles.

Gibson, Strickland and M. A. "An index to Rawlinson's collections (*circa* 1700-50) for a new edition of Wood's *Athenæ Oxonienses.*" *Proceedings and papers of the Oxford Bibliographical society,* Vol. I, Part II (Oxford, 1925), pp. 67-95.

A valuable tool for biographical research.

Greenlaw, Edwin. "Modern English romanticism." *SP,* XXII (1925), 538-50.

Notes on a number of recent studies, several of them pertaining to the eighteenth century.

Hawkes, A. J. *Lancashire printed books: a bibliography of all the books printed in Lancashire down to the year 1800.* Wigan: Printed for the Public Libraries Committee, 1925.

Rev. by A. W. P[ollard] in *Library,* 4th series, VI (1925), 203-04.

Kaye, F. B. [Review of Henry R. Plomer, *A dictionary of the printers and booksellers who were at work in England, Scotland and Ireland from 1668 to 1725.*] *MLN*, XL (1925), 164-71.

Points out grave deficiencies in method and documentation.

McKerrow, R. B. "Bibliographical terms." *TLS*, Oct. 29, 1925, p. 719.

Sensible remarks on the use of "edition," "issue," and "impression."

Madan, Falconer. "The Oxford Press, 1650-75: the struggle for a place in the sun." *Library*, 4th series, VI (1925), 113-47.

Contains a list of "Some notable books, printed at Oxford, 1650-75."

Murphy, Gwendolen. *A bibliography of English character-books, 1608-1700.* Printed at the Oxford University Press for the Bibliographical Society, 1925.

Lists "regular character-books" (Part I), "controversial characters" (Part II), and "books, other than character-books, which contain characters" (Appendix). An admirable example of careful bibliographical method.

Northup, Clark Sutherland, and others. *A register of bibliographies of the English language and literature.* New Haven: Yale University Press; London: Humphrey Milford, Oxford University Press, 1925.

Rev. by R. S. Crane in *MP*, XXIII (1926), 501-05; by A. W. P[ollard] in *Library*, 4th series, VI (1926), 393-94; by A. W. Reed in *RES*, II (1926), 368-69; by H. B. Van Hoesen in *Library journal*, Feb. 15, 1926, pp. 179-82.

Restoration books to be sold by Birrell and Garnett. London: Birrell and Garnett, 1925. Catalogue No. 11.

Contains 727 items.

Van Tieghem, Paul. "Principaux ouvrages récents de littérature générale et comparée." *RSH*, XL (1925), 113-52.

An excellent annual review, now in its ninth year. Section II (pp. 124-38) deals with publications relating to the "Renaissance et âge classique." Van Tieghem's reviews are particularly notable for their numerous and usually very penetrating remarks on method.

Williams, Judith B. *A guide to the printed materials for English social and economic history, 1750-1850.* New York: Columbia University Press, 1925.

II. GENERAL STUDIES

Andreae, G. *The dawn of juvenile literature in England.* Amsterdam: H. J. Paris, 1925.

Berger, Pierre. *Les poètes préromantiques anglais; introduction, traduction et notes.* Paris: La Renaissance du Livre, [1925].

Rev. by L. Cazamian in *RAA,* III (1925), 137-38; by R. Galland in *Les langues modernes,* XXIII (1925), 343-44.

Birkhead, Edith. "Sentiment and sensibility in the eighteenth century novel." *Essays and studies by members of the English Association,* XI (Oxford, 1925), 92-116.

A useful brief synthesis which, though it does not modify current notions regarding the rôle of "sensibility" in eighteenth-century fiction, nevertheless brings together a certain number of unfamiliar facts and texts. Apropos of the change in the meaning of "sentiment" discussed on pp. 93-95, reference might have been made to Johnson's *Dictionary* (see also the definitions of "feeling" and "sensibility"). With regard to Richardson's attitude toward sentiment (pp. 101-04), an illuminating commentary, not noted by Miss Birkhead, is to be found in his letter to Miss Highmore of July 20, 1750 (see *Correspondence,* ed. Barbauld, II, 252).

Bissell, Benjamin. *The American Indian in English literature of the eighteenth century.* New Haven: Yale University Press, 1925.

Rev. by B. V. Crawford in *PQ,* V (1926), 188-89; in *RLC,* VI (1926), 185.

Contains chapters on "The Indian as represented by historians and travellers," "Theories of savage life and the state of nature," "Civilization as seen by the savage," "The Indian in fiction," "The Indian in drama," and "The Indian in poetry." A rather superficial piece of work. The documentation, though fairly extensive for the period after 1750, is very scanty for the first half of the century. There is no indication that Bissell has gone systematically through the periodicals, the travel books, or the miscellanies for any portion of his field; for the most part he confines himself to texts that were already fairly well known to scholars (though we miss a discussion of Defoe), with occasional references to less familiar writings. He is particularly unsatisfactory in dealing with the philosophical background of the conception of the "noble savage." He refers (p. 41n) to Lovejoy's important article in *MP* for Nov. 1923; but he has clearly not taken its conclusions to heart in what he has to say (pp. 42 ff) of Rousseau as the "great originator" of the "pure state of nature." The organization of the book, too, leaves much to be desired. Surely in a monograph dealing with a movement of ideas, distinctions of literary genres are of little significance: what is essential is that we should be able to follow easily the historical unfolding of the conception that is being studied. Finally, it is unpardonable that in a book containing so much detail as this there should be no bibliography.

Bracey, Robert. *Eighteenth century studies.* Oxford: Blackwell, 1925.

Rev. by P. Yvon in *RAA,* III (1926), 348-49.

Contains essays on Boswell, Johnson, Hannah More, and Psalmanazar. The author is an English Catholic.

Bredvold, Louis I. "The religious thought of Donne in relation to medieval and later traditions." *Studies in Shakespeare, Milton and Donne by members of the English department of the University of Michigan* (New York: Macmillan, 1925), pp. 193-232.

Contains much of value to the student of religious ideas after the Restoration.

Burtt, Edwin Arthur. *The metaphysical foundations of modern physical science.* London: Kegan Paul; New York: Harcourt, Brace and Company, 1925.

Rev. by H. T. Costello in the *Journal of philosophy,* XXIII (1926), 47-50; by J. W. N. Sullivan in the *Calendar of modern letters,* I (1925), 400-03.

No student of the history of ideas in English literature during the seventeenth and eighteenth centuries can afford to miss this book. It is a serious study, written in a style that is at once clear and lively, of the gradual formation in the seventeenth century of the mechanistic world-view characteristic of modern physical science. In a half-dozen long and closely packed chapters Burtt passes in review the metaphysical doctrines of Copernicus and Kepler, of Galileo, of Descartes, of the English philosophers (Hobbes, More, etc.), of Gilbert and Boyle, and of Newton. How trustworthy a guide he is through this vast field it is impossible for a mere literary historian to say, but there can be no denying either the importance of the field or the skill with which he has wrought his difficult materials into an illuminating historical synthesis. Whoever undertakes hereafter to deal with such questions as the rise of classical critical theory or the conception of nature in eighteenth-century poetry is bound to incur a large debt to this solid and informing book.

C., J. Z. "*The Norwich Gazette,* 1730." *N & Q,* CXLVIII (1925), 21-23, 43-45.

Clark, A. F. B. *Boileau and the French classical critics in England (1660-1830).* Paris: Champion, 1925. ("Bibliothèque de la Revue de littérature comparée," No. 19.)

Rev. by E. Audra in *RLC,* VI (1926), 162-70; by L. Cazamian in *RAA,* III (1925), 150-51; by C. H. C. Wright in *MLN,* XLI (1926), 275-77.

In four substantial "books" the author deals with the history of Boileau's reputation in England, with the translations and imitations of his works, with the reputation of the principal other French classical critics, and with Boileau's "influence on English literature." Six appendices, comprising various *pièces justificatives,* and an elaborate bibliography conclude the volume. The result is one of the half-dozen most important publications of the year in the field of eighteenth-century studies, a book which throws much new light, not only on the specific problem of the action of Boileau and other French critics in England, but also on a number of questions of possibly more general interest to the historian of English taste in the eighteenth century. On such matters as the vogue of burlesque and the mock-heroic (pp. 150-68, 327-36), the attitude toward Italian Renaissance poetry (pp. 337-60), the conception of the "sublime" (pp. 361-79), the change in poetic style after the Restoration (pp. 407-17), and the development of formal satire (pp. 418-48), Clark has given us some of the most intelligent and discriminating pages that have so far been written. He is less satisfactory in his account of the school of "good sense" (pp. 380-89), for here he is largely content to follow Spingarn, and in consequence, I think, unduly neglects the philosophical background of the critical theories involved; and it would not be difficult to find *lacunae* here and there in his documentation (he does relatively little, for example, with periodical criticism). But when all is said, his information is surprisingly complete and exact, and what is more important, he knows how to transmute his facts into illuminating ideas.

The most serious reservation suggested by a reading of the book concerns the general point of view from which the study is conducted. The task which Clark has set himself—to determine the extent and nature of Boileau's influence on English literature—is fundamentally an impossible one: no scholar, be he ever so critical, can escape that insidious "hypnotism of the unique source" which is inseparable from studies of this sort. And Clark is nothing if not critical. He is so critical, indeed, so admirably sophisticated in all that concerns method, that his book, especially in its later pages, constitutes one of the clearest demonstrations I know of the essential futility of the type of investigation to which he has devoted himself. For after loyally mentioning all the difficulties and alternative possibilities, he ends, almost in spite of himself, by brushing them aside and seeing Boileau everywhere!

Closs, Karl. "Jakob Böhmes Aufnahme in England." *Archiv,* CXLVIII (1925), 18-27.

A convenient collection of texts referring to Böhme from 1644 to 1761.

Crane, Verner W. *The promotion literature of Georgia.* Cambridge [Mass.], 1925. Reprinted from *Bibliographical essays: a tribute to Wilberforce Eames.*

The writer deals briefly (pp. 15-16) with the part played by Thomson, Savage, Aaron Hill, and other poets in promoting enthusiasm for Georgia. *Tomochachi, an ode* (1736), here ascribed to Samuel Wesley, Jr., was probably the work of the Rev. Thomas Fitzgerald. See I. A. Williams in the *London mercury,* XII (1925), 86.

De Maar, Harko G. *A history of modern English romanticism. Volume I: Elizabethan and modern romanticism in the eighteenth century.* London: Humphrey Milford, Oxford University Press, 1924.

Rev. by L. Cazamian in *RAA,* III (1925), 72-74; by Bernhard Fehr in *Beiblatt,* XXXVI (1925), 129-33.

Dobrée, Bonamy. *Essays in biography, 1680-1726.* London: Humphrey Milford, Oxford University Press, 1925.

Rev. by K. A. Esdaile in *Library,* 4th series, VI (1926), 386-88; in *TLS,* Dec. 10, 1925, p. 855.

Stracheyesque essays on Etherege, Vanbrugh, and Addison (who is characterized as "the first of the Victorians").

Dobrée, Bonamy. *Restoration comedy, 1660-1720.* Oxford: Clarendon Press, 1924.

Rev. by L. Cazamian in *RAA,* II (1925), 546-47; by Allardyce Nicoll in *Litteris,* II (1925), 102-04.

Doughty, Oswald. "Eighteenth-century song." *English studies,* VII (1925), 161-69.

Fehr, B. "Ein Wort zur englischen Empfindsamkeitsliteratur des 18. Jahrhunderts." *Anglica: Untersuchungen zur englischen Philologie Alois Brandl. . . . überreicht,* II (Leipzig, 1925), 295-312.

An interesting synthesis of recent studies of eighteenth-century sentimentalism.

Fenn, Percy Thomas, Jr. "The Latitudinarians and toleration." *Washington University studies,* Vol. XIII, Humanistic series, No. 1, Oct., 1925, pp. 181-245.

Fries, Charles C. "The periphrastic future with *shall* and *will* in modern English." *PMLA,* XL (1925), 963-1024.

Suggestive remarks on the eighteenth-century attitude toward linguistic usage.

Graham, Walter. "Some predecessors of the *Tatler.*" *JEGP,* XXIV (1925), 548-54.

Greenlaw, Edwin. "The new science and English literature in the seventeenth century." *Johns Hopkins alumni magazine,* XIII (1925), 331-59.

The main purpose of this address (delivered before the Tudor-Stuart Club at the Johns Hopkins University, Jan. 16, 1925) is to point out that "we shall not arrive at a just valuation of seventeenth century literature . . . . until we study to better purpose the intellectual soil out of which it sprang," and in particular the "philosophical aspects of the scientific movement of the period 1543-1662, from Copernicus to the foundation of the Royal Society." There can of course be no dispute as to the soundness of this general position. What is not so certain is that Greenlaw, in the program of research which he outlines, has laid stress on those aspects of the scientific movement which are most significant for an understanding of the literary development. It is impossible, for example, to comprehend the rise of neo-classicism, particularly on its doctrinal side, without reference to the gradual establishment in the seventeenth century of a characteristic world-view, in the formation of which the new science played a fundamental part. Of this phase of his subject Greenlaw has little or nothing to say. On the other hand, many of his observations—notably those on Bacon's idea of nature (p. 340), on Sprat (pp. 342-43, 347), and on the conception of the place of natural science in poetry (pp. 348-55)—are both fresh and suggestive, and the paper as a whole exhibits that feeling for the larger perspectives of literary history which distinguishes all of its author's writings.

Grierson, H. J. C. *The background of English literature and other collected essays and addresses.* London: Chatto and Windus, 1925.

Contains essays on "The Metaphysical Poets," "Blake and Gray," and "Classical and romantic: a point of view."

Gunther, R. T. *Early science in Oxford.* Volume IV: *The Philosophical Society.* Oxford: For subscribers only, 1925.

Rev. in *TLS,* June 18, 1925, p. 415.

Hittmair, Rudolf. "Die Arbeit bei Langland, Locke, Carlyle. I." *GRM,* XIII (1925), 94-101.

Interesting generalizations on seventeenth-century theories of labor, with special attention to Locke.

Hölzle, Erwin. *Die Idee einer altgermanischen Freiheit vor Montesquieu.* Munich and Berlin: Oldenbourg, 1925.

Rev. by Henri Sée in *RH,* CLI (1926), 281-82.

Valuable for students of English because of its careful discussion of seventeenth- and eighteenth-century ideas on liberty among the Anglo-Saxons.

Howard, Claud. "Coleridge's idealism in its relation to Kant and to the English Platonists of the seventeenth century." *University of Chicago Abstracts of theses,* Humanistic series, I (1925), 385-89.

Howell, Almonte C. "Sir Thomas Browne and seventeenth-century scientific thought." *SP,* XXII (1925), 61-80.

Jones, Richard F. "Eclogue types in English poetry of the eighteenth century." *JEGP,* XXIV (1925), 33-60.

Kaufman, Paul. "Defining romanticism: a survey and a program." *MLN,* XL (1925), 193-204.

Ker, W. P. *Collected essays.* London: Macmillan, 1925. 2 vols.

Rev. in *TLS,* Nov. 19, 1925, p. 768.

Contains papers on Dryden, Horace Walpole, Thomas Warton, Joseph Ritson, and Burns and a general essay on "The eighteenth century."

King, R. W. "Italian influence on English scholarship and literature during the 'Romantic revival.'" *MLR,* XX (1925), 48-63, 295-304; XXI (1926), 24-43.

Should be supplemented, for the eighteenth century, by Clark, *Boileau . . . . in England,* pp. 337-60. An adequate study of the subject is badly needed.

Krutch, Joseph Wood. *Comedy and conscience after the Restoration.* New York: Columbia University Press, 1924.

Rev. by J. W. Draper in *MLN,* XLI (1926), 332-34; by G. H. Nettleton in *SRL,* Feb. 28, 1925, p. 561; by Allardyce Nicoll in *MLR,* XX (1925), 473-74; by Jacob Zeitlin in the *Nation,* Feb. 4, 1925, p. 124.

Legouis, Pierre. "Deux thèmes de la poésie lyrique au XVIIe siècle: *La plainte escrite de sang* et *La belle gueuse.*" *RLC,* V (1925), 139-52.

A study of two borrowings from the Italian sonneteer Claudio Achillini in the *Lyric poems* (1687) of Philip Ayres, with a postscript on the sources of Lovelace in "The faire begger."

Liddell, M. F. "Der Stil der englischen Geschichtsschreibung im 18. Jahrhundert." *Anglica,* II (1925), 313-85.

A useful study of the art of historical exposition as practiced by White Kennett, John Oldmixon, Hume, Robertson, and Gibbon. The writer seems not to know Fueter's important chapter on the English historians of the eighteenth century in his *Geschichte der neueren Historiographie* (1911).

McCutcheon, R. P. "Notes on the occurrence of the sonnet and blank verse." *MLN,* XL (1925), 513-14.

A few gleanings from periodicals before 1725 supplementing R. D. Havens's *Influence of Milton.*

McIntyre, Clara F. "The later career of the Elizabethan villain-hero." *PMLA,* XL (1925), 874-80.

Rather obvious parallels between the "villain-heroes" of Elizabethan romantic tragedy and typical characters in the romances of Mrs. Radcliffe and Monk Lewis.

Manwaring, Elizabeth Wheeler. *Italian landscape in eighteenth century England: a study chiefly of the influence of Claude Lorrain and Salvator Rosa on English taste, 1700-1800.* New York: Oxford University Press, American Branch, 1925.

Rev. by A. Digeon in *RAA,* III (1925), 152-53; by B. Fehr in *Beiblatt,* XXXVI (1925), 295-304; by R. D. Havens in *MLN,* XLI (1926), 132-33; by E. B. Smith in *SRL,* Aug. 29, 1925, p. 80; in *TLS,* Aug. 13, 1925, pp. 525-26.

The main conclusion which this book endeavors to establish is stated clearly at the beginning of the Preface: "the landscape which was taken as a model by Thomson and Dyer, by Kent and Shenstone, by Mrs. Radcliffe, was Italian, the landscape of the seventeenth century painters, Claude Lorrain, Salvator Rosa, the Poussins, and the long line of their followers and imitators, French, Dutch, and English." It is an interesting thesis, and Miss Manwaring develops it with a wealth of learning in the texts of the period which makes her volume an extremely valuable storehouse of materials for the history of eighteenth-century taste. As is nearly always the case, however, with studies which attempt to explain a complex development by reference to a single cause, she does not quite succeed in convincing us of the truth of her central contention. We read and are instructed; we carry away with us an impression that the vogue of Salvator and Claude was indeed very considerable; we gain a fairly clear understanding of the qualities for which each of these painters was prized; but we cannot persuade ourselves in the end that their influence was as far-reaching or as decisive as is here implied. To a certain extent Miss Manwaring has herself to blame for our skepticism. Her book is not well composed. She is too much dominated by her *fiches;* her chapters are not built firmly on a basis of general ideas; her organization shows little evident progression from the beginning of the book to the end; she rather bewilders us by her habit of skipping irresponsibly back and forth over the whole century. It is a pity, for with her extensive knowledge of the whole field of eighteenth-century landscape art, she might have given us a book which would have been an illuminating rather than a merely informing treatment of the subject.—Pp. 163-65: The account of the English garden in France suffers from Miss Manwaring's failure to consult Mornet's fundamental study of the question in his *Sentiment de la nature en France de J.-J. Rousseau à Bernardin de Saint-Pierre* (Paris, 1907).

Muddiman, J. G. "The second newspaper of English news." *TLS,* April 9, 1925, p. 253.

Comment by Alfred Robbins, *ibid.,* April 23, 1925, p. 285.

Murphy, Gwendolen. *A cabinet of characters.* London: Humphrey Milford, Oxford University Press, 1925.

A useful anthology of seventeenth-century "characters," with a few from the eighteenth and nineteenth centuries added to show the persistence of the genre. The Introduction deals in a rather sketchy way with the nature of the "character," its rise in modern England, and its relation to such forms as the epigram, the essay, the sermon, satire, and comedy.

Murphy, Gwendolen. "'England's Helicon.'" *TLS,* May 14, 1925, p. 335.

On punctuation and rhythm in seventeenth-century "characters."

Nethercot, A. H. "The attitude toward 'metaphysical' poetry in neo-classical England." *University of Chicago Abstracts of theses,* Humanistic series, I (1925), 395-97.

Nethercot, A. H. "The reputation of the 'metaphysical poets' during the age of Pope." *PQ,* IV (1925), 161-79.

Nethercot, A. H. "The reputation of the 'metaphysical poets' during the age of Johnson and the 'Romantic revival.'" *SP,* XXII (1925), 81-132.

Nicoll, Allardyce. *British drama: an historical survey from the beginnings to the present time.* London: Harrap, 1925.

Good chapters on the Restoration and eighteenth century.

Nicoll, Allardyce. *A history of early eighteenth century drama, 1700-1750.* Cambridge: University Press, 1925.

Rev. by L. Cazamian in *RAA,* III (1925), 70-72; by A. Koszul in *Les langues modernes,* XXIII (1925), 573-74; by Edith J. Morley in *RES,* I (1925), 364-66; by D. H. Stevens in *MP,* XXIII (1925), 250-51; by A. S. Turberville in *History,* X (1926), 345; in *TLS,* March 12, 1925, p. 169.

In method and plan of treatment this volume follows closely its author's *History of Restoration drama.* There are four main chapters, dealing respectively with "The Theatre," "Tragedy," "Comedy," and "Miscellaneous forms of drama," and three appendices, the last of which contains an invaluable "Hand-list of plays, 1700-1750" (pp. 293-407).

Nicoll, Allardyce. "The rights of Beeston and D'Avenant in Elizabethan plays." *RES,* I (1925), 84-91.

Cf. reply by Hazelton Spencer, *ibid.,* I, 443-46.

Perry, Henry Ten Eyck. *The comic spirit in Restoration drama.* New Haven: Yale University Press, 1925.

Rev. by F. W. Chandler in *MLN,* XLI (1926), 408-09; by J. Isaacs in *RES,* II (1926), 108-09.

Potter, George R. "Coleridge and the idea of evolution." *PMLA,* XL (1925), 379-97.

Valuable to students of the eighteenth century for the incidental light it throws on the transition from a mechanistic to an organic conception of nature.

Praz, Mario. "Stanley, Sherburne and Ayres as translators and imitators of Italian, Spanish and French poets." *MLR,* XX (1925), 280-94, 419-31.

"The Prelude to romanticism." *TLS,* Aug. 13, 1925, pp. 525-26.

Prinsen, J. *De roman in de 18e eeuw in West-Europa.* Groningen: Wolters, 1925.

Rev. by P. Van Tieghem in *RSH,* XL (1925), 131-32.

Raleigh, Sir Walter. *Some authors, a collection of literary essays (1896-1916).* Oxford: Clarendon Press, 1925.

Contains essays on Dryden and political satire, the "battle of the books," Halifax, Burke, Burns, and Blake. The studies of Dryden and Burke are here printed for the first time.

Reed, Amy Louise. *The background of Gray's Elegy: a study in the taste for melancholy poetry, 1700-1751.* New York: Columbia University Press, 1924.

Rev. by Roger Martin in *RAA,* III (1925), 155-56; by C. A. Moore in *MLN,* XL (1925), 431-35.

Reichwein, Adolf. *China and Europe: intellectual and artistic contacts in the eighteenth century.* Translated by J. C. Powell. New York: Knopf, 1925.

Rev. by K. S. Latourette in *AHR,* XXXI (1925), 129-30.

Robertson, J. G. *The reconciliation of classic and romantic.* Cambridge: Bowes & Bowes, 1925. ("Publications of the Modern Humanities Research Association," No. 8.)

Rev. by P. Van Tieghem in *RSH,* XL (1925), 117-19.

One of the least helpful of the many recent attempts to reinterpret the relations of classicism and romanticism. It abounds in contradictory statements, as when we are told on a single page first that "The essential criterion of Classicism may . . . . be narrowed down to dependence on the Latin ideals of a definite age" and second that "the spiritual essence of Classicism in literature is not imitation of the ancients, although this may be its outward form, but the avoidance of the immediate poetic expression of an experience" (p. 10). It is full of such dubious and sterile generalizations as the following: "It seems to me that all Romantic manifestations . . . are, in their ultimate elements, products of inter-racial fertilisation. . . . On the other hand, Classicism is nurtured, or, at least, not hampered, by inbreeding and by the absence of extraneous fertilising elements" (pp. 12-13). But the most striking example of Robertson's confused and essentially unhistorical thinking is his comment on the notion of a "return to nature" (p. 6). At a time when we are coming to realize more and more clearly the profound differences in philosophical outlook which separated the "nature" of Wordsworth (for example) from that of Boileau or Pope, it is disconcerting to find a scholar of Robertson's reputation naïvely assuming an identity of meaning. "Look again," he writes, "at the pioneers of the great age—the greatest age—of Classicism in modern Europe, the French seventeenth century. The initiators of that brilliant age were men who insisted that literature must return to nature and reality—a demand which, again, corresponds to that made by the heralds of every Romantic age. The movement of the seventeenth century is, in its inception at least, quite as Romantic as that of 1828."

Smith, Logan Pearsall. *Words and idioms.* Boston: Houghton Mifflin, 1925.

Contains an essay on "Four romantic words" (*romantic, originality, creative, genius*).

Spencer, Hazelton. "The Restoration play lists." *RES*, I (1925), 443-46.

A criticism of Allardyce Nicoll's article, *ibid.*, I, 84-91.

Studies in the history of ideas. Volume II. Edited by the Department of Philosophy, Columbia University. New York: Columbia University Press, 1925.

Contains essays on Descartes, Malebranche, and Hume.

Van Tieghem, Paul. *Précis d'histoire littéraire de l'Europe depuis la Renaissance.* Paris: Alcan, 1925.

Rev. by F. Baldensperger in *RLC*, VI (1926), 159-62; by G. Rudler in the *French quarterly*, VIII (1926), 66-67.

Written primarily for beginners in literary history and for general readers, this little book deserves to be mentioned here if only because of the novelty of its method. It is, I believe, the first general survey of modern European literature which has had the courage to abandon the traditional organization by countries and to attempt a grouping of facts calculated to bring into relief the traits common to the literatures of all Europe in a given period. The *cadres* chosen are in the main, though not exclusively, literary genres. Thus the section on the "âge classique" includes, after a few pages of generalities, chapters on tragedy, comedy, non-dramatic poetry, prose (theologians, moralists, essayists), the "mouvement philosophique," the novel in the eighteenth century, and the "préromantiques." The volume may be heartily recommended to American graduate students, many of whom could profit from such a rearrangement of perspectives.

Van Tieghem, Paul. *Le préromantisme: études d'histoire littéraire européenne.* Paris: Rieder, 1924.

Rev. by G. Ascoli in *RSH*, XXXIX (1925), 154-55; by F. Baldensperger in *RLC*, VI (1926), 159-62; by L. Cazamian in *RAA*, II (1925), 461-63; by J. G. Robertson in *MLR*, XX (1925), 482-83; by G. Toffanin in *Litteris*, II (1925), 131-41.

This volume contains three studies: "La notion de vraie poésie dans le Préromantisme européen," "La découverte de la mythologie et de l'ancienne poésie scandinave," and "Ossian et l'Ossianisme au XVIIIe siècle." All three of them have appeared in print before; but, to say nothing of the fact that they have been retouched in various places, it is good to have them assembled in a single volume. For they are models of a type of study of which we have had all too few examples and of which Van Tieghem, in these and other similar monographs published during the last few years, has approved himself a master. The conception of "littérature générale" which underlies their construction is set forth briefly but persuasively in the Preface, which contains, among other things, some excellent remarks on the relation between analysis and synthesis in literary history: "On ne peut attendre, pour tenter une synthèse partielle, que le travail d'analyse soit terminé: il ne le sera jamais. La synthèse doit se construire progressivement, et parallèlement à l'analyse dont elle utilise au fur et à mesure les résultats" (p. 13). Of the three monographs, the first is possibly the least satisfying. It is, for one thing, too brief for the enormous complexity of its subject; but in addition Van Tieghem seems to me to miss certain fundamental aspects of the change in literary theory which he is tracing, through insufficient attention both to the seventeenth-century background and to the concurrent changes in philosophical outlook. He is much more successful in the two other studies, both of which—and the second in particular—are admirably clear and well-informed syntheses.

Vaughan, C. E. *Studies in the history of political philosophy before and after Rousseau.* Edited by A. G. Little. Manchester: University Press, 1925. 2 vols.

Rev. by C. D. B. in *International journal of ethics,* XXXVI (1925), 107; by A. H. Lloyd in *AHR,* XXXI (1926), 776-78; by H. W. Schneider in *Journal of philosophy,* XXIII (1926), 155-56.

Contains studies of Hobbes, Spinoza, Locke, Vico, Montesquieu, Hume, and Burke.

Walker, Hugh. *English satire and satirists.* London: J. M. Dent; New York: E. P. Dutton, 1925.

Rev. by A. Digeon in *RAA,* III (1926), 362-63; in *TLS,* Dec. 10, 1925, p. 854.

Whitehead, Alfred North. *Science and the modern world.* New York: Macmillan, 1925.

Suggestive chapters on the seventeenth and eighteenth centuries.

Williams, S. T. "The English sentimental drama from Steele to Cumberland." *Sewanee review,* XXXIII (1925), 405-26.

III. STUDIES OF AUTHORS

Joseph Addison

Beatty, Joseph M., Jr. "Joseph Addison's ancestry." *N & Q,* CXLIX (1925), 459.

Mark Akenside

Chapman, R. W. "A note on the first edition of *The Pleasures of imagination.*" *RES,* I (1925), 346-48.

Christopher Anstey

Williams, Iolo A. [Bibliography of the first editions of Anstey.] *London mercury,* XI (1925), 300-02, 414-17, 526-28, 643-44; XII (1925), 194, 300-01.

John Arbuthnot

The History of John Bull. For the first time faithfully re-issued from the original pamphlets, 1712, together with an investigation into its composition, publication, and authorship by H. Teerink. Amsterdam: H. J. Paris, 1925.

Richard Baxter

The Autobiography of Richard Baxter, being the Reliquiae Baxterianae abridged from the folio (1696). Edited by J. M. Lloyd Thomas. London: J. M. Dent; New York: E. P. Dutton, 1925.

Rev. by Walther Fischer in *Beiblatt*, XXXVII (1926), 36-38; in *TLS*, Dec. 17, 1925, p. 887.

Chapters from Richard Baxter's Christian directory. Selected by Jeannette Tawney. London: Bell, 1925.

Rev. by K. N. Bell in *History*, X (1925), 264.
An attempt to illustrate the economic ideas of a seventeenth-century Puritan.

George Berkeley

Metz, Rudolf. *George Berkeley: Leben und Lehre.* Stuttgart: Frommanns Verlag, 1925.

Hugh Blair

Cowling, G. H. "The English teaching of Dr. Hugh Blair." *Anglica*, II (1925), 281-94.

William Blake

The Writings of William Blake. Edited by Geoffrey Keynes. London: The Nonesuch Press, 1925. 3 vols.

Rev. by P. Berger in *Les langues modernes*, XXIII (1925), 575-76; by S. C. Chew in the *Nation*, June 2, 1926, pp. 611-12; by Thomas Wright in the *New Statesman*, Aug. 22, 1925, pp. 527-28; in *TLS*, Oct. 8, 1925, pp. 645-46.
The first complete scholarly edition.

Bruce, Harold. "William Blake in a brown coat." *TLS*, Aug. 27, 1925, p. 557.

Bruce, Harold. *William Blake in this world.* New York: Harcourt, Brace and co., 1925.

Figgis, Darrell. *The paintings of William Blake.* London: Ernest Benn, 1925.

Rev. in *TLS*, Dec. 3, 1925, p. 827. Cf. *ibid.*, Dec. 17, 1925, p. 883, for comment by Geoffrey Keynes, who questions the authenticity of two plates.

Mabbott, T. O. "Blake's designs for Blair's *Grave*: American edition." *N & Q*, CXLVIII (1925), 98.

Plowman, Max. "Blake and Hayley." *TLS*, April 30, 1925, p. 300.

Plowman, Max. "The incomplete 'Marriage of heaven and hell.'" *TLS*, Oct. 22, 1925, p. 698.

Gives reasons for thinking *A song of liberty* an integral part of *The marriage of heaven and hell.*

Redgrove, H. Stanley. "Blake and Swedenborg." *New-Church magazine*, Jan., 1925.

Saurat, Denis. "Blake et les Celtomanes." *MP*, XXIII (1925), 175-88.

An interpretation of the primitive British history in Blake's *Jerusalem* and *Descriptive catalogue* in the light of eighteenth-century theories about the Celts from Pezron and Stukeley to Williams and Davies. A very important article, in which, for almost the first time, the problem of Blake's thought is approached in a really historical spirit, quite free from the uncritical enthusiasm which down to the present has vitiated most writing on the subject. Saurat has in preparation other studies of a similar character, which, if we may judge from the present sample of his method, should go far toward replacing Blake in his proper eighteenth-century milieu.

Short, Ernest H. *Blake.* London: Philip Allen, 1925. ("British Artists series.")

James Boswell

Boswell's note book, 1776-1777, now first published from the unique original in the collection of R. B. Adam, Esq. London: Humphrey Milford, Oxford University Press, 1925.

Rev. by A. Dupuis in *RAA,* III (1925), 156; by R. D. Havens in *MLN,* XL (1925), 518.

"Boswell's letters." *TLS,* Jan. 15, 1925, pp. 29-30.

Leading article suggested by C. B. Tinker's edition (1924).

Chapman, R. W. [Note on a cancel in Boswell's *Hebrides.*] *Bodleian quarterly record,* IV (1925), 257.

Pottle, Frederick A. "Boswellian myths." *N & Q,* CXLIX (1925), 4-6.

Pottle, Frederick A. "Boswellian notes." *N & Q,* CXLIX (1925), 113-14.

Pottle, Frederick A. "Boswell's 'Miss W—— T.'" *N & Q,* CXLVIII (1925), 80.

Pottle, Frederick A. "Boswell's 'Observations on *The Minor.*'" *Bulletin of the New York Public Library,* XXIX (1925), 3-6.

Pottle, Frederick A. "Bozzy and Yorick." *Blackwood's magazine,* CCXVII (1925), 297-313.

Interesting evidence of a meeting between the two in 1760, with sidelights on Boswell's admiration for Sterne.

Pottle, Frederick A. "'Bozzy' was a bold young blade: the story of his Lady Mackintosh episode based upon unpublished material." *New York Times Book review,* Aug. 23, 1925, pp. 1, 13.

Pottle, Frederick A. "The incredible Boswell." *Blackwood's magazine,* CCXVIII (1925), 149-65.

An account of Boswell's contributions to the *London chronicle* especially between 1767 and 1775, based on Boswell's annotated file of that newspaper now in the Yale Library. A very amusing supplement to Tinker's *Young Boswell.*

Pottle, Frederick A. "James Boswell the younger." *N & Q,* CXLIX (1925), 49.

Henry Brooke

C[hapman], R. W. "Brooke's *Gustavus Vasa.*" *RES,* I (1925), 460-61.

On a copy containing the list of subscribers, among whom were Chesterfield, Johnson, and Swift.

Edmund Burke

Pottle, Frederick A. [Query as to the date of the first edition of Burke's *Sublime and beautiful.*] *N & Q,* CXLVIII (1925), 80.

Replies by Edward Bensly and Theodore Prince, *ibid.,* p. 140.

Tomlinson, F. W. "Burke and the Revolution." *TLS,* Dec. 10, 1925, p. 862.

Announcement of a study in preparation on this subject.

Fanny Burney

Morley, Edith J. *Fanny Burney.* English Association pamphlet, No. 60 (April, 1925).

The essay itself is of little value, but an appendix contains four inedited letters between Miss Burney and Mrs. Thrale, printed from the originals in Dr. Williams's Library.

Robert Burns

Wilson, Sir James. *Scottish poems of Robert Burns in his native dialect.* London: Humphrey Milford, Oxford University Press, 1925.

Rev. by F. Mossé in *Les langues modernes,* XXIII (1925), 266-68.

Mary Chandler

Doughty, Oswald. "A Bath poetess of the eighteenth century." *RES,* I (1925), 404-20.

An essay on Mary Chandler (1687-1745) which should have been published in the *London mercury.* The author informs us (p. 412) that lines 267-80 of the first epistle of the *Essay on Man* were indebted to one of her poems, but he does not think it necessary to name the poem or to offer any evidence for his assertion!

Thomas Chatterton

Meyerstein, E. H. W. "Chatterton, a correction." *TLS,* July 16, 1925, p. 480.

A correction of a note in *TLS* for July 21, 1921.

Meyerstein, E. H. W. "Lydgate and Chatterton." *TLS,* April 16, 1925, p. 268.

Chesterfield

Coxon, Roger. *Chesterfield and his critics.* London: G. Routledge & sons, 1925.

Rev. by P. Yvon in *Les langues modernes,* XXIV (1926), 156-59; in *TLS,* May 14, 1925, p. 331.

Contains hitherto unpublished personal letters.

Colley Cibber

An Apology for the life of Colley Cibber . . . . written by himself. Waltham St. Lawrence, Twyford: Golden Cockerel Press, 1925.

Bateson, F. W. "*The Double gallant* of Colley Cibber." *RES,* I (1925), 343-46.

A study of the sources.

Mary Collyer

Hughes, Helen Sard. "The life and works of Mary Mitchell Collyer." *University of Chicago Abstracts of theses,* Humanistic series, I (1925), 391-94.

William Congreve

Comedies by William Congreve. Edited, with introduction and notes, by Bonamy Dobrée. London: Humphrey Milford, Oxford University Press, [1925]. ("The World's Classics.")

A convenient new edition, containing the four comedies (in the text of the 1710 edition) and the essay "Concerning humour in comedy." The editor's contribution consists of a few explanatory notes, a list of the more important dates in Congreve's life, and a brief introduction on Restoration comedy in general and on Congreve's prose style.

William Cowper

The Unpublished and uncollected letters of William Cowper. Edited by Thomas Wright. London: C. J. Farncombe, 1925.

Rev. in the *New Statesman,* July 25, 1925, pp. 424-25.

Richard Cumberland

Landa, M. J. "The grandfather of melodrama." *Cornhill magazine,* N. S., LIX (1925), 476-84.

Sir William Davenant

Spencer, Hazelton. "D'Avenant's *Macbeth* and Shakespeare's." *PMLA,* XL (1925), 619-44.

Daniel Defoe

Brandl, Leopold. "Krinke Kesmes und Defoes *Robinson.*" *Neophilologus,* XI (1925), 28-40.

Dottin, Paul. *Daniel De Foe et ses romans.* Paris: Presses universitaires, 1924. 3 vols.

Rev. by R. S. C[rane] in *MP,* XXIII (1925), 231-32; by Oliver Elton in the *French quarterly,* VII (1925), 89-92; by E. Pons in *RELV,* XLII (1925), 220-22; by Hermann Ullrich in *ES,* LX (1926), 364-69.

Dottin, Paul. *Vie et aventures de Daniel De Foe, auteur de Robinson Crusoé.* Paris: Perrin, 1925.

Rev. by Camille Cé in *RELV,* XLIII (1926), 166-67; by H. Servajean in *RAA,* III (1926), 256-57.

A condensation of the preceding work.

Gudde, Erwin Gustav. "Grimmelshausen's *Simplicius Simplicissimus* and Defoe's *Robinson Crusoe.*" *PQ,* IV (1925), 110-20.

Gückel, W. and E. Günther. *D. Defoes und J. Swifts Belesenheit und literarische Kritik.* Leipzig: Meyer & Müller, 1925.

Rev. by S. B. Liljegren in *Beiblatt,* XXXVII (1925), 134-35.

Useful so far as it goes, but very incomplete on Defoe: the compilers have restricted themselves, for the most part, to works accessible in modern editions (only a small portion of the *Review,* for example, has been examined).

Hutchins, Henry Clinton. *Robinson Crusoe and its printing, 1719-1731: a bibliographical study.* New York: Columbia University Press, 1925.

Rev. by Harold Williams in the *Library Association record,* N.S., IV (1926), 24-25; in *TLS,* Oct. 22, 1925, p. 695.

An important bibliographical investigation, which only collectors, unfortunately, can afford to buy. The substance of the book consists of a minute and painstaking examination of the English editions of *Robinson Crusoe* published in Defoe's lifetime. The first chapter contains some brief and rather rambling remarks on printing conditions in England, 1700-1725; and there is an interesting discussion (pp. 56-61) of the meaning of the terms "edition" and "issue," though it is doubtful whether the use of the latter term in the analysis of the third and fourth editions (pp. 88-96) will appeal to scholars who are primarily concerned with textual criticism rather than with descriptive bibliography.

Parker, George. "The allegory of *Robinson Crusoe.*" *History,* X (1925), 11-25.

A fantastic elaboration of the old theory that *Robinson Crusoe,* Part I, was intended by Defoe as an allegorical history of his own career. The writer argues, evidently with entire seriousness, that "Crusoe's tame goats are his [Defoe's] publications, that the footprint in the sand represents the *Shortest way with the dissenters,* and that the "enclosure in the woods for his [Crusoe's] goats seems to be the *Review.*" Etc., etc.

Secord, Arthur Wellesley. *Studies in the narrative method of Defoe.* Urbana: University of Illinois Press, 1924.

Rev. by Paul Dottin in *RAA,* II (1925), 444-45; by S. B. Liljegren in *Beiblatt,* XXXVI (1925), 340-43; by H. Ullrich in *ES,* LIX (1925), 457-67.

Ullrich, Hermann. *Defoes Robinson Crusoe: die Geschichte eines Weltbuches.* Leipzig: Reisland, 1924.

Rev. by Paul Dottin in *RAA,* III (1925), 153-54; by Walther Fischer in *Beiblatt,* XXXVI (1925), 133-35; by H. Schöffler in *ES,* LIX (1925), 452-57.

John Dryden

MacFlecknoe, 1682. [Reproduced in type-facsimile.] London: Humphrey Milford, Oxford University Press, 1925.

Bondurant, A. L. "The *Amphitruo* of Plautus, Molière's *Amphitryon,* and the *Amphitryon* of Dryden." *Sewanee review,* XXXIII (1925), 455-68.

Eliot, T. S. *Homage to John Dryden: three essays on poetry of the seventeenth century.* London: Hogarth Press, 1925.

Rev. by John Freeman in the *London mercury,* XI (1925), 663-64; by Edwin Muir in the *Calendar of modern letters,* I (1925), 242-44.

Ellis, Amanda M. "Horace's influence on Dryden." *PQ,* IV (1925), 39-60.

Emerson, Oliver Farrar. "Dryden and the English Academy." *MLR,* XX (1925), 189-90.

Comment on an article by E. Freeman, *ibid.,* XIX (1924), 291-300.

Havens, Raymond D. "Dryden's visit to Milton." *RES,* I (1925), 348-49.

Low, D. M. "An error in Dryden." *TLS,* April 30, 1925, p. 300.

On *Theodore and Honoria,* l. 58.

Lubbock, Alan. *The character of John Dryden.* London: Hogarth Press, 1925.

Rev. in the *Calendar of modern letters,* I (1925), 488; in *TLS,* July 9, 1925, p. 460.

Lynch, Kathleen M. "D'Urfé's *L'Astrée* and the 'proviso' scenes in Dryden's comedy." *PQ,* IV (1925), 302-08.

Smith, John Harrington. "Dryden's critical temper." *Washington University studies,* Vol. XII, Humanistic series, No. 2, 1925, pp. 201-20.

Thorn-Drury, G. "Some notes on Dryden." *RES,* I (1925), 79-83, 187-97, 324-30.

The most important notes are those on Dryden and Milton (pp. 80-81; cf. the note by R. D. Havens, pp. 348-49), on Dryden and Shadwell (pp. 187-92), on the popularity of the Absalom and Achitophel theme before Dryden (pp. 326-27), and on "Dryden and the opera on *The Tempest*" (pp. 327-30).

John Dunton

Moore, C. A. "John Dunton, pietist and impostor." *SP,* XXII (1925), 467-99.

An interesting study of the treatises on death published by Dunton between 1682 and 1704, in which Moore finds "an important link of connection between the poets of death in the pre-Restoration period and their grave-yard successors in the eighteenth century." The article is less significant for the new light it throws on the career and publishing practices of Dunton than for the vivid glimpse it affords into the still little-known world of lower middle-class pietism out of which proceeded so many important impulses during the next hundred years.

Elizabeth Elstob

Ashdown, Margaret. "Elizabeth Elstob, the learned Saxonist." *MLR*, XX (1925), 125-26.

John Evelyn

Squire, W. Barclay. "Evelyn and music." *TLS*, May 14, 1925, p. 333; Dec. 10, 1925, p. 857.

Cf. *ibid.*, May 28, 1925, p. 368.

Robert Fergusson

Fergusson, Robert. *Scots poems.* Reprinted from the *Weekly magazine* and the editions of 1773 and 1779. London: Porpoise Press, 1925.

Henry Fielding

Blanchard, Frederic T. *Fielding the novelist: a study of the novelist's fame and influence.* New Haven: Yale University Press, 1925.

Digeon, A. *The novels of Fielding.* London: Routledge; New York: E. P. Dutton, 1925.

Rev. by W. L. Cross in *SRL*, July 18, 1925, pp. 905-06; by R. M. Lovett in the *New republic*, Aug. 26, 1925, pp. 22-23.

A translation of the author's *Les romans de Fielding* (1923). Digeon writes of Fielding primarily as a literary critic—an excellent critic, be it said, with a rare gift of subtle and penetrating analysis and a genuine sympathy for an author whom we are accustomed to look upon as peculiarly English in both his qualities and limitations. Yet he does not entirely neglect the historical aspects of his subject. No one, for example, has defined more clearly, in relation to the general movement of English taste in the mid-eighteenth century, the transformation in feeling and attitude which led from the parody and humor of *Joseph Andrews* and the irony of *Jonathan Wild* to the moralized sentiment of *Amelia.* On one or two points his conclusions seem open to question. He does not, for example, give sufficient emphasis to what may be called the Mandevillian element in Fielding's conception of human nature—an element that plays a curiously paradoxical rôle throughout the series of novels and accounts in part at least for the intensified religious atmosphere in *Amelia.* Nor can we subscribe to his theory that at some time between 1743 and 1751 Fielding underwent a "conversion" from Deism to Christianity. There can be no doubt that the religious note is more prominent in the later writings, but an examination of such texts as the papers in the *Champion* for Jan. 22 and March 27, 1740, or the essay "On the loss of our friends," is sufficient to dispose of the notion that Fielding, at that early stage of his career, was in any sense sympathetic toward Deism.

Jensen, Gerard E. "*An address to the electors of Great Britain* .... possibly a Fielding tract." *MLN*, XL (1925), 57-58.

Stonehill, Charles. "Fielding's *The Miser.*" *TLS*, Oct. 22, 1925, p. 698.

Thomas Flatman

T[horn]-D[rury], G. "St. Cecilia's day, 1686." *RES,* I (1925), 220.

Notes the existence of *A song for St. Cecilia's day, Nov. 22, 1686,* by Thomas Flatman.

Richard Flecknoe

The Life of Tomaso the wanderer: an attack upon Thomas Killigrew by Richard Flecknoe. Reprinted from the original of 1667. Edited by G. Thorn-Drurv. London: Dobell, 1925.

Rev. in *TLS,* Dec. 3, 1925, p. 829.

David Garrick

Three farces [*The lying valet; A peep behind the curtain; Bon ton*]. Edited by Louise B. Osborn. New Haven: Yale University Press; London: Humphrey Milford, Oxford University Press, 1925.

Rev. by Paul Dottin in *RAA,* III (1925), 155.

Clark, Ruth. "D'Holbach et Garrick." *RLC,* V (1925), 671-73.

Text of a letter from d'Holbach to Garrick, April 20, 1765, written on the occasion of the latter's departure from Paris for London.

John Gay

Poems by John Gay. With an introduction by Francis Bickley. London: Simpkin and Marshall, 1925. ("Abbey classics.")

Edward Gibbon

Robertson, J. M. *Gibbon.* London: Watts, 1925.

Tronchon, Henri. "Gibbon en Hongrie: premières traces." *MLN,* XL (1925), 385-96.

Charles Gildon

T[horn]-D[rury], G. "*A comparison between the two stages . . . 1702.*" *RES,* I (1925), 96.

Shows that the traditional ascription of this work to Gildon (accepted, for example, by Paul Dottin in his *Robinson Crusoe examin'd and criticis'd* [London and Paris, 1923], p. 50) cannot be correct.

Oliver Goldsmith

McKerrow, R. B. and I. A. Williams. [Notes on sheets L and M of the first edition of Goldsmith's *She stoops to conquer.*] *London mercury,* XI (1925), 302-03.

Cf. *ibid.,* XI (1924), 82-86.

Marcus, Hans. "Goldsmith über Deutschland." *Archiv,* CXLIX (1925-26), 1-32, 177-211.

Williams, Iolo A. [Note on the French translation of the *Vicar of Wakefield.*] *London mercury,* XIII (1925), 192.

Thomas Gray

Strachey, J. St. Loe. [On the *Ode on a distant prospect of Eton College.*] *New York Times Book review,* Mar. 1, 1925, p. 10.

Toynbee, Paget. "A Gray-Mason enigma solved." *TLS,* Sept. 17, 1925, p. 600.

Toynbee, Paget. "Gray's letters." *TLS,* Oct. 8, 1925, p. 656.

Announces that he is "engaged on an edition of the correspondence of Gray, based as far as possible on the original manuscripts, in which will be embodied the new letters published ten years ago in the 'Correspondence of Gray, Walpole, West, and Ashton,' together with a few others not included in Mr. Tovey's edition, and as many as can be traced of the letters written to Gray."

Whibley, Leonard. "A correction in Gray's letters." *TLS,* Oct. 1, 1925, p. 639.

James Harrington

James Harrington's Oceana. Edited with notes by S. B. Liljegren. Heidelberg: Winter, 1924.

Rev. by A. J. Carlyle in *EHR,* XLI (1926), 131-32; by F. Liebermann in *Archiv,* CXLVIII (1925), 116-18; by A. O. Lovejoy in *MLN,* XL (1925), 245-46.

The notes in this excellent edition are a treasure-house of facts and texts on the history of English ideas in the seventeenth century.

Liljegren, S. B. "Some notes on the name of James Harrington's *Oceana.*" *Probleme der englischen Sprache und Kultur: Festschrift für Johannes Hoops* (Heidelberg, 1925), pp. 231-49.

Very curious and interesting details on the diffusion of Utopian ideas in England on the eve of the Restoration. Supplements his edition, pp. 227-31.

Thomas Hobbes

Hönigswald, Richard. *Hobbes und die Staatsphilosophie.* Munich: Reinhardt, 1924.

Tonnies, F. *Thomas Hobbes: Leben und Lehre.* Stuttgart: Frommanns Verlag, 1925.

Thomas Holcroft

The Life of Thomas Holcroft. Written by himself, continued to the time of his death by William Hazlitt, and now newly edited by Elbridge Colby. London: Constable, 1925.

Rev. in *TLS,* Aug. 13, 1925, p. 531.

John Houghton

Fussell, G. E. "John Houghton, F. R. S. (b. 1640, d. 1705)." *N & Q,* CXLVIII (1925), 345-46.

David Hume

Hendel, Charles W. *Studies in the philosophy of David Hume.* Princeton: Princeton University Press, 1925.

Rev. by S. P. Lamprecht in the *Journal of philosophy,* XXII (1925), 411-18.

Mure, B. G. "Some unpublished letters of David Hume." *Nineteenth century,* XCVIII (1925), 293-306.

Four letters to William Mure of Caldwell written between 1764 and 1769.

Samuel Johnson

Lives of the English poets. With introduction by L. Archer-Hind. London: J. M. Dent; New York: E. P. Dutton, [1925]. ("Everyman's Library.")

Selected letters of Samuel Johnson. London: Humphrey Milford, Oxford University Press, 1925. ("The World's Classics.")

Introduction by R. W. Chapman. A few letters are included that were not in the Birkbeck Hill edition.

Johnson's *Prologue to Comus,* 1750. [Reproduced in type-facsimile.] London: Humphrey Milford, Oxford University Press, 1925.

Belloc, Hilaire. "Mrs. Piozzi's *Rasselas.*" *SRL,* Aug. 15, 1925, pp. 37-38.

Bloxsome, H. E. "Dr. Johnson and the medical profession." *Cornhill magazine,* N. S., LVIII (1925), 455-71.

Brémond, Henri, Jean, and André. *Le charme d'Athènes et autres essais.* Paris: Bloud et Gay, 1925.

Rev. by A Brulé in *RAA,* III (1926), 263-65.
Contains an essay by André Brémond on the religious element in Johnson's work and influence.

Chapman, R. W. "Johnson and the longitude." *RES,* I (1925), 458-60.

Chapman, R. W. "Johnson's letters." *TLS,* Oct. 1, 1925, p. 639.

Emendations in letters of Oct. 5, 1769 (to Taylor) and April 12, 1783 (to Reynolds).

Collison-Morley, L. "Dr. Johnson and the modern languages." *Cornhill magazine,* N.S., LIX (1925), 572-77.

Courtney, William Prideaux and David Nichol Smith. *A bibliography of Samuel Johnson.* Oxford: Clarendon Press, 1925.

Rev. by A. W. Reed in *RES,* II (1926), 105-07; by I. A. Williams in *London mercury,* XII (1925), 298.
A reissue of the edition of 1915 with the welcome addition of thirty-eight facsimiles. These include, besides the titlepages of most of Johnson's publications, the very rare *Proposals* of 1745 (already reproduced by Karl Young in *University of Wisconsin studies,* No. 18 [1924], opposite p. 172),

the original state of the cancelled p. 48 of the *Journey to the Western Islands,* and the two lists of errata in the same work.

Evans, A. W. *A catalogue of books by or relating to Dr. Johnson & members of his circle, offered for sale by Elkin Matthews, Ltd.* London: Elkin Matthews, 1925.

Rev. in *New York Times Book review,* July 19, 1925, p. 18; in *TLS,* April 23, 1925, p. 288.

Forman, W. Courthope. "Dr. Johnson and Isaac Walton." *N & Q,* CXLIX (1925), 79, 80.

Cf. Edward Bensly, *ibid.,* p. 170.

Gennadius, Joannes. *Dr. Johnson and Homer.* London: Privately printed, 1925.

O'Brien, George. "Dr. Samuel Johnson as an economist." *Studies: an Irish quarterly review,* XIV (1925), 80-101.

Powys, A. R. "Dr. Johnson on a Thames bridge." *London mercury,* XIII (1925), 199.

Roscoe, E. S. "The friendship of Dr. Johnson and Windham." *National review,* July, 1925, pp. 767-74.

Rypins, Stanley. "Johnson's Dictionary reviewed by his contemporaries." *PQ,* IV (1925), 281-86.

Thomas Jordan

T[horn]-D[rury], G. "Jordan's *Money is an asse,* 1668." *RES,* I (1925), 219-20.

George Lord Lyttleton

Roberts, S. C. "An eighteenth-century gentleman." *London mercury,* XI (1925), 290-97.

James Macpherson

Fraser, G. M. "The truth about Macpherson's 'Ossian.'" *Quarterly review,* CCXLV (1925), 331-45.

Moore, John Robert. "Wordsworth's unacknowledged debt to Macpherson's *Ossian.*" *PMLA,* XL (1925), 362-78.

Peers, E. Allison. "The influence of Ossian in Spain." *PQ,* IV (1925), 121-38.

Bernard Mandeville

The Fable of the bees: or private vices, publick benefits. By Bernard Mandeville. With a commentary critical, historical, and explanatory by F. B. Kaye. Oxford: Clarendon Press, 1924. 2 vols.

Rev. by Ch. Bastide in *Revue critique,* XCII (1925), 299-300; by G. Binz in *Beiblatt,* XXXVI (1925), 270-74; by L. I. Bredvold in *JEGP,* XXIV (1925), 586-89; by L. Cazamian in *RAA,* II (1925), 441-42; by B. Croce in *Critica,* XXIII (1925), 298-300; by Sir Edmund Gosse in the *Sunday Times,* Feb. 1, 1925; by E. Greenlaw in *MLN,* XLI (1926), 341-44; by H. J. L[aski] in the *Manchester Guardian,* Jan. 29, 1925; by R. M. Lovett in the *New Republic,* May 6, 1925, pp. 295-96; by R. B. McKerrow in the *Library,* 4th series, VI (1925), 109-11; by G. C. Moore-Smith in *MLR,* XX (1925), 474-76; by C. M. Perry in *International journal of ethics,* XXXVI (1926), 431-35; by A. W. Reed in *RES,* I (1925), 366-70; by J. M. Robertson in the *Literary guide,* April 1925, pp. 73-74; by S. P. Sherman in the *New York Herald-Tribune Books,* March 29, 1925.

After all the notice which this edition has received, it is unnecessary to dwell upon the contribution which it makes to our understanding of an important and undeservedly neglected writer. Two points, however, seem to me to have been given insufficient attention. One of these is the value of Kaye's introduction and notes for students whose interest is not primarily in Mandeville but in the general movement of ideas in the seventeenth and early eighteenth centuries. In calling attention to the current of moral and psychological analysis to which he gives, not altogether happily perhaps, the name of "anti-rationalism," Kaye has done pioneer work of the highest importance for the interpretation of this period. Thanks to his researches, a whole series of new studies is made possible on such writers as Butler, Dryden, Rochester, Wycherley, Steele, Swift, Pope, and Fielding, the general result of which should be to give us a fresh insight into an aspect of the eighteenth century which has been largely obscured hitherto by exaggerated assumptions concerning the predominance of rationalism in the classic age.

The other point is one of method. It is clear that Kaye has learned much from the brilliant school of historical editing which has arisen in France in recent years as a result of the example and stimulus of Lanson; it is clear also that he has profited from the active discussion of "bibliographical" methods which has been going on in England under the leadership of McKerrow, Chapman, and others. His edition deserves to take its place among the most distinguished products of these two schools. Nor is this all. In his chapter on Mandeville's "Background" (I, lxxvii-cxiii), he has given us one of the best models we have of a type of study which is bound to be increasingly prominent in future work on this period, and in his attempt (I, cxiv-cxlvi) to measure Mandeville's influence on later thought, he has treated a difficult and perhaps impossible subject with a prudence and ingenuity which cannot but be instructive.

Rogers, A. K. "The ethics of Mandeville." *International journal of ethics,* XXXVI (1925), 1-17.

A sympathetic, intelligent, and well-written interpretation, which can be read with profit even after Kaye's Introduction. Its weakness is its neglect of Mandeville's predecessors.

William Mason

Draper, John W. *William Mason: a study in eighteenth-century culture.* New York: New York University Press, 1924.

Rev. by B. V. Crawford in *PQ,* IV (1925), 382; by Roger Martin in *RAA,* III (1925), 75-77; by G. C. Moore-Smith in *MLR,* XX (1925), 476-78; by Edith J. Morley in *RES,* I (1925), 497-98; in *TLS,* March 12, 1925, p. 168.

Lady Mary Wortley Montagu

Melville, Lewis [pseud. for Lewis Benjamin]. *Lady Mary Wortley Montagu: her life and letters.* Boston: Houghton Mifflin, 1925.

Rev. by P. Dottin in *RAA,* III (1926), 445-46.

Henry More

The Philosophical writings of Henry More. Edited with an introduction and notes by Flora Isabel Mackinnon. New York: Oxford University Press, American Branch, 1925.

Rev. by S. P. Lamprecht in the *Journal of philosophy,* XXIII (1926), 158-60.

Nicolson, Marjorie H. "The spirit world of Milton and More." *SP,* XXII (1925), 433-52.

The Earl of Orrery

Flood, W. H. Grattan [with comment by F. W. Payne]. "Orrery's *Black Prince.*" *RES,* I (1925), 341-43.

Payne, F. W. "The question of precedence between Dryden and the Earl of Orrery with regard to the English heroic play." *RES,* I (1925), 173-81.

Thomas Otway

Ham, Roswell G. "The portraits of Thomas Otway." *N & Q,* CXLIX (1925), 111-13.

Ham, Roswell G. "Thomas Otway, Rochester, and Mrs. Barry." *N & Q,* CXLIX (1925), 165-67.

Robert Paltock

The Life and adventures of Peter Wilkins. London: Dulau, 1925.

Rev. in *TLS,* May 7, 1925, p. 312.

Skinner, A. J. P. "The author of 'Peter Wilkins.'" *TLS,* May 14, 1925, p. 335.

Samuel Pepys

Dubreton, J. Lucas. *Samuel Pepys, a portrait in miniature.* New York: G. P. Putnam's sons, 1925.

Shipley, A. E. "Mr. Pepys as a man of science and President of the Royal Society." *Quarterly review,* CCXLV (1925), 219-37.

Tanner, J. R. *Mr. Pepys: an introduction to the Diary, together with a sketch of his later life.* London: G. Bell and sons, 1925.

Rev. by W. C. Abbott in *SRL,* Oct. 3, 1925, p. 172; by W. Fischer in *Beiblatt,* XXXVI (1925), 336-37; by G. Nigot in *RAA,* III (1925), 144-47. Probably the best short study of Pepys yet published.

Hester Lynch Piozzi

Anecdotes of the late Samuel Johnson, LL.D., during the last twenty years of his life. Edited by S. C. Roberts. Cambridge: University Press, 1925.

Rev. by R. W. Chapman in *RES,* I (1925), 372-73.

Piozzi marginalia, comprising some extracts from the manuscripts of Hester Lynch Piozzi and annotations from her books. Cambridge [Mass.]: Harvard University Press, 1925.

Rev. by R. W. Chapman in *RES,* II (1926), 356; by R. D. Havens in *MLN,* XLI (1926), 212.

Alexander Pope

Case, Arthur E. "The new poems by Pope." *London mercury,* XI (1925), 411-12.

Hillhouse, J. T. "Teresa Blount and 'Alexis.'" *MLN,* XL (1925), 88-91.

Shows, on the basis of an examination of the correspondence at Mapledurham, that the "Alexis" who corresponded with Teresa and Martha Blount in 1713 was not, as certain students of Pope have supposed, James Moore-Smythe, who was eleven years old in 1713, but one of the Moores of Fawley Court in Berkshire near Mapledurham. The importance of the letters as an explanation of Pope's later animosity to Moore-Smythe is thus destroyed.

Sherburn, George. [Review of R. H. Griffith, *Alexander Pope, a bibliography.*] *MP,* XXII (1925), 327-36.

Many additional items.

Strachey, Lytton. *Pope.* The Leslie Stephen lecture for 1925. Cambridge: University Press, 1925.

Rev. by A. Digeon in *RAA,* III (1925), 154; by A. W. Reed in *RES,* II (1926), 113-14.

Matthew Prior

Chapman, R. W. "A poem attributed to Prior." *RES,* I (1925), 92-93.

Concerns *An epistle from the Elector of Bavaria to the French King* (1706), which, on the basis of manuscript notes in an eighteenth-century copy, is attributed to one Stephen Clay.

Doughty, Oswald. "The poet of the 'familiar style.'" *English studies,* VII (1925), 5-10.

Firth, C. H. "Two poems attributed to Prior." *RES,* I (1925), 456-58.

The poems, both of which are printed in the Appendix to Waller's edition of Prior (II, 380-84, 408), are *A fable of a widow and her cat,* 1712 (three stanzas of which Firth shows are by Swift) and *When the cat's away the mice may play,* 1712 (a Whig piece and so certainly not by Prior).

Williams, Iolo A. [A note on Prior and Philip Ayres.] *London mercury,* XI (1925), 525-26.

Ann Radcliffe

Thompson, L. F. "Ann Radcliffe's knowledge of German." *MLR,* XX (1925), 190-91.

Samuel Richardson

Nairn, J. A. "Samuel Richardson and the Merchant Taylor's school." *N & Q,* CXLIX (1925), 421.

Price, Lawrence Marsden. "Richardson in the moral weeklies of Germany." *University of Wisconsin studies in language and literature,* No. 22 (1925), pp. 169-83.

Thomas Russell (see *Cuthbert Shaw*)

Thomas Shadwell

Walmsley, D. M. "New light on Thomas Shadwell." *TLS,* April 16, 1925, p. 268.

Cf. *ibid.,* May 7, 1925, p. 316 (Montague Summers); May 14, p. 335 (D. M. Walmsley); May 21, 1925, p. 352 (Montague Summers).

Walmsley, D. M. "Two songs ascribed to Thomas Shadwell." *RES,* I (1925), 350-52.

Cuthbert Shaw

The Poems of Cuthbert Shaw and Thomas Russell. Edited by Eric Partridge. London: Dulau, 1925.

Rev. by L. Cazamian in *RAA,* III (1926), 450; by R. D. Havens in *MLN,* XL (1925), 443; by I. A. Williams in *London mercury,* XII (1925), 640; in *TLS,* July 16, 1925, p. 476.

Williams, Iolo A. [Cuthbert Shaw's *The four farthing candles,* 1762.] *London mercury,* XII (1925), 640-42.

Description of a rare copy, unknown to Partridge, of Shaw's poetical attack on Churchill, Lloyd, Colman, and Shirley.

R. B. Sheridan

Rhodes, R. Crompton. "The early editions of Sheridan." *TLS,* Sept. 17, 24, 1925.

On the *Duenna* and the *School for scandal.*

Roberts, W. "Sheridan's *School for scandal.*" *TLS,* Oct. 15, 1925, p. 675.

On a surreptitious Dublin edition of 1786.

Adam Smith

Benians, E. A. "Adam Smith's project of an empire." *Cambridge historical journal,* I (1925), 248-83.

Davenport, H. J. and Glenn R. Morrow. "The ethics of the *Wealth of nations.*" *Philosophical review,* XXXIV (1925), 599-611.

Tobias George Smollett

The Expedition of Humphry Clinker. London: Humphrey Milford, Oxford University Press, [1925]. ("The World's Classics.")

The Expedition of Humphry Clinker. Oxford: Blackwell, 1925. 2 vols. ("The Shakespeare Head edition of Smollett's novels," Vols, I and II.)

Based on the text of the two issues of the second edition of 1771, with occasional corrections from other editions.

The Works of Tobias Smollett. Edited by George Saintsbury. London: Navarre Society, 1925. 12 vols.

A reprint of an edition first issued in 1895.

Buck, Howard Swazey. *A study in Smollett, chiefly "Peregrine Pickle," with a complete collation of the first and second editions.* New Haven: Yale University Press, 1925.

Rev. by E. A. Baker in *RES,* II (1926), 360-63.

This study covers a well defined area of Smollett's life and work with admirable acuteness and thoroughness. Taking *Peregrine Pickle* as a starting-point, Buck brings to light again the fact that the revision for the second edition was made not in 1751 but in 1758, probably as a result of Smollett's reconciliation with Garrick. It should have been added that the author of an article on Smollett in the *Quarterly* (CIII [1858], 68-108) had already used a copy of the second edition and quoted from the Advertisement, though he erroneously implied that the date of the revision was 1757. This evidence, however, passed unnoticed, and Buck has made the point his own by working out the artistic and personal significance of Smollett's revisions. Chapter ii examines the scanty evidence concerning the interpolated "Memoirs of a lady of quality": Smollett, it appears, made the acquaintance of Lady Vane through a common friend, Daniel Mackercher, and was perhaps paid to insert her story in his novel; the lady herself seems to have written the "Memoirs," which were slightly revised by Shebbeare and by Smollett himself. Chapter iii studies the quarrels arising from the *Regicide,* and rewrites important parts of Smollett's life from 1740 to about 1760, by giving a closely knit statement of Smollett's relations with Fleetwood, Lacy, Quin, Garrick, Rich, Chesterfield, Lyttleton, and Fielding. The most striking results here are the convincing argument that Smollett returned from Jamaica about the end of 1742; the account of Quin's part in the rejection of the *Regicide* at Covent Garden; the analysis of Smollett's attacks on Garrick; the proof that Chesterfield, not Lyttleton, was the first patron of Smollett's play; and the demonstration that the feud with Fielding developed from the feud with Lyttleton. Buck's terse and vigorous style controls the material logically without obscuring the broad human interest of his subject. It is not too much to say that his book marks a new period in the study of an author whom modern scholarship his hitherto neglected.—A.D.McK.

"Tobias Smollett." *TLS,* Nov. 19, 1925, pp. 761-62.

Whitridge, Arnold. *Tobias Smollett: a study of his miscellaneous works.* Published by the author, [1925].

This monograph, the Introduction tells us, is a *Vorarbeit* for an extended critical biography of Smollett. It touches on the whole field of Smollett's life and writings exclusive of the novels, and gives an agreeably written but cursory survey of his work in poetry, history, drama, journalism, political controversy, and satire. Only in slight detail does it modify the available biographies and studies. A closer analysis of Smollett's relations with his contemporaries and his manifold literary activities will have to be made before the biography can be profitably rewritten. For example, Miss Tupper's article (*PMLA*, XXXIX [1924], 325-42) on the "Belles lettres" papers in the *British magazine*, disproving Goldsmith's authorship and (though not so convincingly) claiming the essays for Smollett, probably appeared too late to be used by Whitridge, but supersedes his discussion of the *British magazine* (p. 54). Buck's work on the revision of *Peregrine Pickle* makes Whitridge's comments on Smollett's personal feuds inadequate. Interesting clues are suggested and then dropped: thus the letters from Smollett to Richardson, briefly noted on p. 48, might have been analyzed for the light they throw on Smollett's methods as a hack-writer. The analysis of the political satire in the *History and adventures of an atom* is valuable, but must be supplemented by the newly compiled key in the Shakespeare Head edition of Smollett's novels (Oxford, 1926). The accounts of obscure pamphlets, such as Shebbeare's *Occasional critic* and the anonymous *Battle of the reviews*, will be of considerable help to the student. There is no index! —A.D.McK.

Laurence Sterne

Cross, Wilbur L. *The life and times of Laurence Sterne.* A new edition. New Haven: Yale University Press; London: Humphrey Milford, Oxford University Press, 1925. 2 vols.

Rev. by J. M. Turnbull in *RES*, II (1926), 356-60.

The first edition of this excellent biography appeared in 1909. In reissuing it now the author has subjected his text to a considerable revision in the light of recent discoveries, and has incorporated a good deal of new material, including a complete transcript of Sterne's Letter Book from the manuscript in the Morgan Library. Students of Sterne will be especially grateful for the admirable bibliography of Sterne's published works and manuscripts which closes the second volume.

DeFroe, A. *Laurence Sterne and his novels studied in the light of modern psychology.* Groningen: P. Noordhoff, 1925.

Rev. by L. Cazamian in *RAA*, III (1926), 448-50; by B. Fehr in *Beiblatt*, XXXVI (1925), 289-94.

In seven chapters DeFroe studies "The instinctive basis of Sterne's mental constitution," "The working of the instincts on the imaginative plane," "Sterne's temper," "Sterne and religion," "The sentiments," "Pathological phenomena," and "Sterne's psyche as revealed in the novels." His method involves principally an application to Sterne of the analysis of instinct developed by MacDougall in his *Outline of psychology.* He is not unaware, however, of psycho-analysis, and in Chapter ii he makes somewhat free use, on certain points, of Elinor Glyn's *Philosophy of love!* As might be expected from this list of authorities, the result is a rather crude piece of work, the chief value of which lies in the abundance of psychologically significant texts which it brings conveniently together. There can be no question that Sterne lends himself in an unusual measure to psychological analysis, and DeFroe deserves our gratitude for directing attention to the possibilities of the subject. But a more subtle technique than his is necessary, and surely in such matters MacDougall is not the safest guide.

Fluchère, Henri. "Sterne documents." *TLS*, Feb. 12, 1925, p. 104.

Announces that he is engaged on a new study of Sterne.

Matthew Stevenson

T[horn]-D[rury], G. "Matthew Stevenson." *RES*, I (1925), 95.

Supplements and corrects the article in the *D.N.B.*

Jonathan Swift

Swift's Journal to Stella. Newly deciphered and edited by J. K. Moorhead. London: J. M. Dent; New York: E. P. Dutton, [1925]. ("Everyman's Library.")

Goulding, Sybil. *Swift en France.* Paris: Champion, 1924.

Rev. by E. Pons in *RAA,* II (1925), 348-50; by J. G. Robertson in *MLR,* XX (1925), 93; by G. Rudler in the *French quarterly,* VIII (1926), 69-70; by A. Thibaudet in the *London mercury,* XI (1925), 532-34.

Gückel, W. and E. Günther. *D. Defoes und J. Swifts Belesenheit und literarische Kritik.* Leipzig: Meyer & Müller, 1925.

Much more nearly complete for Swift than for Defoe. A partial checking, however, reveals a number of errors and omissions. P. 96: The *Dialogues des morts* which Swift read in 1697 were Fontenelle's and not Fénelon's (the latter's collection did not begin to appear until 1699). P. 96: Reference should have been made here to another French work which Swift includes in his list of reading for 1697—"Œvres Melées 5 Vol.:" (see *A Tale of a tub,* ed. Guthkelch and Nichol Smith [Oxford, 1920], p. liv). This may be almost certainly identified as the *Œuvres meslées de Mr. De Saint-Evremont* (Paris: Claude Barbin, 1697). P. 97: It should not be asserted positively that the phrase "The moderns were much the more ancient of the two" came from Fontenelle's *Entretiens*: the idea was a commonplace throughout the seventeenth century.—The compilers refer to a number of modern studies of Swift's sources, but they seem to be ignorant of W. A. Eddy's *Gulliver's Travels, a critical study* (Princeton, 1923), which would have enabled them to add several items to their list, notably D'Ablancourt's continuation of Lucian and the works of Tom Brown.

James, M. R. "Swift's copy of Dampier." *TLS,* Feb. 26, 1925, p. 138.

Pons, Émile. *Swift: les années de jeunesse et le "Conte du tonneau."* Strasbourg: Istra; London: Humphrey Milford, Oxford University Press, 1925.

Rev. by L. Cazamian in *RAA,* III (1925), 68-70; by R. S. C[rane] in *MP,* XXIII (1925), 232-33; by P. Dottin in *RELV,* XLII (1925), 361-62 (cf. *ibid.,* XLII, 298-307); by A. Koszul in *Les langues modernes,* XXIII (1925), 563-68; by Harold Williams in *RES,* I (1925), 487-92; in *RLC,* V (1925), 541-42.

"Swift's Journal to Stella." *TLS,* Sept. 24, 1925, pp. 605-06.

Williams, Harold. "The Motte editions of *Gulliver's Travels.*" *Library,* 4th series, VI (1925), 229-63.

James Thomson

Hirsch, André. "James Thomson: ses traducteurs et ses critiques en France." *RELV,* XLII (1925), 66-75, 105-12, 160-72.

Marcus, Hans. "Die Entstehung von 'Rule Britannia.' Ein Beitrag zur Psychologie der Engländer." *Beiblatt,* XXXVI (1925), 21-32, 54-64, 78-89, 155-59.

Rev. by Karl Brunner in *Archiv,* CXLIX (1925), 120-21.

Horace Walpole

Reminiscences written in 1788 for the amusement of Miss Mary and Miss Agnes Berry. Now printed in full from the original manuscript, with notes and index by Paget Toynbee. London: Humphrey Milford, Oxford University Press, 1924.

Rev. in *EHR,* XL (1925), 637. Cf. Toynbee's note in *TLS,* Aug. 20, 1925, p. 545.

Pottle, Frederick A. "The part played by Horace Walpole in the quarrel between Rousseau and Hume." *PQ,* IV (1925), 351-63.

William Walsh

Arundell, Dennis. "*The Gordian knot untied.*" *TLS,* June 4, 1925, p. 384.

Cf. *ibid.,* June 11, 1925, p. 400 (W. J. Lawrence and Felix White); June 18, 1925, p. 416 (Dennis Arundell).

Identification with *Trelooby* by Walsh, Congreve, and Vanbrugh.

Nathaniel Wanley

Martin, L. C. "A forgotten poet of the seventeenth century." *Essays and studies by members of the English Association,* XI (1925), 5-31.

Edward Ward

The London spy, compleat in eighteen parts. With an introduction by Ralph Straus. London: The Casanova Society, 1924.

Rev. in *TLS,* Feb. 5, 1925, p. 83.

John Wesley

Henderson, Bernard W. "John Wesley's last university sermon." *Cornhill magazine,* N.S., LVIII (1925), 93-100.

On his sermon at St. Mary's, August 24, 1744.

Simon, John S. *John Wesley and the advance of Methodism.* London: J. Alfred Sharp, 1925.

Rev. in *London quarterly review,* Jan., 1926, p. 127; in *TLS,* Oct. 1, 1925, p. 633.

Covers the years 1747-1756.

Arthur Young

Amery, G. D. *The writings of Arthur Young.* Royal Agricultural Society of England, 1925.

Edward Young

Ibershoff, C. H. "Bodmer and Young." *JEGP,* XXIV (1925), 211-18.

McKillop, Alan D. "Richardson, Young, and the *Conjectures.*" *MP,* XXII (1925), 391-404.

A valuable study of the genesis of the *Conjectures on original composition* in the light of a hitherto neglected Young-Richardson correspondence published in the *Monthly magazine* between 1813 and 1819. McKillop makes clear for the first time the important rôle which Richardson played in the gradual elaboration of the *Conjectures* from 1756 to 1759. P. 403: Young's undated letter (No. CXXVI), quoted in note 3, followed, rather than preceded, Richardson's letter of May 29, 1759 (No. CXLVII), to which it was in part an answer.

IV. STUDIES RELATING TO THE POLITICAL AND SOCIAL ENVIRONMENT

NOTE: In this and the following section I have attempted to list only those publications which seemed especially significant for the historian of English literature.

Beer, Max. *Social struggles and thought (1750-1860).* London: Leonard Parsons, 1925.

Rev. in *TLS,* Aug. 20, 1925, p. 538.
Volume IV of the author's well known *History of socialism.*

Bell, Walter George. *The great plague in London in 1665.* London: John Lane, 1924.

Rev. by J.G.S.C. in the *Dublin review,* CLXXVI (1925), 316-20; by C. L. Kingsford in *EHR,* XL (1925), 435-37; G. E. F. Stammers in *History,* X (1925), 65-66.
Important for students of Defoe.

Blair, D. O. Hunter and others. "James's powders." *N & Q,* CXLVIII (1925), 390-91, 412, 425-26, 448; CXLIX (1925), 11-12.

Bowden, Witt. *Industrial society in England towards the end of the eighteenth century.* New York: Macmillan, 1925.

Rev. by W. T. Laprade in *AHR,* XXX (1925), 808-09.

Brett-James, Norman G. "London traffic in the seventeenth century." *Nineteenth century,* XCVIII (1925), 728-40.

Broxap, Henry. *The later Non-jurors.* Cambridge: University Press, 1925.

Rev. in *TLS,* July 30, 1925, p. 504.

Chancellor, E. Beresford. *London pleasure haunts during four centuries.* London: Constable, 1925.

deCastro, J. Paul. "London coffee-houses in the eighteenth century." *N & Q,* CXLVIII (1925), 426.

On Robin's and the Garter coffee-houses.

Feiling, Keith. *A history of the Tory party, 1640-1714.* Oxford: Clarendon Press, 1924.

Rev. by W. C. Abbott in *AHR,* XXX (1925), 355-56; by Wallace Notestein in *History,* XI (1926), 69-70; by Kenneth Pickthorn in the *London mercury,* XI (1925), 557-59; by G. M. Trevelyan in *EHR,* XL (1925), 132-34.

An important study, which should be known to all students of the literary history of the period.

Feiling, Keith and F. R. D. Needham. "The journals of Edmund Warcup, 1676-84." *EHR,* XL (1925), 235-60.

New light on the activities of Shaftesbury.

Fordham, Sir Herbert George. *John Cary, engraver, map, chart, and print seller and globe-maker, 1754-1835: a bibliography with an introduction and biographical notes.* Cambridge: University Press, 1925.

Rev. by S. W. Wooldridge in *RES,* II (1926), 367-68.

Fordham, Sir Herbert George. "John Ogilby (1600-1676): his *Britannia,* and the British itineraries of the eighteenth century." *Library,* 4th series, VI (1925), 157-78.

Fordham, Sir Herbert George. "'Paterson's Roads.' Daniel Paterson, his maps and itineraries, 1738-1825." *Library,* 4th series, V (1925), 333-56.

George, M. Dorothy. *London life in the eighteenth century.* London: Kegan Paul; New York: Knopf, 1925.

Rev. by W. P. Hall in *AHR,* XXXI (1925), 127-28; by J. L. Hammond in the *New Statesman,* Mar. 21, 1925, pp. 693-94; by A. S. Turberville in *History,* X (1926), 345-46.

Deals mainly with life among the poorer classes. An important first-hand study.

Hoskins, H. L. "The overland route to India in the eighteenth century." *History,* IX (1925), 302-18.

Hotson, J. Leslie. "Bear gardens and bear-baiting during the Commonwealth." *PMLA,* XL (1925), 276-88.

Jeudwine, J. W. *Religion, commerce, liberty, 1683-1793.* London: Longmans, Green and co., 1925.

Cf. *TLS,* Nov. 19, 1925, p. 772.

Kelly, Francis M. and Randolph Schwabe. *Historic costume, 1490-1790.* London: Batsford, 1925.

Rev. in *TLS,* Nov. 26, 1925, p. 782.

"Life in the eighteenth century." *TLS,* April 30, 1925, pp. 289-90.

Apropos of books by Witt Bowden and M. Dorothy George.

Machen, Arthur. *The Canning wonder.* London: Chatto and Windus, 1925.

Rev. by A. Digeon in *RAA,* III (1926), 446-47; in *TLS,* Nov. 26, 1925, p. 791.

Magrath, John R. "Oxford in the eighteenth century." *N & Q*, CXLVIII (1925), 263-64.

On certain public exercises required of candidates for the B.A.

Mallet, Sir Charles Edward. *A history of the University of Oxford.* Volume II: *The sixteenth and seventeenth centuries.* London and New York: Longmans, Green and co., 1924.

Rev. by R. B. Merriman in *AHR,* XXXI (1925), 109-11; by C. Oman in *Edinburgh review,* CCXLI (1925), 103-15.

Moffit, Louis W. *England on the eve of the Industrial Revolution: a study of economic and social conditions from 1740 to 1760, with special reference to Lancashire.* London: P. S. King, 1925.

Rev. by Henri Sée in *RH,* CLII (1926), 93-94; in *TLS,* Dec. 10, 1925, pp. 841-42.

Newton, Lady. *Lyme letters, 1660-1760.* London: Heinemann, 1925.

Rev. in *TLS,* Nov. 12, 1925, p. 753.

Parkes, Joan. *Travel in England in the seventeenth century.* London: Humphrey Milford, Oxford University Press, 1925.

Rose, J. Holland. *A short life of William Pitt.* London: Bell, 1925.

Rev. by G. B. H. in *EHR,* XLI (1926), 312.

Sée, Henri. "Le grand commerce maritime et le système colonial dans leurs relations avec l'évolution du capitalisme (du XVIe au XIXe siècle)." *RSH,* XXXIX (1925), 15-35.

Sée, Henri. "L'évolution du capitalisme en Angleterre du XVe siècle au commencement du XIXe." *RSH,* XL (1925), 31-49.

Stokes, Hugh. *Thomas Gainsborough.* London: Philip Allan, 1925.

Rev. in *TLS,* Dec. 3, 1925, p. 836.

The Diary of Thomas Turner, of East Hoathly, 1754-1765. Edited by Florence Maris Turner (Mrs. Charles Lamb). With an introduction by J. B. Priestley. London: John Lane, 1925.

Rev. in *TLS,* Nov. 12, 1925, p. 751.

Contains interesting notes on the reading of a Sussex shopkeeper in the mid-eighteenth century.

Vaucher, Paul. *La crise du Ministère Walpole en 1733-1744.* Paris: Plon-Nourrit, 1924.

Rev. by W. T. Morgan in *AHR,* XXXI (1926), 515-17.

Vaucher, Paul. *Robert Walpole et la politique de Fleury, 1731-1742.* Paris: Plon-Nourrit, 1924.

Rev. by Richard Lodge in *EHR*, XL (1925), 438-41; by W. T. Morgan in *AHR*, XXXI (1926), 515-17; by Eugène Welvert in *Revue critique*, XCII (1925), 413-15; in *TLS*, July 2, 1925, p. 439.

Verney, Frances Parthenope and Margaret M. *Memoirs of the Verney family during the seventeenth century.* 3rd edition. London: Longmans, Green and co., 1925.

Rev. by W. C. Abbott in *AHR*, XXXI (1925), 571-72.

Wainewright, J. B. "Suicides in England, XVIII century." *N & Q*, CXLVIII (1925), 87.

V. STUDIES RELATING TO THE CONTINENTAL BACKGROUND

Ascoli, Georges. "Le 'Misanthrope' de Molière et la sagesse libertine." *Revue universitaire*, XXXIV (1925), 229-34.

Ascoli, Georges. "Revue de quelques ouvrages récents relatifs à la littérature française." *RSH*, XXXIX (1925), 127-64.

An important review. Pp. 144-55 deal with works on the eighteenth century.

Ascoli, Georges. "Voltaire." *RCC*, XXV[1] (1923-24), 673-87; XXV[2] (1924), 16-27, 128-44, 275-87, 302-15, 417-28, 616-30; XXVI[1] (1924-25), 262-73, 501-14, 703-21; XXVI[2] (1925), 153-67, 373-84, 619-39.

This series of articles constitutes a thorough, an intelligent, and an impartial study of Voltaire's life and work. Without adding much that can exactly be called new, it represents a sound and very valuable *mise au point* of the old. Special attention should be paid to the first two articles, "Les années de formation" and "L'état d'esprit philosophique de Voltaire avant le séjour en Angleterre." In order to determine Voltaire's thought before the English journey of 1726 and in that way to be able to estimate more accurately the extent of the English influence upon him, Ascoli has studied carefully Voltaire's early poems, the 1723 edition of *La Ligue* (later *La Henriade*), and *Le pour et le contre* (known also as *L'Epître à Julie* and *L'Epître à Uranie*). In regard to the English influence, without attempting a detailed study of the relation of individual authors to Voltaire's thought, Ascoli takes a sane position about mid-way between the two extremes of Morley on the one hand and of Brunetière on the other. Since the earliest extant text of *Le pour et le contre* dates, however, from as late as 1738, or at the very earliest from 1732, conclusions based upon it regarding Voltaire's theology before 1726 must remain strictly hypothetical. Ascoli's appreciations of Voltaire's "Œuvre poétique" and particularly of "L'art du conteur" are also especially worthy of note in a series of which *tout est à lire.* —G. R. H.

Atkinson, Geoffrey. *Les relations de voyages du XVIIe siècle et l'évolution des idées: contribution à l'étude de la formation de l'esprit du XVIIIe siècle.* Paris: Champion, 1925.

Rev. by G. Ascoli in *RSH*, XXXIX (1925), 144-46; by P. Dottin in *RAA*, III (1926), 443-44; by A. H. Nethercot in *MP*, XXIII (1925), 242-43; in *TLS*, Nov. 5, 1925, p. 732.

This interesting little book is a by-product of its author's recent investigations in the history of the "extraordinary voyage" in French literature of the seventeenth and early eighteenth centuries. Atkinson has extracted from the "real" travel narratives of the seventeenth century a considerable number of texts in which it is possible to see anticipations of eighteenth-century thought on such matters as the "noble savage," the "philosophical Chinese," political liberalism, Deism, relativism, the idea of progress, and the like. His range of documentation is not very great, and a good many of the sources he uses had already been exploited, from a similar point of view, by Chinard and others. But it is useful to have the question treated as a whole, and Atkinson's volume, commendably modest in its pretensions but intelligently conceived and written, can be read with profit by all students of the eighteenth century. A parallel study of English travel literature during the same period is in preparation.

Bellessort, André. *Essai sur Voltaire. Cours professé à la société des conférences.* Paris: Perrin, 1925.

Rev. by Henri Sée in *RH,* CLI (1926), 266.

Bira, C. *La croyance à la magie au XVIIIe siècle en France, dans les contes, romans et traités.* Paris: J. Gamber, 1925.

Brou, A. *Le dix-huitième siècle littéraire.* II: *L'Encyclopédie; Voltaire.* Paris: P. Téqui, 1925.

Published with the authorization of the Archbishop of Paris.

Busnelli, M. D. *Diderot et l'Italie: reflets de vie et de culture italienne dans la pensée de Diderot.* Paris: Champion, 1925.

Rev. in *TLS,* Dec. 3, 1925, p. 822.

Cazenave, Jean. "Le roman hispano-mauresque en France." *RLC,* V (1925), 594-640.

Cf. *ibid.,* V, 239-45.

Cohen, Gustave. "Le séjour de Saint-Évremond en Hollande (1665-1670)." *RLC,* V (1925), 431-54.

The first of what promises to be an important series of articles.

Crump, P. E. "The theme of solitude: an aspect of the 'sentiment de la nature' in the seventeenth century." *French quarterly,* VII (1925), 158-69.

Descartes, René. *Discours de la méthode.* Texte et commentaire par Étienne Gilson. Paris: Librairie philosophique, J. Vrin, 1925.

On the method of this edition see the *Bulletin de la société française de philosophie,* XXIV (1924), 135-50.

Dijkshoorn, J. A. *L'influence française dans les mœurs et les salons des Provinces-Unies.* Paris: Louis Arnette, 1925.

Dufour, Théophile. *Recherches bibliographiques sur les œuvres imprimées de J.-J. Rousseau, suivies de l'inventaire des papiers de Neufchâtel.* Avec une introduction de P.P.Plan. Paris: Giraud-Badin, 1925. 2 vols.

Rev. by H. Buffenoir in *Revue critique,* XCII (1925), 407-08.
A fundamental work.

Evans, D. O. "Un problème d'histoire littéraire: l'évolution du théâtre social en France de 1750 à 1850." *RSH,* XXXIX (1925), 51-63.

Faÿ, Bernard. *L'esprit révolutionnaire en France et aux États-Unis à la fin du XVIIIe siècle.* Paris: Champion, 1925.

Rev. by A. Aulard in *La Révolution française,* LXXVIII (1925), 83-85; by Carl Becker in *AHR,* XXX (1925), 810-12; by C. Cestre in *RAA,* II (1925), 370-73.

This is an exhaustive study of the current of ideas in eighteenth-century France and America in the period 1770-1800. Faÿ divides these thirty years into five epochs: (1) 1770-1775, a period of religious revival and social optimism; (2) 1775-1782, the formation of the Franco-American alliance; (3) 1783-1789, the discovery of America by French radicals and *philosophes*; (4) 1789-1794, democratic movements in both countries; and (5) 1795-1800, *le grand schisme,* caused by a conservative reaction in the United States and by Bonapartism abroad. Of these five divisions, the first, third, and fourth are especially distinguished by the presentation of much new material from comparatively inaccessible sources. There is a long bibliography, which needs, however, to be checked, and an analytic summary for each chapter. The work is basic for the history of eighteenth-century ideas.

Certain defects appear. Although Faÿ cites his sources with reasonable care, there are many errata not noticed on pp. 377-78, so that the book must be constantly checked. Since he fails to take into account the service of French manners in spreading ideas before 1770, he over-estimates the American hostility to France. His most serious defect is a willingness to generalize from insufficient instances, a characteristic which leads him to see movements and tendencies as more sharply developed than they really were. Moreover, he does not define the varying milieus, French and American, in which particular ideas were potent. No work in the field of Franco-American relationship has appeared, however, comparable in organization or thoroughness to this one; and there are few which treat so lucidly of the political and social ideas of the pre-Revolutionary period in France, and consequently in Europe. —H. M. J.

Folkierski, W. *Entre le classicisme et le romantisme: étude sur l'esthétique et les esthéticiens du XVIIIe siècle.* Paris: Champion, 1925.

Fransen, J. *Les comédiens français en Hollande au XVIIe et au XVIIIe siècles.* Paris: Champion, 1925.

Funk, Philipp. *Von der Aufklärung zur Romantik: Studien zur Vorgeschichte der münchener Romantik.* Munich: Kösel & Pustet, 1925.

Gilman, Margaret. *Othello in France.* Paris: Champion, 1925.

Rev. by J. Derocquigny in *RAA,* III (1926), 340-43.

Giraud, Victor. *Le Christianisme de Chateaubriand.* I. *Les origines.* Paris: Hachette, 1925.

Rev. by Marc Citoleux in *Revue critique,* XCII (1925), 391-93.
A study of the history of religious ideas in France from the seventeenth century to Chateaubriand.

Giraud, Victor. "Les étapes du XVIIIe siècle." *Revue des deux mondes,* July 15, 1924, pp. 344-75 ("Du 'Dictionnaire' de Bayle à l'"Encyclopédie' "); October 15, 1924, pp. 882-917 ("Voltaire et les Encyclopédistes"); November 15, 1924, pp. 393-426 ("Jean-Jacques Rousseau et son école"); January 1, 1925, pp. 79-114 ("La Révolution française et les idées religieuses").

Green, F. C. "Further evidence of realism in the French novel of the eighteenth century." *MLN,* XL (1925), 257-70.

Supplementary to the author's article in *MLN,* XXXVIII (1923), 321-29.

Green, F. C. "Montesquieu the novelist and some imitations of the 'Lettres persanes.'" *MLR,* XX (1925), 32-42.

Haines, C. M. *Shakespeare in France: criticism, Voltaire to Victor Hugo.* London: Humphrey Milford, Oxford University Press, 1925.

Rev. by A. W. Reed in *RES,* II (1926), 109-11; in *Library,* 4th series, VI (1925), 194-95.

Havens, George R. "The nature doctrine of Voltaire." *PMLA,* XL (1925), 852-62.

Havens, George R. "La théorie de la bonté naturelle de l'homme chez J.-J. Rousseau." *RHL,* XXXI (1924), 629-42; XXXII (1925), 24-37, 212-25.

An important series of articles, which should be read by all students of the history of ideas in the eighteenth century.

Havens, George R. *Selections from Voltaire, with explanatory comment upon his life and works.* New York and London: Century co., 1925.

An excellent volume of selections. For the English reader there is no better introduction to the subject.

Hubert, René. *Les sciences sociales dans l'Encyclopédie: la philosophie de l'histoire et le problème des origines sociales.* Paris: Alcan, 1925.

Rev. by G. Ascoli in *RSH,* XXXIX (1925), 152-53; by R. Lenoir, *ibid.,* pp. 113-25.

Hunter, Alfred C. *J. B. A. Suard: un introducteur de la littérature anglaise en France.* Paris: Champion, 1925.

Rev. by P. Van Tieghem in *RSH,* XL (1925), 134-35.

Inklaar, D. *Baculard d'Arnaud, ses imitateurs en Hollande et dans d'autres pays.* The Hague: Smits; Paris: Champion, 1925.

Jan, Eduard von. "Der französische Freimaurerroman im 18. Jahrhundert." *GRM*, XIII (1925), 391-403.

Mainly concerned with Ramsay's *Les voyages de Cyrus* (1728) and Terrasson's *Sethos* (1731).

Jones, Howard Mumford. "Albrecht von Haller and English philosophy." *PMLA*, XL (1925), 103-27.

Important especially for the influence of Newton and Shaftesbury on the continent.

Köster, Albert. *Die deutsche Literatur der Aufklärungsarbeit. Fünf Kapitel aus der Literaturgeschichte des 18. Jahrhunderts mit einem Anhang: Die allgemeinen Tendenzen der Geniebewegung.* Heidelberg: Winter, 1925.

Rev. by A. Ludwig in *Archiv*, CXLIX (1925), 91-94; by J. G. Robertson in *Litteris*, II (1925), 161-62.

Lachèvre, Frédéric. *Le libertinage au XVIIe siècle: les derniers libertins.* Paris: Champion, 1925.

Rev. in *TLS*, Oct. 22, 1925, p. 690.

Lanson, G. *Notes pour servir à l'étude des chapitres 35-39 du "Siècle de Louis XIV" de Voltaire.* Paris: Istra; London: Humphrey Milford, 1924. Reprinted from *Mélanges de littérature et de philologie germaniques offerts à Charles Andler.*

Rev. by G. Rudler in *French quarterly*, VIII (1926), 70-71.

Lanson, R. "Le Moyen âge dans l'art français du XVIIIe siècle." *Bulletin de la société d'histoire moderne*, Feb. 1, 1925.

Legouis, Émile. *G. G. de Beaurieu et son "Elève de la nature," 1763.* Oxford: Clarendon Press, 1925. ("The Taylorian lecture," 1925.)

Rev. by G. Rudler in *French quarterly*, VIII (1926), 74.

Lods, Adolphe and Paul Alphandéry. *Jean Astruc et la critique biblique au XVIIIe siècle.* Paris: Istra, 1924.

An important monograph.

McMahon, Sister Mary Catherine. *Aesthetics and art in the "Astrée" of Honoré d'Urfé.* Washington, 1925.

A Catholic University dissertation.

Magendie, M. *La politesse mondaine et les théories de l'honnêteté en France au XVIIe siècle, de 1600 à 1660.* Paris: Alcan, 1925.

Rev. by J. E. Spingarn in *Romanic review*, XVII (1926), 71-73.

Martin, Gaston. *La franc-maçonnerie et la préparation de la*

Révolution de 1789 en France et spécialement en Bretagne. Toulouse: Falandry, 1925.

Rev. by Henri Sée in *RH,* CXLIX (1925), 263.

Martin, S. G. "Kant as a student of natural science." *Monist,* XXXV (1925), 248-58.

Maugain, Gabriel. [Review of J. G. Robertson, *Studies in the genesis of romantic theory.*] *RLC,* V (1925), 522-29.

Valuable remarks on the attitude toward the "rules" and on conceptions of "taste" and "verisimilitude" in seventeenth-century France and Italy.

"Divers propos du Chevalier de Méré en 1674-1675." Edited by Ch.-H. Boudhors. *RHL,* XXXII (1925), 68-78, 432-56.

Meyer, Eugène. "Diderot moraliste." *RCC,* XXVI[1] (1924-25), 375-81, 469-80, 641-49; XXVI[2] (1925), 521-37, 742-60.

Micard, Étienne. *Antoine Léonard Thomas (1732-1785).* Paris: Champion, 1925.

Rev. in *TLS,* Sept. 10, 1925, p. 580.

Monglond, A. *Vies préromantiques.* Paris: Belles-lettres, 1925.

Murris, R. *La Hollande et les Hollandais au XVIIe et au XVIIIe siècles vus par les français.* Paris: Champion, 1925.

Rice, Richard Ashley. "Rousseau and the poetry of nature in eighteenth-century France." *Smith College studies in modern languages,* Vol. VI, Nos. 3 and 4, April and July, 1925.

Rousseau, J. J. *Correspondence générale de J.-J. Rousseau.* Collationnée sur les originaux, annotée et commentée par Théophile Dufour et publiée par P.-P. Plan. Tomes I-IV. Paris: A. Colin, 1924-25.

Rev. by H. Buffenoir in *Revue critique,* XCII (1925), 245-46, 406-07; by L. Roustan, *ibid.,* XCII (1925), 47-49, 123-24; by A. Schinz in *New York Times Book review,* Jan. 11, 1925, p. 18; in *TLS,* Jan. 29, 1925, p. 64. Cf. A. Schinz in *MP,* XXIII (1925), 167-73.

Rousseau, J. J. *La nouvelle Héloïse.* Nouvelle édition . . . par Daniel Mornet. Paris: Hachette, 1925. 4 vols. ("Les grands écrivains de la France," 2e série.)

Rev. by H. Buffenoir in *Revue critique,* XCII (1925), 429-30; by G. Rudler in *French quarterly,* VIII (1926), 72-74; in *RLC,* VI (1926), 184-85.

An excellent edition, which may be recommended to students of English literature and ideas in the eighteenth century by reason both of the richness of its information and of the maturity and suggestiveness of its method. Of the four volumes, three contain the text and commentary, while the whole of Volume I is devoted to an introductory study of the chief questions raised by Rousseau's novel—the literary and social milieu out of which it sprang, its genesis and composition, the history of its publication (including a bibliographical and critical account of the eighteenth-century editions), and its success and influence in France to the close of the century. The specialist in English literature will regret that Mornet did not extend his researches in Rousseau's background and influence beyond the limits of France (there are, it is true, some excellent pages [I, 93-96] on the influence of Richardson); but all things considered, the Introduction is an extremely valuable and interesting piece of writing, quite the most elaborate and exhaustively documented monograph that has ever been published on an eighteenth-century work of fiction. The commentary in Volumes II-IV is equally deserving of praise. A few examples selected at random will indicate something of its interest for students of eighteenth-century ideas: II, 44-46 (the relation of the good and the beautiful [one misses here a reference to Shaftesbury]), 49-50 (the enthusiasm for ancient history), 130 (the "style marotique"), 154-55 (the "naturalness" of modesty), 190-92 (the question of the duel); III, 145-47 (the attitude toward China); IV, 62-63 (reason in children), 65-66 (Helvétius' doctrine of equality), 103-04 (toleration), 252 (Jansenists and Methodists), 341-42 (truth in art).

Those who have read the articles which Mornet published in the *Revue des cours et conférences* for 1913-14 and 1921-22 will not need to be told that the present edition is a model of careful and self-conscious method. Exception may be taken, it is true, to certain features of the execution: I am not sure, for example, that the best place for a critical-bibliographical discussion of editions is in an Introduction, the point of view of which is primarily historical; and there can be no question that the lack of an index is a grave defect. On the other hand, in dealing with such matters as the relation of the *Nouvelle Héloïse* to its milieu, the difference in the character of its reception by professional men of letters and by the general public (a striking demonstration of the danger of generalizing as to the vogue of a book from the evidence of reviews alone), and the nature and limits of its influence on French fiction, Mornet displays a grasp of the conditions of his problem and an ingenuity in devising new methods of attack which are in the highest degree suggestive.

Schöffler, Herbert. *Das literarische Zürich (1700-1750)*. Leipzig: H. Haessel, 1925.

Rev. by Walther Fischer in *ES*, LX (1926), 363-64.

Schütze, Martin. "The cultural environment of the philosophy of Kant." *Monist*, XXXV (1925), 200-23.

Schütze, Martin. "Herder's psychology." *Monist*, XXXV (1925), 507-54.

Sée, Henri. *L'évolution de la pensée politique au XVIIIe siècle.* Paris: Marcel Giard, 1925.

Rev. by A. Aulard in *La Révolution française*, LXXIX (1926), 70.

Chapters on the origins (Locke and the English influence), on the liberals (Montesquieu, d'Argenson, Voltaire), on the democrats (Rousseau, Diderot), on the reformers (the physiocrats, Helvétius, d'Holbach, Turgot), and on the formation of the revolutionary doctrine (Mably, Condorcet, Raynal, etc.).

Stadler, H. *Paul-Henri Mallet (1730-1807)*. Lausanne: Imprimerie commerciale, 1924.

Rev. in *RLC*, VI (1926), 185.

Strowski, Fortunat. "La philosophie de l'homme dans la littérature française." *RCC*, XXVI^{1} (1924-25), 3-14, 233-42, 395-403, 490-500, 682-94; XXVI^{2} (1925), 13-25, 289-303.

For contents see the following title. A disappointing treatment of an excellent subject.

Strowski, Fortunat. *La sagesse française (Montaigne, St. François de Sales, Descartes, La Rochefoucauld, Pascal).* Paris: Plon-Nourrit, 1925.

Van Roosbroeck, Gustave L. "Persian letters before Montesquieu." *MLR,* XX (1925), 432-42.

New facts on the early history of the "foreign-observer" genre.

Vermeil, M. "La musique de J.-S. Bach et la civilisation allemande au début du XVIIIe siècle." *RCC,* XXVI[1] (1924-25), 108-22, 404-19, 591-605.

Vézinet, F. *Autour de Voltaire, avec quelques inédits.* Paris: Champion, 1925.

Rev. by G. Chinard in *MLN,* XLI (1926), 352; by Henri Sée in *RH,* CLI (1926), 266-67.

1927

ENGLISH LITERATURE OF THE RESTORATION AND EIGHTEENTH CENTURY: A CURRENT BIBLIOGRAPHY

By Ronald S. Crane
University of Chicago

This bibliography undertakes to provide a classified list of the books, articles, and reviews relating to the period 1660-1800 which were published during the year 1926, together with a few bearing a 1925 imprint which came to my attention too late to be included in the bibliography for that year (*PQ,* V, 341-83). Though I have made a serious effort to examine all the more important periodicals and other bibliographical sources significant for this field of study, a selective rather than an exhaustive list has been my aim; I have, for example, excluded most of the purely commercial reprints of eighteenth-century texts now being issued in increasing numbers, especially by English publishers, and I have likewise omitted a good many articles or notes that seemed to me to contain nothing new in the way either of facts or of ideas. Even within these limits, however, I cannot hope that I have not overlooked items that deserved to be included, and I shall be grateful to anyone who will inform me of such oversights. Professors V. B. Heltzel, F. B. Kaye, Baldwin Maxwell, and George Sherburn have contributed the reviews signed with their respective initials.

LIST OF ABBREVIATIONS

AHR=*American historical review.*
Archiv=*Archiv für das Studium der neueren Sprachen und Literaturen.*
Beiblatt=*Beiblatt zur Anglia.*
EHR=*English historical review.*
ES=*Englische Studien.*
GRM=*Germanisch-romanische Monatsschrift.*
JEGP=*Journal of English and Germanic philology.*
LM=*London mercury.*
MLN=*Modern language notes.*
MLR=*Modern language review.*
MP=*Modern philology.*
N&Q=*Notes and queries.*
PMLA=*Publications of the Modern Language Association of America.*
PQ=*Philological quarterly.*
RAA=*Revue anglo-américaine.*
RC=*Revue critique.*
RCC=*Revue des cours et conférences.*

RELV=*Revue de l'enseignement des langues vivantes.*
RES=*Review of English studies.*
RH=*Revue historique.*
RHL=*Revue d'histoire littéraire de la France.*
RLC=*Revue de littérature comparée.*
RSH=*Revue de synthèse historique.*
SP=*Studies in philology.*
SRL=*Saturday review of literature.*
TLS=*Times* [London] *literary supplement.*

I. BIBLIOGRAPHICAL AIDS

Annual bibliography of English language and literature. Volume VI, 1925. Edited for the Modern Humanities Research Association by D. Everett. Cambridge: Bowes & Bowes, 1926.

Baugh, Albert C. "American bibliography for 1925. I. English language and literature." *PMLA,* XLI (1926), 1-23.

See especially pp. 14-18.

Bock, Hellmut. "Die philosophischen Buchveröffentlichungen des englischen Sprachgebietes 1925." *Literarische Berichte aus dem Gebiete der Philosophie* (Erfurt: Kurt Stenger, 1926), pp. 78-93.

"Catalogue of records at Stationers' Hall." *Library,* 4th series, VI (1926), 349-57.

A useful synopsis of the extant records of the Company to the end of the eighteenth century.

Classification of London literature based upon the collection in the Guildhall library. London: The Guildhall library, 1926.

Crane, Ronald S. "English literature of the Restoration and eighteenth century: a current bibliography." *PQ,* V (1926), 341-83.

Halkett, Samuel, and John Laing. *Dictionary of anonymous and pseudonymous English literature.* New and enlarged edition by James Kennedy, W. A. Smith, and A. F. Johnson. Volumes I-II, A-G. London and Edinburgh: Oliver and Boyd, 1926.

To be completed in seven or eight volumes, which will contain between three and four times as many entries as were in the first edition.

Jahresbericht über die Erscheinungen auf dem Gebiete der germanischen Philologie. Berlin: W. de Gruyter, 1926.

Bibliography for 1923.

Morgan, A. E. "Emphasis capitals." *TLS,* Jan. 28, 1926, pp. 62-63.

Light on seventeenth-century usage from a passage in the *Rehearsal.*

Stonehill, Charles A., Andrew Block, and H. W. Stonehill. *Ano-*

nyma and pseudonyma. Part I, A-E. London: C. A. Stonehill, 1926.

Rev. by I. A. Williams in *LM,* XIV (1926), 635-36; in *TLS,* Sept. 9, 1926, p. 600.

Van Tieghem, P. "Principaux ouvrages d'histoire littéraire générale et comparée (dixième compte rendu annuel)." *RSH,* XLII (1926), 121-42.

The Works of Alexander Pope, Dean Swift, Joseph Addison, Sir Richard Steele, Daniel Defoe, Henry Fielding, Samuel Richardson and many other important writers. London: Birrell & Garnett, 1926. Catalogue No. 12.

Contains 796 items.

The Year's work in English studies. Volume V, 1924. Edited for the English Association by F. S. Boas and C. H. Herford. London: Humphrey Milford, Oxford University Press, 1926.

II. STUDIES DEALING WITH CURRENTS OF IDEAS AND TASTE, THE CONDITION OF WRITERS, AND LITERARY FORMS

Baron, Hans. "'Christliches Naturrecht' und 'Ewiges Recht': eine Erwiderung." *Historische Zeitschrift,* CXXXIII (1926), 413-32.

Baskervill, Charles Read. "Play-lists and afterpieces of the mid-eighteenth century." *MP,* XXIII (1926), 445-64.

Bellot, Hugh H. L. "The rule of law." *Quarterly review,* CCXLVI (1926), 346-65.

Suggestive considerations concerning the relation between "natural law" and Parliamentary law in the legal and political thought of the seventeenth and eighteenth centuries.

Black, J. B. *The art of history: a study of four great historians of the eighteenth century.* London: Methuen; New York: F. S. Crofts, 1926.

Rev. by Carl Becker in *AHR,* XXXII (1927), 295-96; by Alice Gardner in *EHR,* XLI (1926), 460-61; by N. Sykes in *History,* XI (1926), 265-66.

"This book," says Black in his preface, "does not profess to be a discussion of eighteenth century historiography in general; its object is specific, viz., to examine sympathetically and critically, the ideas entertained by Voltaire, Hume, Robertson, and Gibbon, with respect to the theory and practice of the historical art." This restriction of aim accounts for the absence of certain features which we should have the right to expect in a more systematic treatment of the subject. Thus neither the conditions which made the eighteenth century a period of active historical writing nor those which explain the characteristic limitations of this writing are anywhere adequately set forth. The Introduction, which undertakes among other things to describe the general intellectual atmosphere in which eighteenth-century historiography developed, is a superficial compilation based mainly upon Leslie Stephen. No account, moreover, is given of the minor historians, and little attempt is made to put the ideas of the major writers clearly and precisely into their setting.

If the reader is interested chiefly in matters like these, he had best leave the book unread. At the same time, within the limits defined in the author's opening statement, the volume deserves much praise. For a modern professional historian, Black has an unusually well developed literary sense: his comparison of Robertson and Prescott (pp. 123-28) and his concluding remarks on the art and style of Gibbon (pp. 173-83) are admirable bits of criticism. He has a sure eye, too, for what is characteristic in the general thinking of his four historians. It would be hard, for example, in the same space, to better his analysis of the relation of Hume's historiography to his theories of knowledge and of politics. Of the four portraits, the best, because the freshest, are those of Hume and Robertson. It was less easy, no doubt, to find anything new to say of either Voltaire or Gibbon, and as a matter of fact in these chapters Black rather suffers by comparison with certain of his recent predecessors, notably Lanson and Fueter. His Voltaire, however, is on the whole an intelligent and discriminating piece of work (if he misses the full significance of the *Lettres philosophiques* in the formation of the theory of history that resulted in the *Essai sur les mœurs,* he at least sins in good company), and his Gibbon, though hardly adequate to the importance of the subject, can nevertheless be read with profit.

Bluestocking letters. Selected, with an introduction, by R. Brimley Johnson. London: John Lane, 1926.

Rev. in *TLS,* Apr. 15, 1926, p. 281.

Selections from the letters of Mrs. Montagu, Mrs. Vesey, Mrs. Boscawen, Mrs. Chapone, and Mrs. Carter.

A Book of English verse satire. Chosen and annotated by A. G. Barnes. London: Methuen, 1926.

Rev. in *TLS,* June 24, 1926, p. 429.

Bradley, L. J. H. "Le Fevre's 'Chymistry.'" *TLS,* July 22, 1926, p. 496.

Comment by David Murray, *ibid.,* Aug. 5, p. 525; by L. J. H. Bradley, *ibid.,* Aug. 12, p. 537.

Bibliographical details of interest to students of the scientific literature of the Restoration.

Bragg, Marion K. *The formal eclogue in eighteenth-century England.* Orono, Maine: University Press, 1926. ("University of Maine studies," 2nd series, No. 6.)

For an American Master's dissertation this monograph shows unusually wide reading and careful formulation of conclusions. One is rather surprised to find no mention of the vogue and influence of Gessner.

Brinton, Crane. *The political ideas of the English romanticists.* London: Humphrey Milford, Oxford University Press, 1926.

Rev. by Agnes Brown in *Economica,* Nov. 1926, pp. 357-59; in *SRL,* Nov. 6, 1926, p. 281; in *TLS,* Aug. 19, 1926, p. 543.

Calverton, V. F. "Social change and the sentimental comedy." *Modern quarterly,* III (1926), 169-88.

Rather crude Marxism.

Campbell, Oscar James, and Paul Mueschke. "'Guilt and sorrow': a study in the genesis of Wordsworth's aesthetic." *MP,* XXIII (1926), 293-306.

Valuable hints for the student of literary ideas in the second half of the eighteenth century.

Child, Harold. "Revivals of English dramatic works, 1919-1925." *RES,* II (1926), 177-88.

Pp. 185-87 list revivals of Restoration and eighteenth-century plays.

Clark, A. F. B. *Boileau and the French classical critics in England (1660-1830).* Paris: Champion, 1925. Cf. *PQ,* V (1926), 345-46.

Rev. by J. G. Robertson in *MLR,* XXI (1926), 324-25; in *TLS,* Jan. 7, 1926, p. 9.

Collins, A. S. "The growth of the reading public during the eighteenth century." *RES,* II (1926), 284-94, 428-38.

The marked increase in the size of the English reading public during the eighteenth century is a phenomenon with which all students of the period are of course familiar. It was an excellent idea, however, to bring together, as Collins has done in this well written article, the principal facts which either illustrate this growth or help to account for it. His method is perhaps a bit too impressionistic for a serious study, and some of his generalizations are certainly excessive. Consider, for example, his opening remarks (p. 284) on the public of Addison's time: "It was confined to London, and mostly to fashionable London. . . . There was no demand for literature from the 'gross, uneducated, untravelled country gentleman,' and the country clergyman's books were limited to the few dusty and long-untouched volumes which he had brought from college and still respected, though past reading them. There was little intellectual life outside London, and there was not much within." Statements like these are not uncommon in books about the eighteenth century, and they have behind them the authority of Macaulay and, more recently, of Beljame; but it is hard to reconcile them with the facts concerning the provincial book-trade given in Plomer's two *Dictionaries,* or with the sales of private libraries recorded in the British Museum *List of catalogues of English book sales,* or—to take a chance example—with such evidence of the intellectual resources of a country town as is contained in *A catalogue of books in the Library at Bedford, the foundation whereof was laid in the year 1700, by the contributions of the clergy and gentry* (London, 1706). That there was an enormous increase in the number of habitual readers between 1700 and 1800 is of course indubitable. Statistics of the growth of periodicals and newspapers—a type of evidence neglected by Collins—put the matter beyond debate (see the "Chronological index" in Crane and Kaye, *A census of British newspapers and periodicals, 1620-1800,* Chapel Hill, N. C., 1927). The point is that the level of development reached by 1700 was much higher than Macaulay or Collins would have us suppose.

Collins, A. S. "Patronage in the days of Johnson." *Nineteenth century,* C (1926), 608-22.

An interesting sketch of the decline of patronage in the eighteenth century, with illustrative details from the careers of Pope, Young, Thomson, Gay, and Johnson. The main points, however, are not new and the basis of fact is rather narrow.

Collins, A. S. "Some aspects of copyright from 1700 to 1780." *Library,* 4th series, VII (1926), 67-81.

A brief analysis of the controversy over perpetual copyright in its bearing upon (1) the relations of "the Trade" to other booksellers, (2) the income of authors, and (3) the growth of the reading public. No account is taken of earlier treatments of the subject; for example, the article of J. W. Draper in *MLN,* XXXVI (1921), 146-54.

Colman, Francis. "Opera register, 1712-34." *The mask,* XII (1926), 110-14.

Cox, Harold. "England's treasure by trade." *Edinburgh review,* CCXLIII (1926), 385-401.

The first few pages deal with seventeenth-century ideas about commerce.

C[rane], R. S. [Review of J. G. Robertson, *Studies in the genesis of romantic theory in the eighteenth century,* Cambridge, 1923.] *MP,* XXIII (1926), 361-63.

Crawford, Bartholow V. "Questions and objections." *PMLA,* XLI (1926), 110-25.

Various forms of this device in the literature of the sixteenth and seventeenth centuries.

Creighton, J. E. "Eighteenth and nineteenth century modes of thought." *Philosophical review,* XXXV (1926), 1-21.

Somewhat stale generalities.

Doughty, Oswald. "The English malady of the eighteenth century." *RES,* II (1926), 257-69.

A collection of passages from writers of the later seventeenth and eighteenth centuries dealing with the "Spleen." As such the article will be useful, but unfortunately it does even less to satisfy our curiosity concerning the significance of the phenomena with which it deals than the mediocre dissertaiton of F. Kalkühler, *Die Natur des Spleens bei den englischen Schriftstellern in der ersten Hälfte des 18. Jahrhunderts* (Leipzig, 1920), which is not mentioned.

Flood, W. H. Grattan. "Early Shakespearean representations in Dublin." *RES,* II (1926), 92-95.

A list of performances extending from 1662 to 1738.

Folkierski, W. *Entre le classicisme et le romantisme: étude sur l'esthétique et les esthéticiens du XVIII*[e] *siècle.* Cracow: Académie polonaise des sciences et des lettres; Paris: Champion, 1925.

Rev. by F. Baldensperger in *RLC,* VI (1926), 368-71; by S. Etienne in *Revue belge de philologie et d'histoire,* V (1926), 583-85; by Abel Lefranc in *RH,* CLIII (1926), 267-68; by J. G. Robertson in *Litteris,* III (1926), 182-84.

This book, which arrived too late to be noticed in the bibliography for 1925, is the work of a professor in the University of Cracow who has also published, in Polish, studies on the aesthetics of Shaftesbury and on the relations between Shaftesbury and Diderot. The specific subject with which it deals is thus defined in the preface: "Le classicisme du grand siècle finissait que le romantisme, même dans son germe, n'était pas né. Entres les deux se trouve une distance ne présentant rien qui puisse ressortir en relief entre les noms éclatants de romantisme et classicisme, ne portant donc point d'appellation historique. Cet intervalle est rempli par la pensée propre du XVIIIe siècle; c'est à celle-ci que nous consacrons cette étude. . . ." The exposition falls into three parts. In the first and longest of these (pp. 5-352), Folkierski attempts to characterize the thought of the eighteenth century before 1770 on such problems as the nature of taste, the definition of the beautiful, the meaning of "imitation of nature," the authority of the ancients and the rules, the relations of poetry and painting, and the theory of literary genres. In the second part (pp. 355-516) he studies the contribution of Diderot to the discussion of these same problems, and in the third part (pp. 519-78), that of Lessing.

It is evident that Folkierski has chosen a subject of the highest interest—a subject, moreover, on which little serious writing of a synthetic sort has hitherto been done. And there can be no doubt that on many point his enquiry has resulted in valuable additions to our knowledge. His chapters on Diderot are particularly fresh; they constitute, in fact, the first comprehensive study of the aesthetic doctrine of that writer. Much of what he has to say, too, about Burke, about Jonathan Richardson, about Condillac, is both penetrating and new. Nor is it the least of his merits that he has approached more closely than any of his predecessors to a conception of his subject in terms of "littérature générale." He has unduly neglected Italian criticism, it is true, and his chapters on the theory of poetry and drama are perhaps too exclusively French in their emphasis; but in the main he has succeeded in exhibiting the movement of aesthetic thought in the eighteenth century in its true perspective as an essentially European phenomenon.

This is of course all to the good. Unfortunately the shortcomings of the book—shortcomings both in method and in substance—greatly outweigh its merits, considerable as these no doubt are. I shall not dwell upon the heavy and diffuse style nor upon the distressingly bad proofreading which appears in nearly all the quotations from English writers. The really serious defects of the work lie deeper than this. Consider, in the first place, the choice of writers for analysis. Those chosen are all, doubtless, worthy of inclusion; the trouble is that there are too few of them: it is obviously impossible to give a just idea of the "pensée générale du siècle"—and that not in one country merely but in all Europe—on the basis of a study of no more than twenty-one authors. Some of the omissions are rather startling. To mention only English examples, there is not a word about Pope, except as a poet, not a word about Young, not a word about Reynolds, not a word about Johnson, though all of these writers had important things to say concerning the critical problems with which the book attempts to deal. The result of this limitation of the study to a few individuals is that the reader is inevitably given a misleading impression of their importance in the general development; a false illusion of uniqueness comes to attach to the writers selected, and doctrines which were in reality the common property of a generation end by being identified with a Shaftesbury or a Richardson.

Nor is this the most serious weakness of the book. An even more fundamental defect is Folkierski's almost total indifference to "background." Apart from passing allusions to Aristotle, to Horace, to Boileau, and to a few other individual critics, the past history of the doctrines he discusses remains entirely outside his picture. One could never gather, for example, from his treatment of the concept of "la belle nature" (I, iii) or of the question of the rules (I, iv) that there lay back of the eighteenth century an immense body of reflection on both of these points that must be mastered in detail and at first hand before it is possible to say anything significant about the contribution of the eighteenth century itself. The principle of course is elementary, but Folkierski's systematic neglect of it leads to really serious consequences. So also does his failure to recognize the importance, for the history of aesthetic ideas, of the development of thought in other fields. Over and over again he discusses theories of literature or of art that would take on new meaning if brought into relation with current or earlier psychological doctrines (the "anti-rationalism" of Dubos [p. 41] is a case in point) or with conceptions prevalent in science or in law (see I, iv, *passim*); but not once, so far as I recall, does he make the requisite connection. As a consequence of this indifference to background—in the twofold sense of the past of aesthetic theory and of the general "climate of opinion"—his conclusions often involve a serious deformation of perspective. An instance is his treatment of Shaftesbury, to whom, following the example of certain recent German historians, he attributes a peculiarly important rôle in the evolution of eighteenth-century aesthetic ideas. The question is too large to permit of discussion here; I can only say that the texts which he quotes in the course of his study (see, for example, pp. 102-05) seem to me to contain no doctrines to which the most self-conscious and convinced of neo-classicists—a Pope, a Dennis, a Johnson—could possibly have taken exception. Folkierski has erred, in short, here as throughout, by applying a purely descriptive or analytical method to a subject which can be studied fruitfully only from a historical-genetic point of view.

Graham, Walter. *The beginnings of English literary periodicals: a study of periodical literature, 1665-1715.* New York: Oxford University Press, American Branch, 1926.

Rev. by R. S. C[rane] in *MP,* XXIV (1926), 245-47; by R. P. McCutcheon in *MLN,* XLII (1927), 126; in *TLS,* Oct. 14, 1926, p. 687.

Haferkorn, Reinhard. *Gotik und Ruine in der englischen Dictung des 18. Jahrhunderts.* Leipzig: B. Tauchnitz, 1924.

Rev. by H. Flasdieck in *ES,* LXI (1926), 95-97; by G. Hübener in *Beiblatt,* XXXVII (1926), 74-76.

Hembdt, P. H. "The influence of early science on formative English." *Journal of chemical education,* III (1926), 1051-57.

The familiar story of the stylistic innovations of the Royal Society. Negligible.

Hesselgrave, Ruth A. *Lady Miller and the Batheaston circle.* New Haven: Yale University Press, 1926.

Hughes, Helen Sard. "The middle-class reader and the English novel." *JEGP,* XXV (1926), 362-78.

An interesting brief discussion of the relation between the improved status of the middle class in the eighteenth century and the growth of the realistic novel. The texts which Miss Hughes brings together in illustration of the rising prestige of the commercial classes could easily have been added to from other sources (e.g., Defoe's *Review*), but they are perhaps sufficient for her purpose, and some of them—notably the quotations from the successive editions of Chamberlayne's *Magna Britanniae notitia* (pp. 366-67)—are highly suggestive.

Janney, F. Lamar. *Childhood in English non-dramatic literature, from 1557 to 1798.* Greifswald: Abel, 1925.

Kaufman, Paul. "Heralds of original genius." *Essays in memory of Barrett Wendell, by his assistants* (Cambridge: Harvard University Press, 1926), pp. 191-217.

This paper contains a well written and suggestive study of the genealogy of the concept of "original genius" and a brief account of the principal expressions of the idea in English literature from Young to Blake. The subject is an exceedingly complex one, and though Kaufman has exhibited some of its essential aspects—for example, the rôle of seventeenth-century theories of the humours and of the "ruling passion" in intensifying the feeling for individuality—he has left out of account, no doubt because of lack of space, a number of other aspects which seem to me equally important. One of these is the religious factor suggested by Young in the sentence quoted by Kaufman as a motto: "With regard to the moral world, conscience—with regard to the intellectual world, genius—is that god within.'' Another aspect, also hinted at in the *Conjectures* (see Morley ed., pp. 12, 31, 33), is the Baconian and Cartesian rejection of authority, with its basic assumption of a nature whose laws had not all been discovered by the ancients; that this idea, carried over into literary criticism by such writers as Gildon (in his first phase) and Blackmore, had an important effect in preparing the eighteenth-century insistence upon originality is, I believe, indubitable. Influential also, no doubt, was the growth of the historico-relativist point of view, which, by undermining the rationalistic doctrine that the rules had their basis outside the individual poet in the ''invariable constitution of things,'' made it possible to regard the great writer as creative in a new sense. A few statements in the paper call for particular comment. Kaufman (Section II) exaggerates, I think, the novelty of the idea of the ''ruling passion'' at the beginning of the eighteenth century; it had been familiar in French psychological discussions, many of which were known in England, for over a generation. He also errs in saying that ''after Addison's pioneer and unquestionably influential defence of the superiority of genius and originality [*Spectator*, No. 160], nothing comparable in extent or emphasis appears for nearly half a century.'' If space permitted, a fairly long series of texts could be cited (from Saint-Evremond, Le Clerc, Blackmore, Welsted, Blackwell, Melmoth, and others) in which, before 1759, imitation of models is denounced and originality exalted with a definiteness of conviction and a vigor of expression equalled only by Young.

Lamprecht, Sterling P. ''Innate ideas in the Cambridge Platonists.'' *Philosophical review,* XXXV (1926), 553-73.

A useful and suggestive article. The importance of the doctrine of innate ideas in the Cambridge Platonists is clearly established on the basis of numerous well selected texts, and an interesting attempt is made to indicate a background for the doctrine in the efforts of the group to find a rationalistic *via media* between Anglican authoritarianism on the one hand and Puritan insistence upon the corruption of human powers and the necessity of divine inspiration through the Scriptures on the other. To an amateur in such matters it would seem that more might have been done to make clear the relation of the doctrine of innate ideas as it appears in the Cambridge Platonists to earlier thought. Descartes is of course mentioned, but, beyond the briefest allusion to Grotius and Herbert of Cherbury, there is no suggestion of any other possible antecedents. Reference might at least have been made to Etienne Gilson's study, ''L'innéisme cartésien et la théologie,'' in his *Etudes de philosophie médiévale* (Strasbourg, 1921), pp. 146-90.

Loria, G. ''Il periodo di storia delle scienze dalla morte di Galileo a Newton. Parte II[a]: Da Bacone all'alba del XVIII secolo.'' *Scientia,* XL (1926), 205-16.

Lynch, Kathleen M. *The social mode of Restoration comedy.* New York: Macmillan, 1926.

A well written and interesting attempt to trace the gradual formation of the social attitude characteristic of Restoration comedy from Fletcher to Congreve.

Manwaring, Elizabeth Wheeler. *Italian landscape in eighteenth century England.* New York: Oxford University Press, American Branch, 1925. Cf. *PQ,* V (1926), 349.

Rev. by H. Flasdieck in *Literaturblatt für germ. u. rom. Phil.,* XLVII (1926), 353-54; by R. P. McCutcheon in *South Atlantic quarterly,* XXV (1926), 324-25; by Clarissa Rinaker in *JEGP,* XXV (1926), 277-81.

Manwaring, G. E. "Journalism in the days of the Commonwealth." *Edinburgh review,* CCXLIII (1926), 105-20.

Mainly concerned with John Dillingham, editor of the *Moderate intelligencer* and other news-books.

Moore, C. A. "*Midnights meditations* (1646): a bibliographical puzzle." *MLN,* XLI (1926), 220-26.

On a seventeenth-century precursor of Young's *Night thoughts.*

Moore, C. A. "Whig panegyric verse, 1700-1760: a phase of sentimentalism." *PMLA,* XLI (1926), 362-401.

After studying in two well known articles the rôle of philosophical influences in the genesis of English sentimentalism, Moore deals in this paper with the effect of the political movement, especially the triumph of Whiggism, in inspiring poets to expressions of humanitarian feeling. The result is a fresh approach to a movement which we have tended hitherto to consider exclusively from a literary or ideological point of view. Moore shows very clearly on the basis of a characteristically solid documentation how certain features of the Whig program, notably the promotion of overseas trade and the effort to protect the English woolen industry, were seized upon by poets like Young, Thomson, Savage, Shenstone, Dyer, and others, and rationalized in terms of "universal benevolence" and sympathy with the lot of the poor. It is the obverse of the picture drawn by R. H. Tawney in his recent *Religion and the rise of capitalism*—an example of historical "compensation" which is not unamusing to contemplate. The article also contains valuable discussions of the theme of liberty in early eighteenth-century poetry, of the attitude of the sentimental poets to the slave trade, and of the part played by literary men in promoting the Spanish war of 1738. Altogether a very interesting and important study.

Muddiman, J. G. "Robert Yard, third editor of the *London gazette.*" *TLS,* Mar. 11, 1926, p. 182.

The Oxford book of eighteenth century verse. Chosen by David Nichol Smith. Oxford: Clarendon Press, 1926.

Platt, Joan. "The development of English colloquial idiom during the eighteenth century." *RES,* II (1926), 70-81, 189-96.

Poems on several occasions written in the eighteenth century. Edited by Kathleen W. Campbell. Oxford: Basil Blackwell, 1926. ("Percy reprints," No. 9.)

Pons, E. "Le 'voyage' genre littéraire au XVIIIe siècle." *Bulletin de la Faculté des lettres de Strasbourg,* IV (1926), 97-101, 144-49, 201-07.

Useful outlines and bibliographies addressed to students preparing for the "Agrégation d'Anglais." The topics treated are (1) "Voyages imaginaires," including a brief general survey of the subject and more detailed remarks on *Gulliver's travels* and *Robinson Crusoe,* and (2) "Récits authentiques de voyages."

Powicke, F. J. *The Cambridge Platonists.* London: J. M. Dent, 1926.

Prinsen, J. *De Roman in de 18e eeuw in West-Europa.* Groningen: Wolters, 1925. Cf. *PQ,* V (1926), 351.

Rev. by J. G. Robertson in *MLR*, XXI (1926), 89-90; by P. Van Tieghem in *RLC*, VI (1926), 709-13.

Randall, John Herman, Jr. *The making of the modern mind: a survey of the intellectual background of the present age.* Boston: Houghton Mifflin, 1926.

Rev. by F. A. Christie in *AHR*, XXXII (1926), 79-81.

A survey, intended primarily for general readers, of the intellectual history of the Western World from the thirteenth century to the present day. Portions of Book II—especially the chapters on the beginnings of modern science—, the whole of Book III ("The order of nature—the development of thought in the seventeenth and eighteenth centuries"), and the first chapter of Book IV ("The romantic protest against the age of reason") can be used with advantage in introducing students to the intellectual background of eighteenth-century literature.

Schücking, L. L. "Die Familie als Geschmacksträger in England im 18. Jahrhundert." *Deutsche Vierteljahrsschrift für Literaturwissenschaft und Geistesgeschichte,* IV (1926), 439-58.

Schücking, L. L. "Literatur und Familie zu Anfang des 18. Jahrhunderts in England." *Probleme der englischen Sprache und Kultur: Festschrift Johannes Hoops* (Heidelberg, 1925), pp. 184-94.

Seventeenth century essays from Bacon to Clarendon. Selected and edited with an introduction by Jacob Zeitlin. New York: Charles Scribner's Sons, [1926].

Useful selections from nineteen essayists, with an excellent introduction. A similar collection for the remainder of the century would be welcome.

Snow, A. J. *Matter & gravity in Newton's physical philosophy: a study in the natural philosophy of Newton's time.* London: Humphrey Milford, Oxford University Press, 1926.

Rev. in *TLS*, Nov. 25, 1926, p. 836.

The historian of ideas in eighteenth-century literature will be mainly interested in the fresh light which Snow casts on the efforts of such thinkers as More, Boyle, Clarke, and especially Newton, to offset the mechanistic conception of the world developed by Descartes (see pp. 55, 63, 79-82, 165-68, 169-210, 226-28).

Spencer, Hazelton. "Improving Shakespeare: some bibliographical notes on the Restoration adaptations." *PMLA,* XLI (1926), 727-46.

Spencer, Hazelton. "The Blackfriars mystery." *SP,* XXIV (1926), 173-80.

Sprague, Arthur Colby. *Beaumont and Fletcher on the Restoration stage.* Cambridge: Harvard University Press, 1926.

In the first part of this volume the author traces the stage history of the Beaumont and Fletcher plays from 1660 to the death of Betterton in 1710; in the second part he discusses with fair detail twenty adaptations or alterations of the plays during the same period. There are two short appendices, in which Sprague questions the composition of "an opera called *The Mad*

Lover," and gives us reason to believe that the oft-mentioned alteration of *The Beggars Bush* by H. N. in 1705 was nothing more than a reprint of the text of the First Folio. He does not discuss the influence of Beaumont and Fletcher on Restoration drama or the minor borrowings. Within the limits set, the volume is highly satisfactory.—B. M.

Stokoe, F. W. *German influences in the English romantic period, 1788-1818*. Cambridge: University Press, 1926.

Rev. in *TLS,* July 29, 1926, p. 508.

Turner, F. Mc D. C. *The element of irony in English literature.* Cambridge: University Press, 1926.

Rev. by J. Douady in *RC,* LX (1926), 358; in *N & Q,* CL (1926), 287-88; in *TLS,* Mar. 18, 1926, p. 207.

Van Tieghem, P. "La sensibilité et la passion dans le roman européen au XVIIIe siècle." *RLC,* VI (1926), 424-35.

The introductory lecture of a course on this subject given at Paris during the year 1925-26.

Waterhouse, Francis A. "Romantic 'originality.'" *Sewanee review,* XXXIV (1926), 40-49.

Second-hand Irving Babbitt.

Westerfrölke, Hermann. *Englische Kaffeehäuser als Sammelpunkte der literarischen Welt im Zeitalter von Dryden und Addison.* Jena: Verlag der Frommannschen Buchhandlung, [1926].

Rev. by B. Fehr in *Beiblatt,* XXXVII (1926), 354-55; by H. Lüdeke in *Deutsche Literaturzeitung,* Dec. 18, 1926, cols. 2522-23.

Williams, Iolo A. [Miscellaneous notes on eighteenth-century poetry.] *LM,* XIII (1926), 418-19, 528; XIV (1926), 72-73, 521, 635-36; XV (1926), 79, 184-85.

Wood, Paul Spencer. "Native elements in English neo-classicism." *MP,* XXIV (1926), 201-08.

An interesting brief study of the affinities between the literary spirit of the Restoration, particularly as regards its exaltation of restraint, decorum, and tradition, and the political, religious, and social ideals of the period. A good selection of illustrative texts.

Zilsel, E. *Die Entstehung des Geniebegriffes: ein Beitrag zur Ideengeschichte der Antike und des Frühkapitalismus.* Tübingen: J. C. B. Mohr, 1926.

Rev. in *Archiv,* CL (1926), 271; in *RLC,* VI (1926), 542-43.

III. STUDIES RELATING TO INDIVIDUAL AUTHORS

Joseph Addison

McCutcheon, Roger P. "Another burlesque of Addison's ballad criticism." *SP,* XXIII (1926), 451-56.

Reprints a humorous essay on the *Dragon of Wantley* from Mist's *Weekly journal* for Sept. 2, 1721.

S[herburn], G[eorge]. [Note on the contents of *Miscellaneous works in verse and prose of the late Right Honourable Joseph Addison,* London, 1726.] *MP,* XXIII (1926), 361.

Mark Akenside

Potter, George Reuben. "Mark Akenside, prophet of evolution." *MP,* XXIV (1926), 55-64.

An intelligent and clearly written study, furnishing interesting sidelights on eighteenth-century science and philosophy. Perhaps, however, Akenside is made to seem too exceptional. There were evolutionists before Akenside. Charles Blount, for instance, notes that "Some Authors are of an opinion, that Man is nothing but an Ape cultivated . . ." (*Anima mundi* [1679], p. 45, in *Miscellaneous works,* 1695). Cf. also Cardano, *De rerum varietate,* bk. 7, ch. 26, and Vanini, *De admirandis naturæ . . . arcanis,* dialogue 37, ed. Paris, 1616, pp. 233-34. Compared with Akenside's, however, these conceptions are mere adumbrations.—F. B. K.

John Aubrey

"John Aubrey (born March 12, 1626-died June, 1697)." *TLS,* Mar. 11, 1926, pp. 169-70.

Richard Baxter

"The Reverend Richard Baxter's last treatise [*The poor husbandman's advocate to rich racking landlords,* 1691]." Edited by Frederick J. Powicke, with an introduction by George Unwin. *Bulletin of the John Rylands Library,* X (1926), 163-218.

William Beckford

Grimsditch, Herbert B. "William Beckford's minor works." *LM,* XIV (1926), 599-605.

George Berkeley

Dunlop, Robert. "Bishop Berkeley on Ireland." *Contemporary review,* CXXIX (1926), 763-71.

Metz, Rudolf. "Berkeleys philosophisches Tagebuch." *Kant-Studien,* XXXI (1926), 344-51.

Metz, Rudolf. "Berkeley und Hume. Erster Teil: Berkeley." *Literarische Berichte aus dem Gebiete der Philosophie* (Erfurt: Kurt Stenger, 1926), pp. 35-46.

Meyerstein, E. H. W. "The first London edition of 'The Querist.'" *TLS,* May 20, 1926, p. 339.

Isaac Bickerstaff

Macmillan, Ethel. "The plays of Isaac Bickerstaff in America." *PQ,* V (1926), 58-69.

Thomas Blackwell

Whitney, Lois. "Thomas Blackwell, a disciple of Shaftesbury." *PQ,* V (1926), 196-211.

An excellent brief article. In her careful discrimination of the contradictory elements in the thought of both Blackwell and Shaftesbury, Miss Whitney has made one of the first really intelligent contributions to the study of primitivistic ideas in eighteenth-century English literature. I am not sure that she does not exaggerate somewhat the completeness of Blackwell's discipleship, and it may be that she takes for granted too readily the primitivistic implication of certain of Shaftesbury's statements (e.g., pp. 208-09). But on the whole her method is admirable.

William Blake

The Prophetic writings of William Blake. Edited with a general introduction, glossarial index of symbols, commentary, and appendices, by D. J. Sloss and J. P. R. Wallis. Oxford: Clarendon Press, 1926. 2 vols.

Rev. by P. Berger in *RAA,* IV (1926), 66-68; by S. Foster Damon in *SRL,* Dec. 4, 1926, pp. 357-58; in *TLS,* July 22, 1926, p. 493.

Ba-Han, Maung. *The evolution of Blakean philosophy.* Freiburg i. B., [1926].

A Freiburg dissertation.

Berger, Pierre. "L'état actuel des études sur Blake d'après quelques livres récents." *RAA,* IV (1926), 55-70.

A useful and interesting summary.

Bruce, Harold L. "William Blake and Gilchrist's remarkable coterie of advanced thinkers." *MP,* XXIII (1926), 285-92.

Burdett, Osbert. *William Blake.* London: Macmillan, 1926. ("English men of letters.")

Rev. by S. Foster Damon in *SRL,* Dec. 4, 1926, pp. 357-58; in *TLS,* Nov. 11, 1926, p. 791.

Fehr, Bernhard. [Notes on recent Blake literature.] *Beiblatt,* XXXVII (1926), 321-32.

Deals particularly with Keynes's edition of the *Writings of William Blake* (1925) and with Maung Ba-Han's *William Blake: his mysticism* (1924), but discusses incidentally a number of other recent publications. A valuable review by a student of Blake whose opinions are always suggestive.

Perugini, Mark E. "Blake's Prophetic books." *TLS,* July 29, 1926, p. 512.

An interesting letter, calling attention to some curious parallels between Blake's early prophetic books and passages in the *Conjuror's magazine* (1791-94) and in Francis Barrett's *Magus* (1801), and urging a systematic exploration of the "occult" publications of the period for further light on Blake's ideas and symbols.

Pierce, Frederick E. "Two notes on Blake." *MLN,* XLI (1926), 169-70.

Plowman, Max. "Blake drawings." *TLS,* Apr. 1, 1926, p. 249.

Comment by J. P. R. Wallis, *ibid.,* May 27, 1926, p. 355.

Plowman, Max. "Blake's 'Infant sorrow.'" *TLS,* Nov. 18, 1926, p. 819.

Povey, K. "Blake's 'Heads of the poets.'" *N&Q,* CLI (1926), 57-58.

Wallis, J. P. R. "Blake's 'Milton.'" *TLS,* Mar. 11, 1926, p. 182.

Winslow, Ola Elizabeth. "William Blake and the century test." *South Atlantic quarterly,* XXV (1926), 25-44.

Largely concerned with Blake's relations to eighteenth-century thought. Little that had not already been said by Berger or Damon.

James Boswell

The Hypochondriack. Edited by Margery Bailey. Stanford University, 1926.

Chapman, R. W. "Boswell's proof-sheets." *LM,* XV (1926), 50-58, 171-80.

An interesting article, based on a collection of revises and re-revises of the first edition of the *Life of Johnson* belonging to Mr. R. B. Adam of Buffalo.

William Lisle Bowles

A Wiltshire parson and his friends: the correspondence of William Lisle Bowles. Edited by Garland Greever. London: Constable; Boston: Houghton Mifflin, 1926.

Rev. in *TLS,* Sept. 23, 1926, p. 629.

Contains, besides the correspondence of Bowles, two unpublished letters and four hitherto unidentified reviews by Coleridge.

Robert Boyle

Davis, Tenney L. "The first edition of the *Sceptical chymist.*" *Isis,* VIII (1926), 71-76.

Henry Brooke

C[hapman], R. W. "Brooke's *Gustavus Vasa.*" *RES,* II (1926), 99.

A postscript to his note in *RES,* I (1925), 460.

Sir Thomas Browne

Dunn, William P. *Sir Thomas Browne: a study in religious philosophy.* Menasha, Wis.: George Banta, 1926.

This study, a Columbia doctor's thesis, attempts "to explain some of the philosophical conceptions of [Browne's] books, to trace their historic antecedents, to set them against the background of contemporary modes of thought, and on such basis to give Browne his proper place in English philosophy of the seventeenth century" (p. 32). It is concerned particularly with those aspects of Browne's thought which have a religious significance—with his treatment of the problem of faith and reason (ch. II), with his "philosophy of nature" (ch. III), and with his speculations on the soul, death, and immortality (ch. IV). The great merit of the book—a merit almost startling in an American doctoral dissertation—is its fine literary sense. Dunn never allows us to forget the poetic quality of Browne's thought; he is constantly alive to its subtly shifting shades of implication; and he gives us as a result many pages which are models of delicate and sympathetic interpretation. Such passages as his commentary on Sections XIV-XVIII of the *Religio medici* (pp. 90-103) or his analysis of the Puritan and Stoic elements in Browne's feeling about death (pp. 165-75) are extremely able bits of writing, as good as anything in the previous literature of the subject from Pater to Sir Edmund Goose or Lytton Strachey.

The defects of the book are to some extent the consequence of these merits. Thus Dunn's concern for the nuance results occasionally in a blurring of the larger point, as, for example, in his discussion of "philosophical skepticism" (pp. 155-58). Again, his very commendable desire to make things easy for the reader leads frequently to an unfortunate concealment of the foundation of fact upon which his historical interpretations are built. Sometimes, indeed, one suspects that the foundation is not as solid as it should be: certain of his allusions to the scholastics, in particular, suggest the disquieting thought that his command of the original texts and of the best modern scholarship on the subject is less extensive than we have a right to expect. In any case, we should be grateful for more precise references; discreetly relegated to the footnotes, these would have subtracted nothing from the charm and ease of the exposition, and they would have added immensely to the usefulness of a very interesting book.

James Buchanan

Kennedy, Arthur G. "Authorship of *The British grammar.*" *MLN,* XLI (1926), 388-91.

Ascription to Buchanan.

John Bunyan

Hodgson, J. E. "Bunyan's 'Book for boys and girls.'" *TLS,* Nov. 4, 1926, p. 770.

Greg, W. W. "The 'issues' of 'The pilgrim's progress.'" *TLS,* Aug. 19, 1926, p. 549.

Valuable remarks on bibliographical method.

Edmund Burke

Cobban, A. B. C. "Edmund Burke and the origins of the theory of nationality." *Cambridge historical journal,* II (1926), 36-47.

O'Brien, William. *Edmund Burke as an Irishman.* Second edition. Dublin: M. H. Gill, 1926.

First published in 1924.

Fanny Burney

Fanny Burney and the Burneys. Edited by R. Brimley Johnson. London: Stanley Paul, 1926.

Rev. in *TLS,* Nov. 25, 1926, p. 840.

Robert Burns

Miller, Frank. "The original of Burns's song, 'The battle of Sherra-Moor.'" *Scottish historical review,* XXIII (1926), 158-59.

Shows that the song was in circulation as early as 1745.

Joseph Butler

Taylor, A. E. "Some features of Butler's ethics." *Mind,* XXXV (1926), 273-300.

Townsend, H. G. "The synthetic principle in Butler's ethics." *International journal of ethics,* XXXVII (1926), 81-87.

George Campbell

Bryan, W. F. "A late eighteenth-century purist." *SP,* XXIII (1926), 358-70.

An interesting study of the rationalistic bias in Campbell's *Philosophy of rhetoric* (1776).

Thomas Chatterton

Meyerstein, E. H. W. "Wordsworth and Chatterton." *TLS,* Oct. 21, 1926, p. 722.

Philip Dormer Stanhope, Earl of Chesterfield

The Poetical works of Lord Chesterfield. London: Elkin Mathews & Marrot, 1926.

Baldensperger, F. [Review of R. Coxon, *Chesterfield and his critics,* London, 1925.] *Litteris,* III (1926), 241-43.

Charles Churchill

Beatty, Joseph M., Jr. "Mrs. Montagu, Churchill, and Miss Cheere." *MLN,* XLI (1926), 384-86.

William Collins

Williams, Iolo A. [Notes on the bibliography of *The passions.*] *LM,* XIII (1926), 644; XIV (1926), 293.

William Congreve

Lawrence, W. J. "A Congreve holograph." *RES,* II (1926), 345.

Evidence that Congreve was a holder of South Sea stock.

Abraham Cowley

The Mistress, with other select poems of Abraham Cowley, 1618-1667. Edited by John Sparrow. London: Nonesuch Press, 1926.

Rev. in *TLS,* Nov. 18, 1926, pp. 805-06.

"Cowley's lyrics." *TLS,* Nov. 18, 1926, pp. 805-06.

A sympathetic and rather penetrating essay.

Nethercot, Arthur H. "Abraham Cowley's *Discourse concerning style.*" *RES,* II (1926), 385-404.

The starting-point of this interesting paper is Sprat's statement that Cowley planned "to publish a discourse concerning style," but died without completing it. By bringing together the rather numerous remarks on poetry and style scattered through Cowley's published works, Nethercot attempts first to reconstruct the probable content of this proposed essay, and then to "place" Cowley in the movement of seventeenth-century critical thought. The article illuminates helpfully a neglected side of Cowley's mind, and should prove useful to students of neo-classical literary theory.

William Cowper

Whiting, Mary Bradford. " 'A burning bush': a new light on the relations between William Cowper and John Newton." *Hibbert journal,* XXIV (1926), 303-13.

Daniel Defoe

Lovett, Robert Morss. "Franklin and Defoe." *New republic,* Nov. 3, 1926, pp. 303-04.

Pompen, Fr. A. "Defoe en zijn bronnen." *Neophilologus,* XII (1926), 31-34.

Apropos of A. W. Secord's *Studies in the narrative method of Defoe,* Urbana, 1924.

Staverman, W. H. [Review of P. Dottin, *Daniel De Foe et ses romans,* Paris, 1924.] *English studies,* VIII (1926), 189-93.

Ullrich, Hermann. [Review of H. C. Hutchins, *Robinson Crusoe and its printing,* New York, 1925.] *Literaturblatt für germ. u. rom. Phil.,* XLVII (1926), cols. 281-85.

White, A. S. "Defoe's military career." *TLS,* Jan. 28, 1926, p. 63.

Correction of an error in Dalton's *English army lists and commission registers.*

Sir John Denham

Banks, Theodore H., Jr. "Denham's supposed authorship of *Directions to a painter,* 1667." *MLN,* XLI (1926), 502-05.

Arguments, in the main fairly cogent, against Denham's authorship.

Banks, Theodore H., Jr. "Sir John Denham and *Paradise lost.*" *MLN,* XLI (1926), 51-54.

Banks, Theodore H., Jr. "Sir John Denham's *Cooper's Hill.*" *MLR,* XXI (1926), 269-77.

A useful presentation of the known facts about Denham's poem—its originality, its style, the history of its text, the celebrated apostrophe to the Thames, and the fame of the poem—with a few new details.

Stephen Duck

Davis, Rose Mary. *Stephen Duck, the thresher-poet.* Orono, Maine: University Press, 1926. ("University of Maine studies," 2nd series, No. 8.)

The mature and extensive documentation of this work is most unusual in dissertations submitted for the M.A. degree. The biography is carefully assembled and the literary criticism has the merit, rare in specialized studies, of not being too enthusiastic. In general, the source material is well chosen.

There may be some doubt if the article by Attenborough is on the whole wisely depended upon; and Lounsbury's *Text of Shakespeare* proves, as usual, a morass. Miss Davis tries to be rational about Pope, but Lounsbury is always breaking in—and the result is that what was merely politics in the attitude of Pope and Swift towards Queen Caroline's poet is at times ascribed to that natural malignity which the last century unjustly imputed to the satirists of the eighteenth century. Anyone must doubt if Duck would be indiscreetly sent to Pope without a note from the Queen. The privilege of consulting the original manuscripts of Alured Clarke's letters (Add. MSS 20,102) might have aided Miss Davis. The "undated" letter which she quotes on p. 46 is in the MS dated (at the end) "Oct. 6, 1730."

But this is unimportant. A more significant matter, the interpretation of which it seems possible to question is the true nature of the interest lords and wits felt in Stephen Duck in 1730. Was it sociological—an interest in proletarian bards, as Professor Draper assumes it to be in his Foreword? If so, why did Clarke and Spence hasten to efface all traces of the soil? Why did they train Duck according to "the Neo-classical formulae of the aristocracy"? The true key to the 1730 attitude towards Duck seems to lie not in the social ideas but in the literary criticism of the day. The quest was not for the peasant-poet but for the natural genius. Such a genius could not be surely detected in the educated classes; but in uneducated circles was found Stephen Duck—untrained, but with a true taste and a natural genius, "superior even to Mr. Pope"—potentially such a genius as Addison had described in *Spectator*, No. 160. Spence and Clarke believed in Duck, but they also believed in Addison's second type of great genius, that which was formed and trained. They show great interest in Duck's untrained creative processes; and yet, comically enough, when it becomes apparent that Duck is to go to court, their confidence wavers, and they make sure that he does some reading before appearing in the great world. For modern students the most amusing thing Miss Davis' book does is to throw light on the 1730 attitude toward natural genius—and on the irreducible minimum of reading which it was felt a natural genius should do before going to court.—G. S.

John Evelyn

Memoires for my grand-son. Transcribed and furnished with a preface and notes by Geoffrey Keynes. London: Nonesuch Press, 1926.

The *Memoires* were begun in 1704. They are notes of advice, run together. The passage recommending certain authors (pp. 38-50) is of interest to students of the history of ideas and taste. At the close is a section called "Promiscuous advices"—a short collection of maxims (also by Evelyn). The text seems careful.—F. B. K.

Segrè, Carlo. "L'Evelyn a Roma nel 1645." *Nuova antologia*, April, 1926, pp. 217-45.

Squire, W. Barclay. "Evelyn and music, 1650-1653." *TLS*, Oct. 14, 1926, p. 695.

Comment by J. W. Kirby, *ibid.*, Oct. 21, p. 722. Cf. *PQ*, V (1926), 360.

Henry Fielding

An Apology for the life of Mrs. Shamela Andrews. With an introduction by R. Brimley Johnson. The Golden Cockerel Press, 1926.

Rev. by A. Digeon in *RAA*, IV (1926), 73.

This beautiful reprint, limited to 450 copies, is very welcome. It purports to reproduce the second issue of the pamphlet (Nov., 1741) "with the original spelling, punctuation, capitals, and abbreviations," except for specified correction of misprints. This difficult attempt is creditably carried out, though in twenty-five pages examined nine small deviations from the second issue have been noted—see pp. 24, 27, 29(2), 33, 41(2), 45, and 47. The Introduction hardly does more than assemble facts about *Shamela* printed in standard works on Fielding, but they are usefully assembled. It would be interesting to argue the case of Fielding's authorship further by comparing the ideas of the author of *Shamela* with those of Fielding. The attitude towards Whitefield and "good works," for example, is exactly that seen in Fielding's novels. —G. S.

Blanchard, Frederic T. *Fielding the novelist.* New Haven: Yale University Press, 1925. Cf. *PQ,* V (1926), 360.

Rev. by Paul Dottin in *RELV,* XLIII (1926), 450-55; by E. S. Noyes in *SRL,* Oct. 16, 1926, p. 198; in *TLS,* July 29, 1926, p. 509.

Digeon, A. *The novels of Fielding.* London: Routledge; New York: E. P. Dutton, 1925. Cf. *PQ,* V (1926), 360.

Rev. by F. T. Blanchard in *University of California chronicle,* XXVIII (1926), 105-07; by S. B. Liljegren in *Litteris,* III (1926), 103-04.

"Fielding's 'Charge to the jury,' 1745." *TLS,* Mar. 4, 1926, p. 168.

Radtke, Bruno. *Henry Fielding als Kritiker.* Leipzig: Mayer & Müller, 1926.

A German dissertation. It is a painstaking collection of citations from Fielding organized on the principle of a dictionary rather than of a systematic exposition of ideas. No real attempt is made to get at Fielding's *basic* attitudes. The possibility of change or development in his opinions is not considered. The background furnished consists only of well-worn quotations from a few celebrated critics. Neo-classical terminology is not sufficiently understood—e.g., that frequently misinterpreted word "invention." The dissertation should, however, be of use to someone attempting a more philosophical analysis of Fielding's critical theories and pronouncements.—F. B. K.

John Gay

Poetical works. Edited by G. C. Faber. Oxford: Clarendon Press, 1926.

Sherburn, George. "The fortunes and misfortunes of *Three hours after marriage.*" *MP,* XXIV (1926), 91-109.

William Godwin

An Enquiry concerning political justice and its influence on general virtue and happiness. Edited and abridged by Raymond A. Preston. New York: Alfred A. Knopf, 1926. 2 vols. ("Political science classics.")

Rev. in *TLS,* Sept. 23, 1926, p. 628.

A reprint of the first edition (1793), with the omission—which the student of the general history of ideas will greatly deplore—of eleven chapters.

Brown, Ford K. *The life of William Godwin.* London: J. M. Dent; New York: E. P. Dutton, 1926.

Rev. by W. R. Dennes in *University of California chronicle,* XXVIII (1926),

460-62; by H. J. Laski in *SRL*, Oct. 16, 1926, p. 191; by R. A. Preston in the *Nation*, Sept. 15, 1926, p. 249; in *TLS*, Apr. 15, 1926, p. 273.

A narrative of Godwin's career based mainly on published and easily accessible sources. It contains little that is likely to interest the historian of ideas. The analysis of *Political justice* (ch. VI) is perfunctory, and the account of the reaction against Godwin (chs. XIV, XV) suffers from the author's failure to make sufficient use of previous studies, particularly those of Henri Roussin and B. S. Allen.

Oliver Goldsmith

Balderston, Katharine C. *A census of the manuscripts of Oliver Goldsmith.* New York: Brick Row Book Shop, 1926.

Rev. in *TLS*, Feb. 24, 1927, p. 122.

Balderston, Katharine C. *The history & sources of Percy's memoir of Goldsmith.* Cambridge: University Press, 1926.

Rev. by Marguerite L. Rocher in *RAA*, IV (1926), 75; in *N & Q*, CL (1926), 395; in *TLS*, June 3, 1926, p. 371.

These two little books are examples of the careful biographical research which we have come to expect from the pupils of C. B. Tinker. Modest in their pretensions, thorough and precise in their method, they will help materially to lighten the task of the future biographer of Goldsmith. In her *Census* Miss Balderston has undertaken to discover and to describe every scrap, however insignificant, that remains in existence of Goldsmith's writing. The intelligent care with which she has pursued the enquiry appears on every page; and if the results in the way of new material seem somewhat disproportionate to the effort which the search must have cost, that is of course not her fault. Of the unpublished manuscripts which she has unearthed, nearly all are letters. She has succeeded in locating the autographs of all but fourteen of the forty-two letters now accessible in print, and in addition she has turned up eleven not hitherto known. (One of these, the first in her list, was printed in part by Sir Ernest Clarke in the *Transactions of the Bibliographical society*, XV [1920], 20—a fact which she does not note.) Her descriptions of the manuscripts are clear and full enough for all practical purposes; it is regrettable, however, that she did not see fit to give for the "receipts, agreements, bills, etc." and for the "literary manuscripts" the precise information regarding previous publication which she gives for the letters.

Her second book is a critical study of the first important biography of Goldsmith—the memoir undertaken by Percy shortly after Goldsmith's death and published in the *Miscellaneous works* of 1801. Of the long and very curious history of this document, Miss Balderston gives a competent and useful account, based in part upon unpublished materials. Her most valuable contribution, however, is her discussion of the sources out of which Percy and his collaborators constructed the memoir. It is an excellent piece of work, and the table of sources which she prints on pages 52-61 will be welcomed by all students of Goldsmith. She has had the good fortune to have access to the manuscripts of Percy now in the possession of his descendant, Miss Constance Meade, of London. From this important collection she prints for the first time *in extenso* (pp. 12-17) the memorandum which Goldsmith dictated to Percy on April 28, 1773, and which Percy used in the preparation of his biography. Other documents from this same collection, including the narrative of Mrs. Hodson, will appear in her forthcoming edition of Goldsmith's letters.

Brown, Joseph E. "Goldsmith's indebtedness to Voltaire and Justus Van Effen." *MP*, XXIII (1926), 273-84.

Further evidence of plagiarism, especially in the *Bee* and the *Citizen of the world.*

Milner-Barry, Alda. "A note on the early literary relations of Oliver Goldsmith and Thomas Percy." *RES*, II (1926), 51-61.

The main points of this article are (1) that the beginnings of Goldsmith's interest in China coincided with his meeting in February, 1759, with Percy, who was then in London trying to find a published for his Chinese novel; (2) that this preoccupation of Percy's may have had some share in determining Goldsmith to adopt a Chinese medium for his letters in the *Public ledger;* and (3) that certain features of the *Chinese letters,* notably the use of Du Halde, may have been due to a reading of Percy's manuscript. The evidence offered for the last of these points is very meager, and the first can hardly be maintained in view of Goldsmith's letter to Robert Bryanton of August, 1758 (*Works,* ed. Gibbs, I, 437). That Percy's influence may have counted for something in the genesis of the *Citizen of the world* is, of course, more than possible, but it could scarcely have been more potent than that of d'Argens or of Voltaire, and in any case the problem hardly admits of definite solution. See below under *Thomas Percy.*

Smith, Hamilton Jewett. *Oliver Goldsmith's The citizen of the world: a study.* New Haven: Yale University Press; London: Humphrey Milford, Oxford University Press, 1926.

Williams, Iolo A. [A cancel in Goldsmith's *Life of . . . Bolingbroke.*] *LM,* XIII (1926), 527.

Williams, Iolo A. [Continental editions and translations of the *Vicar of Wakefield.*] *LM,* XIV (1926), 193.

Richard Graves

The Spiritual Quixote: or, The summer's ramble of Mr. Geoffry Wildgoose. A comic romance. With an introduction by Charles Whibley. London: Peter Davies, 1926.

Rev. in *TLS,* Nov. 11, 1926, p. 789.

Hutton, W. H. "Richard Graves and Bath." *TLS,* Dec. 2, 1926, p. 888.

Reply by B. T. K. Smith, *ibid.,* Dec. 9, p. 913.

Thomas Gray

Beresford, John. "The poet Gray and the Rev. Henry Etough." *TLS,* July 22, 1926, pp. 495-96.

Roe, F. C. "Le voyage de Gray et Walpole en Italie." *RLC,* VI (1926), 189-206.

The first part of this article—a résumé of the experiences of Gray and Walpole in Italy, based upon their published correspondence—contains nothing that had not already been said with greater fullness and precision by such writers as Northup (*Studies in language and literature in celebration of the seventieth birthday of James Morgan Hart,* New York, 1910, pp. 390-439) and Yvon (*La vie d'un dilettante: Horace Walpole,* Paris, 1924, pp. 48-76). The second part—an attempt to define "les résultats tangibles de ce voyage" —is more interesting, but its main conclusions can hardly be said to be very new or, for that matter, entirely true. Certainly no one supposes nowadays that enthusiasm for mountains in English literature really dates from Walpole and Gray. "The greatest objects of Nature," Thomas Burnet had written in 1681, "are, methinks, the most pleasing to behold; . . . there is nothing that I look upon with more pleasure than the wide sea and the Mountains of the Earth. There is something august and stately in the Air of these things, that inspires the Mind with great Thoughts and Passions; we do naturally, upon such occasions, think of God and his Greatness'' (quoted by C. A. Moore in *SP,* XIV [1917], 252). Again, there is the ''rhapsody'' which another traveller in Italy, Shaftesbury, published in 1709—the striking passage in the *Moralists* beginning, ''But behold! through a vast tract of sky before us, the mighty Atlas rears his lofty head covered with snow above the clouds'' (*Characteristics,* ed. Robertson, II, 122-24). Did space permit, a fair number of other texts similar to these could be cited from the half-century before 1740; they would show beyond any doubt, I believe, that no such special historical importance attaches to the mountain descriptions of Gray and Walpole as Roe, following the earlier writers on English romanticism, seems to think.

Stokes, Francis Griffin. ''Gray's 'Elegy': the fourth edition.'' *TLS,* Dec. 16, 1926, p. 935.

Toynbee, Paget. ''Gray and the Regius Professorship: a misplaced letter.'' *TLS,* Oct. 14, 1926, p. 698.

Toynbee, Paget. ''Gray's 'Proposal' as to the professorship of modern history.'' *TLS,* Mar. 4, 1926, p. 163.

Toynbee, Paget. ''Some Gray notes.'' *TLS,* Aug. 26, 1926, p. 564.

Comment by R. M. Robinson, *ibid.,* Sept. 2, p. 580.

Matthew Green

The Spleen and other poems. With a preface by Richardson King Wood. London: Cayme Press, 1926.

Rev. by I. A. Williams in the *Observer,* Aug. 22, 1926, p. 4.

Thomas Hobbes

Nicolson, Marjorie H. ''Milton and Hobbes.'' *SP,* XXIII (1926), 405-33.

The thesis of this most interesting and important article is that in his doctrine of human nature, in his conception of the relation between God and the universe, and in his essentially intellectualistic idea of God, Milton showed marked affinities with such contemporary thinkers as More, Cumberland, Cudworth, and, in general, the whole group of ''English Platonists''; that, like them, he is best interpreted as an opponent of Hobbes. Miss Nicolson leaves it somewhat uncertain how far she thinks Milton was conscious of this opposition (the positive evidence [see p. 413] is rather slight); apart from this, her interpretation seems to me entirely convincing, and besides to have the rare merit of placing a much studied writer in a new and illuminating perspective. It should be impossible henceforth to think of Milton after the Restoration merely as an isolated survival from an age that was past. On the contrary, by virtue of his mature philosophy, he stood in the closest relation to a current of thought that continued to gather force throughout the rest of the century and that, through its effect on such writers as Shaftesbury and Thomson, helped to determine some of the most interesting developments of the century that followed.

Thomas Holcroft

Benn, T. Vincent. ''Holcroft en France.'' *RLC,* VI (1926), 331-27.

David Hume

Carlini, A. "L'attualismo scettico del trattato su la natura umana di D. Hume." *Giornale critico della filosofia italiana,* VII (1926), 104-28.

Laing, B. M. "Hume and the contemporary theory of instinct." *Monist,* XXXVI (1926), 645-66.

Samuel Johnson

"The Authority of Johnson." *TLS,* Sept. 2, 1926, pp. 569-70.

Brown, Joseph Epes. *The critical opinions of Samuel Johnson.* Princeton: Princeton University Press, 1926.

Rev. by R. W. Chapman in *RES,* II (1926), 354-56; by R. S. C[rane] in *MP,* XXIII (1926), 497-98; by R. D. Havens in *MLN,* XLI (1926), 420-21; by F. A. Pottle in *Yale review,* XV (1926), 819.

C[hapman], R. W. "Dr. Johnson and Dr. Taylor." *RES,* II (1926), 338-39.

On Taylor's *Letter to Samuel Johnson, L.L.D. on the subject of a future state* (1787).

C[hapman], R. W. "Johnson's letters to Perkins." *RES,* II (1926), 97-98.

Chapman, R. W. "Johnson's letters to Taylor." *RES,* II (1926), 89-92, 466.

Chapman, R. W. "Johnson's *Plan of a dictionary.*" *RES,* II (1926), 216-18.

Mainly concerned with the two states of sheet A.

Chapman, R. W. "Proposals for a new edition of Johnson's letters." *Essays and studies by members of the English Association,* XII (Oxford, 1926), 47-62.

Gissing, Algernon. "Appleby School: an extra-illustration to Boswell." *Cornhill magazine,* April, 1926, pp. 404-14.

Presents extracts from the Minute Book of Appleby School, June 11, 16, 1739.

MacKinnon, F. D. "Samuel Johnson, undergraduate." *Cornhill magazine,* October, 1926, pp. 444-58.

Powell, L. F. "Johnson and the *Encyclopédie.*" *RES,* II (1926), 335-37.

Borrowings from Johnson's *Dictionary* in the article "Anglois."

Reade, Aleyn Lyell. "The duration of Johnson's residence at Oxford." *TLS,* Sept. 16, 1926, pp. 615-16.

Important.

Reade, Aleyn Lyell. "Johnson's ushership at Market Bosworth." *TLS,* June 10, 1926, p. 394.

Tinker, Chauncey Brewster. *The Wedgewood medallion of Samuel Johnson: a study in iconography.* Cambridge, Mass.: Harvard University Press, 1926.

Rev. in *SRL,* Jan. 8, 1927, p. 507.

Vicesimus Knox

Partridge, Eric. "Vicesimus Knox: his 'Essays moral and literary.' " *A critical medley,* Paris: Champion, 1926, pp. 39-54.

A rather pointless résumé of Knox's opinions, culminating in the pronouncement that "To Professor Saintsbury's stricture that Knox 'is but a Johnson without the genius,' we must subjoin the statement that he is a Johnson in earnestness and talent."

George Lillo

Benn, T. Vincent. "Notes sur la fortune du *George Barnwell* de Lillo en France." *RLC,* VI (1926), 682-87.

James Macpherson

Black, George F. "Macpherson's Ossian and the Ossianic controversy: a contribution towards a bibliography." *Bulletin of the New York Public Library,* XXX (1926), 424-39, 508-24.

Important.

Christiansen, R. T. "Macphersons Ossian og folkedigtningen." *Edda,* XXV (1926), 161-209.

Bernard Mandeville

The Fable of the bees: or, private vices, publick benefits. Edited by F. B. Kaye. Oxford: Clarendon Press, 1924. Cf. *PQ,* V (1926), 364-65.

Rev. by Hermann M. Flasdieck in *Literaturblatt für germ. u. rom. Phil.,* XLVII (1926), cols. 354-55; by Denis Saurat in *Litteris,* III (1926), 78-80; by P. Van Tieghem in *RSH,* XLI (1926), 135-37.

Lamprecht, Sterling P. *"The Fable of the bees." Journal of philosophy,* XXIII (1926), 561-79.

William Mason

Satirical poems published anonymously by William Mason, with notes by Horace Walpole. Now first published from his manuscript. Edited with an exposé of the mystification, notes and index by Paget Toynbee. Oxford: Clarendon Press, 1926.

Rev. by W. S. Lewis in *SRL,* Aug. 7, 1926, p. 24; in *TLS,* May 27, 1926, p. 352.

Draper, John W. *William Mason: a study in eighteenth-century culture.* New York: New York University Press, 1924. Cf. *PQ,* V (1926), 365.

Rev. by Odell Shepard in *JEGP,* XXV (1926), 99-102.

Milton: see *Hobbes*

Hannah More

Knox, E. V. "'Percy' (the tale of a dramatic success)." *LM,* XIII (1926), 509-15.

On Hannah More's tragedy (1777).

Roger Boyle, Earl of Orrery

Clark, William S. "The Earl of Orrery's play *The Generall.*" *RES,* II (1926), 459-60.

A supplement to his note in *RES,* II (1926), 206-11.

Clark, William S. "Further light upon the heroic plays of Roger Boyle, Earl of Orrery." *RES,* II (1926), 206-11.

Clark, William S. "The published but unacted 'heroic plays' of Roger Boyle, Earl of Orrery." *RES,* II (1926), 280-83.

Wagner, Bernard M. "Restoration heroic drama." *TLS,* Sept. 2, 1926, p. 580.

Thomas Otway

Ham, Roswell G. "Additional material for a life of Thomas Otway." *N & Q,* CL (1926), 75-77.

Ham, Roswell G. "New facts about Otway." *TLS,* Jan. 14, 1926, p. 28.

Ham, Roswell G. "Otway's duels with Churchill and Settle." *MLN,* XLI (1926), 73-80.

Samuel Pepys

Private correspondence and miscellaneous papers of Samuel Pepys, 1679-1703, in the possession of J. Pepys Cockerell. Edited by J. R. Tanner. London: Bell; New York: Harcourt, Brace, 1926. 2 vols.

Rev. by W. C. Abbott in *SRL,* July 10, 1926, p. 916; by A. B. in *History,* XI (1926), 280; by K. G. Feiling in *EHR,* XLI (1926), 448-49; by R. M. Lovett in the *New republic,* June 2, 1926, p. 64; in *TLS,* Jan. 28, 1926, p. 59. Correction by Paget Toynbee in *TLS,* Apr. 22, 1926, p. 303.

Samuel Pepys's naval minutes. Edited by J. R. Tanner. Clowes: for the Navy Record Society, 1926.

Rev. in *TLS,* Nov. 4, 1926, p. 763.

Bensly, Edward. "Pepys's eyesight." *N & Q,* CL (1926), 49.

McCutcheon, Roger P. "Pepys in the newspapers of 1679-1680." *AHR,* XXXII (1926), 61-64.

Sidelights on the charges against Pepys of sending naval information to France.

Thomas Percy

Powell, L. F. "Hau Kiou Choaan." *RES,* II (1926), 446-55.

Inspired by Miss Milner-Barry's article on Goldsmith and Percy in *RES,*

II (1926), 51-61. The author gives a rather full account, from Percy's correspondence and diary, of the negotiations leading to the publication of *Hau Kiou Choaan,* and corrects some of Miss Milner-Barry's statements. His discussion (pp. 452-54) "of the nationality of the language from which the Wilkinson-Percy translation was made" carries the problem several steps nearer solution, but it leaves a number of important questions unanswered. Nothing is said, for instance, of the illustrations in the 1761 edition, which seem to indicate that Percy had access to a copy of the Chinese original. This and other problems relating to the novel are discussed in a forthcoming paper by one of my students, Mr. Shau Yi Chan.

Reeve, C. R. "Notes on Percy's *Reliques.*" *TLS,* June 10, 1926, p. 394.

Supplementary notes by Alda Milner-Barry, *ibid.,* July 1, p. 448, and George Gordon, July 8, p. 464.

Hester Lynch Piozzi

M. "Piozzi on Boswell and Johnson." *Harvard Library notes,* No. 17, April, 1926, pp. 104-11.

Notes on annotated copies of the *Life of Johnson* and of the *Journal of a tour to the Hebrides* formerly belonging to Mrs. Piozzi and now in the Harvard Library.

Alexander Pope

Selected poems of Alexander Pope. Edited with an introduction by Louis I. Bredvold. New York: F. S. Crofts, 1926.

This volume of selections from Pope, though designed primarily for use in college classes, deserves to be mentioned here for the sake of the introductory essay on "The element of art in eighteenth century poetry." It is an admirable bit of writing, less courageous in its defence of eighteenth-century poetry than it would have been had it appeared ten years ago, but welcome none the less. The pages on the theory of poetic diction (pp. xvi-xvii) and on the Stoic and Platonic elements in neo-classicism (pp. xix-xxiv) are especially good.

Case, Arthur E. "Pope and Mary Chandler." *RES,* II (1926), 343-44, 466.

Objections to the statement of Oswald Doughty (*RES,* I, 412) that Pope, in the *Essay on man,* borrowed from one of Mary Chandler's poems. Doughty's reply (II, 344-45) begs the question.

Ann Radcliffe

Wieten, A. A. S. *Mrs. Radcliffe—her relation towards romanticism.* Amsterdam: H. J. Paris, 1926.

James Ralph

Dibble, R. F. "James Ralph, Jack of all literary trades." *Nation,* Oct. 13, 1926, pp. 361-63.

Samuel Richardson

Price, Lawrence Marsden. "On the reception of Richardson in Germany." *JEGP,* XXV (1926), 7-33.

John Wilmot, Earl of Rochester

Collected works of John Wilmot, Earl of Rochester. Edited by John Hayward. London: Nonesuch Press, 1926.

A welcome reprint of Rochester's poems, plays, and letters, with a biographical introduction and textual and explanatory notes. Unfortunately, the editor seems not to have taken the literary and historical part of his task very seriously. In his notes on the *Satyr against mankind,* for example, he not only has nothing to say about the place of that extraordinary poem in the thought of the time, but is content to repeat without verification Johnson's misleading statement concerning its relation to Boileau (p. 356). He would have done better had he quoted Rochester's first editor, Thomas Rymer, whose statement of the case in his preface to *Poems, (&c.) on several occasions* (1696) is much nearer the truth. See also Clark, *Boileau . . . in England* (Paris, 1925), pp. 7-8, 114-15.

Thomas Shadwell

Walmsley, D. M. "Shadwell and the operatic *Tempest.*" *RES,* II (1926), 463-66.

Anthony Ashley Cooper, Earl of Shaftesbury

Bandini, Luigi. "Morale e religione nello Shaftesbury." *Rivista di filosofia,* XVII (1926), 221-49.

Extract from a forthcoming book on *La dottrina morale di Shaftesbury.*

Richard Brinsley Sheridan

The Plays of Richard Brinsley Sheridan. Edited with an introduction by Iolo A. Williams. London: Herbert Jenkins; New York: Dial Press, 1926.

Rev. in *TLS,* Oct. 28, 1926, p. 741.

Panter, George W. "Early editions of Sheridan." *TLS,* Apr. 15, 1926, p. 283.

Rhodes, R. Crompton. "Sheridan apocrypha." *TLS,* Aug. 26, 1926, p. 564.

Rhodes, R. Crompton. "Sheridan bibliography." *TLS,* June 17, 1926, p. 414.

Thomas Sheridan

Flood, W. H. Grattan. "Thomas Sheridan's *Brave Irishman.*" *RES,* II (1926), 346-47.

The date of the first performance (Feb. 21, 1736-7).

Christopher Smart

Gosse, Sir Edmund. "Christopher Smart." *TLS,* May 27, 1926, p. 355.

Comment by G. J. Gray, *ibid.,* July 1, p. 448.

Adam Smith

Bonar, J. "'The theory of moral sentiments,' by Adam Smith, 1759." *Journal of philosophical studies,* I (1926), 333-53.

Tobias Smollett

The Letters of Tobias Smollett, M.D. Collected and edited by Edward S. Noyes. Cambridge, [Mass.]: Harvard University Press, 1926.

Rev. in *N & Q*, CLI (1926), 377-78; in *TLS*, Dec. 9, 1926, p. 903.

This beautifully printed edition presents the texts of seventy-two of Smollett's letters. Of these, fifteen have never appeared in print before, and thirteen others are given in a more complete form than in any previous edition. Not much can be said for Smollett's letters considered as literature; as biographical records, however, their value is considerable, and Noyes has spared no pains to make it possible for the scholar to use them easily and intelligently. His notes are unusually full; a few of them offer information which he might possibly have taken for granted in his readers, but, on the other hand, he seldom evades difficulties, and he has usually been successful in finding satisfactory answers to the questions raised by his texts. Among the more interesting notes are those which discuss Smollett's relations to his cousins (pp. 114 and 118); they should be meditated by all who are tempted to supply the lack of trustworthy records concerning the lives of eighteenth-century novelists by extracting autobiographical meanings from their fictions.

Buck, Howard Swazey. *A study in Smollett, chiefly "Peregrine Pickle," with a complete collation of the first and second editions.* New Haven: Yale University Press, 1925. Cf. *PQ*, V (1926), 369.

Rev. by A. Digeon in *RAA*, IV (1926), 73-74; in *N & Q*, CL (1926), 323-24; in *TLS*, Apr. 22, 1926, p. 299.

Melville, Lewis. *The life and letters of Tobias Smollett.* London: Faber and Gwyer, 1926.

Rev. in *TLS*, Dec. 9, 1926, p. 903.

Noyes, E. S. "A note on *Peregrine Pickle* and [Shaw's] *Pygmalion.*" *MLN*, XLI (1926), 327-30.

William Somervile

Havens, Raymond D. "William Somervile's earliest poem." *MLN*, XLI (1926), 80-86.

On the *Wicker chair* (written between 1708 and 1710), an earlier version of *Hobbinol, or the rural games* (1740).

Laurence Sterne

Bensly, Edward. "Sterne and Lord Aboyne." *N & Q*, CL (1926), 65-66.

Cross, Wilbur L. *The life and times of Laurence Sterne.* A new edition. New Haven: Yale University Press, 1925. Cf. *PQ*, V (1926), 370.

Rev. by Edith Birkhead in *MLR*, XXI (1926), 322-24; by J. B. Priestley in *SRL*, Feb. 20, 1926, pp. 569-70.

Ollard, S. L. "Sterne as a young parish priest." *TLS*, Mar. 18, 1926, p. 217.

Ryan, M. J. "An edition of Sterne." *TLS,* Sept. 16, 1926, p. 616.

Sellers, H. "A Sterne problem." *TLS,* Oct. 21, 1926, p. 722.

Comment by C. Wanklyn, *ibid.,* Nov. 4, p. 770.

Turnbull, John M. "The prototype of Walter Shandy's *Tristrapædia.*" *RES,* II (1926), 212-15.

Discloses extensive pilferings by Sterne from Obadiah Walker's *Of education especially of young gentlemen* (1673).

Jonathan Swift

Gulliver's travels. The text of the first edition, with an introduction, bibliography, and notes by Harold Williams. London: The First Edition Club, 1926.

Rev. in *TLS,* Feb. 10, 1927, p. 88.

Bradley, L. J. H. "Swift's 'Directions to servants.'" *TLS,* Feb. 11, 1926, p. 99.

Digeon, Aurélien. "'Gulliver' et La Bruyère." *RAA,* III (1926), 245-47.

Argues that the passages on war in *Gulliver,* Parts II and IV, were indebted to a development on the same theme in the twelfth chapter of *Les caractères.* The correspondences are close enough to make the conclusion fairly probable.

Eddy, William A. "*The Anatomist dissected*—by Lemuel Gulliver." *MLN,* XLI (1926), 330-31.

A satire on the Royal Society in imitation of Swift.

Firth, Sir Charles H. "Dean Swift and ecclesiastical preferment." *RES,* II (1926), 1-17.

An important article.

Firth, Sir Charles H. "A story from *Gulliver's travels.*" *RES,* II (1926), 340-41.

The source of the story of the Prime Minister's wife in *Gulliver,* III, ii.

"Gulliver's travels (October 28, 1726)." *TLS,* Oct. 28, 1926, pp. 729-30.

Mezger, F. "Swift's 'Gulliver's travels' und irische Sagen." *Archiv,* CLI (1926), 12-18.

Wedel, T. O. "On the philosophical background of *Gulliver's travels.*" *SP,* XXIII (1926), 434-50.

This is an unusually interesting article—a storehouse of information and suggestion concerning the history of ideas in the seventeenth and eighteenth centuries; and it is written with genuine gusto. It seems to me, however, open to a fundamental objection: because of defective historical method the perspective is distorted. Wedel makes sharper distinctions than history does; and he plays rather dangerously with chronology, illustrating a postulated intellectual development by opinions uttered a generation later and a generation earlier (e.g., pp. 435 and 439, n. 18). More specifically:

(1) Wedel sees Swift as an almost lone opponent of the growing "optimism" of the time as regards the goodness of human nature. This is distortion. It is reading into the first quarter of the century the benevolism which was more common in the second and third quarters—mistaking tendency for

accomplishment. It involves also a misunderstanding of what "optimism" really was. Optimism did not hold that human nature was good; it argued that no matter how bad it might be, it did not contradict the grand, beneficent plan of God. When Pope wrote (*Essay on man*, I, 155-56),

> If plagues or earthquakes break not heaven's design,
> Why then a Borgia or a Catiline?

he was maintaining that Nature was perfect, not that Borgia or Catiline were. In other words, he was a cosmological, not a humanitarian optimist. Since, therefore, optimism was committed to no brief for the goodness of human nature (and was in fact a way of reconcilement to evil), optimism offers no such contrasting background to Swift as Wedel supposes. Wedel forgets, also, the mass of "Puritan" literature, such as Defoe sometimes turned out: Moll Flanders and Mrs. Veal were no apologists for human nature. It should be noted, too, that *Gulliver's travels* apparently had its inception in the Scriblerus Club, whose members held opinions in good part like Swift's.

(2) As a part of his thesis that Swift was philosophically an exceptional figure—a survival of an earlier unfavorable attitude towards human nature in the midst of a new favorable attitude—Wedel maintains that there was a sudden shift in opinion at about the turn of the century. I do not believe this was so. As indicated above, the derogatory opinions of human nature which Wedel associates with the "old" attitude persisted prominently after the postulated change; and the points of view which he identifies with the "new" attitude—rationalism, deism, optimism—were all commonplace long before the "change": the latter would have been familiar to Plato, Aquinas, and Milton. What happened was no sudden peripety, but a very gradual shifting of emphasis.

I am more than skeptical, too, of Wedel's interpretation of Descartes. And I doubt, finally, the wisdom of the moralistic close, summed up in the words that "Swift's view of man . . . is essentially the view of the classical and Christian tradition." As a matter of history, I question the unqualified implication that there was only one "classical and Christian" tradition; and as a matter both of history and of logic, I object to the begging of the question in assuming the identity of the two traditions.—F. B. K.

Williams, Harold. "The canon of Swift: a late addition." *RES*, II (1926), 322-28.

Arguments—not very cogent in themselves—in support of Scott's ascription of *Jack Frenchman's lamentation* (1708) to Swift.

Sir William Temple

Moore Smith, G. C. "Temple and Hammond families and the related families of Nowell and Knollys." *N & Q*, CLI (1926), 237-39.

Moore Smith, G. C. "Temple and Hammond families and the related family of Harrison." *N & Q*, CLI (1926), 452-53.

Genealogical details of no great interest.

James Thomson

Potter, G[eorge] R[euben]. "James Thomson and the evolution of spirits." *ES*, LXI (1926), 57-65.

An interesting and luminously written study. The article demonstrates incidentally that Thomson was not just a sensitive barometer of the intellectual atmosphere of his day, but consciously wrought out his own philosophy.—F. B. K.

Joseph Trapp

Herrick, Marvin T. "Joseph Trapp and the Aristotelian 'catharsis.'" *MLN*, XLI (1926), 158-63.

Elizabeth Vesey

The Library of Mrs. Elizabeth Vesey, 1715-1791, . . . with other literature of the eighteenth century. Newcastle-on-Tyne: William H. Robinson, 1926. Catalogue No. 14.

Horace Walpole
(See also *William Mason*)

Hieroglyphic tales. By Horace Walpole. London: Elkin Mathews and Marrot, 1926.

Rev. in *TLS*, Dec. 9, 1926, p. 907.

A Selection of the letters of Horace Walpole. Edited by W. S. Lewis. New York: Harper & Brothers, 1926.

Rev. by Percival Merrick in *SRL*, Jan. 1, 1927, p. 481.

Supplement to the letters of Horace Walpole, Fourth Earl of Oxford, together with upwards of 150 letters addressed to Walpole between 1735 and 1796. Chronologically arranged and edited with notes and indices by Paget Toynbee. Vol. III: 1744-1797. Oxford: Clarendon Press, 1926.

Rev. by R. R. S. in *EHR*, XLI (1926), 633; by Lytton Strachey in the *New republic*, June 16, 1926, pp. 110-12; by Paul Yvon in *RAA*, III (1926), 550-53; in *N & Q*, CL (1926), 233-34; in *SRL*, May 1, 1926, p. 759; in *TLS*, Feb. 18, 1926, p. 115.

C[hapman], R. W. [Note on the plates in Walpole's *Anecdotes of painting.*] *Bodleian quarterly record,* V (1926), 55-56.

Smith, Horatio E. "Horace Walpole anticipates Victor Hugo." *MLN*, XLI (1926), 458-61.

The anticipation, which Smith is careful not to call a "source," is in the discussion of the "grotesque" in tragedy in the preface to the second edition of the *Castle of Otranto.*

Yvon, Paul. "En relisant Horace Walpole." *RELV*, XLIII (1926), 456-65.

IV. STUDIES RELATING TO THE POLITICAL AND SOCIAL ENVIRONMENT

NOTE: In this and the following section I have listed only those publications which seemed to me especially important for the historian of English literature and ideas.

Bémont, Charles. "Histoire de Grande-Bretagne." *RH*, CLIII (1926), 101-38.

A general review of recent publications, many of them relating to the period covered by this bibliography. See especially pp. 119-22, 133-36.

Beresford, John. *The godfather of Downing Street: Sir George Downing, 1623-1684.* London: Richard Cobden-Sanderson, 1925.

Rev. by G. O. Sayles in *Scottish historical review,* XXIII (1926), 225.

Buer, M. C. *Health, wealth, and population in the early days of the Industrial Revolution.* London: Routledge, 1926.

The Complete Newgate calendar. Collated and edited with some appendices by J. L. Rayner and G. T. Crook. London: Navarre Society, 1926. 5 vols.

Rev. in *TLS,* June 10, 1926, p. 388.

deCastro, J. Paul. *The Gordon riots.* London: Humphrey Milford, Oxford University Press, 1926.

Rev. in *N & Q,* CLI (1926), 305; in *TLS,* Oct. 7, 1926, p. 667.

Dimond, Sydney G. *The psychology of the Methodist revival.* London: Oxford University Press, 1926.

Drinkwater, John. *Mr. Charles, King of England.* London: Hodder and Stoughton; New York: George H. Doran, 1926.

Rev. in *TLS,* Jan. 13, 1927, p. 22.

Frequent extracts from unpublished manuscripts in the Hinchinbroke collection give to Drinkwater's pages a certain air of erudition. But the documents in question are usually quite unimportant, and the narrative, which deals chiefly with the personal life of Charles, is based in the main upon a few well known sources. The style is agreeable but not distinguished; the later chapters, in particular, leave an unfortunate impression of incoherence. The chief value of the book is that, along with some special pleading, it gives to readers brought up on the traditional Whig interpretation of the Restoration a more sympathetic, and probably truer, conception of Charles' character.

Esdaile, Katharine A. "English sculpture in the later XVIIth and XVIIIth centuries." *LM,* XIV (1926), 170-79, 262-71.

Faber, Harald. *Caius Gabriel Cibber, 1630-1700: his life and work.* Oxford: Clarendon Press, 1926.

Rev. in *N & Q,* CLI (1926), 161-62; in *TLS,* Aug. 5, 1926, p. 521. Comment by Katharine A. Esdaile in *TLS,* Aug. 12, 1926, p. 537.

Firth, Sir Charles H. "The Dictionary of national biography." *Bulletin of the Institute of historical research,* III (1926), 186-95; IV (1926), 48-61, 123-26.

Corrections and additions.

Firth, Sir Charles H. "London during the Civil War." *History,* XI (1926), 25-36.

An interesting commentary on Macaulay's remark (*History of England,* ch. III) that "but for the hostility of the City, Charles I would never have been vanquished, and that without the help of the City, Charles II could scarcely have been restored."

The Foundling Hospital and its neighbourhood. With an introduction by W. R. Lethaby. London: The Foundling Estate Protection Association, 1926.

Grant, Colonel Maurice Harold. *A chronological history of the old English landscape painters (in oil).* London: Published by the author, 1925.

Rev. in *TLS,* Feb. 18, 1926, p. 113.

Hinkhouse, F. J. *The preliminaries of the American Revolution as seen in the English press, 1763-1775.* New York: Columbia University Press, 1926.

Horwood, R. "Plan of the cities of London and Westminster, the Borough of Southwark, and parts adjoining, 1792-1799." *The mask,* XII (1926), 49-65, 100-03.

Sixteen plates.

Johnson, Captain Charles. *A general history of the pirates.* Edited with a preface by Philip Gosse. London: Cayme Press, 1926.

Johnson, Captain Charles. *A general history of the robberies and murders of the most notorious pirates.* Edited by Arthur L. Hayward. London: Routledge, 1926.

Rev. in *TLS,* Nov. 25, 1926, p. 860.

Klingberg, Frank J. *The anti-slavery movement in England: a study in English humanitarianism.* New Haven: Yale University Press, 1926.

McMurray, William. "London taverns in the XVIIth century." *N & Q,* CLI (1926), 438-40.

A list of taverns and coffee-houses flourishing in 1663.

Marshall, Dorothy. *The English poor in the eighteenth century: a study in social and administrative history from 1662 to 1782.* London: Routledge, 1926.

Morgan, William Thomas. "The Five Nations and Queen Anne." *Mississippi Valley historical review,* XIII (1926), 169-89.

Morse, Hosea Ballou. *The chronicles of the East India Company trading to China, 1635-1834.* Oxford: Clarendon Press; Cambridge [Mass.]: Harvard University Press, 1926. 4 vols.

Rev. by John Easton in *Scottish historical review,* XXIV (1926), 61-62; by K. S. Latourette in *AHR,* XXXII (1926), 105-06.

Piette, Maximin. *La réaction Wesléyenne dans l'évolution protestante: étude d'histoire religieuse. Brussels: La Lecture au Foyer,* 1925.

Rev. by Charles Bémont in *RH,* CLIII (1926), 135-36; by J. H. Faulkner in *AHR,* XXXI (1926), 315-16; by Alfred Loisy in *RC,* LX (1926), 81-83; by George Milligan in *Scottish historical review,* XXIII (1926), 216-17.

Sée, Henri. *Les origines du capitalisme moderne.* Paris: Armand Colin, 1926.

Rev. by Albert Mathiez in *Annales historiques de la Révolution française,* III (1926), 502-03.

Smith, Captain Alexander. *A complete history of the lives and robberies of the most notorious highwaymen, footpads, shoplifts, and cheats of both sexes.* Edited by Arthur L. Hayward. London: Routledge, 1926.

Rev. in *TLS,* Oct. 28, 1926, p. 735.

Sykes, Norman. *Edmund Gibson: Bishop of London, 1669-1748: a study in politics and religion in the eighteenth century.* Oxford: Clarendon Press, 1926.

Rev. in *TLS,* Jan. 6, 1927, p. 7.

Tawney, R. H. *Religion and the rise of capitalism: a historical study.* London: Murray; New York: Harcourt, Brace, 1926.

Rev. by Bartlett Brebner in *SRL,* Jan. 8, 1927, p. 495; by Stuart Chase in the *Nation,* Dec. 1, 1926, pp. 563-64; by E. S. Furniss in the *Yale review,* XVI (1927), 385-87; by George O'Brien in *Studies: an Irish quarterly review,* XV (1926), 217-29; by Henri Sée in *Revue d'histoire moderne,* I (1926), 388-89; by Preserved Smith in *AHR,* XXXII (1927), 309-11; in *TLS,* Apr. 29, 1926, p. 311.

The subject of this very important book may be described in general terms as the shifting relations between religious and moral ideals on the one hand and economic practice on the other, from the end of the Middle Ages to the beginning of the eighteenth century. More specifically, Tawney seeks to show how the characteristic medieval notion of a society in which all human activities were at least nominally subject to moral control gradually gave place to the modern "capitalistic" conception of the life of profit-seeking as an autonomous realm in which the only valid laws are mechanical. The forces which operated in bringing about this transformation were in the main, he recognizes, economic—the irresistible march of the commercial and financial middle class. But he seeks to make clear also that the rise within this class of the religious movement of Puritanism, though in its earlier phases it involved a reassertion of the medieval attitude (see especially pp. 216-24), eventually in the period after the Restoration gave an enormous stimulus to the new spirit of profiteering (see pp. 240-47). This thesis, of course, is not altogether new. Tawney himself gave a sketch of it in a series of articles in the *Journal of political economy* for 1923, and in a slightly different form the same thesis has had considerable vogue in Germany ever since the publication of Max Weber's famous study, "Die protestantische Ethik und der Geist des Kapitalismus." Tawney, however, seems to me to mark an advance over Weber (of whose theory he has written a penetrating criticism, pp. 315-17) in two ways: first in his more realistic insistence upon the primacy of economic as distinguished from ideological causes, and second in his recognition of the double character of the Puritan influence. For students of English literature in the seventeenth and eighteenth centuries, his book contains hints which should result in a number of new interpretations of the writers and movements of that period. He himself has some suggestive remarks on Baxter (pp. 220-24) and on Bunyan (p. 307); and it would be easy, and, I believe, illuminating, to study certain later writers from the same point of view. Defoe is an especially good case. Could anything be more "capitalistic," in Tawney's sense of the word, than the following sentences from the *Review* for July 29, 1710: "The *Dutch* are our Neighbours; in the Confederacy they are our Friends; they join with us in defending the Protestant Interest, and the Cause of Liberty; they are our good Allies against the *French,* and I shall be the last that shall speak, or write a Word in prejudice of our Friendship with the *Dutch.*—But Trade knows no Friends, in Commerce there is Correspondence of Nations, but no Confederacy; he is my Friend in Trade, who I can Trade with, *that is,* can get by; but he that would get *from me,* is my Mortal Enemy in Trade, tho' he were my Father, Brother, Friend, or Confederate.'' (I owe this text to one of my students, Mr. H. H. Andersen, who is preparing a study of Defoe's economic and social ideas.) Finally, not the least of the merits of Tawney's book is its excellent and at times brilliant style. It is perhaps too brilliant in places, but that is a fault which, after a prolonged diet of dissertations and articles in learned journals, one is easily tempted to forgive.

Thomas, P. J. *Merchantilism and East India Trade: an early phase of the protection and free trade controversy.* London: P. S. King, 1926.

Tipping, H. Avray. *English homes: Period VI.* Volume I: *Late Georgian, 1760-1820.* London: *Country life,* 1926.

Rev. by Christopher Hussey in *Observer,* Sept. 5, 1926, p. 4; in *TLS,* Sept. 16, 1926, p. 609.

Turberville, A. S. *English men and manners in the eighteenth century: an illustrated narrative.* Oxford: Clarendon Press, 1926.

Rev. in *N & Q,* CLI (1926), 468; in *TLS,* Oct. 21, 1926, p. 711.

An attempt to describe English society in the eighteenth century through a series of portraits of representative personalities—statesmen and politicians (chs. IV-VIII), divines (ch. IX), philanthropists (ch. X), writers, artists, actors, and musicians (chs. XI-XIII), ''empire builders'' (ch. XIV), and soldiers and admirals (chs. XV-XVI). The volume also has an introductory chapter on the general spirit of the period, an ''outline of events'' (ch. II), and an analysis of the structure of society (ch. III). It should prove very useful in giving to students a conception of the social background of eighteenth-century literature. The illustrations are numerous and well selected.

The Diary of a country parson: the Reverend James Woodforde. Edited by John Beresford. Volume II, 1782-1787. London: Humphrey Milford, Oxford University Press, 1926.

Rev. by G. B. H. in *EHR,* XLI (1926), 634-35; in *N & Q,* CL (1926), 251-52; in *TLS,* Mar. 11, 1926, p. 179.

V. STUDIES RELATING TO THE CONTINENTAL BACKGROUND

''John Adams on Rousseau: his comments on Rousseau's 'Inequality among mankind,' written in 1794, and now first published.'' *More books, being the Bulletin of the Boston Public Library,* I (1926), 53-64.

Marginal comments in a copy of the English translation of 1761.

Bernoulli, C., and H. Kern. *Romantische Naturphilosophie.* Jena: Diederichs, 1926.

Bouvier, Auguste. J. G. Zimmerman: un représentant suisse du cosmopolitisme littéraire au XVIIIe siècle. Geneva: Georg et Cie., 1925.

Rev. by Henri Lichtenberger in *Revue germanique,* XVII (1926), 377.

Brunet, P. *Les physiciens hollandais et la méthode expérimentale en France au XVIIIe siècle.* Paris: Blanchard, 1926.

Brunot, Ferdinand. *Histoire de la langue française des origines à 1900.* Tome VII: *La propagation du français en France jusqu'à la fin de l'ancien régime.* Paris: A. Colin, 1926.

Rev. by E. Bourciez in *RC,* LX (1926), 311-14; Louis Brandin in *Modern languages,* VII (1926), 174-76; by Lucien Febvre in *RSH,* XLII (1926), 19-40; by Ch. Guerlin de Guer in *Revue du Nord,* XII (1926), 227-33; by Albert Mathiez in *Annales historiques de la Révolution française,* III (1926), 287-89.

Chase, Cleveland B. *The young Voltaire.* New York: Longmans, Green & Co., 1926.

Rev. in *New York Times Book review,* Oct. 31, 1926, p. 9; in *TLS,* Dec. 16, 1926, p. 931.

A study of Voitaire's stay in England with particular reference to the English influence on his outlook and ideas. A popular restatement of points already well known to specialists.

Cherel, A. *Un aventurier religieux au XVIIIe siècle: André-Michel Ramsay.* Paris: Perrin, 1926.

"Le Classicisme français à l'étranger." *RLC,* VI (1926), 347-50.

Notes on recent studies.

Cohen, Gustave. "Le séjour de Saint-Evremond en Hollande (1665-1670)." *RLC,* VI (1926), 28-78, 402-23.

An important series of articles (see *PQ,* V, 377). Of special interest is the discussion of Saint-Evremond's relations with Vossius, Huygens, and Spinoza.

Dubosq, Y. Z. *Le livre français et son commerce en Hollande de 1750 à 1780* Amsterdam: H. J. Paris, 1926.

Ducros, Louis. *French society in the eighteenth century.* Translated from the French by W. de Geijer, with a foreword by J. A. Higgs-Walker. London: G. Bell, 1926.

Rev. by David Ogg in *Scottish historical review,* XXIV (1926), 70; in *TLS,* June 10, p. 387.

Dugas, L. "Une théorie physiologique du rire au XVIIIe siècle." *Revue bleue,* Jan. 16, 1926, pp. 45-49.

DuPeloux, Charles. *Répertoire général des ouvrages modernes relatifs au XVIIIe siècle français (1715-1789).* Paris: Grund, 1926.

Rev. in *RLC,* VI (1926), 695.

Ernst, Fritz. "La tradition médiatrice de la Suisse aux XVIIIe et XIXe siècles." *RLC,* VI (1926), 549-607.

Etienne, S. "La méthode en histoire littéraire à propos d'une publication récente sur le roman français au XVIIIe siècle" [Mornet's edition of Rousseau's *Nouvelle Héloïse*]. *Revue belge de philologie et d'histoire,* V (1926), 351-80.

Gaffiot, Maurice. "La théorie du luxe dans l'œuvre de Voltaire." *Revue d'histoire économique et sociale,* XIV (1926), 320-43.

A useful summary in four parts: (1) "La définition du luxe"; (2) "Les causes du luxe"; (3) "Les effets du luxe"; and (4) "Les lois somptuaires."

The writer seems not to know the important study of André Morize, *L'apologie du luxe au XVIIIe siècle* (Paris, 1909).

Gaquère, Abbé François. *La vie et les œuvres de Claude Fleury (1640-1723).* Paris: J. de Gigord, 1925.

Rev. by A. Cherel in *RHL*, XXXIII (1926), 634-35; in *TLS*, Mar. 4, 1926, p. 154.

Günther, Hans R. G. "Psychologie des deutschen Pietismus." *Deutsche Vierteljahrsschrift für Literaturwissenschaft und Geistesgeschichte*, IV (1926), 144-76.

Hazard, Paul. "Romantisme italien et romantisme européen." *RLC*, VI (1926), 224-45.

The opening lecture of a course at the Collège de France.

Kies, Paul P. "The sources and basic model of Lessing's *Miss Sara Sampson.*" *MP*, XXIV (1926), 65-90.

An attempt to show that Lessing began by constructing a "plot outline" from elements supplied by Shadwell's *Squire of Alsatia*, and then deliberately inserted into this framework characters and motifs taken now from Mrs. Centlivre's *Perjur'd husband* and now from Charles Johnson's *Caelia*, keeping this latter play "constantly before him during the composition of his own" (p. 89). But as the characters and motifs in question are of a rather conventional type, and as *Miss Sara Sampson* is a play and not a doctor's dissertation, the argument is not entirely convincing.

Lion, H. "Rousseau et d'Argens." *RHL*, XXXIII (1926), 415-18.

Magendie, M. *La politesse mondaine et les théories de l'honnêteté, en France, au XVIIe siècle, de 1600 à 1660.* Paris: Alcan, [1925]. 2 vols.

Rev. by René Bray in *RHL*, XXXIII (1926), 271-72; by J. E. Spingarn in *Romanic review*, XVII (1926), 71-73; in *TLS*, Apr. 15, 1926, p. 276.

In this dissertation of 943 pages Magendie has done pioneer work in an early period of our richest literature of courtesy. In confining his treatment almost exclusively to French writers, however, he has considered in isolation a body of ideas that were very often indifferent to national boundaries. He is not unaware of the indebtedness of France to Italy for theories of *honnêteté*, but in evaluating the debt he examines—rather skeptically—only Castiglione, Della Casa, and Guazzo as possible sources. He might have considered such other representative writers as Machiavelli, Nenna, Romei, Ringhieri, Bargagli, and Ducci in an effort to determine the extent of the Italian influence in general. It is possible, also, that he has given insufficient attention to that important Spanish writer, Gracian, whose influence he appears to minimize (II, 720). The relation of seventeenth-century French courtesy to the general humanistic movement is almost wholly neglected, and if Magendie had formed but the slightest acquaintance with the various medieval books of courtesy (e.g., Caxton's) he would hardly have made the bold statement that "Erasme fut le créateur de la civilité puérile, et ne semble pas avoir eu de devancier" (I, 150).

Magendie might have made his work more useful to students of the *honnête homme* and at the same time have given to his ideas a better emphasis and proportion if he had chosen to treat the theories of *honnêteté* as a tradition by organizing his materials according to ideas rather than according to authors and works.

Nevertheless, in spite of these criticisms as to perspective and method, Magendie has put into his work the results of much careful reading in an extensive and difficult field. Students of the conception of the gentleman in every modern European literature must feel grateful to him for his many careful distinctions (e.g., I, 150), for his warnings concerning the pitfalls that lie ahead of the student in this field (e.g., I, 339 ff), and for his valuable bibliography and his numerous abstracts of books that are practically inaccessible to most of us.—V. B. H.

Martin, Gaston. *La francmaçonnerie française et la préparation de la Révolution.* Paris: Presses universitaires, 1926.

Rev. by A. Aulard and R. Vivier in *La Révolution française,* LXXIX (1926), 173-76; by Albert Mathiez in *Annales historiques de la Révolution française,* III (1926), 498-502; by Henri Sée in *RH,* CLII (1926), 94-96.

Morel, Jean-Emile. "Jean-Jacques Rousseau lit Plutarque." *Revue d'histoire moderne,* I (1926), 81-102.

An interesting study of Rousseau's debt to Plutarch, especially in the *Discours sur l'inégalité,* based on a MS note-book (1753-1754) in which Rousseau recorded passages which had interested him in his reading.

Mornet, Daniel. *La pensée française au XVIIIe siècle.* Paris: Armand Colin, 1926.

Rev. by Gilbert Chinard in *MLN,* XLII (1927), 124-25; in *TLS,* Dec. 23, 1926, p. 946.

Pagès, G. "Histoire de France de 1660 à 1789." *RH,* CLII (1926), 66-86.

A systematic survey of recent publications.

Pflaum, Heinz. "Rationalismus und Mystik in der Philosophie Spinozas." *Deutsche Vierteljahrsschrift für Literaturwissenschaft und Geistesgeschichte,* IV (1926), 127-43.

Price, Lawrence Marsden. "Albrecht von Haller and English theology." *PMLA,* XLI (1926), 942-54.

Questions the importance of Newton's influence (cf. H. M. Jones, *ibid.,* XL [1925], 103-27) and suggests as possible alternative influences William King and Samuel Clarke.

Ranscelot, Jean. "Les manifestations du déclin poétique au début du XVIIIe siècle." *RHL,* XXXIII (1926), 497-520.

An informing and suggestive article on various phases of the rationalistic attack on poetry, discussing what seventeenth- and eighteenth-century theorists thought concerning the cramping influence of verse, whether poetry can be written in prose, and the origins of poetry and of rime. Certain subjective interjections of Ranscelot raise the question whether in studies of this type it is worth arguing with dead authors. Is it not at once better method and more dramatic to let their contemporary adversaries answer, if there must be an answer?—F. B. K.

Ratner, Joseph. "In defense of Spinoza." *Journal of philosophy,* XXIII (1926), 121-33.

A general review of the *Chronicon Spinozanum,* vols. I-III (1921-1923).

Roustan, M. *The pioneers of the French Revolution.* Translated by Frederic Whyte, with an introduction by Harold J. Laski. London: Benn; Boston: Little, Brown, 1926.

Rev. by Henry E. Bourne in *Political science quarterly,* XLI (1926), 635-37; by Kingsley Martin in *Economica,* No. 18, Nov., 1926, pp. 345-47; in the *Nation,* July 28, 1926, p. 83; in *TLS,* Mar. 18, 1926, p. 200.

Schaffer, Aaron. "Chateaubriand's reading during his 'Emigration.'" *PQ,* V (1926), 258-72.

Contains a useful list of the literary references in the *Essai sur les révolutions.* Among the titles which the writer has not been able to identify (p. 272), "Laf.: *Mœurs des sauvages*" is of course the well known work of Lafitau, *Mœurs des sauvages amériquains comparées aux mœurs des premiers temps* (Paris, 1724).

Schinz, Albert. "Bibliographie critique de Jean-Jacques Rousseau dans les cinq dernières années." *MLN,* XLI (1926), 423-38.

Schinz, Albert. "Fénelon, critique littéraire, précurseur." *RCC,* XXVII[1] (1926), 587-601.

Schomann, Emilie. "Des Feminismus während der französischen Revolution." *Zeitschrift für französischen und englischen Unterricht,* XXV (1926), 13-31, 101-17.

Schütze, Martin. "Herder's conception of 'Bild.'" *Germanic review,* I (1926), 21-35.

Stieler, Georg. "Bibliographie der Malebranche-Literatur." *Literarische Berichte aus dem Gebiete der Philosophie* (Erfurt: Kurt Stenger), pp. 93-100.

Teggart, Frederick J. "Turgot's approach to the study of man." *University of California chronicle,* XXVIII (1926), 129-42.

Toinet, Raymond. "Les écrivains moralistes au XVIIe siècle." *RHL,* XXXIII (1926), 395-407.

Additions and corrections to the bibliography published in the same journal between 1916 and 1918.

Vier, J.-A. "L'activité d'une académie provinciale au XVIIIe siècle: l'Académie de Stanislas de 1750 à 1766." *RHL,* XXXIII (1926), 337-54.

Wade, Ira O. *The "philosophe" in the French drama of the eighteenth century.* Princeton: Princeton University Press, 1926. ("Elliott monographs in the Romance languages and literatures," No. 18.)

Willoughby, L. A. *The classical age of German literature, 1745-1805.* London: Oxford University Press, 1926.

Rev. in *RLC,* VI (1926), 523.

1928

ENGLISH LITERATURE, 1660-1800: A CURRENT BIBLIOGRAPHY

By Ronald S. Crane
University of Chicago

This bibliography attempts to list the more significant books, articles, and reviews published during the year 1927, together with a few bearing the date 1926 which came to my attention too late to be included in the bibliography for that year (*PQ*, VI, 161-200). Professors G. R. Havens, F. B. Kaye, Marjorie H. Nicolson, and George Sherburn have contributed the reviews signed with their respective initials.

LIST OF ABBREVIATIONS

AHR=American historical review.
Archiv=Archiv für das Studium der neueren Sprachen und Literaturen.
Beiblatt=Beiblatt zur Anglia.
EHR=English historical review.
ES=Englische Studien.
GRM=Germanisch-romanische Monatsschrift.
JEGP=Journal of English and Germanic philology.
LM=London mercury.
MLN=Modern language notes.
MLR=Modern language review.
MP=Modern philology.
N & Q=Notes and queries.
PMLA=Publications of the Modern Language Association of America.
PQ=Philological quarterly.
RAA=Revue anglo-américaine.
RC=Revue critique.
RCC=Revue des cours et conférences.
RELV=Revue de l'enseignement des langues vivantes.
RES=Review of English studies.
RH=Revue historique.
RHL=Revue d'histoire littéraire de la France.
RLC=Revue de littérature comparée.
RSH=Revue de synthèse historique.
SP=Studies in philology.
SRL=Saturday review of literature.
TLS=Times [London] literary supplement.

I. BIBLIOGRAPHICAL AIDS

Annual bibliography of English language and literature. Volume VII, 1926. Edited for the Modern Humanities Research Association by D. Everett and E. Seaton. Cambridge: Bowes & Bowes, 1927.

The Ashley library: a catalogue of printed books, manuscripts and autograph letters collected by Thomas James Wise. Volume VIII. London: Printed for private circulation only, 1926.

Rev. in *TLS,* March 17, 1927, p. 182.

Baugh, A. C. "American bibliography for 1926. I. English language and literature." *PMLA,* XLII (1927), 1-39.

See especially pp. 27-33.

Bernbaum, Ernest. "Recent works on prose fiction before 1800." *MLN,* XLII (1927), 281-93.

An admirable survey, refreshingly outspoken, which should be continued. The present article deals with publications of 1925 and 1926.

Chapman, R. W. "Cancels and stubs." *Library,* N. S., VIII (1927), 264-68.

Chapman, R. W. "An inventory of paper, 1674." *Library,* N. S., VII (1927), 402-08.

Chapman, R. W. "The numbering of editions in the eighteenth century." *RES,* III (1927), 77-79.

C[hapman], R. W. "'Picked' copies." *RES,* III (1927), 79.

A Collection of books illustrating the literary history of Great Britain during the last fifty years of the eighteenth century. London: Birrell & Garnett, 1927.

Contains 877 items.

Crane, Ronald S. "English literature of the Restoration and eighteenth century: a current bibliography." *PQ,* VI (1927), 161-200.

Crane, R. S. and F. B. Kaye, with the assistance of M. E. Prior. *A census of British newspapers and periodicals, 1620-1800.* Chapel Hill, N. C.: University of North Carolina Press, 1927. Reprinted from *SP,* XXIV (1927), 1-205.

Rev. by G. Binz in *Beiblatt,* XXXVIII (1927), 349-54 (some additional titles, mostly almanacs, which were expressly excluded from the *Census*); by L. Cazamian in *RAA,* V (1928), 266; by W. T. Laprade in *South Atlantic quarterly,* XXVII (1928), 96; by I. A. Williams in *LM,* XVI (1927), 532-34; in *RLC,* VII (1927), 759; in *TLS,* Oct. 20, 1927, p. 739 (cf. also Dec. 15 and 22).

Kennedy, Arthur G. *A bibliography of writings on the English language from the beginning of printing to the end of 1922.* Cambridge and New Haven: Harvard University Press and Yale University Press; London: H. Milford, 1927.

Rev. by A. Mawer in *MLR,* XXII (1927), 466-67.

McKerrow, Ronald B. *An introduction to bibliography for literary students.* Oxford: Clarendon Press, 1927.

Rev. in *N & Q,* CLIII (1927), 377-78; in *TLS,* Nov. 3, 1927, p. 787.

A greatly enlarged edition of the author's "Notes on bibliographical evidence for literary students and editors of English works of the sixteenth and seventeenth centuries" (*Transactions of the Bibliographical Society,* XII

[1914], 213-318). The plan has been improved; many new topics and illustrations have been introduced; and the scope of the work has been broadened so as to take in the whole history of English book-production down to about 1800. Of the value of the book in its new form for editors of Restoration and eighteenth-century no less than of Elizabethan texts it is difficult to speak with moderation. It is true that comparatively few illustrations are drawn from the period after 1640; but this is not a serious criticism even from the point of view of specialists in the later field, for the fundamental practices of compositors and pressmen seem to have changed but little from the days of Elizabeth to those of Victoria, with the result that, as Mr. McKerrow points out, ''a student who is familiar with the methods of book-production in the years during which Shakespeare was writing will need only a little experience with the books themselves to understand the methods of any other period up to the middle of the nineteenth century.'' And nowhere will one find a fuller or more lucid exposition of these methods than in the present book.

I add a few remarks on particular points, mainly by way of confirmation or supplementary illustration. Pp. xiv-xv: the ''short list of some books of special utility to students'' given here includes, besides various standard modern works, two early treatises on printing methods—Moxon's *Mechanick exercises* (1683) and Johnson's *Typographia* (1824). It may be useful to record the titles of a few other books of this sort published in the interval between Moxon and Johnson (there are copies of all of them in the Newberry Library, Chicago): John Smith, *The printer's grammar* (1755); Philip Luckombe, *A concise history of . . . . printing, with practical instructions to the trade in general* (1770); *The printer's grammar, chiefly compiled from Smith's edition* (1787); and C. Stower, *The printer's grammar; or, introduction to the art of printing* (1808). It is perhaps worth noting that the description of the process of composition given by Johnson goes back in large part, through Stower, to Smith. There is a useful account of these treatises in the introduction to T. C. Hansard's *Typographia* (1825). P. 12, n. 2: that leads *were* sometimes inserted after and not during composition is shown by the curious proof-sheets of Goldsmith's *Traveller*, now in the British Museum (C.58.g.7). In these the process of leading has been carried out for the first three sheets (B-D); the four pages of sheet E, however, remain as originally composed, without leads, page-numbers, or running-heads. Pp. 65-66: there is ample support in the treatises referred to above for the statement made here that until the nineteenth century books were regularly arranged directly in pages, without the intervention of long galleys. See, for example, Smith, *The printer's grammar*, p. 201. Proofs were apparently taken after the pages had been put in forms and locked up (*ibid.*, p. 271). P. 91: Wither's testimony as to the responsibility of publishers for the titles of books is echoed by a writer in the *British magazine* for April, 1761 (II, 199): ''Another grievance, of which, like Mons. Bayle, I must say, *animus meminisse horret*, is that practice of booksellers, who, among other invasions of the prerogative of us authors, assume a right to dub a book with a title of their own invention.'' P. 168: for other examples of 12mos sewn in alternate gatherings of eight and four leaves, see A. E. Case in *MP*, XXIV (1927), 297, 309. P. 250: on the question of how far the punctuation of an eighteenth-century book represented the author's wishes it is impossible to generalize until someone has made a systematic study from this point of view of such surviving manuscripts of the period as have passed through printers' hands. Smith says (*The printer's grammar*, p. 199) that it is the business of the printer to ''point'' an author's copy. Most authors, he adds, expect it.

Sawyer, Charles J. and F. J. Harvey Darton. *English books, 1475-1900: a signpost for collectors.* London: C. J. Sawyer, 1927. 2 vols.

Rev. in *TLS*, Nov. 3, 1927, p. 796.

Van Tieghem, Paul. "Principaux ouvrages d'histoire littéraire générale et comparée (onzième compte rendu annuel)." *RSH*, XLIV (1927), 103-37.

The Year's work in English studies. Volume VI, 1925. Edited for the English Association by F. S. Boas and C. H. Herford. London: H. Milford, Oxford University Press, 1927.

Rev. by L. Cazamian in *RAA*, IV (1927), 471-72; in *TLS*, Mar. 17, 1927, p. 182.

Chapters IX and X, by Allardyce Nicoll and Edith J. Morley respectively, cover the period of the Restoration and eighteenth century. The method employed in them is that with which we have become familiar in earlier volumes of the series: a succession of loosely organized appreciations of the principal books and articles published in the course of the year. The chapters represent much devoted and useful labor on the part of their compilers, but the result is hardly as satisfactory as it would be if a clearer understanding prevailed as to the purpose to be served by the work. As it is, the chapters are both too incomplete and too inconveniently arranged to compete as bibliographies with (say) the annual volume of the M.H.R.A.; and on the other hand, they do not quite come up to the ideal of a systematic and critical survey of the state of scholarship which would mark out general tendencies and fit particular works into the scheme of a developing exploration of the field. They suffer, too, from the fact that their writers seem to hesitate between two publics—that of general readers and that of serious investigators.

II. THE SOCIAL AND POLITICAL ENVIRONMENT

NOTE: I include here only such publications as appear to have a fairly direct bearing on the problems of literary and intellectual history.

Austen-Leigh, R. A. *The Eton College register, 1698-1752.* Eton: Spottiswoode, 1927.

Rev. in *TLS*, June 9, 1927, p. 401.

Belasco, Philip S. "Note on the Labour Exchange idea in the seventeenth century." *Economic journal*, Economic history series, No. 2 (1927), pp. 275-79.

Bleackley, Horace. "Eighteenth century Newgate." *N & Q*, CLIII (1927), 167-68.

Constable, W. G. *John Flaxman, 1755-1826.* London: University of London Press, 1927.

Rev. in *TLS*, Aug. 18, 1927, p. 558.

Gosse, Philip. *A bibliography of the works of Capt. Charles Johnson.* London: Dulau, 1927.

Rev. by I. A. Williams in *LM*, XVI (1927), 203.

Griffith, G. Talbot. *Population problems of the age of Malthus.* Cambridge: University Press, 1926.

Rev. by Elie Halévy in *RAA*, V (1927), 79-80.

Imbert-Terry, Sir H. M. *A constitutional king: George I.* London: John Murray, 1927.

Rev. in *TLS*, May 5, 1927, p. 311.

Knight, M. M. "Recent literature on the origins of modern capitalism." *Quarterly journal of economics,* XLI (1927), 520-33.

Lives of the most remarkable criminals who have been condemned and executed for murder, the highway, housebreaking, street robberies, coining, or other offences. Collected from original papers and authentic memoirs and published in 1735. Edited by Arthur L. Hayward. London: Routledge, 1927.

Rev. in *TLS,* Oct. 13, 1927, p. 714.

The Correspondence of James Logan and Thomas Story, 1724-1741. Edited by Norman Penney. London: Friends Book Centre, 1927.

Lower, A. R. M. "The evolution of the sentimental idea of empire: a Canadian view." *History,* XI (1927), 289-303.

Mallet, Sir Charles Edward. *A history of the University of Oxford.* Volume III. London: Methuen, 1927.

Rev. in *TLS,* Oct. 20, 1927, p. 735.

Marcus, Hans. "Friedrichs des Grossen literarische Propaganda in England: eine Sammlung bisher unveröffentlichten Archivmaterials aus den Jahren 1756-1763." *Archiv,* CLI (1927), 161-243.

Letters to Prussian agents in London.

Namier, L. B. "Brice Fisher, M. P.: a mid-eighteenth-century merchant and his connexions." *EHR,* XLII (1927), 514-32.

Ollivant, Alfred. "An eighteenth-century cleric." *Nineteenth century,* CI (1927), 432-40.

Riddell, William Renwick. "Why not give Titus Oates a chance?" *Journal of the American Institute of Criminal Law and Criminology,* XVIII (1927), 17-23.

Riddell, William Renwick. "William Penn and witchcraft." *Journal of the American Institute of Criminal Law and Criminology,* XVIII (1927), 11-16.

Sée, Henri. "Dans quelle mesure Puritains et Juifs ont-ils contribué aux progrès du capitalisme moderne?" *RH,* CLV (1927), 57-68.

A critical discussion of the views of Weber, Troeltsch, Sombart, and Tawney.

Shaw, Wm. A. "Lives of English painters: a bibliographical note." *TLS,* June 2 and Oct. 27, 1927, pp. 391, 765.

Sykes, Norman. "Historical revisions. XL.—Queen Caroline and the Church." *History,* XI (1927), 333-39.

Taylor, Overton H. "Tawney's Religion and capitalism, and

eighteenth-century liberalism." *Quarterly journal of economics,* XLI (1927),718-31.

The Diary of Henry Teonge. Edited by G. E. Manwaring. London: Routledge, 1927.

Light on the navy under Charles II. Teonge was a naval chaplain.

Turberville, A. S. *The House of Lords in the eighteenth century.* Oxford: Clarendon Press, 1927.

Rev. in *TLS,* Oct. 13, 1927, p. 703.

Turner, E. R. "The excise scheme of 1733." *EHR,* XLII (1927), 34-57.

A study in the public opinion of the early eighteenth century and its expression through pamphlets and newspapers.

Turner, E. R. *The Privy Council of England in the seventeenth and eighteenth centuries.* Volume I. Baltimore: The Johns Hopkins University Press, 1927.

Rev. in *TLS,* Oct. 6, 1927, p. 691.

Webb, Sidney and Beatrice. *English Poor Law history.* Part I: *The old Poor Law.* London: Longmans, Green and Co., 1927.

Rev. in *TLS,* Mar. 24, 1927, p. 203.
A detailed study of the period from 1660 to 1834.

Williams, Judith Blow. *A guide to the printed materials for English social and economic history, 1750-1850.* New York: Columbia University Press, 1926.

Rev. by W. T. Laprade in *South Atlantic quarterly,* XXVII (1928), 96-98; by H. S. in *RH,* CLV (1927), 193-94.

The Diary of a country parson: the Reverend James Woodforde. Edited by John Beresford. Volume III, 1788-1792. London: H. Milford, Oxford University Press, 1927.

Wright, W. J. Payling. "Humanitarian London from 1688 to 1750." *Edinburgh review,* CCXLVI (1927), 287-302.

A popular and rather rambling account of the work of such early philanthropists as Thomas Firmin and Robert Nelson and of the rise of charity schools and hospitals in the period before 1750. The latter part of the article is hardly relevant to the main theme.

III. CURRENTS OF IDEAS AND LITERARY FORMS

Binz-Winiger, Elisabeth. *Erziehungsfragen in den Romanen von Samuel Richardson, Henry Fielding, Tobias Smollett, Oliver Goldsmith und Laurence Sterne.* Zürich dissertation, 1926.

Bissell, Benjamin. *The American Indian in English literature of the eighteenth century.* New Haven: Yale University Press, 1925. Cf. *PQ,* V, 344.

Rev. by F. E. Farley in *MLN,* XLII (1927), 335-38 (severe criticism); by H. Schöffler in *Beiblatt,* XXXVIII (1927), 77-82.

Brie, Friedrich. *Englische Rokoko-Epik (1710-1730).* Munich: Max Hueber, 1927.

Rev. by W. F. Schirmer in *Literaturblatt für germ. und rom. Philologie,* XLVIII (1927), cols. 108-111; by G. C. M. S[mith] in *MLR,* XXII (1927), 361-62; in *TLS,* Aug. 11, 1927, p. 548.

The poems studied in this interesting little book are Pope's *Rape of the lock,* Gay's *Fan,* and various other minor pieces in the same genre, such as Breval's *Petticoat* (1716) and *Art of dress* (1717), Jacob's *Rape of the smock* (1727?), Jenyns's *Art of dancing* (1729), and an anonymous *Clarinda, or the fair libertine* (1729). Herr Brie is impatient of the common opinion that sees behind these poems only the tradition of the mock epic inaugurated by Boileau in the preceding century. The *Rape of the lock* "ist ein Gebilde des Rokoko und somit vom stilkritischen Standpunkte aus etwas ganz anderes als die Epen von Boilleau in Frankreich oder Garth in England, die beide noch dem Barock angehören" (p. 7). So too with the others: they form a distinctively English genre, without significant parallels in French literature, but closely related in their themes and general spirit to the social essays of Addison and Steele. On this last point Herr Brie has much to say that is both interesting and new (see especially pp. 38-46, 54-64, 79-86), though he certainly draws too sharp a line between the *Rape of the lock* and the poems of Boileau and Garth. He has some very suggestive remarks also on the relations between English rococo literature and the spread of luxury in early eighteenth-century society (see particularly Chapter III, "Englischer Luxus und englische Rokoko-Literatur").

P. 19: I do not understand what is meant by the statement that "Popes *Essay on Man* ist reine Rokoko-Philosophie." P. 19, n. 1: for "Alberigo Nicola" read "Allardyce Nicoll." P. 30, n. 1: for an earlier defence of luxury by Defoe see the *Review* for May 26, 1712, pp. 739-40. P. 51: to Gildon's statement of the differences between Pope and Boileau should be added that of Dennis in his *Remarks on Mr. Pope's Rape of the lock* (1728).

Brinton, Crane. *The political ideas of the English romanticists.* London: H. Milford, Oxford University Press, 1926. Cf. *PQ,* VI, 164.

Rev. by Irving Babbitt in *Political science quarterly,* XLII (1927), 441-44; by L. Cazamian in *RAA,* V (1927), 67-68; by A. Koszul in *Les langues modernes,* XXV (1927), 561-62.

Bush, Douglas. "Some allusions to Spenser." *MLN,* XLII (1927), 314-16.

Three from the eighteenth century.

Cazamian, Louis. *A history of English literature.* Volume II, *Modern times (1660-1914).* New York: Macmillan, 1927.

Extended discussion of this translation may be dispensed with here as the original is by this time familiar to all serious students of the history of modern English literature. Slightly over half of the volume is concerned with the period from 1660 to 1798. Professor Cazamian is perhaps less intimately familiar with this period than he is with the nineteenth century, but he knows it far better than many specialists, and the four "books" in which he traces the main tendencies of literary taste from the Restoration to the French Revolution form without doubt the most satisfactory synthesis of the period that has yet appeared—the most up-to-date in its information, the most intelligently organized, the most discriminating in its analysis of movements and of individual writers and works.

Collins, A. S. *Authorship in the days of Johnson.* London: Robert Holden & Co., 1927.

Rev. in TLS, May 26, 1927, p. 371.

Collins, A. S. "The growth of the reading public (1780-1800)." *Nineteenth century,* CI (1927), 749-58.

Colman, Francis. "Opera register, 1712-1734." *The mask,* XIII (1927), 18-23.

Continued from XII, 110-14.

Covent Garden drollery, 1672. Edited by the Rev. Montague Summers. London: The Fortune Press, 1927.

Cox, James E. *The rise of sentimental comedy.* Published by the author, Drury College, Springfield, Mo., 1926.

Dentice di Accadia, C. "Il preilluminismo." *Giornale critico della filosofia italiana,* VIII (1927), 1-22, 81-106, 170-89, 256-82.

A sketch of the history of theories of knowledge, ethics, and religion in English philosophy before Locke, with special attention to the influence of Italian Renaissance thought.

"The eighteenth century in verse." *TLS,* Nov. 10, 1927, pp. 797-98.

Folkierski, W. *Entre le classicisme et le romantisme.* Paris: Champion, 1925. Cf. *PQ,* VI, 166-68.

Rev. by L. Cazamian in *RAA,* IV (1927), 452-54; by D. Mornet in *Romanic review,* XVIII (1927), 106-11.

Foster, Herbert D. "International Calvinism through Locke and the Revolution of 1688." *AHR,* XXXII (1927), 475-99.

Foster, James R. "The Abbé Prévost and the English novel." *PMLA,* XLII (1927), 443-64.

A well-documented and discriminating study of the part played by Prévost and his French imitators in the development of the English novel of "sentimental adventure" from the middle of the century to Mrs. Radcliffe. P. 446: it will hardly do to say that Prévost's characters "were embodiments of Shaftesbury's æsthetic morality."

Freeman, Edmund L. "Bacon's influence on John Hall." *PMLA,* XLII (1927), 385-99.

Interesting side-lights on intellectual currents in England on the eve of the Restoration.

Freeman, Edmund L. "A note on Bacon's influence." *MLN,* XLII (1927), 239-40.

As shown by the *Reliquiae Gethinianae* (1699), a posthumous publication based on the commonplace-book of Lady Grace Gethin (1676-1697).

Fries, Charles C. "The rules of common school grammars." *PMLA,* XLII (1927), 221-37.

An interesting study of their origin in the later eighteenth century, illustrating the predominance of rationalistic thinking among the grammarians of that period.

Frost, Walter. *Bacon und die Naturphilosophie.* Munich, 1927.

Rev. by A. E. Taylor in *Mind,* XXXVI (1927), 244-45.

Gertsch, Alfred. *Der steigende Ruhm Miltons: die Geschichte einer*

Heteronomie der literarischen Urteilsbildung. Leipzig: Tauchnitz, 1927.

See H. Schöffler in *ES,* LXII (1927), 234-37.

Gooch, G. P. *English democratic ideas in the seventeenth century.* Second edition, with supplementary notes by H. J. Laski. Cambridge: University Press, 1927.

Graham, Walter. *The beginnings of English literary periodicals: a study of periodical literature, 1665-1715.* New York: Oxford University Press, American Branch, 1926. Cf. *PQ,* VI, 168.

Rev. by F. Baldensperger in *Litteris,* IV (1927), 108-09; by L. F. Powell in *RES,* III (1927), 368-70; by D.N.S. in *MLR,* XXII (1927), 361.

Gregory, Joshua C. "The animate and mechanical models of reality." *Journal of philosophical studies,* II (1927), 301-14.

Contains a suggestive brief sketch of the transition in the seventeenth century "from the animate to the mechanical model in versions of physical nature."

Haller, William. "Before *Areopagitica.*" *PMLA,* XLII (1927), 875-900.

Milton's place in the controversy concerning freedom of thought and expression, 1643-44. An important new chapter in the history of the idea of toleration.

Harbeson, William Page. *The Elizabethan influence on the tragedy of the late eighteenth and early nineteenth centuries.* Lancaster, Pa.: Wickersham Printing Co., 1927. University of Pennsylvania dissertation.

Havens, Raymond D. "An earlier and a later *Rolliad.*" *RES,* III (1927), 218-20.

Mainly concerned with *Extracts from the album, at Streatham. . . .* (1788), which Professor Havens regards as "not so much an imitation as a continuation of the *Rolliad* group of satires."

Hesselgrave, Ruth A. *Lady Miller and the Batheaston literary circle.* New Haven: Yale University Press, 1927.

Rev. in *TLS,* Mar. 31, 1927, p. 227.

Isaacs, J. "English men of letters at Padua in the seventeenth century." *RES,* III (1927), 75.

The list includes John Evelyn, Edmund Waller, Kenelm Digby, Thomas Killigrew, Thomas Vaughan, Bolingbroke, and Addison.

Jones, Henry Broadus. "The death song of the 'noble savage': a sketch in the idealization of the American Indian." University of Chicago *Abstracts of theses,* Humanistic series, III (1927), 339-45.

Lovejoy, Arthur O. " 'Nature' as aesthetic norm." *MLN,* XLII (1927), 444-50.

A most useful tabulation of the manifold senses attaching to the term "nature" in the literary and artistic criticism of the seventeenth and eighteenth centures. The all-too-brief concluding "Remarks" are very suggestive, particularly on the often misunderstood matter of the relation between aesthetic primitivism and neo-classicism.

Lovejoy, Arthur O. "Optimism and romanticism." *PMLA*, XLII (1927), 921-45.

An interpretation of eighteenth-century "optimism" designed to show the significance of that movement in the transformation of standards that led to romanticism. It is a very important article; I know, in fact, of few studies in the history of ideas during this period that are more provocative of thought, or more vivaciously written. I have only one reservation, and that concerns a matter of detail. It is not, I believe, nearly so certain as Professor Lovejoy thinks (see p. 926, n. 9) that Pope in writing the *Essay on Man* had before him anything corresponding to the *Fragments or minutes of essays* later printed in Bolingbroke's *Works*. The testimony of Lord Bathurst is certainly too late to be of any value. And aside from this, it may be noted (1) that Bolingbroke in the "Advertisement" prefixed to the *Fragments* does not expressly say that the notes communicated to Pope "in scraps, as they were occasionally writ," were intended to be utilized in the writing of the *Essay*; (2) that the discussion in Fragment I of "Dr. Cudworth's posthumous treatise concerning eternal and immutable morality, which you [Pope] sent me long ago," must have been written some time after 1731, when the *Treatise* was published; and (3) that Bolingbroke in his *Letter to . . . . Mr. Pope* (1753 ed., pp. 425-26, 431-33), writing after the publication of the *Epistle to Burlington* (Dec. 1731), speaks as if his promise to compose something on the philosophical questions that interested the two friends was still unfulfilled. This is not of course conclusive, and I do not mean in any case to cast doubt on the reality and importance of Bolingbroke's contribution to the genesis of the *Essay*; but I do not think the case for a *written* contribution is quite as clear as Professor Lovejoy seems to believe.

Lowes, John Livingston. *The road to Xanadu: a study in the ways of the imagination.* Boston and New York: Houghton Mifflin Company, 1927.

Rev. by Emile Legouis in *RAA*, V (1928), 269-73.

Detailed discussion of this work—surely one of the great books of our generation—must be left to specialists in Coleridge and the Romantic Movement. It is for them to do justice to its amazing erudition, to its brilliant insight into poetic psychology, and to the beauty and vitality of its style. I cannot list it here, however, without a word about its value to students of the later eighteenth century. For the magnificent sweep of Professor Lowes' research has caught up an extraordinary number of facts of the greatest interest to anyone who would reconstruct the curious ferment of ideas which characterized that age. The popularity of voyages, the revival of Neoplatonism, the spell of a newly discovered Germany, mesmerism and animal magnetism, the vogue of the Wandering Jew and of the myths of the antediluvian world, new fashions in poetic diction—whoever is curious about these and other little known aspects of the world of Coleridge's youth will find them discussed, often brilliantly and always with an abundance of precise information, in Professor Lowes' text and notes. Chapter XVII, on the elements which entered into the style of the *Ancient mariner*, is a particularly fine piece of work—a model of discriminating analysis which should set a new standard in studies of this sort.

Mackintosh, Donald T. " 'New dress'd in the habits of the times.' " *TLS*, Aug. 25, 1927, p. 575.

New facts on eighteenth-century attempts to establish historic dressing on the English stage.

Mirabent, F. *La estetica inglesa del siglo XVIII.* Barcelona: Editorial Cervantes, 1927.

Rev. by Charles Lalo in *Revue d'histoire de la philosophie,* I (1927), 465-66.

Moore, C. A. "Miltoniana (1679-1741)." *MP,* XXIV (1927), 321-39.

Contains among other things interesting details on the earlier history of "graveyard poetry."

Muirhead, J. H. "The Cambridge Platonists." *Mind,* XXXVI (1927), 158-78, 326-41.

Mainly on Cudworth.

Nicoll, Allardyce. *A history of late eighteenth century drama, 1750-1800.* Cambridge: University Press, 1927.

Rev. by J. H. Caskey in *JEGP,* XXVII (1928), 122-25; by Dougald MacMillan in *MLN,* XLII (1927), 472-74; by Paul Meissner in *Deutsche Literaturzeitung,* Oct. 22, 1927, cols. 2104-07; by G. H. Nettleton in *SRL,* Oct. 22, 1927, p. 238; in *TLS,* Mar. 17, 1927, p. 182.

Paull, H. M. "The ethics of plagiarism." *Fortnightly review,* CXXII (1927), 202-16.

A few details on the attitude toward plagiarism in the seventeenth and eighteenth centuries.

Powicke, Frederick J. *The Cambridge Platonists.* London: J. M. Dent & Sons, 1926; Cambridge: Harvard University Press, 1927.

Rev. by P. E. More in *SRL,* Nov. 12, 1927, p. 299.

Mr. Powicke in his preface has protected himself against otherwise inevitable criticism, when he says of this study that "it makes no pretence at all to be complete, and aims at nothing more than to express those aspects of the subject which struck me most and have seemed most relevant to my own needs." His book is admittedly a personal evaluation of a group of divines to whom he has gone, as he says more than once, for "spiritual nutriment." As personal appreciation, one cannot quarrel with it; one may indeed welcome it—and particularly the inclusion of Peter Sterry, too infrequently mentioned elsewhere—as one welcomes any study which helps to draw attention to this remarkable group of philosophers, theologians, and "latitude-men."

Yet the critic must regret that in a work which promised so well, Mr. Powicke has been content, on the whole, to follow in the footsteps of Campagnac, and particularly (for all his disagreement on a few points in the last chapter) of Principal Tulloch, in insisting that the chief, perhaps the only, importance of these Cambridge men lay in their divinity. Such a recent study as E. A. Burtt's *Metaphysical foundations of modern physical science* has done much to reëvaluate the position of some of the number in metaphysics and science; briefer studies which have appeared during the last half-dozen years in connection with such men as Shaftesbury, Sir Thomas Browne, and Milton, have served to establish their peculiar position in the history of ethics. Yet, these more technical matters aside, the real importance of the group can be appreciated only when its members are seen in their historical perspective, when the reader is made aware of the position they maintained in connection with both the liberalizing and the reactionary movements of thought of their century—for example, in regard to such problems as the acceptance of Copernicanism, the quarrel of *ancient* and *modern,* the idea of *progress,* the beginnings of the new scientific movement as exemplified in Bacon or in Descartes. It is not enough to generalize about such matters, or, as Mr. Powicke too often does, to "suppose" relationships; to possess any validity, such relationships must be proved; and they are all capable of proof. The "Platonism" of these men, too, must be more sharply defined and distinguished. By which of the many Renaissance "Platonisms" were they affected? In what matters of great moment did they consciously deny, or unconsciously depart from the tenets of Neoplatonism? On these subjects Mr. Powicke's treatment is unsatisfactory, because he has been content to draw his biographical facts, and to accept his historical relationships from Tulloch; and Tulloch is not only often misleading, but frequently actually wrong both in his statements and in his implications. Sympathetic, therefore, as are Mr. Powicke's appreciations of these men as individuals, his general statements, particularly in his introductory and closing chapters, are too often either vague or incorrect. Had he gone back to the period itself, he could hardly have failed, for instance, to be aware of the true significance of those terms which trouble him—"reason" and "natural light" (cf. pp. 21-22, 31-32, 46-47). He is quite right in believing them of great significance in the systems of the Cambridge men; but careful discrimination of the uses and of the sources of the terms is necessary before their real meaning emerges. Only through study of the men in their own period is their position and contribution to be understood; and for such study mere *selections* from their works are not enough; for a highly significant phase of the movement is to be found in the changing position taken by these individuals as the century advances, to the radical changes both in science and in philosophy.

Finally, it is curious that, in spite of Mr. Powicke's interest in the question of the "influence" of this group, he should have been unaware of the part they played in the nineteenth century in the Romantic Movement, of their effect upon Coleridge, and, through him and directly, upon such New England Transcendentalists as James Marsh, Theodore Parker, and Ralph Waldo Emerson.—M. H. N.

Railo, Eino. *The haunted castle: a study of the elements of English romanticism.* London: Routledge; New York: E. P. Dutton, 1927.

Rev. by W. L. Phelps in *SRL,* Oct. 15, 1927, p. 194; in *TLS,* July 21, 1927, p. 500.

Raysor, Thomas M. "The downfall of the three unities." *MLN,* XLII (1927), 1-9.

An interesting paper, which places Johnson's attack in its immediate setting by describing the renewal of attacks on the unities in the decade before 1765, and shows, on the basis of some new material, how complete was the "downfall" of the dogma in English criticism between 1765 and 1800.

Raysor, Thomas M. "The study of Shakespeare's characters in the eighteenth century." *MLN,* XLII (1927), 495-500.

Adds a number of studies of Shakespeare's characters to the list given by Nichol Smith in his *Eighteenth-century essays on Shakespeare.*

Schelling, Felix E. *Shakespeare and "demi-science": papers on Elizabethan topics.* Philadelphia: University of Pennsylvania Press, 1927.

Contains a rewritten version of his well known paper on "Ben Jonson and the classical school."

Seeger, O. *Die Auseinandersetzung zwischen Antike und Moderne in England bis zum Tode Dr. Samuel Johnsons.* Leipzig: Mayer und Müller, 1927.

Spencer, Hazelton. *Shakespeare improved.* Cambridge: Harvard University Press, 1927.

Stokoe, F. W. *German influences in the English romantic period, 1788-1818.* Cambridge: University Press, 1926. Cf. *PQ,* VI, 172.

Rev. by R. F. Arnold in *Die Literatur,* May, 1927, pp. 488-89; by F. Baldensperger in *RLC,* VII (1927), 784-90; by L. Cazamian in *RAA,* V (1927), 66-67; by A. Koszul in *Les langues modernes,* XXV (1927), 232-33; by Edna Purdie in *MLR,* XXIII (1927), 80-82; by Helene Richter in *Die neueren Sprachen,* XXXV (1927), 214-18; by William Rose in *RES,* III (1927), 245-46.

Straus, Ralph. *The unspeakable Curll. Being some account of Edmund Curll, bookseller; to which is added a full list of his books.* London: Chapman and Hall, 1927.

Rev. in *TLS,* Dec. 15, 1927, p. 945.

This book contains a great mass of valuable information, which in the hands of the inexperienced will certainly tend to subvert history. Pages 201-314 are headed, "A Handlist (1706-1746)." The assumption would naturally be that Curll was in some way connected with the books here handlisted—one might even assume that he was concerned in their publication. The sad truth is that while most of the entries might belong in a handlist of books sold by Curll, many are included simply because at some time and for some reason (unstated) Mr. Straus suspected Curll of possibly having an interest in them. No one, I trust, forced Mr. Straus to make this Handlist; if he chose to make it, he should have played the game as good bibliographical method demands. The trouble is that he feels superior to his task. He feels pleasure in it, but fears someone may call him a pedant. From the title (which is possibly a bit severe) to the sprightly comments on entries in the Handlist (such as "So there!" or "Which is vague, but I can't help it") the author indulges constantly his desire to cut a literary caper. At the same time he shows, as he himself confesses (p. 202), a habit of "letting things go" as far as drudgery is concerned. He writes (p. 249): "About Charles Ancillon I can find nothing, or, rather, I have found nothing, because I have not worried myself." Since in the British Museum it ought not to have taken more than two minutes to consult the printed catalogue of the Bibliothèque Nationale on Ancillon, such a statement rather worries the reader, who may suspect that he is not always thus warned when Mr. Straus "lets things go." The volume contains a wealth of invaluable detail, however, and for that we must be grateful. It will be a blessing if the price (42 *s*) and the small number of copies printed (535) keep the volume out of the hands of the inexperienced; for, alas! there are people who will take Mr. Straus's guesses or hypotheses or even his witticisms as sober statements of solid fact.—G.S.

Thompson, Elbert N. S. *The seventeenth century English essay.* Iowa City: University of Iowa, 1927.

Rev. by Morris W. Croll in *MLN,* XLII (1927), 563-64; by G. C. Moore Smith in *MLR,* XXIII (1928), 77-78.

Thüme, Hans. *Beiträge zur Geschichte des Geniebegriffs in England.* Halle (Saale): Max Niemeyer, 1927.

An attempt to show that the conception of genius expressed by such writers as Addison and Young represented not a new development but rather the culminating phase of a tradition that had been continuous in English criticism since its rise in the sixteenth century. The book consists of a fairly long Introduction on the "Vorbereitung des Geniebegriffs in der italienischen Renaissance" and of four short chapters entitled respectively "Die Elisabethanischen Kritiker," "Von Jonson bis Dryden," "Der Klassizismus," and "Der Naturalismus." For specialists in the eighteenth century the most valuable part is undoubtedly the opening analysis of Renaissance ideas on the divine inspiration of the poet and on his power of free imaginative creation. The later sections, which attempt to trace the fortune of these ideas in England from Sidney to Young, are much less satisfactory. They contain a good many facts and texts which it will be useful to have assembled in one place, but as the author has seldom gone beyond the most obvious and easily accessible sources, they add little to what we already knew about the subject.

Van Tieghem, Paul. "Les droits de l'amour et l'union libre dans le roman français et allemand (1760-1790)." *Neophilologus,* XII (1927), 96-103.

Van Tieghem, Paul. "Quelques aspects de la sensibilité préromantique dans le roman européen au XVIIIe siècle." *Edda,* XXVI (1927), 146-75.

These two articles are preparatory studies for a more complete account of the history of the sentimental novel in eighteenth-century Europe which the author intends to publish soon. The first paper is limited to a description of the "roman sentimental passionné, parfois sensuel, et hardi" as it developed, particularly in France and Germany, after 1760. The second article is broader in scope: it contains (1) an interesting study of the vocabulary of sentimentalism in France, England, and Germany, and (2) an excellent analysis of the principal internal characteristics and external manifestations of "sensibilité" in the novel of these and other countries during the whole of the eighteenth century. In the space at my disposal I can comment on only a few of the writer's points. P. 147: to the bibliography of works on the vocabulary of sentimentalism given here, add Anna Wüstner, " 'Sentiment' und 'sentimental' in der engl. Prosaliteratur des XVIII. Jahrhunderts," in *Bausteine: Zeitschrift für neuenglische Wortforschung,* I (1906), 249-95. P. 152: on Sterne's use of "sentimental" in 1740 (not 1741) see a recent controversy in *TLS,* June 23 and July 21, 1927, pp. 440 and 504. P. 159: "Pope et après lui Voltaire ont enseigné qu'il faut, non arracher de l'âme les passions comme le veut une morale ascétique, mais s'en servir, en les combinant, pour être heureux en restant vertueux." The attitude toward the passions described here was very much older than Pope. It was, in fact, a stock position of the anti-Stoic moralists of the seventeenth century. I give a few references—many others might be added: Edward Reynolds, *A treatise of the passions* (1640), pp. 57-60; John Hartcliffe, *A treatise of moral and intellectual virtues* (1691), pp. 17-18, 294-96; James Lowde, *A discourse concerning the nature of man* (1694), p. 24; M. Burghope, *The government of the passions* (1701), pp. 3-5; and Richard Steele in the *Lover,* No. 32, May 8, 1714.

Whiting, George W. "The condition of the London theaters, 1679-83: a reflection of the political situation." *MP,* XXV (1927), 195-206.

Zilsel, E. *Die Entstehung des Geniebegriffs.* Tübingen: J. C. B. Mohr, 1926.

Rev. by H. Gmelin in *Die neueren Sprachen,* XXXV (1927), 396-98.

IV. INDIVIDUAL AUTHORS

John Arbuthnot

Pons, Émile. [Review of H. Teerink, *The history of John Bull. . . ,* Amsterdam, 1925.] *RAA,* IV (1927), 354-56.

One of the few sane evaluations of Teerink's arguments for Swift's authorship.

Jane Austen

The Novels of Jane Austen. Edited with introduction and notes by R. W. Chapman. Second edition. London: H. Milford, Oxford University Press, 1926. 5 vols.

Rev. by Léonie Villard in *RAA,* V (1927), 63-66.

Sadleir, Michael. *The Northanger novels. A footnote to Jane Austen.* English Association pamphlet, No. 68 (Nov., 1927).

Expanded and revised from an article published in the *Edinburgh review,* CCXLVI (1927), 91-106.

Richard Baxter

Powicke, Frederick J. *The Reverend Richard Baxter: under the cross (1662-1691).* London: Jonathan Cape, 1927.

Rev. in *TLS,* Apr. 28, 1927, p. 288.

William Blake

Poetry and prose of William Blake. Edited by Geoffrey Keynes. Complete in one volume. London: Nonesuch Press, 1927.

An excellent edition, based on the three volume Blake published by the Nonesuch Press in 1925, but without variants or notes.

The Poems and prophecies of William Blake. Edited by Max Plowman. London: J. M. Dent & Sons; New York: E. P. Dutton & Co., [1927]. "Everyman's Library."

Binyon, Laurence. *The engraved designs of William Blake.* London: Benn, 1927.

Rev. in *TLS,* Feb. 3, 1927, p. 71.

Herford, C. H. "William Blake." *Hibbert journal,* XXVI (1927), 15-30.

Lindsay, J. *William Blake: creative will and the poetic image.* London: Fanfrolico Press, 1927.

Pierce, Frederick E. "The genesis and general meaning of Blake's *Milton.*" *MP,* XXV (1927), 165-78.

Plowman, Max. *An introduction to the study of Blake.* London: J. M. Dent & Sons, 1927.

White, Helen C. *The mysticism of William Blake.* Madison: University of Wisconsin Press, 1927. ("University of Wisconsin studies," No. 23.)

Rev. by Pierre Berger in *RAA,* V (1927), 62-63.

"William Blake." *TLS,* Aug. 11, 1927, pp. 537-38.

Wilson, Mona. "Blake and Bedlam." *TLS,* Dec. 15, 1927, p. 961.

Disposes conclusively of the statement in the *Revue britannique* for July, 1833, that Blake was an inmate of Bedlam.

Wilson, Mona. *The life of William Blake.* London: Nonesuch Press, 1927.

Rev. by Pierre Berger in *RAA,* V (1928), 267-68; in *TLS,* Aug. 11, 1927, pp. 537-38.

Wright, Herbert G. "Henry Crabb Robinson's 'Essay on Blake.'" *MLR,* XXII (1927), 137-54.

Wright, Herbert. "William Blake and Sir Joshua Reynolds." *Nineteenth century,* CI (1927), 417-31.

Henry Saint-John, Viscount Bolingbroke

Ratchford, Fannie E. "Pope and the *Patriot King.*" University of Texas *Studies in English,* No. 6, Dec., 1926, pp. 157-77.

Torrey, Norman L. "Bolingbroke and Voltaire—a fictitious influence." *PMLA,* XLII (1927), 788-97.

James Boswell

"Original Boswell papers." *SRL,* Oct. 1, 1927, p. 163.

A brief note on the important collection of papers recently brought to America by Col. Ralph Isham.

Pottle, Frederick A. "Portraits of James Boswell." *N & Q,* CLII (1927), 80-81.

A list of portraits, with queries as to their present whereabouts.

Tinker, C. B. and F. A. Pottle. *A new portrait of James Boswell.* Cambridge: Harvard University Press, 1927.

Thomas Brown

Amusements, serious and comical, and other works. By Tom Brown. Edited, with notes, by Arthur L. Hayward. London: Routledge, 1927.

Rev. in *TLS,* July 14, 1927, p. 483.

Sir Thomas Browne

Sir Thomas Browne's Christian morals. The second edition, with the life of the author, by Samuel Johnson. Edited with an introduction and notes, by S. C. Roberts. Cambridge: University Press, 1927.

Tempest, Norton R. "Rhythm in the prose of Sir Thomas Browne." *RES,* III (1927), 308-18.

Michael Bruce

Life and complete works of Michael Bruce. The Cottage edition. By John Guthrie Barnet. London: Chas. J. Thynne & Jarvis, 1927.

A work of piety rather than of scholarship.

John Bunyan

Draper, John W. "Bunyan's Mr Ignorance." *MLR,* XXII (1927), 15-21.

Starting from the obvious fact that in creating the characters of *Pilgrim's progress* Bunyan had his eye on contemporary groups and types, Mr. Draper argues that in the person of Ignorance he intended to symbolize "the evolution of bourgeois thought of the late seventeenth century from Calvinism to Deism and Sentimentalism." Ignorance, we are told, like the third Earl of Shaftesbury, having been "freed by the deistic tendencies of his time from a pessimistic view of human nature, renounces the old theology with all its ethical and metaphysical implications, and embraces a 'new ethics' of optimism and emotion, an ethics that can best be described as essentially Sentimental." And when Christian analyzes for Hopeful the reasons why such persons as Ignorance lack "right fear," the discourse is said to constitute "Bunyan's psychological explanation of the rise of Sentimentalism" among the English middle classes. This is not very convincing. There is plainly only one way of discovering what Bunyan had in mind in the passages about Ignorance, and that is to bring them into relation with other texts both in Bunyan himself and in his contemporaries or predecessors in which the same doctrines appear. What is needed, in other words, is a historical interpretation. But Mr. Draper's method is the reverse of historical: he seeks the clue to Bunyan's meaning, not in the concrete facts of his intellectual environment, but in a set of abstract formulae, some of them only doubtfully true, which he has found in the books of modern students of eighteenth-century sentimentalism. The result is curiously artificial. "Gentlemen," says Ignorance, "ye be utter strangers to me, I know you not: be content to follow the religion of your country, and I will follow the religion of mine. I hope all will be well." This Mr. Draper labels, parenthetically, "optimism." On a later occasion Ignorance remarks that he prefers to "walk alone." This is "individualism." Christian, again, refers to persons holding the views of Ignorance as religiously "in a natural condition." Ignorance is therefore "clearly a disciple of Natural Religion." He says: "I know my Lord's will, and I have been a good liver; I pay every man his own; I pray, fast, pay tithes, and give alms, and have left my country for whither I am going." He has consequently "an humanitarian faith in justification by philanthropic works." And so on. I regret that I cannot take these interpretations more seriously, for Mr. Draper has shown on many occasions that he has a high standard of scholarly method, and he has both done and inspired good work on the eighteenth century. But the most that can be said for the present article is that it calls attention to an interesting text and suggests the need of a new edition of *Pilgrim's progress* which will place Bunyan's thought in its true historical setting.

Golder, Harold. "John Bunyan's hypocrisy." *North American review,* CCXXIII (1926-27), 323-32.

An interesting popular discussion of the effect of Bunyan's early reading of chivalric romances on *Pilgrim's progress.*

Edmund Burke

Newman, Bertram. *Edmund Burke.* London: G. Bell and Sons, 1927.

Rev. by J. Vallette in *Les langues modernes,* XXV (1927), 558-61; in *TLS,* May 5, 1927, p. 315.

Fanny Burney

Masefield, Muriel (Mrs. Charles Masefield). *The story of Fanny*

Burney: an introduction to the diary and letters of Madame d'Arblay. Cambridge: University Press, 1927.

Rev. in *TLS*, June 30, 1927, p. 452.

John Byrom : see *William Law*

Philip Dormer Stanhope, Earl of Chesterfield

Yvon, Paul. "Chesterfield et les français: est-il pour nous un ami compromettant?" *RAA*, V (1927), 146-57.

Charles Churchill

Beatty, Joseph M., Jr. "Churchill's influence on minor eighteenth century satirists." *PMLA*, XLII (1927), 162-76.

Contains a long and useful list of publications "occasioned by Churchill's works or influenced by them" between 1761 and 1783.

Colley Cibber

Sprague, Arthur Colby. "A new scene in Colley Cibber's *Richard III.*" *MLN*, XLII (1927), 29-32.

Reprints the scene, later omitted, from the first edition (1700).

William Collins

Ode occasion'd by the death of Mr. Thomson, 1749. By William Collins. Oxford: Clarendon Press, 1927.

A type-facsimile reprint.

White, H. O. "The letters of William Collins." *RES*, III (1927), 12-21.

Notes on the two surviving letters: (1) to John Gilbert Cooper, Nov. 10, 1747, concerning Collins' plans for a literary review; and (2) to Dr. William Hayes, Nov. 8, 1750, concerning the latter's music for *The Passions* and the Oxford edition of that poem. The letter to Cooper, discovered in 1924 (see *LM*, X, 525), is the more important of the two. The reference in it to Collins' scheme for printing in his paper "any Poetical fragments of our best writers, such as some MSS. of Fairfax which I can procure" helps to illuminate the later tribute to Fairfax in the *Ode on the popular superstitions of the Highlands* (stanza XII).

William Congreve

Isaacs, J. "Congreve and America." *RES*, III (1927), 79.

On an accident to Congreve at Bath, as recorded in the *Daily post* for Oct. 1, 1728.

Abraham Cowley

Sparrow, John. "The text of Cowley's *Mistress.*" *RES*, III (1927), 22-27.

The results of a collation of the editions of 1647, 1656, and 1668.

William Cowper

"Cowper's spiritual diary." Edited by Kenneth Povey. *LM,* XV (1927), 493-96.

The text of a fragmentary diary written in 1795. For corrections see *ibid.,* XV, 640.

"The Hurdis-Cowper letters. Unpublished letters addressed by James Hurdis, the Sussex poet, to William Cowper." *Sussex county magazine,* April, 1927, pp. 223-25.

Martin, L. C. "Vaughan and Cowper." *MLR,* XXII (1927), 79-84.

Suggests the probability that a reading of Vaughan may have been partly responsible for the change in Cowper's attitude toward external nature which appears first in his *Retirement* (1782). An intelligent bit of source-study.

Povey, K. "The text of Cowper's 'Letters.'" *MLR,* XXII (1927), 22-27.

Evidence of the incompleteness and inaccuracy of all of the existing collections.

Spiller, Robert E. "A new biographical source for William Cowper." *PMLA,* XLII (1927), 946-62.

A diary of the Rev. John Johnson relating to Cowper and Mrs. Unwin during their residence with him in Norfolk from 1795 to 1800.

Taffe, Valentine. "Le sentiment de la nature chez Cowper." *RAA,* IV (1927), 308-19.

Daniel Defoe

A Tour thro' the whole island of Great Britain. By Daniel Defoe. With an introduction by G. D. H. Cole. London: Peter Davies, 1927. 2 vols.

Rev. in *TLS,* Jan. 12, 1928, p. 25.
A reprint of the first edition, 1724-26.

Dottin, Paul. "Les sources de la *Roxana* de Daniel de Foë." *RAA,* IV (1927), 531-34.

Elissa-Rhaïs, Roland. "Une influence anglaise dans *Manon Lescaut,* ou une source du réalisme." *RLC,* VII (1927), 619-49.

The "source" is *Moll Flanders.*

Hutchins, H. C. "Two hitherto unrecorded editions of *Robinson Crusoe.*" *Library,* N. S., VIII (1927), 58-72.

Sir John Denham

Baldwin, T. W. "Sir John Denham and *Paradise lost.*" *MLN,* XLII (1927), 508-09.

Supplements T. H. Banks's article (*ibid.,* XLI, 51-54) by showing that Denham was in attendance on Parliament in 1667 at the time he is supposed to have uttered his praise of *Paradise lost.*

Banks, Theodore H. "The personal relations between Denham and Waller." *MLN,* XLII (1927), 372-78.

Hutchinson, F. E. "Sir John Denham's translations of Virgil." *TLS,* July 7, 1927, p. 472.

John Dryden

Annus mirabilis: the year of wonders, 1666. By John Dryden. Type-facsimile reprint of the first edition, 1667. Oxford: Clarendon Press, 1927.

Clark, William S. "Dryden's relations with Howard and Orrery." *MLN,* XLII (1927), 16-20.

Prints a hitherto unpublished letter which seems to show that Dryden was living with Sir Robert Howard in 1663. On the basis of this document the writer builds up a plausible, though largely speculative, argument that it was through this intimacy with Howard that Dryden was introduced to Roger Boyle, Earl of Orrery (a first cousin by marriage of Howard), and that "the example of the pioneer plays of the Earl of Orrery plus the direct, personal relations existing between Dryden, Howard, and Orrery, seem the chief influences that occasioned the writing of *The Indian Queen* in rimed verse."

Harder, Franz. "Eine deutsche Anregung zu Drydens 'Alexander's Feast'?" *ES,* LXI (1927), 177-82.

A poem in Morhof's *Unterricht von der teutschen Sprache und Poesie* (1682).

Hughes, Merritt Y. "Dryden as a statist." *PQ,* VI (1927), 335-50.

An interesting though structurally rather confused article, in which the attempt is made to demonstrate a certain consistency of attitude in Dryden's political thinking and to show that in the transition from the absolutism of Hobbes to the theory of constitutional monarchy his place is with Halifax in "the last stage before Locke." The treatment of this second point is brief and not altogether satisfactory, and the greater part of the paper is devoted to exhibiting Dryden's contempt for the populace and his reflection of Hobbesian points of view in his plays. The paper as a whole is somewhat lacking in precision and leaves one with the impression that Mr. Hughes is not any too familiar either with the details of Restoration political history or with all of the pertinent facts about Dryden himself. He makes no reference, for example, to the interesting statement in Aubrey's *Brief lives* concerning Dryden's attitude toward Hobbes or to the testimony on the same point in the *Censure of the Rota.* And he leaves out of account the whole complicated question, which is not without a bearing on the points at issue, of the influence of Hobbes on Dryden's general philosophy. On this problem I may refer to an important paper by L. I. Bredvold on "Dryden, Hobbes, and the Royal Society," to be published in an early number of *Modern philology.*

Sir George Etherege

The Works of Sir George Etherege. Edited by H. F. B. Brett-Smith. Volumes I and II, *Plays.* Oxford: Blackwell, 1927.

Foster, Dorothy. "Sir George Etherege: collections." *N & Q,* CLIII (1927), 417-19, 435-40, 454-59, 472-78.

Notes on a lawsuit of 1656 in which Etherege was concerned, on the date of his death, and on his library.

John Evelyn

Vellacott, Paul. "Evelyn and Cosin?" *TLS*, Apr. 21, 1927, p. 280.

A note on a passage in his *Memoires for my grand-son.*

Henry Fielding

Blanchard, F. T. *Fielding the novelist.* New Haven: Yale University Press, 1925. See *PQ*, VI, 180.

Rev. by E. A. Baker in *RES*, III (1927), 227-32; by F. Baldensperger in *Litteris*, IV (1927), 222-25; by Oliver Elton in *MLR*, XXII (1927), 225-28; by A. Digeon in *RAA*, V (1927), 57-59; by H. Schöffler in *Beiblatt*, XXXVIII (1927), 65-68; in *RLC*, VII (1927), 395-96.

Digeon, A. "La condemnation de *Tom Jones* à Paris." *RAA*, IV (1927), 529-31.

Disposes of the tradition that *Tom Jones* was condemned for its immorality.

McCutcheon, Roger P. "'Amelia, or the distressed wife.'" *MLN*, XLII (1927), 32-33.

A "piece of secret personal history" published in May, 1751. No trace of influence on Fielding.

David Garrick

Nicoll, Allardyce. "Garrick's lost 'Jubilee': a manuscript copy." *Times* [London], June 25, 1927, pp. 13-14.

John Gay

The Poetical works of John Gay, including 'Polly,' 'The Beggar's opera,' and selections from the other dramatic works. Edited by G. C. Faber. London: Oxford University Press, 1926.

Rev. by Harold Williams in *RES*, III (1927), 358-61.

An excellent edition. The Introduction contains some sound remarks on the treatment of spelling and punctuation in modern editions of eighteenth-century poets.

Oliver Goldsmith

The Noel Douglas replicas. Oliver Goldsmith, *The Deserted village.* London: Noel Douglas, 1927.

A reproduction of the British Museum copy of the first edition.

New essays by Oliver Goldsmith. Now first collected and edited with an introduction and notes by Ronald S. Crane. Chicago: University of Chicago Press, 1927.

Rev. in *N & Q*, CLIV (1928), 72.

Balderston, Katharine C. *A census of the manuscripts of Oliver Goldsmith.* New York: E. B. Hackett, The Brick Row Book Shop, 1926. Cf. *PQ*, VI, 181.

Rev. by I. A. Williams in *LM*, XV (1927), 641-43; in *TLS*, Feb. 24, 1927, p. 122.

Balderston, Katherine C. "Goldsmith's supposed attack on Fielding." *MLN*, XLII (1927), 165-68.

Shows that Goldsmith could not have intended Letter LXXXIII of the *Citizen of the World* as an attack on Fielding or any other contemporary since the discussion of romances in this essay was borrowed almost literally from the translation of Du Halde's *Description of the Empire of China*, published by Edward Cave in 1738-41.

Balderston, Katharine C. *The history & sources of Percy's memoir of Goldsmith.* Cambridge: University Press, 1926. Cf. *PQ*, VI, 181.

Rev. by H. V. D. Dyson in *MLR*, XXII (1927), 465; by Alda Milner-Barry in *RES*, III (1927), 232-34; by H. T. Price in *Beiblatt*, XXXVIII (1927), 139-40.

Brown, Joseph E. "Goldsmith and Johnson on biography." *MLN*, XLII (1927), 168-71.

Borrowings at the beginning of the *Life of Richard Nash* from the *Idler*, No. 84.

Crane, R. S. "The 'Deserted village' in prose (1762)." *TLS*, Sept. 8, 1927, p. 607.

Crane, R. S. "Goldsmith's 'Essays': dates of original publication." *N & Q*, CLIII (1927), 153.

Seitz, R. W. "Goldsmith and 'A concise history of England.'" *N & Q*, CLIII (1927), 3-4.

Identifies the history of England for "writing and compiling" which Goldsmith received thirty guineas from Dodsley on Aug. 8, 1764, as the second part (pp. 247-397) of a work entitled *The geography and history of England*, published by Dodsley in March, 1765. The evidence is mainly internal: the second part of Dodsley's volume, which bears the title *A concise history of England; or, the revolutions of the British constitution*, is "little more than an abridgement" of Goldsmith's *History of England in a series of letters*, which Newbery had published in 1764. Mr. Seitz gives only two parallels in support of this statement, but an independent comparison of the two works leaves no doubt as to the correctness of his conclusion. And the existence of the receipt of Aug. 8, 1764, makes it equally certain that the abridger was Goldsmith himself.

Smith, H. J. *Oliver Goldsmith's The citizen of the world: a study.* New Haven: Yale University Press, 1926. Cf. *PQ*, VI, 182.

Rev. by H. V. D. Dyson in *MLR*, XXII (1927), 465-66; by Caroline F. Tupper in *JEGP*, XXVI (1927), 269-71; by L. F. Powell in *RES*, IV (1928), 111-13.

Thomas Gray

Bradner, Leicester. "Dr. Wharton's translations of Gray's Latin poems." *MP*, XXV (1927), 124-27.

Toynbee, Paget. "Gray's imitation of Cowley." *TLS*, Oct. 20, 1927, p. 742.

Toynbee, Paget. "Gray's visit to Oxfordshire in 1760." *TLS*, July 21 and 28, 1927, pp. 504 and 520.

Toynbee, Paget. "The text of Norton Nicholls's 'Reminiscences of Gray.'" *TLS*, Sept. 1, 1927, p. 592.

Whibley, Leonard. "Thomas Gray and Norton Nicholls." *TLS*, May 5, 1927, p. 318.

Comment by R. Martin, *ibid.*, May 12, 1927, p. 336.

George Savile, Lord Halifax

The Lady's New Year gift; or advice to a daughter. By the late Lord Marquis of Halifax. Edited and with a preface by Bonamy Dobrée. London: Cayme Press, 1927.

"George Savile, Lord Halifax." *TLS*, Dec. 15, 1927, pp. 941-42.

David Hume

Taylor, A. E. *David Hume and the miraculous.* The Leslie Stephen lecture for 1927. Cambridge: University Press, 1927.

Samuel Johnson
(See also *Sir Thomas Browne*)

Samuel Johnson: writer. A selection. Edited, with an introduction, by S. C. Roberts. London: Herbert Jenkins, 1927.

The History of Rasselas, Prince of Abissinia, a tale. By Samuel Johnson. Edited by R. W. Chapman. Oxford: Clarendon Press, 1927.

An excellent edition. Typographically it is beyond praise: *Rasselas* has been reprinted many times but surely never in a more beautiful form. Nor is the work of the editor within the limits which he has set for himself (there is no literary or historical commentary) any less admirable in its precision and sobriety. The text followed is that of the second edition (June, 1759), corrected by the restoration of the reading or punctuation of the first edition (April, 1759) in a few places where these had been altered "not deliberately but by inadvertence." An appendix lists all variations "of the slightest consequence" between these two editions, including a few not noted by O. F. Emerson in his paper on "The text of Johnson's *Rasselas*" (*Anglia*, XXII [1899], 499-509). There is no reason to think that Johnson ever reviewed the text after the second edition, but for the sake of completeness all variations "of any possible importance" between the second edition and the fourth (1766) are likewise included. The text is preceded by a brief Introduction dealing with the history of the composition and publication of *Rasselas* and with Johnson's habits of revision. Some of the facts given here are new, and the deductions are for the most part sound. On a few points, however, it is possible to add supplementary information from sources not consulted by Mr. Chapman. P. xi, n. 2: Strahan *was* the printer. The evidence is given by R. A. Austen Leigh in his article on "William Strahan and his ledgers" in the *Library*, N. S., III (1923), 283-84. From this same source we also learn that the first edition comprised 1,500 copies and that there was a charge of £2 4*s* 6*d* for extra corrections. P. xv: for *Morning chronicle* read *London chronicle*. The earliest advertisement of *Rasselas* I have noted is in the *Public advertiser* for Friday, Mar. 30, 1759, where it is announced for publication "next Thursday." This announcement is repeated in the issue for the following day; after that there is no further mention of the work until April 13, when it is announced for "next week." P. xvi: I do not understand the following comment on Boswell's remarks concerning the relations of *Rasselas* and *Candide*: "Now *Candide* was published before the end of February; and it is hardly necessary to point out that a book which was written in a week *might* have been imitated from one which was published some six weeks earlier. Boswell's report is perhaps not quite correct." But all the evidence points to the fact that *Rasselas,* begun toward the end of January, was in press by the end of March, and that, although *Candide* was printed in Geneva in February, no copies seem to have been known in England until J. Nourse brought out an edition of the French text on April 26 (see the *Public advertiser* for that date). The first translation did not appear until May 19 (*ibid.*). P. xxi: apropos of the tradition, here shown to be without foundation, that Johnson's tale was not originally called *Rasselas,* it may be noted that the first edition was regularly advertised as *Rasselas, Prince of Abbissinia, a tale.* See the *London chronicle* for April 10-12, 12-14, and 19-21.

Papers written by Dr. Johnson and Dr. Dodd in 1777. Printed from the originals in the possession of A. Edward Newton, Esq. With an introduction and notes by R. W. Chapman. Oxford: Clarendon Press, 1927.

The Vanity of human wishes, 1749. Oxford: Clarendon Press, 1927.

A type-facsimile of the first edition, with a record of the variant readings of the edition of 1755.

Babbitt, Irving. "Dr. Johnson and imagination." *Southwest review,* XIII (1927), 25-35.

This article is an instance of what Professor Babbitt calls "judicial scholarship." It does not merely describe Johnson's attitude towards the imagination, but judges that attitude according to its distance from what Professor Babbitt considers—here and in his other works—the proper use of the imagination: the employment of it, "disciplined to normal human experience," to achieve an illusion through which a higher reality may be grasped—the use of illusion to obtain truth. Professor Babbitt finds that, though Johnson condemned the wrong use of the imagination to day-dream and delude, he did not understand its right use and condemned it in both literature and life. In this he was in harmony with his age, for "the imagination was under suspicion in the neo-classic period." Like other neo-classicists, too, he failed to see how fiction could aid the discovery of truth.

Professor Babbitt points out some interesting illustrations of Johnson's resistance to illusion, but his sweeping statements concerning neo-classic distrust of imagination are, I think, exaggerated. The neo-classicist distrusted only the undisciplined use of the faculty; the disciplined imagination he required. The following is a typical neo-classic statement: "In a good poem, whether it be *epic* or *dramatic*; as also in *sonnets, epigrams,* and other pieces, both judgment and fancy are required. . . ." (Hobbes, *Of man,* pt. I, sect. 8). This was a doctrine preached by Pope and Addison.

That the neo-classicists could hardly help respecting the imagination is shown by their conceptions of the creative act. The central psychological theory was that of Hobbes and Locke, according to which the judgment separates the impressions stored in the memory by the senses and the imagination joins and relates them. Imagination, therefore, was as necessary to controlled thinking as judgment and shared in its good repute. When not thus mechanically conceived the same or greater respect was granted to controlled imagination, and, whether mechanically conceived or not, to the cognate faculty of "original genius" and the power of "invention."

One wonders in retrospect whether this indicting of the dead for lacking a concept which their age had not does not distort the focus of history.—F. B. K.

Cuming, A. "A copy of Shakespeare's Works which formerly belonged to Dr. Johnson." *RES,* III (1927), 208-12.

The set was used by Johnson in preparing his *Dictionary* and his edition of Shakespeare.

Hawkins, L. M. *Gossip about Dr. Johnson and others, being chapters from the memoirs of Miss Laetitia Matilda Hawkins.* Edited by F. H. Skrine. London: Nash and Grayson, 1927.

Powell, L. F. "Johnson's part in *The Adventurer.*" *RES,* III (1927), 420-29.

Much fresh light on the literary and financial history of the paper, including fairly convincing evidence that Johnson wrote the four papers subscribed "Misargyrus" (Nos. 34, 41, 53, 62), which were not accepted as his by Boswell, Malone, or Hill.

Reade, Aleyn Lyell. "The duration of Johnson's residence at Oxford." *TLS,* Sept. 15, 1927.

Roberts, S. C. "Johnson's books." *LM,* XVI (1927), 615-24.

Roberts, S. C. "*On the death of Dr. Robert Levet*—a note on the text." *RES,* III (1927), 442-45.

"The text . . . . of the *Gentleman's Magazine* [Aug., 1783] should be restored, subject to the correction of what is certainly a printer's error in 1. 17, and of what may very likely be a similar error in 1. 36."

Tinker, C. B. "Flaxman's medallion of Dr. Johnson." *TLS,* Mar. 10, 1927, p. 160.

Whibley, Charles. "Samuel Johnson: man of letters." *Blackwood's magazine,* CCXXI (1927), 663-72.

William King

Williams, George G. "Dr. William King, humorist." *Sewanee review,* XXXV (1927), 2-14.

Discursive remarks on King's life and writings.

William Law

Hobhouse, Stephen. *William Law and eighteenth-century Quakerism, including some unpublished letters and fragments of William Law and John Byrom.* London: Allen and Unwin, 1927.

Rev. in *TLS,* Oct. 6, 1927, p. 679.

John Locke

The Correspondence of John Locke and Edward Clarke. Edited, with a biographical study, by Benjamin Rand. Cambridge: Harvard University Press; London: Oxford University Press, 1927.

Rev. by W. R. S. in *Mind,* XXXVI (1927), 507-09; in *TLS,* Aug. 11, 1927, p. 544.

The correspondence extends from 1672 to 1704.

Lamprecht, Sterling P. "Locke's attack upon innate ideas." *Philosophical review,* XXXVI (1927), 145-65.

Rev. by E. B. in *Revue d'histoire de la philosophie,* II (1928), 109-10 (a very important article).

Andrew Marvell

The Poems and letters of Andrew Marvell. Edited by H. M. Margoliouth. Oxford: Clarendon Press, 1927. 2 vols.

Rev. in *N & Q,* CLIII (1927), 232-33; in *TLS,* Sept. 22, 1927.

William Mason

Satirical poems published anonymously by William Mason, with notes by Horace Walpole. Now first printed from his manuscript. Edited, with an exposé of the mystification, notes and index, by Paget Toynbee. Oxford: Clarendon Press, 1926. Cf. *PQ,* VI, 185.

Rev. by Oswald Doughty in *RES,* III (1927), 363-66; by John W. Draper in *MLN,* XLII (1927), 468-71 (points out numerous errors in the text); by G. C. M. S[mith] in *MLR,* XXII (1927), 117.

Whibley, Leonard. "William Mason, poet and biographer." *Blackwood's magazine,* CCXXII (1927), 514-27.

John Milton: see *Henry More*

Edward Moore

Caskey, John Homer. *The life and works of Edward Moore.* New Haven: Yale University Press; London: H. Milford, Oxford University Press, 1927.

Rev. in *N & Q,* CLIII (1927), 414.

This Yale dissertation is a useful addition to the list of monographs dealing with minor men of letters of the eighteenth century. It is based on wide reading and it deals in a workmanlike way with the problems raised by Moore's early life and education and by his brief career as poet, dramatist, political writer, and editor. It is clearly superior to its only predecessor in the field—the German dissertation of Hugo Beyer (1889). I have noted a few slips, none of them very important. P. 157: it is hardly accurate to speak of "the *new* interest in 'graveyard poetry' " apropos of a song published in 1752. P. 163: I know of no evidence that Goldsmith, whose literary career did not begin until after Moore's death, was ever one of his friends. P. 164: the reference here to the "poverty in which he [Moore] had lived and died" is hard to reconcile with the statement on p. 92 that "in 1753, Moore came into good fortune that was to last for the rest of his life" (cf. also p. 153).

Henry More

Nicolson, Marjorie H. "Milton and the *Conjectura cabbalistica.*" *PQ,* VI (1927), 1-18.

An admirably lucid study of the likenesses between Milton and More in their conceptions of the creation of the universe, the creation and nature of man, and the fall. It is not contended that Milton borrowed from More, although, as the *Conjectura cabbalistica* was published in 1653, borrowing was of course possible, but merely that the two men were affected in a similar way by the same current of ideas. When the hypothesis of a cabbalistic strain in *Paradise lost* was first stated by Denis Saurat in 1922, it was greeted with some incredulity; Miss Nicolson makes clear that, considering the intellectual atmosphere in which Milton's epic was written, such an influence need surprise no one. Incidentally she helps us to understand why it was that the Cabbala appealed so strongly to idealistic Englishmen like More during the second quarter of the seventeenth century.

Sir Isaac Newton

Dunn, S. G. "Newton and Wordsworth." *TLS,* Aug. 25, 1927, p. 576.

Isaac Newton, 1642-1727: a memorial volume. Edited for The Mathematical Association by W. J. Greenstreet. London: Bell, 1927.

"Isaac Newton (December 25, 1642—March 20, 1727)." *TLS,* Mar. 17, 1927, pp. 167-68.

Comment by G. M. Trevelyan, *ibid.,* Mar. 24, 1927, p. 215.

Snow, A. J. "The rôle of mathematics and hypothesis in Newton's physics." *Scientia,* XLII (1927), 1-10.

Roger Boyle, Earl of Orrery

(See also *John Dryden*)

Clark, William S. "The early stage history of the first heroic play." *MLN,* XLII (1927), 381-83.

A performance at Dublin on Oct. 18, 1662 of the Earl of Orrery's *The General.*

Thomas Otway

The Complete works of Thomas Otway. Edited by Montague Summers. London: Nonesuch Press, 1927. 3 vols.

Rev. in *TLS,* Mar. 3, 1927, pp. 133-34.

Thomas Paine

Best, Mary Agnes. *Thomas Paine: prophet and martyr of democracy.* New York: Harcourt, Brace, and Co., 1927.

The writer of this book has an ardent admiration for Paine and an intense conviction that justice has not been done him by posterity. Otherwise she has no qualifications whatever for the task of writing a new biography. She does nothing toward fitting Paine into his historical setting, and her narrative of events is incoherent and badly written, interrupted by long undigested quotations and passages of hysterical hero-worship. In short, a worthless compilation.

Samuel Pepys

Whitear, Walter H. *More Pepysiana: being notes on the Diary of*

Samuel Pepys and on the genealogy of the family, with corrected pedigrees. London: Simpkin, Marshall, 1927.

Rev. in *TLS,* July 21, 1927, p. 500.

Thomas Percy

Milner-Barry, Alda and L. F. Powell. "A further note on *Hau Kiou Choaan.*" *RES,* III (1927), 214-18.

Bibliographical notes on the two issues (1761 and 1774), with a brief discussion of Percy's part in the translation.

Sir William Petty

The Petty papers: some unpublished writings of Sir William Petty. Edited from the Bowood papers by the Marquis of Lansdowne. London: Constable, 1927. 2 vols.

Rev. in *TLS,* Nov. 10, 1927, p. 803.

John Philips

The Poems of John Philips. Edited by M. G. Lloyd Thomas. Oxford: Blackwell, 1927.

Rev. in *TLS,* Nov. 17, 1927, p. 835.

Alexander Pope

Case, Arthur E. "Notes on the bibliography of Pope." *MP,* XXIV (1927), 297-313.

Details supplementary to the first volume of R. H. Griffith's *Alexander Pope: a bibliography* (1922) and to G. Sherburn's review of that work in *MP,* XXII (1925), 327-36.

Griffith, Reginald Harvey. *Alexander Pope: a bibliography.* Volume I, Part II, *Pope's own writings, 1735-1751.* Austin: Published by the University of Texas, 1927.

Professor Griffith continues the good work admirably. Here he examines and describes, with the care that we now expect from him, 325 books. The volume completes a survey of the field of first editions of all important works, and unless he turns immediately to Popiana, Professor Griffith's next volume will be more perfunctory than the two now completed. The great puzzle here is the tangle of editions of the poet's letters. One can now study as never before this problem and its implications as to Pope's character.

The Introduction to the volume is especially illuminating on various complications in book-making and marketing in the period. The comment on Pope as a business man (pp. xlvi, xlvii) is likewise valuable for an understanding of the poet's personality.—G. S.

Lotspeich, C. M. "The metrical technique of Pope's illustrative couplets." *JEGP,* XXVI (1927), 471-74.

An interpretation of lines 364-73 of the *Essay on criticism.* Rather obvious points.

Matthew Prior

Occasional verses, 1702-1719. By Matthew Prior. Oxford: Clarendon Press, 1927.

C[hapman], R. W. "Prior's poems, 1709." *RES,* III (1927), 76.
Four cancels in this edition.

Allan Ramsay

Chapman, R. W. "Allan Ramsay's *Poems,* 1720." *RES,* III (1927), 343-46.

Sir Joshua Reynolds

Johnson and Garrick: two dialogues. By Sir Joshua Reynolds. With an introduction by R. Brimley Johnson. London: The Cayme Press, 1927.

Samuel Richardson

Wilcox, Frank Howard. "Prévost's translations of Richardson's novels." *University of California Publications in modern philology,* XII (1927), 341-411.

Rev. by Georges Ascoli in *RC,* LXI (1927), 455-56; by M. E. I. R. in *MLR,* XXIII (1928), 114-115.

"This study," says the author, "is an attempt to illustrate certain characteristics of French taste in the eighteenth century by an examination of the changes which Prévost introduced into his versions of Richardson's novels." It contains five chapters and a conclusion. Chapter I is of doubtful value: the facts which it presents concerning Prévost's rôle as an interpreter of England in his novels and in the *Pour et contre* are familiar to all students of the period and should probably have been taken for granted; the last section of the chapter—on standards of translation in eighteenth-century France—is based on too scanty a documentation to be of much utility. Chapter II, which gives a general account of Prévost's translations of Richardson and in particular disposes of the tradition that he translated *Pamela* as well as *Clarissa* and *Sir Charles Grandison,* is more satisfactory. The best of the book, however, is in Chapters III-V. Here the author describes at length and with well selected illustrations the changes which Prévost made in the text of Richardson in order (1) to adapt it to the reigning French dislike of vulgarity, extravagance, and unrestrained expression of feeling, (2) to attenuate the realism, especially in the descriptions of mental states, in the interest of the story, and (3) to lessen the amount of moralizing. Thanks to the precision of the analysis, one cannot read these chapters without an enhanced understanding not only of "certain characteristics of French taste in the eighteenth century" but of the distinguishing qualities of Richardson himself. They are excellent examples of a type of study which could be applied with profit to other writers, both French and English, of the eighteenth century.

John Wilmot, Earl of Rochester

Isaacs, J. "The Earl of Rochester's Grand Tour." *RES,* III (1927), 75-76.

Prinz, Johannes. *John Wilmot Earl of Rochester, his life and writings, with his Lordship's private correspondence, various other documents, and a bibliography of his works and of the literature on him.* Leipzig: Mayer & Müller, 1927.

Williamson, George. "The Restoration Petronius." *University of California chronicle,* XXIX (1927), 273-80.

A sympathetic essay on Rochester. Negligible from a scholarly point of view.

Sir Charles Sedley

Pinto, V. de Sola. *Sir Charles Sedley, 1639-1701: a study in the life and literature of the Restoration.* London: Constable, 1927.

Rev. in *TLS,* Aug. 18, 1927, p. 559.

Thomas Shadwell

The Complete works of Thomas Shadwell. Now first collected and edited by the Rev. Montague Summers. London: Fortune Press, 1927. 5 vols.

Ham, Roswell G. "Shadwell and 'The Tory poets.'" *N & Q,* CLII (1927), 6-8.

Thorn-Drury, G. "Shadwell and the operatic *Tempest.*" *RES,* III (1927), 204-08.

A reply to the note by D. M. Walmsley, *ibid.,* II, 463-64.

Walmsley, D. M. "Shadwell and the operatic *Tempest.*" *RES,* III (1927), 451-53.

A rejoinder to the preceding.

Anthony Ashley Cooper, Earl of Shaftesbury

Bandini, Luigi. "Bene, virtù et 'senso morale' nello Shaftesbury." *Logos: rivista internazionale di filosofia,* X (1927), 28-42, 182-210.

Extract from a forthcoming volume on *La dottrina morale di Shaftesbury.*

William Shenstone

Men and manners. By William Shenstone. Selected and introduced by Havelock Ellis. London: Golden Cockerel Press, 1927.

Rev. in *TLS,* Aug. 11, 1927, p. 545.

Williams, Marjorie. "Shenstone and his friends." *TLS,* Sept. 1, 1927, pp. 591-92.

Richard Brinsley Sheridan

An Ode to Scandal, together with A portrait. By Richard Brinsley Sheridan. Edited by R. Crompton Rhodes. Oxford: Blackwell, 1927.

Rev. in *TLS,* Apr. 14, 1927, p. 263. See *ibid.,* Apr. 28, May 12, and May 26, pp. 299, 336, and 375, for a discussion of the authenticity of the *Ode to Scandal.*

Rhodes, R. Crompton. "Sheridan: a study in theatrical bibliography." *LM,* XV (1927), 381-90.

Christopher Smart

Abbott, Charles David. "The date of Christopher Smart's confinement." *TLS,* Nov. 3, 1927, p. 790.

Whibley, Leonard. "The jubilee at Pembroke Hall in 1743." *Blackwood's magazine,* CCXXI (1927), 104-15.

New facts concerning this celebration, for which Smart wrote "A secular ode on the jubilee at Pembroke College, Cambridge, in 1743."

Adam Smith

Hollander, Jacob H. "Adam Smith, 1776-1926." *Journal of political economy,* XXXV (1927), 153-97.

An interesting paper on Smith's background and influence.

Morrow, Glenn R. "Adam Smith: moralist and philosopher." *Journal of political economy,* XXXV (1927), 321-42.

Viner, Jacob. "Adam Smith and laissez faire." *Journal of political economy,* XXXV (1927), 198-232.

This is a very expert piece of work, scholarly and penetrating. Professor Viner starts with the statement that "Smith's major claim to fame . . . seems to rest on his elaborate and detailed application to the economic world of the concept of a unified natural order, operating according to natural law, and if left to its own course producing results beneficial to mankind." Of this contribution of Adam Smith's he traces the development through the *Theory of moral sentiments* and the *Wealth of nations,* finding Smith's economic "optimism" unqualified in the earlier book, but much modified in the *Wealth of nations.* This modification he studies in detail and shows convincingly that in this work Smith was no such complete advocate of *laissez faire* as is often supposed. Incidentally, light is thrown on the development of "optimism" in the later eighteenth century.

When stating Smith's originality in developing the concept of *laissez faire* Professor Viner might perhaps have mentioned Mandeville's earlier presentation of this philosophy in his *Fable of the bees.*—F. B. K.

Tobias Smollett

The Letters of Tobias Smollett, M. D. Collected and edited by Edward S. Noyes. Cambridge: Harvard University Press, 1926. Cf. *PQ,* VI, 189.

Rev. by E. A. Baker in *RES,* III (1927), 361-63; by A. W. Secord in *MLN,* XLIII (1928), 138-40; by G. S[herburn] in *MP,* XXIV (1927), 380.

Buck, Howard Swazey. *Smollett as poet.* New Haven: Yale University Press; London: H. Milford, Oxford University Press, 1927.

Rev. in *TLS,* Sept. 8, 1927, p. 603.

Buck, Howard Swazey. *A study in Smollett.* New Haven: Yale University Press, 1925. Cf. *PQ,* V, 369; VI, 189.

Rev. by H. Schöffler in *Beiblatt,* XXXVIII (1927), 137-38; by G. S[herburn] in *MP,* XXIV (1927), 380.

Noyes, Edward S. "Another Smollett letter." *MLN*, XLII (1927), 231-35.

A letter to John Moore, Aug. 19, 1762, printed in the *New Scots magazine* for Dec., 1829. Throws light on Smollett's connection with the *Critical review*.

Stein, Harold. "Smollett's imprisonment." *TLS*, May 5, 1927, p. 318.

Fixes the exact dates.

Thomas Spence

Rudkin, Olive D. *Thomas Spence and his connections*. London: Allen and Unwin, 1927.

Rev. in *TLS*, June 9, 1927, p. 398.

Laurence Sterne

The Shakespeare Head edition of the works of Laurence Sterne. Oxford: Blackwell, 1927. 7 vols.

Caskey, J. Homer. "Two notes on Uncle Toby." *MLN*, XLII (1927), 321-23.

Possible borrowings from Edward Moore.

Curtis, Lewis P. "Sterne and 'sentimental.'" *TLS*, June 23, 1927, p. 440.

Reply by Margaret R. B. Shaw, *ibid.*, July 21, 1927, p. 504.

Glaesener, Henri. "Laurence Sterne et Xavier de Maistre." *RLC*, VII (1927), 459-79.

"Laurence Sterne." *TLS*, May 26, 1927, pp. 361-62.

Jonathan Swift

Gulliver's travels. The text of the first edition, with an introduction, bibliography, and notes by Harold Williams. London: The First Edition Club, 1926. Cf. *PQ*, VI, 190.

Rev. by H. C. Hutchins in *RES*, III (1927), 466-73; by E. Pons in *RAA*, V (1927), 158-60.

Gulliver's travels (*extraits*). Avec une introduction et des notes par Émile Pons. Paris: Hachette, [1927].

This book is an abridgment of *Gulliver* intended primarily for the use of French lycées. But it is far from being an ordinary text-book. The editor, who is one of the most distinguished of living students of Swift, has included a commentary which not only sums up admirably the most important results of recent scholarship on the sources of *Gulliver* but on a number of points—for example, the meaning of the Lilliputian language, the continuity of inspiration between *Gulliver* and Swift's earlier works, and the Irish background of the last two books—adds something new. Among the longer and more interesting notes may be mentioned those on pp. 114 (Swift's conception of relativity), 251 (the academy of Lagado), 264 (the identification of political vices with diseases), 279 (the Struldbrugs), and 303 and 306 (the Yahoos). The Introduction contains an excellent brief sketch of Swift's life to 1726 and a useful synopsis of the relations between *Gulliver* and earlier imaginary voyages. P. 251: the William King who wrote the *Transactioneer* was not Archbishop King.

Firth, C. H. "The canon of Swift." *RES,* III (1927), 73-74.

Calls attention to a contemporary ascription of *Jack Frenchman's lamentation* (see *RES,* II, 322-28) to Congreve.

Hearsey, Marguerite. "New light on the evidence for Swift's marriage." *PMLA,* XLII (1927), 157-61.

White, Newport B. "Bibliography of Dean Swift." *TLS,* June 9, 1927, p. 408.

Williams, Harold. "A misplaced paragraph in 'Gulliver's travels.'" *TLS,* July 28, 1927, p. 520.

Cf. *ibid.,* June 30, 1927, p. 460, and *RES,* III (1927), 471-73.

Williams, Harold. "The canon of Swift." *RES,* III (1927), 212-14.

Further discussion of the authorship of *Jack Frenchman's lamentation,* with remarks on other doubtful pieces.

James Thomson

Cameron, Margaret M. *L'influence des Saisons de Thomson sur la poésie descriptive en France (1759-1810).* Paris: Champion, 1927. ("Bibliothèque de la Revue de littérature comparée," No. 37.)

Case, Arthur E. "Aaron Hill and Thomson's *Sophonisba.*" *MLN,* XLII (1927), 175-76.

C[hapman], R. W. "*The Castle of indolence.*" *RES,* III (1927), 456.

John Toland

Lantoine, Albert. *Un précurseur de la franc-maçonnerie, John Toland.* Paris: Emile Nourry, 1927.

Rev. by A. Mathiez in *Annales historiques de la Révolution française,* V (1928), 74.

Sir Samuel Tuke

The Adventures of five hours. By Sir Samuel Tuke. Reprinted from the folio of 1663 and the third impression of 1671, together with Coello's *Los empeños de seis horas.* Edited by A. E. H. Swaen. Amsterdam: Swets & Zeitlinger, 1927.

Rev. by A. Nicoll in *MLR,* XXIII (1928), 78-79; by Mario Praz in *English studies,* IX (1927), 118-22.

The Adventures of five hours. By Sir Samuel Tuke. With an introduction by the Rev. Montague Summers. London: Holden, 1927. (The "Covent Garden" series of Restoration plays, edited by B. van Thal.)

Rev. in *TLS,* Jan. 5, 1928, p. 15.

Edmund Waller

(See also *Sir John Denham*)

Grierson, H. J. C. "Poems by Waller." *TLS*, Dec. 29, 1927, p. 989.

Horace Walpole

(See also *William Mason*)

Strawberry Hill accounts, kept by Mr. Horace Walpole from 1747 to 1795. Now first printed by Paget Toynbee. Oxford: Clarendon Press, 1927.

Rev. by Sir Edmund Gosse in the *Sunday Times*, June 26, 1927, p. 8; in *TLS*, May 19, 1927, p. 350.

Dobson, Austin. *Horace Walpole, a memoir, with an appendix of books printed at the Strawberry Hill press.* Fourth edition, revised and enlarged by Paget Toynbee. London: Oxford University Press, 1927.

The third edition of this book appeared in 1910. Since then many new documents relating to Walpole have come to light, notably the letters of Madame du Deffand, first published by Mrs. Paget Toynbee in 1912, and the early correspondence with Gray, West, and Ashton, edited by Mr. Toynbee in 1915. In the light of this fresh material the text of Dobson's *Memoir* has been corrected and in a few places enlarged, and many additions have been made to the notes. The revision greatly enhances the value of a book which, by reason of its charm of manner, has long had a place among the best short biographies of eighteenth-century men of letters.

Stuart, Dorothy Margaret. *Horace Walpole.* London: Macmillan, 1927. ("English men of letters series.")

Toynbee, Paget. "Horace Walpole's 'Delenda est Oxonia.' " *EHR*, XLII (1927), 95-108.

Contains the text of a suppressed pamphlet by Walpole, 1749.

The Wartons

The Three Wartons: a choice of their verse. Edited with a note and a select bibliography by Eric Partridge. London: The Scholartis Press, 1927.

Rev. in *TLS*, Jan. 5, 1928, p. 9.

Smith, Audley L. "The primitivism of Joseph Warton." *MLN*, XLII (1927), 501-04.

An interesting study of Warton's use of Lucretius in *The Enthusiast*.

John Wesley

Hutton, William Holden. *The life of John Wesley.* London: Macmillan, 1927.

Rev. in *TLS*, Apr. 21, 1927, p. 274.

Simon, John. *John Wesley, the master builder.* London: The Epworth Press, 1927.

Rev. in *TLS,* Sept. 8, 1927, p. 600.
Covers the period from 1757 to 1772.

Anne Finch, Countess of Winchilsea

Murry, J. Middleton. "Anne Finch, Countess of Winchilsea (1661-1720)." *New Adelphi,* I (1927), 145-53.

Mary Wollstonecraft

Godwin, William. *Memoirs of Mary Wollstonecraft.* Edited, with a preface and a supplement, by W. Clark Durant. London: Constable, 1927.

Rev. in *TLS,* June 23, 1927, p. 434.

Arthur Young

Gay, Edwin F. "Arthur Young on English roads." *Quarterly journal of economics,* XLI (1927), 545-51.

Sée, Henri. "La valeur historique des 'Voyages en France' d' Arthur Young." *Mélanges d'histoire offerts à Henri Pirenne,* Brussels, 1926.

V. THE CONTINENTAL BACKGROUND

Ascoli, Georges. "Histoire littéraire, XVIIIe siècle." *RSH,* XLIII (1927), 150-54.

Notes on recent publications relating to French literature in the eighteenth century.

Aubignac, L'Abbé d'. *La pratique du théatre.* Nouvelle édition, avec des corrections et des additions inédites de l'auteur, une préface et des notes par Pierre Martino. Paris: Champion, 1927.

Bray, René. *La formation de la doctrine classique en France.* Paris: Hachette, 1927.

Rev. by H. C. Lancaster in *MLN,* XLII (1927), 414-16; by W. A. N[itze] in *MP,* XXV (1927), 246; by Arthur Tilley in *MLR,* XXIII (1928), 88-91; in *RLC,* VII (1927), 554.

This book is a study of literary theory in France from about 1600 to about 1670—an important period, of which previous investigators have given only an incomplete or one-sided account. The matter is arranged in four parts. The first deals with the origins of the classical doctrine, with special emphasis on the Italian influence and the cult of Aristotle; the second, with the fundamental principles of the doctrine (the utilitarian aims of poetry, the respective parts of genius and art in the poet's inspiration, the necessity of rules and their foundation in reason, the imitation of nature, and the imitation of the ancients); the third, with the rules common to various genres (verisimilitude, decorum, the unities, etc.); and the fourth, with the rules peculiar to particular genres (tragedy, tragicomedy, comedy, heroic poetry, pastoral, lyric, and satire). So far as one can judge who is not a specialist in the field, the author has done a thorough and careful piece of work. He has read extensively—his bibliography contains the names of close to a hundred writers; he has asked, in the main, the right questions; and he has built his results into a clearly organized and well-proportioned volume, which no one who is interested in the doctrinal aspects of neo-classicism can afford to neglect. The only quarrel I have with the book is that its method is perhaps too exclusively descriptive. It is not enough to be told what the theorists of literature thought about such matters as the rules, the obligation to imitate nature, or the relations between the imagination and the reason. We want to know why it was natural for them to think as they did—why, in fact, they could hardly have thought otherwise. In a word, we want an *explanatory* study of literary theory, in which the doctrines of the critics are interpreted in the light of the basic assumptions and points of view dominant in other fields of speculation at the time. Such a study, at once precise in its analysis and comprehensive in its scope, is, I believe, one of the outstanding desiderata in the domain with which M. Bray's book is concerned. I regret that he has not undertaken it. But the lack can be supplied in the future, and in the meantime he has written a book which, within the limits of its plan, contains a vast amount of well digested and useful information, much of which is accessible in no other place.

Brewer, Edward V. "Lessing and 'the corrective virtue in comedy.'" *JEGP,* XXVI (1927), 1-23.

Lessing studied in the light of the controversy, precipitated by Shaftesbury, over laughter as a "test of truth."

Brunschvicg, Léon. "Mathématique et métaphysique chez Descartes." *Revue de métaphysique et de morale,* XXXIV (1927), 277-324.

Apropos of Gilson's edition of the *Discours de la méthode.*

Croce, Benedetto. "Il pensiero italiano nel seicento, V-VI." *La Critica,* XXV (1927), 1-37, 69-84.

Croce, Benedetto. "La poesia e la letteratura italiana nel seicento." *La Critica,* XXV (1927), 133-57, 197-224, 269-99, 341-59.

Daudin, Henri. *De Linné à Jussieu: méthodes de la classification et idée de série en botanique et en zoologie (1740-1790).* Paris: Alcan, 1926.

Rev. by Emile Bréhier in *Revue d'histoire de la philosophie,* I (1927), 359-61; by Lucien Febvre in *RSH,* XLIII (1927), 37-60; by W. K. Gregory in *Journal of philosophy,* XXIV (1927), 633-35; in *TLS,* July 14, 1927, p. 482.

Eggli, Edmond. *Schiller et le romantisme français.* Paris: J. Gamber, 1927. 2 vols.

Rev. by J. G. Robertson in *MLR,* XXIII (1928), 91-94.

Ermatinger, Emil. *Barock und Rokoko in der deutschen Dichtung.* Leipzig: Teubner, 1926.

Rev. by Karl Viëtor in *Deutsche Literaturzeitung,* June 18, 1927, cols. 1201-07.

Green, Frederick C. "The critic of the seventeenth century and his attitude toward the French novel." *MP,* XXIV (1927), 285-95.

Grossman, Mordecai. *The philosophy of Helvétius, with special emphasis on the educational implications of sensationalism.* New York: Teachers College, Columbia University, 1926.

Rev. by E. N. Henderson in *Journal of philosophy,* XXIV (1927), 498-99.

Gurvitch, Georges. "La philosophie du droit de Hugo Grotius et la théorie moderne du droit international." *Revue de métaphysique et de morale,* XXXIV (1927), 365-91.

Hayes, Carlton J. H. "Contributions of Herder to the doctrine of nationalism." *AHR,* XXXII (1927), 719-36.

Hubert, René. "La formation des idées politiques de Rousseau du Premier au Second Discours." *Revue d'histoire de la philosophie,* I (1927), 406-36.

An extract from a forthcoming book on *Rousseau et l'Encyclopédie.*

Hubert, René. "Revue critique de quelques ouvrages récents relatifs à la philosophie de Malebranche." *Revue d'histoire de la philosophie,* I (1927), 269-93.

Jacoubet, Henri. "Comment on lisait au XVIIIe siècle le roman de Tristan et Iseut." *RHL,* XXXIV (1927), 517-44.

Jacquart, Jean. *Un témoin de la vie littéraire au XVIIIe siècle: l'abbé Trublet, critique et moraliste (1697-1770).* Paris: Picard, 1926.

Rev. by A. Brulé in *RAA,* V (1927), 175-76.

Johansson, J. Viktor. *Études sur Denis Diderot: recherches sur un volume-manuscrit conservé à la Bibliothèque publique de l'État à Leningrad.* Göteborg: Wettergren & Kerbers; Paris: Champion, 1927.

Lanson, Gustave. *Esquisse d'une histoire de la tragédie française.* Nouvelle édition revue et corrigée. Paris: Champion, 1927.

Lanson, René. *Le goût du moyen âge en France au XVIIIe siècle.* Paris: G. Vanoest, 1927.

Laporte, J. "Le cœur et la raison selon Pascal." *Revue philosophique,* CIII (1927), 93-118, 255-99, 421-51.

An important article.

Lenoir, Raymond. *Les historiens de l'esprit humain: Fontenelle, Marivaux, Lord Bolingbroke, Vauvenargues, La Mettrie.* Paris: Alcan, 1926.

Lenoir, Raymond. "Le mesmérisme et le système du monde." *Revue d'histoire de la philosophie,* I (1927), 192-218, 294-320.

Lévy-Bruhl, L. "Les tendances générales de Bayle et de Fontenelle." *Revue d'histoire de la philosophie,* I (1927), 49-68.

Looten, C. *La première controverse internationale sur Shakespeare entre l'abbé Leblanc et W. Guthrie, 1745-1747-1748.* Lille: Facultés catholiques, 1927.

Magendie, Maurice. *Du nouveau sur l'Astrée.* Paris: Champion, 1927.

Minderhoud, H. J. *La Henriade dans la littérature hollandaise.* Paris: Champion, 1927. ("Bibliothèque de la Revue de littérature comparée," No. 34.)

Moorhead, M. Dorothy. "*Les Ruines* de Volney." *French quarterly,* IX (1927), 138-46.

A rather superficial analysis of the content of Volney's book, with some indication of its significance.

Mornet, Daniel. "Philosophie de la littérature ou histoire de la littérature." *Romanic review,* XVIII (1927), 103-13.

A discussion of method in literary history inspired by Spingarn's review of Magendie's *La Politesse mondaine* (*Romanic review,* XVII, 71-73) and by Folkierski's *Entre le classicisme et le romantisme.* Under the name of "philosophie de la littérature" the writer attacks two tendencies in current literary study—hasty and over-ambitious syntheses and attempts to organize the interpretation of literary or intellectual developments on an international basis. The second of these tendencies he seems to look upon as a specific case of the first. Folkierski's book perhaps affords some warrant for this view, and M. Mornet makes some excellent points in criticism of that author's unhistorical treatment of Diderot (pp. 109-10) and of his haphazard selection of writers for study (p. 111). But the case for the historical study of common trends in European thought and literature is too solid to be disposed of by a single instance of defective method, and I cannot help thinking that much of M. Mornet's argument is beside the point. At the same time he has written a provocative article, which should lead to a more precise definition of the aims and technique of "littérature générale."

Mornet, Daniel. [Reviews of F. Brunot, *Histoire de la langue française,* t. VII (1926), of Joseph Dedieu, *Histoire politique des protestants français* (1925), and of Henri Sée, *L'évolution de la pensée politique en France au XVIIIe siècle* (1925).] *RHL,* XXXIV (1927), 444-51.

These three reviews contain interesting remarks on the history of ideas in eighteenth-century France and especially on the methods proper to their investigation.

Mornet, Daniel. "La véritable signification du *Neveu de Rameau.*" *Revue des deux mondes,* Aug. 15, 1927, pp. 881-908.

Nitze, W. A. "Molière et le mouvement libertin de la Renaissance." *RHL,* XXXIV (1927), 356-76.

An interesting study of the origins of Molière's "naturalism" and of the forms which it takes in his comedies. Professor Nitze perhaps makes too much of Pierre Charron. After all, as he himself acknowledges (pp. 361-63), the leading ideas of *De la sagesse* had been expressed by Montaigne and others in the preceding century, and they could, consequently, have reached Molière through other channels. But the article is a valuable contribution to our understanding not only of Molière but of the history of ethical naturalism in the Renaissance and seventeenth century.

Prévost, L'Abbé. *Mémoires et aventures d'un homme de qualité qui s'est retiré du monde.* Tome V: *Séjour en Angleterre.* Édition critique par Mysie E. I. Robertson. Paris: Champion, 1927. ("Bibliothèque de la Revue de littérature comparée," No. 38.)

Rev. by G. S[herburn] in *MP,* XXV (1927), 246-48; in *RLC,* VII (1927), 600-01; in *TLS,* Oct. 20, 1927, p. 732.

Volume V of the Abbé Prévost's *Mémoires d'un homme de qualité* reflects largely the author's desire to spread among his own countrymen knowledge and appreciation of England. This is what gives significance to the ninety-two pages of text for which Miss Robertson has provided a preface and numerous "notes explicatives."

The highlight of the preface is undoubtedly the attempt, by means of newly discovered documents, to show Prévost guilty, as had been previously charged by more or less hostile contemporaries, of trying to obtain money by means of a false draft, subject in consequence, according to the English law of the time, to capital punishment, and barely escaping this fate through the favor of the Eyles family against whom the fraud had been directed. In identifying the "Chevalier Ey . . .," of whose son Prévost was the tutor, with Sir John Eyles rather than with Sir Robert Eyre, Miss Robertson departs from her predecessors and follows the lead of new testimony which, as she herself admits, establishes her theory only "avec une quasi-certitude" (p. 8). On the more important question of Prévost's guilt or innocence, she has discovered in the Sessions Rolls of Middlesex a document reading as follows: "Marc Anthony Prevost, Committed 13th December by Thos. de Veil, Esq. on Oath of Francis Eyles Esq. upon a strong Suspicion of feloniously and falsely making a Promisary Note of the Sum of fifty pounds signed Francis Eyles payable to Mr. Prevost or Order and Uttering the same, knowing it to be false and with an Intent to Defraud him of the said sum of fifty pounds" (p. 14). On the margin is the notation "Discharged." Items in various newspapers of the time confirm the testimony of this document. The difference in name, Marc-Antoine instead of Antoine-François, while raising some doubt, is not conclusive in favor of Prévost. Moreover, the period in question is a time when Prévost, for reasons which he does not definitely explain, abandoned temporarily the editorship of the *Pour et contre.* Again the matter remains in doubt, but Miss Robertson has made a very strong case, which the vagueness of Prévost's denials rather supports than refutes and which is bound to be taken into consideration by his future biographers.

The extensive notes on the text are in general sane and remarkably complete. They show the background of Prévost's England, his occasional anachronisms, the way in which his observations generally check with those of other travellers or guide books, in short whatever is necessary for understanding or controlling his text. Rarely does Miss Robertson exaggerate, but she appears to me to do so in regard to Prévost's attitude toward Thomson: "Quoi qu'il en soit, ce tribut français à Thomson, publié dès 1731, est d'un intérêt qu'on ne saurait exagérer" (p. 156). Since, however, Prévost merely mentions Thomson's name and links him with Prior and Addison as not in any way inferior "aux meilleurs Poètes de tous les tems" (p. 69), and since the sentence is absolutely lacking in definiteness or any sign of personal appreciation, the passage appears entirely undeserving of Miss Robertson's enthusiasm. It is significant also that Prévost does not discuss Thomson in his *Pour et contre,* where there was every reason for him to do so if he really appreciated him. In her preface (p. 31), Miss Robertson praises Prévost for avoiding the anachronism of speaking in his novel, whose action is supposed to be laid in 1716, of three important works which came after that time—*Robinson Crusoe* (1719), *Gulliver's travels* (1726), and the *Beggar's opera* (1728). The plausibility of this praise disappears, however, when we consider that in the *Pour et contre* Prévost did not treat *Robinson Crusoe* at all, that he depreciated *Gulliver's travels* in favor of Swift's epistles, poems, and "petites pièces," and that he treated the *Beggar's opera* as merely "une turlupinade, assez ingénieuse à la vérité, mais pleine de traits bas et obscènes." One would like proof for so important a statement as the following: "Le ton plus modéré de la critique subséquente (cf. Le Blanc) est dû dans une grande mesure à l'influence de Prévost" (p. 154).

But the occasional statements which may be questioned are few in comparison with the many which are thoroughly sound, giving evidence of painstaking research intelligently interpreted. This critical edition is a valuable addition, not only to our knowledge of the Abbé Prévost, but also to that of Anglo-French literary relations during the eighteenth century. It will be frequently consulted by students of the period.—G. R. H.

Ravier, E. *Le système de Leibniz et le problème des rapports de la raison et de la foi.* Caen: J. Robert, 1927.

Reynaud, Louis. *Le romantisme: ses origines anglo-germaniques; influences étrangères et traditions nationales; le réveil du génie français.* Paris: A. Colin, 1926.

Rev. by L. Cazamian in *RAA,* V (1927), 176-79; by G. Chinard in *MLN,* XLII (1927), 188-94 (cf. also pp. 398-400); by H. Tronchon in *RLC,* VII (1927), 776-84.

Rousseau, J. J. *Correspondance générale de J.-J. Rousseau.* Collationée sur les originaux, annotée et commentée par Théophile Dufour et publiée par P.-P. Plan. Tomes V-VIII. Paris: A. Colin, 1926-27.

Sée, Henri. *Economic and social conditions in France during the eighteenth century.* Translated from the French by E. H. Zeydel. New York: Knopf, 1927.

Sonet, E. *Voltaire et l'influence anglaise.* Rennes: Ouest-Eclair, 1926.

1929

ENGLISH LITERATURE, 1660-1800: A CURRENT BIBLIOGRAPHY

By Ronald S. Crane
University of Chicago

This bibliography attempts to list the more significant books, articles, and reviews published during the year 1928, together with a few bearing the date 1927 that were inadvertently omitted from the bibliography for that year (*PQ,* VII, 155-94). Professors Godfrey Davies, A. O. Lovejoy, A. D. McKillop, and Napier Wilt have contributed the reviews signed with their respective initials.

LIST OF ABBREVIATIONS

AHR=American historical review.
Archiv=Archiv für das Studium der neueren Sprachen und Literaturen.
Beiblatt=Beiblatt zur Anglia.
EHR=English historical review.
ES=Englische Studien.
GRM=Germanisch-romanische Monatsschrift.
JEGP=Journal of English and Germanic philology.
LM=London mercury.
MLN=Modern language notes.
MLR=Modern language review.
MP=Modern philology.
N & Q=Notes and queries.
PMLA=Publications of the Modern Language Association of America.
PQ=Philological quarterly.
RAA=Revue anglo-américaine.
RC=Revue critique.
RCC=Revue des cours et conférences.
RELV=Revue de l'enseignement des langues vivantes.
RES=Review of English studies.
RH=Revue historique.
RHL=Revue d'histoire littéraire de la France.
RLC=Revue de littérature comparée.
RSH=Revue de synthèse historique.
SP=Studies in philology.
SRL=Saturday review of literature.
TLS=Times [London] literary supplement.

I. BIBLIOGRAPHICAL AIDS

Annual bibliography of English language and literature. Volume VIII, 1927. Edited for the Modern Humanities Research Association by D. Everett and E. Seaton. Cambridge: Bowes & Bowes, 1928. Pp. vi+201.

Baugh, Albert C. "American bibliography for 1927. I. English language and literature." *PMLA,* XLIII (1928), 1-39.

See especially pp. 26-33.

Bernbaum, Ernest. "Recent works on prose fiction before 1800." *MLN,* XLIII (1928), 416-25.

An excellent general review.

Bibliography of British history: Stuart period, 1603-1714. Edited by Godfrey Davies. Oxford: Clarendon Press, 1928. Pp. x+459.

Rev. in *N & Q,* CLV (1928), 323-24; in *TLS,* Oct. 18, 1928, p. 746.

This is the first volume to appear of the Bibliography of modern British history which was undertaken in 1909 by the Royal Historical Society and the American Historical Association. It is designed to give a selective list, with descriptive and critical notes, of the most important and useful bibliographies, printed sources, and "later works" now available for the study of the Stuart period. The titles, which number altogether close to 5,800, are grouped in sixteen chapters, as follows: "English political and constitutional history," "Military history," "Naval history," "Religious history," "Economic history," "Social," "Literature, ballads, and journalism," "Fine arts and music," "Science and medicine," "Political science," "Local history," "Scotland," "Ireland," "Wales," "Voyages and travels," and "Colonial history." There are two indexes, one of the authors and books referred to and one of subjects.

The test of a tool of research is of course in the using. It is safe to say, however, that for all those students of the literary history of this period who concern themselves with the interrelations between their subject and other phases of contemporary British life, this book will be a godsend. It will save them from much loss of time and, what is still more important, from that weakness for out-of-date or untrustworthy authorities which seems to be the besetting vice of most of us who venture unaided into the difficult fields of political, social, or religious history.

I add the titles of a few works, most of them fairly well known, which ought perhaps to be inserted in a second edition. Chapter IV: William Stephens, *An account of the growth of deism in England,* London, 1696; John Leland, *A view of the principal deistical writers,* London, 1754; John Hunt, *Religious thought in England from the Reformation to the end of the last century,* London, 1870-73; J. M. Robertson, *A short history of freethought, ancient and modern,* 2nd ed., rewritten and greatly enlarged, London and New York, 1906; S. G. Hefelbower, *The relation of John Locke to English deism,* Chicago, 1918. Chapter V: Auguste Dubois, *Précis de l'histoire des doctrines économiques dans leurs rapports avec les faits et avec les institutions,* Tome premier: "L'époque antérieure aux physiocrates," Paris, 1903. Chapter VI: J. Paul de Castro, "Principal London coffee-houses, taverns, and inns in the eighteenth century," *N & Q,* 12, VI and VII (1920). Chapter IX: E. A. Burtt, *The metaphysical foundations of modern physical science,* London and New York, 1925.—P. 230: the name of the author, A. F. B. Clark, should be supplied in No. 2354.

Chapman, R. W. "Elementary exercises in bibliography." *Library,* Fourth series, IX (1928), 197-201.

Deals with "Imposition in half-sheets," "erroneous perfecting," and "simple inference from watermarks." The examples are all taken from eighteenth-century books.

Chapman, R. W. "Guessing in bibliography." *TLS,* Apr. 12, 1928, p. 272.

Cooper, Lane and Alfred Gudeman. *A bibliography of the "Poetics" of Aristotle.* New Haven: Yale University Press; London: Humphrey Milford, Oxford University Press, 1928. Pp. x+193. ("Cornell studies in English," XI.)

Crane, Ronald S. "English literature, 1660-1800: a current bibliography." *PQ,* VII (1928), 155-94.

Crane, R. S. and F. B. Kaye. *A census of British newspapers and periodicals, 1620-1800.* Chapel Hill, N.C.: University of North Carolina Press, 1927. Cf. *PQ,* VII, 156.

Rev. by E. A. Baker in *MLR,* XXIII (1928), 357-58; by R. D. H[avens] in *MLN,* XLIII (1928), 212-13; by J. H[oops] in *ES,* LXIII (1928), 326; by L. C. Wroth in *Library,* Fourth series, IX (1928), 75-76.

Esdaile, Arundell. *The sources of English literature: a guide for students.* Cambridge: University Press, 1928. Pp. vii+131.

Much valuable information and advice by one who knows the tools of the literary historian from long personal use. I have noted only one serious slip: on p. 95, after mentioning several bibliographies of individual authors, he says, "It is perhaps significant that all four of these works come from America, that spacious land, where Universities have staffs large enough to allow them some leisure"!

Firth, Sir Charles Harding. *A bibliography of the writings of Sir Charles Firth.* Oxford: Clarendon Press, 1928. Pp. 45.

The items are arranged by subject.

Fordham, Sir Herbert George. *Hand-list of catalogues and works of reference relating to carto-bibliography for Great Britain and Ireland, 1720 to 1927.* Cambridge: University Press, 1928. Pp. 25.

Halkett, Samuel, and John Laing. *Dictionary of anonymous and pseudonymous English literature.* New and enlarged edition by James Kennedy, W. A. Smith, and A. F. Johnson. Volumes III-IV, H-P. London and Edinburgh: Oliver and Boyd, 1928. Cf. *PQ,* VI, 162.

McKerrow, Ronald B. *An introduction to bibliography for literary students.* Oxford: Clarendon Press, 1927. Cf. *PQ,* VII, 156-57.

Rev. by A. T. P. Byles in *MLR,* XXIII (1928), 223-26; by R. S. C[rane] in *MP,* XXV (1928), 372-74; by Charles Sisson in *Library,* Fourth series, VIII (1928), 478-82.

Simpson, Percy. "Proof-reading by English authors of the sixteenth and seventeenth centuries." Oxford Bibliographical Society, *Proceedings & papers,* Vol. II, Part I, 1927 (Oxford, 1928), pp. 5-24.

"Some eighteenth-century trifles." *TLS,* Aug. 30, 1928, p. 620.

Notes on recent sales at Sotheby's; they concern especially Swift and Fielding.

Van Tieghem, Paul. "Histoire littéraire générale et comparée (douzième compte rendu annuel)." *RSH,* XLVI (1928), 127-52.

Williams, Iolo A. *The elements of book-collecting.* London: Elkin Mathews & Marrot; New York: F. A. Stokes, 1927. Pp. 171.

Rev. by R. B. McKerrow in *Library,* Fourth series, VIII (1928), 488-91.

A sensible and charmingly written little book. The parts that will particularly interest the readers of this bibliography are Chapters II-VI, which deal with such matters as the determination of format, the make-up of a book, the detection of imperfections in a book, the discrimination of issues and editions (including a brief discussion of cancels), and the technique of bibliographical description. What is said on these points admirably supplements the more elaborate *Introduction to bibliography* of R. B. McKerrow, and for students of the eighteenth century has the additional merit of being based very largely on the typographical practice of that period. P. 16, l. 21: for "two-three-three" read "two-three-two."

The Year's work in English studies. Volume VII, 1926. Edited for the English Association by F. S. Boas and C. H. Herford. London: H. Milford, Oxford University Press, 1928. Pp. 321.

II. THE SOCIAL AND POLITICAL ENVIRONMENT

NOTE: I include here only such publications as have a fairly direct bearing on the problems of literary and intellectual history.

Belloc, Hilaire. *James the Second.* London: Faber and Gwyer, 1928. Pp. 304.

Rev. in *TLS,* Apr. 26, 1928, p. 301.

Besterman, Theodore. "A bibliography of Lord Macartney's Embassy to China, 1792-1794." *N & Q,* CLIV (1928), 201-04, 221-25.

A specimen of a forthcoming larger bibliography of voyages and travels (1600-1800).

The Correspondence of King George the Third, from 1760 to December, 1783. Printed from the original papers in the Royal Archives at Windsor Castle. Arranged and edited by Sir John Fortesque. London: Macmillan, 1927-28. 6 vols.

Cox, Nicholas. *The gentleman's recreation.* With a preface by E. D. Cuming. London: Cresset Press, 1928. Pp. xxiv+136.

Rev. in *TLS,* June 28, 1928.
First published in 1674.

Crane, Verner W. *The Southern frontier, 1670-1732.* Durham, N.C.: Duke University Press, 1928. Pp. xi+391.

Chapter XIII throws new light on the connections between early eighteenth-century English philanthropy and the genesis of Georgia.

Eden, Sir Frederic Morton. *The state of the poor: a history of the labouring classes in England, with parochial reports.* Abridged and edited by A. G. L. Rogers. London: Routledge, 1928. Pp. li+383.

Rev. in *TLS,* Dec. 20, 1928, p. 998.
First published in 1797.

Edwards, F. A. "Narratives of the great plague." *N & Q,* CLIV (1928), 422-23.

Some plague books earlier than Defoe's.

"A Forerunner of Whitaker's almanack." *TLS,* July 26, 1928, pp. 541-42.

An essay on Edward Chamberlayne's *Angliae notitia.* Comment by Roger Howson, *ibid.,* Sept. 6, 1928, p. 632.

Forsythe, Robert Stanley. *A noble rake. The life of Charles, Fourth Lord Mohun, being a study in the historical background of Thackeray's Henry Esmond.* Cambridge [Mass.]: Harvard University Press, 1928. Pp. xviii+310.

Rev. in *TLS,* Dec. 27, 1928, p. 1027.

George, M. Dorothy. *England in Johnson's day.* London: Methuen, 1928. Pp. xvi+239.

Rev. in *TLS,* May 31, 1928, p. 408.
An anthology of extracts from literary sources designed to illustrate English social life in the middle eighteenth century.

Gothein, Marie Luise. *A history of garden art.* Edited by Walter P. Wright. Translated from the German by Mrs. Archer-Hind. London: Dent, 1928. 2 vols.

Rev. in *TLS,* Nov. 1, 1928, p. 797.

Graham, Henry Grey. *The social life of Scotland in the eighteenth century.* London: Black, 1928. Pp. xii+545.

Rev. in *TLS,* Feb. 23, 1928, p. 133.

Grundy, C. Reginald. *English art in the XVIIIth century.* London: The Studio, 1928. Pp. xii+82, with plates.

Rev. in *TLS,* Nov. 8, 1928, p. 819.

Interior decoration of the eighteenth century (woodwork, wall treatments, staircases, chimney-pieces, and other details). From the designs by Abraham Swan. Selected by Arthur Stratton. London: Tiranti, 1928. 64 plates.

Rev. in *TLS,* July 5, 1928, p. 505.

"Jeffreys and the 'Bloody Assize.'" *TLS,* July 12, 1928, pp. 509-10.

For discussion see correspondence in the issues for July 19, 26, Aug. 2, 9, 16, 23, and Sept. 6, 1928.

Laprade, William T. "The power of the English press in the

eighteenth century." *South Atlantic quarterly,* XXVII (1928), 426-34.

A brief but suggestive article based on an intimate knowledge of the ways of politicians with journalists in the eighteenth century.

Lenygon, Francis. *Decoration in England, 1640 to 1760.* Second ed. London: Batsford, 1928.

Rev. in *TLS,* May 17, 1928, p. 376.

Mantoux, Paul. *The industrial revolution in the eighteenth century.* Revised edition translated by Marjorie Vernon. London: J. Cape; New York: Harcourt, Brace, 1928.

Namier, L. B. *The structure of politics at the accession of George III.* London: Macmillan, 1928. 2 vols.

Rev. in *TLS,* Jan. 31, 1929, pp. 69-70.

Oxford in 1710 from the Travels of Zacharias Conrad von Uffenbach. Edited by W. H. Quarrell and W. J. C. Quarrell. Oxford: Blackwell, 1928.

The Portledge papers: Being extracts from the letters of Richard Lapthorne, Gent., of Hatton Garden, London, to Richard Coffin, Esq. of Portledge, Bideford, Devon, from December 10, 1687 to August 7, 1697. Edited by R. J. Kerr and Ida C. Duncan, with a preface by Sir Edmund Gosse. London: J. Cape, 1928. Pp. 280.

Rev. in *TLS,* Mar. 8, 1928, p. 163.
Many references to books.

Shaw, William A. "Burnet and the 'characters' of John Macky." *TLS,* June 14 and 21, 1928, pp. 449, 466. Cf. also June 28 and July 5, pp. 486, 504.

Shaw defines his purpose as follows: "To show that the often-quoted 'Characters' in Macky's *Memoirs* were more or less finished drafts by Burnet and were intended by him to be worked up in the later part of the *History of his own Time*; and that the manuscript was purloined and published as another man's production, and was deliberately mangled in the process of publication." According to this view Burnet kept a rough-book in which he sketched the principal personages of the day, and constantly changed them. This volume was borrowed or purloined or came into the possession of Macky in some other way, and he added what Shaw calls "Scotland Yard details," probably obtained from brief personal descriptions of particular personages officially supplied to Customs officers "for the purposes of espionage and arrest." The last suggestion may be rejected without hesitation, inasmuch as the government of Queen Anne is hardly likely to have contemplated the arrest of its own members (e.g., Marlborough, Godolphin, etc.). If Burnet wrote these characters, he could surely know what their originals looked like, since nearly all sat in the House of Lords with him. The only evidence Shaw adduces to prove that he kept a rough-book of characters is contained in Dartmouth's note that Burnet's cousin said that after a debate in the House of Lords the bishop usually went home and altered everybody's character, as they had pleased or displeased him that day (Preface to *History,* ed. Airy, p. xxxv). This may refer, however, to the many revisions of the text of the *History.* Even if the existence of the rough-book be conceded, it need not have been the basis of Macky's characters. The internal evidence is not convincing. Shaw writes: "It is next door to demonstrable that the character of Johnston in Macky's volume is from Burnet's pen, and likewise that of Carstares; and it is fully demonstrable that neither of these two characters could have been written by Macky." Nevertheless the characters of Johnston in Burnet's original memoirs (Foxcroft, *Supplement*, pp. 370, 392, 415) and in Macky (pp. 204-07) do not seem by the same writer. In the former he is said to have "great dexterity in managing business," in the latter to be "something too credulous and suspicious." Moreover, what possible service to Burnet would it be to record commonplace details about Johnston whom he had known all his life? In spite of Shaw's positive statement that the character of Carstares "emanated from Burnet and could only have emanated from Burnet," there is no reason why the bishop should have drafted it for insertion in a later volume of his *History,* because he studiously ignores Carstares in his earlier work and would have no occasion to mention him afterwards. On the other hand, if Shaw's suggestion is correct that Macky's troubles may have been "perfidiously instigated by Carstares himself," Macky may well have sought revenge by describing him as "the cunningest subtle dissembler," etc. The similarity between Macky's characters and those in the Hyndford manuscript scarcely needed demonstration, inasmuch as the editor of the *Carstares State papers,* in which the latter is printed, pointed this out in 1774. Yet the strongest argument against the theory that Burnet wrote these characters in order to work them up into the later part of his *History* is that they would be useless for such a purpose. To take an example, what conceivable use would Burnet have for the sketch of the previous life of Marlborough (pp. 4-7). He had already described the general's early life (*Supplement,* pp. 291-92, etc.), and when he wished to revise it in the light of later events he changed it into the form printed in the *History.* Neither version corresponds to Macky except in the details which were common knowledge. On the other hand, if Macky drew up these characters for the benefit of Sophia of Hanover, as the dedication asserts, a brief account to date of the lives of the most important contemporaries—her future subjects, as she hoped—and a description of their appearance, habits, etc., would be very useful to her, a stranger. Finally, it may be asked whether Burnet is supposed to have written the character of himself (Macky, pp. 138-40) in which he is described as "a man neither of prudence nor temper"?—G. D.

Tanner, J. R. *English constitutional conflicts of the seventeenth century, 1603-1689.* Cambridge: University Press, 1928. Pp. x+315.

Rev. by H. J. Laski in *Economica,* Dec. 1928, p. 388; in *TLS,* Dec. 6, 1928, p. 948.

Tipping, H. Avray and Christopher Hussey. *English homes.* Period IV, Volume II, *The Work of Sir John Vanbrugh and his school, 1699-1736.* London: "Country Life," 1928. Pp. lxiv+333.

Rev. in *TLS,* Aug. 9, 1928, p. 579.

Turner, Edward Raymond. *The Privy Council of England in the seventeenth and eighteenth centuries, 1603-1784.* Volume II. Baltimore: The Johns Hopkins University Press, 1928. Pp. xi+507.

Rev. by A. L. Cross in *AHR,* XXXIV (1928), 117-19; in *TLS,* Oct. 4, 1928, p. 709.

Whitley, William T. *Artists and their friends in England, from 1700 to 1799.* London: Medici Society, 1928. 2 vols.

Rev. in *TLS,* Nov. 1, 1928, p. 799.

Whitley, W. T. *The Baptists of London, 1612-1928: their fellowship, their expansion, with notes on their 850 churches.* London: Kingsgate Press, 1928. Pp. 331.

Rev. in *TLS,* Dec. 20, 1928, p. 1013.

Wright, Charles and C. Ernest Fayle. *A history of Lloyd's.* London: Macmillan, 1928.

Rev. in *TLS,* May 17, 1928, p. 371.

III. CURRENTS OF IDEAS AND LITERARY FORMS

Anderson, Marjorie. "Interest in the Scottish highlands in eighteenth-century English literature and its relation to the work of Sir Walter Scott." University of Chicago *Abstracts of theses,* Humanistic series, IV (1928), 313-16.

Bond, Richmond P. "Some eighteenth-century Chaucer allusions." *SP,* XXV (1928), 316-35. Additions by J. F. Royster, pp. 336-39.

Allusions which escaped Miss Spurgeon. The collection does not modify appreciably our notion of Chaucer's place in the period.

Brauchli, Jakob. *Der englische Schauerroman um 1800 unter Berücksichtigung der unbekannten Bücher: ein Beitrag zur Geschichte der Volksliteratur.* Weida i. Thür: Thomas & Hubert, 1928. Pp. 260.

Rev. by L. Cazamian in *RAA,* VI (1928), 174-75.

The most valuable part of this monograph is the list of more than three hundred "novels of terror," published chiefly between 1790 and 1830, which Brauchli prints as an appendix. It might easily have been made more nearly complete. One misses entirely, for example, the names of Sophia Lee and Charlotte Smith, and Clara Reeve is represented only by the familiar *Old English baron.* But it will save the future bibliographer of romantic fiction an immense amount of labor, and meanwhile, thanks to the threefold classification of the titles under period of publication, theme, and author, it furnishes solid support to the author's generalizations, in the body of his study, concerning the characteristics and diffusion of the type. On these points Brauchli has much to say that is both interesting and new; especially illuminating are his chapters on the composition of the public to which the "novels of terror" were addressed and on the importance of long established popular tastes as factors in their success. His chief limitations as a historian of romantic fiction are two: as a result of his predominantly analytical method of treatment he fails, I think, to take sufficient account of the significant differences in tone and method between the earlier and the later phases of the development; and, for the same reason perhaps, he tends to isolate the "novel of terror" of the late eighteenth century too completely from the earlier forms of sentimental fiction. He is less open to criticism on this last point than many of his predecessors, but a comparison of his treatment of "influences" (pp. 80-131) with the recent suggestions of J. R. Foster (*PMLA,* XLII, 443-

64 and XLIII, 463-75) will indicate how far he is from seeing his subject in its full historical perspective.

Bush, Douglas. "Musaeus in English verse." *MLN*, XLIII (1928), 101-04.

A list of versions.

A Century of broadside elegies, being ninety English and ten Scotch broadsides illustrating the biography and manners of the seventeenth century. Photographically reproduced and edited with an introduction and notes by John W. Draper. London: Ingpen and Grant, 1928. Pp. xviii+229.

Rev. in *TLS*, Nov. 29, 1928, p. 925.

Clark, Kenneth. *The Gothic revival, an essay in the history of taste.* London: Constable & Co., 1928. Pp. xvi+308.

Rev. in *TLS*, Nov. 8, 1928, p. 823.

An interesting sketch of the Gothic revival in architecture from the beginnings to the end of the nineteenth century. The chapters dealing with the early phases of the Revival (I-V) contain, along with much that is commonplace (especially on the literary affiliations of the movement) a number of fresh details and suggestive discriminations. They fail to give us, however, what we need most in this field—a careful analytical study, fully documented, of the aesthetic presuppositions involved in "Gothicism" and of their background in the general thought of the period.

Clark, William S. "The sources of the Restoration heroic play." *RES*, IV (1928), 49-63.

Clark's main argument is directed against those modern scholars—he mentions specifically J. W. Tupper, F. E. Schelling, and Allardyce Nicoll—who have interpreted the heroic play as primarily a "legitimate development" of pre-Restoration romantic drama. In opposition to this view, still widely accepted, he insists once more on the importance of the debt to France: "The rimed verse, in which these heroic plays were written, was introduced by the Earl of Orrery as a new dramatic fashion in frank imitation of the French mode. The historical theme, the names and types of the characters, the situations and incidents of the plots, the sentimental motives in the action, even the lofty love [*sic*] of the dialogue—all these were in the main derived from the contemporary French heroic romances. Finally, the extremely bombastic language, which was not an original characteristic of the species, but developed subsequently, was inspired by fresh critical ideas on Dryden's part, stimulated by the outburst of enthusiasm for the heroic poem, generated in France" (p. 62). "In the face of this extensive dependence upon French suggestions," he concludes, "the resemblances between the heroic plays and the English drama of earlier periods come to have much less significance."

Clark, I think, exaggerates somewhat the opposition between his views and those of the critics mentioned above. Neither Tupper nor Nicoll, for example, excludes the hypothesis of French influence quite so completely as he leads us to suppose, and, on the other hand, he himself in his final summary (p. 63) makes allowance—rather grudgingly, it is true—for the continued working of native tradition after the Restoration. He falls into some confusion, too, when he attempts (see p. 50) to differentiate his point of view from that of these earlier scholars. "An *historical* study of sources for the heroic play," he says, "tends to modify profoundly the conclusions to which a broad, *critical* survey of the serious drama before and after the interregnum might easily lead" (italics mine). But this distinction of method becomes meaningless when we realize that the revivals of Beaumont and Fletcher and other early dramatists on the Restoration stage—to say nothing of their currency in print

—made them just as organic a part of the environment in which the heroic play developed as the romances themselves. The truth is no doubt that suggestions from the one source mingled in the minds of Dryden and his contemporaries with suggestions from the other and that it is impossible with the facts at our disposal to settle in any precise way the proportion of iniquity between them. Clark, however, deserves our thanks for his able and vigorous restatement of the case for a French influence. To the evidence presented by H. W. Hill in his monograph on La Calprenède, he adds several valuable points of his own, notably a demonstration that *The Indian Queen* was indebted in several important ways to Gomberville's *Polexandre* (pp. 55-57) and a suggestive discussion of the effect of Dryden's interest in the heroic poem on the style and imagery of his later heroic plays (pp. 60-61).

Collins, A. S. *The profession of letters: a study of the relation of author to patron, publisher, and public, 1780-1832.* London: Routledge, 1928. Pp. 279.

Rev. in *TLS,* Dec. 13, 1928, p. 985.

Covent Garden drollery. Edited by the Rev. Montague Summers. London: Fortune Press, 1927. Pp. vii+124.

Rev. in *TLS,* Jan. 26, 1928, p. 57.

Covent Garden drollery: a miscellany of 1672. Edited by G. Thorn-Drury. London: Dobell, 1927. Pp. xxi+154.

Rev. by V. de Sola Pinto in *RES,* IV (1928), 468-72; in *TLS,* Jan. 26, 1928, p. 57.

Das, Praphulla Kumar. *Evidences of a growing taste for nature in the age of Pope.* Calcutta: Calcutta University Press, 1928. Pp. 64.

Nothing new.

Dent, Edward J. *Foundations of English opera: a study of musical drama in England during the seventeenth century.* Cambridge: University Press, 1928. Pp. xi+242.

Rev. in *TLS,* June 21, 1928, p. 464.

Elton, Oliver. *A survey of English literature, 1730-1780.* London: Edward Arnold, 1928. 2 vols.

Rev. by E. E. Kellett in *New statesman,* Dec. 8, 1928, pp. 291-92; in *TLS,* Jan. 17, 1929, p. 41.

Fairchild, Hoxie Neale. *The noble savage: a study in romantic naturalism.* New York: Columbia University Press, 1928. Pp. ix+535.

Rev. by F. A. Pottle in *SRL,* Aug. 25, 1928, p. 67; in *TLS,* Sept. 6, 1928, p. 629.

An important contribution to the historiography of ideas. Doubtless a few "noble savages" in English literature between the sixteenth century and 1830 have eluded the author's inquisition; but his census is far more comprehensive than any previously made, and his accounts of individual specimens are full, lively, usually exact, and instructively contrasted and correlated. In the more philosophical part of his task—his attempts to show the relation of the conception to other ideas, to trace, historically and psychologically, its sources and effects, to distinguish and account for the successive phases of its history—Fairchild, though often illuminating, has not, I think, been wholly successful. The subject is pervaded by the ambiguities and confusions attaching to the term "nature"; while much more alert to these than most previous writers, the author does not altogether escape them, and does not sufficiently point out the part they played in the processes with which he deals. Nor does he clearly bring out certain of the most important *general* facts concerning the idealization of the "savage." I can mention here only two of these. (1) The characteristic quest of the "rationalism" of the late Renaissance and the Enlightenment was for truths which could be supposed discoverable by each man for himself by "the pure light of nature"; i.e., by the reason identical in all. Such truths must be uniform and obvious, and the knowledge of them dependent upon no socially mediated tradition. The creeds and codes actually current showed no such uniformity, simplicity, and self-evidence to the plain man. This was explained in the prevalent philosophy of history as the result of a long series of unhappy sophistications due to "pride" or ambition. Strip these off and primitive man—or the savage, as his approximate equivalent—is disclosed as the embodiment of what is uniform and fundamental in all men. The savage conceived as the model of humanity was thus primarily an expression of the central idea of this anti-intellectualistic rationalism. Now much that is called (even by Fairchild) "romantic naturalism" is essentially this idea-complex of the *Aufklärung* or a development from it. (2) An assumption impressed upon sixteenth-century writers by several traditions, but especially by the influence of Stoicism, was the superiority of things as "Nature" made them over things as "art," i.e., human design, had transformed them. But man himself *tel qu'il a dû sortir des mains de la nature* was supposed to be exemplified by the savage. The sources, motives, ambiguities, implications, and immense influence of this fundamental antithesis of "nature" and "art" Fairchild has not sufficiently analyzed, though many of his citations illustrate it. The *locus classicus* for the idea in English literature—Shakespeare's reply to Montaigne in *Winter's tale,* IV, iv—is not mentioned. The special theme of the book is, in these and some other respects, too little brought into relation with what may be called the general logic of primitivism. And its historical perspective seems to me partly false; it is only half-emancipated from certain common confusions about "Romanticism" which I have tried to point out elsewhere (see *PMLA,* June, 1924). The author seems to have started with the notion that "naturalism" and primitivism are of the essence of Romanticism, and at the same time with a traditional classification of certain authors as Romantics. Much of the evidence which he himself faithfully presents tends to correct these confusions; but the odd result is that the greater part of the volume deals with a period in which true primitivism was being overcome by ideas antithetic to it, and with writers who are shown to have had little or no belief in the nobility of the real savage and who, in most senses of the vague term, were not representative of "naturalism." Though open to criticism in these points, the book is a very welcome addition to our knowledge of an extremely important phase of the history of thought and taste.—A. O. L.

Flasdieck, Hermann M. *Der Gedanke einer englischen Sprachakademie in Vergangenheit und Gegenwart.* Jena: Verlag der Frommannschen Buchhandlung, 1928. Pp. viii+246.

Rev. in *Archiv,* CLIV (1928), 142.

Traces the idea of an academy for the regulation of the English language from the Renaissance to the present day. The first four chapters (pp. 1-143) deal with the period before the end of the eighteenth century. A richly documented study.

Gotô, Souéo. "Les premiers échanges de civilisation entre l'Extrême-Orient et l'Occident dans les temps modernes." *RLC,* VIII (1928), 401-19, 601-18.

An interesting general survey of the subject. Section II deals with "Les idées morales de la Chine introduites en Occident"; Section III with "La doctrine de Confucius introduite en Occident."

Haas, C. E. de. *Nature and the country in English poetry of the first half of the eighteenth century.* Amsterdam: H. J. Paris, 1928. Pp. 301.

Rev. in *TLS,* July 26, 1928, p. 549.

Hadley, Frances W. "The theory of milieu in English criticism from 1660 to 1801." University of Chicago *Abstracts of theses,* Humanistic series, IV (1928), 321-24.

Halévy, Elie. *The growth of philosophical radicalism.* Translated by Mary Morris. With a preface by A. D. Lindsay. London: Faber and Gwyer, 1928. Pp. xvii+554.

Rev. in *TLS,* Jan. 10, 1929, p. 19.

Heltzel, Virgil B. "*The rules of civility* (1671) and its French source." *MLN,* XLIII (1928), 17-22.

Hillhouse, James T. *The Grub-street journal.* Durham, N.C.: Duke University Press, 1928. Pp. vii+354.

A valuable monograph on one of the most interesting periodicals of the Walpole era. Hillhouse begins (Chapter I) by investigating its external history, including the hitherto obscure question of the identity of its editors, on which he is able to throw new light. He then deals at some length (Chapter II) with the problem of Pope's connection with the *Journal;* as to this see a review by George Sherburn, *MP,* XXVI, 361-67. His other chapters (III-VI) are devoted to an account of the numerous controversies in which the paper was engaged and in general to an analysis of its extremely miscellaneous contents. A useful appendix lists by numbers "all essays, letters, poems, epigrams, etc., which appeared in the first main section of the *Grub-street Journal* and in the *Literary Courier of Grub-street,* and in the column called 'From the Pegasus in Grub-street,' which ran from number 16 of the *Journal* to the end, number 418." Altogether a very welcome contribution to our knowledge of eighteenth-century journalism.

Hotson, Leslie. *The commonwealth and Restoration stage.* Cambridge [Mass.]: Harvard University Press, 1928. Pp. ix+424.

Rev. by S. C. Chew in *Books,* Oct. 21, 1928, p. 25; in *TLS,* Nov. 15, 1928, p. 853.

Hussey, Christopher. *The picturesque: studies in a point of view.* London and New York: G. P. Putnam's Sons, 1927. Pp. 308.

Rev. by B. Sprague Allen in *MLN,* XLIV (1929), 121-23; in *TLS,* Dec. 1, 1927, p. 905.

McKillop, Alan D. "The first English translator of *Werther.*" *MLN,* XLIII (1928), 36-38.

Cf. his note, *ibid,* p. 467.

Muddiman, J. G. "Fictitious newspapers." *N & Q,* CLV (1928), 101-02.

Cf. *ibid,* CLIV, 333, 408, and CLV, 12.

Nicoll, Allardyce. *A history of late eighteenth century drama,*

1750-1800. Cambridge: University Press, 1927. Cf. *PQ,* VII, 165.

Rev. by M. St. Clare Byrne in *RES,* IV (1928), 355-56; by L. Cazamian in *RAA,* V (1928), 367; by F. H. Schwartz in *Beiblatt,* XXXIX (1928), 74-77.

Nicoll, Allardyce. *A history of Restoration drama, 1660-1700.* Second edition. Cambridge: University Press, 1928. Pp. ix +410.

O'Leary, John Gerard. *English literary history and bibliography.* A thesis accepted for the diploma of the Library Association. With a foreword by R. A. Peddie. London: Grafton & Co., 1928. Pp. xii+192.

Chapters II-V contain a brief and rather superficial account of the development of literary history in the seventeenth and eighteenth centuries.

Ornstein, Martha. *The rôle of scientific societies in the seventeenth century.* Chicago: University of Chicago Press, 1928. Pp. xiv +308.

Rev. by J. H. Randall, Jr. in *AHR,* XXXIV (1929), 386-87 (reservations as to the author's conception of the history of early modern science); in *TLS,* Sept. 27, 1928, p. 679.

First published in 1913 and now reprinted without revision.

Partridge, Eric. "The 1762 efflorescence of poetics." *SP,* XXV (1928), 27-35.

This article deals with four works the "accumulative importance" of which, we are told, "makes of 1762 an *annus mirabilis artis poeticae.*" They are John Foster's *Essay on the different nature of accent and quantity,* John Newbery's (?) *Art of poetry on a new plan,* James Ogden's *Epistle on poetical composition,* and Daniel Webb's *Remarks on the beauties of poetry.* Partridge's treatment of them is extremely amateurish. Foster's book he has apparently only glanced at; he completely obscures its main intention and gives an altogether misleading statement of its position on the question of quantity in English verse. His discussion of the *Art of poetry,* which he regards as the most important book of the four and to which he devotes nearly half his space, is likewise unsatisfactory in nearly every respect. He mentions the fact that this work "has sometimes been attributed to Goldsmith," but he dismisses the matter without examination, unaware of the evidence that Goldsmith really did have a hand in it (see Prior's *Life,* I, 416-17), and goes on to suggest, in a note, that "the author may have been Francis Newbery, the publisher's son"—though he was only a schoolboy of nineteen in 1762! The truth is that the *Art of poetry* was a revision, with considerable additions from various other sources, of a small text-book for young children first published by Newbery in 1746—*The art of poetry made easy. . . . Being the seventh volume of the Circle of the sciences, &c.* Partridge might have spared us same absurdity in his account of the ideas of the book had he known this fact, the clue to which was provided by Gibbs as long ago as 1886 (see his edition of *The Works of Oliver Goldsmith,* V, 409-10, 412). For of the passages which he quotes in order to convince us that the *Art of poetry* had a "very significant" place in the "efflorescence" of 1762 (pp. 31-33), two of the longest—the first and the fifth—were taken over almost verbatim from the school-book of 1746. I have not succeeded yet in tracing all the rest, but at least three of them, including one which is said to show that even "in the matter of style in poetry, Newbery appears in accord with the new movement for freedom and picturesqueness,'' had their source in the *Traité des études* (1726-31) of the good but certainly not very romantic Rollin. The *Art of poetry* is an interesting book, but its value does not lie in the novelty of its ideas: in none of the passages, in fact, that Partridge quotes from it is there a single point of view that had not been a commonplace of criticism for at least a century. The remainder of the article is of a piece with what has gone before. Ogden's *Epistle* is dismissed briefly; it is, thinks Partridge, the least ''significant'' of the group, though he admits that he has never seen a copy. His analysis of Webb is accurate as far as it goes, but it does not go nearly far enough: of the brilliant defense of Shakespeare's artistry and penetrating study of his use of metaphor—passages which make of the *Remarks* one of the most original critical productions of the day—there is scarcely a word; Partridge can see only the platitudes with which these insights are mixed.

Perry, Charner Marquis. ''The genesis and operation of moral judgments: a study of British theories from Hobbes to Adam Smith.'' University of Chicago *Abstracts of theses,* Humanistic series, V (1928), 27-32.

Powicke, F. J. *The Cambridge Platonists.* London: J. M. Dent & Sons, 1926; Cambridge [Mass.]: Harvard University Press, 1927. Cf. *PQ,* VII, 165-66.

Rev. by Émile Bréhier in *Revue d'histoire de la philosophie,* II (1928), 429-31; by S. P. Lamprecht in *Philosophical review,* XXXVII (1928), 187-89.

Praz, Mario. ''Poets and wits of the Restoration.'' *English studies,* X (1928), 41-53.

Suggestive remarks occasioned by recent studies of Etherege, Sedley, Rochester, and Marvell.

Richardson, Caroline Frances. *English preachers and preaching, 1640-1670: a secular study.* London: S.P.C.K.; New York: Macmillan, 1928. Pp. xii+359.

Rev. by Austin Warren in *MLN,* XLIII (1928), 545-46; in *TLS,* Aug. 2, 1928, p. 560.

Saurat, Denis. *Milton et le matérialisme chrétien en Angleterre.* Paris: Rieder, 1928. Pp. 243.

Rev. by Ch. B[émont] in *RH,* CLVII (1928), 407-08; by Paul Chauvet in *RAA,* VI (1928), 172-74; by André Leroy in *Revue d'histoire de la philosophie,* II (1928), 427-29; by S. Reinach in *RC,* LXII (1928), 231-32; in *TLS,* Oct. 11, 1928, p. 735.

Three parts: ''Robert Fludd,'' ''De Fludd à Milton: les Mortalistes,'' and ''Le système de Milton.'' Much of the matter of the book appeared, in English, in *Milton, man and thinker* (1925), but there are additions, particularly in the first two parts, and the order of treatment has been changed in order to throw the chief emphasis on the successive phases in the development of ''le matérialisme occultiste'' during the seventeenth century.

Schneider, Rudolf. *Der Mönch in der englischen Dichtung bis auf Lewis's ''Monk'' 1795.* Leipzig: Mayer & Müller, 1928. Pp. ix+204.

Chapters VII-X deal with the Restoration and eighteenth century.

Smith, David Nichol. *Shakespeare in the eighteenth century.* Oxford: Clarendon Press, 1928. Pp. 91.

Rev. by Oswald Doughty in *MLR,* XXIV (1929), 86-88; in *TLS,* Sept. 27, 1928, p. 683.

The three lectures which make up this book were delivered. in Birkbeck College, London, in November, 1927. They describe, in lucid and flexible prose, the general movement of Shakespearean acting, scholarship, and criticism from the Restoration to the end of the eighteenth century. The specialist will not carry away from them any great number of new facts, but he will find many pages of fresh interpretation and appreciation, and an admirably clear statement of the changing ideals of editors and critics. The discussion of Johnson (pp. 47-52, 68-84) is particularly illuminating; if any better brief characterization of his place in the development of Shakespearean scholarship and criticism has been written, I have not seen it.

The Social and political ideas of some English thinkers of the Augustan age, A. D. 1650-1750. A series of lectures delivered at King's College, University of London, during the session of 1927-28. Edited by F. J. C. Hearnshaw. London: Harrap, 1928. Pp. 247.

Rev. in *TLS,* Nov. 15, 1928, p. 846.

Contains studies of Filmer, Halifax, Locke, Hoadly, Defoe, Swift, Bolingbroke, and the "Jacobites and Non-Jurors."

Spencer, Hazelton. *Shakespeare improved.* Cambridge [Mass.]: Harvard University Press, 1927. Pp. xii+406. Cf. *PQ,* VII, 167.

Rev. by B. V. Crawford in *PQ,* VII (1928), 318-19; by W. H. Durham in *University of California chronicle,* XXX (1928), 259-61; by G. Kitchin in *MLR,* XXIV (1929), 82-84; by Allardyce Nicoll in *MLN,* XLIII (1928), 400-02; by D. M. Walmsley in *RES,* IV (1928), 472-74; in *TLS,* July 5, 1928, pp. 493-94.

Stones, G. B. "The atomic view of matter in the XVth, XVIth, and XVIIth centuries." *Isis,* X (1928), 445-65.

Thornton, Richard H. "The periodical press and literary currents in England, 1785-1802." University of Chicago *Abstracts of theses,* Humanistic series, IV (1928), 347-52.

Thorp, Willard. "The stage adventures of some Gothic novels." *PMLA,* XLIII (1928), 476-86.

How far were the characteristic themes and effects of Gothic romance naturalized on the English stage before 1800? This question Thorp seeks to answer by analyzing seven plays produced between 1781 and 1798, the sources of which were novels of the "Gothic" type, together with two other productions of which the Gothicism appears to have been the invention of their writers. He concludes that "an examination of these dramatized versions discloses the curious fact that their authors seem to have taken pains to minimize the horrors of their originals rather than to utilize them for dramatic effect," and that they "frequently perverted the terrors into comedy, by the way of concession to a public which was not yet willing to suffer a romanticized theater." So far as I can judge, his generalizations fit the facts which he presents sufficiently well, though in his treatment of Boaden's dramatization of *The Romance of the forest* he perhaps stresses unduly the "timidity" of the playwright in the ghost scene. The chief weakness of the article is the too sharp contrast which it establishes between the taste of novelists and their readers and that of contemporary dramatists and their public. For Thorp "Gothicism" is more or less equivalent to the cult of the supernatural (cf., for example, his reason for not considering Boaden's dramatic version of Mrs. Radcliffe's *Italian*, p. 485). Consequently, when he finds his dramatists either omitting the supernatural from their plays or giving it a comic turn, he concludes that theater-goers of the late eighteenth century were less hospitable to romantic themes than the novel readers of the same period. There is doubtless some truth in this view, especially for the last few years of the century, but it certainly exaggerates the importance of supernaturalism in the works of the school of "Gothic" novelists that culminated in Mrs. Radcliffe. As we have been recently reminded (see J. R. Foster in *PMLA*, XLII, 443 ff), these writers tended, precisely as did the dramatists whom Thorp has studied, to reduce the supernatural element in their themes to a minimum and to rationalize it whenever it appeared; they were followers not so much of Walpole as of Prévost, and their Gothicism was less an affair of ghosts and enchantments than of sentimental adventures amid a romantic *mise en scène.*

Trevelyan, G. M. "'Artificial' comedy." *TLS*, Jan. 5, 1928, p. 12.

Comment by Elmer Edgar Stoll, Mar. 1, 1928, p. 150; by G. M. Trevelyan, Mar. 8, p. 170; by T. A. Lacey, Mar. 15, p. 188.

Tricks of the town: eighteenth-century diversions. Being reprints of three eighteenth-century tracts. With an introduction by Ralph Straus. London: Chapman and Hall, 1928. Pp. xxv +256.

Three pamphlets describing aspects of London life shortly before the middle of the century.

Walmsley, D. M. "The influence of foreign opera on English operatic plays of the Restoration period." *Anglia*, LII (1928), 37-50.

Whitford, Robert C. "Juvenal in England, 1750-1802." *PQ*, VII (1928), 9-16.

Whiting, George W. "Political satire on the London stage, 1675-90." University of Chicago *Abstracts of theses*, Humanistic series, IV (1928), 353-56.

Wilson, John Harold. *The influence of Beaumont and Fletcher on Restoration drama.* Columbus, Ohio: Ohio State University Press, 1928. Pp. 164.

Wood, Paul Spencer. "The opposition to neo-classicism in England between 1660 and 1700." *PMLA*, XLIII (1928), 182-97.

Wood discusses briefly a number of the obstacles that interfered with "the complete dominance of the neo-classical movement after 1660," especially the characteristic individualism of the English people, "the prestige of Elizabethan literature," and the tendency in various quarters to object to "the strict rules of Aristotelian formalism." His main object is to combat the view that these phenomena were manifestations of a "romantic" spirit. He makes some sensible points, which doubtless still need to be emphasized in introductory courses on this period, though hardly, one would think, in the pages of a learned journal. That his own perspective is still somewhat old-fashioned is indicated by his statement (p. 182) that "1660 definitely begins the classical period.''—P. 190: the passage quoted here from Oldham's poem ''Upon the works of Ben Johnson'' is not a protest against the ''rules''; it is concerned, as the context shows, merely with various forms of affectation and pedantry in style.

Wray, Edith. ''English adaptations of French drama between 1780 and 1815.'' *MLN,* XLIII (1928), 87-90.

A useful hand-list of plays.

Wright, Louis B. ''Notes on Thomas Heywood's later reputation.'' *RES,* IV (1928), 135-44.

IV. INDIVIDUAL AUTHORS

Richard Baxter

Richard Baxter and Margaret Charlton: a Puritan love-story. Being the breviate of the life of Margaret Baxter, 1681. With an introductory essay, notes and appendices by John T. Wilkinson. London: Allen and Unwin, 1928. Pp. 204.

Rev. in *TLS,* June 7, 1928, p. 425.

William Beckford

The Travel-diaries of William Beckford of Fonthill. Edited with a biographical introduction by Guy Chapman. London: Constable, 1928. 2 vols.

Rev. in *TLS,* May 3, 1928, p. 331. Cf. *ibid.,* May 10, 1928, p. 358.

May, Marcel. *La jeunesse de William Beckford et la genèse de son ''Vathek.''* Paris: Presses universitaires, 1928. Pp. 437.

Rev. by L. Cazamian in *RAA,* VI (1928), 69-70; by Léon Lemonnier in *Les langues modernes,* XXVI (1928), 457-58.

The eight chapters of this book are divided equally between a sketch of Beckford's early life and a psychological and literary study of *Vathek.* May displays considerable insight and sympathy in dealing with the biographical aspects of his subject, but being restricted for the most part to printed documents, he has been unable to add much of importance to what we have known since the publication of Melville's *Life and letters* in 1910. He has been much more successful in his efforts to explain the genesis and to penetrate the meaning of *Vathek.* Of the sources to which he calls attention for the first time, the most important are probably two Oriental tales published in the *Bibliothèque des romans* at the time of Beckford's first visit to the Continent. The discussion of the literary influences is conducted with much finesse, in close connection with a study of the psychological forces that determined the inner content and meaning of the novel, and the effect of the whole is greatly to enhance our understanding of one of the most interesting productions in the history of English Pre-romanticism.—P. 331: a more likely source than Dante for the motif of the flaming hearts in the Hall of Eblis is Gueullette's *Mogul tales.* See M. P. Conant, *The Oriental tale in England* (New York, 1908), pp. 36-38. Miss Conant also notes the influence of *Les aventures d'Abdalla* (pp. 38-41, and cf. May, pp. 253-57). P. 433: May's bibliography of the literature relating to *Vathek* contains no mention of *The episodes of Vathek,* ed. Lewis Melville, London, 1912. Nor are these tales, long supposed to be lost, discussed anywhere in his book.

Jeremy Bentham

A Comment on the Commentaries: a criticism of William Blackstone's Commentaries on the laws of England. By Jeremy Bentham. Now first printed from the author's manuscript with introduction and notes by Charles Warren Everett. Oxford: Clarendon Press, 1928. Pp. vii+253.

Rev. in *TLS,* May 10, 1928, p. 357.

The manuscript of the *Comment* was discovered among Bentham's papers in the library of University College, London. Everett's introduction deals with the circumstances that led to the writing of the work and with the chief questions at issue between Bentham and Blackstone.

William Blake

Fairchild, Hoxie Neale. "Unpublished references to Blake by Hayley and Lady Hesketh." *SP,* XXV (1928), 1-10.

Herford, C. H. *William Blake.* Manchester: University Press; London: Longmans, 1928. Pp. 16.

Pierce, Frederick E. "Blake and Klopstock." *SP,* XXV (1928), 11-26.

It is possible that Blake was familiar with *The Messiah* by 1803, but the evidence given by Pierce is far from decisive, and it certainly does not warrant the statement (p. 12) that "if we find seeming traces of *The Messiah's* influence on Blake's poetry from 1803 on, even if these traces seem at times a little vague, it is right that we should be impressed by them." The "traces" which Pierce has found consist of nineteen scattered parallels between the Prophetic Books and Collyer's translation of Klopstock's poem. Some of them (e.g., b2, d, f, h, j, l) are extremely far-fetched; not one of them involves a resemblance that could not be explained equally well by supposing either coincidence or a common acquaintance with Milton or the Bible. Pierce, indeed, recognizes their inadequacy as proofs of influence and falls back in the end upon general impressions, "a haunting sense that there is something common" between the two poets—which is only another way of saying that the problem is not susceptible of scholarly investigation.

Pierce, Frederick E. "Blake and Thomas Taylor." *PMLA,* XLIII (1928), 1121-41.

Wicksteed, Joseph H. *Blake's Innocence and Experience: a study of the songs and manuscripts "shewing the two contrary states of the human soul."* London: Dent, 1928. Pp. 301.

Rev. in *TLS,* Sept. 13, 1928, p. 644.

James Boswell

The Hypochondriack. Being the seventy essays by the celebrated biographer, James Boswell, appearing in the London Magazine, from November, 1777, to August, 1783, and here first reprinted. Edited by Margery Bailey. Stanford University, Cal.: Stanford University Press, 1928. 2 vols.

Rev. by R. W. Chapman in *MLN,* XLIV (1929), 109-13; by R. S. C[rane] in *MP*, XXVI (1929), 375-76; by B. R. Redman in *Books*, July 15, 1928, p. 10; in *RLC*, VIII (1928), 741; in *TLS*, Sept. 6, 1928, p. 629.

Pleadwell, Frank Lester. "Lord Mountstuart—Boswell's *Maecenas.*" *American collector*, V (1928), 233-41.

Five letters from Lord Mountstuart to William Hamilton, 1764-67. No references to Boswell.

Henry Brooke

Scurr, Helen Margaret. *Henry Brooke.* A thesis submitted to the Graduate Faculty of the University of Minnesota . . ., May, 1922. [Minneapolis, Minn., 1927]. Pp. vi+128.

Stevenson, Lionel. "Brooke's *Universal beauty* and modern thought." *PMLA*, XLIII (1928), 198-209.

John Bunyan

The Pilgrim's progress. By John Bunyan. London: Noel Douglas, 1928. Pp. 233.

A facsimile of the British Museum copy of the first edition.

The Pilgrim's progress and The Life and death of Mr. Badman. Edited by G. B. Harrison. London: Nonesuch Press, 1928. Pp. 450.

The Church book of Bunyan Meeting, 1650-1821. Being a reproduction in facsimile of the original folio in the possession of the Trustees of Bunyan Meeting at Bedford, entitled A Booke containing a record of the Acts of a congregation of Christ in and about Bedford, and a brief account of their first gathering. With an introduction by G. B. Harrison. London: Dent, 1928. Pp. xii+260.

Brown, John. *John Bunyan (1628-1688): his life, times and work.* The tercentenary edition revised by Frank Mott Harrison, with marginal notes, addenda and appendices. London: Hulbert Publishing Co., 1928. Pp. xxiv+515.

Rev. in *TLS*, Mar. 22, 1928, p. 227.

Harrison, G. B. *John Bunyan: a study in personality.* London: Dent, 1928. Pp. 191.

These two books seem to be the most important of the numerous biographies and appreciations called forth by the tercentenary.

"The Spirit of Bunyan." *TLS*, Nov. 29, 1928, pp. 917-18.

Edmund Burke

Gwynn, Denis. "Dr. Hussey and Edmund Burke." *Studies, an Irish quarterly review*, XVII (1928), 529-46.

Robert Burns

Journal of a tour in the Highlands made in the year 1787. By Robert Burns. Reproduced in facsimile from his original manuscript in the possession of Mr. William K. Bixby. With introduction and transcript by J. C. Ewing. London: Gowans and Gray, 1927.

Rev. in *TLS,* Jan. 19, 1928, p. 37.

The Letters of Robert Burns. Selected, with an introduction, by R. Brimley Johnson. London: John Lane, 1928. Pp. ix+188.

Rev. in *TLS,* Nov. 22, 1928, p. 888 (points out errors in the text).

Anderson, Harry B. "Robert Burns, his medical friends, attendants, and biographer." *Annals of medical history,* X (1928), 47-58.

The chief point of the article is that Burns's death was due, not to alcoholism, but to endocarditis. "In his correspondence the symptoms Burns describes and the information he furnishes are sufficiently definite to place the diagnosis of his disease beyond reasonable doubt." The same conclusion had been reached by Sir James Crichton-Browne in his *Burns in a new light.*—I owe this summary to F. B. Snyder.

Dewar, R. "Two Burns relics." *TLS,* Oct. 25, 1928, p. 783.

Comment by Davidson Cook, Nov. 8, 1928, p. 834.

Ferguson, J. De Lancey. "Cancelled passages in the letters of Robert Burns to George Thomson." *PMLA,* XLIII (1928), 1110-20.

Schroder, J. H. E. "Burns and Rudel." *TLS,* Apr. 19, 1928, p. 290.

The source of "Sae far awa." The discussion is continued in the issues of *TLS,* for May 31, June 7, Sept. 6, and 27, pp. 412, 430-31, 632, and 687.

Snyder, Franklyn Bliss. "Burns and his biographers." *SP,* XXV (1928), 401-15.

Snyder, Franklyn Bliss. "A note on Burns's language." *MLN,* XLIII (1928), 511-18.

Samuel Butler

Satires and miscellaneous poetry and prose. By Samuel Butler. Edited by René Lamar. Cambridge: University Press, 1928. Pp. xxi+504.

Rev. in *TLS,* Aug. 16, 1928, p. 591.

deBeer, E. S. "The later life of Samuel Butler." *RES,* IV (1928), 159-66.

A somewhat over-condensed but generally clear statement of what is definitely known from contemporary sources concerning Butler's life from the Restoration to his death in 1680. A few details are given for the first time, but the value of the article is in the main that of a full and precisely documented *mise au point.* Two minor oversights should perhaps be pointed out. The author refers in his introduction to René Lamar's important paper on Butler's early life, but when he comes (p. 163) to discuss the poet's connection with the Duke of Buckingham in 1673 he neglects to state that it was Lamar who discovered and utilized for the first time the document on which our knowledge of this fact rests (*RAA,* I, 217). And it is not quite correct to say (p. 165) that the gifts of Charles II to Butler "were not known to Aubrey or to other contemporaries." Aubrey's words are: "They [Charles and Clarendon] both promised him great matters, but to this day he haz got *no* employment, only the king gave him . . . *li*" (*Brief lives,* ed. Andrew Clark, I [Oxford, 1898], 136). Aubrey, in short, did know the fact of the gifts; what he did not know was the precise amount.

Greg, W. W. "Hudibrastics." *TLS,* Aug. 23, 1928, p. 605.

Criticism of Lamar's edition of the *Satires and miscellaneous poetry and prose.*

Susanna Centlivre

Bowyer, John Wilson. "Susanna Freeman Centlivre." *MLN,* XLIII (1928), 78-80.

Mainly additions to the bibliography of her works in the *Cambridge history.*

Philip Dormer Stanhope, Earl of Chesterfield

Heltzel, Virgil B. "Chesterfield and the anti-laughter tradition." *MP,* XXVI (1928), 73-90.

Heltzel, Virgil B. "Chesterfield and the tradition of the ideal gentleman." University of Chicago *Abstracts of theses,* Humanistic series, IV (1928), 325-28.

Charles Churchill

Whitford, Robert C. "Gleanings of Churchill bibliography." *MLN,* XLIII (1928), 30-34.

Supplements and corrects Beatty's article in *PMLA,* XLII, 162-76.

Colley Cibber

Habbema, D. M. E. *An appreciation of Colley Cibber, actor and dramatist, together with a reprint of his play "The Careless husband."* Amsterdam: H. J. Paris, 1928. Pp. 190.

Rev. in *TLS,* July 12, 1928, p. 517.

"The study here presented," says the author, "is the outgrowth of a desire to claim for Colley Cibber a rather higher place in the history of the literature of the eighteenth century than has been allotted to him." The exposition of this thesis fills seventy-eight pages and includes chapters on Cibber's life, on his career and merits as actor and theatrical manager, on the morals of Restoration comedy, on the relation of Cibber's plays to the movement for dramatic reform, and on the stage-history and literary qualities of *The Careless husband.* There is little in this part of the book that need detain the specialist: few of the facts are new and the treatment is amateurish in the extreme. Nor is the edition of *The Careless husband* which occupies the second half of the volume a much more satisfactory piece of work. I pass over the question whether Habbema should not have reprinted the text of 1721, which was revised by Cibber, rather than that of the first edition (1705). A more serious fault is his neglect to give any exact description of the seven editions he has collated, or any clear statement of the bibliographical relations existing between them. He does, it is true, remark (p. 80) that editions "A, B, D, were evidently based on the editio princeps . . ., whereas E and F were based on C, which forms part of the complete edition of Cibber's works [1721], revised by himself." Something more precise than this, however, is needed if we are to form a true picture of the evolution of the text. As to the accuracy of his reproduction of the first edition, a collation of a few scattering pages shows a number of slight variations from the original, mostly in details of capitalization and punctuation.

Senior, F. Dorothy. *The life and times of Colley Cibber.* London: Constable, 1928. Pp. xvi+286.

Rev. in *TLS,* July 12, 1928, p. 517.

Miss Senior's statement in her "Prologue" that she has not in any respect "shed new light on my subject" should prepare one for what follows. The author recounts in a light and superficial fashion the outstanding events and all the well known gossip about Cibber; gives brief pictures of some of the people closely connected with him, his son Theophilus, his daughter Charlotte, Mrs. Barry, Nance Oldfield, and Peg Woffington; and takes all of Cibber's enemies, especially Pope, to task for attacking him. The discussion of Cibber's plays is more than superficial. Among the appendices are a list of the parts played by Cibber, the chronology of his plays, a reprint of the first edition of *The Careless husband,* and some extracts from Fielding's *The Tryal of Colley Cibber.* There are a number of excellent illustrations.—N. W.

Jeremy Collier

Bradley, L. J. H. "Jeremy Collier's 'Marcus Aurelius.'" *TLS,* Jan. 19, 1928, p. 44.

Comment by Michael Holland, *ibid.,* Jan. 26, 1928, p. 62.

Freeman, Edmund L. "Jeremy Collier and Francis Bacon." *PQ,* VII (1928), 17-26.

Borrowings from Bacon in Collier's *Essays.*

William Collins

Garrod, H. W. *Collins.* Oxford: Clarendon Press, 1928. Pp. 123.

Rev. in *N & Q,* CLV (1928), 432; in *TLS,* Feb. 7, 1929, p. 95.

Garrod interprets Collins, in contrast with Gray, as an "inheritor of unfulfilled renown," a poet more interesting for his potentialities than for his accomplishment. But vexation at Swinburne's "over-pitched praises" leads the critic to dwell on Collins's actual failures rather than on his successes, possible or actual. A keen analysis of the text of the *Odes* yields some brilliant emendations, and much, we gather, that cannot be corrected. After a close scrutiny of the *Ode occasion'd by the death of Mr. Thomson,* Garrod says candidly: "I am left with a perplexed sense that this is a better poem than I seem to have allowed—I had almost said, a better poem than it should be." One is tempted to generalize this comment and make it the conclusion of the book: Collins is a better poet than he should be—if judged by his lapses in punctuation, rhetoric, and scholarship.—A. D. McK.

Garrod, W. H. "Errors in the text of Collins." *TLS,* Mar. 15, 1928, p,. 188.

The discussion is continued by various hands in the issues for Mar. 22, 29, Apr. 5, and 12, pp. 221, 243, 257, and 272.

McKillop, Alan Dugald. "A lost poem by Collins." *TLS,* Dec. 6, 1928, p. 965.

The poem is *An Epistle to the editor of Fairfax his translation of Tasso,* which was advertised in February and March, 1750, but apparently never published. Interesting remarks on its place in Collins's work.

Woodhouse, A. S. P. "Collins and Martin Martin." *TLS,* Dec. 20, 1928, p. 1011.

Borrowings from *A late voyage to St. Kilda* in Stanza X of the *Ode on the popular superstitions of the Highlands.*

Abraham Cowley

Nethercot, A. H. "Abraham Cowley as dramatist." *RES,* IV (1928), 1-24.

Nethercot, A. H. "The letters of Abraham Cowley." *MLN,* XLIII (1928), 369-75.

William Cowper

Fairchild, Hoxie Neale. "Additional notes on John Johnson's diary." *PMLA,* XLIII (1928), 571-72.

Cf. *PMLA,* XLII, 946-62.

Fausset, Hugh I'Anson. *William Cowper.* London: Jonathan Cape, 1928. Pp. 219.

Rev. in *TLS,* Oct. 25, 1928, p. 776.

Daniel Defoe

The Shakespeare Head edition of the novels and selected writings of Daniel Defoe. Oxford: Blackwell, 1927-28. 14 vols.

A Tour thro' the whole island of Great Britain. By Daniel Defoe. With an introduction by G. D. H. Cole. London: Peter Davies, 1927. 2 vols. Cf. *PQ,* VII, 173.

A very attractive reprint of the first edition. The text is an exact reproduction of the original except that Herman Moll's maps of the counties of England and Wales are inserted *in loco.* The introduction is hardly adequate, and does little more than point out the general importance of the *Tour* to the economic historian. Its great defect is that it leaves untouched the question of Defoe's sources, apart from the assertions that "he borrowed freely from guide-books and works of reference in supplementing what he knew by direct observation," and that he "unblushingly borrowed a good many particulars" from Macky's *A Journey through England in familiar letters.* The first statement is too vague to be very helpful, and the second is very dubious. Usually Defoe mentions Macky only to refute him, and when his descriptions are similar to those of the earlier writer, it is probable that both authors were borrowing from a common source. Defoe frequently mentions his indebtedness to Gibson's edition of Camden, and his debt is even greater than he acknowledges. Before the value of the *Tour* as historical evidence can be determined it is essential that it be compared with earlier descriptions of England. This would reveal the new information incorporated, which in its turn could be partially tested at least by sources not available when Defoe was writing. At present it is impossible for the student of the *Tour* to tell whether a passage is merely a rehash of what had already appeared in print, an accurate description of what Defoe actually witnessed, or whether a fertile imagination is supplying the place of observation. Unfortunately Cole's introduction will furnish little guidance toward the solution of these difficult problems. His suggestion that Defoe "had as little scruple in writing about places to which he had never been as . . . in issuing, from his confinement in Newgate, his narrative of the *Great Storm*" is not likely to lead astray anyone who is familiar with W. P. Trent's valuable contributions to our knowledge of that author.—G. D.

Flasdieck, H. M. "Robinson Crusoe im Lichte der neueren Forschung." *Deutsche Rundschau,* Jan., 1928.

Hubbard, L. L. "Text changes in the Taylor editions of *Robinson Crusoe.*" *Papers of the Bibliographical society of America,* XX (1928), 1-76.

Pollert, Hubert. *Daniel Defoes Stellung zum englischen Kolonialwesen.* Phil Diss. Münster, 1928. Pp. 210.

Secord, A. W. "Defoe's release from Newgate." *TLS,* Jan. 26, 1928, p. 62.

Sir John Denham

The Poetical works of Sir John Denham. Edited with notes and introduction by Theodore Howard Banks, Jr. New Haven: Yale University Press; London: Humphrey Milford, Oxford University Press, 1928. Pp. xi+362.

Rev. in *TLS,* July 5, 1928, p. 501.

The first edition of Denham with any pretensions to completeness or scholarship. The text, except for eight pieces, is based on the *Poems and translations* of 1668. It is accompanied by an introductory study of Denham's life and place in the history of poetry, by notes both textual and historical, and by six appendices, which include, among other things, a discussion of various writings falsely attributed to Denham, a useful collection of allusions to *Cooper's hill,* and a bibliography. The work on the text seems to be very competently done, and the commentary brings together much precise and pertinent information. As a matter of editorial technique one could wish that Banks had not included parallels with later writers among his explanatory notes on the poems; it would have been better, I think, to group them by themselves in a comprehensive appendix on Denham's influence.

John Dryden

Bredvold, Louis I. "Dryden, Hobbes, and the Royal Society." *MP,* XXV (1928), 417-38.

After outlining briefly the dilemma in which the early leaders of the Royal Society, disciples of the new mathematical philosophy but at the same time good Christians, found themselves placed by the "atheistical" tendencies associated with the extreme mechanism of Hobbes, Bredvold proceeds to show (1) how their desire to combat materialism led to the formulation of "a critique of the very science they were promoting, a critique which varied all the way from timidity in generalization to philosophical skepticism," and (2) how the attitude of Dryden to Hobbes, shown chiefly in his plays, and his early praises of the Royal Society reflect at once an awareness of the characteristic views of the scientists and a sympathy with their position. From this he concludes that "when we look for the meaning and importance of [Dryden's] distrust of the reason in *Religio laici* and *The Hind and the panther,* or for the interpretation of his ingenuous changeableness in literary opinions, we must go, among other places, to his intellectual experiences with the new science, with Hobbes, and with the Royal Society."

The article is a well written and extremely suggestive contribution to our understanding of Dryden's relation to his age. I am not sure, however, that in thus linking Dryden's point of view in his religious poems with that of the scientists, Bredvold has not overlooked one important distinction. That the avowals of ''skepticism'' quoted on pages 434 and 436 from the *Defense of the Essay of dramatic poesy* and the *Preface to Sylvae* imply an attitude very similar to the anti-dogmatism of Glanvill and Boyle there can of course be no doubt, and Bredvold is certainly right in seeing in them an effect of the poet's association with the Royal Society. What is not so certain is that the ''skepticism'' of the *Religio laici* and *The Hind and the panther* is of the same type or that it can be derived from the same source. After all, as Bredvold himself recognizes (see p. 430), the *scepsis scientifica* of Glanvill and Boyle stopped far short of genuine philosophical skepticism. Its import was chiefly methodological; Glanvill well described its essence when he wrote that the ''*Free Philosophers* are by other accounted *Scepticks* from their way of enquiry, which is not to continue still poring upon the Writings and Opinions of Philosophers, but to seek Truth in the Great Book of Nature; and in that search to proceed with wariness and circumspection without too much forwardness in establishing Maxims, and positive Doctrines: To propose their Opinions as *Hypotheseis,* that *may probably* be the true accounts, without peremptorily affirming that *they are.*'' ''This,'' he added, ''is *Scepticism* with some; and if it be so indeed, 'tis such Scepticism, as is the only way to sure and grounded Knowledge'' (*Essays* .... [London, 1676], p. 44). Bredvold does not, I think, sufficiently stress this point, nor does he recognize—what is even more important—that this brand of ''skepticism'' coexisted, in the writings of both Boyle and Glanvill, with religious rationalism of a somewhat pronounced type. Now when Dryden described himself in the Preface to *Religio laici* as one ''naturally inclin'd to skepticism in philosophy,'' he was using these words to define an attitude that was only superficially similar to that of the scientists. He was not concerned with the same issues or with the same antagonists. His problem was neither scientific method nor materialism; what preoccupied him was the question of the ability of man's unaided reason to attain religious truth, and his attack was directed against, not the Hobbists, but the rationalists, both the deists and those orthodox rationalists who numbered, in his time, most of the so-called ''skeptics'' of the Royal Society. It is clearly of this last group that he is thinking when he complains that ''our modern philosophers, *nay, and some of our philosophizing divines,* have too much exalted the faculties of our souls, when they have maintain'd that by their force mankind has been able to find out that there is one supreme agent or intellectual being which we call God; that praise and prayer are his due worship; and the rest of those deducements, which I am confident are the remote effects of revelation, and unattainable by our discourse; I mean as simply consider'd, and without the benefit of divine illumination'' (italics mine). And the language in which, in the same passage, he insists on the complete impotence of man's reason to ascertain any of the fundamental dogmas of religion indicates more plainly still the sharp opposition between his attitude in 1682 and that of Glanvill or Boyle: ''They who would prove religion by reason do but weaken the cause which they endeavour to support: 't is to take away the pillars from our faith, and to prop it only with a twig; 't is to design a tower like that of Babel, which, if it were possible (as it is not) to reach heaven, would come to nothing by the confusion of the workmen. For every man is building a several way; impotently conceited of his own model and his own materials: reason is always striving, and always at a loss; and of necessity it must so come to pass, while 't is exercis'd about that which is not its proper object. Let us be content at last to know God by his own methods; at least, so much of him as he is pleas'd to reveal to us in the sacred Scriptures; to apprehend them to be the word of God is all our reason has to do; for all beyond it is the work of faith, which is the seal of heaven impress'd upon our human understanding.'' This is a very different sort of ''skepticism'' from that which appears in the *Defense of the Essay* and the *Preface to Sylvae*; and it cannot, I think, be wholly or even mainly accounted for as a product of the same set of influences. Its sources must probably be sought in various places, for it is merely a new manifestation of a very old theological attitude—the "fidéisme" of a long line of apologists in the sixteenth and seventeenth centuries, Catholics many of them, running unbroken through Montaigne and Charron to La Mothe Le Vayer and Pascal (see the recent work of Henri Busson, *Les sources et le développement du rationalisme dans la littérature française de la Renaissance* [Paris, 1922], especially pp. 52-56, 97-109, 420-23, 428, 434-49, 458-89, 619-21).

"Cleopatra and "that Criticall warr." *TLS,* Oct. 11, 1928, pp. 717-18.

Contains an interesting appreciation of *All for love.*

Diffenbaugh, Guy Linton. *The rise and development of the mock heroic poem in England from 1660 to 1714: Dryden's "Mac Flecknoe."* Urbana, Illinois, 1926. Pp. 28.

A chapter from a University of Illinois dissertation.

Ham, Roswell G. "Dryden versus Settle." *MP,* XXV (1928), 409-16.

Ham, Roswell G. "Uncollected verse by John Dryden." *TLS,* Dec. 27, 1928, p. 1025.

Items in the Huntington Library and the Bodleian.

Havens, Raymond D. "An adaptation of one of Dryden's plays." *RES,* IV (1928), 88.

Wild, B. Josef. *Dryden und die römische Kirche.* Leipzig: Robert Noske, 1928. Pp. ix+90.

Students familiar with Dryden's works and the chief studies relating to him will find little in this brief sketch of his religious development that will be new to them. Wild is convinced of the sincerity of the conversion to Rome, but his account of the influences, particularly those of an intellectual order, that helped to bring it about is superficial and confused. He sees in Dryden's avowal of "skepticism in philosophy," for example, only a confession of doubt as to the dogmas of revealed religion, and he uses it as a warrant for placing him, at all events before 1682, in the company of such "deists" and "rationalists" as Herbert of Cherbury and Charles Blount (see pp. 14-16, 58-59). And though he notes the passage in *Religio laici* in which Dryden mentions his reading of Simon's *Histoire critique du Vieux Testament* (pp. 54, 55), he neglects altogether the important question of the effect of that epoch-making work upon the poet's thought.

John Dunton

McCutcheon, Roger P. "John Dunton's connection with book-reviewing." *SP,* XXV (1928), 346-61.

Sir George Etherege

The Works of Sir George Etherege. Edited by H. F. B. Brett-Smith. Volumes I and II, *Plays.* Oxford: Blackwell, 1927. Cf. *PQ,* VII, 174.

Rev. by A. Digeon in *RAA*, V (1928), 475-76; by V. de Sola Pinto in *RES*, IV (1928), 341-49.

The Letterbook of Sir George Etherege. Edited with an introduction and notes by Sybil Rosenfeld. Oxford: University Press; London: Humphrey Milford, 1928. Pp. ix+441.

Foster, Dorothy. "Sir George Etherege." *TLS*, May 31, 1928, p. 412.

Foster, Dorothy. "Sir George Etherege: collections. Addenda." *N & Q*, CLIV (1928), 28. Cf. *PQ*, VII, 174.

"Sir George Etherege." *TLS*, Mar. 1, 1928, pp. 137-38.

David Garrick

The Diary of David Garrick, being a record of his memorable trip to Paris in 1751. Now first printed from the original manuscript and edited by Phyllis Clair Alexander. Oxford: University Press; London: Humphrey Milford, 1928. Pp. x+117.

Rev. in *TLS*, July 19, 1928, p. 533. Comment by R. W. Chapman, *ibid.*, July 26, 1928, p. 552.

[Notes on the sale of two Garrick collections.] *TLS*, June 28, 1928, p. 492.

John Gay

Irving, William Henry. *John Gay's London.* Cambridge [Mass.]: Harvard University Press, 1928. Pp. xviii+459.

Though Irving has something to say about Gay's career and reputation and though most of the topics he treats are brought into at least a vague connection with *Trivia*, the subject of his book is really the life of London in Gay's time, or rather those aspects of the life of London that are mirrored in the verse of the period. He discusses in his second chapter some of the literary influences that helped to mould the treatment of London in poetry, and then hastens on to accumulate passages describing the life of the streets, the habits of rakes and whores, and popular London amusements. The fullness of his documentation in these chapters reflects at once his own antiquarian zest and the richness of the Harvard library. What he gives us is indeed rather an anthology than a serious social history. To attempt to reconstruct "the way ordinary people lived" in the past from a single class of literary documents is at best a questionable procedure, and one's doubt as to the value of the result is increased in Irving's case by the fact that his documents are almost all the work of satirists. To this reservation must be added another: Irving has a habit of playing fast and loose with chronology. As an example of his method we may take his discussion of the English merchant in Chapter III (pp. 205-08). "The English merchant of that time," he says, "was lazy." The context makes clear that by "that time" he means the early eighteenth century; yet he proceeds to illustrate his assertion by a passage from Sorbière, who wrote in 1667, and to this he adds, for other traits of the picture, bits from poems dating respectively 1663, 1615, 1598, and 1597! The distortion of history which results from such a method is all too common throughout his book; time and again texts from the early seventeenth century or from the middle or later eighteenth are treated as if they had equal value for his purpose with texts written during the period with which he is specially concerned. This is plainly a false assumption, and it detracts seriously from the historical value of a book which shows much out-of-the-way reading and which is written, for the most part, entertainingly and with gusto.

Joseph Glanvill

Nicolson, Marjorie. "The real Scholar Gipsy." *Yale review,* XVIII (1928), 347-63.

An admirably written sketch of Francis Mercury Van Helmont.

Oliver Goldsmith

The Collected letters of Oliver Goldsmith. Edited by Katharine C. Balderston. Cambridge: University Press, 1928. Pp. lii+190.

Rev. by A. W. P[ollard] in *Library,* Fourth series, IX (1928), 335-36; in *TLS,* Nov. 8, 1928, pp. 813-14.

A very careful and intelligent piece of work, probably the most important single contribution to our knowledge of Goldsmith's life that has appeared for nearly a century.

The materials which Miss Balderston makes accessible for the first time in print include nine genuine letters, a number of forgeries, inserted "merely to safeguard future students of the letters from imposition," the full text of Mrs. Hodson's narrative of Goldsmith's youth, and a group of documents relating to the *Threnodia Augustalis* and to *She stoops to conquer.* In addition she has been able to furnish new and in several cases more complete texts, based on an independent collation of the originals, for thirty-one letters already in print, and, in a number of instances, to rectify the dates adopted by previous editors. Finally, in an Introduction designed to illustrate the letters, she gives us studies of five important biographical problems—Goldsmith's relations with his family, the authenticity of his Fiddleback escapade, the circumstances that led to the abandonment of his intended voyage to India, the occasion of his composition of the *Threnodia Augustalis,* and the history of the revision and production of *She stoops to conquer.* On all these topics, as well as on numerous smaller points that arise in the course of her commentary on the texts, she has much that is both new and important to say.

Of the high quality of her editing there can be no question. Her accuracy, judged by the letters she has reproduced from printed sources, is exemplary; in a collation of eleven of these, I have noted only one slip—a brief postscript is omitted from Letter IX (see p. 41 and cf. Prior, *Life,* I, 267). The same painstaking care is exhibited in her notes on the text. These are for the most part models of precision and sobriety. It was, perhaps, unnecessary to tell us, apropos of an allusion to "an old Saxon poem" in a letter of 1772 (p. 109) that "Goldsmith, as is obvious, made no distinction between Saxon and Middle English." But this is exceptional: Miss Balderston, in general, keeps close to her text, and seldom writes a note merely to display her own learning. Occasionally, indeed, she errs on the other side by withholding information, especially of a bibliographical sort, which most of her readers will need, as when she alludes, without references, to Monro's class books (p. 5, n. 2), to the recently discovered proof of Goldsmith's part in a *Geography and history of England* published by Dodsley in 1765 (p. 73, n. 3), to a lawsuit against Colman involving *The Good-natured man* (p. 97, n. 1), or to Reynolds' note-books (p. 103, n. 3; but cf. p. 110, n. 2). These, however, are insignificant defects in an edition which is distinguished throughout by tact and good sense and which does high honor both to Miss Balderston herself and to her teacher, C. B. Tinker.

I add a few notes on details. P. 39, n. 3: Goldsmith's remark to Bryanton —"you see I use Chinese names to show my own erudition, as I shall soon make our Chinese talk like an Englishman to show his''—can hardly be used as proof that ''he was already [in August, 1758] actively planning *The Citizen of the World.*'' The allusion is plainly to the next paragraph of the letter, in which Goldsmith gives the substance of the Chinese scholar's ''lecture.'' P. 73, n. 2: further proof that Goldsmith had lodgings in Gray's Inn in the early part of 1764 is contained in the MS Register of Members of the Society of Arts, where his address is given as ''No. 9 Holbourn Court, Grays Inn.'' P. 110, n. 1: Miss Balderston omits to state that Letter XXXVI, like letter XXXV, was first printed in *N & Q*, 5, VII, 102. P. 110, n. 2: that Goldsmith had begun to go to Edgeware as early as 1768 appears from an entry in Percy's diary for May 7 of that year: ''Then went to Edgeware & dined with Goldsmith'' (B. M. Addit. MS, 32,336, fol. 117).

New essays by Oliver Goldsmith. Now first collected and edited with an introduction and notes by Ronald S. Crane. Chicago: University of Chicago Press, 1927. Cf. *PQ*, VII, 175.

Rev. by K. C. Balderston in *MLN*, XLIII (1928), 404-05; by L. I. Bredvold in *MP*, XXVI (1928), 113-15; by L. Cazamian in *RAA*, V (1928), 476-78; by Caroline F. Tupper in *JEGP*, XXVII (1928), 571-72; in *RLC*, VIII (1928), 350; in *TLS*, Nov. 8, 1928, p. 813-14.

The Vicar of Wakefield. By Oliver Goldsmith. Edited with introduction and notes by Oswald Doughty. London: Scholartis Press, 1928. Pp. liv+243.

An Exhibition in the Yale University Library of the works of Oliver Goldsmith in connection with the bicentenary of his birth. New Haven: Printed for the Yale University Library, 1928. Pp. 7.

Bonner, Willard Hallam. '' 'Poems for young ladies.' A bibliographical note.'' *N & Q*, CLV (1928), 129-32.

Notes on the editions of 1767, 1770, and 1785, and on the text of *Edwin and Angelina.*

''Oliver Goldsmith. 1728(?)-1774.'' *TLS*, Nov. 8, 1928, pp. 813-14.

Smith, H. J. *Oliver Goldsmith's The citizen of the world: a study.* New Haven: Yale University Press, 1926. Cf. *PQ*, VI, 182; VII, 176.

Rev. by K. C. Balderston in *MLN*, XLIII (1928), 403-04; by Hans Marcus in *Archiv*, CLIII (1928), 123-26; by L. F. Powell in *RES*, IV (1928), 111-13.

Thomas Gray

Toynbee, Paget. ''An alleged holograph of Gray.'' *TLS*, Nov. 8, 1928, p. 834.

Comment by Leonard Whibley, *ibid.*, Nov. 15, 1928, p. 859.

Toynbee, Paget. ''Gray and the Bedingfields.'' *TLS*, Mar. 15, 1928, p. 188.

Toynbee, Paget. '' 'Jack' and 'Johnny' in Gray's letters.'' *TLS*, Sept. 13, 1928, p. 648.

Whibley, Leonard. ''Manuscripts of Thomas Gray and William Mason at York.'' *TLS*, Apr. 5, 1928, p. 257.

Thomas Hobbes

The Elements of law, natural and politic. By Thomas Hobbes. Edited with a preface and critical notes by Ferdinand Tönnies. To which are subjoined selected extracts from unprinted MSS. of Thomas Hobbes. Cambridge: University Press, 1928. Pp. xviii+195.

Rev. in *N & Q*, CLIV (1928), 214-15; in *TLS*, Jan. 3, 1929, p. 8.

Charles Hopkins

Maxwell, Baldwin. "Notes on Charles Hopkins' *Boadicea.*" *RES*, IV (1928), 79-83.

Samuel Johnson

Chapman, R. W. "Dr. Johnson and Dr. James." *TLS*, Dec. 13, 1928, p. 991.

Comment by S. M. Ellis, Dec. 20, 1928, p. 1011, and by L. F. Powell, Jan. 3, 1929, p. 12.

Flood, W. H. Grattan. "*On the death of Dr. Robert Levet.*" *RES*, IV (1928), 88 89.

A note on the text as published in Thomas Parks' edition of Johnson's *Poetical works* (1805). Cf. *RES*, III, 442-45.

Hollis, Christopher. *Dr. Johnson.* London: Victor Gollancz, 1928. Pp. 203.

Rev. in *TLS*, Sept. 20, 1928, p. 663.

Lynd, Robert. *Dr. Johnson and company.* London: Hodder and Stoughton; New York: Doubleday, Doran, 1928. Pp. 248.

Powell, L. F. "Samuel Johnson: an early 'Friend of the Bodleian.'" *Bodleian quarterly record*, V (1928), 280-81.

Reade, Aleyn Lyell. *Johnsonian gleanings.* Part V, *The Doctor's life, 1728-1735.* London: Privately printed for the author by Percy Lund, Humphries & Co., Ltd., 1928. Pp. xii+314.

Rev. by R. S. C[rane] in *MP*, XXVI (1928), 245-46; by J. C. S[quire] in *LM*, XVIII (1928), 543-45; in *N & Q*, CLV (1928), 143; in *TLS*, Oct. 4, 1928, p. 708. Cf. also *TLS*, Apr. 26 and Nov. 29, 1928, pp. 313, 938.

Roberts, S. C. "Johnson in Grub street." *Cornhill magazine*, Oct., 1928, pp. 440-51.

Roscoe, E. S. *Aspects of Dr. Johnson.* Cambridge: University Press, 1928.

Rev. by Sylva Norman in *Nation and Athenaeum*, July 14, 1928, pp. 502, 503; in *N & Q*, CLV (1928), 126.

Small, Miriam R. "The source of a note in Johnson's edition of *Macbeth.*" *MLN*, XLIII (1928), 34-35.

A borrowing from the *Lady's museum.*

Squire, J. C. "Johnson's contributions to other people's works." *LM,* XVII (1928), 273-85.

"Junius"

The Letters of Junius. Edited with an introduction by C. W. Everett. London: Faber and Gwyer, 1927. Pp. lviii+410.

Rev. in *TLS,* Mar. 8, 1928, p. 161.

Sir William Killigrew

Lawrence, W. J. "Sir William Killigrew's *The siege of Urbin.*" *TLS,* Oct. 18, 1928, p. 755.

Comment by B. M. Wagner, *ibid.,* Nov. 1, 1928, p. 806.

John Locke

Zobel, Arthur. "Darstellung und kritische Würdigung der Sprachphilosophie John Lockes." *Anglia,* LII (1928), 289-344.

Henry Mackenzie

The Anecdotes and egotisms of Henry Mackenzie, 1745-1831. Now first published. Edited with an introduction by Harold William Thompson. Oxford: University Press; London: Humphrey Milford, 1928. Pp. xxxiv+303.

Rev. by M. Y. Hughes in *University of California chronicle,* XXX (1928), 488-90; by J. A. Inglis in *Scottish historical review,* XXV (1928), 204-05; by C. Wilkinson in *LM,* XVII (1928), 599-600; in *SRL,* May 26, 1928, p. 917; in *TLS,* Mar. 1, 1928, p. 145.

The Man of Feeling. By Henry Mackenzie. Edited, with an introduction, by Hamish Miles. London: Scholartis Press, 1928. Pp. 208.

Rev. by H. W. Husbands in *MLR,* XXIII (1928), 490-91; in *TLS,* Aug. 9, 1928, p. 579.

Andrew Marvell

The Poems and letters of Andrew Marvell. Edited by H. M. Margoliouth. Oxford: Clarendon Press, 1927. 2 vols. Cf. *PQ,* VII, 180.

Rev. by Pierre Legouis in *RAA,* V (1928), 472-75.

Legouis, Pierre. *André Marvell, poète, puritain, patriote, 1621-1678.* Paris: Henri Didier; London: Oxford University Press, 1928. Pp. xi+514.

Rev. by L. Cazamian in *RAA,* VI (1928), 65-67; by Mario Praz in *English studies,* XI (1929), 33-40; by G. C. Moore Smith in *MLR,* XXIV (1929), 78-80; in *TLS,* Jan. 3, 1929, p. 9.

Some may question whether Marvell deserves, either as man or as poet, the patient and exhaustive scrutiny to which Legouis has subjected him in this excellent book. From the point of view of the historian, the answer cannot be in doubt: in few figures of the middle seventeenth century can we study more profitably the complex play of tendencies out of which came the moral and aesthetic ideals of the Restoration. And Legouis, without losing sight of the purely individual aspects of his subject, has omitted no pains to characterize and interpret those traits of Marvell that make him symptomatic of his generation. To read the chapters (I, IV, V) in which he traces the course of the poet's political views and attachments from the outbreak of the Civil War to his death is to gain a new understanding not only of Marvell himself but incidentally also of some of the forces that affected Englishmen in general during those years. The same thing is true to an even greater degree of the chapters on Marvell's lyric poetry (II, III) and on his later satires and controversial pamphlets (VI, VII). These constitute a series of literary studies of a type that we seldom meet with outside the school of French critics to which Legouis belongs. Admirably planned and written, they give us at once a just and sympathetic estimate of Marvell's talent and a body of materials which will be of the greatest value to the historian of taste and style. I have no space for an inventory of their riches; suffice it to say that they cannot be neglected by any one who is interested in such questions as the influence of Donne, the intermingling of ''baroque'' and ''classical'' styles in mid-century verse and prose, or the technique of early Restoration satire.

William Mason: see *Thomas Gray*

Lady Mary Wortley Montagu

Hughes, Helen Sard. ''A letter from Lady Mary to Mr. Wortley Montagu.'' *RES,* IV (1928), 327-30.

''Lady Mary W. Montagu's fiction.'' *TLS,* Aug. 16, 1928, p. 596.

Dorothy Osborne

The Letters of Dorothy Osborne to William Temple. Edited .... by G. C. Moore Smith. Oxford: Clarendon Press, 1928. Pp. li+331.

Rev. in *N & Q,* CLV (1928), 341-42; in *TLS,* Oct. 25, 1928, p. 777.

Thomas Otway

Moore, John Robert. ''Contemporary satire in Otway's *Venice preserved.*'' *PMLA,* XLIII (1928), 166-81.

The author's contention is that this play, first acted in February, 1682, is full of satire against Shaftesbury and his supporters. ''In six respects,'' he asserts, ''contemporary allusions may be traced farther and more precisely than previous students have done,'' and his claim seems justified. His first argument deals with the ''vast amount of offering and taking of formal oaths of loyalty and of truth,'' which is regarded as a reference to the perjury of the witnesses in the Popish Plot trials. There is no reason to question this, but possibly Otway had also in mind the prevalent fondness for imposing oaths as tests on all occasions—during the Commonwealth and Protectorate or in the Test Act of 1673. His second and third points identify Shaftesbury as Renault and then as Antonio. These may be safely accepted. The fourth point consists of explicit references to the Popish Plot, though these mainly occur in the Prologue and Epilogue, and the fifth is the reduction of the conspiracy to a mere bubble although in Otway's source (Saint-Réal's romance, *Conjuration des Espagnols contre la rêpublique de Venise en 1618*) it was of considerable consequence. These two points might be further developed with the aid of the notes in Montague Summers, *Complete works of Thomas Otway* (London, 1927), III, 272-74. The sixth argument concerns the scorn heaped on the senate "apparently with reference to parliament." There are several allusions which make this identification seem more certain. In the Epistle Dedicatory Otway expresses the wish that the Duke of Richmond, son of Charles II and the Duchess of Portsmouth, may live to defend his father's right "against the encroachments of Republicans in his Senate." Pierre is angry because when he drove Renault away from Aquilina,

> The matter was complain'd of in the Senate,
> I summon'd to appear, and censur'd basely,
> For violating something they call priviledge.

He is obviously referring to privilege of parliament often invoked by members of both houses against those anxious to call them to account. On the whole this article, though the best on the subject, might have been improved if the political history of the time had been studied more carefully. This would have prevented a few errors, such as 1678 instead of 1679 as the date of the dissolution of the cavalier parliament, or Shaftesbury's protest against so "prolonged a session" instead of so long a prorogation in 1675-77, and would also have enabled the author to give a clearer background to the play.—G. D.

John Ozell

Hodges, John C. "The authorship of *Squire Trelooby.*" *RES,* IV (1928), 404-13.

Ascribed to Ozell.

Samuel Pepys

Further correspondence of Samuel Pepys, 1662-1679. From the family papers in the possession of J. Pepys Cockerell. Edited by J. R. Tanner. London: Bell, 1928. Pp. xx+381.

Rev. in *TLS,* Jan. 24, 1929, p. 57.

Ponsonby, Arthur. *Samuel Pepys.* London: Macmillan, 1928. Pp. xiii+160. ("English men of letters series.")

Rev. in *TLS,* Oct. 18, 1928, p. 752.

"Reports of Pepys's speech in the House of Commons, March 5th, 1668." Communicated by E. S. deBeer. *Mariner's mirror,* XIV (1928), 55-58.

Thomas Percy

Powell, L. F. "Percy's *Reliques.*" *Library,* Fourth series, IX (1928), 113-37.

An excellent bibliographical study.

Sir William Petty

Petty-Southwell correspondence, 1676-1687. Edited from the Bowood papers by the Marquis of Lansdowne. London: Constable, 1928. Pp. xxxii+343.

Rev. in *TLS,* Nov. 8, 1928, p. 821.

Edward Phillips

Albrecht, Walter. *Ueber das "Theatrum poetarum" von Miltons Neffen Edward Phillips (1675).* Leipzig: Mayer & Müller, 1928. P. vii+108.

Hester Lynch Piozzi

Merritt, Percival. *The true story of the so-called love letters of Mrs. Piozzi.* Cambridge [Mass.]: Harvard University Press, 1928. Pp. 85.

Rev. in *TLS,* Mar. 22, 1928, p. 211.

Alexander Pope

Bond, Donald F. "The *Essay on man,* Epistle II, lines 31-34." *MLN,* XLIII (1928), 326.

A parallel in the *Spectator,* No. 621.

Case, Arthur E. "The model for Pope's verses *To the author of a poem intitled 'Successio.'*" *MLN,* XLIII (1928), 321-22.

The model is a poem by Dorset.

Havens, George R. "Voltaire's marginal comments upon Pope's *Essay on man.*" *MLN,* XLIII (1928), 429-39.

Helsztyński, Stanislaw. "Pope in Poland: a bibliographical sketch." *Slavonic review,* VII (1928), 230-40.

Hillhouse, J. T. "The man of taste." *MLN,* XLIII (1928), 174-76.

Poems inspired by Pope's *Epistle on taste.*

Hughes, Helen Sard. "Pope to Bathurst: an unpublished letter." *SP,* XXV (1928), 462-67.

Krumpelmann, John T. "Schiller's 'Hoffnung' and Pope's *Essay on man.*" *Germanic review,* III (1928), 128-33.

Ann Radcliffe
(See also *Charlotte Smith*)

Sadleir, Michael. "Poems by Ann Radcliffe." *TLS,* Mar. 29, 1928, p. 242.

Allan Ramsay

Gibson, Andrew. *New light on Allan Ramsay.* Edinburgh: William Brown, 1927. Pp. x+152.

Thomas Reid

Jones, Olin McKendree. *Empiricism and intuitionism in Reid's common sense philosophy.* Princeton: Princeton University Press, 1927. Pp. xxv+134.

Samuel Richardson

Familiar letters on important occasions. By Samuel Richardson. With an introduction by Brian W. Downs. London: Routledge, 1928. Pp. xl+252.

Rev. in *TLS,* Jan. 31, 1929, p. 77.

Dottin, Paul. "Du nouveau sur Richardson (documents inédits)." *RAA,* V (1928), 557-61.

The first of a series of extracts from the Richardson manuscripts in the South Kensington Museum. The letter printed here is one written early in August, 1741, to Richardson's brother-in-law, James Leake of Bath, concerning the continuation of *Pamela.* It is an interesting document, but unfortunately Dottin's transcription of the text seems not to be entirely trustworthy. A. D. McKillop, who has examined the original, sends me the following note: "In the manuscript a page of the text has been lost near the last, but there follows a conclusion which clearly belongs to this letter. Dottin, however, substitutes another conclusion, properly belonging to the next letter in the collection, which happens to be to Dr. George Cheyne, n. d., but evidently written in January, 1742. He switches in the middle of a sentence without realizing that he is getting into another letter."

Downs, Brian W. *Richardson.* London: Routledge, 1928. Pp. 248.

Rev. in *TLS,* Jan. 31, 1929, p. 77.

A skilfully condensed account of Richardson's life, works, and influence, combining a rapid restatement of the familiar facts with fresh material drawn from recent special studies and, to a smaller extent, from the MSS at South Kensington and from original investigation. The book disposes lightly of some of the stock topics, such as the origin of *Pamela* and Richardson's relations with Fielding, and dwells on others which have been comparatively neglected, e.g., Richardson's work as a printer and the literature about *Pamela.* Downs's own comments are valuable, and he does not make the common mistake of letting Richardson's failings as a man obscure his importance as a writer. The lively style of the book and its pungent criticism will make it acceptable to the general reader; some of the new material will make it useful to the student as a supplement to the standard lives by Dobson and Clara Thomson.

One reservation must be made. Was it in the interest of the unpedantic public that footnotes were tabooed? There are many unplaced quotations and unauthenticated details. Surely any one who is interested in such subjects as the Anti-Pamelas, Lady Bradshaigh, and the Dutch imitations of Richardson would not balk at a few footnotes. Students will need to know which of the extracts from the MS letters have been printed before, and how far Downs relies on the work of the scholars named in his bibliography. The bibliography itself, select though it is, should not have omitted the works of Cross, Digeon, and Blanchard on Fielding, Whicher's *Eliza Haywood,* Dorothy Brewster's *Aaron Hill,* and Schücking's articles in *GRM,* XII (1924). These defects in method are a serious blemish in an otherwise competent and tactful book.—A. D. McK.

Joseph Ritson

Hopkins, Annette B. "Ritson's *Life of King Arthur.*" *PMLA,* XLIII (1928), 251-87.

A careful study of the methods and value of Ritson's contributions to Arthurian scholarship.

Sir Charles Sedley

The Poetical and dramatic works of Sir Charles Sedley. Collected and edited from the old editions. With a preface on the text, explanatory and textual notes, an appendix containing works of doubtful authenticity, and a bibliography. By V. de Sola Pinto. London: Constable, 1928. 2 vols.

Rev. in *TLS,* Nov. 1, 1928, p. 800.

Pinto, V. de Sola. *Sir Charles Sedley, 1639-1701: a study in the life and literature of the Restoration.* London: Constable, 1927. Cf. *PQ,* VII, 184.

Rev. by Paul Birdsall in *SRL,* May 26, 1928, p. 913; by R. Warwick Bond in *MLR,* XXIII (1928), 234-38; by R. H. Case in *RES,* IV (1928), 474-79.

Thomas Shadwell

Borgman, Albert S. *Thomas Shadwell: his life and comedies.* New York: New York University Press, 1928. Pp. x+269.

W[almsley], D. M. "A song of D'Urfey's wrongly ascribed to Shadwell." *RES,* IV (1928), 431.

Richard Brinsley Sheridan

The Plays and poems of Richard Brinsley Sheridan. Edited, with introduction, appendices and bibliographies, by R. Crompton Rhodes. Oxford: Blackwell, 1928. 3 vols.

Rev. in *TLS,* Jan. 3, 1929, pp. 1-2.

Gabriel, Miriam and Paul Mueschke. "Two contemporary sources of Sheridan's *The Rivals.*" *PMLA,* XLIII (1928), 237-50.

The two "sources" are Garrick's *Miss in her teens* and Colman's *Deuce is in him,* the first of which is said to have been responsible for the outlines of Sheridan's main plot, the second for the motivation of his sub-plot. Except in one instance (see pp. 246-47), the similarities pointed out are not very striking. The article is much too long.

Hinton, Percival F. "A Sheridan pamphlet." *TLS,* June 28, 1928, p. 486.

Rhodes, R. Crompton. "Some aspects of Sheridan bibliography." *Library,* Fourth series, IX (1928), 233-61.

Ryan, M. J. "The text of *The School for scandal.*" *TLS,* Mar. 22 and 29, 1928, pp. 212 and 240.

For the discussion provoked by these articles see the issues of *TLS* for Apr. 5, p. 257, Apr. 19, p. 290, Apr. 26, pp. 313-14, May 10, p. 358, May 17, p. 379, May 24, p. 396, and June 7, p. 430.

Charlotte Smith

Foster, James R. "Charlotte Smith, pre-romantic novelist." *PMLA,* XLIII (1928), 463-75.

An attempt to show that Charlotte Smith "was the first [novelist] in England to give an appreciable attention to romantic landscape description" and that her early romances—*Emmeline* (1788), *Ethelinde* (1789), and *Celestina* (1791)—had an important influence on the *Romance of the forest* (1792) and the other later novels of Mrs. Radcliffe. The first of these conclusions is made to seem fairly plausible; the second needs far more precise support from the texts than Foster gives it. The whole article, indeed, though it contains some useful suggestions, impresses one as a rather hasty first draft, much inferior to the author's brilliant study in *PMLA* for 1927 (XLII, 443-64) of the influence of Prévost on the English novel of sentimental adventure. There are too many sentences like the following: "The modern critics are wont to dismiss the sentimental adventure novel that flourished in the 1780's and 90's with a disdainful smile and the epithet of 'cheap' sentimentality, but their knowledge of this literature is often inexact as is often seen in their having to argue a German influence or, what is just as faulty, to make *Otranto* the sole parent of this body of narratives."

Tobias Smollett

The Letters of Tobias Smollett, M.D. Collected and edited by Edward S. Noyes. Cambridge [Mass.]: Harvard University Press, 1926. Cf. *PQ,* VI, 189; VII, 185.

Rev. by L. I. Bredvold in *JEGP,* XXVII (1928), 140-41; by A. W. Secord in *MLN,* XLIII (1928), 138-40 (points out inaccuracies in the text).

Buck, Howard. "A *Roderick Random* play, 1748." *MLN,* XLIII (1928), 111-12.

McKillop, Alan D. "Notes on Smollett." *PQ,* VII (1928), 368-74.

Sir Richard Steele

The Letters of Richard Steele. Selected and collated with the original MSS. With an introduction by R. Brimley Johnson. London: John Lane, [1927]. Pp. xii+202.

Rev. in *TLS,* Feb. 23, 1928, p. 127.

Blanchard, Rae. "Richard Steele as a moralist and social reformer." University of Chicago *Abstracts of theses,* Humanistic series, V (1928), 447-51.

Laurence Sterne

Bensly, Edward. "A debt of Sterne's." *TLS,* Nov. 1, 1928, p. 806.

Clark, Edwin. "Sterne's letters are a mystery." *New York Times Book review,* Jan. 15, 1928, pp. 1, 25.

Jonathan Swift

Bennett, R. E. "A note on the Cyrano-Swift criticism." *MLN,* XLIII (1928), 96-97.

Hubbard, Lucius L. *Notes on The adventures and surprizing deliverances of James Dubourdieu and his wife. A source for Gulliver's travels. Also The adventures of Alexander Vend-*

church [*London, 1719*]. [Ann Arbor, Mich.]: Ann Arbor Press, 1927.

Le Fanu, T. P. "Catalogue of Dean Swift's library in 1715, with an inventory of his personal property in 1742." *Proceedings of the Royal Irish academy,* Vol. XXXVII, Section C, No. 13 (July, 1927), pp. 263-75.

Moore, John Brooks. "The rôle of Gulliver." *MP,* XXV (1928), 469-80.

Williams, Harold. "*Gulliver's travels*: further notes." *Library,* Fourth series, IX (1928), 187-96.

James Thomson

Hughes, Helen Sard. "Thomson and the Countess of Hertford." *MP,* XXV (1928), 439-68.

An important article, based on researches in the Percy family papers at Alnwick Castle.

Sir Samuel Tuke

Clark, William S. "George and Samuel Tuke." *TLS,* May 3, 1928, p. 334.

Reply by A. E. H. Swaen, *ibid.,* May 24, 1928, p. 396.

Sir John Vanbrugh

The Complete works of Sir John Vanbrugh. The Plays edited by Bonamy Dobrée. The Letters edited by Geoffrey Webb. London: Nonesuch Press, 1927-28. 4 vols.

Rev. in *TLS,* Apr. 19, 1928, p. 287.

Edmund Waller

Lloyd, Claude. "Edmund Waller as a member of the Royal Society." *PMLA,* XLIII (1928), 162-65.

Merely collects the references to Waller in Birch's *History of the Royal Society.* An error in the date of the *Panegyric to My Lord Protector* (1658 for 1655) is pointed out by Ella T. Riske in *PMLA,* XLIII, 1201-02.

Horace Walpole

Manuscript commonplace book. By Horace Walpole. New York: W. E. Rudge, 1927.

Rev. in *TLS,* Mar. 8, 1928, p. 161.

Hughes, Helen Sard. "Another letter by Horace Walpole." *MLN,* XLII (1928), 319-20.

An unpublished letter to the Duchess of Northumberland, Apr. 2, 1760.

Lewis, W. S. "Walpole's Xo Ho." *TLS,* Aug. 30, 1928, p. 617.

Sources and number of editions.

Nathaniel Wanley

The Poems of Nathaniel Wanley. Edited by L. C. Martin. Oxford: Clarendon Press, 1928. Pp. xx+88.

Thomas Warton, Sr.

Williams, Iolo A. [Note on Thomas Warton Sr.'s *Poems on several occasions,* 1748.] *LM,* XVII (1928), 306-07.

Thomas Warton, Jr.

Havens, Raymond D. "Thomas Warton and the eighteenth-century dilemma." *SP,* XXV (1928), 36-50.

It is no longer so common as it was a decade ago to write enthusiastically of Thomas Warton as a "rebel" against neo-classical taste, but this essay, in which the limitations of his "romanticism" are set forth with much skill and knowledge of the texts, is none the less welcome. The discussion of Warton's views on the plan of the *Faerie Queene* (pp. 38-43) is especially notable for its careful discrimination of shifting aesthetic standards. Altogether a very sane appraisal.

Wecter, Dixon. "Thomas Warton's poems." *TLS,* June 14, 1928, p. 450.

Comment by Percival F. Hinton, *ibid.,* July 12, 1928, p. 520.

Gilbert White

Johnson, Walter. *Gilbert White, pioneer, poet, and stylist.* London: Murray, 1928. Pp. xvi+340.

Rev. in *TLS,* Nov. 15, 1928, p. 852.

Edward Young

C[hapman], R. W. "Young's *Night thoughts.*" *RES,* IV (1928), 330.

Dates of publication of Nights IV-VI, VIII.

Sherburn, George. "Edward Young and book advertising." *RES,* IV (1928), 414-17.

V. THE CONTINENTAL BACKGROUND

NOTE: The few studies listed here are selected either because they bear directly on some phase of English relations with the Continent or because they deal with some movement of thought or taste that was common to both the Continent and England.

Bouillier, V. "Silvain et Kant, ou les antécédents français de la théorie du sublime." *RLC,* VIII (1928), 242-57.

Bray, René. *La formation de la doctrine classique en France.* Paris: Hachette, 1927. Cf. *PQ,* VII, 189-90.

Rev. by G. Ascoli in *RC,* LXII (1928), 549-52; by Albert Cahen in *RHL,* XXXV (1928), 267-69; by P. Van Tieghem in *RSH,* XLV (1928), 154-55.

Brulé, André. "Les hommes de lettres au dix-huitième siècle." *Revue de France,* VIII[2] (1928), 684-711; VIII[3] (1928), 63-90.

Chinard, Gilbert. "Quelques origines littéraires de *René.*" *PMLA,* XLIII (1928), 288-302.

Interesting light on late eighteenth-century "naturalism" and the reaction against it.

Cobb, Lillian. *Pierre-Antoine de La Place: sa vie et son œuvre (1707-1793).* Paris: E. de Boccard, 1928. Pp. 226.

Especially valuable for its full and careful treatment of La Place as a translator of Shakespeare, Fielding, and other English writers.

Crump, Phyllis E. *Nature in the age of Louis XIV.* London: Routledge, 1928. Pp. 324.

Rev. in *TLS,* Sept. 27, 1928, p. 683.

Dubeux, Albert. *Les traductions françaises de Shakespeare.* Paris: "Les Belles Lettres," [1928]. ("Études françaises," no. 15.)

Fusil, C. A. "Lucrèce et les philosophes du XVIIIe siècle." *RHL,* XXXV (1928), 194-210.

The conclusion is that the appeal of Lucretius to the "philosophes" has been greatly exaggerated: "on est même tenté d'aller jusqu'à dire que, dans l'ensemble, les philosophes n'approuvent guère Lucrèce et n'usent que très modérément du poème *De la nature.*"

Green, F. C. "The eighteenth-century French critic and the contemporary novel." *MLR,* XXIII (1928), 174-87.

Havens, George R. and Norman L. Torrey. "The private library of Voltaire at Leningrad." *PMLA,* XLIII (1928), 990-1009.

Jacoubet, Henri. "A propos de 'Je-ne sais-quoi." *RHL,* XXXV (1928), 73-77.

Reproduces an interesting text of 1693 which throws light on the connotations of the expression in the seventeenth century.

Jan, Eduard von. "Voltaire und das Problem der religiösen Toleranz." *GRM,* XVI (1928), 49-61.

Jouglard, Madeleine. "L' 'imitation inventrice' ou les contradictions d'André Chénier." *RLC,* VIII (1928), 640-53.

Suggestions for the history of ideas on "imitation" in the eighteenth century.

Koch, Franz. "Lessing und der Irrationalismus." *Deutsche Vierteljahrschrift,* VI (1928), 114-43.

Larat, P and J. "Les 'Lettres d'une religieuse portugaise' et la sensibilité française." *RLC,* VIII (1928), 619-39.

Laurila, K. S. *Les premiers devanciers français de la théorie du milieu.* Helsinki: Société de littérature finnoise, 1928. Pp. 50.

Deals with Bodin, Chardin, Fontenelle, Fénelon, and Dubos.

McKeon, Richard. *The philosophy of Spinoza: the unity of his thought.* New York and London: Longmans, Green & Co., 1928. Pp. ix+345.

Rev. in *TLS,* Jan. 24, 1929, p. 54.

Mornet, Daniel. *La Nouvelle Héloïse de J.-J. Rousseau. Etude et analyse.* Paris: Mellotté, 1928. Pp. 340.

Rev. by Louis Cons in *MLN,* XLIII (1928), 560-61.

Oliver, Thomas Edward. *The "Merope" of George Jeffreys as a source of Voltaire's "Mérope."* Urbana [Illinois]: University of Illinois, 1927. Pp. 111. ("University of Illinois studies in language and literature," Vol. XII, No. 4.)

Rev. by H. Carrington Lancaster in *MLN,* XLIII (1928), 561-62 (Oliver's conclusions unconvincing).

Rovillain, Eugène E. "Sur le *Zadig* de Voltaire; quelques influences probables." *PMLA,* XLIII (1928), 447-55.

Storer, Mary Elizabeth. *Un épisode littéraire de la fin du XVIIe siècle: la mode des contes de fées (1685-1700).* Paris: Champion, 1928. Pp. 289. ("Bibliothèque de la Revue de littérature comparée," No. 48.)

Rev. by J. Roche-Mazon in *RC,* LXII (1928), 464-69 (serious reservations).

Tchao-Ts'ing, Ting. *Les descriptions de la Chine par les Français, 1650-1750.* Paris: Geuthner, 1928.

Teeter, Lura May. "Albrecht von Haller and Samuel Clarke." *JEGP,* XXVII (1928), 520-23.

Torrey, Norman L. "A note on Voltaire's *Commentaire historique.*" *MLN,* XLIII (1928), 439-42.

Notes on a copy in the Public Library at Leningrad.

Torrey, Norman L. "Voltaire and Peter Annet's *Life of David.*" *PMLA,* XLIII (1928), 836-43.

Tresnon, Jeannette. "The paradox of Rousseau." *PMLA,* XLIII (1928), 1010-25.

An attempt, by a disciple of Irving Babbitt, to show that G. R. Havens in his recent articles on Rousseau's theory of "natural goodness" presents "an essentially false interpretation of Rousseau's writings; and, further, that his articles leave with his readers a totally false impression of what is Rousseau's relation to the philosophic thought and speculation of his age." Miss Tresnon shares not only the moral bias but the exegetical methods of her teacher. Her treatment of Rousseau's ideas of *bonté* and *vertu* is based on a mosaic of passages from his complete works brought together without reference to date or context and interpreted in the light of a background that consists merely of vague generalizations about "the older humanistic (*i.e.,* non-religious) view of life."

Viatte, Auguste. *Les sources occultes du romantisme: illuminisme-théosophie, 1770-1820.* Paris: Champion, 1928. 2 vols. ("Bibliothèque de la Revue de littérature comparée," Nos. 46, 47.)
Rev. by Pierre Martino in *RC,* LXII (1928), 415-16.

Wade, Ira O. "Middle-class philosophes, middle-class philosophy, in the drama of the eighteenth century." *MP,* XXVI (1928), 215-29.

1930

ENGLISH LITERATURE, 1660-1800: A CURRENT BIBLIOGRAPHY

By Ronald S. Crane
University of Chicago

This bibliography attempts to list the more significant books, articles, and reviews published during the year 1929, together with a few bearing the date 1928 that were inadvertently omitted from the bibliography for that year (*PQ*, VIII, 165-206). I am indebted to several of my students and in particular to Mr. W. K. Chandler for much valuable assistance in the collection and verification of material.

LIST OF ABBREVIATIONS

AHR=American historical review.
Archiv=Archiv für das Studium der neueren Sprachen und Literaturen.
Beiblatt=Beiblatt zur Anglia.
EHR=English historical review.
ES=Englische Studien.
GRM=Germanisch-romanische Monatsschrift.
JEGP=Journal of English and Germanic philology.
JMH=Journal of modern history.
LM=London mercury.
MLN=Modern language notes.
MLR=Modern language review.
MP=Modern philology.
N & Q=Notes and queries.
PMLA=Publications of the Modern Language Association of America.
PQ=Philological quarterly.
RAA=Revue anglo-américaine.
RC=Revue critique.
RCC=Revue des cours et conférences.
RELV=Revue de l'enseignement des langues vivantes.
RES=Review of English studies.
RH=Revue historique.
RHL=Revue d'histoire littéraire de la France.
RHP=Revue d'histoire de la philosophie.
RLC=Revue de littérature comparée.
RSH=Revue de synthèse historique.
SP=Studies in philology.
SRL=Saturday review of literature.
TLS=Times [London] literary supplement.

I. BIBLIOGRAPHICAL AIDS

Annual bibliography of English language and literature. Volume IX, 1928. Edited for the Modern Humanities Research Association by E. Seaton and M. S. Serjeantson. Cambridge: Bowes & Bowes, 1929. Pp. vi+228.

Babcock, R. W. "A preliminary bibliography of eighteenth-century criticism of Shakespeare." *SP,* Extra series, No. 1 (1929), pp. 58-98.

A useful check-list of contemporary texts and modern studies. The compiler will welcome additions and corrections.

Baugh, Albert C. "American bibliography for 1928. II. English language and literature." *PMLA,* XLIV (1929), 9-45.

See especially pp. 30-39.

Bémont, Ch. "Histoire de Grande-Bretagne." *RH,* CLX (1929), 88-127, 359-74.

For reviews of recent works on the seventeenth and eighteenth centuries see pp. 117-27, 359-69.

Bibliography of British history: Stuart period, 1603-1714. Edited by Godfrey Davies. Oxford: Clarendon Press, 1928. Cf. *PQ,* VIII, 166.

Rev. by Keith Feiling in *EHR,* XLIV (1929), 305-07; by Wallace Notestein in *AHR,* XXXV (1929), 101-02; by Frances H. Relf in *JMH,* I (1929), 296-98.

Bradner, Leicester. "A finding list of Anglo-Latin anthologies." *MP,* XXVII (1929), 97-102.

Many of these are from the seventeenth and eighteenth centuries.

Cooper, Lane and Alfred Gudeman. *A bibliography of the "Poetics" of Aristotle.* New Haven: Yale University Press, 1928. Cf. *PQ,* VIII, 167.

Rev. by Gustav Binz in *Beiblatt,* XL (1929), 296-99; by E[mile] B[réhier] in *RHP,* III (1929), 485-86; by R. S. Crane in *MLN,* XLIV (1929), 548-49; by A. H. Gilbert in *Philosophical review,* XXXVIII (1929), 610-12.

Crane, Ronald S. "English literature, 1660-1800: a current bibliography." *PQ,* VIII (1929), 165-206.

Crane, R. S. and F. B. Kaye. *A census of British newspapers and periodicals, 1620-1800.* Chapel Hill, N. C.: University of North Carolina Press, 1927. Cf. *PQ,* VII, 156; VIII, 167.

Rev. by Walter Graham in *JEGP,* XXVIII (1929), 303-07; by L. F. Powell in *RES,* V (1929), 241-43.

Early newspapers from 1625 to 1850. Offered for sale by Birrell and Garnett. Catalogue, No. 26. [London, 1929.] Pp. 32.

A few items not in Crane and Kaye. Cf. *TLS,* Feb. 6, 1930, p. 108.

Eighteenth century books. Offered for sale by Birrell and Garnett. Catalogue No. 24. [London, 1929.]

Contains 797 items.

Halkett, Samuel and John Laing. *Dictionary of anonymous and pseudonymous English literature.* New and enlarged edition by James Kennedy, W. A. Smith, and A. F. Johnson. Volume V. London and Edinburgh: Oliver and Boyd, 1929. Cf. *PQ,* VI, 162; VIII, 167.

Contains the letters Q, R, and S.

The Year's work in English studies. Volume VIII, 1927. Edited for the English Association by F. S. Boas and C. H. Herford. Oxford: Oxford University Press; London: H. Milford, 1929. Pp. 386.

Rev. in *TLS,* May 2, 1929, p. 356.

II. THE SOCIAL AND POLITICAL ENVIRONMENT

Abbott, Wilbur Cortez. *A bibliography of Oliver Cromwell: a list of printed materials relating to Oliver Cromwell, together with a list of portraits and caricatures.* Cambridge, [Mass.]: Harvard University Press; London: H. Milford, 1929. Pp. xxviii+540.

Rev. in *TLS,* Nov. 14, 1929, p. 921.

Ashton, Thomas Southcliffe and Joseph Sykes. *The coal industry of the eighteenth century.* Manchester: Manchester University Press, 1929. Pp. ix+268.

Rev. by T. H. Marshall in *Economica,* Nov. 1929, pp. 367-69; by A. P. Usher in *AHR,* XXXV (1930), 399-400; in *TLS,* June 13, 1929, p. 465.

Beales, H. L. "The industrial revolution." *History,* XIV (1929), 125-29.

Indicates some of the newer trends in the interpretation of this movement.

The Bloody assizes. Edited by J. G. Muddiman. Edinburgh and London: William Hodge, 1929. Pp. 250.

Rev. in *Saturday review,* Nov. 30, 1929, p. 648; in *TLS,* Dec. 5, 1929, p. 1018. Comment by M. C. Balfour, *ibid.,* Dec. 12, 1929, p. 1058; by J. G. Muddiman, *ibid.,* Dec. 19, 1929, p. 1081; by M. C. Balfour, *ibid.,* Jan. 2, 1930, p. 12.

The editor has traced the evolution of this famous tract from its first appearance in 1689 as *The Protestant martyrs: or, The bloody assizes* to its final form in 1705 when the fifth and enlarged edition was published as *The Western martyrology; or, The bloody assizes.* He reprints the latter with a few trivial omissions, and adds comments and corrections mainly from newsletters. The appendixes contain a valuable analysis of the judges' lists of rebels executed or transported. Absolute certainty is unattainable, but there were apparently about 250 of the former and more than twice as many of the latter.—G. Davies.

Bowen, Marjorie. *The third Mary Stuart, Mary of York, Orange and England, being a character study with memoirs and letters of Mary II of England, 1662-1694.* London: John Lane, 1929. Pp. xxi+319.

Rev. in *New statesman,* Dec. 7, 1929, p. x; in *TLS,* Dec. 19, 1929, p. 1080.

Bunn, L. H. "The enthusiasm of the Methodist revival." *London quarterly review,* Oct., 1929, pp. 257-60.

Consists mainly of extracts from Wesley showing his antipathy to enthusiasm and the practical and unemotional character of his teaching.

Clark-Kennedy, A. E. *Stephen Hales, D.D., F.R.S., an eighteenth century biography.* Cambridge: Cambridge University Press, 1929. Pp. xii+256.

Rev. in *N & Q,* CLVII (1929), 71; in *TLS,* Sept. 12, 1929, p. 693.

Cock, F. William. "A list of Non-jurors." *N & Q,* CLVI (1929), 39-43.

Cf. *ibid.,* CLVI, 141.

Dorn, Walter L. "Frederic the Great and Lord Bute." *JMH,* I (1929), 529-60.

Feiling, Keith. "Clarendon and the Act of Uniformity." *EHR,* XLIV (1929), 289-91.

Firth, Sir Charles. *Modern languages at Oxford, 1724-1929.* Oxford: Oxford University Press; London: H. Milford, 1929. Pp. vi+151.

Rev. in *TLS,* June 20, 1929, p, 485.

An account of the development of their study. Prior to 1724 there was no systematic instruction in any modern foreign language in the schools of England and none at all in the universities. The government of George I tried to effect such a change as would make the two universities of Oxford and Cambridge a nursery for men acquainted with living tongues who might then be employed by the state in its relations with foreign countries. Accordingly a Professor of Modern History was endowed with a salary of £400 a year, out of which he was to pay two teachers of modern language to work under his supervision. Twenty students at each university were to be nominated by the government and to receive their tuition free. If they mastered foreign languages they might hope that the secretaries of state would find them employment. Out of the twenty original scholars, however, only three were found posts. The scheme failed, therefore, because it was idle to train civil servants when there was no organized civil service. The result was the bitter comment of Gibbon that had he remained at Oxford he would have "grown to manhood ignorant of the life and language of Europe." It is true that the Professor continued to draw his salary, but no modern languages were taught until a century had elapsed, when the establishment of the Taylorian Institution in 1848 witnessed their revival. Further details of the experiment under George I may be found in *EHR,* XXXII (1917), 1-21.—G. Davies.

Fordham, Sir Herbert George. *Some notable surveyors and map-makers of the sixteenth, seventeenth, and eighteenth centuries and their work.* Cambridge: Cambridge University Press, 1929.

Rev. in *N & Q,* CLVI (1929), 161-62.

Fry, Roger, and others. *Georgian art (1760-1820): an introductory review of English painting, architecture, sculpture, ceramics, glass, metal-work, furniture, textiles, and other arts during the reign of George III.* London: Batsford, 1929.

Rev. in *TLS,* Aug. 22, 1929, p. 647.

Fussell, G. E. and Constance Goodman. "Travel and topography in eighteenth-century England: a bibliography of sources for economic history." *Library,* 4th series, X (1929), 84-103.

A valuable list.

Games and gamesters of the Restoration. With an introduction by Cyril Hughes Hartmann. London: Routledge, 1929. Pp. xxx+282.

Rev. in *New statesman,* Dec. 7, 1929, p. xii; in TLS, Dec. 12, 1929, p. 1047. A reprint of Charles Cotton's *The Compleat gamester* (1674) and of Theophilus Lucas' *Lives of the gamesters* (1714).

Gonnard, René. "Les doctrines de la population avant Malthus." *Revue d'histoire économique et sociale,* XVII (1929), 58-84, 213-39.

Gothein, Marie Luise. *A history of garden art.* New York: Dutton, 1929. 2 vols. Cf. *PQ,* VIII, 169.

Rev. by M. P. Smith in *SRL,* May 25, 1929, p. 1052 (the review contains interesting general views on the subject).

Hamilton, Earl J. "American treasure and the rise of capitalism (1500-1700)." *Economica,* Nov., 1929, pp. 338-57.

Hauser, Henri. "Réflexions sur l'histoire des banques à l'époque moderne, de la fin du XVe à la fin du XVIIIe siècle." *Annales d'histoire économique et sociale,* I (1929), 335-51.

Hawkins, L. M. *Allegiance in Church and State.* London: Routledge, 1928.

Rev. by N. S. in *EHR,* XLIV (1929), 685-86; in *TLS,* Dec. 5, 1929, p. 1012. A study of the Nonjurors.

Jayne, R. Everest. *James Hanway, philanthropist, politician and author, 1712-1786.* London: Epworth Press, 1929. Pp. 143.

Kramer, Stella. *The English craft gilds: studies in their progress and decline.* New York: Columbia University Press, 1927. Pp. xi+228.

Rev. by A. V. Judges in *Economica,* Nov., 1929, pp. 384-87; by R. H. Tawney in *History,* XIV (1929), 261-62.

Maps of seventeenth-century London (circa 1603, 1660, 1702). Prepared and drawn by Norman G. Brett James. London: the Author, Ridgeway House, Mill Hill School, N. W. 7, 1929.

Rev. in *TLS,* Apr. 4, 1929, p. 278.

Marshall, D. "The domestic servants of the eighteenth century." *Economica,* April, 1929, pp. 15-40.

Marshall, J. N. "Jethro Tull and the 'new husbandry' of the eighteenth century." *Economic history review,* II (1929), 41-66.

Marshall, T. H. "Capitalism and the decline of the English gilds." *Cambridge historical journal,* III (1929), 23-33.

Inspired by Stella Kramer's *The English craft gilds* (1927).

Morgan, William Thomas. "The origins of the South Sea Company." *Political science quarterly,* XLIV (1929), 16-38.

Namier, L. B. *The structure of politics at the accession of George III.* London: Macmillan, 1929. 2 vols.

Rev. by A. L. Cross in *JMH,* I (1929), 473-77; by Richard Lodge in *History,* XIV (1929), 269-70; by T. C. P. in *AHR,* XXXIV (1929), 824-26; by J. Vallette in *Les langues modernes,* XXVII (1929), 237-39; by D. A. Winstanley in *EHR,* XLIV (1929), 657-60; in *Blackwood's magazine,* CCXXV (1929), 422-29; in *TLS,* Jan. 31, 1929, pp. 69-70.

Oliver, F. S. *The endless adventure.* London: Macmillan, 1929. Pp. xii+428.

Rev. in *TLS,* Jan. 16, 1930, p. 37.

The first volume of a new work on Robert Walpole and the politics of his time.

Osborn, Max. *Die Kunst des Rokoko.* Berlin: Propyläen Verlag, 1929.

Rev. in *TLS,* Nov. 28, 1929, p. 993.

Parry, Sir Edward. *The bloody assize.* London: Ernest Benn; New York: Dodd, Mead and company, 1929. Pp. 301.

Rev. by H. S. Commager in *Books,* Aug. 18, 1929, pp. 5-6; in *TLS,* June 6, 1929, p. 444.

Richards, R. D. *The early history of banking in England.* London: King, 1929.

Richards, R. D. "The pioneers of banking in England." *Economic journal,* Economic history series, Jan., 1929, pp. 485-502.

Select documents for Queen Anne's reign down to the Union with Scotland, 1702-7. Selected and edited by G. M. Trevelyan. Cambridge: Cambridge University Press, 1929. Pp. xiii+250.

Rev. by Ch. B[émont] in *RH,* CLXI (1929), 397-98; in *Nation & Athenæum,* June 1, 1929, pp. 309-10; in *N & Q,* CLVI (1929), 416; in *TLS,* Jan. 2, 1930, p. 2.

This selection of excerpts from sources is intended for students reading for a special subject in the Cambridge Historical Tripos. Its six sections deal with foreign treaties of alliance, home politics, Gibralter, Blenheim and Ramillies, the Marlborough papers (to illustrate the connection between home and foreign politics), and Scotland and the Union. The design is doubtless largely responsible for the selection, which is well calculated to interest novices in historical research. Most of the material is reprinted from volumes readily accessible, but there are several valuable citations from British Museum MSS on military operations. There are two obvious criticisms: that the very modest scope of the work tends to give rather a one-sided view of the period covered—the two *Examiners* of 1711 and the *Lockhart papers,* covering about twenty pages (out of two hundred and fifty), alone represent the views of the opposition—; and that social history is only incidentally treated and economic history not at all.—G. Davies.

Stratton, Arthur. *Introductory handbook to the styles of English architecture.* Part II, *Tudor and Renaissance (end of fifteenth to end of eighteenth centuries).* London: Batsford, 1929. Pp. 32.

Sykes, Norman. "Bishop Gibson and Sir Robert Walpole." *EHR,* XLIV (1929), 628-33.

Symonds, R. W. *English furniture from Charles II to George II.* With over 260 illustrations from examples in the collection of Percival D. Griffiths. London: "Connoisseur," 1929. Pp. xviii +322.

Rev. in *TLS,* Oct. 31, 1929, p. 865.

Wead, Eunice. "British opinion of the peace with America, 1782." *AHR,* XXXIV (1929), 513-31.

Wilkinson, Clennell. *William Dampier.* London: John Lane, 1929. Pp. xii+257.

Rev. by Francis Clarke in *LM,* XX (1929), 440-42; in *Spectator,* July 6, 1929, pp. 25-26; in *TLS,* Sept. 5, 1929, p. 675.

Williams, Ethyn Morgan. "Women preachers in the Civil War." *JMH,* I (1929), 561-69.

An interesting chapter in the early history of English feminism.

III. CURRENTS OF IDEAS AND LITERARY FORMS

Bateson, F. W. *English comic drama, 1700-1750.* Oxford: Clarendon Press, 1929. Pp. 158.

Rev. by Eduard Eckhardt in *Deutsche Literaturzeitung,* L (1929), cols. 1915-17; by Paul Meissner in *Beiblatt,* XL (1929), 306-09; by Allardyce Nicoll in *MLR,* XXIV (1929), 477-78; in *N & Q,* CLVI (1929), 380; in *TLS,* Apr. 11, 1929, p. 291.

Contains an introductory essay on the qualities which distinguish the early eighteenth century from the Restoration, essays on the comedies of Cibber, Steele, Mrs. Centlivre, Gay, Carey, and Fielding, and brief remarks, by way of conclusion, on the "decline" in English comedy after 1700.

Blanchard, Rae. "The French source of two early English feminist tracts." *MLN,* XLIV (1929), 381-83.

Bond, Richmond P. "*-Iad*: a progeny of the *Dunciad.*" *PMLA,* XLIV (1929), 1099-1105.

The author has been impressed by the fact that for more than a century after the *Dunciad* "an extraordinary number of productions had titles ending in *-iad* (*-ead, -ad, -ade*)." Of these he has collected over two hundred specimens ranging from the *Popiad* of 1728 to a skit in the *Harvard lampoon* for February 9, 1928. By diligent study he is able to show that most of the works bearing titles of this kind were satires, especially of the mock-heroic variety; that the favorite verse form was the heroic couplet, "with blank verse a poor second"; that they varied greatly in length; that the same title was occasionally used more than once; that some of the "*-iads*" embalmed "the names of prominent people"; that "History and geography also entered the mode"; that "practically every kind of word was considered available'' in the formation of the titles; and so on. *Parturient montes.*

Boswell, Eleanore. ''The library of the Royal College of Physicians in the Great Fire.'' *Library,* 4th series, X (1929), 313-26.

Contains a contemporary list of the books rescued from the Fire.

Boswell, Eleanore. '' 'Young Mr. Cartwright.' '' *MLR,* XXIV (1929), 125-42.

An account of a Restoration actor.

Brie, Friedrich. *Imperialistische Strömungen in der englischen Literatur.* Zweite durchgesehene und erweiterte Auflage. Halle: Niemeyer, 1928. Pp. xiv+285.

Rev. by Karl Ehrke in *Die neueren Sprachen,* XXXVII (1929), 424-28; by J. A. Falconer in *English studies,* XI (1929), 116-18; by A. K[oszul] in *Les langues modernes,* XXVII (1929), 231-33.

A Century of broadside elegies. Photographically reproduced and edited with an introduction and notes by John W. Draper. London: Ingpen and Grant, 1928. Cf. *PQ,* VIII, 173.

Rev. by Hyder E. Rollins in *MLN,* XLIV (1929), 398-400; by E. N. S. Thompson in *PQ,* IX (1930), 96.

Clark, Kenneth. *The Gothic revival, an essay in the history of taste.* London: Constable & Co., 1928. Cf. *PQ,* VIII, 173.

Rev. by A. Digeon in *RAA,* VII (1929), 180-81; by P. Yvon in *Les langues modernes,* XXVII (1929), 546-50.

Crawford, Bartholow V. ''High comedy in terms of Restoration practice.'' *PQ,* VIII (1929), 339-47.

Croll, Morris W. ''The baroque style in prose.'' *Studies in English philology, a miscellany in honor of Frederick Klaeber* (Minneapolis: University of Minnesota Press, 1929), pp. 427-56.

This article is the latest of a series of papers, all of them very distinguished pieces of interpretative literary scholarship, in which Croll has studied various aspects of the Anti-Ciceronian movement in prose style which developed in the principal literary centers of Europe from the last quarter of the sixteenth century. In his earlier articles he was concerned mainly with the aims and theories of the Anti-Ciceronian leaders (Muret, Lipsius, Montaigne, Bacon), with their preferred models in antiquity, and with the connection between their stylistic ideals and their general program of intellectual reform. He now supplements these more theoretical studies by a masterly analysis of one important element in the prose technique of the Anti-Ciceronians—their handling of the rhetorical period. His examples are drawn from a fairly wide range of authors, both English and French: Montaigne, Bacon, Sir Henry Wotton, Balzac, Pascal, Burton, Sir Thomas Browne, and La Bruyère. His description of the two chief forms assumed by the period in these writers—''the période coupé'' and the ''loose period''—is one of the most convincing attempts I know to deal with the actual phenomena of ''style'' in modern prose; it is a model of subtle and discriminating analysis, which deserves the careful study not only of specialists in the authors in question but of all those who are interested in the reform of prose technique which took place after the middle of the seventeenth century and which was at once a reaction against and a prolongation of the movement here described.

Dobrée, Bonamy. *Restoration tragedy, 1660-1720.* Oxford: Clarendon Press, 1929. Pp. 189.

Rev. in *TLS,* Dec. 5, 1929, p. 1025.

Draper, John W. *The funeral elegy and the rise of English romanticism.* New York: New York University Press, 1929. Pp. xv+358.

Rev. by Paull F. Baum in the *South Atlantic quarterly,* XXVIII (1929), 331; by Merritt Y. Hughes in the *University of California chronicle,* XXXI (1929), 321-23; in *TLS,* May 16, 1929, p. 399.

The main point which Draper seeks to clarify in this large and imposing book is the origins of eighteenth-century "graveyard poetry." To one familiar with recent scholarship on the question his major conclusions will hardly seem very new. Both Amy Reed in her *Background of Gray's "Elegy"* and C. A. Moore in a series of papers which Draper unduly neglects (*SP,* XX, 467-99; *MLN,* XL, 431-35, XLI, 220-26; *MP,* 326-31) have prepared us to look upon Blair's *Grave,* Young's *Night thoughts,* Gray's *Elegy,* and other similar works of the same period, not as "new departures," but as the culminating manifestations in polite literature of a fashion of lugubrious meditation which had descended to the eighteenth century from the Puritan seventeenth. The main lines of the picture as thus sketched remain unchanged in Draper's book. What he adds is chiefly a mass of new details drawn from sources hitherto neglected by students of the subject—the "funeral elegies" of the Commonwealth, the Restoration, and the early eighteenth century. In the tone and imagery of these popular laments, many of them published as broadsides with suitable funereal borders and woodcuts, he sees not only an expression of the religious feeling of the Puritan middle classes in the days of Cromwell and later, but also "the origin of the graveyard poetry that ushered in Romanticism" (p. ix). Accordingly, and at great length, he studies the formation of the genre, its use by "Cavaliers" and then by "Puritans," its place in the funeral rites of Anglicans and dissenters, its diffusion in the American colonies and in Scotland, and its fortunes and influence—chronicled reign by reign—from the Restoration to the death of George II.

Despite one's gratitude for many of the new facts and texts which Draper brings to light and for his illuminating discussions of such points as the iconography of the broadside elegies (pp. 47-48), the elegiac elements in Blair, Young, and Gray (pp. 226-30, 306-09, 310-12), or the development of the "mortuary landscape" (pp. 255-61), one cannot help feeling that his book is badly conceived. The problem as stated in the first chapter obviously called for an essay in the history of religious sentiment—a comprehensive study, based on all the pertinent sources, of the peculiar feeling about death which lay back of the melancholy poetry of the early and middle eighteenth century. In such a study "funeral elegies" would naturally find a place, along with sermons, manuals of piety, and non-elegiac poems, as one element—but one only—in an adequate documentation. Draper, unfortunately, has chosen to concentrate on them to the virtual exclusion of all the rest, and to treat them, not as so many documents, but as manifestations of a literary genre the life-history of which deserved to be traced, through all its phases, with exhaustive detail. The result reflects great credit on his patience and industry in research, but the profit to the student is slight, since the history of the funeral elegy is of little interest in itself and since many of the examples of the form which he lists or describes have no real significance for the main question at issue—the origin of the moods and themes of eighteenth-century graveyard poetry. Then, too, his neglect of the other types of popular literature which drew their inspiration from the current of Puritan religious melancholy inevitably leads to unwarranted dogmatism concerning the specific influence of the funeral elegy on the later and more generalized types of melancholy verse. Some influence there undoubtedly was, but before one has a right to feel sure of it in any given case—before one can say, for example, that when Young calls himself a ''frail Child of Dust'' and a ''Worm,'' he is borrowing ''the verbiage of the elegy'' (pp. 307-08)—there is needed a broader knowledge of the *memento mori* tradition as a whole than Draper, preoccupied with a single class of sources, has been able to acquire.

His method is even more questionable in those portions of the book which deal with the ''deeper things'' of which the funeral elegy is for him merely ''the outward symbol.'' His theme here is the old problem of the rise of English romanticism. Believing that ''the crux and basis of Romanticism lies in emotionalism cultivated as an end in itself'' (p. 330), he explains its appearance in the eighteenth century as a result of ''the rise of the trading-classes to wealth, their consequent return to artistic patronage and their re-interpretation of Protestantism on a Sentimental, instead of a Calvinistic, basis'' (p. 22). Or, to quote another of his formulae, ''Sentimentalism developed in the funeral elegy as it developed in the middle classes, in the reign of Charles II, and grew apace during the generations that followed, as the main by-product of disintegrating Calvinism and the main element of the middle class mental life that could not enter into the sublimation of Neo-classicism'' (p. 328).

Something like this has of course often been suggested before, and within limits the hypothesis has its uses in the interpretation of the period. Draper's handling of it, however, comes perilously close to caricature. To regard ''sentimentalism'' as ''peculiarly the characteristic of the trading classes'' (p. 189) and to explain it chiefly as a ''by-product of disintegrating Calvinism'' is obviously to exclude from view a whole set of other forces, widely operative among educated persons, Anglicans and dissenters alike, in the later seventeenth century, without a consideration of which it is impossible to understand either the rise of the movement at this particular time or its rapid spread during the next generation. The facts in the case are to be had for the looking; to discover them, however, requires a properly genetic method and a mind free, as Draper's is not, from the hypnotism of a single theory.

Through all his discussion of this topic, moreover, there runs a vein of reckless generalization that leaves the reader frequently aghast. We are told, for example, that deism arose in response to Locke's demonstration ''that the senses were the sole source of mental data'' (p. 183); that the majority of educated persons in the reign of Queen Anne gained their knowledge of Roman literature ''from the efficient interlinear translations and other devices then in vogue in the schools and universities'' (p. 234); that the public which read the (anonymous) essays of Steele was ''of a lower social degree'' than that which read the (equally anonymous) essays of Addison (p. 241); that ''in the third quarter of the century, all idea of imitation was abandoned in favor of Original Genius'' (p. 242); and that the literary patronage of the Church was ''rather suddenly removed'' in the reign of George I (p. 265). For none of these statements does Draper give any adequate proof, and it is not too much to say that every one of them is at variance with facts known to most students of the period. When he ventures into the domain of political and social history the results are even worse, for here his knowledge is largely drawn from secondary and, for the most part, out-of-date sources. Otherwise, he could hardly have repeated the long exploded notion that Virginia and the Carolinas ''were settled by aristocrats'' (pp. 155-56), or asserted that the philosophy of the Declaration of Independence ''was derived by Jefferson from French sources'' (p. 176), or perpetuated the illusion that there was a ''Tory Party'' in the reign of George II (p. 287). His strangest error is the statement, several times repeated (see pp. 121-23, 178, 314), that the status of the commercial classes had been steadily declining in England since the fifteenth century until, after a temporary revival during the Commonwealth, they reached under Charles II ''the lowest point to which they have ever fallen since the

Mediæval towns first wrested charters from their reluctant suzerains'' (p. 314). It is needless to show how completely this distorts history; the important point is that we are asked to accept the generalization merely on the strength of a few statements by writers like Lecky and the late S. N. Patten and of a confused inference from the ecclesiastical position of the Puritan clergy after the Act of Uniformity to the social and economic status of their flocks (see pp. 122-23).

But perhaps the most disturbing feature of Draper's method is his excessive fondness for abstractions. Some of these are comparatively harmless; when he speaks of ''Puritanism,'' of ''the bourgeoisie,'' of ''Deism,'' we have at least a notion of what he means, though the terms are sometimes given a sense which unduly simplifies the realities for which they are intended to stand. When, however, it is a question, not, as in these cases, of collective names applied at the time to groups of persons having in common certain clearly realized habits or ideas, but of abstract formulae devised by modern literary critics in order to unify the confused facts and tendencies of the period, the results are all too frequently fatal to any kind of historical precision. Even the most critical student can hardly employ terms like ''Sentimentalism'' or ''the Neo-classical Compromise'' without falling into either vagueness or allegory. Draper does both: not only does he fail to give to these expressions any fixed or clear-cut signification, but again and again he treats them as if they were, not formulae merely, but facts in their own right, institutions no less real and self-acting than Parliament or the Church of England. Thus he sums up what is to him the crucial point of his history in the words, ''Exclusion of Puritan emotionalism from the Neo-classical compromise, and its survival and development into Sentimentalism'' (p. xiii). To translate this into concrete and intelligible terms is impossible; it is verbalism pure and simple—an arrangement of pseudo-historical entities that exhibits a certain logical pattern but has little relation to any realities observable in the texts. And it is typical: the whole interpretation of the movement that led from ''Puritanism'' to ''Romanticism'' is worked out on this plane of scholastic abstraction.

It is apparent, in short, that except for a certain number of new facts which help us to see the eighteenth-century cult of melancholy in a fuller perspective, Draper's book hardly justifies the enormous pains it must have cost. It contains a good deal that will be useful to the historian of taste and ideas, but these real contributions are buried beneath a mass of undocumented speculation and irrelevant erudition which can only try the patience of the critical reader. In spite of the statement in the Preface that the author ''has tried to write in a packed and pithy manner that might assuage somewhat the reader's elegiac pains as he surveys the flat pastures of prolixity and skirts the tear-drenched bogs of mortuary bathos,'' little effort at compression is visible anywhere in the three hundred and fifty pages and over twelve hundred notes that make up the volume. It is clear that Draper has set out to tell us all he knows, not merely about the funeral elegy, but about everything else that he can find an excuse for dragging into either his text or his notes, from the use of the *Rig Veda* in Brahman ceremonials (p. 94) to the vogue of gambling in eighteenth-century England (p. 296, n. 44). The opening sentences of his chapter on ''The Funeral Elegy in Liturgic Use'' (p. 93) will give some impression of his method: ''How the fine arts are related to general utility and whether they flourish best when cultivated as an end in themselves or when developed as an auxiliary to some social need, constitute intricate problems; but the fact that they have a social side and that they minister on occasion to a well defined psychological, and at times even to an obviously material human requirement, is inherent in the very nature of art-creation: the individual artist cannot shape and delineate without some urge from within—an urge that he must surely have in common with at least some of his fellows—and usually he cannot spare from the routine of daily necessity the time and energy for this exhilarating but wearisome labor unless compensated by social recognition and reward. Architecture has its obvious physical use; and music, its emotional effect, Apollonian or Dionysiac, which the human mind craves for rest or for stimulation. Sometimes the arts have lent support to some social institution. . . . Thus, also, much literature has been brought into being to laud and magnify some social institution, the Church, the State, or the noble house: Homer and the Bible and such poetry of Christian tradition as the Mediæval hymns to the Virgin, are religious; the Æneid was intended to lend grandeur and perspective to the Roman people as a political entity; and the *Song of Roland*, according to the latest opinion, is an encomium of the crusading exploits in Spain of certain Norman families. Elizabethan drama shows all these tendencies. . . .'' All this lest we be surprised at the ''great volume of elegiac composition of one sort or another during the seventeenth and eighteenth centuries.''

Elton, Oliver. *A survey of English literature, 1730-1780.* London: Edward Arnold, 1928. 2 vols. Cf. *PQ*, VIII, 174.

Rev. by R. S. Crane in *New republic*, Oct. 16, 1929, p. 248.

Fairchild, Hoxie Neale. *The Noble savage: a study in romantic naturalism.* New York: Columbia University Press, 1928. Cf. *PQ*, VIII, 174-75.

Rev. by H. W. Husbands in *MLR*, XXV (1930), 105-06; by Paul Meissner in *ES*, LXIV (1929), 131-35; by A. Perdeck in *Neophilologus*, XV (1929), 60-61; by H. Schöffler in *Beiblatt*, XL (1929), 168-73.

Freund, Michael. *Die Idee der Toleranz im England der grossen Revolution.* Halle: Niemeyer, 1927. Pp. xvi+293.

Rev. by Harris Fletcher in *JEGP*, XXVIII (1929), 574-77; by G. P. G. in *EHR*, XLIV (1929), 162; by André Leroy in *RHP*, III (1929), 358-64; by E. W. Nelson in *Philosophical review*, XXXVIII (1929), 84-88.

Grierson, H. J. C. *Cross currents in English literature of the XVIIth century; or the world, the flesh & the spirit, their actions & reactions.* London: Chatto & Windus, 1929. Pp. xiv+344.

Rev. in *Saturday review*, Dec. 7, 1929, pp. 680, 682; in *TLS*, Jan. 16, 1930, p. 41.

Nine lectures delivered at Cornell University in 1926-27. ''I thought I might venture,'' says Grierson, ''to set forth to my sympathetic American audience what I had come to think, viz. that the conflict between the spirit or temper of the Renaissance and that of the Reformation, seen in its full power in the fanaticism of English Puritanism, had affected our literature in a deeper and more complex manner than our histories always made quite clear. . . .'' (p. ix). It is an old theme, but it serves here to organize an unusually fresh and thoughtful study of the chief writers and movements in English literature from Spenser to Dryden. Grierson is thoroughly at home in the period, and he writes of all aspects of it with a sensitiveness and a largeness of view that go far toward disarming criticism of his occasional dubious generalizations and his rather too pronounced religious bias.

Haas, C. E. de. *Nature and the country in English poetry of the first half of the eighteenth century.* Amsterdam: H. J. Paris, 1928. Cf. *PQ*, VIII, 176.

Rev. by E. C. B. in *RES*, V (1929), 486-87; by J. H. Caskey in *JEGP*, XXVIII (1929), 441-42; by R. S. C[rane] in *MP*, XXVII (1929), 242-43; by A. Digeon in *RAA*, VI (1929), 364-65.

Havens, Raymond D. ''Changing taste in the eighteenth century:

a study of Dryden's and Dodsley's miscellanies." *PMLA,* XLIV (1929), 501-36.

An important and interesting article.

Heidler, Joseph Bunn. *The history, from 1700 to 1800, of English criticism of prose fiction.* Urbana, Illinois, 1928. Pp. 187. ("University of Illinois Studies in language and literature," Vol. XIII, No. 2.)

Hillhouse, James T. *The Grub-street journal.* Durham, N. C.: Duke University Press, 1928. Cf. *PQ,* VIII, 176.

Rev. by Walter Graham in *MLN,* XLIV (1929), 271-73; by George Sherburn in *MP,* XXVI (1929), 361-67; in *TLS,* May 23, 1929, p. 416.

Hotson, Leslie. *The commonwealth and Restoration stage.* Cambridge [Mass.]: Harvard University Press, 1928. Cf. *PQ,* VIII, 176.

Rev. by W. M. Clyde in *RES,* V (1929), 221-24; by B. V. Crawford in *PQ,* VIII (1929), 319-20; by A. Digeon in *RAA,* VI (1929), 441-42; by H. N. Hillebrand in *JEGP,* XXVIII (1929), 312-14; by Allardyce Nicoll in *MLN,* XLIV (1929), 395-96; by Charles Sisson in *MLR,* XXIV (1929), 347-49; in *N & Q,* CLVI (1929), 35-36.

Howe, Earle Barton. "The idealized bard of the eighteenth century: a study in origins." University of Chicago *Abstracts of theses,* Humanistic series, VI, (1929), 367-71.

Hussey, Christopher. *The picturesque: studies in a point of view.* London and New York: G. P. Putnam's Sons, 1927. Cf. *PQ,* VIII, 176.

Rev. by B. C[roce] in *La critica,* XXVII (1929), 362-65; by J.-J. Mayoux in *RAA,* VI (1929), 365-66.

"The Jubilee in honour of Shakespeare" [at Stratford, 1769]. *TLS,* April 18, 1929, pp. 301-02.

Comment by F. M. Parsons, *ibid.,* Apr. 25, p. 338; by L. F. Powell, *ibid.,* May 16, p. 403; by A. H. Westwood, *ibid.,* May 2, p. 362.

Kittredge, George Lyman. *Witchcraft in Old and New England.* Cambridge [Mass.]: Harvard University Press, 1929. Pp. viii+641.

Rev. by George L. Burr in *AHR,* XXXIV (1929), 814-17 (dissents from many of Kittredge's interpretations); by M. W. Jernegan in *Mississippi Valley historical review,* XVI (1929), 405-06; by F. G. Marcham in *Yale review,* XIX (1929), 190-91.

Lawrence, W. J. "A Restoration opera problem." *TLS,* Sept. 26, 1929, p. 737.

Leonard, S. A. *The doctrine of correctness in English usage, 1700-1800.* Madison, 1929. Pp. 361. ("University of Wisconsin studies in language and literature," No. 25.)

Loria, Gino. "La scienza nel secolo XVIII." *Scientia,* XLV (1929), 1-12.

Lynch, Kathleen. "Conventions of Platonic drama in the heroic plays of Orrery and Dryden." *PMLA,* XLIV (1929), 456-71.

A criticism of W. S. Clark's recent effort (see *RES,* IV, 49-63, and cf. *PQ,* VIII, 173-74) to stress French influences on Restoration heroic drama at the expense of native traditions. To the evidence which has hitherto been the chief support of the thesis attacked by Clark—the appearance in the heroic drama of traits already clearly marked in the plays of Beaumont and Fletcher and others—Miss Lynch adds a new set of parallels: similarities in the treatment of the theme of love between the plays of Orrery and Dryden and those of the "Platonic" dramatists of Charles I's time, notably Carlell, Cartwright, Suckling, Killigrew, and D'Avenant. Her analysis of these similarities, though somewhat disorderly in presentation, is convincing as far as it goes, and she is able to point to a few facts which indicate that Dryden and Orrery were familiar with some of the earlier expressions of the tradition. Her general conclusion, however, seems to me slightly excessive: "In all heroic drama. . . ., although other features may be introduced, the Platonic emphasis is of fundamental importance. Platonic enthusiasm is the impelling force which determines and justifies every great career" (p. 471). The facts presented certainly warrant no such sweeping claims.

If the present discussion of the origins of the heroic drama is to be continued, it is desirable that the question should be shifted to a somewhat broader ground than has been taken by most recent students of the subject. So long as the problem is posed merely in terms of one literary genre and so long as it involves chiefly a decision as to the relative importance of two sets of influences, English and French, both of which were admittedly operative, little further progress can be made. What is needed is a comprehensive study, conceived according to the methods of *littérature générale,* of the origins, the chief manifestations both in creative art and in theory, and the diffusion throughout Western Europe of the "heroic" mode. Some of the materials for such a study now exist in scattered monographs, and a suggestive, though superficial, attempt at synthesis has been made by B. J. Pendlebury in the first chapter of his *Dryden's heroic plays* (1923). But much remains to be done both in bringing together the essential texts—Miss Lynch's paper should be of value here—and in disengaging their meaning. The enquiry, it is needless to say, should embrace all the literary forms in which the "heroic" themes found expression, and it might be profitable to extend it to some of the other arts as well. It is not a task to be lightly undertaken, but the results could hardly help throwing light not only on the specific question at issue in the present article but also on some of the most important and distinctive features of seventeenth-century taste.

Metzger, Helène. "Newton et l'évolution de la théorie chimique" [in the eighteenth century]. *Archeion,* IX (1928), 243-56, 433-61; XI (1929), 13-25.

Montgomery, Franz. "Early criticism of Italian opera in England." *Musical quarterly,* XV (1929), 415-25.

Nicolson, Marjorie. "Christ's College and the latitude-men." *MP,* XXVII (1929), 35-53.

An important paper, based in large part on unpublished documents.

Nicolson, Marjorie. "The early stage of Cartesianism in England." *SP,* XXVI (1929), 356-74.

An interesting series of notes for a future history of the beginnings of Cartesianism in England. Section I prints for the first time an important letter from Sir Kenelm Digby to Hobbes, written at Paris, October 4, 1637, to accompany a gift of the recently published *Discours de la méthode*—possibly the first copy to reach English readers. It also calls attention to several translations published between 1649 and 1653, the prefaces to which testify eloquently to the high esteem in which Descartes was held in England at this time. Section II attempts to illustrate the fortunes of Cartesian ideas in the university world by outlining the course of Henry More's attitude toward Descartes from the early enthusiasm which could pronounce the new doctrine "the most admirable Philosophy that has appeared in these European parts since Noah's floud" (1650) to the sweeping disparagement of the *Enchiridion metaphysicum* (1671). This part of the article professes to be merely a sketch, and though it utilizes some fresh material, it does not change materially the picture of More's development already familiar to scholars. I am not sure that Miss Nicolson does not exaggerate somewhat the disfavor into which Descartes had fallen by the middle seventies when she writes: "Such was More's development; and it was on the whole characteristic of the development of much of the academic Cartesianism in England. In the 1640's and 1650's the liberal theologians and philosophers saw in Descartes a savior; by 1675 his philosophy was more often condemned than praised" (p. 369). One would have to qualify this statement even more than Miss Nicolson does to make it apply either to Glanvill, whose high estimate of Descartes remained substantially unchanged between the *Vanity of dogmatizing* (1661) and the *Essays* (1676), or to Boyle, who in an eloquent passage in his *Hydrostatical discourse* (1672) objected strongly to the charges of irreligion brought against the Cartesian metaphysics by More (see *Works* [London, 1772], III, 597-98). In the last section of her article Miss Nicolson undertakes "to suggest tentatively some of the possible results upon contemporary literature and contemporary thought of early Cartesianism as it was interpreted in England." Her most valuable points concern the rôle which the Cartesian idea of indefinite extension played in the formation of "one of the most significant of all seventeenth-century conceptions: the idea of infinity"—a theme which she proposes to study more fully elsewhere—and the prominence of Cartesian elements in the program of the Royal Society for the reform of prose style. Some of her other suggestions seem to me less fruitful. It may be that a popular reading of Descartes was partly responsible for "a new introspection, a new realiaztion of the individual self as the important thing in the universe" which she finds in later seventeenth-century autobiography, in the early novel, and subsequently in "the steadily growing tendency to self-analysis and self-glorification in pre-Romantic literature." But though these are matters that tempt conjecture, I do not see how they can ever be subjected to serious historical investigation. Over a quarter of a century ago the question was discussed for French literature in an important article by Gustave Lanson, and the conclusion which he reached then holds good today and for England: "Si l'analyse psychologique tient tant de place dans les ouvrages de tout genre au XVIIe siècle, ce peut être parce que Descartes a séparé absolument l'esprit de la matière, et déclaré le monde intérieur de la pensée plus facile à connaître que le monde extérieur de l'étendue: la concordance est frappante et l'explication séduisante. Mais que d'autres causes se présentent pour rendre compte de l'effet!" (*Revue de métaphysique et de morale,* IV [1896], 518).

Proper, C. B. A. *Social elements in English prose fiction between 1700 and 1832.* Amsterdam: H. J. Paris, 1929. Pp. 302.

Rey, A. "An English imitation attributed to Quevedo." *Romanic review,* XX (1929), 242-44.

Deals with *The travels of Don Francisco de Quevedo through Terra Australis incognita. . . . A novel* (London, 1684).

Rhodes, R. Crompton. "The King's players at Oxford, 1661-1712." *TLS*, Feb. 21, 1929, p. 140.

Comment by W. J. Lawrence, *ibid.*, Feb. 28, 1929, p. 163; by F. S. Boas, *ibid.*, Mar. 14, p. 206; by R. Crompton Rhodes, *ibid.*, Apr. 11 p. 293.

Saurat, Denis. *Milton et le matérialisme chrétien en Angleterre.* Paris: Rieder, 1928. Cf. *PQ,* VIII, 178.

Rev. by R. S. Crane in *MP,* XXVII (1930), 362-64; by A. Koyré in *Revue philosophique,* LIV (1929), 145-48.

Schücking, L. L. *Die Familie im Puritanismus. Studien über Familie und Literatur in England im 16., 17. und 18 Jahrhundert.* Leipzig: Teubner, 1929. Pp. xii+220.

Rev. by S. B. Liljegren in *Litteris,* V (1928), 243-49; by G. C. Moore Smith in *MLR,* XXIV (1929), 222-23; by H. Schöffler in *Beiblatt,* XL (1929), 129-33.

Selections from the pre-romantic movement. Selected and edited by Ernest Bernbaum. New York: Nelson and Sons, 1929. Pp. 470.

A useful collection of texts, for the most part brief, illustrating the principal aspects of English Pre-romanticism.

Taylor, O. H. "Economics and the idea of natural law." *Quarterly journal of economics,* XLIV (1929), 1-39.

A suggestive article.

Thorndike, Ashley H. *English Comedy.* New York: Macmillan, 1929. Pp. vi+635.

A history of English comedy from the beginnings to the present day which has the same qualities of solid learning, clear organization, and sane judgment as the author's earlier volume on English tragedy. The six chapters (XIII-XVIII) which deal with the period from 1660 to 1800 form an admirably clear-cut survey of the subject. The bibliographies contained in the "Notes" give a brief but useful selection of authorities.

Ustick, W. Lee. "The courtier and the bookseller: some vagaries of seventeenth-century publishing." *RES,* V (1929), 143-54.

Deals with English translations or adaptations of Eustache du Refuge's *Traité de la cour.*

Ustick, W. Lee. "Seventeenth century books of conduct: further light on Antoine de Courtin and *The rules of civility.*" *MLN,* XLIV (1929), 148-58.

Supplements and corrects the article by V. B. Heltzel, *MLN,* XLIII, 17-22.

Wallas, Ada. *Before the Bluestockings.* London: Allen and Unwin, 1929. Pp. 223.

Rev. by Dorothy M. Stuart in *Nation & Athenaeum,* June 29, 1929, pp. 436, 438; in *TLS,* June 20, 1929, p. 489.

Sketches of Hannah Woolley, Lady Elizabeth Savile, Damaris Masham, Mary Astell, and Elizabeth Elstob.

Williams, Iolo A. "Some poetical miscellanies of the early eighteenth century." *Library,* 4th series, X (1929), 233-51.

The chief purpose of Williams in this article is to call the attention of librarians to the most important poetical miscellanies published in the first thirty years of the eighteenth century. His list exhibits both the breadth of his knowledge and the excellence of his taste: his notes, brief though they necessarily are, prove conclusively the value of every book he includes.

Williams' collations are valuable, not only for their fulness and accuracy, but because he has had access to a number of unusual or unique variants of the books he describes. Among such variants are the cancel titlepage of *A new miscellany* (1701), and the rare original leaves A5, E6, E7, and E8 in the same collection. It may be noted that one of the two copies of this book in the Yale Library provides a still earlier titlepage, and the other has the original leaves B2-B4, so that only the original leaf B is still to seek.

Williams also gives the correct date (1707-8) to Fenton's *Oxford and Cambridge miscellany,* usually assigned to the year 1709 on the authority of Nichols' *Literary anecdotes.* The evidence of the presentation copy described by Williams is confined by a series of advertisements in the *Daily courant* of January, 1707-8, fixing the actual day of publication as either the seventh or eighth of that month.—ARTHUR E. CASE.

Williamson, Margaret. *Colloquial language of the Commonwealth and Restoration.* Oxford: Oxford University Press, 1929. Pp. 32. (English Association pamphlet No. 73.)

Rev. in *TLS,* Oct. 31, 1929, p. 872.

IV. INDIVIDUAL AUTHORS

Joseph Addison

Bateson, F. W. 'The *errata* in *The tatler.*'' *RES,* V (1929), 155-66.

Argues that Addison wrote Nos. 104 (in part), 151, 221, 222, and 227.

Bond, Richmond P. ''A fragment by Addison.'' *RES,* V (1929), 203-05.

Prints a fragment of an essay on friendship from B. M. Addit. MS. 33,441, fols. 1-2.

William Beckford

Vathek, with the Episodes of Vathek. By William Beckford of Fonthill. Edited, with a historical introduction and notes, by Guy Chapman. London: Constable, 1929. 2 vols.

Rev. by T. Earle Welby in *Saturday review,* Feb. 23, 1929, p. 249; in *TLS,* July 18, 1929, p. 572.

Hodgkin, John. ''The Nonesuch 'Vathek.' '' *TLS,* Dec. 26, 1929, p. 1097.

Comment by Guy Chapman, *ibid.,* Jan. 2, 1930, p. 12; by Guy Chapman, *ibid.,* Jan. 16, p. 44; by John Hodgkin, *ibid.,* Jan. 23, p. 60; by Herbert B. Grimsditch, *ibid.,* Feb. 20, p. 142.

May, Marcel. *La jeunesse de William Beckford et la genèse de son ''Vathek.''* Paris: Presses universitaires, 1928. Cf. *PQ,* VIII, 181.

Rev. by Ernest A. Baker in *RES,* V. (1929), 235-41; by J. Douady in *RC,* LXIII (1929), 133-35.

George Berkeley

Hone, J. M. "Berkeley at Cloyne." *LM,* XIX (1929), 593-602.

Maheu, René. "Le catalogue de la bibliothèque des Berkeley." *RHP,* III (1929), 180-99.

Mead, George H. "Bishop Berkeley and his message." *Journal of philosophy,* XXVI (1929), 421-30.

William Blake

Saurat, Denis. *Blake & modern thought.* London: Constable; New York: Lincoln MacVeagh, Dial Press, 1929. Pp. xv+200.

Rev. in *New statesman,* Aug. 3, 1929, pp. 529-30; in *Saturday review,* Aug. 3, 1929, pp. 134-35; in *TLS,* Aug. 22, 1929, p. 649.

Saurat, Denis. [Review of Helen C. White, *The mysticism of William Blake,* Madison, 1927.] *MP,* XXVII (1929), 111-15. Cf. *PQ,* VII, 169.

Webb, Clement C. J. "Blake and Jeremy Taylor." *TLS,* Apr. 11, 1929, p. 296.

Wright, Thomas. *The life of William Blake.* Olney, Bucks: Thomas Wright, 1929. 2 vols.

Rev. by Charles Gardner in *Spectator,* Jan. 26, 1929, pp. 129-30; in *TLS,* Feb. 7, 1929, p. 95.

James Boswell

(See also *Samuel Johnson*)

On the profession of a player. Three essays by James Boswell. Now first printed from the *London Magazine* for August, September, and October, 1770. London: Elkin Mathews and Marrot, 1929. Pp. 43.

Rev. in *TLS,* Dec. 5, 1929, p. 1038.

Private papers of James Boswell from Malahide Castle in the coltection of Lieut.-Colonel Ralph Heyward Isham. Prepared for the press by Geoffrey Scott and now first printed. New York: William Edwin Rudge, 1928-29. Vols. I-VI.

Rev. by F. A. Pottle in *SRL,* Feb. 16, 1929, pp. 677-78, July 20, 1929, pp. 1187-88, Aug. 24, 1929, p. 74; by Sir Andrew Macphail in *Quarterly review,* CCLII (1929), 42-73; by Carl Van Doren in *Books,* Feb. 3, 1929 pp. 1, 6, July 21, 1929, pp. 1-2; in *TLS* Feb. 6, 1930, pp. 85-86.

Pottle, Frederick Albert. *The literary career of James Boswell, Esq., being the bibliographical materials for a life of Boswell.* Oxford: Clarendon Press, 1929. Pp. xliv+335.

Rev. by R. S. Crane in *Yale review,* XIX (1930), 616-19; by Dorothy M. Stuart in *Nation & Anthenæum,* June 15, 1929, p. 374; by E. N. S. Thompson in *PQ*, IX (1930), 87-88; by I A. Williams in *LM*, XX (1929), 618; in *New statesman*, June 8, 1929, pp. 278, 280; in *TLS*, May 16, 1929, p. 408.

John Bunyan

The Pilgrim's progress from this world to that which is to come. By John Bunyan. Edited by James Blanton Wharey. Oxford: Clarendon Press, 1928. Pp. cxiii+352.

Rev. by F. M. H. in *Library*, 4th series, X (1929), 222-29; by G. B. Harrison in *MLR*, XXIV (1929), 472-73; in *N & Q*, CLVI (1929), 254; in *TLS*, Feb. 28, 1929, p. 159.

This work, which appeared too late to be noticed in last year's bibliography, is the first successful attempt to apply modern textual methods to Bunyan's masterpiece. It rests on a painstaking examination of the twelve editions issued during Bunyan's lifetime by his authorized publisher, Nathaniel Ponder; these are all carefully described, and their relations to each other and to the author investigated, in a critical Introduction which is a model of patient and intelligent bibliographical research. For his basic text Wharey has chosen the third edition (1679) as on the whole the nearest to Bunyan's definitive intentions; his notes record "all significant variations" found in the first, second, fourth, and seventh editions and a selection of those found in the fifth, sixth, eighth, and subsequent editions. The total number of variants recorded is not great, but it is swelled unnecessarily by the inclusion of insignificant readings from editions with which, as Wharey himself remarks, there is not the slightest evidence that Bunyan had anything to do. Is it of any value to the student of Bunyan's text, for example, to know that in the eleventh edition "*Christian*" (p. 26, l. 3) was printed in roman instead of italic, that in the same edition and also in the tenth "Then" (p. 35, l. 5) was printed in italic instead of roman, or that "*happened*" (p. 73, l. 1) appeared in the eleventh edition as "hapned"? These, however, are exceedingly minor flaws in an edition which in the main is distinguished no less for economy and restraint than for careful and exhaustive erudition.

Golder, Harold. "Bunyan's Valley of the shadow." *MP*, XXVII (1929), 55-72.

On Bunyan's relations to the chivalric romances popular in the seventeenth century. An interesting and well written paper.

Harris, J. Rendel. "A further note on the fictitious Bunyan books." *Bulletin of the John Rylands Library*, XIII (1929), 123-27.

Hills, Alfred. "Bunyan at Bocking." *Essex review*, XXXVIII (1929), 1-9.

Edmund Burke

B[aumann], A. A. *Burke: the founder of conservatism.* London: Eyre and Spottiswoode, 1929. Pp. 171.

Rev. by Walter Elliot in *Saturday review*, Nov. 30, 1929, pp. 644-45; in *TLS*, Jan. 30, 1930, p. 68.

"The Bicentenary of Burke." *TLS*, Jan. 10, 1929, pp. 17-18.

Cobban, Alfred. *Edmund Burke and the revolt against the eighteenth century: a study of the political and social thinking of Burke, Wordsworth, Coleridge, and Southey.* London: Allen and Unwin, 1929. Pp. 280.

Rev. in *TLS*, Dec. 12, 1929, p. 1052.

Tomlinson, Andrew. "An unpublished letter of Burke's." *TLS*, Jan. 10, 1929, p. 28.

Cf. *TLS*, Jan. 17, 1929, p. 44.

Robert Burns

Ferguson, J. De Lancey. "Burns and the Indies in 1788." *MLN*, XLIV (1929), 303-05.

Ferguson, J. De Lancey. "New light on the Burns-Dunlop estrangement." *PMLA*, XLIV (1929), 1106-15.

Jefferson, Bernard L. " 'The rural lass' and 'Tam Glen.' " *TLS*, Dec. 5, 1929, p. 1032.

Robert Burns and his rhyming friends. Collected and edited by John D. Ross. With bibliographical and biographical notes, and a glossary by George F. Black. Sterling: Eneas Mackay, 1929. Pp. 117.

Rev. in *TLS*, Jan. 31, 1929, p. 82.

Snyder, Franklyn B. "Burns's last years." *SP*, XXVI (1929), 457-69.

Samuel Butler

Satires and miscellaneous poetry and prose. By Samuel Butler. Edited by René Lamar. Cambridge: Cambridge University Press, 1928. Cf. *PQ*, VIII, 184.

Rev. by H. V. D. Dyson in *RES*, V (1929), 479-80; by A. Koszul in *RAA*, VII (1930), 260-61; by J. H. Lobban in *MLR*, XXIV (1929), 352-55.

Curtiss, Joseph Toy. "Butler's *Sidrophel.*" *PMLA*, XLIV (1929), 1066-78.

The author's main contention is that the character of Sidrophel in *Hudibras* Part II (1663) was originally begun, probably before 1649, as a satire on the astrologer William Lilly and was completed and revised after the Restoration as a satire on Sir Paul Neile and the Royal Society.

Quintana, Ricardo, "John Hall of Durham and Samuel Butler: a note." *MLN*, XLIV (1929), 176-79.

Interesting analogies in style and satirical point of view between Hall's *A satire* (1646) and *Hudibras.*

Henry Carey

Wood, F. T. "*The disappointment.*" *RES*, V (1929), 66-69.

Wood, Frederick T. "An eighteenth-century original for Lamb?" *RES*, V (1929), 442-47.

A learned dissertation on dumpling (cir. 1724), which is here assigned to Carey.

Colley Cibber

Habbema, D. M. E. *An appreciation of Colley Cibber, actor and dramatist, together with a reprint of his play "The Careless husband."* Amsterdam: H. J. Paris, 1928. Cf. *PQ*, VIII, 185-86.

Rev. by J. Homer Caskey in *JEGP*, XXVIII (1929), 323-25; by A. Digeon in *RAA*, VI (1929), 268-69; by V. de Sola Pinto in *RES*, V (1929), 229-32.

William Collins

The Poems of William Collins. Edited with an introductory study by Edmund Blunden. London: Frederick Etchells and Hugh Macdonald, 1929. Pp. viii+179.

Rev. in *TLS*, July 18, 1929, p. 573. Comment by Edmund Blunden and H. W. Garrod, *ibid.*, July 25, Aug. 8, 29, 1929, pp. 592, 624, 668-69.

Garrod, H. W. *Collins.* Oxford: Clarendon Press, 1928. Cf. *PQ*, VIII, 186.

Rev. by B. V. Crawford in *PQ*, IX (1930), 94-95; by A. Digeon in *RAA*, VI (1929), 543-44; by Oliver Elton in *MLR*, XXIV (1929), 356-58; by James McLean in *SRL*, June 1, 1929, p. 1074; by A. C. E. Vechtman-Veth in *English studies*, XI (1929), 231-32. Comment by H. W. Garrod, H. O. White, and "Your reviewer" in *TLS*, Feb. 14, 21, 1929, pp. 118, 142.

Woodhouse, A. S. P. "Imitations of the 'Ode to evening.'" *TLS*, May 30, 1929, p. 436.

Cf. H. O. White and Davidson Cook, *ibid.*, Apr. 18, June 6, 1929, pp. 315, 454.

William Congreve

Hodges, John C. "William Congreve in the government service." *MP*, XXVII (1929), 183-92.

A careful study, based on hitherto unexploited documents in the Public Record Office.

"William Congreve." *TLS*, Jan. 17, 1929, pp. 33-34.

Abraham Cowley

Sparrow, John. "Cowley's *Plantarum libri duo*: a presentation copy." *LM*, XX (1929), 398-99.

Note on a copy with an inscription in Latin verse to Sir Alexander Fraizer.

Hannah Cowley

Rhodes, R. Crompton. *"The belle's stratagem."* *RES*, V (1929), 129-42.

William Cowper

Cecil, David. *The stricken deer, or, the life of Cowper.* London: Constable, 1929. Pp. 303.

Rev. in *TLS*, Dec. 19, 1929, p. 1077.

Povey, Kenneth. "Some notes on Cowper's letters and poems." *RES*, V (1929), 167-72.

George Crabbe

Bär, Horst. *George Crabbe als Epiker. Eine Studie zur Technik seiner Verserzählungen.* Leipzig: Bernhard Tauchnitz, 1929. Pp. 135.

Daniel Defoe

Memoirs of Captain Carleton. Edited, with an introduction, by Cyril Hughes Hartmann. London: Routledge, 1929. Pp. xxviii+301.

Rev. in *TLS*, Apr. 18, 1929, p. 306. Comment by A. W. Secord, C. H. Hartmann, and Harold Williams, *ibid.*, Sept. 12, 19, 26, 1929, pp. 704, 723, 746-47.

The appearance of this reprint has revived an old controversy. The reviewer in *TLS* thought that "it appears at least to be probable" that Carleton wrote the *Memoirs* that bear his name. This roused A. W. Secord, who in a long letter in *TLS* for Sept. 12 (p. 704) summed up his view that the *Memoirs* are fictitious and were compiled by Defoe from published sources. On Sept. 19, the editor of the new reprint, C. H. Hartmann, argued that the accurate information available about Carleton himself proved that he must either have been the writer or have collaborated with him. This seems undeniable, for Defoe could not have found anywhere in print all the particulars of Carleton's military services which Charles Dalton and others have verified. On Sept. 26, Harold Williams printed four contemporary notes written in his copy of the first issue of the *Memoirs*, and these lend some support to the theory of Carleton's collaboration. On the whole it is probable that the old methods of studying this perennial question will yield little more. Unless new evidence should come to light, or a better technique be evolved, discussion of Carleton's *Memoirs* may give rise to further ingenious surmises but not yield indisputable results. As a conjecture it is suggested that Carleton supplied some true recollections and in addition may have claimed the exploits and adventures of others as his own. Then someone, probably Defoe, wrote them up and padded them from easily accessible books.—G. DAVIES.

A Tour thro' London about the year 1725, being Letter V and parts of Letter VI of "A Tour thro' the whole island of Great Britain," containing a description of the City of London, as taking in the City of Westminster, Borough of Southwark, and parts of Middlesex. By Daniel Defoe. Reprinted from the text of the original edition (1724-1726). Edited and annotated by Sir Mayson M. Beeton and E. Beresford Chancellor. London: Batsford, 1929. Pp. xxi+115.

Rev. in *TLS*, Dec. 12, 1929, p. 1045.

Burch, Charles Eaton. "*An equivalent for Daniel Defoe.*" *MLN*, XLIV (1929), 378.

On the date and occasion of this attack on Defoe.

Burch, Charles Eaton. "Defoe's connections with the *Edinburgh courant.*" *RES*, V (1929), 437-40.

Dottin, Paul. *The life and strange and surprising adventures of*

Daniel De Foe. Translated by Louise Ragan. New York: Macaulay, 1929.

Rev. by Arthur Colton in *SRL,* Mar. 1, 1930, pp. 769-71.

Hutchins, Henry Clinton. [Review of A. W. Secord, *Studies in the narrative method of Defoe,* Urbana, 1924.] *JEGP,* XXVIII (1929), 443-52.

Jacob, Ernst Gerhard. *Daniel Defoe, Essay on projects (1697): eine Wirtschafts- und Sozialgeschichtliche Studie.* Leipzig: Bernhard Tauchnitz, 1929. Pp. 142.

After a brief sketch of Defoe's life to 1702, which would seem hardly necessary in a work addressed to scholars, Jacob studies the genesis and publication of the *Essay,* points out its general significance as an expression of what Defoe called "the Projecting Age," describes and classifies the various proposals which it contains, discusses their originality, and, finally, attempts a critical evaluation of the work in terms of its subject-matter, its spirit, and the personality of its author. The result is an appreciative and frequently suggestive monograph on a book that has been unduly neglected by students of Defoe and his period. As happens too often in studies of this sort, however, the treatment of the social background leaves much to be desired. Though Jacob has read a number of contemporary economic treatises and other documents, he relies very largely for his facts and conclusions on secondary works—notably on the various writings of Werner Sombart—with the result that much of his book scarcely rises above the level of superficial compilation. Nothing could be more perfunctory, for example, than the pages in which he discusses the historical significance of Defoe's project for an academy for women (pp. 122-24). Here if anywhere wide reading in seventeenth-century literature is indicated; it is not enough to dismiss the subject, as Jacob does, with a few references to Mary Astell (quoted at second hand), to Fénelon, and to Swift.

P. 14: in giving 1661 as the date of Defoe's birth, Jacob takes no account of the arguments in favor of the preceding year set forth by Dottin in his *Daniel De Foe et ses romans,* pp. 10-11.—P. 31: Jacob should have noted that the *Essay* was advertised in the *Term catalogues* for Hilary Term, 1696/7 (ed. Arber, III, 8).—Pp. 34, 104: it might have been added here that the chapter "Of bankrupts" was reprinted in the *Review* during February, 1706 (Vol. III, Nos. 20, 21).

Martin, Burns. "Defoe's conception of poetry." *MLN,* XLIV (1929), 377-78.

Prints a passage from Robert Wodrow's *Analecta* in which Defoe is quoted. Unimportant.

Pastor, Antonio. *The idea of Robinson Crusoe.* Volume I. Watford: Gongora Press, 1929. Pp. xii+391.

Rev. in *TLS,* Jan. 16, 1930, p. 39.

Powell, L. F. "Defoe and Drelincourt." *TLS,* Feb. 7, 1929, p. 98.

Smith, G. C. Moore. "An unrecognized work of Defoe's?" *RES,* V (1929), 64-66.

The work in question is a tract entitled *Reasons humbly offered for a law to enact the castration of Popish ecclesiasticks, as the best way to prevent the growth of Popery in England* (1700).

Ullrich, Hermann. "Zwölf Jahre Defoeforschung (1916-1928)." *GRM,* XVII (1929), 458-69.

Sir John Denham

The Poetical works of Sir John Denham. Edited with notes and introduction by Theodore Howard Banks, Jr. New Haven: Yale University Press, 1928. Cf. *PQ,* VIII, 188.

Rev. by J. Homer Caskey in *JEGP,* XXVIII (1929), 140-42; by Pierre Legouis in *RAA,* VI (1929), 362-64; by H. Lüdeke in *Beiblatt,* XL (1929), 236-38; by George Sherburn in *MLN,* XLIV (1929), 194-95; by G. C. Moore Smith in *RES,* V (1929), 232-35 (cf. also *ibid.,* V, 332).

John Downes

Roscius anglicanus. By John Downes. Edited by the Rev. Montague Summers. London: Fortune Press, 1929. Pp. xiii+286.

Rev. in *TLS,* Jan. 24, 1929, p. 59; comment by Roswell G. Ham, *ibid.,* Aug. 22, 1929, p. 652.

John Dryden

Dryden and Howard, 1664-1668. The text of *An Essay of dramatic poesy, The Indian emperor,* and *The Duke of Lerma,* with other controversial matter. Edited by D. D. Arundell. Cambridge: Cambridge University Press, 1929. Pp. xiv+288.

Rev. in *TLS,* Dec. 19, 1929, pp. 1065-66.

"Dryden and artificial tragedy." *TLS,* Aug. 15, 1929, pp. 629-30.

White, H. O. "Dryden and Descartes." *TLS,* Dec. 19, 1929, p. 1081.

Comment by Louis I. Bredvold, *ibid.,* Jan. 2, 1930, p. 12.

Wild, B. Josef. *Dryden und die römische Kirche.* Leipzig: Robert Noske, 1928. Cf. *PQ,* VIII, 190.

Rev. by A. Eichler in *Beiblatt,* XL (1929), 239-41.

Sir George Etherege

The Letterbook of Sir George Etherege. Edited with an introduction and notes by Sybil Rosenfeld. Oxford: Oxford University Press; London: H. Milford, 1928. Cf. *PQ,* VIII, 191.

Rev. by H. F. B. Brett-Smith in *RES,* V (1929), 224-29; by K. F. in *EHR,* XLIV (1929), 685; by Glenn W. Gray in *AHR,* XXXIV (1929), 584-85; in *TLS,* Mar. 7, 1929, p. 181.

Brett-Smith, H. F. B. "The works of Etherege." *RES,* V (1929), 77-78.

A reply to V. de Sola Pinto's review of his edition (*RES,* IV, 341-49).

Henry Fielding

The Adventures of Joseph Andrews. By Henry Fielding. Edited, with introduction and notes by J. Paul de Castro. London: Scholartis Press, 1929. Pp. 409.

Rev. by A. Digeon in *RAA,* VII (1930), 263; in *N & Q,* CLVI (1929), 342; in *TLS,* Apr. 25, 1929, p. 343.

Parfitt, G. E. *L'influence française dans les œuvres de Fielding et dans le théâtre anglais contemporain de ses comédies.* Paris: Presses universitaires, 1928.

Sarah Fielding

The Lives of Cleopatra and Octavia. By Sarah Fielding. Edited, with introduction, by R. Brimley Johnson. London: Scholartis Press, 1929. Pp. xliv+183.

Rev. in *TLS,* Apr. 4, 1929, p. 273; comment by R. Brimley Johnson, *ibid.,* Apr. 11, 1929, p. 295.

David Garrick

Williams, Charles Riddell. "David Garrick, actor-manager: two unpublished letters" [1765]. *Cornhill magazine,* N. S., LXVI (1929), 289-97.

John Gay

Goulding, Sybil. "Eighteenth century French taste and 'The Beggar's opera.' " *MLR,* XXIV (1929), 276-93.

Irving, William Henry. *John Gay's London.* Cambridge [Mass.]: Harvard University Press, 1928. Cf. *PQ,* VIII, 191-92.

Rev. by Walter Graham in *JEGP,* XXVIII (1929), 573-74; by W. T. Morgan in *AHR,* XXXV (1930), 342-44.

Sherwin, Oscar. *Mr. Gay, being a picture of the life and times of the author of the "Beggar's opera."* New York: John Day, 1929.

Negligible.

Edward Gibbon

Gibbon's journal to January 28th, 1763. My journal, I, II, and III, and ephemerides. With introductory essays by D. M. Low. London: Chatto and Windus, 1929. Pp. cxvii+261.

Rev. by J. C. Squire in *Observer,* May 26, 1929, p. 6; in *TLS,* June 6, 1929, pp. 441-42.

Bell, C. F., "The iconography of Edward Gibbon." *TLS,* June 20, 1929, p. 494.

Comment by D. M. Low, *ibid.,* July 25, 1929, p. 592; by C. F. Bell, Aug. 1, p. 608.

William Gilpin

Templeman, William D. "German translations of William Gilpin." *N & Q,* CLVI (1929), 293-95.

Templeman, William D. "Gilpin's Essay upon prints." *TLS,* Apr. 11, 1929, p. 296.

William Godwin

Koszul, A. and G. Bresch. "Un lettre de William Godwin." *RAA,* VI (1929), 430-32.

A letter to Thomas Holcroft dated Oct. 10, 1819.

Oliver Goldsmith

The Collected letters of Oliver Goldsmith. Edited by Katharine C. Balderston. Cambridge: Cambridge University Press, 1928. Cf. *PQ,* VIII, 192-93.

Rev. by A. K[oszul] in *Les langues modernes,* XXVII (1929), 370-71.

New Essays by Oliver Goldsmith. Now first collected and edited with an introduction and notes by Ronald S. Crane. Chicago: University of Chicago Press, 1927. Cf. *PQ,* VII, 175; VIII, 193.

Rev. by Elise Deckner in *Beiblatt,* XL (1929), 241-43; by A. K[oszul] in *Les langues modernes,* XXVII (1929), 369-70.

Balderston, K. C. "The birth of Goldsmith." *TLS,* Mar. 7, 1929, pp. 185-86.

Comment by James B. Leslie, *ibid.,* Mar. 14, 1929, p. 207.

Goldsmith's only known statements concerning the date of his birth are contained in three documents: the Matriculation Register of Trinity College, Dublin, under date of June 11, 1745; his letter to Henry Goldsmith of January (not February, as Miss Balderston says), 1759; and the memorandum which he dictated to Percy in April, 1773. If the first of these is to be trusted, he was born in 1730; the second seems to assert that he was born in either 1727 or 1728 (Miss Balderston rejects the latter interpretation, I think without sufficient reason); and the third says definitely that the date was either 1731 or 1730. The problem, moreover, is complicated still further by the conflicting information furnished to Percy after Goldsmith's death by members of his family: Mrs. Hodson in her narrative written in 1776 giving 1729 as the birth year, and Maurice Goldsmith at a still later time insisting on 1728, the date accepted by Percy in his Memoir of 1801 and by most subsequent biographers. Miss Balderston attempts to show that "there is more weight for 1730 as the correct birth year than for any other." Her argument is ingenious and commands respect, but I am not sure that she does not unduly minimize some of the difficulties in the way of a clear-cut conclusion. On the one hand, the evidence of the Trinity College records is hardly "incontrovertible" (see the letter by J. B. Leslie mentioned above); and in view of the vagueness or inaccuracy of some of Goldsmith's statements to Percy about less remote events in his life than his birth, it is surely excessive to describe the memorandum of 1773 as a document in which "correctness would most naturally be expected and observed." On the other hand, Miss Balderston's attempt to dispose of the definite assertion in Mrs. Hodson's narrative that the year was 1729 errs equally, I think, on the side of skepticism. In particular, she seems to me to dismiss too easily the possibility that the direct source of this assertion was the Goldsmith family Bible. The possibility is suggested not only, as she recognizes, by the agreement as to the day of the month of Oliver's birth (November 10) between the narrative and the entry in the Bible (as is well known the year date had been torn away when Prior consulted the

Bible in 1830) but also by another passage in the narrative which she overlooks. This passage concerns the birth of Goldsmith's next younger brother, Maurice, and reads as follows: "at this time his fathers family increased by the Byrth of a third Son unexpected as his mother was for seven years without bearing a Child. . . ." (*Collected letters*, ed. Balderston, p. 164). It may be of course that when Mrs. Hodson wrote "seven years" she was relying merely on what Miss Balderston calls her "none too accurate memory," but if so it served her suspiciously well in this case, for the interval between the date which she gave for Oliver's birth and that recorded in the Bible for Maurice's—July 7, 1736 (see Prior, *Life*, I, 14)—was in fact roughly seven years. I grant that this is far from conclusive, but it at least "lends probability to the supposition that the Bible was in her hands at the time that she wrote the narrative of her brother's early life" and that she used it as far as it went for her facts—greater probability certainly than Miss Balderston is willing to allow. At all events, as matters stand, a clear decision in favor of 1730 rather than 1729 would seem to be out of the question. In the meantime Miss Balderston's article has, I think, made one thing plain: of all the dates that have been proposed, the one most widely accepted by the biographers (1728) stands on the weakest foundation of contemporary evidence. For the rest, we may remain content, until fresh testimony is forthcoming, with her final charmingly turned remark: "Whatever may be one's conclusion about the correct solution of this problem, it is at least delightfully clear that Goldsmith, like his own Tony Lumpkin, did not know exactly when he was born, but that, unlike Tony Lumpkin, he did not much care."

Chapman, R. W. "A Goldsmith anecdote." *TLS,* June 13, 1929, p. 474.

On Goldsmith's use of D. Fenning's *The Young man's book of knowledge* in his *History of England in a series of letters.*

Church, R. "Oliver Goldsmith." *Criterion,* VIII (1929), 437-44.

Colum, Padraic. "Young Goldsmith." *Scribner's magazine,* LXXXVI (1929), 555-63.

Dix, E. R. McC. "The works of Oliver Goldsmith: a hand-list of Dublin editions before 1801." *Publications of the Bibliographical Society of Ireland,* III (1928), 93-101.

"Goldsmith and Johnson manuscripts." *TLS,* Oct. 24, 1929, p. 852.

Hale-White, Sir William. *The bicentenary of the birth of Oliver Goldsmith, M. B. Dub. & Oxf.* Reprinted from the *Lancet,* June 8, 1929. Pp. 14.

Mainly about Goldsmith's medical interests.

Ingalls, Gertrude Van Arsdale. "Some sources of Goldsmith's *She stoops to conquer.*" *PMLA,* XLIV (1929), 565-68.

The parallels are not very convincing.

"Prologue written by Goldsmith." *Morning post,* Oct. 22, 1929, p. 9.

On the manuscript of the Prologue to Cradock's *Zobeide.*

Scott, Temple. *Oliver Goldsmith, bibliographically and biographically considered, based on the collection of materials in the library of W. M. Elkins, Esq.* With an introduction by A. Edward Newton. New York: Bowling Green Press; London: Maggs Brothers, 1928. Pp. xix+368.

Rev. by L. L. Mackall in *Books,* June 2, 1929, p. 23; by H. J. Smith in *SRL,* Mar. 16, 1929, p. 788; in *TLS,* Feb. 28, 1929, p. 161.

As the Elkins collection is extremely rich in editions and issues of Goldsmith's works, the catalogue which forms the main excuse for this book—the biography proper offers little that is new—is easily the most nearly complete full-dress bibliography of the subject that has yet been published. The descriptions, though not free from errors, are detailed and clear, and they are accompanied in most cases by useful photographic reproductions of titlepages. Of particular interest and value are the pages dealing with the issues of *The traveller* dated 1764 (pp. 139-42), with the *Vicar* (pp. 173-93), and with the duodecimo editions of *The deserted village* (pp. 242-50). With regard to these last, Scott errs when he calls the three copies in the Elkins collection so many "issues"; they were all printed from separate settings of type, as his own list of variants shows (see pp. 249-50). Nor can I agree with him in feeling sure that they were published before the quarto edition of May, 1770; this is a mere assumption which seems to have grown out of the traditional belief, here justly treated with skepticism, that they formed "a privately printed edition." The frontispiece of the volume is a reproduction in color of the little known portrait of Goldsmith by Benjamin West, and among the most interesting illustrations are a number of pages from the Newbery manuscripts, now in the Elkins collection.

Seitz, R. W. "Goldsmith and the *Literary magazine.*" *RES,* V (1929), 410-30.

Seven articles or series of articles published in the *Literary magazine* between December, 1757, and July, 1758, have been ascribed to Goldsmith—four of them by Prior in 1837, the others by Gibbs in 1885. The group comprises "The history of our own times," "The poetical scale," "The sequel to the poetical balance, being miscellaneous thoughts on English poets," "Phanor: or the butterfly pursuit, a political allegory," "The history of our own language," "On the character of English officers," and "Of the pride and luxury of the middling class of people." In no case were the arguments for their admission to the canon conclusive, and most recent students of Goldsmith have, I believe, felt increasing doubt of their authenticity. Seitz has now crystallized this doubt in a carefully studied paper in which, after effectively discrediting every bit of evidence, internal or external, that has been advanced in support of the attributions, he reduces Goldsmith's connection with the *Literary magazine* to that of a mere reader who, having come upon a set of its numbers in November, 1759, used it occasionally between that date and 1763 as a source of material in the *Bee,* the *Lady's magazine,* the *Public ledger,* the *Political view of the result of the present war with America,* and the *History of England in a series of letters.* The results which he reaches are thus largely negative, but he makes, incidentally, a number of new points of a more positive sort. Among these are the inclusion of John Campbell's *Present state of Europe* among the sources of Goldsmith's *Political view* (pp. 412, 415), the indication of several hitherto unnoted borrowings in the *Citizen of the world* and elsewhere from Johnson's articles in the *Literary magazine* for 1756 (pp. 414-15), and the discovery that the essay in the *Bee* entitled "Custom and laws compared" was a slightly expanded version of a paper with the same title printed in the July, 1758, number of the *Literary magazine,* where it is ascribed to "a great Writer of our own nation now alive" (pp. 422-23). Altogether an able and important article.

Pp. 418-20: a further indication that Goldsmith did not write the central portion of "An account of the Augustan Age of England" (*Bee,* No. VIII) is perhaps to be seen in the contradiction between the judgment of Tillotson expressed here (see *Works,* ed. Gibbs, II, 447) and that set forth in the essay

"Of eloquence" (*Bee,* No. VII; *Works,* II, 427). It is to be noted also that the two papers which immediately preceded this essay in the *Bee* were borrowed from books by other writers—one from the Abbé Le Blanc's *Letters on the English and French nations,* the other from Thomas Gordon's *Humourist.*—P. 430, n. 6: I fail to see how Goldsmith's allusion to "my Chinese Philosopher" in his letter of August 14, 1758, can be supposed to indicate that he "was probably already planning the *Chinese Letters. . . .*" Cf. *PQ,* VIII, 192-93.

Seitz, R. W. "Goldsmith's *Lives of the Fathers.*" *MP,* XXVI (1929), 295-305.

Identifies the *Lives of the Fathers* for which Goldsmith acknowledged the receipt of ten guineas from Newbery in October, 1763.

Smith, Hamilton Jewett. "Goldsmithiana." *University of California chronicle,* XXXI (1929), 429-36.

A review of recent scholarship.

Smith, Hamilton Jewett. "Mr. Tattler of Pekin, China: a venture in journalism." *Essays in criticism by members of the Department of English, University of California* (Berkeley, Cal.: University of California Press, 1929), pp. 155-75.

An essay on the *Citizen of the world.*

Thomas Gray

An Elegy written in a country churchyard. By Thomas Gray. The text of the first quarto with the variants of the MSS and of the early editions (1751-71). A bibliographical and historical introduction and appendices. . . . by Francis Griffin Stokes. Oxford: Clarendon Press, 1929. Pp. 98.

Rev. by A. W. P[ollard] in *Library,* 4th series, X (1929), 112-13; by John Wilks in *MLR,* XXIV (1929), 478-80; in *N & Q,* CLVI (1929), 308; in *TLS,* Apr. 25, 1929, p. 342.

Fothergill, Roy. "An early influence on the poetry of Gray." *RLC,* IX (1929), 565-73.

Notes Gray's admiration for the poetry of Jean-Baptiste Gresset and attempts to show that "Gresset deserves more attention than he has usually received, in a consideration of the influences contributing to the exquisite poetry of Gray." The claim seems to me exaggerated.

Fukuhara, Rintaro. "Mason's edition of Gray." *TLS,* Oct. 17, 1929, p. 822.

Comment by R. Martin, *ibid.,* Oct. 31, 1929, p. 874.

Toynbee, Paget. "Missing letters of Gray." *TLS,* Feb. 7, 1929, p. 98.

Toynbee, Paget. "Some Gray queries." *TLS,* Oct. 3, 1929, p. 766.

Reply by Edward Bensly, *ibid.,* Oct. 10, 1929, p. 794 (cf. also Oct. 17, p. 822).

Whibley, Leonard. "Thomas Gray at Eton." *Blackwood's magazine,* CCXXV (1929), 611-23.

James Harrington

Liljegren, S. B. "Harrington and Leibnitz." *Studies in English philology, a miscellany in honor of Frederick Klaeber* (Minneapolis: University of Minnesota Press, 1929), pp. 414-26.

Throws light incidentally on the relations between Leibnitz and Toland.

James Harris

Funke, Otto. *Studien zur Geschichte der Sprachphilosophie.* Bern: Francke, 1928. Pp. 140.

Rev. by A. Koszul in *Les langues modernes,* XXVII (1929), 215-17; by H. J. Pos in *English studies,* XI (1929), 224-25.

Contains a study of Harris' *Hermes* (1751).

Thomas Hobbes

Baratier, P. "Quelques aspects de la fonction judiciaire d'après Hobbes." *RAA,* VI (1929), 406-11.

Brandt, Frithiof. *Thomas Hobbes' mechanical conception of nature.* Copenhagen: Levin & Munksgaard, 1928. Pp. 399.

Rev. by Emile Bréhier in *Revue philosophique,* LIV (1929), 439-41.

Thomas, J. A. "Some contemporary critics of Thomas Hobbes." *Economica,* June, 1929, pp. 185-91.

Deals with criticisms of Hobbes' political doctrines by Clarendon, Lucy, Lawson, Eachard, Tenison, Filmer, Whitehall, and Rosse.

John Home

MacMillan, Dougald. "The first editions of Home's *Douglas.*" *SP,* XXVI (1929), 401-09.

David Hume

Mertz, Rudolf. "Les amitiés françaises de Hume et le mouvement des idées." *RLC,* IX (1929), 644-713.

Miller, Hugh. "The naturalism of Hume." *Philosophical review,* XXXVIII (1929), 469-82.

Toynbee, Paget. "Mme du Deffand and Hume." *MLR,* XXIV (1929), 447-51.

A number of unpublished letters to Hume.

Samuel Johnson

Johnson, Boswell and Mrs. Piozzi: a suppressed passage restored. Oxford: Oxford University Press; London: H. Milford, 1929. Pp. [12].

Contains a collotype facsimile and a transcript of Johnson's letter to Mrs. Thrale of June 19, 1775, showing a passage in praise of Boswell's journal in the Highlands suppressed by Mrs. Piozzi when she sent the letter to the press, and now restored. The circumstances are set forth in a prefatory note by R. W. Chapman. Cf. *TLS,* Jan. 24, 1929, p. 62.

The R. B. Adam library relating to Dr. Samuel Johnson and his era. London: Oxford University Press, 1929. 3 vols.

Rev. by G. M. T[roxell] in *SRL,* Mar. 8, 1930, p. 812.

It will never again be possible to build up such a collection as this by the methods employed by the two Adams. The books could for the most part be duplicated in more than one library in America, though there are two or three of which no copies are known outside of public libraries, but until the Adam Collection is dispersed (which God forbid) no one can accumulate a body of Johnsonian MSS in any way comparable to Mr. Adam's. These MSS have been, in the truest sense of the word, "collected"; they were not purchased in a lot at the sale of some former library, but were patiently and skilfully assembled from innumerable sources. The first volume of the new catalogue lists (with complete transcripts of the texts) over 225 autograph letters of Johnson to 54 correspondents; 50 letters of Boswell, 20 letters of Burke, 6 of Reynolds, and 16 of Garrick. Besides letters, the collection also contains other autograph MSS of the highest importance, including some which may have served as printer's copy. The second volume is a catalogue of the books, and the third lists the miscellaneous autograph letters, of which there are a great many more than one would expect to find in a collection which is content to call itself Johnsonian. The elder Adam formed the gigantic project of extra-illustrating a set of Hill's Boswell with at least one autograph letter of every person mentioned in the Index. How well he succeeded is shown by the fact that there are fifty different names under the letter "A" alone, including (to chose some whose connection with Johnson is remote) John Adams, Ariosto, Roger Ascham, and Jane Austen. I doubt whether anywhere else in the world there exists so full a body of materials for identifying an unknown or suspected handwriting. If one of our learned societies could arrange with Mr. Adam to issue a volume of facsimiles of only eighteenth-century hands it would thereby provide us with a reference book of the greatest utility.

Mr. Adam's former catalogue was printed in an edition of only 50 copies, of which none were for sale, though with his usual generosity he presented copies to many of the more important libraries. Scholars should be very grateful that he has allowed the Oxford University Press to publish for sale a small edition of his new and greatly enlarged catalogue. It will be found indispensable to all institutions conducting research in the eighteenth century. The facsimiles which are lavishly strewn through all three volumes would alone furnish materials to keep a small seminary class in work for a year.—F. A. POTTLE.

Brett, Oliver. "A note on Dr. Johnson's first editions." *Life and letters,* III (1929), 366-68.

C[hapman], R. W. "Bennet's *Ascham.*" *RES,* V (1929), 69-70.

Bibliographical details concerning an edition of Ascham's English works for which Johnson wrote not only a life of Ascham but also many of the notes.

Chapman, R. W. "Dr. Johnson, Dr. Bridges and the B. B. C." *TLS,* Aug. 15, 1929, p. 637.

Chapman, R. W. "Johnson and poetry." *SRL,* Aug. 17, 1929, pp. 49-51.

Powell, L. F. "Dr. Johnson and Dr. James." *TLS,* Jan. 3, 1929, p. 12.

Reade, Aleyn Lyell. "Dr. Johnson's Lichfield origins." *TLS,* June 27, 1929, p. 514.

Roscoe, E. S. "Letters of Dr. Johnson to Sir Robert Chambers." *Cornhill magazine,* October, 1929, pp. 407-21.

Salpeter, Harry. *Dr. Johnson and Mr. Boswell.* New York: Coward-McCann, 1929.

Smith, David Nichol, R. W. Chapman, and L. F. Powell. *Johnson & Boswell revised by themselves and others.* Oxford: Clarendon Press, 1928. Pp. 66.

Rev. by A. W. P[ollard] in *Library,* 4th series, X (1929), 111-12; in *N & Q,* CLVI (1929), 179-80; in *TLS,* Jan. 24, 1929, p. 65.

Three admirable essays on Johnson's revision of his own works, Boswell's "revises" for the *Life of Johnson,* and the forthcoming new edition of Hill's Boswell.

Smith, David Nichol. *Samuel Johnson's "Irene."* Oxford: Clarendon Press, 1929. Pp. 23. (Reprinted in part from *Essays and studies by members of the English Association,* Vol. XIV.)

A clear and convenient presentation of all the known facts about Johnson's tragedy.

Whibley, Leonard. "Dr. Johnson and the universities." *Blackwood's magazine,* CCXXVI (1929), 369-83.

Nathaniel Lee

Fletcher, Harris. "Nathaniel Lee and Milton." *MLN,* XLIV (1929), 173-75.

Ghosh, J. C. "Prologue and epilogue to Lee's *Constantine the Great.*" *TLS,* Mar. 14, 1929, p. 207.

Kies, Paul P. "Lessing and Lee." *JEGP,* XXVIII (1929), 402-09.

Andrew Marvell

Legouis, Pierre. *André Marvell, poète, puritain, patriote, 1621-1678.* Paris: Henri Didier, 1928. Cf. *PQ,* VIII, 195-96.

Rev. by B. Fehr in *Beiblatt,* XL (1929), 133-38; by René Galland in *RELV,* XLVI (1929), 258-62; by Mario Praz in *English studies,* XI (1929), 33-40.

Roger Boyle, Earl of Orrery

Clark, William S. "Notes on two Orrery manuscripts." *MLN,* XLIV (1929), 1-6.

Samuel Pepys

Tanner, J. R. "Samuel Pepys and the Trinity House." *EHR,* XLIV (1929), 573-87.

Thomas Percy

Thomas, P. G. "Bishop Percy and the Scottish ballads." *TLS,* July 4, 1929, p. 538.

Comment by Marjorie Williams and C. A. Stonehill, *ibid.*, July 11, 1929, p. 558; by P. G. Thomas, *ibid.*, July 25, p. 592.

John Philips

The Poems of John Philips. Edited by M. G. Lloyd Thomas. Oxford: Blackwell, 1927. Cf. *PQ*, VII, 182.

Rev. by L. I. Bredvold in *MLN*, XLIV (1929), 66-67; by V. de Sola Pinto in *RES*, V (1929), 360-62.

Alexander Pope

The Dunciad variorum with the prolegomena of Scriblerus. By Alexander Pope. Reproduced in facsimile from the first issue of the original edition of 1729. With an introductory essay by Robert Kilburn Root, Princeton: Princeton University Press, 1929. Pp. 42+124.

This photographic facsimile of the first edition of the *Dunciad variorum* makes available to modern students for the first time an accurate text of this important form of Pope's poem.

Root's introductory essay is written in an easy and polished manner. While he has contributed nothing new to the history of the poem, he has admirably condensed into forty-two pages most of the significant facts concerning its composition, publication, and reception that have so far been established. The specific details are too often incorrect. Root writes, for instance, that in April of 1729 "Any one who made inquiry at Stationers' Hall would have learned that technically the publishers were three powerful noblemen. . . ." (p. 2); as a matter of fact, the lords' ownership of the copyright was not recorded until November 21 of that year. On p. 3 we are told that "Pope's name does not appear upon the title page, nor is his authorship declared quite explicitly anywhere in the volume"; but on p. 7 of the "Letter to the publisher" appears the statement that Pope "has laugh'd and written the *Dunciad.*" After accepting Griffith's argument that the duodecimo (No. 198) is the *princeps* (p. 9), Root gives the reading of the first line "BOOK and the man. . . .," of the octavo (No. 199) to support his statement that "The *Dunciad* of 1728 was deliberately intended to be an 'imperfect' copy" (p. 12). There are numerous other errors, such as the obviously incorrect grouping of the various issues of the 1728 *Dunciad* into "four editions" (p. 11); but these errors, while disappointing to the Pope specialist, are not of sufficient importance to detract seriously from the value of the volume—a volume which is obviously prepared in order to make the *Dunciad variorum* in its earlier form available to the student. Root can almost lay claim to being the first editor of the *Dunciad* free from the intense prejudice against Pope which has for so long characterized the attitude of scholars. He justifies Pope's judgment against the "dunces" (pp. 13-18); he presents clearly the attitude of Pope and his friends towards the Bentley-Theobald type of scholarship (pp. 24-31); and his critical discussion of the poem (pp. 31-36), while brief, is free from bias.—W. K. CHANDLER.

Selections from Alexander Pope. Edited with an introduction by George Sherburn. New York: Thomas Nelson and Sons, [1929]. Pp. xli+467.

Seldom has a book of this sort been done with more sympathy, skill in presentation, or genuine scholarship. Modestly masquerading as a text-book for college students, it puts at our disposal more fresh ideas concerning Pope and his work—the fruit of long research and meditation—than have appeared in print for many years. The introduction of thirty-five pages, in which Sherburn reviews Pope's life and defines with great sensitiveness the distinguishing qualities of his poetry, is undoubtedly one of the best essays yet written on its subject. High praise must likewise be given to the notes on the separate poems which are grouped at the end of the volume: models of condensation, they not only bring together conveniently whatever the student needs to know of the genesis of the various pieces and their dominant intentions but on many points offer corrections of traditional errors or suggestive new hypotheses. The reader will note particularly the heretical view which Sherburn expresses on the old problem of Bolingbroke's part in the composition of the *Essay on man* (pp. 406-09). I do not think he settles the question, but his points cannot be neglected when the next editor of the *Essay* comes to study the matter in detail.

Hughes, Helen Sard. "More Popeana: items from an unpublished correspondence." *PMLA*, XLIV (1929), 1090-98.

Warren, Austin. *Alexander Pope as critic and humanist.* Princeton: Princeton University Press, 1929. Pp. viii+289.

Of the eight chapters which make up this book, four (I, III, IV, and V) are devoted to an analysis of Pope's chief critical productions—the *Essay on criticism,* the commentary on Homer, the edition of Shakespeare, and the *Dunciad*; one (II) to a summary of his theory of poetry; and three (VI, VII, VIII) to a survey of his reading in classical, continental, and English writers.

The freshest part of the work is undoubtedly the last. Warren would probably be the first to admit that his study of Pope's culture is incomplete on many points. He has himself shown the possibilities of further research in an interesting note, just published, on Pope's copy of Ben Jonson (*MLN,* XLV [1930], 86-88); and other omissions, whether of writers or of references, will certainly be noted by readers familiar with Pope and with the scholarship concerning him. Thus a glance at Spence's *Anecdotes* yields several names missing from his list; for example, Balzac (ed. Singer, p. 176), Hutcheson (pp. 177-78), Saint-Evremond (pp. 178-79), Lillo (p. 215). (See also a review by George Sherburn to appear shortly in *MP.*) But the value of these chapters even as they stand is considerable: for the first time the chief materials for an appraisal of Pope's varied reading are brought together in one place and interpreted, on the whole, in a clear and discriminating way. Of special interest is the revelation of the important place occupied in Pope's culture by the great writers of pre-Augustan England. The point is perhaps not quite so new as Warren thinks, but it has never been illustrated by such an impressive assemblage of details, some of which at least—notably the praise of Spenser quoted from the *Observations on the Iliad* (p. 231)—will be unfamiliar to many students.

It is Warren's misfortune that the topics treated in his other chapters have been more often worked over by editors and critics of Pope. To say anything really new about the sources of the *Essay on criticism,* the methods of the edition of Shakespeare, or the literary satire of the *Dunciad* is now, after the labors of Elwin and Courthope, Lounsbury, and others, no easy task. And Warren, for the most part, has been content to build his study of these questions out of generally familiar materials. A less hackneyed subject is the criticism of Homer, and on this he makes a number of suggestive remarks, especially as to Pope's relation to the contemporary Homeric controversy in France (pp. 83-95). He deserves credit, too, for being one of the first to emphasize in print the interest of the critical dicta scattered through the *Observations on the Iliad.* But in general it cannot be said that this part of the book adds greatly to the knowledge or understanding of Pope's critical doctrine and practice already possessed by specialists in the subject.

The result might have been different had Warren allowed his study to mature longer before publishing it or had he confined himself to one or another of its special aspects—for instance, Pope's reading, or his rôle as a critic of Homer. For the faults of his work are due to no inability to think clearly or to appreciate the significance of facts; they are in the main the faults inevitable in any book that attempts to treat so large a subject in the time usually given to dissertations for the American Ph.D. To deal freshly or even adequately with Pope's literary theories, for example, demands an extensive first-hand acquaintance with Renaissance and seventeenth-century criticism and philosophy which no one could be expected to acquire in the few years of graduate study. Warren has done what most persons would do under the circumstances: he has fallen back on the obvious secondary guides—Spingarn, Durham, Brunetière, Nisard, and the like, for the background of the *Essay on criticism*; Vial and Denise (chiefly) for the background of the remarks on Homer. Even among works of this type his reading has not been particularly thorough. Had he known the important article of W. L. Bullock in *MP*, XXV (1928), 293-312, he might have modified at least slightly his rather sweeping generalizations concerning the status of "imitation" in the Renaissance (p. 47). Had he consulted Gillot's *La querelle des anciens et des modernes en France* (1914) he would have been able to write somewhat more precisely than he does (pp. 83-84) about the issues of that not always clearly understood controversy. And he would certainly have found in René Bray's *La formation de la doctrine classique* (1927) an abundance of ideas and texts which he could have used with advantage in his discussion of Pope's relations to neo-classical theory. So likewise with the portions of the book that concern Pope's own writings: in attempting to cover so much ground he has frequently neglected to push his researches as far as the available means would permit. His account of the publication of the *Iliad* (p. 77) would have been somewhat different had he looked at what Griffith has to say on the subject in his *Alexander Pope: a bibliography* (Vol. I, Part I, pp. 41-42). A glance at the *Dictionary of national biography* would have saved him from writing (p. 166, n. 27): "I am unable to identify General Codrington." His paragraph on p. 171 about attacks on Pope immediately preceding the *Dunciad* would have been modified had he relied for his information on Griffith (*MP*, XIII [1915], 3-6) rather than on Lounsbury. He would have felt obliged to give some specific evidence for his ascription of the *Virgilius restauratus* to Pope (p. 181) had he considered Aitken's remarks in his *Life and works of John Arbuthnot* (p. 121). And so on.

All this is regrettable, for in one respect at least Warren is admirably equipped to give us a valuable book on Pope as a critic. He has, what so many previous students have lacked, sympathy with his subject. "This book," he remarks in his Preface, "attempts to take the eighteenth century somewhat more at its own valuation, to apprehend more sympathetically its aims and standards." It is in this spirit that he has analyzed Pope's tastes and critical utterances, and the portrait, which rightly stresses "a certain largeness of attitude, a certain catholicity . . . . to which adequate justice has never been done," is on the whole, and in spite of weaknesses of detail, perhaps the most convincing that has yet been drawn.

Matthew Prior

"Letters of Matthew Prior." *TLS*, Apr. 25, 1929, p. 344.

Ann Radcliffe

Tompkins, J. M. S. "Ramond de Carbonnières, Grosley and Mrs. Radcliffe." *RES*, V (1929), 294-301.

Isaac Reed

Powell, L. F. "George Steevens and Isaac Reed's *Biographia dramatica*." *RES*, V (1929), 288-93.

Sir Joshua Reynolds

Letters of Sir Joshua Reynolds. Collected and edited by Frederick Whiley Hilles. Cambridge: Cambridge University Press, 1929. Pp. xxii+274.

Rev. in *TLS,* Dec. 5, 1929, p. 1023.

Samuel Richardson

Dottin, Paul. "Du nouveau sur Richardson (documents inédits)." *RAA,* VI (1929), 258-61; VII (1929), 55-59.

Dottin, Paul. [Review of B. W. Downs, *Richardson,* London, 1928.] *RELV,* XLVI (1929), 164-67.

William Richardson

Babcock, R. W. "William Richardson's criticism of Shakespeare." *JEGP,* XXVIII (1929), 117-36.

Nicholas Rowe

Three plays by Nicholas Rowe. Edited by J. R. Sutherland. London: Scholartis Press, 1929. Pp. 353.

Rev. by Alfred Jackson in *MLR,* XXIV (1929), 475-76; in *TLS,* Oct. 10, 1929, pp. 773-74.

Thomas Shadwell

Borgman, Albert S. *Thomas Shadwell: his life and comedies.* New York: New York University Press, 1928. Cf. *PQ,* VIII, 200.

Rev. in *N & Q,* CLVII (1929), 161; in *TLS,* May 2, 1929, pp. 345-46. An excellent monograph.

Lloyd, Claude. "Shadwell and the virtuosi." *PMLA,* XLIV (1929), 472-94.

Richard Brinsley Sheridan

The Plays and poems of Richard Brinsley Sheridan. Edited, with introduction, appendices and bibliographies, by R. Crompton Rhodes. Oxford: Blackwell, 1928. 3 vols. Cf. *PQ,* VIII, 200.

Rev. by F. W. Bateson in *RES,* V (1929), 482-84; by G. H. Nettleton in *SRL,* June 8, 1929, p. 1090.

Bateson, F. W. "The text of Sheridan" [*The rivals* and *The school for scandal*]. *TLS,* Nov. 28, Dec. 5, 1929, pp. 998, 1029.

For the discussion provoked by these articles see the issues of *TLS* for Dec. 5, p. 1032, Dec. 19, pp. 1081-82, Dec. 26, 1929, p. 1097, Jan. 2, 1930, p. 12, Jan. 16, p. 44, and Jan. 23, p. 60.

Christopher Smart

Abbott, Charles Davis. "The date of Christopher Smart's confinement." *TLS,* Jan. 24, 1929, p. 62.

Piggott, Stuart. "New light on Christopher Smart." *TLS,* June 13, 1929, p. 474.

Tobias Smollett

Ellison, Lee Monroe. "Elizabethan drama and the works of Smollett." *PMLA,* XLIV (1929), 842-62.

Sir Richard Steele

Blanchard, Rae. "'The Christian hero,' by Richard Steele: a bibliography." *Library,* 4th series, X (1929), 61-72.

Blanchard, Rae. "Richard Steele and the status of women." *SP,* XXVI (1929), 325-55.

Laurence Sterne

Second journal to Eliza. By Laurence Sterne. Hitherto known as Letters supposed to have been written by Yorick and Eliza, but now shown to be a later version of the Journal to Eliza. Transcribed from the copy in the British Museum and presented with an introduction by Margaret R. B. Shaw, together with a foreword by Charles Whibley. London: Bell, 1929. Pp. xxxix+165.

Rev. by E. E. K. in *New statesman,* Nov. 9, 1929, p. viii; by Wilbur Cross in *SRL,* Dec. 21, 1929, p. 587 (rejects the ascription); in *TLS,* Oct. 31, 1929, p. 867.

Curtis, Lewis Perry. *The politicks of Laurence Sterne.* Oxford: Oxford University Press; London: H. Milford, 1929. Pp. xiii+139.

Rev. by Wilbur Cross in *Yale review,* XIX (1929), 181-82; in *TLS,* Mar. 28, 1929, p. 253.

Eddy, William A. "Tom Brown and *Tristram Shandy.*" *MLN,* XLIV (1929), 379-81.

Tompkins, J. M. S. "Triglyph and Tristram." *TLS,* July 11, 1929, p. 558.

Allusions to Sterne by Richard Griffith.

Jonathan Swift

Ball, F. Elrington. *Swift's verse, an essay.* London: John Murray, 1929. Pp. xv+402.

At the death of the author in January, 1928, this book was complete except for the index; it has been seen through the press by E. M. Walker with the expert assistance of D. Nichol Smith and Harold Williams. Its eleven chapters attempt to place Swift's poems in their biographical setting and to exhibit the development of his characteristic style. In the notes are gathered many useful facts concerning the bibliography of the various pieces, and the appendices contain the texts of upwards of twenty poems which are here added to the canon. It is clear that much more work will need to be done before we can have a satisfactory critical edition of Swift's verse; but the task of the editor has been materially lightened by the publication of this volume.

Eddy, William A. "*Gulliver's travels* and *Le théâtre italien.*" *MLN,* XLIV (1929), 356-61.

Rovillain, Eugène E. "Jonathan Swift's *A voyage to Lilliput* and *The thousand and one quarters of an hour, Tartarian tales* of Thomas Simon Gueulette." *MLN,* XLIV (1929), 362-64.

"The Poems of Swift." *TLS,* July 4, 1929, pp. 521-22.

Williams, Harold. "A sentence of 'Gulliver's travels' in Swift's hand." *TLS,* Jan. 10, 1929, p. 28.

Thomas Taylor

Johnson, Franklin P. "Neo-Platonic hymns by Thomas Taylor." *PQ,* VIII (1929), 145-56.

William Johnston Temple

Diaries of William Johnston Temple, 1780-1796. Edited with a memoir by Lewis Bettany. Oxford: Clarendon Press, 1929. Pp. lxxvi+197.

Rev. by F. A. Pottle in *SRL,* Jan. 18, 1930, p. 657; in *TLS,* Oct. 3, 1929, p. 763.

James Thomson

Das, P. K. "James Thomson's appreciation of mountain scenery." *ES,* LXIV (1929), 65-70.

Williams, George G. "Who was 'Cenus' in the poem *To the memory of Mr. Congreve.*" *PMLA,* XLIV (1929), 495-500.

Thomas Traherne

Thompson, Elbert N. S. "The philosophy of Thomas Traherne." *PQ,* VIII (1929), 97-112.

Horace Walpole

The Castle of Otranto. By Horace Walpole. Edited with an introductory essay and notes by Oswald Doughty. London: Scholartis Press, 1929. Pp. lxxx+111.

Rev. by A. Digeon in *RAA,* VII (1929), 68-69; by Herbert G. Wright in *MLR,* XXIV (1929), 480-81; in *TLS,* Sept. 12, 1929, p. 699.

deKoven, Anna. *Horace Walpole and Madame du Deffand: an*

eighteenth century friendship. New York: Appleton, 1929. Pp. xii+199.

Rev. in *TLS,* Dec. 12, 1929, p. 1062.

Holzknecht, K. L. "Horace Walpole as dramatist." *South Atlantic quarterly,* XXVIII (1929), 174-89.

Thomas Warton

Woodhouse, A. S. P. "Thomas Warton and the 'Ode to horror.'" *TLS,* Jan. 24, 1929, p. 62.

Comment by P. Parker, *ibid.,* Mar. 7, 1929, p. 186; by A. S. P. Woodhouse, *ibid.,* May 23, p. 420.

Anne Finch, Countess of Winchilsea

Hughes, Helen Sard. "Lady Winchilsea and her friends." *LM,* XIX (1929), 624-35.

Based on a MS volume of her poems in the library of Wellesley College and on gleanings from the papers of the Countess of Hertford at Alnwick Castle.

William Wycherley

Hargest, W. G. "Wycherley and the Countess of Drogheda." *TLS,* Nov. 21, 1929, p. 960.

Comment by Eleanore Boswell, *ibid.,* Nov. 28, 1929, pp. 1001-02.

Arthur Young

Travels in France during the years 1787, 1788, and 1789. By Arthur Young. Edited by Constantia Maxwell. Cambridge: Cambridge University Press, 1929. Pp. lvi+428.

Rev. by A. J. Grant in *History,* XIV (1929), 270-71; by Henri Sée in *Revue d'histoire moderne,* March-April, 1929, pp. 138-39; in *New statesman,* May 4, 1929, pp. vii-viii; in *N & Q,* CLVI (1929), 343-44; in *TLS,* May 2, 1929, p. 357.

Edward Young

Clark, Harry Hayden. *The romanticism of Edward Young.* Reprinted from the *Transactions of the Wisconsin Academy of sciences, arts and letters,* Vol. XXIV (1929). Pp. 45.

"In order to ascertain in what ways Young is romantic," says the author, "I propose simply to discover which of his doctrines he held in common with those later nineteenth century writers generally referred to as romanticists" (p. 1). The result of the study is a list of twelve "major traits" which Clark thinks are to be found both in Young and in the typical spokesmen of the romantic movement: "(1) scorn for the commonplace and the actual world; (2) praise of a solitude unique and distinctive; (3) apotheosis of the lawless, creative, idyllic imagination; (4) indeterminate expansiveneses in the guise of religious aspiration; (5) praise of art as a means of play and escape; (6) contempt for rules and restrictions; (7) preference for native genius rather than culture and the classics; (8) recognition of nature as 'the felt presence of the deity'; (9) hostility to imitation and praise of militant individualism; (10) glorification of the master-passion and the hope of progress; (11) praise of a unique and idiosyncratic subjectivity; (12) the parading of a personal and singular melancholy.''

The article shows a wide range of reading and makes some points with which all students of Young will agree, but like most writings on the eighteenth century inspired by the teaching of Irving Babbitt it is based on a thoroughly unsound conception of scholarly method. I do not refer to the constant intrusion of moral preoccupations in phrases like ''True Christian aspiration'' (p. 12), ''that poisonous heresy 'art for art's sake' '' (p. 16), ''the fatal weakness of the romanticists, the inability to mediate between extremes'' (p. 30), or to the naïve philosophy of history which inspires the pronouncement that ''It is scarcely necessary to remark that here we stand at the headwaters of a current which was to sweep with devastating violence over the war-torn fields of France in 1917'' (p. 32). All this is annoying enough to one who wishes to get on with the matter in hand, but it is no more objectionable in itself than any of the other forms of rhetorical embroidery in which critics indulge. A more fundamental weakness results from Clark's unhistorical approach to his central theme. Two things are obviously necessary before it is possible to define intelligently Young's place in the history of ideas: a careful analysis of the various strains of thought and sentiment that are combined in his work, and an interpretation of these by reference to the ruling presuppositions, points of view, and standards of value of the period in which his ideas were formed. This would seem to be self-evident; but it has never been done in any thoroughgoing way, and Clark does not do it. Instead he takes as his term of comparison a set of general formulae (see the first paragraph above) devised originally to describe—and to condemn—what seemed to Babbitt, their inventor, tendencies characteristics of the extremer forms of nineteenth-century ''romanticism.'' It would be easy to show that some of them (for example, Nos. 4, 5, 8, 10) are so vaguely expressed that they could be made to cover a number of essentially distinct and even opposing ideas. It is obvious, too, that the list as a whole lumps together without discrimination ideas which were really new and revolutionary in the eighteenth century (e.g., Nos. 9, 11) and conceptions which in one form or another had been current among ''unromantic'' thinkers since at least the Renaissance (e.g., No. 7). But the point I wish to make here is that the particular connotations which all of these formulae have in Clark's mind are derived from their association, in Babbitt and elsewhere, with phenomena observed in a period much later than that of Young. To use them, therefore, for the interpretation of the *Night thoughts* or the *Conjectures on original composition* is inevitably to distort history. It is to impose on those ideas of Young to which they seem to apply a coloring not warranted by the context—to read into them a meaning subtly different from that which they have when one studies them in the light both of Young's total thought and of the peculiar climate of opinion in which they took form.

Two illustrations will have to suffice. On p. 3, after quoting a passage from the discussion of immortality in Night VI, Clark says: ''His [Young's] attitude toward the here and now is clear; he calls it this 'miry vale'; 'this nest of pains'; 'this dark, incarcerating colony'; 'this night of frailty, change, and death'; 'this dismal scene'; 'this vapour'; this 'prison'; this 'pestilential earth.' No wonder he longed to escape to 'that vast Unseen!' '' As a description of Young's characteristic ''otherworldliness'' this will pass muster, but the interpretation which Clark places on the expressions quoted will surprise any one who has been accustomed to seeing in them merely the *clichés* of traditional ascetic Christianity. Without pausing to consider, for example, what such a phrase as ''The vast Unseen'' must have meant to Young and his contemporary public, he immediately proceeds to read into it implications of a highly romantic sort. ''This attitude toward the actual world was the groundwork of much of the later romantic idealism. It is interesting to find it predominating in Germany,—where Young's influence was strongest—as illustrated in the phantasies of Tieck and Novalis.'' We may see it also, he tells us, in the contrast which Shelley draws between the ''sad reality'' of *The Cenci* and his earlier dreams of what ought to be, or what may be''; in the Poictesme of the ''arch-romantic American'' James Branch Cabell; and in the ''Charmed magic casements'' of Keats. Another instance of the subtle distortion of Young's literal meaning to which Clark's method inevitably leads him appears in his treatment of the familiar passage in the *Conjectures* beginning ''In the fairy-land of fancy genius may wander wild. . . .'' This passage, it is now known (see McKillop in *MP*, XXII, 393-94), was supplied to Young by Richardson; and as can easily be seen if it is read in its immediate context, it is introduced by way of concession in a paragraph intended to qualify in the interest of religion the preceding exaltation of ''genius'' over ''learning.'' Clark, therefore, seems to me to be exaggerating its importance as a reflection of Young's basic thought when he uses it to support the generalization that Young's ''yearning for novelty, expansion, infinitude finds expression through the glorification of an imagination emancipated from all purpose, restraint, and reality'' (p. 14). Young—and Richardson—would have been horrified at this, and they would have been even more disturbed could they have read the discussion that follows (pp. 15-16), in which Clark sees in this and another, still more harmless, passage of the *Conjectures* an adumbration of the ''romantic'' conception of art as play. It is not by this method that the history of ideas in the eighteenth century is to be written.

V. THE CONTINENTAL BACKGROUND

NOTE: I list here a few studies which seem to me of particular importance for the specialist in English literature and ideas.

Baldensperger, F. ''Voltaire anglophile avant son séjour d'Angleterre.'' *RLC,* IX (1929), 25-61.

This article sums up various facts and possibilities affecting Voltaire's Anglomania, in an endeavor to show that certain English *penchants* were active in his mind before 1726. Most of these center round the personality and influence of Bolingbroke. Accepting the conclusions of Reynald and Torrey as Baldensperger stresses the latter's rôle as host, guide, and friend to the young Arouet. Lady Bolingbroke also kindly forwarded his English interests and contacts. In their circle were people as diverse as Lord Peterborough and Levesque de Pouilly. These and other visitors may well have set Voltaire on the trail of Locke and Newton; his host may have stimulated an interest in Deism, though not an acceptance of that creed. The general ''Brittanic'' atmosphere at La Source doubtless disposed a young and mobile mind toward a belief in England's sterling qualities and prepared Voltaire for spontaneously choosing that country as a refuge in exile. Another result of frequenting the Bolingbroke circle, encouraged also by Voltaire's incipient friendship with the merchant Falkener, was perhaps his tendency to associate England's greatness with her commercial supremacy. Other contacts still, for example with Atterbury and Lord Stair, would add accretions to the Frenchman's growing Anglomania. And the author of the article uses various outlying correspondences to show that Voltaire was already flattering the House of Hanover and was already known, through *La Ligue,* to Alexander Pope.

The value of the article is in massing such facts rather than in its conjectures as to a possible acquaintance with Prior or as to what the young Arouet may have learned about England in Holland. But the assembled evidence proves that Voltaire was strongly drawn to England before he went there. One must demur at the further conclusions that he had little to discover in the island and that what he did discover was more of a disillusionment than a satisfaction. That the general trend was otherwise is borne out both by the *Lettres philosophiques* and by his subsequent writings, including most of the *Correspondance.*—E. P. DARGAN.

Bray, René. "L'esthétique classique." *RCC,* XXX (1929), 97-111, 211-26, 363-78, 434-49, 673-84.

A series of lectures covering some of the same ground as the author's book, *La formation de la doctrine classique* (1927).

Brulé, André. *La vie aux dix-huitième siècle.* Tome I: *Les gens de lettres.* Paris: Editions Marcel Seheur, 1929.

Rev. in *TLS,* Aug. 8, 1929, p. 618.

Clement, N. H. "Nature and the country in sixteenth and seventeenth century French poetry." *PMLA,* XLIV (1929), 1005-47.

Croce, Benedetto. *Storia della età barocca in Italia: pensiero—poesia e letteratura—vita morale.* Bari: Laterza & Figli, 1929. Pp. x+508.

Rev. by E. G. Gardner in *MLR,* XXIV (1929), 494-97.

François, Alexis. *Les origines lyriques de la phrase moderne. Etude sur la prose cadencée dans la littérature française au dix-huitième siècle.* Paris: Presses universitaires, 1929. Pp. 61.

Rev. by H. P. Thieme in *Books abroad,* III (1929), 208.

Gilson, Etienne. "Recherches sur la formation du système cartésien". *RHP,* III (1929), 113-64.

Green, F. C. *Eighteenth-century France. Six essays.* London: Dent, 1929. Pp. vii+221.

Rev. by A. J. Grant in *History,* XIV (1929), 270; in *N & Q,* CLVI (1929), 200; in *TLS,* June 27, 1929, p. 508.

Green, F. C. *French novelists: manners and ideas from the Renaissance to the Revolution.* London: Dent; New York: Appleton, 1929. Pp. xi+239.

Rev. by A. Brulé in *RAA,* VII (1929), 164-65; by Urban T. Holmes in *JMH,* I (1929), 463-65; in *TLS,* Feb. 7, 1929, p. 94.

Grubbs, H. A. "The originality of La Rochefoucauld's Maxims." *RHL,* XXXVI (1929), 18-59.

Havens, George R. "Rousseau's doctrine of goodness according to nature." *PMLA,* XLIV (1929), 1239-45.

An interesting and convincing reply to the article by Jeannette Tresnon in *PMLA,* XLIII (1928), 1010-25.

Havens, George R. and Norman L. Torrey. "Voltaire's books: a selected list." *MP,* XXVII (1929), 1-22.

Havens, George R. and Norman L. Torrey. "Voltaire's library." *Fortnightly review,* CXXVI (1929), 397-405.

Hazard, Paul, et ses étudiants americains. *Etude critique sur "Manon Lescaut."* Chicago: University of Chicago Press, 1929. Pp. ix+113.

Rev. by Gilbert Chinard in *MLN,* XLV (1930), 184-85.

Admirably written studies on various aspects of Prévost's inspiration and art in *Manon Lescaut,* concluding with a useful chapter on "L'Abbé Prévost et l'Angleterre: état des travaux" and a valuable "Bibliographie critique pour servir à l'étude de *Manon Lescaut.*"

Hubert, René. *Rousseau et l'Encyclopédie: essai sur la formation des idées politiques de Rousseau (1742-1756).* Paris: Gamber, 1928. Pp. 137.

Rev. by Emile Bréhier in *RHP,* III (1929), 503-04, and in *Revue philosophique,* LIV (1929), 444-45.

Jacoubet, Henri. *Le genre troubadour et les origines françaises du romantisme.* Paris: "Belles lettres," 1929. Pp. 288.

Kies, Paul P. "Lessing's early study of English drama." *JEGP,* XXVIII (1929), 16-34.

Lancaster, Henry Carrington. *A history of French dramatic literature in the seventeenth century.* Part I: *The pre-classical period.* Baltimore: The Johns Hopkins Press, 1929. 2 vols.

Rev. by Louis Cons in *MLN,* XLV (1930), 179-83.

Lancaster, H. Carrington. "The introduction of the unities into the French drama of the seventeenth century." *MLN,* XLIV (1929), 207-17.

Martin, Kingsley. *French liberal thought in the eighteenth century.* London: Benn; Boston: Little, Brown and Company, 1929. Pp. xviii+313.

Rev. by Albert Guerard in *Books,* Jan. 12, 1930, p. 10; in *TLS,* Aug. 22, 1929, p. 644.

Monglond, A. *Histoire intérieure du préromantisme français de l'abbé Prévost à Joubert.* Grenoble: Arthaud, 1929. 2 vols.

Moreau-Rendu, S. *L'idée de bonté naturelle chez J.-J. Rousseau.* Paris: Marcel Rivière, 1929.

Mornet, Daniel. *French thought in the eighteenth century.* Translated by Lawrence M. Levin. New York: Prentice-Hall, 1929. Pp. x+336.

Mornet, Daniel. *Histoire de la clarté française: ses origines, son évolution, sa valeur.* Paris: Payot, 1929. Pp. 358.

Pienaar, W. J. B. *English influences in Dutch literature and Justus Van Effen as intermediary: an aspect of eighteenth century achievement.* Cambridge: Cambridge University Press, 1929. Pp. x+260.

Rev. by Georges Roger in *Les langues modernes,* XXVII (1929), 242-44; in *Neophilologus,* XV (1929), 63-64; in *N & Q,* CLVI (1929), 470.

Schinz, Albert. "The concept of Nature in philosophy and literature; a consideration of recent discussions." *Proceedings of the American Philosophical society,* LXVIII (1929), 207-225.

Schinz, Albert. *La pensée de Jean-Jacques Rousseau: essai d'interprétation nouvelle.* Paris: Alcan; Northampton, Mass.: Smith College, 1929. 2 vols.

Rev. by Emile B[réhier] in *RHP,* III (1929), 504-05; by Albert Feuillerat in *SRL,* Sept. 28, 1929, p. 190; by C. H. C. Wright in *AHR,* XXXV (1930), 344-45.

Silz, Walter. *Early German romanticism: its founders and Heinrich von Kleist.* Cambridge [Mass.]: Harvard University Press, 1929.

Stadelmann, Rudolf. "Die Angfänge einer Kulturphilosophie in Rousseaus erstem Discours." *Deutsche Vierteljahrschrift,* VII (1929), 29-50.

Tilley, Arthur. *The decline of the Age of Louis XIV; or French literature, 1687-1715.* Cambridge: Cambridge University Press, 1929. Pp. xviii+458.

Rev. by H. Carrington Lancaster in *MLN,* XLV (1930), 183-84; in *TLS,* June 27, 1929, p. 508.

Torrey, Norman L. "Voltaire's English notebook." *MP,* XXVI (1929), 307-25.

Wright, Ernest Hunter. *The meaning of Rousseau.* Oxford: Oxford University Press; London: H. Milford, 1929. Pp. vi+168.

Rev. by P. Descamps in *RAA,* VII (1929), 166-67; by C. H. C. Wright in *AHR,* XXXV (1930), 344-45; in *TLS,* May 23, 1929, p. 416.

This is a brief, compact, clear-cut book on the leading ideas of Rousseau, which has the rare merit of interpreting him, not by quotation of isolated paradoxes, but by following closely and consecutively his thought in its main outlines from fundamental premises to conclusions. Instead of flaunting before us some pet thesis of his own, Wright sticks modestly to his subject. He is careful to observe the necessary precaution of noting the sometimes unusual meaning of Rousseau's terms, which need to be considered, not only in their context, but in the ideological background of their times. The four chapters of the book deal with Rousseau's ideas on the "Natural man," the "Natural education," the "Natural society," and the "Natural religion." The open-minded reader can easily convince himself that Rousseau's language is more paradoxical, from the modern point of view, than his ideas and that, if we have not in general yet found out the truth about Rousseau, it is mainly, as Wright says, because "we have not *wanted* to find it" (pp. 5-6). While there are a few critics—for example, Lanson—who have *wanted* to find, and have found, the truth about Rousseau's ideas, it is unfortunately true that too much so-called Rousseau "criticism" has been enthusiastic praise or violent blame. Wright has avoided Scylla and Charybdis and produced an honest book which will be welcomed by all equally honest readers as a valuable aid to the accurate understanding of Rousseau's ideas.—George R. Havens.

1931

ENGLISH LITERATURE, 1660-1800: A CURRENT BIBLIOGRAPHY

By Ronald S. Crane
University of Chicago

This bibliography attempts to list the more significant books, articles, and reviews published during the year 1930, together with some bearing the date 1929 that were inadvertently omitted from the bibliography for that year (*PQ*, IX, 165-208). I am indebted to Professor M. E. Prior of Northwestern University and to Mr. Charles Kerby-Miller of the University of Chicago for much valuable assistance in the collection and verification of material.

LIST OF ABBREVIATIONS

AHR=*American historical review.*
Archiv=*Archiv für das Studium der neueren Sprachen und Literaturen.*
Beiblatt=*Beiblatt zur Anglia.*
DVLG=*Deutsche Vierteljahrsscrift für Literaturwissenschaft u. Geistesgeschichte.*
EHR=*English historical review.*
ES=*Englische Studien.*
GRM=*Germanisch-romanische Monatsschrift.*
JEGP=*Journal of English and Germanic philology.*
JMH=*Journal of modern history.*
LM=*London mercury.*
MLN=*Modern language notes.*
MLR=*Modern language review.*
MP=*Modern philology.*
N & Q=*Notes and queries.*
PMLA=*Publications of the Modern Language Association of America.*
PQ=*Philological quarterly.*
RAA=*Revue anglo-américaine.*
RC=*Revue critique.*
RCC=*Revue des cours et conférences.*
RELV=*Revue de l'enseignement des langues vivantes.*
RES=*Review of English studies.*
RH=*Revue historique.*
RHL=*Revue d'histoire littéraire de la France.*
RHP=*Revue d'histoire de la philosophie.*
RLC=*Revue de littérature comparée.*
RSH=*Revue de synthèse historique.*
SP=*Studies in philology.*
SRL=*Saturday review of literature.*
TLS=*Times literary supplement* (London).

I. BIBLIOGRAPHIES AND BIBLIOGRAPHICAL STUDIES

Annual bibliography of English language and literature. Volume X, 1929. Edited for the Modern Humanities Research Association by M. S. Serjeantson. Cambridge: Bowes & Bowes, 1930. Pp. viii+238.

Baugh, Albert C. "American bibliography for 1929. VIII. Seventeenth century. IX. Eighteenth century." *PMLA,* XLV (1930), 35-42.

Bosanquet, Eustace F. "English seventeenth-century almanacks. 1. Their history. 2. As books of reference. 3. As a medium for advertisement. 4. The MS. notes in them by contemporary owners." *Library,* 4th series, X (1930), 361-97.

Carlton, W. J. "Bibliography of shorthand." *TLS,* Nov. 13, 1930, p. 942.

Caskey, J. Homer. "The two issues of *The World.*" *MLN,* XLV (1930), 29-31.

A Catalogue of XVIIIth century verse. Part I, "Addison-Jerningham." Part II, "Johnson-Scott." London: P. J. & A. E. Dobell, [1930]. Catalogues 99, 102.

Rev. in *TLS,* Nov. 13, 1930, p. 948.
The two parts of this valuable catalogue contain 1591 items.

Chapman, R. W. *Cancels.* London: Constable; New York: R. R. Smith, 1930. Pp. 70.

Rev. in *TLS,* Dec. 10, 1930, p. 1039.

Crane, Ronald S. "English literature, 1660-1800: a current bibliography." *PQ,* IX (1930), 165-208.

Doughty, Oswald. "Romanticism in eighteenth-century England." *English studies,* XII (1930), 41-44.

Brief notices of several recent studies.

Early newspapers from 1625 to 1850. Offered for sale by Birrell & Garnett. Catalogue No. 26. [London, 1929.] Pp. 32.

Rev. in *TLS,* Feb. 6, 1930, p. 108.
It is understood that the entire collection described in this catalogue has been acquired by the library of Duke University.

Grose, Clyde L. "Thirty years' study of a formerly neglected century of British history, 1660-1760." *JMH,* II (1930), 448-71.

A valuable critical bibliography.

Hayward, John. "Reader's bibliography. Life and letters after the Restoration." *Life and letters,* IV (1930), 485-91.

Heawood, Edward. "Papers used in England after 1600. I. The seventeenth century to c. 1680." *Library,* 4th series, XI (1930), 263-99.

Johnson, A. F. "The evolution of the modern-face roman." *Library,* 4th series, XI (1930), 353-77.

Morison, Stanley. *John Bell, 1745-1831, bookseller, printer, publisher, typefounder, journalist.* Cambridge: Cambridge University press, 1930. Pp. x+167.

Rev. in *TLS,* June 26, 1930, p. 531.

Mumby, Frank Arthur. *Publishing and bookselling: a history from the earliest times to the present day.* With a bibliography by W. H. Peet. London: Johnathan Cape, 1930. Pp. 480.

Rev. in *TLS,* Nov. 27, 1930, p. 1006.

Novels and romances from Petronius to Wells. Offered for sale by Birrell & Garnett. Catalogue No. 29. [London, 1930.]

A good many eighteenth-century titles.

"Oriental tales." *TLS,* Apr. 10, 1930, p. 324.

Comment by Duncan B. Macdonald, *ibid.,* May 15, 1930, p. 414.

Ricci, Seymour de. *English collectors of books & manuscripts (1530-1930) and their marks of ownership.* Cambridge: Cambridge University press, 1930. Pp. x+238.

Sadleir, Michael. *The evolution of publishers' binding styles, 1770-1900.* London: Constable; New York: R. R. Smith, 1930. Pp. x+96.

Rev. by I. A. Williams in *LM,* XXII (1930), 58; in *TLS,* May 22, 1930, p. 427.

Sée, Henri. "Histoire économique et sociale." *RH,* CLXV (1930), 109-58.

Spencer, Hazelton. "A caveat on Restoration play quartos." *RES,* VI (1930), 315-16.

Van Tieghem, Paul. "Histoire littéraire générale et comparée (treizième compte rendu annuel)." *RSH,* XLVIII (1929), 79-112.

See especially pp. 86-103.

Wood, Frederick T. "Pirate printing in the XVIII century." *N & Q,* CLIX (1930), 381-84, 400-03.

II. THE SOCIAL AND POLITICAL ENVIRONMENT

Abbott, Wilbur Cortez. *A bibliography of Oliver Cromwell.* Cambridge, [Mass.]: Harvard University press, 1929. Cf. *PQ,* IX, 167.

Rev. by Clyde L. Grose in *JMH,* II (1930), 305-07.

Barnes, Donald Grove. *A history of the English corn laws, 1660-*

1846. London: Routledge; New York: F. S. Crofts & co., 1930. Pp. xv+336.

Rev. by Jacob Viner in *Journal of political economy,* XXXVIII (1930), 710-12; in *TLS,* Apr. 10, 1930, p. 309.

Brailsford, Mabel Richmond. *The making of William Penn.* London: Longmans, 1930. Pp. xxiv+368.

Rev. in *TLS,* Oct. 30, 1930, p. 877.

The Diary and letter book of the Rev. Thomas Brockbank, 1671-1709. Edited by Richard Trappes-Lomax. Manchester: The Chetham society, 1930. Pp. xi+417.

Rev. in *TLS,* Aug. 28, 1930, p. 679.

Carruthers, Sir Joseph. *Captain James Cook, R. N.: 150 years after.* London: Murray, 1930. Pp. xx+316.

Rev. in *TLS,* July 3, 1930, p. 549.

Chauvet, Paul. "L'Angleterre et la Corse." *RAA,* VII (1930), 418-31.

A brief discussion of English interest in Corsica from Boswell to the present time.

Clark, Dora Mae. *British opinion and the American Revolution.* New Haven: Yale University press; London: Humphrey Milford, Oxford University press, 1930. Pp. viii+308.

Rev. by Holden Furber in *JMH,* III (1931), 119-20; by A. C. McL[aughlin] in *AHR,* XXXVI (1930), 167-68; in *TLS,* July 24, 1930, p. 613.

This study explores a field already covered in part by F. J. Hinkhouse, *Preliminaries of the American Revolution as seen in the English press, 1763-1775* (1926); but it covers a longer period, to 1783, and it differs even more importantly in method. Newspapers and magazines are supplemented as sources by pamphlets, correspondence, memoirs, etc. Moreover, instead of seeking to penetrate to actual public opinion solely through the haze of propaganda in letters to the editor and press paragraphs, the views of various groups—merchants, manufacturers, country gentlemen, political radicals, crown officials, lawyers, clergy, parliament men—are discovered in their activities, and in petitions and memorials, associations, resolutions, and the like, in the face of specific issues. Though Miss Clark covers a good deal of familiar ground, she has made a fuller analysis than we have had of the varieties of opinion which existed in England on American questions, such as the Sugar Act, the Stamp Act, the Townshend duties, the tea affair, coercion, the war and its conduct and objects, and upon the broader issues of mercantilism and imperialism. She also shows pretty convincingly that these clashing and changing opinions were in each instance based upon distinctively British interests and preconceptions. To some extent she demonstrates the influence of such opinions upon the course of events. The most serious defect is the omission of any detailed consideration of the views of the nonconformists.—V. W. Crane.

Clark, G. N. *The seventeenth century.* Oxford: Clarendon press, 1929. Pp. xii+372.

Rev. by Violet Barbour in *AHR,* XXXV (1930), 848-49; by M. M. Knappen in *JMH,* II (1930), 484-86; by W. F. Reddaway in *EHR,* XLV (1930), 311-13; by R. H. Tawney in *History,* XV (1930), 265-66.

Ewen, C. L'Estrange. *Witch hunting and witch trials: the in-*

dictments for witchcraft from the records of 1373 assizes held for the Home Circuit, A. D. 1559-1736. London: Kegan Paul; New York: Dial press, 1929. Pp. xiii+345.

Rev. by G. L. Burr in *AHR*, XXXV (1930), 844-45.

Feiling, Keith. *British foreign policy, 1660-1672.* London and New York: Macmillan, 1930. Pp. xii+385.

Rev. in *New statesman*, Nov. 15, 1930, pp. 180-81.

Fussell, G. E. "Eighteenth century agricultural dictionaries." *Bulletin of the Institute of historical research*, VII (1930), 144-48.

A brief survey with bibliography.

George, M. Dorothy. "Elections and electioneering, 1679-81." *EHR*, XLV (1930), 552-78.

Grubb, Isabel. *Quakerism and industry before 1800.* London: Williams and Norgate, 1930. Pp. 192.

Rev. in *TLS*, Apr. 24, 1930, p. 342.

Hamilton, Alexander. *A new account of the East Indies.* Now edited with introduction and notes by Sir William Foster. London: Argonaut press, 1930. 2 vols.

Rev. in *TLS*, June 19, 1930, p. 505.

Horn, D. B. *Sir Charles Hanbury Williams and European diplomacy (1747-58).* London: Harrap, 1930. Pp. 314.

Rev. in *TLS*, May 15, 1930, p. 403.

James, Margaret. *Social problems and policy during the Puritan revolution, 1640-1660.* London: Routledge, 1930.

Rev. in *Nation & Athenæum*, Nov. 1, 1930, pp. 170, 172; in *New statesman*, Nov. 22, 1930, p. 210.

Laprade, William T. "The Stamp Act in British politics." *AHR*, XXXV (1930), 735-57.

Larkin, Paschal. *Property in the eighteenth century, with special reference to England and Locke.* With a preface by J. L. Stocks. London: Longmans, 1930. Pp. xiii+252.

Rev. in *TLS*, Dec. 4, 1930, p. 1024.

Lodge, Sir Richard. *Studies in eighteenth-century diplomacy, 1740--1748.* London: Murray, 1930. Pp. xiii+421.

Lodge, Sir Richard. "The word 'premier.'" *TLS*, March 6, 1930, p. 190.

Comment by various persons, *ibid.*, March 13, 1930, p. 214; March 20, 1930, p. 247; March 27, 1930, p. 274.

Marillier, H. C. *English tapestries of the eighteenth century. A handbook to the post-Mortlake productions of English weavers.* London: Medici society, 1930. Pp. xxiii+128, with 48 plates.

Rev. in *TLS,* Oct. 16, 1930, p. 826.

Markun, Leo. *Mrs. Grundy: a history of four centuries of morals intended to illuminate present problems in Great Britain and the United States.* New York: Appleton, 1930. Pp. 665.

Rev. by Preserved Smith in *SRL,* Aug. 9, 1930, p. 34.

Memoirs of Sarah, Duchess of Marlborough, together with her characters of contemporaries and her opinions. Edited, with an introduction, by William King. London: Routledge, 1930. Pp. xxv+340.

Rev. in *TLS,* May 1, 1930, p. 363.

Morini-Comby, J. *Mercantilisme et protectionisme. Essai sur les doctrines interventionnistes en politique commerciale, du XVe au XIXe siècle.* Paris: Alcan, 1930. Pp. xx+217.

Rev. by Henri Hauser in *RH,* CLXV (1930), 363-64; in *TLS,* Nov. 27, 1930, p. 1015.

Mullet, C. F. "English imperial thinking, 1764-1783." *Political science quarterly,* XLV (1930), 548-79.

Namier, L. B. *England in the age of the American Revolution.* [Book I, "Government and Parliament under the Duke of Newcastle."] London: Macmillan, 1930. Pp. viii+518.

Rev. by G. M. Trevelyan in *Nation & Athenæum,* Nov. 15, 1930, p. 238.

Newton, E. E. "Twining's coffee house in Devereux Court." *N & Q,* CLVIII (1930), 147-48.

Nicholson, T. C. and A. S. Turberville. *Charles Talbot, Duke of Shrewsbury.* Cambridge: Cambridge University press, 1930. Pp. vii+250.

Rev. in *TLS,* Dec. 4, 1930, p. 1031.

Letters of Sarah Byng Osborn, 1721-1773, from the collection of the Hon. Mrs. McDonnel. With an introduction and further notes by John McClelland. Stanford University: Stanford University press, 1930. Pp. xix+148.

The interest of Mrs. Osborn's letters is chiefly personal and human, but they are not without value for the history of English social life in the middle of the eighteenth century.

Pinchbeck, Ivy. *Women workers and the Industrial revolution, 1750-1850.* London: Routledge, 1930. Pp. x+342.

Rev. in *TLS,* March 20, 1930, p. 227.

Postgate, Raymond. *"That devil Wilkes."* London: Constable, 1930. Pp. 288.

Rev. by F. W. Hilles in *SRL,* Nov. 29, 1930, p. 384; by A. P. Nicholson in

Saturday review, CXLIX (1930), 456-57; by William Seagle in *Nation,* March 12, 1930, p. 299; in *TLS,* May 15, 1930, pp. 401-02.

Sacret, J. H. "The Restoration government and municipal corporations." *EHR,* XLV (1930), 232-59.

Sanderson, William. *Two hundred years of Freemasonry: a history of the Britannic Lodge No. 33, A. D. 1730-1930.* London: George Kenning, 1930. Pp. 168.

Sherrard, O. A. *A life of John Wilkes.* London: Allen and Unwin, 1930. Pp. 319.

Rev. by M. D. George in *History,* XV (1930), 273-74; by Arthur Waugh in *Fortnightly review,* CXXXIII (1930), 580; in *TLS,* May 15, 1930, pp. 401-02.

Trevelyan, George Macaulay. *England under Queen Anne: Blenheim.* London and New York: Longmans, 1930. Pp. xii+477.

Rev. in *TLS,* Sept. 25, 1930, pp. 741-42.

Trevelyan, Mary Caroline. *William the Third and the defence of Holland,* 1672-4. London: Longmans, 1930. Pp. xiii+359.

Rev. in *TLS,* Oct. 30, 1930, p. 876.

Turberville, A. S. "The House of Lords under Charles II. Part II." *EHR,* XLV (1930), 58-77.

Turner, Edward Raymond. *The cabinet council of England in the seventeenth and eighteenth centuries, 1622-1784.* Volume I. Baltimore: Johns Hopkins press, 1930. Pp. xiii+469.

Rev. by A. L. Cross in *AHR,* XXXVI (1930), 124-26; in *TLS,* Sept. 18, 1930, p. 723.

Verney letters of the eighteenth century from the manuscripts at Claydon House. Edited by Margaret Maria, Lady Verney. London: Ernest Benn, 1930. 2 vols.

Rev. in *TLS,* Nov. 6, 1930, p. 911.

Walters, Thomas B. *Robert Raikes, founder of Sunday schools.* London: Epworth press, 1930. Pp. 128.

Warner, Wellman J. *The Wesleyan movement in the Industrial revolution.* London and New York: Longmans, 1930. Pp. x+299.

Rev. by K. E. Barnhart in *American journal of sociology,* XXXVI (1930), 494-95; by H. Sée in *Revue d'histoire moderne,* mai-juin 1930, pp. 225-26; by Harris E. Starr in *AHR,* XXXVI (1930), 127-28; by Gilbert Thomas in *Nation & Athenæum,* July 26, 1930, p. 540; in *London quarterly review,* July, 1930, pp. 113-15; in *New statesman,* Aug. 23, 1930, pp. 625-26; in *TLS,* May 15, 1930, p. 404.

Wilson, P. W. *William Pitt the younger.* Garden City: Doubleday, Doran and co., 1930.

Rev. by Ford K. Brown in *New York Herald-Tribune Books,* May 18, 1930, p. 7.

III. MOVEMENTS OF IDEAS AND LITERARY FORMS

An Anthology of English poetry: Dryden to Blake. Compiled by Kathleen Campbell. London: Thornton Butterworth, 1930. Pp. 252.

Babcock, R. W. "The attack of the late eighteenth century upon alterations of Shakespeare's plays." *MLN,* XLV (1930), 446-51.

Babcock, R. W. "The attitude toward Shakespeare's learning in the late eighteenth century." *PQ,* IX (1930), 116-22.

Babcock, R. W. "The direct influence of late eighteenth century Shakespeare criticism on Hazlitt and Coleridge." *MLN,* XLV (1930), 377-87.

Babcock, R. W. "The English reaction against Voltaire's criticism of Shakespeare." *SP,* XXVII (1930), 609-25.

Baker, Ernest A. *The history of the English novel.* Volume III, *The later romances and the establishment of realism.* Pp. 278. Volume IV, *Intellectual realism from Richardson to Sterne.* Pp. 297. London: H. F. & G. Witherby, 1929-30.

Rev. by A. Digeon in *RAA,* VII (1930), 445-47 (Vol. III); by J. E. G. de M. in *Contemporary review,* CXXXVII (1930), 793-95; by E. G. Twitchett in *LM,* XXI (1930), 373 (Vol. III); in *TLS,* July 17, 1930, pp. 581-82 (Vols. III, IV).

Batchelor, Grace E. "A study of the manuscripts of theatrical and dramatic interest preserved in the British Museum, 1660-1720" [abstract of dissertation]. *Bulletin of the Institute of historical research,* VIII (1930), 37-38.

Bateson, F. W. *English comic drama, 1700-1750.* Oxford: Clarendon press, 1929. Cf. *PQ,* IX, 171.

Rev. by De Witt C. Croissant in *MLN,* XLV (1930), 406-07; by V. de Sola Pinto in *RES,* VI (1930), 366-68.

Behner, Albert Jacob. "The theology of the early Evangelical movement in England as influenced by contemporary economic and political change." University of Chicago *Abstracts of theses,* Humanistic series, VII (1930), 589-95.

Bernbaum, Ernest. *Guide through the romantic movement.* New York: Thomas Nelson and sons, 1930. Pp. 480.

This book is the result of an attempt to make accessible to students the "facts, judgments, and documents" which recent scholarly study of the romantice movement has brought to light. In the opening chapters on "The pre-romantic movement" and on William Blake—the only portions of the volume that fall within the scope of this bibliography—the effort to condense in a few pages the best contemporary knowledge and opinion is on the whole unusually successful. The chief exception I have noted is the parargraph on Shaftesbury (p. 20), which not only gives to that writer a position of primacy in the development of "sentimental" ethics which I cannot believe he deserves, but describes his ideas in a way that is likely to be somewhat misleading to the students for whom the volume is intended. Thus while texts could no doubt be found in the *Characteristics* to support the statement that for Shaftesbury "man instinctively and without instruction or discipline had a 'moral sense' which recognized virtuous conduct and delighted in it" and that in his view nothing "except 'force of custom and education in opposition to Nature' stood in the way of morality," one would like to have the formula qualified by a recognition of those other passages in the same work which insist on the necessity of discipline, decorum, and self-control.

Bonar, James. *Moral sense.* London: Allen and Unwin; New York: Macmillan, 1930. Pp. 304.

Rev. in *TLS,* Oct. 9, 1930, p. 800.

An exposition and criticism of the views of that school of eighteenth-century British moralists "which derived our moral perceptions from a special Moral Sense, interpreted on the analogy of the Five Bodily Senses." The twelve chapters discuss in an agreeable though at times somewhat perfunctory way the psychological and ethical ideas of Shaftesbury and his critics (especially Mandeville, Berkeley, and Butler), of Hutcheson, of the "minor critics of the theory" in the middle of the century (Brown and Price), of Hume, of Adam Smith, and of Kant. Except for a brief passage (pp. 27-30) on Shaftesbury's relations to Cudworth, Spinoza, and Hobbes, Bonar neglects the problem of the origins of the school almost entirely, and in general he is indifferent to various aspects of the subject which would interest the historian of "ideas" as distinguished from the professional student of moral philosophy.

Bosker, A. *Literary criticism in the age of Johnson.* Groningen: J. B. Wolters, 1930. Pp. ix+294.

The announced subject of this book is the conflict, in English literary criticism of the middle eighteenth century, between "rationalism" and the various doctrines that undermined its sway. After a brief Introduction on "The chief critical tendencies of the seventeenth and the beginning of the eighteenth century," Bosker develops his theme in four "Parts": I, "Some general aspects of literary criticism during the age of Johnson"; II, "The believers in the doctrine of reason" (Johnson, Fielding, Sterne, Kames, etc.); III, "The champions of taste" (Goldsmith, Reynolds, Shenstone, Blair, Beattie); and IV, "The revolt against the supremacy of reason" (Joseph Warton, Thomas Warton, Young, Hurd, Twining, Hoole, etc.).

For the specialist in the eighteenth century the chief value of Bosker's work will undoubtedly lie in its illustrative quotations, particularly those from such relatively unfamiliar writers as Stockdale, Pye, Harris, Twining, Hoole, Belsham, Hayley, Aikin, and Pinkerton. On the doctrines of the more important critics he has little to say that is either penetrating or new; his chapters on Johnson, Fielding, Reynolds, the Wartons, and Young, for example, are, in point of knowledge and insight, hardly above the capacity of a beginning graduate student. In his interpretation of the general movement of literary theory in the period he does, it is true, display occasionally a certain vigor of mind and a capacity for large views; but the formulae he proposes seem to me to give a distorted and in the main unreal impression of the phenomena with which his book attempts to deal.

The difficulty is that he has come to the study of mid-eighteenth-century criticism with a set of prepossessions about the ruling aesthetic philosophy of the immediately preceding period which, though still widely held, are nevertheless open to serious doubt. The basis of "neo-classicism," he implies more than once (e.g., pp. 43-44, 63-64), was the acceptance, in a thoroughly authoritarian spirit, of "Aristotelian and Horatian precepts"; and its ideal both for the writer and his public was that of "unimpassioned reason" and "the repression of the higher qualities of poetry: emotion and imagination" (p. 24; cf. also p. 34). Hence his disposition to interpret as signs of an essentially "new" attitude those texts in Johnson, Fielding, Kames, and many others in the middle of the century which find the source of literary rules in the "natural and invariable constitution of things" rather than in the "arbitrary edicts of legislators, authorised only by themselves." Hence the importance he gives to those pages in Goldsmith, Shenstone, Blair, the Wartons, Hurd, and others which recognize the necessity of emotion and imagination in the genius of poets and in the taste of their readers: the supposed revolt of these men against the tyranny of "unimpassioned reason" is for him their most significant contribution to the change in literary ideas that was taking place in the age of Johnson.

This is not a new interpretation, and properly qualified it has, of course, a certain validity. The tendency to regard the traditional rules as partaking more of "custom" than of "nature" was undoubtedly more marked in the middle and later eighteenth century than it had been in the seventeenth; and there can be no question that a greater value was commonly attached to "sensibility," both in genius and in taste, after 1740 than had been the case before. But it is only on the basis of an over-simplified and even distorted conception of earlier "neo-classical" doctrine that these changes can be considered revolutionary in any real sense. For in the first place, however great may have been the veneration of writers like Rapin or Pope for the precepts of Aristotle and Horace, their adherence to them was always justified on rationalistic and not on authoritarian grounds. "The Rules laid down by those great Criticks are not to be valu'd, because they are given by *Aristotle, Horace,* &c. but because they are in Nature and in Truth": this formula of Oldmixon's (*An essay on criticism* [London, 1728], p. 3) expressed succinctly a point of view that would have been accepted by all the representative and influential theorists of the later seventeenth and early eighteenth centuries. And in the second place, though it is of course true that these men continually insisted on the importance of "reason" and "judgment" in the creation and valuation of poetry, it is a serious misunderstanding of their meaning to suppose that they failed to recognize the necessity of feeling—controlled feeling—and of imagination—controlled imagination—in the equipment of writers and readers. In aesthetics no more than in ethics was the ideal of the neo-classical period a Stoic ideal of "unimpassioned reason." What was meant in fact by "reason," in the normal and characteristic uses of the word, was something quite different from the antithesis of intellect and feeling which seems to Bosker the most significant aspect of the prevailing doctrine. Much of the time at least the term derived its connotations from the belief, which was of course one of the chief ruling assumptions of the period, that the business of the poet is to express and to appeal to "the general sentiments of men." Not "the supremacy of the unimpassioned understanding" (p. 34) but the primacy of the universal element in human nature was the distinctive trait of the rationalism which dominated criticism during the seventeenth century and the greater part of the eighteenth.

To analyze the complex manifestations and implications of this idea and to make clear the causes and progress of the revolt against it which set in around 1750 should be one of the main tasks of the historian of aesthetic theory in this period. Bosker is not unaware of the presence of a uniformitarian strain in neo-classic criticism (see, for example, pp.62-70, 75-85, 134, 154, 161-62), and he touches here and there in the latter part of his book on a few phases of the opposition to it (e.g., pp. 194-95, 221-22, 255-59). But his treatment is fragmentary and inadequate, and he nowhere shows any realization of its major importance among the developments he is attempting to study.

Bréhier, Emile. *Histoire de la philosophie.* Tome II, *La philoso-*

phie moderne. I, "Le dix-septième siècle." II, "Le dix-huitième siècle." Paris: Alcan, 1929-30. Pp. 576.

Rev. by Maurice Halbwachs in *RC,* LXIV (1930), 353-55; by Albert Mathiez in *Annales historiques de la Révolution française,* VII (1930), 282-83.

These two fascicules of Bréhier's remarkable general history of European philosophy contain chapters on the following topics: the general characteristics of the seventeenth century; Bacon and experimental philosophy; Descartes and Cartesianism; Pascal; Hobbes; Spinoza; Malebranche; Leibniz; Locke; Bayle and Fontenelle; the masters of the eighteenth century: Newton and Locke; deism and the ethics of sentiment; Christian Wolff; Vico; Montesquieu; Condillac; Hume and Adam Smith; Vauvenargues; theories of physical nature; Voltaire; Rousseau; sentimentalism and pre-romanticism; the persistence of rationalism; Kant and the critical philosophy. Each chapter is followed by a selective bibliography of editions and modern studies.

Broadside ballads of the Restoration period from the Jersey collection known as the Osterley Park ballads. With an introduction and notes by F. Burlington Fawcett. London: John Lane, 1930. Pp. xxvii+248.

Rev. in *TLS,* Jan. 22, 1931, pp. 49-50.

Caskey, J. Homer. "Truth and fiction in eighteenth-century newspapers." *MLN,* XLV (1930), 438-40.

Calls attention to interesting passages in Foote's *Bankrupt* and Murphy's *News from Parnassus.*

A Century of broadside elegies. Photographically reproduced and edited with an introduction and notes by John W. Draper. London: Ingpen and Grant, 1928. Cf. *PQ,* VIII, 173; IX, 172.

Rev. by H. Winifred Husbands in *MLR,* XXV (1930), 353-54.

Chan, Shau Yi. "The influence of China on English culture during the eighteenth century." University of Chicago *Abstracts of theses,* Humanistic series, VII (1930), 537-41.

Clark, Kenneth. *The Gothic revival, an essay in the history of taste.* London: Constable, 1928. Cf. *PQ,* VIII, 173; IX, 172.

Rev. by Bernhard Fehr in *Beiblatt,* XLI (1930), 264-67; by P. Yvon in *Les langues modernes,* XXVII (1929), 546-50; XXVIII (1930), 108-13.

Clark, William S. and Kathleen M. Lynch. "The Platonic element in the Restoration heroic play." *PMLA,* XLV (1930), 623-26.

Cf. *PMLA,* XLIV (1929), 456-71, and *PQ,* IX, 178.

Cole, F. J. *Early theories of sexual generation.* Oxford: Clarendon press, 1930. Pp. x+230.

Rev. in *TLS,* Jan. 15, 1931, p. 36.

Conway letters. The correspondence of Anne, Viscountess Conway, Henry More, and their friends, 1642-1684. Collected from manuscript sources & edited with a biographical account by

Marjorie Hope Nicolson. New Haven: Yale University press; London: Humphrey Milford, Oxford University press, 1930. Pp. xxvii+517.

Rev. in *TLS*, Jan. 29, 1931, p. 71.

This volume of letters is undoubtedly one of the most interesting publications of the year, and its appeal extends beyond the group of serious students of the seventeenth century. In the present collection the central figures are the learned, eager, and long suffering Anne, Viscountess Conway, and Henry More, Platonist philosopher and divine of Cambridge, who for many years was her devoted correspondent and friend; but numerous letters have been included from other members of the circle of which these two were the center, and they make up a colorful background for the main study. It is due, however, only to the careful selection and neat arrangement of these by the editor that a unified and progressive narrative has been achieved; from the wealth of manuscript materials which her ingenious curiosity and tireless industry have uncovered, she has picked out only those which would give the completest possible picture of this friendship within practicable limits. This aim has, of course, necessitated the omission of a great number of letters which, to the student of the intellectual temper of the times, would have been more interesting than many which have been included; but one must agree that the sacrifice was legitimate and necessary for purely artistic reasons, and the present loss may be philosophically accepted since Miss Nicolson has promised to include the omitted letters in a later study.

Even with the care which has been shown in the arrangement and ordering of the letters, however, much of the significance of these documents would have been lost to the modern reader were it not for the useful explanatory notes throughout the volume, and especially for the admirably written essays that precede each of the eight sections into which the letters are divided. In these Miss Nicolson has filled up gaps which the letters leave open, given the important features of each section their proper emphasis, provided brief studies of the characters who figure in the various episodes, suggested the philosophic importance of certain of the developments, and in general dramatized the facts in the letters which follow into a fascinating and moving story. With much tact and skill she has described the character and significance of some very important and even strange and romantic figures from this century of great changes and striking paradoxes. It is this feature, in fact, which most impresses the reader of the volume—the clear-cut impressions he carries with him of such people, to mention only a few, as Sir Kenelm Digby, Greatrakes, Van Helmont, the Quakers, More, and the heroic Viscountess.

It would have been quite impossible for any one who had studied these letters to have treated the personality of Lady Conway with anything short of profound sympathy and admiration. In harmony with this characterization, Miss Nicolson has elevated all the other figures to the same high plane. The reader leaves the book with the feeling of having had a privileged glimpse into the lives and thoughts of men and women more intense and noble and heroic than, unfortunately, are likely to be met with again, and he is grateful to capricious fate that once allowed such a group to assemble intimately together, and that preserved such generous traces of its activities. The cautious reader may indeed wonder, on occasion, whether he has not allowed himself to be carried too far, but he merely admits in that case that Miss Nicolson has performed her task with cleverness and vigor. Under the circumstances only a Momus would suggest that in the somewhat idealized and glorified portraits sketched for us by the editor we see perhaps only too clearly—to use the phrase which she applies to the characters in More's *Divine dialogues*—the superiority of art over life.—M. E. PRIOR.

Dampier-Whetham, William Cecil Dampier. *A history of science and its relations with philosophy and religion.* Cambridge: Cambridge University press, 1930. Pp. xxi+514.

Rev. by J. E. G. deM. in *Contemporary review,* CXXXVII (1930), 801-04; in *Saturday review,* CXLIX (1930), 231-32; in *TLS,* June 12, 1930, p. 490.

Dennis, Leah A. "The attitude of the eighteenth century toward the medieval romances." *Abstracts of dissertations, Stanford University,* III (1929), 68-72.

"Dictionary of national biography." *Bulletin of the Institute of historical research,* VII (1930), 193-94; VIII (1930), 41-43.

Additions or corrections to the articles on Defoe, Nathaniel Mist, and James Boswell.

Dobrée, Bonamy. *Restoration tragedy, 1660-1720.* Oxford: Clarendon press, 1929. Cf. *PQ,* IX, 173.

Rev. by L. Cazamian in *RAA,* VII (1930), 444; by W. S. Clark in *MLN,* XLVI (1931), 202-04; by Eduard Eckhardt in *Beiblatt,* XLI (1930), 197-202.

Draper, John W. *The funeral elegy and the rise of English romanticism.* New York: New York University press, 1929. Cf. *PQ,* IX, 173-76.

Rev. by Carroll D. Clark in *American journal of sociology,* XXXV (1930), 672-73; by Paul Dottin in *RELV,* XLVII (1930), 115-16; by Erna Fischer in *Beiblatt,* XLI (1930), 296-301; by H. Winifred Husbands in *MLR,* XXV (1930), 351-53; by William O. Raymond in *JEGP,* XXX (1931), 122-26; by G. C. M. S[mith] in *EHR,* XLV (1930), 503-04.

F., S. *"The Daily universal register."* *N & Q,* CLVIII (1930), 219.

Possible origin of the first title of the London *Times.*

Fairchild, Hoxie Neale. *The Noble savage: a study in romantic naturalism.* New York: Columbia University press, 1928. Cf. *PQ,* VIII, 174-75; IX, 176.

Rev. by Camillo von Klenze in *Archiv,* CLVII (1930), 93-98.

Flasdieck, Hermann M. *Der Gedanke einer englischen Sprachakademie in Vergangenheit und Gegenwart.* Jena: Verlag der Frommannschen Buchhandlung, 1928. Cf. *PQ,* VIII, 175.

Rev. by P. Gurrey in *MLR,* XXV (1930), 356-58; by Émile Pons in *RAA,* VII (1930), 347-49.

Freund, Michael. *Die Idee der Toleranz im England der grossen Revolution.* Halle: Niemeyer, 1927. Cf. *PQ,* IX, 176.

Rev. by Harris Fletcher in *JEGP,* XXVIII (1929), 574-77; by Ernest W. Nelson in *Philosophical review,* XXXVIII (1929), 84-88; by Alfred Stern in *Litteris,* VII (1930), 37-41.

Funke, Otto. *Zum Weltsprachenproblem in England in 17. Jahrhundert: G. Dalgarno's "Ars signorum" (1661) und J. Wil-*

kins' "Essay towards a real character and a philosophical language" (1668). Heidelberg: Carl Winter, 1929. Pp. 163.

Rev. by O. Jespersen in *Beiblatt*, XLI (1930), 65-69.

Gaddis, Merrill Elmer. "Christian perfectionism in America." University of Chicago *Abstracts of theses*, Humanistic series, VII (1930), 625-33.

The thesis of which this is a summary contains sections on the English and continental background.

Graham, Walter. *English literary periodicals*. New York: Thomas Nelson & sons, 1930. Pp. 424.

A valuable survey of the whole field, which brings together more precise and verified information than any earlier work on the subject. I hope to be able to speak of the book at greater length elsewhere.

Granger, Frank. "'Magnificance' as a term of art." *TLS*, Aug. 14, 1930, p. 653.

Suggestive notes on the use of the term in the seventeenth and early eighteenth centuries.

Grierson, H. J. C. *Cross currents in English literature of the XVIIth century*. London: Chatto & Windus, 1929. Cf. *PQ*, IX, 176.

Rev. by Marjorie Nicolson in *MLN*, XLVI (1931), 205-06; by Mario Praz in *English studies*, XII (1930), 117-19.

Gunther, R. T. *Early science in Oxford*. Volume VI, *The life and work of Robert Hooke*, Part I. Pp. xxiv+396. Volume VII, *The life and work of Robert Hooke*, Part II. Pp. vii+397-806. Magdalen College, Oxford: The author, 1930.

Rev. in *TLS*, Apr. 10, 1930, p. 313.

Habel, Ursula. *Die Nachwirkung des picaresken Romans in England (von Nash bis Fielding und Smollett)*. Breslau: Priebatsch, 1930. Pp. 77.

Havens, Raymond D. "More eighteenth-century sonnets." *MLN*, XLV (1930), 77-84.

Harwood, Dix. *Love for animals and how it developed in Great Britain*. New York: [Privately printed], 1928. Pp. 381.

Heidler, Joseph Bunn. *The history, from 1700 to 1800, of English criticism of prose fiction*. Urbana, Illinois, 1928. Cf. *PQ*, IX, 177.

Rev. by A. Koszul in *RC*, LXIV (1930), 178-79; by Herbert Schöffler in *Beiblatt*, XLI (1930), 194-96.

Heinrich, Joachim. *Die Frauenfrage bei Steele und Addison*. Leipzig: Mayer & Müller, 1930. Pp. xv+261. ("Palaestra," 168.)

Rev. by H. Jantzen in *Beiblatt,* XLI (1930), 340-42; by Paul Meissner in *Archiv,* CLVIII (1930), 286-88.

Heinrich has attempted to present the views of Steele and Addison concerning women in the light of seventeenth-century opinion. The first half of his book is a survey of this opinion under three heads: woman in general, the education of women, and the problem of marriage. The second half is an analysis of Steele's and Addison's ideas with reference to their background, under the following headings: woman as reader; woman as authoress; woman in society, courtship, and marriage. The contribution of Steele and Addison to the woman question is the subject of the brief conclusion.

In view of the aim and scope of Heinrich's study, his accomplishment is disappointing. No hitherto unknown documents have been brought to light. The imposing list of seventeenth-century texts tabulated as the basis of the opening discussion of the background proves to be mainly an enumeration of titles obtainable from the *Term catalogues,* Hazlitt's *Hand-book* and the British Museum *Catalogue.* As many of these texts were unfortunately not accessible to Heinrich, who had to infer their contents from titles or from secondhand information, they contribute little solid substance to his synthesis of seventeenth-century opinion. Not only is no important new document included, but the well-known writings of Halifax, Mary Astell, Defoe, Hickes, and others are not presented with fresh perspective. The extensive bibliography of women authors in Chapter VI does not go beyond Myra Reynolds' valuable work, *The learned lady in England, 1650-1760* (1920).

The feminist views of Steele and Addison have been gleaned, thoroughly and successfully, from the *Tatler, Spectator,* and *Guardian* papers, nearly half of which, Heinrich estimates, deal with women (420 out of 1081). Conspicuous omissions, however, are the first expression of Steele's views in *The Christian hero* and his delightful application of them in the heroines of his plays—Lady Sharlot, Biddy Tipkin, and Indiana. During the entire twenty years of his career Steele wrote unremittingly on this problem (two-thirds of the papers considered are his). Heinrich's title puts undue emphasis on Addison, who, like Budgell, Hughes, and other contributors to the periodicals, followed in his papers on women the editorial policy of Steele. The analysis of this body of opinion presents clearly, but without new accents, Steele's well-known position: his genuine respect for woman and his efforts to improve her manners and morals; and on the question of social reform, his extreme conservatism in limiting her interests to the home, her education to conventional ethical instruction, and her position in marriage to one of dignified subordination.

The interpretation of these ideas—which the reader hopes will be made by reference to the prevailing points of view of the period—is superficial. Heinrich's very general conclusion is that Steele and Addison fuse the liberal feminist ideals of the Renaissance with the more repressive ideals of the Reformation. Immediate and relevant questions on which we should like enlightenment are not considered at all: What intellectual or social animus dominates Steele's reform? How may his conservatism regarding education for women be explained? From what intellectual, social, or religious ideals is his conception of marriage and family life derived? How far was he aware of contemporary reformers who in the spirit of rationalism, often specifically Cartesian, advocated for woman a liberal education, equality in marriage with her husband, and, if unmarried, economic independence?

The relation of Steele's reforming ideas to the feminist movement of the eighteenth century—their sources in earlier social, economic, and cultural currents and their contribution to the progress of the movement—is a question well worth investigation. But a more penetrating analysis of their seventeenth- and eighteenth-century background than Heinrich has made is required to explain Steele's innovations and his conservatism. The Puritan ideal of a "family hierarchy" recently studied by L. L. Schücking may explain the complex of ideas involved in the doctrine of woman's inferiority and her legal and social subordination. Changes in the economic structure of society, the influence of French feminist opinion at the close of the seventeenth century, the rôle of the literature of gallantry, the mingled spirit of rationalism and empiricism underlying the proposed innovations—all these matters must be taken into account. And only a synthesis of these various elements will give us the needed perspective for an understanding of Steele's ideas.—RAE BLANCHARD.

Herrick, Marvin Theodore. *The Poetics of Aristotle in England.* New Haven: Yale University press; London: Humphrey Milford, Oxford University press, 1930. Pp. 196. ("Cornell studies in English," XVII.)

Hillhouse, James T. *The Grub-street journal.* Durham, N.C.: Duke University press, 1928. Cf. *PQ,* VIII, 176; IX, 177.

Rev. by R. F. Jones in *JEGP,* XXIX (1930), 311-12.

Hoevel, Ernst Felix. *Die soziale Herkunft der neuzeitlichen Dialekt-literatur Englands.* Leipzig: Tauchnitz, 1929. Pp. 67.

Rev. by Harold Whitehall in *PQ,* IX (1930), 219-20.

Horner, Joyce M. *The English women novelists and their connection with the feminist movement (1688-1797).* Northampton, Mass., 1929-30. Pp. xiii+152. ("Smith College studies in modern languages," Vol. XI, Nos. 1-3.)

Huscher, Herbert. *Über Eigenart und Ursprung des englischen Naturgefühls.* Leipzig: Bernhard Tauchnitz, 1929. Pp. 39.

Rev. by A. C. E. Vechtman-Veth in *English studies,* XII (1930), 199-200.

Jones, Richard F. "Science and English prose style in the third quarter of the seventeenth century." *PMLA,* XLV (1930), 977-1009.

The outlines of the history of seventeenth-century prose style are not obscure. At the beginning of the century, or a little before, the retarded rationalism of the Renaissance won its first *general* success in the victory of the Anti-Ciceronian movement of Muret, Lipsius, Montaigne, and Bacon. The program of this movement included the rehabilitation in literary favor of the Anti-Ciceronians of the first century, especially Seneca and Tacitus; and the form and structure of seventeenth-century English prose is largely determined by the imitation of these two authors and of Lipsius and Montaigne, their modern disciples, though, of course, it derives qualities of its own from the fantastic genius of the age that produced it. Then, about the middle of the century, a movement of clarification and "enlightenment" began to be self-conscious, working, however, within the limits set by the Anti-Ciceronian model, now so well established. In this several elements combined to a single end: the mathematical genius of the Cartesian philosophy, the ideal of *mondanité* emerging in French civilized society, and the "practical" aims of Baconian science.

It is with the later of these two movements that Jones is concerned, and specifically with the part that science played in it. The story he tells is not unfamiliar. It is chiefly an account of the successful attempts of the Royal Society, through its spokesman, Thomas Sprat, to make the prose of scientific study as bare of imagination, reverie, and eloquence as it is possible for written discourse to be. But if the story is not new, Jones has enriched it with new detail, longer quotations, and revealing illustrations. Best of all there is his illustration by parallel passages of Glanvill's re-writing (in 1676) of his *Vanity of dogmatizing,* "so alter'd as to be in a manner new." This is delightfully illuminating. The citations from the earlier work show that Glanvill, like so many others, was then trying awkwardly and amusingly to shoot in Browne's bow. The parallels from the later version reveal and justify the new vision of a clear, lighted prose. They give the reader the same impression that he may receive when he walks from dark vaulted halls into the Library of Trinity College, which is perhaps a work of Wren's.

Jones's essay is a valuable marshalling of facts; but his readers are likely to be puzzled by his attempts to place them in their relations with the general movement of seventeenth-century prose. His statements on this subject are uncertain and even inconsistent; but his conclusion seems to be that Anti-Ciceronian prose and the bare prose of scientific study run parallel throughout the century unaware of each other's existence and character. The real history is somewhat more complex, but also more understandable. The scientific cult of unrhetorical speech from 1650 onward is a second, later stage in the history of the same naturalistic tendency that shows itself in the Anti-Ciceronian victory at the end of the preceding century. It did not create a new, a rival style to the Anti-Ciceronian; it only introduced certain changes within the *cadres* of that style. It was an attempt, a successful attempt, to take the heat and fever out of the imaginative naturalism of Montaigne, Bacon, and Browne, to prune their conceits and metaphors, to restrain the wild motions of their eloquence. But it did not change the form and structure of the prose of its time. That this is the relation between the Anti-Ciceronians and the clarifiers is made clear and explicit in contemporary French criticism; but it is equally clear in English practice. Glanvill's later style is a *revision* of Browne's; and Sprat's easy periods have almost exactly the form of Bacon's harder and knottier ones. Seventeenth-century prose is and remains Anti-Ciceronian and predominantly Senecan; and Shaftesbury's statement, in the last years of the century, that English ears were so accustomed to the Senecan pace in prose that they were scarcely aware of any other is borne out by the facts.—MORRIS W. CROLL.

I add brief notes on two points not discussed in the preceding review.

1. In describing the program of stylistic reform urged by Sprat and other members of the Royal Society, Jones rightly emphasizes the strong anti-rhetorical bias of these men, their antipathy to "Tropes and Figures," their insistence on "a close, naked, natural way of speaking. . . . bringing all things as near the Mathematical plainness, as they can." But he does not, I think, make sufficiently clear that in these and similar declarations they were recommending a special type of style suitable for use primarily in "philosophical," that is in scientific works, and were not attempting to impose a universal model of style to be followed in all kinds of writing. A more complete analysis of their theory would make clear the important rôle played in their thinking by the idea, so prominent in ancient rhetoric, that different audiences and different subjects require different manners of treatment. It was on this idea that they normally based their pleas for unmetaphorical plainness in "philosophical" exposition (see, for example, Bacon, *Advancement of learning,* in *Works,* ed. Spedding, Ellis, and Heath [Boston, 1860-64], VI, 120-21; Boyle, *Works* [London, 1772], I, 304-05, 462; II, 254), and in so doing they were following a tradition as old as Aristotle. But it is a mistake to imply, as Jones seems to do, that they also demanded the same extreme bareness in all other forms of prose writing. Sprat certainly did not, as appears from what he has to say of the value of "experiments" in providing writers with "beautiful *Conceptions,* and inimitable *Similitudes,*" "an inexhaustible Treasure of *Fancy* and *Invention* (*History of the Royal Society* [London, 1722], pp. 413, 416-17); and as for Boyle, his comments on the "eloquence" of the Scriptures (*Works* [London, 1772], II, 301-02), as well as some of his remarks on his own manner of writing (e.g., *ibid.,* I, 462; II, 254), reflect a conception of style that can by no means be confined within the narrow limits of the official program of the Royal Society.

2. In his attempt to show that the development with which he is concerned

had no real connection with the earlier Anti-Ciceronian movement, Jones remarks (p. 1004): "The Anti-Ciceronian style found its theories in Aristotle. . . .; science renounced Aristotle and all his works. . . ." To realize how imperfectly this generalization fits the facts one need only recall that an important element in Bacon's discussion of rhetoric springs directly from Aristotle (see *Works* [Boston, 1860-64], VI, 301; IX, 131, 134, 135ff, 219; and cf. Croll, *PMLA,* XXXIX [1924], 282); that Hobbes, whose plea for a "plain" style is quoted by Jones (pp. 981-82), wrote *The whole art of rhetorick in English, being a translation of Aristotle's*; that Cowley mentioned Aristotle's *Rhetoric* as an authority, along with the works of Cicero and Quintilian, in his *Proposition for the advancement of experimental philosophy*; and that Glanvill, in spite of his many attacks on Aristotle, announced in *Plus ultra* (1668) that he was quite willing "to give chearful Acknowledgements to his *Rhetorick, History of Animals,* and *Mechanicks,* and could wish that these were more studied by his *devoted* Admirers" (sig. [B5]).

Kittredge, George Lyman. *Witchcraft in Old and New England.* Cambridge [Mass.]: Harvard University press, 1929. Cf. *PQ,* IX, 177.

Rev. by Lois Oliphant Gibbons in *JEGP,* XXX (1931), 126-28; in *TLS,* Oct. 23, 1930, p. 850.

Lalande, André. *Les théories de l'induction et de l'expérimentation.* Paris: Boivin & cie, 1929. Pp. vi+287.

Rev. by P. P. Wiener in *Journal of philosophy,* XXVII (1930), 668-69.

Lawrence, W. J. "Oxford Restoration prologues." *TLS,* Jan. 16, 1930, p. 43.

Leonard, S. A. *The doctrine of correctness in English usage, 1700-1800.* Madison, 1929. Cf. *PQ,* IX, 177.

Rev. by Paul Dottin in *RELV,* XLVII (1930), 403; by Bert Emsley in *PQ,* IX (1930), 222-24; by H. M. Flasdieck in *Beiblatt,* XLI (1930), 372-76.

McGrew, J. Fred. "A bibliography of the works on speech composition in England during the 16th and 17th centuries." *Quarterly journal of speech,* XV (1929), 381-412.

A very useful bibliographical account of books on rhetoric and oratory published between 1479 and 1700.

McMahon, A. Philip. "Seven questions on Aristotelian definitions of tragedy and comedy." *Harvard studies in classical philology,* XL (1929), 97-198.

The last two "questions" concern the seventeenth and eighteenth centuries.

Martin, Abbott C. "The love of solitude in eighteenth century poetry." *South Atlantic quarterly,* XXIX (1930), 48-59.

Maxfield, Ezra Kempton. "The Quakers in English stage plays before 1800." *PMLA,* XLV (1930), 256-73.

Comment by J. W. Bowyer, *ibid.,* XLV (1930), 957-58.

Metzger, Hélène. *Newton, Stahl, Boerhave et la doctrine chimique.* Paris: Alcan, 1930.

Rev. by Edmond Goblot in *Revue philosophique,* CXI (1931), 134-35.

Mezger, Fritz. *Des Ire in der englischen Literatur bis zum Anfang des 19. Jahrhunderts.* Leipzig: Mayer & Müller, 1929. Pp. viii+214.

Nethercot, Arthur H. "The reputation of native versus foreign 'metaphysical poets' in England." *MLR,* XXV (1930), 152-64.

Considers Marino, Du Bartas, and Góngora.

Newlin, Claude M. "The theatre and the apprentices." *MLN,* XLV (1930), 451-54.

Olschki, Leonardo. "Der geometrische Geist in Literatur und Kunst." *DVLG,* VIII (1930), 516-38.

Papenheim, Wilhelm. *Die Charakterschilderungen in "Tatler," "Spectator," und "Guardian": ihr Verhältnis zu Theophrast, La Bruyère und den englischen character-writers des 17. Jahrhunderts.* Leipzig: Bernhard Tauchnitz, 1930. Pp. 112.

Pawson, G. P. H. *The Cambridge Platonists and their place in religious thought.* London: S. P. C. K., 1930. Pp. 95.

Rev. in *TLS,* March 27, 1930, p. 278.

The Pepys ballads. Edited by Hyder Edward Rollins. Volume III, 1666-1688. Numbers 91-163. Volume IV, 1688-1689. Numbers 164-253. Cambridge, Mass.: Harvard University press, 1930. Pp. xvii+338; xv+353.

Rev. by G. Thorn-Drury in *MLR,* XXV (1930), 198-201; in *TLS,* June 12, 1930, p. 493; Jan. 22, 1931, pp. 49-50.

Perdeck, Albert Adam. *Theology in Augustan literature, being an inquiry into the extent of orthodox Protestant thought in the literature of Pope's time.* Groningen: J. B. Wolters, 1928. Pp. 106.

Unimportant.
Rev. by H. O. Wilde in *Beiblatt,* XLI (1930), 268-69.

Pützer, F. *Prediger des englischen Barock, stilistisch untersucht.* Phil. Diss. Bonn, 1929. Pp. 133.

Rev. by F. Asanger in *Literaturblatt für germ. und rom. Phil.,* LI (1930), cols. 26-27.

Quintana, Ricardo. "Notes on English educational opinion during the seventeenth century." *SP,* XXVII (1930), 265-92.

The purpose of this article is "to show in some detail the nature of English educational opinion during the seventeenth century, and thereby to emphasize the vigorous character of this opinion and its continuity." The writer suggests briefly the change in tone that followed the early humanistic attacks on prevailing methods of education, the growing signs of discontent voiced in England during the late years of the sixteenth and the early years of the seventeenth centuries with current educational practices, the importance in this development of certain views not primarily directed toward educational problems, and the influence of "Baconian naturalism" on educational theory in England.

This statement of the aims of the article, however, conceals its most serious defect; for within this framework Quintana introduces, in roughly chronological order, but in logically bewildering juxtaposition, a number of interesting texts reflecting various strains of thought and often quite opposed assumptions. For example, he quotes several passages illustrating the disparagement of excessive study of books which formed a part of the attack on pedantry carried on by writers who preached the ideal of the *honnête homme.* But he deals with them separately at different points in his plan, and he fails to make entirely clear just how they are peculiarly a part of the argument which they are designed to illustrate (e.g., the quotations on pp. 266-67 [Peacham], 272 [Feltham], 286-87 [Osborn]). The fault, moreover, is not one of careless organization; it is a failure to distinguish the exact significance and direction of the passages used. We are told, for instance, that in "leaving John Webster for Francis Osborn. . . ., one leaves a writer of fanatical tendencies for one who is eminently sane and well balanced" (p. 286). But the essential difference is far more basic than this; one actually leaves a particular ideal of education for an entirely different ideal, and this is just the point that Quintana fails to bring out. Similarly, we are told that "John Hall . . . . takes up a position beside Feltham in the matter of useful as against useless study and writing" (p. 273). But again, what Hall meant by useful study would scarcely accord with the views of Feltham, who held that "company and conversation are the best instructors for a noble behavior." The difference between the two becomes much clearer when one considers a brisk pamphlet of Hall's, which Quintana does not refer to in his section on the influence of Bacon, *An humble motion to the Parliament of England concerning the advancement of learning* (1649); in this work Hall condemns the education in use and urges, as did Webster later, the introduction of experimental and scientific studies after the plan of Bacon. The argument that study should be directed toward the uses of life could be employed to defend either the social ideal of the gentleman or the advancement of the practical sciences; the fact that both Feltham and Hall insist on useful knowledge is therefore no more than a verbal similarity.

In consequence of his plan of procedure, Quintana fails to bring out the force of some of his most interesting observations. In section II, which deals with writers whose "*obiter dicta* were calculated to add great resonance to the charges levelled both by humanistic writers and Baconians against useless scholastic endeavour and arid learning" (p. 268), he quotes passages, charged with Pyrrhonism, from Sir John Davies and Fulke Greville. Now, the importance of Renaissance skepticism can scarcely be overestimated in any study of seventeenth-century theories of education, especially when one considers the prominence of the traditional Pyrrhonistic arguments in the "Idols" of Bacon's *Novum organum* or in the opening statements of Descartes' *Discours* and *Méditations,* all works which exercised a profound influence on many aspects of the thought of their time. But though Quintana points out that this awareness of the limitations of human knowledge led to a concern with "what sort of knowledge is to be received" (p. 271), he makes no effort to show how the skeptical assumptions supported new and different views concerning the aims and possible limits of education; and by immediately following these remarks with texts reflecting very different assumptions and tendencies from such writers as Joseph Hall, Feltham, and Lord North, he completely conceals a very significant suggestion.—M.E. PRIOR.

Reiter, Hildegard. *William Hogarth und die Literatur seiner Zeit: ein Vergleich zwischen malerischer und dichterischer Gestaltung.* Breslau: Priebatsch, 1930. Pp. 105.

Restoration verse, 1660-1715. Chosen and edited by William Kerr. London: Macmillan, 1930. Pp. xxvi+439.

Rev. in *TLS,* Dec. 25, 1930, p. 1098.

This anthology reprints 420 poems from about one hundred writers, and since many of these are little known, the book has a value for students of the period which such collections usually lack. Along with a number of doubtful statements (as that the young men of William III's reign "ignored Milton, just as the young men of to-day ignore Tennyson" [p. xiii]), the Introduction contains some interesting and provocative writing about the general character and temper of the Restoration period. Not so much can be said for most of the notes.

Salvatorelli, L. *From Locke to Reitzenstein: the historical investigation of the origins of Christianity.* Cambridge [Mass.]: Harvard University press, 1930.

Sanford, William P. "English rhetoric reverts to classicism, 1600-1650." *Quarterly journal of speech,* XV (1929), 503-25.

A valuable study of the influence of classical rhetorical theory in England in the first half of the seventeenth century.

Saupe, G. *Die Sophonisbetragödien in der englischen Literatur des 17. und 18. Jahrhunderts.* Phil. Diss. Halle-Wittenberg, 1929. Pp. 78.

Schmid, Paul. "William Hogarth als Maler der Aufklärung und Begründer des englischen Kunstgeschmacks." *Neuphilologische Monatsschrift,* I (1930), 345-61.

Smith, Preserved. *A history of modern culture.* Volume I, *The great renewal, 1543-1687.* New York: Henry Holt and company; London: Routledge, [1930]. Pp. xi+672.

Rev. by David S. Muzzey in *Political science quarterly,* XLV (1930), 633-35; by J. H. Randall, Jr. in *JMH,* II (1930), 648-52; by James Harvey Robinson in *AHR,* XXXV (1930), 840-42; in *TLS,* Oct. 16, 1930, p. 824.

Preserved Smith's subject in this first volume of a projected series of four is the history of Western European culture—"that complex whole that includes knowledge, belief, morals, law, customs, opinions, religion, superstition, and art"—in the period between the Reformation and the eighteenth-century Enlightenment.

Since "the scientific rebirth" is for him the great distinguishing feature of this age, he naturally gives first place in his plan (pp. 17-176) to an account of the various particular sciences—astronomy, physics, chemistry, mathematics, geography, biology, anatomy— and of the more general aspects of scientific method and organization. Next in order come the "humanities" (pp. 179-311), including philosophy, political theory, historiography, and Biblical and classical scholarship; then the institutions of "social control"—education, religion, superstition, persecution and tolerance, and laws (pp. 315-522); and finally, a somewhat miscellaneous group of phenomena—morals and manners, literature, and art—which are grouped under the heading "The spirit of the times" (pp. 525-603). The book ends with an excellent bibliography and an index.

The multiplicity of topics provided for in this scheme and the immense scale on which the treatment is planned might easily have seemed, to a less conscientious scholar than Preserved Smith, a sufficient excuse for writing merely another compilation. Fortunately he has not done so, and in large parts of the book at any rate his exposition has the sharpness of outline and the precision of detail that can come only from direct communion with the sources. His pages on religion are, as might be expected from the author of *The age of the Reformation,* especially notable examples of this quality. But it is to be seen also in his chapters on political theory, on historiography, on Biblical scholarship, on the universities. In dealing with all of these questions he has taken the trouble to read and reflect on the chief contemporary documents and to digest the results of the most important modern studies. How thorough on the whole has been his work of documentation will be apparent to any one who examines the remarkable series of bibliographical chapters at the close of the volume.

It is inevitable of course that in a book of so ambitious a sweep there should be many pages that are either perfunctory or ill-informed. Now and then Smith's usual caution in generalization deserts him, and he permits himself such questionable statements as that (p. 8) the commercial revolution of the sixteenth century ''raised the merchant class into the dominant position in the state'' (see also p. 563, but cf. p. 536) or as that (p. 216) the idea of the law of nature ''lay almost dormant during the Middle Ages.'' Now and then he gives a misleading because over-simple interpretation of a writer or work, as, for example, of Dryden's *Religio laici* (p. 413) or of Glanvill's views on witchcraft (pp. 457-58). Then too, admirable as is his command of the results of modern scholarship, there are certain domains in which one could wish that he had pushed his reading somewhat farther afield. Had he been more familiar, for instance, with recent studies in the history of late medieval science, he would surely have qualified somewhat the impression he gives (e.g., pp. 18, 59) of the suddenness of the ''rebirth'' in the early sixteenth century, and he would surely have enlarged his account of the conditions which favored this rebirth (pp. 145-46) by including some mention of the important rôle played at this time by the revival of Neo-platonism. Similarly, had he mastered more completely the work of such scholars as E. A. Burtt (whose book appears in his bibliography), he would have been able to write a more adequate and better balanced account (pp. 153-64) of the formation of scientific method and especially of the very important metaphysical implications which this method carried with it; he would also, one may suppose, have reduced somewhat the space he gives in this connection to Francis Bacon. For all its abundance and precision of detail, his story of the scientific movement is hardly as modern in its perspectives or as illuminating as its importance in his scheme of the period requires that it should be. And much the same complaint could be made of his treatment of the great philosophers of the seventeenth century, of his analysis of the development of economic thought, and of his chapter on literature.

I must confess to some misgivings also concerning the distribution of space. The chapter on literature (21 pages) is admittedly incomplete (see p. 569); but it contains presumably all that Smith intends to say about Shakespeare, and that all extends to scarcely four pages! But the most striking instance of disproportion appears in the amount of attention devoted to the natural sciences (160 pages) as compared with that given to political theory, psychology, and ethics (approximately 50 pages). In the retrospective eyes of the twentieth century, no doubt, the seventeenth appears to be primarily the ''great century'' of science; but the preoccupations of contemporaries were not so one-sided, and a picture of the intellectual life of that age which dismisses in a bare half-dozen pages its many brilliant attempts ''to trace the passions to their sources, to unfold the seminal principles of vice and virtue, or sound the depths of the heart for the motives of action'' can hardly be accepted as adequate or complete.

Finally, one may question whether Smith has really succeeded in his design of exhibiting the cultural activities of this period ''as a unified whole'' (see p. 3). Except for a few suggestive pages in the ''Epilogue,'' his synthesis largely resolves itself into a series of separate studies of particular themes.

What were the great ruling ideas, the often tacit but nevertheless dynamic assumptions and prepossessions which pervaded and directed the thinking of the seventeenth century on its various special problems? He never tells us, partly because he has organized his materials according to fields of interest rather than according to currents of ideas, and partly, one suspects, because he has not appreciated the importance of the question. Thus he has occasion to deal, at different points in his plan, with the idea of the law of nature in Grotius, the conception of history prevalent in the sixteenth and seventeenth centuries, the theory of natural religion, the ethics of the Cambridge Platonists, and French classical art. But the reader will look in vain for any awareness that these apparently diverse phenomena were so many particular manifestations of a general way of thinking that has to be made clear if we are to understand the distinctive intellectual climate of the age.

It would be unfair, however, to dwell too long on these defects in the content and method of the book. "In this work, when it shall be found that much is omitted, let it not be forgotten that much likewise is performed": the plea of Johnson for his *Dictionary* might well be the motto of all reviewers who write about books of so large a scope and ambition as Smith's. I conclude, therefore, by expressing once more my admiration for a work which, in spite of a certain number of weaknesses, must rank among the most learned and useful contributions to intellectual history made in America for a long time.

Stauffer, Donald A. *English biography before 1700.* Cambridge, Mass.: Harvard University press, 1930. Pp. xvii+392.

Rev. in *N & Q,* CLIX (1930), 323-24; in *TLS,* Dec. 11, 1930, p. 1061.

Stearns, Bertha-Monica. "The first English periodical for women." *MP,* XXVIII (1930), 45-59.

Dunton's experiments with a periodical for women in the *Athenian mercury.*

Stockley, V. *German literature as known in England, 1750-1830.* London: Routledge, 1929. Pp. xiv+339.

Rev. in *TLS,* March 20, 1930, p. 213.

Taylor, O. H. "Economics and the idea of *jus naturale.*" *Quarterly journal of economics,* XLIV (1930), 205-41.

Thomas, Paul Karl. *Die literarische Verkörperung des philanthropischen Zuges in der englischen Aufklärung.* Phil. Diss. Breslau, 1929. Pp. 68.

Rev. by Florian Asanger in *Literaturblatt für germ. und rom. Phil.,* LI (1930), col. 106; by Paul Meissner in *Beiblatt,* XLI (1930), 181-83.

Van Tieghem, Paul. "L'automne dans la poésie ouest-européenne de Brockes à Lamartine (1720-1820)." *Mélanges . . . . Baldensperger* (Paris: Champion, 1930), II, 327-43.

Van Tieghem, Paul. *Les divers aspects du sentiment de la nature dans la littérature ouest-européenne du XVIIIe siècle.* Reprinted from *Omagui lui Ramiro Ortiz,* Bucarest, 1930. Pp. 14.

Van Tieghem, Paul. *Outline of the literary history of Europe since the Renaissance.* Translated from the French by Aimee Leffingwell McKenzie. With a preface by Ronald S. Crane. New York: Century co., 1930. Pp. xvi+361.

The orginal was noticed in *PQ,* V, 352.

Van Tieghem, Paul. *Le préromantisme: études d'histoire littéraire européenne.* [Second series.] Paris: Alcan, 1930. Pp. viii+324.

In this volume Van Tieghem brings together two studies, both of which had appeared in print before, the first—''La poésie de la nuit et des tombeaux''—in the *Mémoires de l'Académie royale de Belgique* in 1921, the second—''Les idylles de Gessner et le rêve pastoral''—in the *Revue de littérature comparée* in 1924. The reader familiar with these earlier publications will note that a number of points which were formerly neglected or passed over with but meager illustration have now been given more adequate treatment as a result either of recent writings by other scholars or of further studies by Van Tieghem himself. In the first essay, for example, he has profited by the work of Moore, Draper, and Miss Reed on the history of melancholy poetry in England before Young to give a much more acceptable interpretation of this aspect of the subject than was contained in the previous edition (see pp. 11ff.).

P. 16: for ''Richard Blair'' read ''Robert Blair.''—P. 123: the statement about the possible relation of Collins' *Ode to evening* to Gray's *Elegy* needs revision in the light of the dates of the two poems.—P. 124: John Duncombe's *An evening contemplation in a college* appeared in 1753.

Viner, Jacob. ''English theories of foreign trade before Adam Smith.'' *Journal of political economy,* XXXVIII (1930), 249-301, 404-57.

Vines, Sherard. *The course of English classicism.* London: Hogarth press; New York: Harcourt, Brace, and company, 1930. Pp. 160.

Rev. in *TLS,* Apr. 24, 1930, pp. 354-55.

Wagner, Bernard M. ''George Jolly at Norwich.'' *RES,* VI (1930), 449-52.

Weber, Max. *The Protestant ethic and the spirit of capitalism.* Translated by Talcott Parsons. With a foreword by R. H. Tawney. London: Allen and Unwin; New York: Charles Scribner's sons, 1930. Pp. xi+292.

Rev. in *TLS,* July 10, 1930, p. 563.

Whiting, George W. ''Political satire in London stage plays, 1680-83.'' *MP,* XXVIII (1930), 29-43.

Wilde, Hans Oskar. *Der Gottesgedanke in der englischen Literatur: das Problem der Entwicklung von puritanischer zu romantischer Literatur.* Breslau: Priebatsch, 1930. Pp. 155.

Williams, George G. ''The beginnings of nature poetry in the eighteenth century.'' *SP,* XXVII (1930), 583-608.

Williamson, George. *The Donne tradition: a study in English poetry from Donne to the death of Cowley.* Cambridge [Mass.]: Harvard University press, 1930. Pp. x+264.

Rev. by Pierre Legouis in *RAA,* VIII (1930), 152-54; by Mario Praz in *English studies,* XII (1930), 195-98; in *TLS,* July 31, 1930, p. 625.

Willoughby, Westel W. *The ethical basis of political authority.* New York: Macmillan company, 1930. Pp. viii+460.

Contains useful and suggestive discussions of the social contract theory and of the political doctrines of Hobbes, Spinoza, Locke, and Rousseau.

Woledge, Geoffrey. "Saint Amand, Fairfax and Marvell." *MLR,* XXV (1930), 481-83.

Interesting remarks on "that little stream of nature poetry, distinguished by its familiar tone and precise observation, which rises in France with Saint Amand and Théophile, and ends perhaps in England with Marvell and Cotton." Evidence that Fairfax, who was Marvell's patron, translated Saint Amand's *Solitude.*

Wood, Frederick T. "Goodman's Fields theatre." *MLR,* XXV (1930), 443-56.

IV. INDIVIDUAL AUTHORS

Joseph Addison

Segrè, Carlo. "Il viaggo dell' Addison in Italia." *Nuova antologia,* CCLXX (1930), 3-20, 164-80.

John Arbuthnot

Mayo, Thomas F. "The authorship of *The history of John Bull.*" *PMLA,* XLV (1930), 274-82.

A criticism of Teerink. Cf. *PQ,* V, 353.

William Beckford

The Vision. Liber veritatis. By William Beckford of Fonthill. Edited, with introduction and notes, by Guy Chapman. London: Routledge; New York, R. R. Smith, 1930. Pp. xxix+166.

Rev. in *TLS,* Aug. 14, 1930, p. 650.

Chapman, Guy, in conjunction with John Hodgkin. *A bibliography of William Beckford of Fonthill.* London: Constable; New York: R. R. Smith, 1930. Pp. xxii+128.

Rev. in *TLS,* Dec. 4, 1930, p. 1034.

Sitwell, Sacheverell. *Beckford and Beckfordism, an essay.* London: Duckworth, 1930. Pp. 39.

Rev. in *TLS,* Dec. 4, 1930, p. 1034.

George Berkeley

Hone, J. M. "A manuscript of Bishop Berkeley." *TLS,* Mar. 13, 1930, p. 211.

Cf. *ibid.,* Apr. 3, 1930, p. 295.

William Blake

Keynes, Geoffrey. "Blake and Hayley, a new letter." *TLS,* July 31, 1930, p. 624.

Keynes, Geoffrey. "William Blake and the Portland vase." *TLS,* July 3, 1930, p. 554.

Pierce, Frederick E. "Taylor, Aristotle, and Blake." *PQ,* IX (1930), 363-70.

Richter, Helene. "Blake und Hamann." *Archiv,* CLVIII (1930), 213-21.

Saurat, Denis. *Blake & modern thought.* London: Constable, 1929. Cf. *PQ,* IX, 182.

Rev. by Pierre Berger in *RELV,* XLVII (1930), 61-63; by G. Lafourcade in *Litteris,* VII (1930), 30-37; by Jean Wahl in *RAA,* VII (1930), 553-54.

Henry St. John, Viscount Bolingbroke

Hayes, Carlton J. H. "The philosopher turned patriot." *Essays in intellectual history presented to James Harvey Robinson* (New York: Harper & brothers, 1929), pp. 189-206.

An able and suggestive analysis of Bolingbroke's nationalism.

James Boswell

(See also *Samuel Johnson*)

Dorando, a Spanish tale. [By James Boswell.] London: Elkin Mathews and Marrot, 1930. Pp. 44.

"Conjugal fidelity. A suppressed dialogue between Boswell and Johnson." *Life and letters,* IV (1930), 164-66.

Reprinted from the very rare uncancelled state of page 302 of Volume II of the first edition of Boswell's *Life.*

Private papers of James Boswell from Malahide Castle in the collection of Lt-Colonel Ralph Heyward Isham. Prepared for the press by Geoffrey Scott and Frederick A. Pottle. New York: Privately printed, 1930. Vols. VII, VIII, IX.

Inge, Charles C. "Two more Boswell letters." *TLS,* March 27, 1930, p. 274.

"The Making of Boswell's 'Johnson.'" *TLS,* Feb. 6, 1930, pp. 85-86.

Comment by Lewis Bettany, *ibid.,* Feb. 13, 1930, p. 122.

An admirable essay, occasioned by the publication of the first six volumes of the *Private papers.*

Pottle, Frederick Albert. *The literary career of James Boswell, Esq.* Oxford: Clarendon press, 1929. Cf. PQ, IX, 182-83.

Rev. by L. Cazamian in *RAA,* VIII (1930), 157-59; by T. B. Simpson in *JEGP,* XXIX (1930), 289-90; by John Wilks in *MLR,* XXV (1930), 488-90; by G. P. Winship in *MLN,* XLV (1930), 254-56; in *N & Q,* CLVIII (1930), 179.

Frances Brooke

Lady Julia Mandeville. By Frances Brooke. London: Scholartis press, 1930. Pp. 219.

Rev. in *TLS,* July 10, 1930, p. 568.

Henry Brooke

Hogl, Hans. *Henry Brooke's Roman "The Fool of quality" und sein Verhältnis su den grossen Romanschriftstellern des 18. Jahrhunderts.* Phil. Diss. Erlangen, 1930. Pp. 81.

Thomas Brown

Eddy, William A. "Tom Brown and Partridge the astrologer." *MP,* XXVIII (1930), 163-68.

John Bunyan

The Pilgrim's progress from this world to that which is to come. By John Bunyan. Edited by James Blanton Wharey. Oxford: Clarendon press, 1928. Cf. *PQ,* IX, 183.

Rev. by Bernhard Fehr in *Beiblatt,* XLI (1930), 43-45; by H. Schöffler in *Literaturblatt für germ. und rom. Phil.,* LI (1930), cols. 435-36; by John Sparrow in *RES,* VI (1930), 219-24.

Golder, Harold. "Bunyan and Spenser." *PMLA,* XLV (1930), 216-37.

Frances Burney

Evelina; or, The history of a young lady's entrance into the world. By Frances Burney. With notes, indexes, and illustrations from contemporary sources. Edited by Sir Frank D. Mackinnon. Oxford: Clarendon press, 1930. Pp. 590.

Rev. in *TLS,* Apr. 17, 1930, p. 333.

Robert Burns

Carswell, Catherine. *The life of Robert Burns.* London: Chatto and Windus, 1930. Pp. xiii+467.

Rev. by Bonamy Dobrée in *Spectator,* Oct. 25, 1930, pp. 601-02; in *TLS,* Nov. 13, 1930, p. 936.

Ferguson, J. De Lancey. "Burns and Hugh Blair." *MLN,* XLV (1930), 440-46.

Ferguson, J. De Lancey. "In defense of R. H. Cromek." *PQ,* IX (1930), 239-48.

Ferguson, J. De Lancey. "Robert Burns and Maria Riddell." *MP,* XXVIII (1930), 169-84.

Ferguson, J. De Lancey. "Some notes on Burns's reading." *MLN,* XLV (1930), 370-77.

Ferguson, J. De Lancey. "The text of Burns's *Passion's cry.*" *MLN,* XLV (1930), 99-102.

Henry Carey

The Poems of Henry Carey. Edited with an introduction and notes by Frederick T. Wood. London: Scholartis press, 1930. Pp. 261.

Rev. by J. R. S. in *MLR,* XXV (1930), 502; in *TLS,* Apr. 24, 1930, p. 349.

Sutherland, James R. "Carey: an ascription." *TLS,* Dec. 25, 1930, p. 1101.

Ascribes to Carey *The records of love: or weekly amusements for the fair sex* (1710).

Wood, Frederick T. "Phillips or Carey?" *TLS,* Feb. 27, 1930, p. 166.

Discussion continued, *ibid.,* Apr. 3, 1930, p. 298; Apr. 10, 1930, p. 318; Apr. 24, 1930, p. 352; May 8, 1930, p. 394; May 22, 1930, p. 434.

Thomas Chatterton

Ellinger, Esther Parker. *Thomas Chatterton, the marvellous boy; to which is added, "The exhibition, a personal satire."* Philadelphia: University of Pennsylvania press; London: Humphrey Milford, Oxford University press, 1930. Pp. 75.

Rev. in *TLS,* July 31, 1930, p. 625.

Meyerstein, E. H. W. *A life of Thomas Chatterton.* London: Ingpen and Grant, 1930. Pp. xix+584.

Rev. by Edmund Blunden in *Nation & Athenæum,* Nov. 1, 1930, p. 165; by Osbert Burdett in *Saturday review,* Nov. 8, 1930, pp. 604-06; by R. A. Scott-James in *New statesman,* Dec. 20, 1930, pp. 337-38; in *TLS,* Nov. 27, 1930, p. 1009.

Philip Dormer Stanhope, Earl of Chesterfield

Private correspondence of Chesterfield and Newcastle, 1744-1746. Part I, "Chesterfield at The Hague." Part II, "Chesterfield at Dublin." Edited with an introduction and notes by Sir

Richard Lodge. London: Royal Historical society, 1930. Pp. 155.

Rev. in *TLS,* Aug. 21, 1930, p. 659.

William Collins

Garrod, H. W. *Collins.* Oxford: Clarendon press, 1928. Cf. *PQ,* VIII, 186; IX, 185.

Rev. by H. O. White in *RES,* VI (1930), 236-40.

Legouis, Pierre. "Les amours de Dieu chez Collins et Milton." *RAA,* VIII (1930), 136-38.

White, H. O. "William Collins and Miss Bundy." *RES,* VI (1930), 437-42.

Woodhouse, A. S. P. "Collins in the eighteenth century." *TLS,* Oct. 16, 1930, p. 838.

William Congreve

The Works of Congreve. Edited by F. W. Bateson. London: Peter Davies, 1930. Pp. xxviii+507.

Rev. in *TLS,* July 24, 1930, p. 606.

John Gilbert Cooper

Addington, Marion H. "The call of Aristippus." *MLN,* XLV (1930), 89-90.

Abraham Cowley

Nethercot, Arthur H. "Abraham Cowley's essays." *JEGP,* XXIX (1930), 114-30.

William Cowper

Förster, M. "Cowpers Ballade 'John Gilpin.' Textgestalt, Verbreitung und Fortsetzungen." *ES,* LXIV (1929), 380-416; LXV (1930), 26-48.

Manning, B. L. "History, politics, and religion in certain poems of William Cowper." *Congregational quarterly,* VII (1929), 326-43.

Probert, G. Carwardine. " 'The stricken deer.' " *N & Q,* CLVIII (1930), 381-82.

Ralph Cudworth

Ralph Cudworth. A sermon preached before the House of Commons, March 31, 1647. Reproduced from the original edition. New York: Facsimile text society, 1930. Pp. 83.

Richard Cumberland

Caskey, J. Homer. "Richard Cumberland's mission in Spain." *PQ,* IX (1930), 82-86.

Charles Davenant

Casper, Willy. *Charles Davenant. Ein Beitrag zur Kenntnis des englischen Merkantilismus.* Jena: G. Fischer, 1930. Pp. viii+140.

Daniel Defoe

Burch, Charles Eaton. "Attacks on Defoe in Union pamphlets." *RES,* VI (1930), 318-19.

Burch, Charles Eaton. "Daniel Defoe's views on education." *London quarterly review,* Oct., 1930, pp. 220-29.

Burch, Charles Eaton. "Wodrow's list of Defoe's pamphlets on the Union." *MP,* XXVIII (1930), 99-100.

Jacob, Ernst Gerhard. *Daniel Defoe, Essay on projects (1697).* Leipzig: Tauchnitz, 1929. Cf. *PQ,* IX, 187.

Rev. by Paul Dottin in *RAA,* VII (1930), 343-44; by E. L. in *Revue d'histoire économique et sociale,* XVIII (1930), 529-30; by A. W. Secord in *MLN,* XLV (1930), 479-80; by A. C. E. Vechtman-Veth in *English studies,* XII (1930), 198-99; in *TLS,* July 3, 1930, p. 555.

Pastor, Antonio. *The idea of Robinson Crusoe.* Volume one. Watford: The Gongora press, 1930. Pp. xii+391.

An elaborate and useful study of the Spanish Arabic romance, *The story of Hayy ibn Yaqzan.*

Roorda, Gerridina. *Realism in Daniel De Foe's narratives of adventure.* Wageningen: H. Veenman & Zonen, 1929. Pp. 142.

Rev. by A. W. Secord in *MLN,* XLV (1930), 480.

John Dryden

Ham, Roswell G. "Some uncollected verse of John Dryden." *LM,* XXI (1930), 421-26.

Lloyd, Claude. "John Dryden and the Royal Society." *PMLA,* XLV (1930), 967-76.

Lloyd has collected the passages in Birch's *History of the Royal Society* which indicate that Dryden was in 1665 and 1666 in arrears in his payments to the Royal Society. These passages are important, but they do not, as Lloyd assumes, necessarily indicate an indifference on the part of Dryden to the ideals of the Society. In 1666 over six hundred pounds in dues were in arrears; in 1671 over fifteen hundred pounds. Other questionable features of the article I shall examine at length elsewhere.—LOUIS I. BREDVOLD.

Newdigate, B. H. "An overlooked ode by John Dryden." *LM,* XXII (1930), 438-42.

On the marriage of the fair and vertuous lady, Mrs. Anastasia Stafford.

T[horn]-D[rury], G. "Dryden's verses 'To the Lady *Castlemain, upon her incouraging his first play.*'" *RES*, VI (1930), 193-94.

Collates the text in the *Examen poeticum* (1693) with that published in *A new collection of poems and songs* (1674).

Wild, B. Josef. *Dryden und die römische Kirche.* Leipzig: Robert Noske, 1928. Cf. *PQ*, VIII, 190; IX, 188.

Rev. by R. S. Crane in *MLN*, XLV (1930), 67; by G. D. Willcock in *RES*, VI (1930), 224-25.

Thomas D'Urfey

Lynch, Kathleen M. "Thomas D'Urfey's contribution to sentimental comedy." *PQ*, IX (1930), 249-59.

John Dyer

Hughes, Helen Sard. "John Dyer and the Countess of Hertford." *MP*, XXVII (1930), 311-20.

Contains a new manuscript draft of *Grongar hill.*

John Evelyn

Fumifugium. By John Evelyn, of Balliol College, Oxford, in 1661. Oxford: R. T. Gunther, Folly Bridge, 1930. ("Old Ashmolean reprints," VIII.)

George Farquhar

The Complete works of George Farquhar. Edited by Charles Stonehill. London: Nonesuch press, 1930. 2 vols.

Rev. in *TLS*, July 17, 1930, p. 589.

Lawrence, W. J. "George Farquhar: Thomas Wilkes." *TLS*, June 26, 1930, p. 534.

Adam Ferguson

Lehmann, William Christian. *Adam Ferguson and the beginnings of modern sociology; an analysis of the sociological elements in his writings with some suggestions as to his place in the history of social theory.* New York: Columbia University press, 1930. Pp. 268. (Columbia "Studies in history, economics and public law," No. 328.)

Henry Fielding

An Apology for the life of Mrs. Shamela Andrews. Attributed to Henry Fielding. With an introduction by Brian W. Downs. Cambridge: St. John's College, Gordon Fraser, 1930. Pp. xi+60.

Banerji, H. K. *Henry Fielding: playwright, journalist and master of the art of fiction, his life and works.* Oxford: Blackwell, 1929. Pp. vi+342.

Rev. by A. Digeon in *RAA,* VII (1930), 62; by E. G. Twitchett in *LM,* XXI (1930), 373-75; in *TLS,* Apr. 3, 1930, p. 293.

This attractively printed volume is a useful introduction to the works of Fielding for those who wish to explore his lesser writings. It is hardly a biography (though it contains much about Fielding's life), for it begins with his first publications in 1728 and stresses the contents of the various works in the order of their appearance. Of the ten chapters not half deal with Fielding's prose fiction.

There are some errors in fact, but I have noted only small ones. In the Preface the *Miscellanies* are spoken of as in *two* volumes, though the Bibliography (p. 299) correctly notes three. On p. 22 *J.* Roberts is expanded into *John* when it should be *James*; on p. 70 one may be led to believe that in 1737 there were two theaters in Lincoln's Inn Fields instead of one; on pp. 108 and 109 a misinterpretation of satire on Cibber in *Shamela* leads to the unwarranted assumption that when *Shamela* was written Fielding thought Cibber the author of *Pamela*; and on p. 244 Banerji assumes that the second edition of *Peregrine Pickle* appeared in 1751, whereas Professor Buck's *Study in Smollett* (1925) shows 1758 to be its year.

The factual side of the book is, however, relatively sound. The critical opinions are in several cases disappointing. The volume gives effective summary treatment of minor works rather than incisive criticism, and in this survey will lie its usefulness. Little is done with such matters as Fielding's taste in reading: Banerji rather shuns the idea that so great an author as Fielding was indebted to others (pp. 111, 195). The longest discussion of any one phase of Fielding's art is that devoted to its ethical aspects in the chapter on *Tom Jones.* This account is strictly Victorian: it neglects the fact that in Fielding's day love and drinking were slight sins; and it also fails to consider that Fielding's reputation was largely sullied by his preference for the society of those who by birth were his social inferiors to that of his social superiors, "the great." This error (social not moral) no century, least of all the eighteenth, will forgive a born aristocrat—especially if in his writings he flaunts a delight in such "low" company as that of country parsons, footmen, tradespeople, and debtors—to go no lower. In 1931 one is shocked at Banerji's slight opinion of Fielding's moralizing. "Some admirers of the novelist [he says], though their number is not very large, have no hesitation in pronouncing Fielding to be an effective and sound moralist" (p. 210).

Lack of understanding of Fielding's social attitudes leads to no profound understanding of *Amelia.* Banerji agrees with most critics that the relative lack of exuberance in this novel is due to Fielding's increasing physical infirmities, but he notes that most of the things written after *Amelia,* when the author's health was even desperate, have something of the old sparkle and verve lacking in the novel. The unnoted truth about *Amelia* is the truth to be seen in the "high" comedies and in the later parts of *Tom Jones*: Fielding had no sympathy for London high society—in fact, not even an artist's interest in it as material. Most of his persons from this class are hard and unattractive even to the point of repulsiveness. They are handled almost dully. There is no lightness in any of the London comedies except *Love in several masques,* and they were all failures. The Lady Bellaston episode in *Tom Jones* is likewise a failure, and all that Fielding gives to materials presented without enthusiasm in *Amelia* is artistic authenticity—without much added charm.

Banerji's method of taking up the works *seriatim* has kept him from making any detailed comparisons between various works. He is somewhat needlessly uninterested in Digeon's ingenious relation of Fielding's work to Richardson's (p. 192), which he dismisses as "curious enough." Not much is too curious in this volume, but it is a useful introduction to the less known works of a very great writer.—GEORGE SHERBURN.

Samuel Foote

Belden, Mary Megie. *The dramatic work of Samuel Foote.* New Haven: Yale University press; London: Humphrey Milford, Oxford University press, 1929. Pp. viii+224.

Rev. by J. Homer Caskey in *JEGP,* XXX (1931), 135-36; by B. V. Crawford in *PQ,* IX (1930), 221; by E. Bradlee Watson in *MLN,* XLV (1930), 469-72; in *TLS,* May 22, 1930, p. 421.

David Garrick

Pineapples of finest flavor, or A selection of sundry unpublished letters of the English Roscius, David Garrick. Edited with an introduction and notes by David Mason Little. Cambridge [Mass.]: Harvard University press, 1930. Pp. xx+101.

Rev. by George P. Baker in *MLN,* XLV (1930), 553-54; in *TLS,* May 8, 1930, p. 389.

William Gifford

Clark, Roy Benjamin. *William Gifford, Tory satirist, critic, and editor.* New York: Columbia University press, 1930. Pp. 294.

Oliver Goldsmith

The Collected letters of Oliver Goldsmith. Edited by Katharine C. Balderston. Cambridge: Cambridge University press, 1928. Cf. *PQ,* VIII, 192-93; IX, 190.

Rev. by L. F. Powell in *RES,* VI (1930), 111-13.

When this edition appeared in 1928, Miss Balderston was unable to include the text of Goldsmith's letter to Boswell of April 4, 1773, replying to the latter's congratulations on the success of *She stoops to conquer.* The letter, a very fine one, is now available in Vol. IX of the *Private papers of James Boswell* (see above, under "*James Boswell*").

New essays by Oliver Goldsmith. Now first collected and edited with an introduction and notes by Ronald S. Crane. Chicago: University of Chicago press, 1927. Cf. *PQ,* VII, 175; VIII, 193; IX, 190.

Rev. by L. F. Powell in *RES,* VI (1930), 232-33.

Balderston, K. C. "A manuscript version of *She stoops to conquer.*" *MLN,* XLV (1930), 84-85.

Notes on the licenser's manuscript copy belonging to the Larpent Collection in the Huntington Library.

Balderston, K. C. "The birth of Goldsmith." *TLS,* March 7, 1929, pp. 185-86.

Miss Balderston has sent me the following comment on my notice of this article in *PQ,* IX, 190-91:

"Mr. Crane's chief objection to 1730 as the best attested date centers in his contention that more value than I allowed should be attached to the testimony of Mrs. Hodson for 1729. The only possible claim for her must be based on the possibility of her having used the family Bible, since her general habit of thought was demonstrably inaccurate. Her statement, for instance, of the year in which Henry Goldsmith entered Trinity College is four years away from the truth, and Oliver's entrance is misstated by two years. She did not attach importance to accuracy, and there is a justifiable room for doubt that in this one particular she would have sought for authentic certainty, even though it was at hand, which cannot be proved. More particularly, if she had the Bible to consult, she would hardly have made two curious errors in her statements about the family: first, that the family consisted of seven children, when the Bible record plainly shows that it consisted of eight, the eldest daughter Margaret having presumably died in infancy; and second, that Henry was the oldest child, when she herself was the oldest, a fact that anyone but a Goldsmith might have been expected to know without documentary proof. Furthermore, if she had used the authority of the Bible record, we might justifiably assume that Maurice, who solicited her to write the Memoir, and who acted as amanuensis for part of it, would have been aware of the fact, and would not have changed the date, as he did later, to 1728. The reviewer's point that she states the interval between Oliver's birth and Maurice's with approximate correctness, according to her own reckoning of the date of the former, loses significance when one remembers that Maurice himself was at hand when she wrote to offer information as to his own birth date, and the Bible record need not be postulated as her authority.

"Let me say in closing, what I have said before, that the reputation for inaccuracy under which the Trinity College records have suffered has been denied by their most competent critic and latest editor, Mr. T. U. Sadleir, who says in the preface to his edition of the records: 'Generally speaking, . . . the records were accurately kept, and careless reference has too often been the cause of unjust criticism.' "

Miss Balderston's objection to my objection to her skepticism concerning Mrs. Hodson's date is very ingeniously argued, and I gladly surrender the point. As to the authority of the Dublin records, I was aware of Sadleir's statement when I wrote the review, and I recognize that it must be given considerable weight; but it is one thing to admit the general trustworthiness of a body of documents and quite another to regard any particular statement contained in them as necessarily acceptable on that account in the absence of supporting evidence. After all, the value of the entry in question depends entirely on the value of Goldsmith's testimony to his own age in 1745, and that can hardly be said to be wholly above suspicion.

Baudin, Maurice. "Une source de *She stoops to conquer.*" *PMLA*, XLV (1930), 614.

Parallels, which could easily be mere coincidences, with the *Galant coureur* of Marc Antoine Le Grand (1722).

Chapman, R. W. "An unconsidered trifle." *Colophon*, Part III, 1930.

On Goldsmith's use of D. Fenning's *The young man's book of knowledge* in his *History of England in a series of letters.* Cf. *TLS*, June 13, 1929, p. 474.

Crane, R. S. "The text of Goldsmith's *Memoirs of M. de Voltaire.*" *MP*, XXVIII (1930), 212-19.

Alterations and omissions in Prior's edition (1837).

Seitz, R. W. "Goldsmith and the *Present state of the British empire.*" *MLN*, XLV (1930), 434-38.

Shows that nearly a hundred pages of this work were borrowed with but little change from Burke's *Account of the European settlements in America* (1757).

Tupper, Caroline F. "Oliver Goldsmith and 'The gentleman who signs D.'" *MLN,* XLV (1930), 71-77.

Shows that Goldsmith's review of Mallet in the *Monthly review* for April, 1757, was a translation of an article in the *Bibliothèque des sciences et des beaux-arts* for October-December, 1756.

Thomas Gray

Jones, W. Powell. "The contemporary reception of Gray's *Odes.*" *MP,* XXVIII (1930), 61-82.

A careful reconsideration of the problem, with some new documents.

Toynbee, Paget. "Gray and 'Lady Bath' in 1769." *TLS,* July 17, 1930, p. 592.

Toynbee, Paget. "A Gray query." *TLS,* Sept. 18, 1930, p. 735.

Replies by Edward Bensly and Lilian E. Elliott, *ibid.,* Sept. 25, 1930, p. 758.

Toynbee, Paget. "A newly discovered draft of Gray's lines, 'William Shakespeare to Mrs. Anne.'" *MLR,* XXV (1930), 83-85.

Whibley, Leonard. "The candidate: by Mr. Gray." *TLS,* Aug. 21, 1930, pp. 667-68.

Whibley, Leonard. "The foreign tour of Gray and Walpole." *Blackwood's magazine,* CCXXVII (1930), 813-27.

Whibley, Leonard. "Gray's satirical poems." *TLS,* Oct. 9, 1930, p. 805.

Whibley, Leonard. "Thomas Gray, undergraduate." *Blackwood's magazine,* CCXXVII (1930), 273-86.

James Harrington

Gough, J. W. "Harrington and contemporary thought." *Political science quarterly,* XLV (1930), 395-404.

Deals with his relations to "the democratic theories of seventeenth-century Puritan England." The writer makes no use of Liljegren's edition or of his article in the *Festschrift für Johannes Hoops* (see *PQ,* V, 362).

Thomas Hobbes

Landry, B. *Hobbes.* Paris: Alcan, 1930. Pp. 278. ("Les grands philosophes.")

Lips, Julius. *Die Stellung des Thomas Hobbes zu den politischen Parteien der grossen englischen Revolution.* Leipzig: Ernst Wiegandt, 1927. Pp. 288.

Rev. by Werner Becker in *Deutsche Literaturzeitung,* LI (1930), cols. 350-53.

Tönnies, Ferdinand. "Die Lehre von den Volksversammlungen

und die Urversammlung in Hobbes' Leviathan.'' *Zeitschrift für die gesamte Staatswissenschaft,* LXXXIX (1930), 1-22.

David Hume

Annand, M. R. ''An examination of Hume's theory of relations.'' *Monist,* XL (1930), 581-97.

Hobart, R. E. ''Hume without scepticism.'' *Mind,* XXXIX (1930), 273-301, 409-25.

Salmon, C. V. *The central problem of David Hume's philosophy: an essay towards a phenomenological interpretation of the First Book of the Treatise of human nature.* Halle (Saale): Max Niemeyer, 1929. Pp. vii+151.

Rev. by Mary E. Clarke in *Journal of philosophy,* XXVII (1930), 575-79.

Robert Jephson

Peterson, Martin Severin. *Robert Jephson (1736-1803): a study of his life and works.* Lincoln, Nebraska, 1930. Pp. 45. (''University of Nebraska Studies in language, literature, and criticism,'' Number 11.)

Samuel Johnson

(See also *James Boswell*)

London, a poem, and The Vanity of human wishes. By Samuel Johnson. With an introductory essay by T. S. Eliot. London: Etchells and Macdonald, 1930. Pp. 44.

Rev. in *TLS,* Nov. 20, 1930, p. 973.

Proposals for The publisher, 1744. Now reprinted in facsimile and for the first time ascribed to Samuel Johnson. [With a prefatory note by R. W. Chapman.] Oxford University press; London: Humphrey Milford, 1930. Pp. 6.

Baker, H. Arthur. ''Chesterfield and Johnson.'' *Contemporary review,* CXXXVII (1930), 353-60.

Chapman, R. W. ''Johnson's works: a lost piece and a forgotten piece.'' *LM,* XXI (1930), 438-44.

On the *Proposals for The publisher* (1744) and the *Life of Zachery Pearce* (1777).

Crane, R. S. ''Johnson and Evan Evans.'' *MLN,* XLV (1930), 31-32.

Fortesque-Brickdale, Charles. ''Dr. Johnson and Mrs. Macaulay: the credibility of Boswell.'' *N & Q,* CLIX (1930), 111-12.

Pottle, Frederick A. "'The character of Dr. Johnson.'" *TLS,* May 22, 1930, p. 434.

On a pamphlet by William Johnston Temple with this title (1792).

Reade, Aleyn Lyell. *Johnsonian gleanings.* Part V. London: Privately printed, 1928. See *PQ,* VIII, 194.

Rev. by L. F. Powell in *RES,* VI (1930), 230-32.

Reade, Aleyn Lyell. "A new admirer for Dr. Johnson." *LM,* XXI (1930), 243-53.

Letters of Mrs. Mary Nicholas.

George Keith

Nicolson, Marjorie. "George Keith and the Cambridge Platonists." *Philosophical review,* XXXIX (1930), 36-55.

Thomas Killigrew

Harbage, Alfred. *Thomas Killigrew, Cavalier dramatist, 1612-83.* Philadelphia: University of Pennsylvania press, 1930. Pp. ix+247.

Rev. by Hazelton Spencer in *MLN,* XLVI (1931), 200-01; in *TLS,* Apr. 10, 1930, p. 315.

John Locke

Jackson, Reginald. "Locke's version of the doctrine of representative perception." *Mind,* XXXIX (1930), 1-25.

Henry More

Henry More. Enchiridion ethicum. The English translation of 1690. Reproduced from the first edition. New York: Facsimile text society, 1930. Pp. 268.

Maurice Morgann

Carver, P. L. "The influence of Maurice Morgann." *RES,* VI (1930), 320-22.

Possible influence of his *Essay on . . . Falstaff* (1777) on Hazlitt. Cf. note by R. W. Chapman, *ibid.,* VI, 455.

Roger Boyle, Earl of Orrery

Clark, William S. "The relation of Shirley's prologue to Orrery's *The generall.*" *RES,* VI, (1930), 191-93.

Samuel Pepys

Drinkwater, John. *Pepys, his life and character.* London: Heinemann; Garden City: Doubleday, Doran and company, 1930.

Rev. by James Laver in *Spectator,* Oct. 25, 1930, p. 599; by G. F. Whicher in *Books,* Nov. 23, 1930, p. 6; in *New statesman,* Nov. 29, 1930, p. 246; in *TLS,* Nov. 13, 1930, p. 936.

Thomas Percy

Priebsch, R. "Two unpublished letters by Joseph Cooper Walker to Bishop Percy." *MLR,* XXV (1930), 90-95.

Alexander Pope

Characters and observations: an eighteenth century manuscript. With a foreword by Lord Gorell. London: Murray; New York: Frederick A. Stokes and co., 1930. Pp. xvi+296.

Rev. by Samuel Chew in *Books,* Nov. 2, 1930, p. 21; in *TLS,* Apr. 24, 1930, p. 349.

One may well shy at reviewing a book like this. According to the Foreword the volume purports to publish a manuscript recently discovered by a junk-man in an old piece of furniture purchased in or near Twickenham. The junk-man admired the wit and wisdom of the *pensées* in the manner of La Rochefoucauld which made up the manuscript, and his wife (done quite in the manner of Jenny Distaff or Poor Richard's wife) tired of hearing him praise these qualities, and eventually sold the manuscript to the present publishers. The manuscript as a whole is nowhere carefully described. From the "Thoughts on various subjects" printed in the Elwin-Courthope edition of Pope's *Works,* X, 550-61, one gets a partial model for its substance. Since the publishers print a facsimile of one page, and since the hand resembles closely that of Alexander Pope, and since the fly leaf has his (?) signature and the word "Twickeam" (if that is a word!) written in what seems to be an eighteenth-century hand, why may not this manuscript be Pope's own? ask the publishers.

The language of the junk-man's wife in the preface sounds fictitious: she as well as the *pensées* tries to be eigtheenth-century: she should be contemporary. "Twickeam" reminds one of Chatterton's attempts at archaic spelling, and the vocabulary of the *pensées* seems not to be quite that of Pope's day—or perhaps of any other day. "Galopino" is used as the name of a dancing master. The word was used before the eighteenth century as a name for a page, who presumably "galoped" about on his errands. The word *galop* in connection with dancing seems to date from the nineteenth century. There are other matters that raise doubts, and one wonders and hesitates to stir what looks like a mare's nest.—GEORGE SHERBURN.

The Dunciad variorum with the prolegomena of Scriblerus. By Alexander Pope. With an introductory essay by Robert Kilburn Root. Princeton: Princeton University press, 1929. Cf. *PQ,* IX, 197.

Rev. by George Sherburn in *MLN,* XLV (1930), 472-74; by Austin Warren in *Sewanee review,* XXXVIII (1930), 507-08; in *TLS,* Apr. 17, 1930, p. 332.

Hughes, Helen Sard. "'Mr. Pope on his grotto.'" *MP,* XXVIII (1930), 100-04.

Sitwell, Edith. *Alexander Pope.* London: Faber and Faber, 1930. Pp. xiii+316.

Rev. in *TLS,* March 20, 1930, pp. 223-24.

Warren, Austin. *Alexander Pope as critic and humanist.* Princeton: Princeton University press, 1929. Cf. *PQ,* IX, 198-99.

Rev. by Arthur E. Case in *MLN,* XLV (1930), 486-87; by M. G. Lloyd Thomas in *RES,* VI (1930), 227-28.

Warren, Austin. "A note on Pope's Preface to Homer." *PQ,* IX (1930), 210-12.

The possible influence of Fontenelle on Pope's discussion of Homer's language.

Warren, Austin. "Pope and Ben Jonson." *MLN,* XLV (1930), 86-88.

Wyld, H. C. "Observations on Pope's versification." *MLR,* XXV (1930), 274-85.

Matthew Prior

Needham, F. R. D. "Verses by Prior." *TLS,* Apr. 10, May 29, 1930, pp. 318, 458.

Thomas Purney

White, H. O. "Thomas Purney: a forgotten poet and critic of the eighteenth century." *Essays and studies by members of the English association,* XV (1929), 67-97.

Cf. *TLS,* Oct. 30, 1930, p. 890.

Samuel Richardson

Pamela, or virtue rewarded. By Samuel Richardson. Oxford: Blackwell, 1930. 4 vols. ("The Shakespeare Head edition of the novels of Samuel Richardson.")

Dottin, Paul. "Du nouveau sur Richardson (documents inédits). IV, Richardson, agent matrimonial." *RAA,* VII (1930), 432-34.

An interesting unpublished letter of Oct. 9, 1750.

Dottin, Paul. "L'accueil fait à Pamela." *RAA,* VII (1930), 505-19.

Dottin prints for the first time (in French translation) some of the eulogies preserved in the Richardson papers at South Kensington, but he does not take account of the opposition to *Pamela,* and probably exaggerates the favor accorded to the book by fastidious readers and professed critics. He fails to realize, for example, that Shenstone's letter to Jago "in the Manner of Pamela" is satirical.—A. D. McKillop.

Dottin, Paul. "Les continuations de 'Pamela.'" *RELV,* XLVII (1930), 444-61.

Krutch, Joseph Wood. "Samuel Richardson." In his *Five masters: a study in the mutations of the novel* (New York: Jonathan Cape & Harrison Smith, 1930), pp. 109-73.

Martin, Burns. "Richardson's removal to Salisbury Court." *MLN,* XLV (1930), 469.

Miller, George Morey. "The publisher of 'Pamela.'" *TLS*, July 31, 1930, p. 628.

Comment by C. J. Longman, *ibid.*, Aug. 28, 1930, p. 684.

"Newbery's edition of 'Pamela,' 1769." *TLS*, March 6, 1930, p. 196.

Nicholas Rowe

Jackson, Alfred. "Rowe's edition of Shakespeare." *Library*, 4th series, X (1930), 455-73.

Jackson, Alfred. "Rowe's historical tragedies." *Anglia*, LIV (1930), 307-30.

Critical estimates of *The royal convert, Jane Shore,* and *Lady Jane Gray.*

Thomas Shadwell

Epsom Wells and The volunteers, or the stock-jobbers. By Thomas Shadwell. Edited by D. M. Walmsley. New York: D. C. Heath and company, 1930. Pp. lxi+387.

Rev. by A. S. Borgman in *MLN*, XLVI (1931), 201-02; in *TLS*, Aug. 7, 1930, p. 638.

Borgman, Albert S. *Thomas Shadwell: his life and comedies.* New York: New York University press, 1928. Cf. *PQ*, VIII, 200; IX, 200.

Rev. by H. N. Hillebrand in *JEGP*, XXIX (1930), 299-300; by J. R. Sutherland in *MLR*, XXV (1930), 216-17; by D. M. Walmsley in *RES*, VI (1930), 362-65.

Bull, A. J. "Thomas Shadwell's satire on Edward Howard." *RES*, VI (1930), 312-15.

Needham, Francis. "A letter of Shadwell's." *TLS*, Oct. 23, 1930, p. 866.

Anthony Ashley Cooper, Earl of Shaftesbury

Bandini, Luigi. *Shaftesbury. Etica e religione. La morale del sentimento.* Bari: Laterza, 1930. Pp. xxxii+232.

Rev. by G. d. R. in *La critica*, XXVIII (1930), 134-36.

Smith, Emma Peters. "The philosophy of Anthony, third Earl of Shaftesbury." *Essays in intellectual history dedicated to James Harvey Robinson* (New York: Harper & brothers, 1929), pp. 21-40.

William Shenstone

Gammans, H. W. "Shenstone's appreciation of Vergil." *Classical weekly*, XXII (1929), 90-91.

Richard Brinsley Sheridan

The School for scandal. By Richard Brinsley Sheridan. Edited, with an introduction, by R. Crompton Rhodes. Oxford: Blackwell, 1930. Pp. xxvii+145.

MacMillan, Dougald. "Sheridan's share in *The stranger.*" *MLN,* XLV (1930), 85-86.

Christopher Smart

Abbott, Charles David. "Christopher Smart's madness." *PMLA,* XLV (1930), 1014-22.

Adam Smith

Fay, C. R. "Adam Smith and the dynamic state." *Economic journal,* XL (1930), 25-34.

Tobias George Smollett

Knapp, C. "The classical element in Smollett, Roderick Random." *Classical weekly,* XXIII (1929), 9-11, 17-19.

Knapp, Lewis M. "Ann Smollett, wife of Tobias Smollett." *PMLA,* XLV (1930), 1035-49.

McKillop, Allan Dugald. "Smollett's first comedy." *MLN,* XLV (1930), 396-97.

Robert South

Mattis, Norman. "Robert South." *Quarterly journal of speech,* XV (1929), 537-60.

On his rhetorical theories and practice.

Roberts, Donald A. "Evelyn and South." *TLS,* July 24, 1930, p. 612.

Sir Richard Steele

Blanchard, Rae. "Steele's *Christian hero* and the *errata* in *The tatler.*" *RES,* VI (1930), 183-85.

Cf. F. W. Bateson in *RES,* V (1929), 155-66. Miss Blanchard's note shows the incorrectness of the belief that Steele did not revise his work once it was in print.

Hazard, Paul. "Une source anglaise de l'abbé Prévost." *MP,* XXVII (1930), 339-44.

Steele's *Conscious lovers* as the source of a narrative in Volume V of Prévost's *Mémoires et aventures d'un homme de qualité.*

Laurence Sterne

A Facsimile reproduction of a unique catalogue of Laurence Sterne's library. With preface by Charles Whibley. London:

James Tregaskis; New York: Edgar H. Wells & co., 1930. Pp. 14+94.

Bensley, Edward. "An alleged source of 'Tristram Shandy.'" *N & Q*, CLIX (1930), 27, 84.

Concerning *The life and memoirs of Mr. Ephraim Tristram Bates* (1756). The article seems to have been written in ignorance of Helen Sard Hughes' study of the same subject in *JEGP*, XVII, 227-51.

Peter Sterry

Pinto, V. de Sola. "Peter Sterry and his unpublished writings." *RES*, VI (1930), 385-407.

Jonathan Swift

Ball, F. Elrington. *Swift's verse, an essay.* London: John Murray, 1929. Cf. *PQ*, IX, 201-02.

Rev. by Emile Pons in *RAA*, VII (1930), 343-45.

Eddy, William A. "Ned Ward and 'Lilliput.'" *N & Q*, CLVIII (1930), 148-49.

Rice, J. A., Jun. "A letter from Stella." *TLS*, May 29, 1930, p. 457.

Comment by Harold Williams, *ibid.*, June 5, 1930, p. 478; by Shane Leslie, *ibid.*, July 24, 1930, p. 611.

Van Doren, Carl. *Swift.* New York: Viking press, 1930. Pp. 279.

Williams, Harold. *"A hue and cry after dismal."* *RES*, VI (1930), 195-96.

Sir William Temple

The Early essays and romances of Sir William Temple, Bt., with the life and character of Sir William Temple by his sister, Lady Giffard. Edited from the original manuscripts by G. C. Moore Smith. Oxford: Clarendon press, 1930. Pp. xxviii+215.

Rev. in *TLS*, Jan. 22, 1931, p. 57.

Chang, Y. Z. "A note on sharawadgi." *MLN*, XLV (1930), 221-24.

Apropos of Temple's description of Chinese gardening.

William Johnston Temple

(See also *Samuel Johnson*)

Diaries of William Johnston Temple. Edited with a memoir by

Lewis Bettany. Oxford: Clarendon press, 1929. Cf. *PQ,* IX, 202.

Rev. by G. Kitchin in *MLR,* XXV (1930), 217-18; by G. C. Moore Smith in *RES,* VI (1930), 368-69; by F. A. Pottle in *MLN,* XLV (1930), 474-76.

James Thomson

Anwander, Erna. *Pseudoklassizistisches und Romantisches in Thomsons "Seasons."* Leipzig: Bernhard Tauchnitz, 1930. Pp. 132.

Drennon, Herbert. "James Thomson and Newtonianism." University of Chicago *Abstracts of theses,* Humanistic series, VII (1930), 523-28.

Williams, George G. "Did Thomson write the poem *To the memory of Mr. Congreve?*" *PMLA,* XLV (1930), 1010-13.

Concludes, largely on evidence of style and structure, that he did.

Thomas Tickell

Butt, J. E. "A 'first edition' of Tickell's 'Colin and Lucy.'" *Bodleian quarterly record,* VI (1930), 103-04.

Horace Walpole

Lewis, W. S. "A library dedicated to the life and works of Horace Walpole." *Colophon,* Part III, 1930.

A description of his own library, of which a *catalogue raisonné* is in preparation.

Needham, Francis. "A Strawberry Hill 'North Briton.'" *TLS,* Nov. 27, 1930, p. 1014.

Comment by John C. Fox, *ibid.,* Dec. 11, 1930, p. 1066.

Thomas Warton, Sr.

Thomas Warton the elder. Poems on several occasions. Reproduced from the edition of 1748. New York: Facsimile text society, 1930. Pp. 228.

Thomas Warton, Jr.

Verses on Sir Joshua Reynolds's painted window at New College, Oxford, 1782. By Thomas Warton. Oxford University press; London: Humphrey Milford, 1930. Pp. 7.

Hinton, Percival. "Thomas Warton's poems." *TLS,* Apr. 24, 1930, p. 352.

On the two editions of 1777. Cf. *TLS,* July 12, 1928, p. 520.

Smith, David Nichol. *Warton's History of English poetry.* London: Humphrey Milford, 1929. Pp. 29. ("Warton lecture on English poetry.")

Rev. by Paul Meissner in *Beiblatt,* XLI (1930), 338-39.

John Wesley

Wade, Donald. *John Wesley.* New York: Coward-McCann, 1930. Pp. 301.

Wright, Louis B. "John Wesley: scholar and critic." *South Atlantic quarterly,* XXIX (1930), 262-81.

Assembles a large number of Wesley's judgments on books and literary questions. Little interpretation.

Helen Maria Williams

Woodward, L. D. *Une adhérente anglaise de la Révolution française, Hélène-Maria Williams et ses amis.* Paris: Champion, 1930. Pp. 283.

Anne Finch, Countess of Winchilsea

Anderson, Paul Bunyan. "Mrs. Manley's text of three of Lady Winchilsea's poems." *MLN,* XLV (1930), 95-99.

William Wycherley

Connely, Willard. *Brawny Wycherley, first master in English modern comedy.* New York: Charles Scribner's sons, 1930. Pp. x+352.

Rev. by G. H. Nettleton in *SRL,* May 24, 1930, p. 1066.

Edward Young

Boas, F. S. "A manuscript copy of Edward Young's *Busiris.*" *TLS,* May 22, 1930, p. 434.

V. THE CONTINENTAL BACKGROUND

NOTE: I list here a few publications which seem to me of special importance for the student of English literature and ideas in the seventeenth and eighteenth centuries.

Ascoli, Georges. *La Grande-Bretagne devant l'opinion française au XVIIe siècle.* Paris: J. Gamber, 1930. Pp. 894.

Barr, Mary-Margaret H. *A century of Voltaire study: a bibliography of writings on Voltaire, 1825-1925.* New York: Institute of French studies, 1929. Pp. xxiii+123.

Brunet, Pierre. *Maupertuis.* Paris: A. Blanchard, 1929. 2 vols.

Rev. by Edmond Goblot in *Revue philosophique,* CX (1930), 469-70.

An important study. The first volume is a biography of Maupertuis; the second deals with his work and its place in the scientific thought of the eighteenth century.

Brunot, Ferdinand. *Histoire de la langue française des origines à 1900.* Tome VI, *Le XVIIIe siècle.* Première partie, "Le mouvement des idées et les vocabulaires techniques." Paris: Colin, 1930. Pp. 860.

A mine of texts and references for the student of eighteenth-century ideas.

Cohen, Gustave. "Le voyage de Samuel Sorbière en Hollande en 1660." *Mélanges . . . . Baldensperger* (Paris: Champion, 1930), I, 148-64.

Dargan, E. Preston. "The question of Voltaire's primacy in establishing the English vogue." *Mélanges . . . . Baldensperger* (Paris: Champion, 1930), I, 187-98.

Dodds, Muriel. *Les récits de voyages, sources de l'"Esprit des lois" de Montesquieu.* Paris: Champion, 1929. Pp. 304.

Rev. by G. L. van Roosbroeck in *Romanic review,* XXI (1930), 259-60.

DuPeloux, Vicomte Charles. *Repertoire biographique et bibliographique des artistes du XVIIIe siècle français.* Paris: Champion, 1930. Pp. viii+456.

François, Alexis. "Où en est 'romantique'?" *Mélanges . . . . Baldensperger* (Paris: Champion, 1930), I, 321-31.

A valuable lexicographical study.

Fusil, C.-A. "Lucrèce et les littérateurs poètes et artistes du XVIIIe siècle." *RHL,* XXXVII (1930), 161-76.

Guilloton, Vincent. "Autour de la *Relation* du voyage de Samuel Sorbière en Angleterre, 1663-1664." *Smith College studies in modern languages,* XI (1930), 1-29.

Interesting new light on the controversy provoked in England by Sorbière's book and especially on the part played in this controversy by the Royal Society.

Hazard, Paul. "'Cosmopolite.'" *Mélanges . . . . Baldensperger* (Paris: Champion, 1930), I, 354-64.

A sketch of the history of the word.

Hazard, Paul. "Qu'est-ce qu'un classique?" *Revue de France,* Nov. 1, 1930, pp. 160-65.

d'Irsay, Stephen. *Albrecht von Haller: eine Studie zur Geistesgeschichte der Aufklärung.* Leipzig: Thieme, 1930. Pp. vi+98.

Kies, Paul Philemon. "The influence of English drama on the early plays of Lessing." University of Chicago *Abstracts of theses,* Humanistic series, VII (1930), 529-33.

Lancaster, Henry Carrington. *A history of French dramatic literature in the seventeenth century.* Part I, *The pre-classical period, 1610-1634.* Baltimore: Johns Hopkins press, 1930. 2 vols.

Lanson, Gustave. *Études d'histoire littéraire.* Réunies et publiées par ses collègues, ses élèves et ses amis. Paris: Champion, 1929. Pp. 333.

Eight of the twelve studies reprinted in this volume concern the history of literature and ideas during the seventeenth and eighteenth centuries. They are: "Programme d'études sur l'histoire provinciale de la vie littéraire en France"; "L'influence de la philosophie cartésienne sur la littérature française"; "Le 'Discours sur les passions de l'amour' est-il de Pascal?"; "Sur une page de Bourdaloue"; "Le déterminisme historique et l'idéalisme social dans l'*Esprit des lois*"; "Le rôle de l'expérience dans la formation de la philosophie du XVIIIe siècle en France"; "Les idées littéraires de Condillac"; "Un manuscrit de *Paul et Virginie.*"

Mathiez, Albert. "La place de Montesquieu dans l'histoire des doctrines politiques au XVIIIe siècle." *Annales historiques de la Révolution française,* VII (1930), 97-112.

Montesquieu as a reactionary spokesman of the "feudal" point of view.

Miller, Minnie May. "The English influence in the *Choix des anciens Mercures et des autres journaux* (1757-64)." University of Chicago *Abstracts of theses,* Humanistic series, VII (1930), 475-80.

Miller, Minnie M. "Science and philosophy as precursors of the English influence in France: a study of the *Choix des anciens journaux.*" *PMLA,* XLV (1930), 856-96.

Moffat, M. *Rousseau et la querelle du théâtre au XVIIIe siècle.* Paris: Boccard, 1930. Pp. 430.

Montesquieu. Lettres persanes. Texte établi et présenté par Elie Carcassonne. Paris: F. Roches, 1929. 2 vols.

Rev. by G. L. van Roosbroeck in *Romanic review,* XXI (1930), 341-43 (adds useful details on the earlier history of the pseudo-"foreign letter" genre).

Morel, Jean-Emile. "Un essai d'interprétation du 'Discours de l'inégalité' d'après un livre récent." *Revue d'histoire moderne,* July-Aug., 1930, pp. 289-302.

A criticism of the views of Schinz in his *La pensée de Jean-Jacques Rousseau.* Suggests some important but often overlooked distinctions on the subject of the "natural goodness of man."

Peyre, Henri. "Pascal et la critique contemporaine." *Romanic review,* XXI (1930), 325-40.

An admirable review of recent scholarship.

Peyre, Henri. "Racine et la critique contemporaine." *PMLA,* XLV (1930), 848-55.

Philips, Edith. "French interest in Quakers before Voltaire." *PMLA,* XLV (1930), 238-55.

Philips, Edith. "Pensylvanie: l'age d'or." *AHR,* XXXVI (1930), 1-16.

Poole, E. Phillips. "Translations of 'Marianne.'" *TLS,* Feb. 20, 1930, p. 142.

Further details by Helen Sard Hughes, *ibid.,* Apr. 17, 1930, p. 336.

Schinz, Albert. *La pensée de Jean-Jacques Rousseau: essai d'interprétation nouvelle.* Paris: Alcan; Northampton, Mass.: Smith College, 1929. 2 vols. Cf. *PQ,* IX, 208.

Rev. by E. Preston Dargan in *MP,* XXVIII (1930), 117-20; by Adolphe-Jacques Dickman in *PQ,* IX (1930), 407-09; by Arthur O. Lovejoy in *MLN,* XLVI (1931), 41-46 (a penetrating and suggestive review).

Sée, Henri. "Le philosophie de l'histoire de Herder." *RSH,* XLVIII (1929), 21-36.

The Social and political ideas of some great French thinkers of the Age of Reason. Edited by F. J. C. Hearnshaw. London: Harrap; New York: Crofts, 1930.

Rev. by Carl Becker in *JMH,* III (1931), 116-18; by E. H. W. Meyerstein in *Saturday review,* Oct. 11, 1930, pp. 458, 460; by Arthur E. Murphy in *International journal of ethics,* XLI (1931), 270-71; by A. Paul in *Revue d'histoire moderne,* July-Aug., 1930, pp. 308-09.

Lectures at King's College, London, 1928-29, on Bossuet, Fénelon, the Abbé de Saint-Pierre, Montesquieu, Voltaire, Rousseau, Helvétius and Holbach, Morelly and Mably.

Terry, Charles Sanford. *John Christian Bach.* Oxford University press; London: Humphrey Milford, 1930. Pp. xvi+373.

Rev. in *TLS,* Apr. 10, 1930, p. 313.

Torrey, Norman L. *Voltaire and the English deists.* New Haven: Yale University press; London: Humphrey Milford, Oxford University press, 1930. Pp. x+224.

Rev. by C. M. Perry in *International journal of ethics,* XLI (1931), 255-56; in *TLS,* July 3, 1930, p. 544.

Voltaire. Zadig ou la destinée, histoire orientale. Edition critique avec une introduction et un commentaire par Georges Ascoli. Paris: Hachette, 1929. 2 vols. ("Société des textes français modernes.")

Besides the text the first volume contains an elaborate introduction on the composition and publication of *Zadig,* the effect which it produced, the later history of the text, the sources of the novel, its philosophy, its oriental coloring, and its art. A learned, though perhaps somewhat overcharged, commentary fills the second volume.

1932

ENGLISH LITERATURE, 1660-1800: A CURRENT BIBLIOGRAPHY

By R. S. CRANE and M. E. PRIOR
University of Chicago and Northwestern University

This bibliography attempts to list the more significant books, articles, and reviews published during the year 1931, together with some bearing the date 1930 that were inadvertently omitted from the bibliography for that year (*PQ*, X, 169-215).

LIST OF ABBREVIATIONS

AHR=*American historical review.*
Archiv=*Archiv für das Studium der neueren Sprachen und Literaturen.*
Beiblatt=*Beiblatt zur Anglia.*
DVLG=*Deutsche Vierteljahrsschrift für Literaturwissenschaft und Geistesgeschichte.*
EHR=*English historical review.*
ES=*Englische Studien.*
GRM=*Germanisch-romanische Monatsschrift.*
JEGP=*Journal of English and Germanic philology.*
JMH=*Journal of modern history.*
LM=*London mercury.*
MLN=*Modern language notes.*
MLR=*Modern language review.*
MP=*Modern philology.*
N & Q=*Notes and queries.*
PMLA=*Publications of the Modern Language Association of America.*
PQ=*Philological quarterly.*
RAA=*Revue anglo-américaine.*
RC=*Revue critique.*
RCC=*Revue des cours et conférences.*
RELV=*Revue de l'enseignement des langues vivantes.*
RES=*Review of English studies.*
RH=*Revue historique.*
RHL=*Revue d'histoire littéraire de la France.*
RHP=*Revue d'histoire de la philosophie.*
RLC=*Revue de littérature comparée.*
SP=*Studies in philology.*
SRL=*Saturday review of literature.*
TLS=*Times literary supplement.*

I. BIBLIOGRAPHIES AND BIBLIOGRAPHICAL STUDIES

Annual bibliography of English language and literature. Volume XI, 1930. Edited for the Modern Humanities Research Association by Mary S. Serjeantson, assisted by L. N. Broughton. Cambridge: Bowes & Bowes, 1931. Pp. ix+232.

Baugh, Albert C. "American bibliography for 1930: English language and literature." *PMLA,* XLVI (1931), 8-38.

See especially pp. 25-33.

Bernbaum, Ernest. "Recent works on prose fiction before 1800." *MLN,* XLVI (1931), 95-107.

Castell, Alburey. "Histories of modern European thought, 1918-1930." *JMH,* III (1931), 242-65.

Deals only with books in English, translations included. So far as it goes, however, it is a useful bibliographical survey, though the critical judgments show no great mastery of the field.

Catalogue of the very extensive and well-known library of English poetry, drama and other literature, principally of the XVII and early XVIII centuries, formed by the late George Thorn-Drury, Esq. K. C. London: Sotheby and co., 1931. 2 parts. Pp. 175.

Chapman, R. W. "Eighteenth-century imprints." *Library,* 4th series, XI (1931), 503-04.

Chapman, R. W. "Numbering of editions." *RES,* VII (1931), 213-15.

Chapman, R. W. "Thoughts on half-titles." *The colophon,* Part VII (1931).

Crane, Ronald S. "English literature, 1660-1800: a current bibliography." *PQ,* X (1930), 169-215.

Draper, John W. *Eighteenth century English æsthetics: a bibliography.* Heidelberg: Carl Winter, 1931. Pp. 140. ("Anglistische Forschungen," Heft 71.)

Rev. by R. S. C[rane] in *MP,* XXIX (1931), 251-52; by R. D. Havens in *MLN,* XLVII (1932), 118-20 (a valuable list of additional titles); by F. T. Wood in *ES,* LXVI (1931), 279-81.

Gabler, Anthony J. "Check list of English newspapers and periodicals before 1801 in the Huntington Library." *The Huntington Library bulletin,* Number 2 (November, 1931), pp. 1-66.

A useful list, especially valuable for the seventeenth century. The statement (p. 3) that the Library possesses two separate printings of Goldsmith's *Bee* (1759) should be corrected in the light of more detailed information supplied by the staff: the two copies vary in certain details, but all the sheets appear to be from the same setting of type.

Heawood, Edward. "Papers used in England after 1600. II. *c.* 1680-1750." *Library,* 4th series, XI (1931), 466-98.

Herrick, Marvin T. "A supplement to Cooper and Gudeman's bibliography of the *Poetics* of Aristotle." *American journal of philology,* LII (1931), 168-74.

Maclehose, James. *The Glasgow University press, 1638-1931, with some notes on Scottish printing in the last three hundred years.* Glasgow: University press, 1931.

Milford, R. T. "Cotes's weekly journal." *TLS,* March 19, 1931, p. 234.

Muddiman, J. G., and others. "The history and bibliography of English newspapers." *N & Q,* CLX (1931), 3-6, 21-24, 40-43, 57-59, 174-75, 207-09, 228-30, 264, 298-300, 336-38, 375, 391, 442-43; CLXI (1931), 337.

"Thirty-first critical bibliography of the history and philosophy of science and of the history of civilization (to March 1931)." *Isis,* XVI (1931), 476-575.

See especially pp. 493-504.

Wood, Frederick T. [Reviews of recent works on the eighteenth century.] *ES,* LXVI (1931), 122-38, 275-87.

The Year's work in English studies. Volume X, 1929. Edited for the English Association by F. S. Boas. Oxford: University press; London: Humphrey Milford, 1931. Pp. 418.

II. THE SOCIAL AND POLITICAL ENVIRONMENT

Anstey, L. M. "The library of a London merchant in the eighteenth century." *N & Q,* CLX (1931), 188-90.

The Diary of John Baker, barrister of the Middle Temple, solicitor-general of the Leeward Islands. . . . Edited by Philip C. Yorke. London: Hutchinson, 1931. Pp. xvii+517.

Rev. in *New statesman and Nation,* Aug. 29, 1931, pp. 256-57; in *TLS,* July 9, 1931, p. 540.

Blum, André. *La gravure en Angleterre au XVIIIe siècle.* Paris, 1930.

Rev. by Emil Waldmann in *Deutsche Literaturzeitung,* July 12, 1931, cols. 1315-17.

Borenius, Tancred. "On collecting Jacobite books and prints." *Book-collector's quarterly,* No. IV (October-December, 1931), pp. 1-22,

Brandenburg, S. J. "The place of agriculture in British national economy prior to Adam Smith." *Journal of political economy,* XXXIX (1931), 281-320.

Brown, Louise Fargo. "The first Earl of Shaftesbury." *Persecution and liberty: essays in honor of George Lincoln Burr* (New York: Century co., 1931), pp. 361-73.

Cahen, Léon. "Le 'diable' Wilkes." *Revue d'histoire moderne,* Jan.-Feb., 1931, pp. 56-61.

A review of the books by Postgate and Sherrard (cf. *PQ,* X, 174-75).

Campbell, Andrew J. *Two centuries of the Church of Scotland, 1707-1929.* Paisley: A. Gardner, 1931. Pp. 317.

Rev. in *TLS,* March 26, 1931, p. 244.

The King of the beggars: Bampfylde-Moore Carew. Edited by C. H. Wilkinson. Oxford: Clarendon press; London: Humphrey Milford, 1931. Pp. xxiv+307.

Rev. in *TLS,* Oct. 8, 1931, p. 767.

Castells, F. de P. *English freemasonry in its period of transition, A. D. 1600-1700.* London: Rider, 1931. Pp. 222.

Rev. in *TLS,* Nov. 5, 1931, p. 870.

The Blecheley diary of the Rev. William Cole, 1765-1767. Edited from the original manuscript in the British Museum by Francis Griffin Stokes. With an introduction by Helen Waddell. London: Constable, 1931. Pp. ix+392.

Rev. in *TLS,* Jan. 14, 1932, p. 23.

A Journal of my journey to Paris in the year 1765. By the Rev. William Cole. Edited from the original manuscript in the British Museum by Francis Griffin Stokes. With an introduction by Helen Waddell. London: Constable, 1931. Pp. xxxii +410.

Rev. by Osbert Burdett in *Saturday review,* Feb. 7, 1931, pp. 203-04; by Paul Yvon in *RAA,* IX (1931), 60-61; in *TLS,* Feb. 19, 1931, p. 127.

deBeer, G. R. *Early travellers in the Alps.* London: Sidgwick and Jackson, 1931. Pp. xx+204.

Rev. in *TLS,* March 5, 1931, p. 169.

Draper, John W. "Social influences once more." *RAA,* VIII (1931), 489-95.

Dutcher, George Matthew. "Further considerations on the origins and nature of the enlightened despotism." *Persecution and liberty: essays in honor of George Lincoln Burr* (New York: Century co., 1931), pp. 375-403.

George, M. Dorothy. *England in transition: life and work in the eighteenth century.* London: Routledge, 1931. Pp. vii+229.

Gill, Doris M. "The treasury, 1660-1714." *EHR,* XLVI (1931), 600-22.

Hervey, John Lord. *Some materials towards memoirs of the reign of King George II.* Printed from a copy of the original manuscript in the Royal Archives at Windsor Castle, and from the original manuscript at Ickworth. Edited by Romney Sedgwick. London: Eyre and Spottiswoode, 1931. 3 vols.

Rev. by A. Birrell in *New statesman,* Nov. 14, 1931, Lit. sup., pp. viii, x;

by Bonamy Dobrée in *English review,* LIII (1931), 748-50; in *TLS,* Sept. 24, 1931, p. 724.

Johnson, Edgar A. J. "The mercantilist concept of 'art' and 'ingenious labour.'" *Economic history,* II, No. 6 (Jan., 1931), 234-53.

Jones, I. Deane. *The English revolution, an introduction to English history, 1603-1714.* London: Heinemann, 1931. Pp. xvi +361.

Rev. in *TLS,* June 11, 1931, p. 457.

Judges, A. V. "The origins of English banking." *History,* XVI (1931), 138-45.

Developments before the foundation of the Bank of England in 1694.

Lee, Umphrey. *The historical backgrounds of early Methodist enthusiasm.* New York: Columbia University press, 1931. Pp. 176.

Rev. by M. E. Graddis in *Journal of religion,* XII (1932), 126-27.

Lipson, E. *The economic history of England.* Volumes II and III: *The age of mercantilism.* London: A. and C. Black, 1931.

Rev. by G. D. H. Cole in *Week-end review,* Aug. 29, 1931, pp. 255-56; by Hugh Massingham in *Observer,* Aug. 2, 1931, p. 4; by C. F. Ray in *Economic journal,* XLI (1931), 624-28.

Lodge, Sir Richard. "English foreign policy, 1660-1715." *History,* XV (1931), 296-307.

A review of recent works.

McLachlan, H. *English education under the Test acts, being the history of the non-conformist academies, 1662-1820.* Manchester: University press, 1931. Pp. xi+344.

Rev. in *TLS,* Nov. 12, 1931, p. 878.

Map of XVII century England, with description, chronological tables, and a map of London, circa 1660. Southampton: Ordnance survey, 1931. Pp. 24.

Maxwell, L. F. *A bibliography of English law from 1651 to 1800.* London: Sweet and Maxwell, 1931. Pp. viii+270.

Rev. by A. R. H. in *Library Association record,* 3d series, I (1931), 433.

Nulle, Stebelton H. *Thomas Pelham-Holles, Duke of Newcastle: his early political career, 1693-1724.* Philadelphia: University of Pennsylvania press; London: Humphrey Milford, 1931. Pp. x+204.

Rev. by W. T. Laprade in *AHR,* XXXVII (1931), 107-08; by the same in *South Atlantic quarterly,* XXX (1931), 319-20; in *TLS,* July 9, 1931, p. 537.

Oliver, F. S. *The endless adventure.* Volume II, 1727-1735. London: Macmillan, 1931. Pp. xiii+333.

Rev. in *TLS,* Apr. 23, 1931, p. 315.
Cf. *PQ,* IX, 170.

The Purefoy letters, 1735-1753. Edited by G. Eland. London: Sidgwick and Jackson, 1931. 2 vols.

Realey, Charles Bechdolt. *The early opposition to Sir Robert Walpole, 1720-1727.* Lawrence, Kansas: University of Kansas, Department of journalism press, 1931. Pp. 280.

Richardson, A. E. *Georgian England.* London: Batsford; New York: Charles Scribner's sons, 1931. Pp. 202.

Rev. by Edwin Clark in *New York Times book review,* June 21, 1931, p. 11; in *TLS,* Jan. 7, 1932, p. 9.

"Rhodon." "Wilkes and the *North Briton.*" *N & Q,* CLXI (1931), 165-66.

Cf. also *ibid.,* pp. 211-12, 268.

Taylor, G. R. Stirling. *Robert Walpole and his age.* London: Jonathan Cape, 1931. Pp. 343.

Rev. by A. Birrell in *New statesman and Nation,* July 18, 1931, pp. 82-83; in *TLS,* Aug. 6, 1931, p. 603.

Terry, Charles Sanford. *Bach: the historical approach.* Oxford: University press; London: Humphrey Milford, 1931. Pp. 157.

Rev. in *TLS,* Apr. 3, 1931, p. 265.

Wadsworth, A. P., and Julia de Lacy Mann. *The cotton trade and industrial Lancashire, 1600-1780.* Manchester: University press, 1931.

Rev. by H. L. Beales in *New statesman and Nation,* Aug. 8, 1931, pp. 174-76; in *Observer,* July 19, 1931, p. 4.

The Eighteenth volume of the Walpole society, 1929-1930. Vertue notebooks. Volume I. Oxford: Printed for the Walpole society at the Oxford University press, 1931. Pp. xxviii+163.

Rev. by I. A. Williams in *LM,* XXIV (1931), 437-43; in TLS, Apr. 9, 1931, p. 283.

Whiting, C. E. *Studies in English puritanism from the Restoration to the Revolution.* London: S.P.C.K., 1931. Pp. 584.

Rev. in *TLS,* Aug. 27, 1931, p. 640.

Zimmermann, Henry. *An account of the third voyage of Captain Cook around the world, 1776-1780.* Translated from the Mannheim edition of 1781 by Elsa Michaelis and Cecil French. Edited with an introduction and notes by F. W. Howay. Toronto: Ryerson press, 1931. Pp. 120.

Rev. in *TLS,* Apr. 30, 1931, p. 334; cf. *ibid.,* May 7, 1931, p. 367, and Nov. 5, 1931, p. 866.

III. MOVEMENTS OF IDEAS AND LITERARY FORMS

Allen, Robert J. "The Kit-cat Club and the theatre." *RES,* VII (1931), 56-61.

An Anthology of Augustan poetry. Compiled and edited by Frederick T. Wood. London and New York: Macmillan, 1931. Pp. lxix+323.

Rev. in *TLS*, Nov. 5, 1931, p. 861.

Babcock, Robert Witbeck. *The genesis of Shakespeare idolatry, 1766-1799: a study in English criticism of the late eighteenth century.* Chapel Hill [N.C.]: University of North Carolina press, 1931. Pp. xxviii+307.

Rev. in *Books*, Nov. 29, 1931, p. 10; in *TLS*, Oct. 22, 1931, p. 823.

Black, A. Bruce, and Robert Metcalf Smith. *Shakespeare allusions and parallels.* Bethlehem, Pennsylvania: Lehigh University, 1931. Pp. viii+59.

Hitherto unnoted allusions from the period 1599-1701.

Blunden, Edmund. *Votive tablets: studies chiefly appreciative of English authors and books.* London: Cobden-Sanderson, 1931. Pp. 367.

Rev. in *TLS*, Nov. 26, 1931, p. 942.
Contains essays on Bunyan, Defoe, Steele, Goldsmith, Churchill, etc.

Bonar, James. *Theories of population from Raleigh to Arthur Young.* London: G. Allen & Unwin, 1931. P. 253.

Rev. by N. E. Himes in *Journal of political economy*, XXXIX (1931), 850-51; by Henry Macrosty in *Economic journal*, XLI (1931), 466-69.

Bond, Richmond P., John W. Bowyer, C. B. Millican, and G. Hubert Smith. "A collection of Chaucer allusions." *SP*, XXVIII (1931), 481-512.

Pp. 486-508 deal with the Restoration and eighteenth century.

Bosker, A. *Literary criticism in the age of Johnson.* Groningen: J. B. Wolters, 1930. Cf. *PQ*, X, 177-78.

Rev. by A. Digeon in *RAA*, IX (1931), 59; by R. D. Havens in *MLN*, XLVII (1932), 137-38; by Harold Jenkins in *MLR*, XXVI (1931), 357-58; by Willem van Doorn in *English studies*, XIII (1931), 30-32.

Boswell, Eleanore. "A playbill of 1687." *Library*, 4th series, XI (1931), 499-502.

Bréhier, Emile. *Histoire de la philosophie.* Tome II, *La philosophie moderne.* II, "Le dix-huitème siècle." Paris: Alcan, 1930. Cf. *PQ*, X, 178-79.

Rev. by D. Mornet in *RHL*, XXXVIII (1931), 323-25.

Buck, Gerhard. *Die Vorgeschichte des historischen Romans in der modernen englischen Literatur.* Hamburg: Friedrichsen, de Gruyter and co., 1931. Pp. 115.

Rev. in *TLS*, Nov. 12, 1931, p. 895.

Burra, Peter. *Baroque and Gothic sentimentalism.* London: Duckworth, 1931. Pp. 35.

A suggestive but rather superficial essay.

Clapp, Sarah L. C. "The beginnings of subscription publication in the seventeenth century." *MP,* XXIX (1931), 199-224.

An able and important study of the period before about 1688.

Cole, F. J. *Early theories of sexual generation.* Oxford: Clarendon press, 1930. Cf. *PQ,* X, 179.

Rev. by Pierre Brunet in *Archeion,* XIII (1931), 271-72; by Charles A. Kofoid in *Isis,* XVI (1931), 463-65.

Conway letters. The correspondence of Anne, Viscountess Conway, Henry More, and their friends, 1624-1684. Collected from manuscript sources & edited with a biographical account by Marjorie Hope Nicolson. New Haven: Yale University press; London: Humphrey Milford, Oxford University press, 1930. Cf. *PQ,* X, 179-80.

Rev. by Edwin Clark in *New York Times book review,* Oct. 4, 1931, p. 20; by Archibald Malloch in *Yale review,* XX (1931), 613-15; by S. P. Lamprecht in *MLN,* XLVI (1931), 541-42; by J. Pelseneer in *Isis,* XVI (1931), 141-43; by G. C. Moore Smith in *RES,* VII (1931), 349-56; by Harold Williams in *MLR,* XXVI (1931), 200-02; in *TLS,* Jan. 29, 1931, p. 71.

Craig, Mary Elizabeth. *The Scottish periodical press, 1750-1789.* Edinburgh and London: Oliver and Boyd, 1931. Pp. vi+113.

Rev. in *TLS,* Oct. 29, 1931, p. 840; cf. J. M. Bulloch, *ibid.,* Nov. 5, 1931, p. 866.

The body of Miss Craig's study consists of a series of precise and useful notes on the newspapers and other periodicals published between 1750 and 1789 in Edinburgh, Glasgow, Aberdeen, Dundee, Perth, Dumfries, Kelso, and Berwick-upon-Tweed. There are also introductory and concluding chapters on the conditions that affected the development of periodicals in Scotland during this period and on the place of the press in the life of the people. The appendixes to the book include a chart of the periodicals running during each of the years covered by the study and an alphabetical list of journals with indications of the libraries of Great Britain and the United States in which copies are to be found. Altogether a capable and thorough piece of work.

Crum, Ralph B. *Scientific thought in poetry.* New York: Columbia University press, 1931. Pp. vi+246.

The author seeks to throw light on "the vexed question of the relationship of science and poetry" by considering how some of the poets of the past have treated the themes afforded by the scientific thought of their day. Since he deals with poets important in this connection from Lucretius to John Davidson, only a part of his book comes within the scope of this bibliography—and what does is not entirely satisfactory. The very extent of the material he covers is responsible for some of his chief weaknesses—his many loose generalizations, his fondness for formulae the implications of which he has not always understood, his sometimes casual use of important normative terms. Here are a few examples: the very loose application of the term "deism" which permits the view that this form of religious rationalism grew almost directly out of the development of mechanistic science (pp. 9, 62); the statement that "the new scientific spirit . . . . had a distinct tendency now to break down the rigorous classification of the genres which pseudo-classicism had prescribed" (p. 90), without any indication of how or why scientific thought effected this change in criticism; the idea that it was Locke who was responsible for the application of mechanistic principles to psychology (pp. 9, 61), a view which leads one to wonder wherein Locke brought this about more completely than Hobbes had done a generation earlier; the assertion that the publication of Newton's *Principia* "opened for the whole field of human thought the mathematical ideal of science" (p. 61), a generalization which completely neglects the great influence of Cartesianism; the discussion of the "anti-rationalism" of such writers as Rochester and Mandeville as if the background of this radical solution of the problem of the reason and the passions were somehow largely scientific (pp. 57, 63); the implication (Chapter IV, *passim*) that "the English poet's respect for tradition in the first half of the eighteenth century is a sufficient explanation of the fact that he does not whole-heartedly praise the conception of a mechanical world" (p. 74), whereas the poets were in this respect consciously following such great English scientists as Boyle and Newton, who were themselves more than reluctant to accept a purely mechanical world. These examples illustrate sufficiently, perhaps, the confusions into which the author frequently falls in his attempt to deal with the history of scientific ideas during this period. His occasional failure to do justice to the poets themselves appears, for example, in his neglect of Thomson's *Seasons*, a poem which can scarcely be paralleled for its passages of versified Newtonianism.—M. E. P.

Deane, Cecil V. *Dramatic theory and the rhymed heroic play.* Oxford: University press; London: Humphrey Milford, 1931. Pp. vii+235.

Rev. in *TLS*, July 16, 1931, p. 561.

Draper, John W. *The funeral elegy and the rise of English romanticism.* New York: New York University press, 1929. Cf. *PQ*, IX, 173-76; X, 181.

Rev. by Maurice Kelley in *ES*, LXV (1931), 401-03; by C. A. Moore in *MLN*, XLVI (1931), 270-71; by W. O. Raymond in *JEGP*, XXX (1931), 122-26.

"Early poetry for children." *TLS*, Nov. 26, 1931, pp. 923-24.

Engel, Claire-Eliane. *La littérature alpestre en France et en Angleterre au XVIIIe et XIXe siècles.* Chambéry: Librairie Dardel, 1930. Pp. xi+287.

Rev. by L. Cazamian in *RAA*, IX (1931), 155-58; by René Galland in *RLC*, XI (1931), 806-09; by Pierre Martino in *RC*, LXV (1931), 277.

Miss Engel's subject is the rise and flourishing of enthusiasm for the Alps—and incidentally for mountains in general—as expressed by English, French, and Swiss writers—and incidentally painters—between 1685 and 1868. Of the five parts into which she divides her exposition, the last three deal almost entirely with the nineteenth century, and, as far as I can judge, they deserve the praise that has been bestowed on them in the reviews listed above. I wish I could feel equally satisfied with the earlier portions of her book. On the whole, however, and aside from a few interesting pages on the awakening of a scientific concern with the Alps after 1750 and fairly substantial studies of H.-B. de Saussure and Ramond de Carbonnières, the chapters in which she treats of the beginning and spread of Alpinism in the eighteenth century are—for a French doctor's thesis at any rate—surprisingly meager in content and feeble in interpretation.

As an indication of the superficiality of her treatment it is sufficient to say that she has built her conclusions concerning English interest in the Alps and in mountains generally before 1801 on a bibliography that includes no more than sixty odd works of all types—books of travel, novels, poems, scientific treatises—and that she nowhere shows any acquaintance with the valuable contributions to her problem made in recent years by scholars like Elizabeth Manwaring and C. A. Moore. The consequence is that she is seldom able to tell us more about the major aspects of her subject than most of us knew already, and that on certain important questions she remains wedded to views that have long since been seriously qualified or rejected outright by specialists in the field. Thus she still seems to believe that until about 1740 the attitude toward mountains entertained by educated Englishmen was almost universally one of repugnance. ''L'animosité qu'inspirent les montagnes domine tout, et se double d'un manque total du sens des proportions: toutes les sommités sont redoutables et tristes, depuis les taupinières de Windsor Forest, que Pope compare pompeusement à l'Olympe, jusqu'aux Alpes'' (p. 9): to this generalization she recognizes only two exceptions, a passage in a letter by Lady Mary Wortley Montagu written in 1747 and a sentence or two by Addison in his *Remarks on several parts of Italy* (1705). Now it cannot of course be denied that enthusiasm for the peculiar beauty of mountains was less widely prevalent among Englishmen at the beginning of the eighteenth century than it became a generation later on. But that is not to say that it was not far more common in the years between 1685 and 1720 than Miss Engel is willing to admit: the striking passages quoted by Moore and Miss Manwaring from writers of as varied temperaments as Burnet, Dennis, Addison, Shaftesbury, and Berkeley should have made that clear beyond question (see *SP,* XIV [1917], 252 n, 262-64; Manwaring, *Italian landscape in eighteenth century England* [1925], pp. 5-12; cf. also the texts referred to below).

The early portions of Miss Engel's book are disappointing in still another respect. Even if one were disposed to accept her contention that there was no significant appreciation of mountain scenery in England or France before 1740, the problem of accounting for its appearance when it did finally arrive would still remain. There are no signs, however, that she has given the question any serious thought. In one place, indeed, she throws out a suggestion that might, had her reading been more extensive and her curiosity stronger, have led to interesting interpretative results. ''Le finalisme chrétien du XVIIe siècle,'' she writes (p. 9), ''chercha avec beaucoup de patience les raisons qui avaient pu amener le Créateur à semer la terre de ces obstacles néfastes.'' But she immediately adds: ''On n'offrit jamais que des solutions très réalistes: . . . . Les montagnes donnent naissance aux pluies, aux fleuves, aux vents. La pluie produit le nitre et le phosphore (?): tout cela est indispensable à la vie humaine'' (pp. 9-10). The truth is that before 1720, in England at least, the popularity of the argument from design had resulted, among orthodox divines and deists alike, in a fairly common insistence not merely upon the utility of mountains but upon their beauty as well. See, for example, Gracián, *The critick,* tr. Rycaut (1681), pp. 37-38; John Ray, *Three physico-theological discourses* (2d ed., 1693), pp. 35-36; Richard Bentley, *Works,* ed. Dyce (1838), III, 193-99 (Bentley's eighth Boyle Lecture, preached Dec. 5, 1692); William Nichols, *A conference with a theist* (3d ed., 1723), II, 472-73 (originally published in 1699); Shaftesbury, *The moralists* (1709), in *Characteristics,* ed. Robertson (1900), II, 122-24; Henry Needler, ''On the beauty of the universe'' (written before 1718), in *Works* (3d ed., 1735), p. 67. Thanks to works like these, some of which carried an unusual weight of authority, the idea was widely disseminated at the beginning of the eighteenth century that the irregular mountainous masses of the earth were intended by God to add to man's aesthetic pleasure as well as to his material comfort.

Of all this Miss Engel gives no hint, and she is equally silent about another current of ideas which became prominent at the same time and which contributed no less directly to the encouragement of the taste for mountain scenery. This was the extension into the field of aesthetic theory of the old notion that things as Nature made them are inherently superior to things shaped and disciplined by human art. When with this idea there was associated, as was frequently the case, the further assumption that the essential attributes of Nature are ''wildness'' and ''irregularity,'' a revolt was inevitable against what Miss Engel calls ''le désir d'ordre, d'équilibre et de raison qui règne, tout puissant, sur les esprits de l'âge classique'' (p. 13). Expressions of such a revolt began to appear very early in the century. ''I shall no longer,'' declared Philocles in *The moralists*, ''resist the passion growing in me for things of a natural kind, where neither art nor the conceit or caprice of man has spoiled their genuine order by breaking in upon that primitive state. Even the rude rocks, the mossy caverns, the irregular unwrought grottos and broken falls of waters, with all the horrid graces of the wilderness itself, as representing Nature more, will be the more engaging, and appear with a magnificence beyond the formal mockery of princely gardens'' (*Characteristics,* ed. Robertson, II, 125). This was in 1709: during the next half century the ideas to which Shaftesbury here gives expression were among the most potent forces making for the reform of landscape gardening and, somewhat later, for the revival of a taste for Gothic architecture. That they also played an important rôle in breaking down the old indifference to mountains is hardly less evident. Addison clearly was thinking in terms of the new aesthetics of irregularity when in 1705 he described the Alps near Geneva as ''broken into so many Steeps and Precipices, that they fill the Mind with an agreeable kind of Horror, and form one of the most irregular misshapen Scenes in the World'' (quoted by Manwaring, pp. 11-12); and the same assumption underlay his remarks in the *Spectator* about the pleasure the imagination derives from ''that rude kind of Magnificence'' which appears in ''a vast uncultivated Desart, ... huge Heaps of Mountains, high Rocks and Precipices . . . .'' (No. 412). So too Shaftesbury, in a passage of *The moralists* immediately preceding the description of mountains cited above: ''The wildness pleases. We seem to live alone with Nature. We view her in her inmost recesses, and contemplate her with more delight in these original wilds than in the artificial labyrinths and feigned wildernesses of the palace'' (*Characteristics,* II, 122).—R. S. C.

Evans, Joan. *Pattern: a study of ornament in Western Europe from 1180 to 1900.* Oxford: Clarendon press, 1931. 2 vols.

Rev. in *TLS,* July 9, 1931, p. 541.

A very important book, which students of literary taste during the seventeenth and eighteenth centuries cannot afford to neglect.

Fairchild, Hoxie Neale. *The romantic quest.* New York: Columbia University press, 1931. Pp. viii+444.

Foster, James R. ''The minor English novelists, 1750-1800.'' *Harvard University summaries of theses,* II (1930), 172-75.

Gabrielson, Arvid. *Edward Bysshe's Dictionary of rhymes (1702) as a source of information on early modern English pronunciation.* Uppsala and Stockholm: Almquist, 1931. Pp. xi+87.

Garofalo, L. ''Il problema dell' infinito dal Rinascimento a Kant.'' *Logos,* XIV (1931), 1-23.

''The Gentleman's magazine, 1731-1907.'' *TLS,* June 11, 1931, pp. 453-54.

Graham, Walter. *English literary periodicals.* New York: Thomas Nelson & sons, 1930. Cf. *PQ,* X, 182.

Rev. by E. A. B. in *MLR,* XXVI (1931), 499; by E. N. S. Thompson in *PQ,*

X (1931), 410-11; by N. I. White in *South Atlantic quarterly*, XXX (1931), 332-33; by D. Willoughby in *Saturday review*, Feb. 28, 1931, p. 316; in *TLS*, June 4, 1931, p. 442.

Gray, Charles Harold. *Theatrical criticism in London to 1795.* New York: Columbia University press, 1931. Pp. vi+333.

Gregory, Joshua C. *A short history of atomism, from Democritus to Bohr.* London: Black, 1931. Pp. 258.

Rev. in *TLS*, Sept. 17, 1931, p. 704.

Hawkins, Aubrey. "Some writers on *The monthly review.*" *RES*, VII (1931), 168-81.

Based on Griffiths' marked copy in the Bodleian Library.

Hayes, Carlton J. H. *The historical evolution of modern nationalism.* New York: Richard R. Smith, 1931. Pp. viii+327.

By "modern nationalism" Hayes means the body of explicitly formulated doctrines about the value of nationality which have been increasingly fashionable in Europe since the middle of the eighteenth century. He makes no attempt to reduce these doctrines to unity; nationalism, he rightly insists, "is plural rather than singular"; and he shows that during the period with which he is concerned there have flourished no less than five major "nationalisms" differing widely from each other in both motives and temper: humaritarian nationalism, Jacobin nationalism, traditional nationalism, liberal nationalism, and "integral" nationalism. Of each of these he gives an admirably clear, though not always very detailed, account, mainly in the form of separate studies of its most influential or representative spokesmen. Thus (to speak only of the period before 1800) he analyzes humanitarian nationalism in terms of Bolingbroke, Rousseau, and Herder; traditional nationalism in terms of Burke; and liberal nationalism in terms of Bentham.

Hayes writes primarily for the general public, and this fact, together with the scale of treatment which he has adopted, prevents him from doing anything like full justice to the various problems presented by the rise of nationalism in the eighteenth century. Eventually we ought to look forward to a work on the subject comparable in scale and similar in method to the *Documentary history of primitivism* now under way at the Johns Hopkins University. Starting with a thorough and richly illustrated analysis of the cosmopolitanism of the Enlightenment, especially in its relation to the prevailing ideals of uniformity and universality, such a work would proceed to describe in detail the various developments in philosophy, political theory, history, and aesthetics before 1800 which involved either the modification or the reversal of this dominant view. It would neglect none of the aspects of the subject touched on by Hayes, but it would add others concerning which he has little or nothing to say. One of its important chapters, for example, would be devoted to tracing the rise of nationalist ideals in the criticism of literature and art, from their appearance in the later seventeenth century in discussions of special *genres* such as oratory and the drama, through the more generalized theories of writers like Condillac and Goldsmith in the middle of the eighteenth century, to the full blown "romantic" nationalism of Herder and Friedrich Schlegel after 1780. Another chapter, even more important, would bring together the many writings of the seventeenth and eighteenth centuries which undertook to set forth (in the words of one of them) "The Reasons of that great Diversity to be observed in the Customs, Manners, and Usages of Nations" (*Civil polity* [1703], titlepage); it would then attempt to explain by what profound transformation of values there ultimately emerged out of this purely speculative concern with the differences separating nations the conviction that these differences were the result, not of human defect or "prejudice," but of the original intent of a beneficent Nature, an instance, as Scott wrote in 1826, "of that general variety which Nature seems to have adopted as a principle through all her works, as anxious, apparently, to avoid, as modern statesmen to enforce, any thing like an approach to absolute 'uniformity' " (*Prose works,* XXI [1839], 374). An adequate treatment of these and other relevant topics would be a work of years and would require the collaboration of specialists in several widely different fields; but I can think of few undertakings in the general history of eighteenth-century ideas which would have greater significance for an understanding of the modern world.—R. S. C.

Heal, Ambrose. *The English writing-masters and their copy-books, 1570-1800: a biographical dictionary and a bibliography.* With an introduction on the development of handwriting by Stanley Morison. Cambridge: University press, 1931. Pp. xl+225.

Rev. in *TLS,* Oct. 15, 1931, p. 793.

Heal, Ambrose. "The projector of circulating libraries." *N & Q,* CLXI (1931), 358.

Hudson, Arthur Palmer. "The hermit and divine providence." *SP,* XXVIII (1931), 750-66.

A study of treatments of the theme by Henry More, Cotton Mather, Parnell, and Voltaire interpreted "as indexes of the intellectual outlooks and artistic powers of the story-tellers." One misses a reference to the latest discussion of the subject—that by G. Ascoli in his edition of *Zadig* (Paris, 1929), II, 136-64.

Jaggard, William. "Literary secrets. Authorship of the 'Whole duty of man' and cognate writings, 1658-84." *Bookman* (London), LXXXI (1931), 66-69.

Jan, Eduard von. "Humanité." *Zeitschrift für französische Sprache und Literatur,* LV (1931), 1-66.

A valuable study of the meanings of the term from classical Rome to the present time.

Jones, Richard F. "The attack on pupit eloquence in the Restoration: an episode in the development of the neo-classical standard for prose." *JEGP,* XXX (1931), 188-217.

The self-conscious attempt to develop a new prose during the seventeenth century was not confined to any single group of writers. The present article, dealing with the efforts of numerous clergymen in England to reform the style of sermons in the direction of greater clarity and avoidance of excessive ornament, supplements Jones's previous study of the movement for a reform in style sponsored by the scientists of the same period; and, with its added material, it gives some indication of how general was the impulse toward a new type of prose. So widespread a movement—and the two groups already mentioned by no means exhaust the list of those who were actively concerned in the matter—argues the presence of general and inclusive causes which left their effects in various fields of writing. After reading this article, one has the impression that, in spite of certain qualifications, Jones considers "science" the principal cause of the change in style, and perhaps the only influence seriously worth considering. His general position is that these "new stylistic values soon spread from the scene of their origin [science], and, owing to the popularity of the new science and to the representative nature of the membership of the Royal Society, were widely disseminated" (p. 189). He considers, accordingly, the possible connections with science of each of the ecclesiastics whom he cites, urging the point at times, as in the case of South

(p. 192 and n. 10), when the connection seems remote and the attitude of the writer in question not wholly sympathetic. In the light of the thoroughgoing manner in which Jones applies this point of view, his suggestions of other possible influencing factors (pp. 204-07) are not felt to have much weight with him.

No one would be willing seriously to dispute the fact that the English scientists made a powerful plea for a plain style adapted to the needs of scientific exposition, or that this program of reform left a definite impression on the attitude toward prose style, and on the actual practice of a modified prose, among their numerous disciples. Nevertheless, Jones's treatment of the problem raises some questions. One of these centers in his use of the word "science," which for him seems to mean only the Baconian spirit of experimentation as exemplified in the Royal Society. This limited interpretation underlies his statement that Glanvill's style "when under the influence of Descartes, remained highly rhetorical, but when he came under the discipline of the scientists, it underwent a remarkable change toward simplicity and directness" (p. 199, n. 27). Does not this opinion, however, disregard completely Descartes' views about the place of rhetoric in philosophical exposition (*Discours*, ed. Gilson, p. 7) and his own practice as a writer? Does it not imply, besides, a definition of the term "science" which, in its virtual exclusion of Descartes and its suggestion that his work was opposed to all that the Royal Society stood for, gives a far too simplified impression of the intellectual movements of the time? On the question, moreover, of the scientists' feelings about style, Jones takes a position that seems again a little uncompromising, as when, for example, he remarks that "the nonconformists would not, like the scientists, sweep away all metaphors" (p. 211). Were the scientists desirous of sweeping away all metaphors? In the writing up of experiments, yes; but they certainly did not deny the appropriateness of the ornaments of style in other forms of discourse (see the references in *PQ*, X [1931], 185). Neglect of this point is at least in part responsible for Jones's (needless) surprise that Glanvill, who is an important support for his general argument, should have defended the use of a certain amount of rhetoric in sermons (p. 212; Glanvill, incidentally, restates this point in *The zealous and impartial Protestant* [1681], pp. 39-41).

If, for a moment, we accept Jones's position without question, we shall find that the facts he presents are not always harmonious among themselves. We are told, for example, that the "reformation of pulpit eloquence began earlier in France than in England" (p. 214), and also that with the French "the scientific movement was not so strong as with the English" (p. 215). The second statement remains to be proved, but if we grant it, we are led to entertain possibilities which will not fit in readily with the logically simple pattern of cause and effect relationships which Jones has set up between science and the reform of pupit eloquence in England. In short, when a movement embraces so many fields, and is found active in so many centers, it seems a little unconvincing to argue that its cause was one—i.e., science—particularly as the cause is usually thought of as operating characteristically in one locality—i.e., England.—M. E. P.

Kastner, L. E. "Saint-Amant and the English poets." *MLR*, XXVI (1931), 180-82.

Cf. *PQ*, X, 193.

Kitchin, George. *A survey of burlesque and parody in English.* Edinburgh and London: Oliver and Boyd, 1931. Pp. xxiv+388.

Rev. by Osbert Burdett in *Saturday review*, May 23, 1931, pp. 263-64; in *TLS*, Sept. 10, 1931, pp. 669-70.

Chapters III-VII deal with the Restoration and eighteenth century.

Longaker, Mark. *English biography in the eighteenth century.* Philadelphia: University of Pennsylvania press, 1931. Pp. ix+519.

Rev. in *TLS,* Dec. 3, 1931, p. 985.

Marcus, Hans. *Friedrich der Grosse in der englischen Literatur.* Leipzig: Mayer & Müller, 1930. Pp. vi+308.

Rev. in *TLS,* March 19, 1931, p. 235.

Meissner, Paul. "Die rationalistische Grundlage der englischen Kultur des 17. Jahrhunderts." *Anglia,* LV (1931), 321-67.

Morison, Stanley. *Ichabod Dawks and his news-letter, with an account of the Dawks family of booksellers and stationers, 1635-1731.* Cambridge: University press, 1931. Pp. viii+41.

Rev. in *N & Q,* CLXI (1931), 340-41; in *TLS,* Nov. 12, 1931, p. 887.

Morris, C. R. *Locke, Berkeley, Hume.* Oxford: Clarendon press, 1931. Pp. 174.

Rev. by S. P. Lamprecht in *Journal of philosophy,* XXVIII (1931), 664-66; in *TLS,* Apr. 23, 1931, p. 320.

Muirhead, John H. *The Platonic tradition in Anglo-Saxon philosophy: studies in the history of idealism in England and America.* London: George Allen & Unwin, 1931. Pp. 446.

Rev. by H. Barker in *Mind,* XL (1931), 483-91; by F. J. Powicke in *History,* XVI (1931), 272-73; in *TLS,* July 23, 1931, p. 574.

Oras, Ants. *Milton's editors and commentators from Patrick Hume to Henry John Todd (1695-1801), a study in critical views and methods.* Dorpat, Estonia: University of Tartu; London: Humphrey Milford, Oxford University press, 1931. Pp. 381.

Papenheim, Wilhelm. *Die Charakterschilderungen im "Tatler," "Spectator," und "Guardian."* Leipzig: Bernhard Tauchnitz, 1930. Cf. *PQ,* X, 187.

Rev. by C. N. Greenough in *MLN,* XLVI (1931), 271-73; by Paul Meissner in *Beiblatt,* XLII (1931), 271-74; in *TLS,* May 14, 1931, p. 391.

The Pepys ballads. Edited by Hyder Edward Rollins. Volume V, 1689-1691. Volume VI, 1691-1693. Volume VII, 1693-1702. Cambridge, Mass.: Harvard University press, 1931.

Plays of the Restoration and eighteenth century as they were acted at the Theatres-royal by their Majesties' servants. Edited by Dougald MacMillan and Howard Mumford Jones. New York: Henry Holt, 1931. Pp. 896.

Proper, Coenraad B. A. *Social elements in English prose fiction between 1700 and 1832.* Amsterdam: H. J. Paris, 1929. Pp. 302.

Sandford, William Phillips. *English theories of public address,*

1530-1828. Columbus, Ohio: Ohio State University, 1929 [issued in 1931]. Pp. 212.

Sawyer, Newell W. *The comedy of manners from Sheridan to Maugham.* Philadelphia: University of Pennsylvania press, 1931. Pp. vi+275.

Schirmer, Walter F. "Die geistesgeschichtlichen Grundlagen der englischen Barockliteratur." *GRM,* XIX (1931), 273-84.

Segar, Mary. "Dictionary making in the early eighteenth century." *RES,* VII (1931), 210-13.

Especially the projects of Addison and Ambrose Philips.

Seymour, Mabel. "*The Museum.*" *N & Q,* CLXI (1931), 355-56.

Notes on Dodsley's periodical of that title.

Smith, M. Ellwood. "Æsop, a decayed personality: changing conception as to Æsop's personality in English writers before Gay." *PMLA,* XLVI (1931), 225-36.

Tsanoff, Radoslav A. *The nature of evil.* New York: Macmillan, 1931. Pp. xvi+447.

Rev. by W. O. Stapledon in *Philosophy,* VII (1931), 107-08.

Van Tieghem, P. "Classique." *Revue de synthèse,* I (1931), 238-42.

An analysis of the meanings of the term.

Walker, E. C. "The history of 'enthusiasm' as a factor in the religious and social problems of the eighteenth century' [summary of thesis]. *Bulletin of the Institute of historical research,* IX, (1931), 123-26.

Watson, Harold Francis. *The sailor in English fiction and drama, 1550-1800.* New York: Columbia University press, 1931. Pp. 241.

In preparation for this study the author has made his way through a large number of English books of travel, plays, and novels written between 1550 and 1800 and has collected from them all the passages which deal with the characters and exploits of sailors. These he analyzes, according to a plan which strikes one as singularly mechanical, in eight chapters: the sailor in travel books, 1550-1660; the sailor in travel books, 1660-1800; the sailor in fiction and drama, 1550-1600; the sailor in drama, 1600-1642; the sailor in fiction, 1660-1760; the sailor in drama, 1660-1760; the sailor in fiction, 1760-1802; the sailor in drama, 1760-1800. Since there is obviously no real unity in his subject, it is not surprising that in the end he reaches no general conclusions of any significance for literary or for social history. If the book is consulted at all by scholars it will be mainly for the sake of its observations on particular works (e.g., some of the less familiar imaginary voyages of the middle of the eighteenth century).—R. S. C.

Webster, C. M. "Prose satires on the Puritans, 1620-1700." *N & Q,* CLXI (1931), 407.

Welker, John J. "The Spectator's notable Jew." *SP*, XXVIII (1931), 519-21.

Argues that the allusion to "a *Jew* of considerable Note" in the *Spectator*, No. 380, is probably a reflection on Sir Solomon de Medina, who had recently testified against Marlborough.

Wellek, René. *Immanuel Kant in England, 1793-1838*. Princeton: Princeton University press, 1931. Pp. vii+317.

An important study.

Wentscher, Else. *Englische Wege zu Kant*. Leipzig: Bernhard Tauchnitz, 1931. Pp. 86.

West, Albert H. *L'influence française dans la poésie burlesque en Angleterre entre 1660 et 1700*. Paris: Champion, 1931. Pp. 219. ("Bibliothèque de la *Revue de littérature comparée*," tome 74.)

White, Arthur F. "The Office of Revels and dramatic censorship during the Restoration period." *Western Reserve bulletin*, N. S., XXXIV (Sept. 15, 1931), 5-45.

Wood, Frederick T. "The beginnings and significance of sentimental comedy." *Anglia*, LV (1931), 368-92.

A rather undiscriminating paper. "The first traces of sentimental comedy are to be found as far back as the Morality Plays."

Wood, Frederick T., and others. "Notes on English provincial playhouses in the eighteenth century." *N & Q*, CLX (1931), 147-50, 165-69, 183-87, 209-10, 226-27, 247-48, 253, 267, 283-84, 301, 317-18, 338-39, 356-57, 388; CLXI (1931), 30-31.

Wood, Frederick T., and Ambrose Heal. "Notes on London booksellers and publishers, 1700-1750." *N & Q*, CLXI (1931), 39-42, 60-64, 76-82, 93-99, 114-18, 130-33, 150-54, 169-73, 185-89, 203-06, 219-21, 240-44, 255-57, 275-77, 291-93, 313-16, 328-29, 347-51, 363-67, 382-85, 400-04, 435-39.

Wood, Frederick T. "Strolling actors in the eighteenth century." *ES*, LXVI (1931), 16-53.

Yvon, Paul. *Le gothique et la renaissance gothique en Angleterre (1750-1880), essai de psychologie littéraire, artistique et sociale.* Caen: Jouan; Paris: Vrin, 1931.

Rev. by A. Brulé in *RAA*, VIII (1931), 546-47; in *TLS*, Feb. 11, 1932, p. 95.

IV. INDIVIDUAL AUTHORS

Joseph Addison

Heilman, Lee W. "Addison's 'The drummer.'" *TLS*, Oct. 1, 1931, p. 754.

John Aubrey

The Scandal and credulities of John Aubrey. Edited by John Collier. London: Peter Davies, 1931. Pp. xli+169.

Rev. by Rose Macaulay in *New statesman and Nation,* July 18, 1931, pp. 86, 88; in *TLS,* July 2, 1931, p. 524.

Gunther, R. T. "The library of John Aubrey, F. R. S." *Bodleian quarterly record,* VI (1931), 230-36.

Jane Austen

Chapman, R. W. "Jane Austen: a reply to Mr. Garrod." *Essays by divers hands, being the transactions of the Royal Society of Literature,* N. S., X (1931), 17-34.

Chapman, R. W. "Jane Austen's letters." *TLS,* Sept. 17, Oct. 29, 1931, pp. 705-06, 842.

Chapman, R. W. "Jane Austen's 'Warren.'" *TLS,* May 7, 1931, p. 367.

Richard Baxter

Powicke, F. J. "Some unpublished correspondence of the Rev. Richard Baxter and the Rev. John Eliot, 'The apostle to the American Indians.'" *Bulletin of the John Rylands library,* XV (1931), 138-76, 442-66.

Jeremy Bentham

Everett, Charles Warren. *The education of Jeremy Bentham.* New York: Columbia University press, 1931. Pp. ix+216.

In spite of the similarity of his title to that of Halévy's classic first volume, *La jeunesse de Bentham,* Everett has had a very different aim in view. He has not concerned himself with the formation of Bentham's ideas in the period before 1789, but rather with the development of his personality and the history of his experiences and contacts during the forty odd years in which his character took shape and most of his fundamental thinking and writing was done. From the Bentham manuscripts at University College he has brought to light a good many documents and facts not known to earlier biographers, and out of these and the materials already in print he has succeeded in building a narrative that is always interesting and at times lively and vivid. His chapters on Bentham as "a man of the world" and on Bentham at Bowood and in Russia are especially well done.—R. S. C.

Greaves, H. R. G. "Bentham on legislative procedure." *Economica,* XXXIII (1931), 308-27.

George Berkeley

Berkeley's commonplace book. Edited with introduction, notes, and index by G. A. Johnston. London: Faber and Faber, 1931. Pp. xxiv+158.

Rev. in *TLS,* March 12, 1931, p. 192.

"An Unpublished sermon of Bishop Berkeley. With a foreword [by John Wild]." *Philosophical review,* XL (1931), 522-36.

Aaron, R. I. "Locke and Berkeley's *Commonplace book.*" *Mind,* XL (1931), 439-59.

Hone, J. M., and M. M. Rossi. *Bishop Berkeley: his life, writings and philosophy.* With an introduction by W. B. Yeats. London: Faber and Faber, 1931.

Rev. in *TLS,* Nov. 5, 1931, p. 858; cf. *ibid.,* Jan. 28, 1932, p. 60.

Mabbott, J. D. "The place of God in Berkeley's philosophy." *Journal of philosophical studies,* VI (1931), 18-29.

Hugh Blair

Chapman, R. W. "Blair on Ossian." *RES,* VII (1931), 80-83.

Correspondence between Blair and the publisher Thomas Becket concerning the former's *Critical dissertation on the poems of Ossian.*

William Blake

Hamblen, Emily S. *On the minor prophecies of William Blake.* With an introduction by S. Foster Damon. New York: E. P. Dutton; London: Dent, 1930. Pp. xiii+395.

Rev. by Mary Siegrist in *New York Times book review,* May 10, 1931, p. 2; in *TLS,* Feb. 12, 1931, p. 112.

Pierce, Frederick E. "Etymology as explanation in Blake." *PQ,* X (1931), 395-99.

Suggests etymologies for the following names: Urizen, Ahania, Urthona, and Vala.

Plunkett, Margaret Louise. "The political philosophy of William Blake." *South Atlantic quarterly,* XXX (1931), 27-39.

Richter, Helene. "Blake und Hamann." *Archiv,* CLIX (1931), 37-45, 195-210.

Saurat, Denis. *Blake and modern thought.* London: Constable, 1929. Cf. *PQ,* IX, 182; X, 194.

Rev. by Bernhard Fehr in *Beiblatt,* XLII (1931), 162-65; by Gustav Hübener in *ES,* LXV (1931), 405-07; by Mario Praz in *RES,* VII (1931), 235-36.

Wright, Herbert G. "Blake and the Welsh triads." *TLS,* March 5, 1931, p. 178.

Comment by Mona Wilson, *ibid.,* March 12, 1931, p. 199.

James Boswell

Private papers of James Boswell from Malahide Castle in the col-

lection of Lt-Colonel Ralph Heyward Isham. Prepared for the press by Geoffrey Scott and Frederick A. Pottle. [New York:] Privately printed, 1931. Volumes X, XI, XII.

These volumes contain Boswell's Journal for the years 1774-1777.

Bostock, J. Knight. *A. E. Klausing's translation of Boswell's "Corsica" with four facsimiles.* January, 1931 [privately printed at the University press, Oxford].

Pottle, Frederick A., and Marion S. Pottle. *The private papers of James Boswell from Malahide Castle . . . . : a catalogue.* London and New York: Oxford University press, 1931.

Sir Thomas Browne

The Works of Sir Thomas Browne. Volume V: *Miscellany tracts, repertorium, miscellaneous writings.* Volume VI: *Letters.* London: Faber and Faber, 1931.

Leroy, O. *Le Chevalier Thomas Browne (1605-1682), médecin, styliste et métaphysicien.* Paris: Gamber, 1931. Pp. xi+422.

Thaler, Alwin. "Sir Thomas Browne and the Elizabethans." *SP,* XXVIII (1931), 87-117.

Critics have at times asserted or implied that Sir Thomas Browne had little appreciation and no very profound knowledge of the English literature of his own or the preceding generation. Thaler attempts first to refute this in general, and next to show that, in the case of Bacon, in particular, Browne was neither ignorant nor unappreciative. For the first point he relies largely on Browne's letters to his sons and, more especially, on the 1711 sale *Catalogue of the libraries of the learned Sir Thomas Browne and Dr. Edward Browne, his son.* He recognizes the difficulty of distinguishing between the items in this list that belonged to the elder and those that belonged to the younger Browne, and on a few titles he supplies additional information which helps to establish their original ownership; but he is also inclined to extend his conclusions in favor of Sir Thomas without supplementary evidence wherever he feels that he should appropriately do so. One is disposed to believe, of course, that Browne was probably familiar with a good deal of Elizabethan literature, but for the most part this belief must rest largely on faith. Incidentally, Thaler has misapplied one of the entries in the *Catalogue.* In his enumeration of the works of Bacon which appear therein, and which were therefore presumably known to Browne, he includes "Ld *Bacon's* Relation of the Sweating Sickness . . . . 1671" (p. 109, n. 119), which is not by Bacon at all but is a critique by Thomas Stubbe, the arch-enemy of the Royal Society.

In discussing Browne's knowledge of Bacon and his indebtedness to him, Thaler relies almost solely on the evidence afforded by parallel passages. Here again he is apparently aware that of all the devices of literary scholarship this one is fraught with the most subtle and seductive dangers; yet one is certain that he has not completely escaped them. His frequent and extensive editorial omissions render some of the passages suspect by making it difficult to detect, offhand, slight but significant differences in color and emphasis. Waiving such objections, however, one is still left with the impression that not all the texts cited are parallel in any basic or conclusive way. This criticism, which Thaler anticipates, cannot, unfortunately, be fully elaborated here. One characteristic illustration, which must suffice, is the second example on page 106. Here Browne is merely stating the fact that commonly accepted errors are impediments to the progress of truth, and that learning therefore needs to be cleansed of them; whereas Bacon is concerned rather with errors in method and with the possibility of remedies for the weaknesses of the human understanding. Thaler's method of demonstration, furthermore, lacks finality even at certain points where fairly close similarity of thought exists (examples through pp. 110-15), since it fails to take into consideration that often where Browne seems to be echoing the ideas of Bacon's "Idols," he may be merely repeating a commonplace of classical or Renaissance Pyrrhonism; for, original as the "Idols" of Bacon were in part, they derived many of their assumptions and arguments from sources of skeptical thought in antiquity or the later sixteenth century which were equally accessible to Browne. But even if all of Thaler's parallels were to be uncritically conceded, and the problem of a common background left out of account, the question would still remain whether he has not, without definitely asserting as much, implied a far greater affinity of thought than actually exists between the two men. External similarities in ideas and even in expressions may appear without in themselves establishing—what is after all of much greater importance and interest—similarity in philosophical assumptions and intentions.—M. E. P.

John Bunyan

Golder, Harold. "Bunyan's Giant Despair." *JEGP*, XXX (1931), 361-78.

Thiel, Gerhard. *Bunyans Stellung innerhalb der religiösen Strömungen seiner Zeit.* Breslau: Priebatsch, 1931. Pp. 158.

Edmund Burke

Barker, Ernest. *Burke and Bristol: a study of the relations between Burke and his constituency during the years 1774-1780.* Bristol: Arrowsmith, 1931. Pp. 132.

Rev. in *Contemporary review*, CXL (1931), 398-400.

Murray, Robert H. *Edmund Burke, a biography.* Oxford: University press; London: Humphrey Milford, 1931. Pp. viii+423.

Rev. in *Contemporary review*, CXL (1931), 661-63; in *TLS*, Oct. 15, 1931, p. 792; cf. *ibid.*, Oct. 22, 1931, p. 820.

Somerset, H. V. F. "Burke's eloquence and Hansard's reports." *English review*, LII (1931), 342-50.

William Burnaby

The Dramatic works of William Burnaby. Edited by F. E. Budd. London: Scholartis press, 1931. Pp. 469.

Rev. in *TLS*, July 30, 1931, p. 595; cf. note by Montague Summers, *ibid.*, Aug. 6, 1931, p. 609.

Robert Burns

The Letters of Robert Burns. Edited from the original manuscripts by J. DeLancey Ferguson. Oxford: Clarendon press, 1931. 2 vols.

Rev. in *TLS,* Nov. 5, 1931, pp. 579-80.

Ferguson, J. DeLancey. "'Against two things I am fixed as fate.'" *MLN,* XLVI (1931), 232-36.

Ferguson, J. DeLancey. "The Reid miniature of Robert Burns." *The colophon,* Part VI (1931).

Jamieson, A. Burns. *Burns and religion.* Cambridge: Heffer, 1931. Pp. xvii+122.

Koszul, A. "Une lettre de Burns." *RAA,* VIII (1931), 237-39.

Text of a letter to William Nicol dated July 29, 1787.

Henry Carey

The Poems of Henry Carey. Edited with an introduction and notes by Frederick T. Wood. London: Scholartis press, 1930. Cf. *PQ,* X, 196.

Rev. by T. H. Banks, Jr. in *MLN,* XLVI (1931), 136-37 (severe criticism of Wood's editorial method); by Harold Williams in *RES,* VII (1931), 356-59.

Thomas Chatterton

Mabbott, T. O. "Two letters of Thomas Chatterton in America." *N & Q,* CLX (1931), 170-71.

Meyerstein, E. H. W. "Chatterton's spelling of *Ælla.*" *N & Q,* CLX (1931), 262-63.

Meyerstein, E. H. W. *A life of Thomas Chatterton.* London: Ingpen and Grant, 1930; New York: Charles Scribner's sons, 1931. Cf. *PQ,* X, 196.

Rev. by Ernest A. Baker in *MLR,* XXVI (1931), 474-76; by Samuel Chew in *Yale review,* XXI (1931), 207-10.

Meyerstein, E. H. W. "Thomas Chatterton." *TLS,* June 25, 1931, p. 504.

Notes supplementary to his book.

Powell, L. F. "Thomas Tyrwhitt and the Rowley poems." *RES,* VII (1931), 314-26.

Shows that when Tyrwhitt undertook his edition he was still a believer in the authenticity of the poems. An important study of the question, with much new detail.

Charles Churchill

"Charles Churchill." *TLS,* Feb. 5, 1931, pp. 85-86.

Colley Cibber

(See also *Henry Fielding*)

MacMillan, Dougald. "The text of *Love's last shift.*" *MLN,* XLVI (1931), 518-19.

William Collins

Delamare, Marcel. "L'originalité de Collins." *RAA,* IX (1931), 16-28.

Woodhouse, A. S. P. "Collins and the creative imagination: a study in the critical background of his odes (1746)." *Studies in English by members of University College, Toronto* (Toronto: University of Toronto press, 1931), pp. 59-130.

This is on the whole an excellent study. Its main thesis, developed at length in section III, is that certain of the most characteristic and original qualities of Collins' *Odes* of 1746—especially their use of personifications for pictorial effects and their creation out of these and other materials of "a world of ideal wonder, touched with terror"—become more intelligible when they are viewed in relation to the ideas about the imagination which had been formulated early in the century by Addison and reiterated during the following decades by writers like Hughes, Mallet, Akenside, and, in Collins' own circle, Joseph Warton. It is an illuminating suggestion, and Woodhouse elaborates it in such a way as greatly to enhance our understanding of Collins' aims and through these of the motives and historical meaning of the new movement in English poetry which emerged during the 1740's and which found in him its most gifted though by no means its only representative.

Such reservations as I have concern, not this central part of the essay, which is a solid and at times brilliant piece of work, but rather the sections in which Woodhouse attempts to place his subject in its wider setting. I cannot quite follow him in his account (pp. 72-77) of "the Neo-classical treatment of the imagination." The few texts he quotes in this connection do indeed suggest something like the "prejudice" or "distrust" which, in common with many earlier students, he assumes to have been the normal attitude of critics during the Restoration and early eighteenth century. But some of these are irrelevant to the question at issue (e.g., the quotations from Hobbes and Johnson, p. 73, n. 14, which merely stress the need of rational control in the affairs of practical life), while most of the others are, I think, to be interpreted simply as rather extreme expressions of a view that implied not so much a positive distrust of the imagination itself as a revolt against fashions in poetry which, in their encouragement of a libertine and purely personal fancy, appeared to have neglected unduly the claims of "judgment" and "nature." It would be easy, moreover, to match all of Woodhouse's quotations from neo-classical critics with other passages, from the same writers or from writers equally typical of the school, which not only admit the necessity of imagination in the poet but insist that it is quite as indispensable as "judgment." Thus Hobbes, who is one of the main supports of his position, could also write: "In a good poem, whether it be *epic* or *dramatic*; as also in *sonnets, epigrams,* and other pieces, both judgment and fancy are required. . . ." (*Leviathan,* Part I, Ch. 8). And nothing certainly could be more categorical than the words of that arch-classicist, Charles Gildon, in 1718: "For Fancy and Judgment must join in every great Poet, as Courage and Judgment in every great General; for where either is wanting, the other is useless, or of small Value. Fancy is what we generally call *Nature,* or a *Genius*; *Judgment* is what we mean by Art, the Union of which in one Man makes a complete Poet" (*The complete art of poetry,* I, 125).

I have strong doubts, also, concerning another point. What makes Woodhouse's paper valuable is the very precise and discerning analysis it contains of an important episode in eighteenth-century poetry viewed in the work of its most distinguished representative. Unfortunately, he is not content with an interpretation of this episode in terms of its immediate antecedents and its most distinctive ruling ideas; the temptation to seek a still larger meaning is too great for him, and he accordingly concludes by bringing both "Collins's creative effort'' and the ''critical protest'' of Warton under a formula which assimilates them almost completely to the ''Romanticism'' of the following century. But the formula itself is of doubtful historical value—the unity it imposes on ''the Romantic movement'' is largely a verbal one—and its use here obscures rather than clarifies the significance of the particular movement with which Woodhouse is concerned—a movement which certainly differed in as many noteworthy ways from the ''Romanticism'' of the early nineteenth century as it did from the ''Classicism'' of the early eighteenth.—R. S. C.

William Congreve

Taylor, D. Crane. *William Congreve.* Oxford: University press; London: Humphrey Milford, 1931. Pp. x+252.

Rev. by P. F. Baum in *South Atlantic quarterly,* XXX (1931), 324-26; by A. Brandl in *Deutsche Literaturzeitung,* June 28, 1931, cols. 1220-21; by A. Digeon in *RAA,* IX (1931), 58; by A. W. P[ollard] in *Library,* 4th series, XII (1931), 121-23; by F. T. Wood in *ES,* LXVI (1931), 133-34; in *TLS,* June 4, 1931, p. 442; cf. comment by Montague Summers, *TLS,* June 11, 1931, p. 467.

Abraham Cowley

Loiseau, Jean. *Abraham Cowley, sa vie, son œuvre.* Paris: Henri Didier, 1931. Pp. xvii+715.

Loiseau, Jean. *Abraham Cowley's reputation in England.* Paris: Henri Didier, 1931. Pp. x+221.

Nethercot, Arthur H. *Abraham Cowley, the muse's Hannibal.* Oxford: University press; London: Humphrey Milford, 1931. Pp. xii+366.

Rev. by Morris W. Croll in *MP,* XXIX (1931), 237-38; by E. S. deB[eer] in *History,* XVI (1931), 284; by John Hayward in *Criterion,* XI (1931), 162-64; by Mario Praz in *English studies,* XIV (1932), 34-35; by John Sparrow in *RES,* VII (1931), 478-82; by E. N. S. Thompson in *PQ,* X (1931), 317-18; by William Troy in *Nation,* CXXXII (1931), 426-27; in *TLS,* March 12, 1931, p. 195.

Nethercot, Arthur H. ''Concerning Cowley's prose style.'' *PMLA,* XLVI (1931), 962-65.

Comment on R. F. Jones's article in *PMLA,* XLV, 977-1009. For Jones's reply see pp. 965-67.

William Cowper

Povey, Kenneth. ''Notes for a bibliography of Cowper's letters.'' *RES,* VII (1931), 182-87.

''Power and gentleness.'' *TLS,* Nov. 19, 1931, pp. 901-02.

Pratt, Robert A. ''Two letters of William Cowper.'' *TLS,* Nov. 19, 1931, p. 916.

Erasmus Darwin

''Dr. Darwin. Born December 12, 1731.'' *TLS,* Dec. 10, 1931, pp. 989-90.

Pearson, Hesketh. *Doctor Darwin.* London: Dent, 1930. Pp. xi+242.

Pearson, Hesketh. "Erasmus Darwin, 1731-1802." *Nineteenth century and after,* CX (1931), 723-34.

Daniel Defoe

Blass, Armin. *Die Geschichtsauffassung Daniel Defoes.* Heidelberg: Carl Winters Universitätsbuchhandlung, 1931. Pp. viii+107.

Blass traces Defoe's philosophy of history to three fundamental biases: his belief in both God's and the devil's intervention in human affairs; his theory (akin to Locke's) that government, established through a social contract, is subject to the will of the people (property owners) and the law of nature; and his conviction that national greatness depends upon a flourishing commerce. The main value of the study lies in this analysis of Defoe's characteristic obsessions, notably his awareness of the devil and his political theories as expressed in the long and somewhat neglected poem *Jure divino.* Blass is incisive, and preserves an alert skepticism, which, he feels, must accompany any interpretation of Defoe. His caution in concluding is unfortunately offset to a certain extent by an uncritical attitude toward the bewildering bibliography of Defoe's works, and by a loose and undiscriminating use of secondary sources (e.g., pp. 8, n. 1; 11, n. 1; 32). His study suffers also from not being comprehensive enough. The treatment of the background of Defoe's ideas, in so far as it pertains to his philosophy of history, is rather sketchy and is partly hidden in the footnotes (pp. 60 ff.); Defoe himself remains vague. Moreover, by restricting his attention to Defoe's observations on history, Blass fails to reveal the depth of the biases. His account of Defoe's commercial aggressiveness (pp. 96-101) is noticeably inadequate. Even the more extensive survey of Defoe's view of the devil's machinations is too limited, since it takes insufficient notice of his conception of evil, particularly his belief in man's natural depravity and irrationality (see *Jure divino,* Introduction and Book VII).—H. H. ANDERSEN.

"Daniel Defoe. April 26, 1731." *TLS,* Apr. 23, 1931, pp. 313-14.

Dottin, Paul. "De Foe et la France." *English studies,* XIII (1931), 69-74.

Firth, C. H. "Defoe's *True relation of the apparition of Mrs. Veal.*" *RES,* VII (1931), 1-6.

Prints a letter dated October 9, 1705, nine months before Defoe's pamphlet was published, which contains substantially the same story of the apparition of Mrs. Veal to Mrs. "Bargrove." Important as confirmation of G. A. Aitken's theory concerning the origin of the *True relation.*

Gardiner, Dorothy. "What Canterbury knew of Mrs. Veal and her friends." *RES,* VII (1931), 188-97.

Further details on the background of Defoe's *True relation.*

"Hermann Ullrich: a bibliography [of his writings on Defoe]." *English studies,* XIII (1931), 87-89.

Harlan, Virginia. "Defoe's narrative style." *JEGP,* XXX (1931), 55-73.

Jacob, Ernst Gerhard. *Daniel Defoe, Essay on projects (1697).* Leipzig: Tauchnitz, 1929. Cf. *PQ,* IX, 187; X, 198.

Rev. by Hans H. Andersen in *MP,* XXIX (1931), 250-51.

Jacob, Ernst Gerhard. "Daniel Defoe im Lichte der neueren Forschung." *English studies,* XIII (1931), 58-68.

Legouis, Pierre. "Marion Flanders est-elle une victime de la société." *RELV*, XLVIII (1931), 289-99.

Praz, Mario. "De Foe and Cellini." *English studies,* XIII (1931), 75-87.

Staverman, W. H. "Robinson Crusoe in Holland." *English studies,* XIII (1931), 49-58.

Temple, R. C. "Daniel Defoe and Thomas Bowrey." *N & Q,* CLX (1931), 39-40.

Wright, Thomas. *The life of Danial Defoe.* Bi-centenary edition, with a great deal of entirely new information respecting Defoe and additional important illustrations and plans. London: C. J. Farncombe, 1931. Pp. 427.

Rev. in *TLS,* Jan. 7, 1932, p. 9.

John Dryden

Dryden. The dramatic works. Edited by Montague Summers. Volumes I and II. London: Nonesuch press, 1931.

Rev. in *TLS,* Feb. 4, 1932, p. 73 (severe criticism of the text).

Boswell, Eleanore. "Chaucer, Dryden and the laureateship: a seventeenth-century tradition." *RES,* VII (1931), 337-39.

Bredvold, Louis I. "Dryden and the University of Oxford." *MLN,* XLVI (1931), 218-24.

Brunner, F. *John Drydens Hymnen.* Phil. Diss. Freiburg, 1931. Pp. 134.

A Dryden library. A catalogue of printed books, manuscripts, and autograph letters by John Dryden. Collected by Thomas James Wise. London: Printed for private circulation only, 1930. Pp. 89.

Rev. by Percy J. Dobell in *Book-collector's quarterly,* No. II (March-May, 1931), pp. 36-39; in *TLS,* May 14, 1931, p. 388.

Ham, Roswell G. "An addition to the works of Dryden." *TLS,* Oct. 8, 1931, p. 778.

A dedication written for Henry Purcell to *The vocal and instrumental musick of the Prophetess* (1691).

Ham, Roswell G. "The date of Dryden's birth." *TLS,* Aug. 20, 1931, p. 633.

Comment by Duncan MacNaughton, *ibid.,* Sept. 3, p. 664 (cf. Sept. 10, p.

683); by Roswell G. Ham, *ibid.*, Sept. 17, p. 706; by Duncan MacNaughton, *ibid.*, Sept. 24, p. 730; by Edward G. Fletcher, *ibid.*, Nov. 12, p. 894.

Hiscock, W. G. "A Dryden epilogue." *TLS,* March 5, 1931, p. 178.

"John Dryden, August 9, 1631-May 1, 1700." *TLS,* Aug. 6, 1931, pp. 601-02.

Jones, Richard F. "The originality of *Absalom and Achitophel.*" *MLN,* XLVI (1931), 211-18.

Lawrence, W. J. "Dryden's abortive opera." *TLS,* Aug. 6, 1931, p. 606.

Comment by Montague Summers, *ibid.*, Aug. 13, p. 621; by Bernard M. Wagner, *ibid.*, Oct. 1, p. 754; by George W. Whiting, *ibid.*, Nov. 24, p. 1041.

Legouis, Pierre. "Quinault et Dryden: une source de *The Spanish fryar.*" *RLC,* XI (1931), 398-415.

Riske, Ella Theodora, Louis I. Bredvold, Thomas B. Stroup, and Claude Lloyd. "Dryden and Waller as members of the Royal Society." *PMLA,* XLVI (1931), 951-62.

Controversy growing out of the articles by Claude Lloyd in *PMLA,* XLIII (1928), 162-65, and XLV (1930), 967-76.

John Dunton

Hatfield, Theodore M. "The true secret history of Mr. John Dunton." *Harvard University summaries of theses,* II (1930), 175-77.

Thomas Ellwood

Fischer, Walther. "Zur Textgeschichte von Thomas Ellwoods 'Davideis' (1712-1796)." *Anglia,* LV (1931), 84-100.

John Evelyn

Keynes, Geoffrey. "John Evelyn as a bibliophile." *Library,* 4th series, XII (1931), 175-93.

Henry Fielding

De Castro, J. Paul. "Fielding and Lyme Regis." *TLS,* June 4, 1931, p. 447.

Digeon, A. "Fielding a-t-il écrit le dernier chapitre de 'A journey from this world into the next.'" *RAA,* VIII (1931), 428-30.

Attributes it to Sarah Fielding.

Du Bois, Arthur E. "A forgotten Salisbury surgeon." *TLS,* March 19, 1931, p. 234.

Comment by J. Paul de Castro, *ibid.*, March 26, p. 252.

McKillop, Alan D. "The personal relations between Fielding and Richardson." *MP,* XXVIII (1931), 423-33.

Nichols, Charles Washburn. "Fielding's satire on pantomine." *PMLA,* XLVI (1931), 1107-12.

Read, Stanley E. "Fielding's *Miser.*" *Huntington Library bulletin,* Number 1 (May, 1931), pp. 211-13.

Shows (against C. Stonehill, *TLS,* Oct. 22, 1925, p. 698) that the folio edition of the play was "a somewhat careless reprint from the octavo."

Seymour, Mabel. "Henry Fielding." *LM,* XXIV (1931), 160.

Bibliographical notes on *A compleat and authentick history of the rise, progress, and extinction of the late rebellion.*

Taylor, Houghton W. "Fielding upon Cibber." *MP,* XXIX (1931), 73-90.

Thornbury, Ethel Margaret. *Henry Fielding's theory of the comic prose epic.* Madison, 1931. Pp. 202. ("University of Wisconsin studies in language and literature," No. 30.)

Voorde, F. P. van der. *Henry Fielding, critic and satirist.* 's Gravenhage: Westerbaan, 1931. Pp. 230.

John Gay

Williams, Harold. "*To a lady on her passion for old china.*" *RES,* VII (1931), 79-80.

Confirmation of Gay's authorship.

William Gilpin

Templeman, W. D. "Three anonymous works by William Gilpin." *N & Q,* CLX (1931), 112-14.

Templeman, W. D. "An unpublished French letter to William Gilpin." *MLN,* XLVI (1931), 107-09.

The writer of the letter, Charles, Baron de Beaulieu, says that Gilpin's writings are well known and respected in Germany. The letter is undated, but was probably written "not long after 1793."

Joseph Glanvill

Joseph Glanvill. The vanity of dogmatizing. Reproduced from the edition of 1661. With a bibliographical note by Moody E. Prior. New York: Columbia University press for the Facsimile text society, 1931. Pp. [viii]+[xxxii]+256.

Oliver Goldsmith

The Grumbler, an adaptation by Oliver Goldsmith. With introduction and notes by Alice I. Perry Wood. Cambridge, Mass.:

Harvard University press, 1931. Pp. xx+33. ("Huntington Library publications.")

Rev. in *TLS*, Dec. 17, 1931, p. 1022.

Paschal, The Rev. Father. "Goldsmith as a social philosopher." *Irish ecclesiastical record*, 5th series, XXXV (1930), 113-24.

Seitz, R. W. "Goldsmith and the 'English lives.'" *MP*, XXVIII (1931), 329-36.

Wright, Edwin M. "Oliver Goldsmith: a study in the theory of 'delightful teaching.'" *Harvard University summaries of theses*, II (1930), 188-91.

James Granger

Powell, L. F. "Granger's biographical history." *TLS*, Apr. 23, 1931, p. 327.

Thomas Gray

Ghosh, P. C. "Gray and Catullus." *Beiblatt*, XLII (1931), 31-32.

The source of *Elegy*, l. 70.

Hazard, Paul. "Foscolo et Gray au Nouveau-monde." *RLC*, XI (1931), 5-12.

On a translation of the *Elegy* by José Antonio Miralla.

Toynbee, Paget. "'Mrs. E' in Gray's letters." *TLS*, Feb. 12, 1931, p. 116.

Comment by E. G. Box, *ibid.*, Feb. 19, p. 135; by Paget Toynbee, *ibid.*, Feb. 26, p. 154.

Thomas Hobbes

Lubienski, Z. "Hobbes' philosophy and its historical background." *Journal of philosophical studies*, V (1930), 175-90.

David Hume

Greig, J. Y. T. *David Hume*. London: Cape, 1931. Pp. 436.

Rev. by Herbert Agar in *New statesman and Nation*, Oct. 10, 1931, p. 448; in *TLS*, Oct. 8, 1931, p. 765.

Johnson, Edgar A. J. "L'économie synthétique de Hume." *Revue d'histoire économique et sociale*, XIX (1931), 225-43.

Kuypers, Mary Shaw. *Studies in the eighteenth century background of Hume's empiricism*. Minneapolis: University of Minnesota press, 1930. Pp. viii+140.

Rev. by S. P. Lamprecht in *Journal of philosophy*, XXVIII (1931), 585-86.

Leroy, André. *La critique et la religion chez David Hume*. Paris: Alcan, [1929]. Pp. xix+376.

Samuel Johnson

Ashmun, Margaret. "Johnson's schoolmaster." *TLS,* July 30, 1931, p. 597.

Comment by G. W. Craig, *ibid.,* Aug. 6, p. 609.
On the Rev. John Hunter.

Christiani, Sigyn. *Samuel Johnson als Kritiker im Lichte von Pseudo-Klassizismus und Romantik.* Leipzig: Bernhard Tauchnitz, 1931. Pp. 120. ("Beiträge zur englischen Philologie," Heft XVIII.)

A mechanical and peculiarly unilluminating piece of work. The author has read in various old-fashioned textbooks or has been told by her professor that such and such opinions or interests or beliefs were essentially "pseudo-classical" and such and such other opinions or interests or beliefs were essentially "romantic." It has not occurred to her to test the historical validity of these formulae, still less to raise the question whether such crude and over-simplified categories are of any value for purposes of scholarly interpretation; she has accepted them without criticism and has proceeded to apply them to one after another of the passages in Johnson's published writings or in his recorded conversations in which he pronounces on the literary, moral, and religious issues of the day. The results to which such a method inevitably leads are exemplified in her answer to the question: "Wie stellt sich nun Johnson im besonderen zur Vernunftkultur der Aufklärungzeit?" "Johnson," she writes (p. 33), "vertrat auch darin die Meinung der Pseudoklassizisten, dass er in der Vernunft einen überaus wichtigen Faktor für das dichterische Schaffen sah. Er verurteilt die Leser '*who draw their principles of judgment rather from books than from reason*' (Lives I 175 f). Trotzdem aber Johnson die Vernunft beim Schaffen eines Kunstwerkes für wichtig hielt, schrieb er an anderer Stelle, dass doch nicht durch die Vernunft allein, sondern nur durch ihre Zussammenarbeit mit '*imagination*' ein Kunstwerk entstehen könne, und damit bewies er, dass er, über das pseudoklassizistische Ideal hinausgehend, der Phantasie eine gewisse Mitwirkung beim küunstlerischen Schaffen zuschrieb: '*Poetry is the art of uniting pleasure with truth, by calling imagination to the help of reason*' (Lives I 170). Damit liess er Forderungen der Romantik unbewusst schon gelten, wenn er auch selbst noch nicht ganz von alten Bindungen sich frei machen konnte. Bezeichnend für Johnsons zur Romantik hinneigende Einstellung ist es, wenn er Nekaya im 'Rasselas' (Ch. XXVIII) bemerken lässt: '*There are a thousand familiar disputes which reason never can decide; questions that elude investigation, and make logick ridiculous. . . .*'" It is a commentary on the state of eighteenth-century studies in at least some quarters in Germany that a work of which the greater part is no less naïve than this should be allowed to appear in so reputable a series as the "Beiträge zur englischen Philologie."—R. S. C.

Gow, A. S. F. "The unknown Johnson." *Life and letters,* VII (1931), 200-15.

Gray, W. Forbes. "Dr. Johnson's publisher." *Fortnightly review,* N. S., CXXXIX (1931), 245-50.

A brief sketch of Millar's relations to prominent writers.

"Johnson and poetry." *TLS,* June 18, 1931, pp. 473-74.

Langenfelt, Gösta. "Patriotism and scoundrels. I." *Neophilologus,* XVII (1931), 32-41.

Johnson's uses of "Whig," "Tory," "liberty," "patriotism."

Powell, L. F. [Review of *The R. B. Adam library relating to Dr. Samuel Johnson and his era,* 1929.] *RES,* VII (1931), 230-35. Cf. *PQ,* IX, 195.

Smith, Frederick M. *Some friends of Doctor Johnson.* London: Henry Hartley, 1931. Pp. 253.

Tyson, Moses. "Unpublished manuscripts, papers and letters of Dr. Johnson, Mrs. Thrale, and their friends, in the John Rylands library." *Bulletin of the John Rylands library,* XV (1931), 467-88.

Contains a brief history of the fate of Mrs. Piozzi's papers and a description, with some excerpts, of a collection of letters and other papers recently acquired by the Library.

William King

Williams, Harold. "The old trumpeter of Liberty Hall." *Book-collector's quarterly,* No. IV (October-December, 1931), pp. 29-56.

Nathaniel Lee: see *Thomas Otway*

John Locke

(See also *George Berkeley*)

An Essay concerning the understanding, knowledge, opinion and assent. By John Locke. Edited with an introduction by Benjamin Rand. Cambridge, Mass.: Harvard University press, 1931. Pp. lix+307.

Rev. by W. R. Sorley in *Mind,* XLI (1932), 126-28.

An early draft of the *Essay concerning human understanding,* written in 1671.

Henry Mackenzie

Thompson, Harold William. *A Scottish man of feeling: some account of Henry Mackenzie, Esq. of Edinburgh and of the golden age of Burns and Scott.* Oxford: University press; London: Humphrey Milford; New York: Oxford University press, 1931. Pp. xvii+463.

Rev. in *TLS,* June 18, 1931, p. 482.

James Macpherson: see *Hugh Blair*

Bernard Mandeville

Ward, H. Gordon. "An unnoted poem by Mandeville." *RES,* VII (1931), 73-76.

Latin verses prefixed to a medical treatise by Joannes Groeneveldt (2d ed., London, 1703) and signed "B. Mandeville, M. D."

Mary de la Rivière Manley

Anderson, Paul Bunyan. "The history and authorship of Mrs. Crackenthorpe's *Female tatler.*" *MP*, XXVIII (1931), 354-60.

Shows that the original Mrs. Crackenthorpe was Mrs. Manley. For further light on the spurious *Female tatler* see R. T. Milford in *MP*, XXIX (1932), 350-51.

William Mason

Whibley, Leonard. "A satirical ode by William Mason." *TLS*, Sept. 24, 1931, p. 727.

James Burnett, Lord Monboddo

Blickensderfer, Joseph P. "A study of Lord Monboddo and his works." *Harvard University summaries of theses*, II (1930), 163-65.

Henry More

The Philosophical poems of Henry More, comprising Psychozoia and minor poems. Edited with an introduction and notes by Geoffrey Bullough. Manchester: University press, 1931. Pp. xc+250.

Rev. in *TLS*, Aug. 27, 1931, p. 644; comment by E. H. W. Meyerstein, *ibid.*, Sept. 17, p. 706; by Geoffrey Bullough, *ibid.*, Sept. 24, p. 730.

MacKinnon, Flora I. [Review of recent publications on More and his group.] *Journal of philosophy*, XXVIII (1931), 466-70.

Peter Motteux

Cunningham, R. N., Jr. "Nine tales by Motteux." *MLN*, XLVI (1931), 93-95.

Motteux' authorship of *A Banquet for gentlemen and ladies* (1701).

Arthur Murphy

Caskey, J. Homer. "Arthur Murphy and the war on sentimental comedy." *JEGP*, XXX (1931), 563-77.

Henry Needler

Drennon, Herbert. "Henry Needler and Shaftesbury." *PMLA*, XLVI (1931), 1095-1106.

This article is another step in the general revaluation of the place of Shaftesbury in eighteenth-century thought. It demonstrates quite satisfactorily the incorrectness of C. A. Moore's view that Needler was an early convert to Shaftesbury's theological views and an early imitator of his rhapsodical style. Drennon shows that the characteristic features of Needler's theology came directly from Newton and from the school of divines who were popularizing the metaphysical suggestions contained in Newton's works. He also finds examples of the rhapsodical treatment of the theme of nature in Needler's writings at an earlier date than his probable introduction to Shaftesbury's works, and concludes that this manner "was a temperamental trait with him." This last suggestion, however, seems unfortunate. It apparently excludes the possibility of finding a historical development in the use and appreciation of this style before Needler that might have affected Needler's style—or even Shaftesbury's for that matter—just as his contact with the spreading Newtonian theology affected his thought. In the absence of better evidence for it than Drennon presents, it would have been preferable, perhaps, to withhold a conclusion based on assumptions quite different from those which determine the method and aims of the rest of the article.—M. E. P.

Sir Isaac Newton

Villamil, R. de. *Newton: the man.* Foreword by Professor Albert Einstein. London: Gordon D. Knox, 1931. Pp. 111.

Rev. in *TLS,* Nov. 19, 1931, p. 905.
Includes important new information about the books in Newton's library.

Roger Boyle, Earl of Orrery

Clark, William S. "Roger Boyle, Earl of Orrery, and his successors in the English heroic play." *Harvard University summaries of theses,* II (1930), 168-70.

Thomas Otway

Ham, Roswell Gray. *Otway and Lee: biography from a baroque age.* New Haven: Yale University press; London: Humphrey Milford, Oxford University press, 1931. Pp. vii+250.

Rev. by P. F. Baum in *South Atlantic quarterly,* XXX (1931), 324-26; in *TLS,* Apr. 9, 1931, p. 285; comment by Graham Greene, *ibid.,* Apr. 16, p. 307.

Samuel Pepys

Boswell, Eleanore. "Footnotes to seventeenth-century biographies. Samuel Pepys." *MLR,* XXVI (1931), 176-78.

Hanford, James H. "Pepys and the Skinner family." *RES,* VII (1931), 257-70.

[Notes on a sale of Pepys manuscripts.] *TLS,* Apr. 9, 1931, p. 292.

Thomas Percy

Dennis, Leah. "'Blandamour' in the Percy-Ritson controversy." *MP,* XXIX (1931), 232-34.

Dennis, Leah. "The text of the Percy-Warton letters." *PMLA,* XLVI (1931), 1166-1201.

Important for the history of the medieval revival.

Katherine Philips

Souers, Philip Webster. *The matchless Orinda.* Cambridge, Mass.: Harvard University press, 1931. Pp. viii+326.

Rev. in *TLS,* July 9, 1931, p. 543.

Hester Lynch Piozzi: see *Samuel Johnson*

Alexander Pope

Audra, E. *L'influence française dans l'œuvre de Pope.* Paris: Champion, 1931. Pp. 649. ("Bibliothèque de la *Revue de littérature comparée,*" tome 72.)

Rev. in *TLS,* Jan. 28, 1932, p. 56.

In many ways this is an impressive book. Audra has examined in detail all the important aspects of Pope's relations with French literature—his youthful study of the language, the stimulus to a reading of French books which he derived from his early friends, his later contacts with French men of letters apropos of the controversies provoked in France by the *Essay on man,* the extent of his familiarity with the French language and of his knowledge of French literature, his borrowings from French critics in the *Discourse on pastoral poetry,* the *Essay on criticism,* and the Homer, his debt to Voiture and to Boileau, his use of French sources in the *Rape of the lock, The dying Christian to his soul,* and *Eloisa to Abelard,* his appropriation of the ideas of French moralists in the *Essay on man* and the *Moral essays,* and finally, his indebtedness in his work as a whole to French ideals of art. On many of these questions, it goes without saying, Audra has been able to do little more than rearrange facts long familiar to students of Pope. He has not, however, written a mere compilation. On the problem of Pope's knowledge of the French language, on his relations with Voltaire, on his admiration for Voiture and the reflection of that admiration in the style of his early letters and in the *Rape of the lock,* on the French sources of many of his writings from the *Discourse on pastoral poetry* to the *Essay on man*—on all these matters and on numerous minor points besides, he has succeeded in making useful additions to our knowledge or our understanding of his subject. Of special interest, among his incidental finds, is his recovery of the English text of the much controverted letter to Louis Racine of September 1, 1742, in which Pope assures his correspondent "that my Opinions [in the *Essay on man*] are intirely different from those of Spinoza, or even of Leibnitz; but on the contrary conformable to those of Mons: Pascal & Mons. Fenelon: the latter of whom I would most readily imitate, in submitting all my Opinions to the Decision of the Church." In short, he has written a book from which we can all learn much and with which students of Pope will long have to reckon.

Of the shortcomings inevitable in so large a work perhaps the most conspicuous is a certain tendency to special pleading, all too common in "comparative" studies of this type and particularly apparent here in the sections in which Audra attempts to deal with the sources of Pope's thought in the *Essay on criticism* and the *Essay on man.* He has discovered (or others have discovered before him) for many of the ideas expressed in these poems parallels in Boileau, in Rapin, in Montaigne, in Pascal, in La Rochefoucauld; and, dominated by the single hypothesis on which his book as a whole is built, he conceives it to be his proper task to persuade us that it was indeed from a reading of these particular authors that Pope acquired the doctrines in question. He does occasionally, it is true, show an awareness that the same doctrines are also to be found in English writers equally familiar to Pope; but if he now and then concedes a possible source in Dryden or Shaftesbury or Locke or Bolingbroke, there is no evidence that he has prepared himself by a systematic reading of all the relevant English texts to be able to say, for the other ideas he considers, that they could have come only from France. And still less is there any evidence that he has carefully considered the possibilities contained in Cicero or other Latin authors, or that he has ever suspected that some of the notions which he seeks to derive from particular French critics or moralists might be after all commonplace assumptions of the age, familiar to Pope long before he read Boileau or Montaigne or Locke. If the results are not always so unsatisfactory as one might expect, it is because Audra's native good sense holds him back at times from conclusions which a less critical "comparatiste" would not have hesitated to draw. All too frequently, however, he falls a victim to the characteristic temptations of his method. A striking instance is his argument (pp. 474-77) that Pope derived his notion of the utility of the passions, together with his comparison of the function of the passions in the moral life to that of the winds at sea (*Essay on man,* Epistle II) from the *Apologie de Ramond Sebond.* The parallel is certainly close; but when one considers that by 1733 the idea and to a somewhat lesser extent the image had become so utter a commonplace of English ethical speculation as to recur with monotonous iteration in nearly every moralist or essayist or preacher that one picks up, whatever force the comparison with Montaigne might seem at first to have largely disappears. So too with the suggestions of specific French origins for other important ideas of Pope—the Chain of Being (pp. 488-90), the harmony of "self-love and social" (p. 500), the Ruling Passion (pp. 519-20), the psychological "anti-rationalism" of the first *Moral essay* (pp. 521-22): no one who is familiar with the history of these conceptions in the seventeenth and early eighteenth centuries but will feel the futility of any attempt to trace Pope's knowledge of them to a particular source.

One may also quarrel with a certain number of Audra's statements both in this and in other sections of the book. P. 143: in ascribing to Pope rather than to Warburton the allusions to Montesquieu's *Esprit des lois* in the edition of 1751, he has forgotten either that Pope died in 1744 or that the *Esprit des lois* was not published until 1748. P. 223-25: when Pope urges the critic to "follow Nature" (*Essay on criticism,* ll. 68-73) he is clearly using the sacred term in the sense of "Light of Nature," i.e., "Reason," and not in any of the senses in which it was commonly employed to designate the object of the poet's imitation. Audra does not appear to be sufficiently aware of this distinction. P. 498: Audra, I think, quite mistakes Pope's meaning in the passage of the *Essay on man* beginning "Nature that tyrant checks" (III, 51-62). The point is not that "les créatures exercent sur l'homme une véritable domination par les passions qu'elles provoquent en lui," but that man, while pursuing his own ends, impelled by interest, by pride, by love of pleasure, at the same time "cares for all"; it is this fact, indeed, that distinguishes him from the other animals: "he only knows, and helps, another creature's wants and woes." The sense of Pope's lines is clarified by a note in Edmund Law's translation of King's *Origin of evil* (3d ed., 1739), pp. 132-33. Pp. 511-20: I cannot see that Audra has produced a single precise or convincing reason to support his hypothesis that Pope's general intention in the Epistle to Cobham was to refute the *Maximes* of La Rochefoucauld.—R. S. C.

Audra, E. *Les traductions françaises de Pope (1717-1825): étude de bibliographie.* Paris: Champion, 1931.

Barnes, F. "Pope and Ovid." *TLS,* May 21, 1931, p. 408.

Comment by Stanley Beverley and C. L. Quinton, *ibid.,* June 4, p. 447.

Chandler, W. K. "The first edition of the *Dunciad.*" *MP,* XXIX (1931), 59-72.

Griffith, R. H. "A piracy of Pope's *Iliad.*" *SP,* XXVIII (1931), 737-41.

Jackson, Alfred. "Pope's epitaphs on Nicholas Rowe." *RES,* VII (1931), 76-79.

Meyer, H. *Studien zur Verskunst Alexander Popes.* Phil. Diss. Göttingen, 1930. Pp. 123.

A Pope library. A catalogue of plays, poems, and prose writings by Alexander Pope. Collected by Thomas James Wise. London: Printed for private circulation only, 1931. Pp. xxiv+113.

Sale, William M., Jr. "Pope and Lord Dysart." *MLN,* XLVI (1931), 109-11.

Warren, Austin. "Pope's index to Beaumont and Fletcher." *MLN,* XLVI (1931), 515-17.

Warren, Austin. "Pope on the translators of Homer." *MP,* XXIX (1931), 229-32.

Webb, Geoffrey. "The letters and drawings of Nicholas Hawksmoor relating to the building of the mausoleum at Castle Howard, 1726-1742." *The Walpole society,* XIX (1931), 111-64.

Interesting for the Earl of Burlington and the background of Pope's epistle.

Joseph Priestley

Holt, Anne. *A life of Joseph Priestley.* With an introduction by Francis W. Hirst. Oxford: University press; London: Humphrey Milford, 1931. Pp. xviii+221.

Rev. in *TLS,* May 14, 1931, p. 377.

Allan Ramsay

Martin, Burns. *Allan Ramsay: a study of his life and works.* Cambridge: Harvard University press, 1931. Pp. vi+203.

Edward Ravenscroft

McManaway, James G. "The copy for *The careless lovers.*" *MLN,* XLVI (1931), 406-09.

Norris, Edward T. "The original of Ravenscroft's *Anatomist,* and an anecdote of Jemmy Spiller." *MLN,* XLVI (1931), 522-26.

Samuel Richardson

(See also *Henry Fielding*)

Clarissa, or the history of a young lady. By Samuel Richardson. Oxford: Blackwell, 1931. 8 vols. ("The Shakespeare Head edition of the novels of Samuel Richardson.")

Rev. in *TLS,* July 16, 1931, p. 561.

Beckstein, J. *Richardsons "Pamela" nach ihrem Gedankengehalt betrachtet. Mit einem Anhang: die Quellenfrage bei der "Pamela."* Bremen: H. Engelke, 1929. Pp. 154.

Beckwith, F. "The 'anti-Pamelas.'" *TLS,* Feb. 19, 1931, p. 135.

Comment by Brian W. Downs, *ibid.,* Feb. 26, p. 154.

Dottin, Paul. *Samuel Richardson, 1689-1761, imprimeur de Londres, auteur de Pamela, Clarissa, et Grandison.* Paris: Perrin et cie, [1931]. Pp. xx+517.

Rev. by L. Cazamian in *RH,* CLXVIII (1931), 395-97; by J. W. Draper in *PQ,* X (1931), 320; by J. A. Falconer in *English studies,* XIV (1932), 37-40; by Emile Legouis in *RAA,* IX (1931), 151-52; by A. D. McKillop in *MLN,* XLVII (1932), 120-22; in *TLS,* July 16, 1931, p. 561.

Reade, Aleyn Lyell. "Samuel Richardson and Christ's hospital." *TLS,* Feb. 5, 1931, p. 99.

Comment by O. H. T. Dudley in *TLS,* Feb. 12, p. 116.

Joseph Ritson

(See also *Thomas Percy*)

Bronson, Bertrand H. "*The Caledonian muse.*" *PMLA,* XLVI (1931), 1202-20.

John Wilmot, Earl of Rochester

Harris, Brice. "'A satyr on the court ladies.'" *TLS,* Aug. 20, 1931, p. 633.

Comment by Geoffrey Bullough, *ibid.,* Feb. 18, 1932, p. 112.

Anna Seward

Ashmun, Margaret. *The singing swan: an account of Anna Seward and her acquaintance with Dr. Johnson, Boswell and others of their time.* With a preface by Frederick A. Pottle. New Haven: Yale University press; London: Humphrey Milford, Oxford University press, 1931. Pp. xiv+298.

Rev. in *TLS,* May 14, 1931, p. 382.

Anthony Ashley Cooper, Third Earl of Shaftesbury

(See also *Henry Needler*)

Mylord Shaftesbury. A letter concerning enthusiasm. Texte anglais et traduction française, avec une introduction et des notes par André Leroy. Paris: Presses universitaires, 1930. Pp. xvi+323.

Alderman, William E. "Shaftesbury and the doctrine of benevolence in the eighteenth century." *Transactions of the Wisconsin academy of sciences, arts and letters,* XXVI (1931), 137-59.

Except for some new illustrative texts, what Alderman gives us here is mainly a rather confused restatement of the thesis advanced in 1916 by C. A. Moore in his article on "Shaftesbury and the ethical poets in England, 1700-1760" (*PMLA,* XXXI, 264-325). The doctrines of *The characteristics* with which he is chiefly concerned are three: that "the natural affections, which lead to the good of the public" are no less fundamental in human nature than self-love, man being "by his original constitution" essentially a social creature; that the chief reward, or one of the chief rewards, of the cultivation of "benevolence" consists in the pleasure which it brings in this life; and that, consequently, there is "no conflict between the good of the individual and the good of the species." He summarizes briefly Shaftesbury's principal expressions of these ideas, and then proceeds to show how widespread was their vogue among English writers of all sorts between 1713 and the end of the century. The conclusion he wishes us to draw is of course that it was Shaftesbury who was mainly responsible for the introduction of this body of principles into English ethical thought.

It will not do! Among the numerous ideas contained in *The characteristics* there were doubtless some that would have impressed an educated contemporary as at least relatively unfamiliar, but the list would not have included any of the doctrines discussed in this study. If Alderman can think otherwise, it is because he has never given special attention to the history of moral ideas in England during the forty years between the Restoration and the publication of Shaftesbury's first book. Had he read as widely in the relevant texts of the seventeenth century as he has done in those of the eighteenth, he would have recognized that most of what was said in the *Enquiry concerning virtue and merit,* in the *Letter concerning enthusiasm,* and in the *Moralists* about the "natural" sociability of man, the pleasures of doing good, and the harmony of self-love and benevolence represented in no sense a new departure in ethics but merely a fresh statement of positions that had been frequently maintained in England since before Shaftesbury was born.

It is impossible in a short review to exhibit all the evidence on which this statement is based. Incomplete as are the following notes, however, they will perhaps serve to suggest to how great an extent the ideas which interest Alderman had become diffused among the educated classes before 1700.

1. The belief that man is "naturally good" in the sense that one of the distinctive traits of his nature is a strong desire for a peaceful social life with his fellows had of course been a commonplace in the writings of various ancient moralists and of certain Fathers of the Church (for an interesting summary of this tradition see Grotius, *De jure belli ac pacis,* Prolegomena). It was an idea congenial to the temper of the liberal Anglican divines of the middle of the seventeenth century, and there wanted only the shock of Hobbes' description of man as an egoistic animal, "naturally" disposed to inflict injury upon his kind, to encourage them to make it, in a somewhat developed form, one of the main articles of their ethical creed. The results can be studied in a long series of texts that run from the Restoration into the eighteenth century; see, for example, Isaac Barrow, "The first sermon" (June 30, 1661), in *Sermons preached upon several occasions* (1678), pp. 24-25; also "Sermon XXVIII" and "Sermon XXX" (before 1677), in *Theological works* (Oxford, 1830), II, 79, 140-42; Thomas Tenison, *The creed of Mr. Hobbes examined* (1671), pp. 140-41; Richard Cumberland, *A treatise of the laws of nature* (1727), p. 164 (the Latin original appeared in 1672); William Gould, *The generosity of Christian love* (1676), pp. 12-13; John Tillotson, "Sermon XX" (December 3, 1678) and "Sermon XXXIII" (March 8, 1689), in *Works* (1728), I, 171, 305; Samuel Parker, *A demonstration of the divine authority of the law of nature* (1681), pp. 25-26, 29-30, 54-56; John Scott, *The Christian life* (1681), p. 176; William Clagett, *Of the humanity and charity of Christians*

(1687), pp. 4-5; also *A discourse of humanity and charity* (1693), p. 76; John Dryden, *The hind and the panther* (1687), I, 245-50; Jeremy Collier, "Of general kindness," in *Miscellanies* (1694), pp. 51-78; James Lowde, *A discourse concerning the nature of man* (1694), pp. 164-66; Benjamin Whichcote, *Select sermons* (1698), especially pp. 155-56, 181-82, 217, 381-82; Sir William Dawes, *Self love the great cause of bad times* (1701), p. 9. As a sample of what was being said by the leaders of the movement even as early as the 1670's I add a short passage from Barrow's "Sermon XXX": "We are indispensably obliged to these duties [charity], because the best of our natural inclinations prompt us to the performance of them, especially those of pity and benignity, which are manifestly discernible in all, but most powerful and vigorous in the best natures; and which, questionless, by the most wise and good Author of our beings were implanted therein both as monitors to direct, and as spurs to incite us to the performance of our duty . . . . Even the stories of calamities, that in ages long since past have happened to persons nowise related to us, yea, the fabulous reports of tragical events, do (even against the bent of our wills, and all resistance of reason) melt our hearts with compassion, and draw tears from our eyes; and thereby evidently signify that general sympathy which naturally intercedes between all men, since we can neither see, nor hear of, nor imagine another's grief, without being afflicted ourselves. Antipathies may be natural to wild beasts; but to rational creatures they are wholly unnatural. . . . . Since nature therefore hath made our neighbour's misery our pain, and his content our pleasure; since with indissoluble bands of mutual sympathy she hath concatenated our fortunes and affections together; since by the discipline of our sense she instructs us, and by the importunity thereof solicits us to the observance of our duty, let us follow her wise directions, and conspire with her kindly motions; let us not stifle or weaken by disuse, or contrary practice, but by conformable action cherish and confirm the good inclinations of nature" (*Theological works* [1830], II. 140-42).

2. If humane and sympathetic feelings are thus "natural" to man, it follows that their exercise will result in happiness to the individual. By many writers of the later seventeenth century this fact was made the basis of a somewhat new type of ethical appeal: let us seek the good of others not merely because it is reasonable to do so or because such conduct will be rewarded in another world, but because nothing brings us so exquisite a pleasure here and now. Cf. H. Lukin, *The chief interest of man* (1670), 3d ed., 1718, pp. 38-39; Richard Kidder, *Charity directed* (1676), p. 12 ("There is a Delight and Joy that Accompanies doing good, there is a kind of sensuality in it"); Isaac Barrow, "Sermon XXX" (before 1677), in *Theological works* (1830), II, 140-42; Samuel Parker, *A demonstration of the divine authority of the law of nature* (1681), pp. 64-65; Hezekiah Burton, *A second volume of discourses* (1685), pp. 564-72; Gregory Hascard, *A sermon* (1685), p. 5; Edward Pelling, *A practical discourse upon charity* (1693), p. 25; Edmund Calamy, *A sermon* (1699), p. 18; Edward Young, *Sermons on several occasions* (1702), I, 391-92.

3. To insist on the pleasures of benevolence is of course to imply a harmony between the individual's good and the good of the species. Cf. also the following texts, in which the reality of such a harmony is urged on somewhat different grounds: Richard Cumberland, *A treatise of the laws of nature* (1727), pp. 128, 164 (first published in Latin in 1672); Samuel Parker, *A demonstration of the divine authority of the law of nature* (1681), pp. 18, 21-22; Hezekiah Burton, *A second volume of discourses* (1685), pp. 515-16; H. Downes, *The excellency of publick charity* (1697), p. 3.—R. S. C.

Alderman, William E. "Shaftesbury and the doctrine of moral sense in the eighteenth century." *PMLA*, XLVI (1931), 1087-94.

This article is open to the same general criticism as the preceding. Although Alderman recognizes that the term "moral sense" had been used by

Henry More in 1668, he proceeds on the assumption that the doctrine of a natural ability to distinguish right from wrong, uniform in all men and operating "exclusive of art, culture, or discipline," was, as developed by Shaftesbury, a new idea in English ethics, and that consequently when we meet with the same or similar notions during the eighteenth century, the presumption is that they derived directly or indirectly from *The characteristics*. But, to begin with, this is to overlook the fact that a conception of moral judgment differing in no essential respect from that which Alderman summarizes in his opening paragraphs had frequently been given popular expression, in the half century before 1699, by writers whose general aims anticipate Shaftesbury's own. Two illustrations will have to suffice. The first is a passage in one of Isaac Barrow's sermons (written before 1677): "The practice of benignity, of courtesy, of clemency at first sight, without any discursive reflection, doth obtain approbation and applause from us; being no less grateful and amiable to the mind than beauty to our eyes, harmony to our ears, fragrancy to our smell, and sweetness to our palate: and to the same mental sense, malignity, cruelty, hardness, all kinds of uncharitable dealing, are very disgustful and loathsome. There wanteth not any commendation to procure a respect for charity, nor any incentive to breed abhorrence of uncharitableness; nature sufficiently prompting to favour the one, and to detest the other" (*Works* [New York, 1845] I, 270). The second illustration is from John Hartcliffe's *A treatise of moral and intellectual virtues* (1691), pp. 352-54: "First there is a secret impression upon the Minds of Men, whereby they are naturally directed to approve some things as *good*, and avoid other things as *evil*; just as the Creatures below Men are by a natural Instinct led to their own preservation, and to take care of their young ones. In like manner we find in human Nature a propensity to some things that are beneficial, and a loathing of other things, that are hurtful to them; the former appear beautiful and lovely, the latter ugly and deformed. Now these inclinations do not proceed from Reason, but from Nature, and are antecedent to all Discourse, as it is manifest from hence, that they are as strong, and do put forth themselves as vigorously in young persons, as in those that are older; they do shew themselves as much in the rude and ignorant sort of People, as in those who are more refined, and better instructed . . . . so that the Providence of God appears herein to be wonderfully careful of the happiness and welfare of Mankind, in that he hath wrought such inclinations into our Natures, as to secure the most material parts of our Duty, in planting in us a natural sense of *good* and *evil*. . . ." It seems to me evident, moreover, that the doctrine expressed in passages like these, and to a considerable extent in Shaftesbury in the next generation, must be regarded as merely a variant, under a new set of names and with special application to ethics, of the idea of "natural reason" or "the light of nature" which, after a long history in antiquity, had come to occupy a ruling position in the "rationalism" of the sixteenth and seventeenth centuries. The connection cannot be doubted by anyone who will compare the texts quoted by Alderman from *The characteristics* with certain passages in Culverwel's *An elegant and learned discourse of the light of nature* (1652), notably those on pages 42 (from Grotius), 50, 58, 71, and 83 of the first edition.

All this is not intended to minimize the importance of Shaftesbury and still less of Hutcheson in reformulating the old doctrine for the uses of the eighteenth century. But it is dangerous to assume, as Alderman tends to do, that whenever writers between 1725 and 1800 speak of "our natural sense of right and wrong" they are necessarily reflecting the influence of one or another of these men. Several of the passages he quotes could just as easily have been written before Shaftesbury published a line, and one of them, as a matter of fact, actually was: I refer to the speech of the philosopher in *Rasselas* about the "universal and unalterable law, with which every heart is originally impressed" (see Alderman, p. 1091), which has long been recognized as merely a paraphrase of a sentence in one of Cicero's orations (*Pro Milone* iv).—R. S. C.

Casati, Ennemond. "Quelques correspondants français de Shaftesbury." *RLC,* XI (1931), 219-36.

Relations of Shaftesbury with Bayle, Leclerc, DesMaizeaux, and Coste.

William Shenstone

Bond, Richmond P. "Shenstone's heroi-comical poem." *SP,* XXVIII (1931), 742-49.

An unpublished poem entitled *The snuff-box* contained in B. M. Addit. MS 15,913. According to the manuscript it was written in 1735.

Fullington, James F. "The dating of Shenstone's letters." *PMLA,* XLVI (1931), 1128-36.

Hughes, Helen Sard. "Shenstone and the Countess of Hertford." *PLMA,* XLVI (1931), 1113-27.

Purkis, E. Monro. *William Shenstone, poet and landscape gardener.* Wolverhampton: Whitehead brothers, 1931. Pp. 143.

Rev. in *TLS,* Dec. 24, 1931, p. 1039.

Richard Brinsley Sheridan

Butler, E. M. *Sheridan: a ghost story.* London: Constable, 1931. Pp. xiii+312.

Rev. by F. T. Wood in *ES,* LXVI (1931), 134; in *TLS,* Apr. 16, 1931, p. 303.

Adam Smith

Scott, W. R. "The manuscript of Adam Smith's Glasgow lectures." *Economic history review,* III (1931), 91-92.

Sommer, Artur. "Das Naturrechtskolleg von Adam Smith." *Archiv für Rechts- und Wirtschaftsphilosophie,* XXIII (1930), 321-41.

Tobias Smollett

Hunter, A. C. "Les livres de Smollett détenus par la douane à Boulogne en 1763." *RLC,* XI (1931), 736-37.

Knapp, Lewis M. "A rare satire on Smollett." *TLS,* Oct. 8, 1931, p. 778.

Knapp, Lewis M. "Smollett's verses and their musical settings in the eighteenth century." *MLN,* XLVI (1931), 224-32.

Laurence Sterne

Fluchère, Henri. "Laurence Sterne et William Combe: vol, plagiat, imitation." *RAA,* VIII (1931), 313-28.

On Margaret R. B. Shaw's *Second journal to Eliza.* Cf. *PQ,* IX, 201.

Hine, Reginald L. "Captain Robert Hinde." *TLS,* May 21, 1931, p. 408.

A supposed original of Uncle Toby.

Jonathan Swift

Darnall, F. M. "Swift's religion." *JEGP,* XXX (1931), 379-82.

Deals with Pons' interpretation of Swift's attitude toward "mysteries" in *A tale of a tub,* criticizing it in the light of the much later sermon "On the trinity."

Davis, Herbert. "Swift's view of poetry." *Studies in English by members of University College, Toronto* (Toronto: University of Toronto press, 1931), pp. 9-58.

Develops the idea that Swift is "in his casual and contemptuous manner the most extreme example that we have ever had in England of reaction against the heroic or romantic view of the poet's function and art." One of the best short studies of Swift's verse I have seen.

Davis, Herbert. "Verses on the death of Dr. Swift." *Book-collector's quarterly,* No. II (March-May, 1931), pp. 57-73.

On the authenticity of *The life and genuine character of Doctor Swift* (1733) and the relation of this poem to *Verses on the death of Doctor Swift* (1739). A valuable article.

Esdaile, Katharine. "The fairy feast." *TLS,* Feb. 12, 1931, p. 116.

Comment by Harold Williams, *ibid.,* Feb. 19, p. 135.

Frantz, R. W. "Swift's Yahoos and the voyagers." *MP,* XXIX (1931), 49-57.

This article proposes an answer to the question where Swift found the revolting details for his picture of the Yahoos. These, Frantz points out, were probably not the pure invention of a degraded imagination, but were suggested to Swift by the descriptions of large apes, and of the Hottentots, to be found in a number of contemporary voyagers' accounts, some of which Swift undoubtedly knew. In the passages which Frantz quotes from books of travel may be found most of the essential features which Swift emphasizes in his picture of the Yahoos. And the voyagers, furthermore, allot a position in the scale of animate nature to the apes, or Hottentots, not unlike that occupied by the Yahoos in the philosophical allegory of the fourth book of *Gulliver's travels.* In spite of his cautions and qualifications, Frantz succeeds in making his proposals, if not finally convincing, certainly very tempting.—M. E. P.

Van Doorn, C. *An investigation into the character of Jonathan Swift.* Amsterdam: Swets & Zeitlinger, 1931. Pp. 152.

On the basis of a questionnaire sent to three thousand Dutch physicians, Professors Heymans and Wiersma classified human temperaments into the nervous, the sentimental, the sanguine, the phlegmatic, the choleric, the passionate, and the amorphous. With more concern for Dr. Heymans' types than for Swift, Van Doorn has graded Swift's standing in each of these groups. The general conclusions are not remarkable: "Swift's interests were chiefly political and ecclesiastical. . . . His tenacious passion and his ebullient activity were two components of his personality. . . . His irritability estranged some of his friends. His pride sometimes stood in his way. . . ." (pp. 133-36). Ninety questions are asked and answered impartially from the original sources and from twentieth-century critics of Swift. The questions are asked, not because they are pertinent, but because they were asked by Dr. Heymans in his medical study. No. 76—"Is the subject an enthusiastic collector?"—reveals that Swift wrote to Stella: "I am resolved to bring over a great deal of china. I loved it mightily today." Moriarty is quoted to prove that Swift was "a good hater" (p. 33), while Whibley and Stephen are used to prove that Swift was a staunch friend (p. 34). No. 77 suggests new approaches to Swift, to enlarge the field for possible theses: "Is the subject an anarchist, socialist, theosophist, vegetarian, teetotaler, or a partisan of 'Kollewijnschen Rechtschreibung'?"

The use of sources is as unscholarly as the conclusions are unprofitable. The recklessness with which the writer uses his materials appears on every page. Mrs. Pilkington's "Memoirs (1748) which bear the stamp of truthfulness," and the statement, "In 1727 appeared 'Gulliver's Travels,'" are characteristic samples of frequent error. In short, the volume is of no use to the student of Swift.—WILLIAM A. EDDY.

Webster, C. M. "Swift and the Royal Society's *Philosophical transactions.*" *N & Q,* CLXI (1931), 99-100.

A note on Swift's use of the word "hamated" in the *Discourse concerning the mechanical operation of the spirit.* Cf. *ibid.,* p. 194, for a communication by "S," who suggests Lucretius as the source of the word.

Webster, C. M. "Temple, Casaubon, and Swift." *N & Q,* CLX (1931), 405.

Webster, C. M. "'The Yahoo's overthrow.'" *TLS,* May 14, 1931, p. 390.

Its significance in the history of Swift's antipathy to freethinkers and fanatics.

Sir William Temple

Bensly, Edward. "The library at Moor Park." *N & Q,* CLIX (1930), 48.

James Thomson

Cronk, Gertrude Green. "Lucretius and Thomson's autumnal fogs." *American journal of philology,* LI (1930), 233-42.

Hughes, Helen Sard. "Thomson and Lady Hertford again." *MP,* XXVIII (1931), 468-70.

Thomas Tickell

Tickell, Richard Eustace. *Thomas Tickell and the eighteenth century poets (1685-1740), containing numerous letters and poems hitherto unpublished.* Compiled from his family papers. London: Constable, 1931. Pp. xv+256.

Rev. in *TLS,* Oct. 29, 1931, p. 837.

Josiah Tucker

Schuyler, Robert Livingston. *Josiah Tucker, a selection from his economic and political writings.* New York: Columbia University press, 1931. Pp. ix+576.

Sir Samuel Tuke

deBeer, E. S. "Sir Samuel Tuke." *N & Q,* CLXI (1931), 345-47.

Thomas Tyrwhitt: see *Thomas Chatterton*

Edmund Waller: see *John Dryden*

Horace Walpole

Horace Walpole's fugitive verses. Edited by W. S. Lewis. New York: Oxford University press; London: Humphrey Milford, 1931. Pp. xxii+188. ("Miscellaneous antiquities," Number five.)
Rev. in *TLS,* Apr. 16, 1931, p. 302.
An excellent edition.

Esdaile, Mrs. [Arundell]. "Walpole's 'Anecdotes of painting.'" *TLS,* March 19, 1931, p. 224.

Lewis, W. S. *The forlorn printer, being notes on Horace Walpole's alleged neglect of Thomas Kirgate.* Farmington, Connecticut: Privately printed, 1931. Pp. 24. ("Miscellaneous antiquities," Number six.)

Lewis, W. S. "Walpole's 'Anecdotes.'" *TLS,* May 7, 1931, p. 367.

Thomas Warton, Sr.

Willoughby, Edwin Elliott. "The chronology of the poems of Thomas Warton, the elder." *JEGP,* XXX (1931), 87-89.

Thomas Warton, Jr.: see *Thomas Percy*

John Wesley

The Letters of the Rev. John Wesley. Edited by John Telford. London: The Epworth press, 1931. 8 vols.
Rev. in *TLS,* Sept. 24, 1931, p. 720.

Vulliamy, C. E. *John Wesley.* London: Geoffrey Bles, 1931. Pp. xii+370.
Rev. in *TLS,* Nov. 5, 1931, p. 857.

Gilbert White

Journals of Gilbert White. Edited by Walter Johnson. London: Routledge, 1931. Pp. xlviii+463.
Rev. in *TLS,* Apr. 30, 1931, p. 337.

John Wilkins

Stimson, Dorothy. "Dr. Wilkins and the Royal Society." *JMH,* III (1931), 539-63.

William Wycherley

The Country Wife. By William Wycherley. Edited with a critical introduction, notes, and appendices, by Ursula Todd-Naylor. Northampton, Mass., 1931. Pp. lix+108. ("Smith College studies in modern languages," Vol. XII, Nos. 1-3.)

Arthur Young

Haslam, C. S. *The biography of Arthur Young, F. R. S. from his birth until 1787.* Rugby, 1930. Pp. 253.

Rev. by Henri Sée in *RH,* CLXVI (1931), 366-67.

Vignols, Léon. "L'anticolonialisme d'Arthur Young." *Revue d'histoire économique et sociale,* XIX (1931), 114-17.

V. THE CONTINENTAL BACKGROUND

Bardon, Maurice. *"Don Quichotte" en France au XVIIe et au XVIIIe siècle, 1605-1815.* Paris: Champion, 1931. Pp. 932. ("Bibliothèque de la *Revue de littérature comparée,* tome 69).

Beckwith, F. "The Bibliothèque britannique, 1733-47." *Library,* 4th series, XII (1931), 75-82.

Brunet, Pierre. *L'introduction des théories de Newton en France au XVIIIe siècle, avant 1738* Paris: Albert Blanchard, 1931.

Rev. by C. Siegel in *Deutsche Literaturzeitung,* July 26, 1931, cols. 1433-36.

Chinard, Gilbert. *"Agatha* et le vœu fatal d'*Atala."* *MLN,* XLVI (1931), 69-77.

Agatha, or a narrative of recent events (1796), a sentimental counter-revolutionary novel, as an anticipation of *Atala.*

Dedieu, J. "Survivances et influences de l'apologétique traditionnelle dans les 'Pensées.'" *RHL,* XXXVII (1930), 481-513; XXXVIII (1931), 1-39.

Ergang, Robert R. *Herder and the foundations of German nationalism.* New York: Columbia University press, 1931. Pp. 288.

Fréville, Henri. "Richard Simon et les protestants d'après sa correspondance." *Revue d'histoire moderne,* Jan.-Feb., 1931, pp. 30-55.

Glaesener, Henri. "Le type d'Ahasvérus aux XVIIIe et XIXe siècles." *RLC,* XI (1931), 373-97.

Haxo, Henry E. "Pierre Bayle et Voltaire avant les *Lettres philosophiques.*" *PMLA,* XLVI (1931), 461-97.

A beginning has here been made in the study of that elusive and often discouraging problem, Bayle's influence on Voltaire.

Haxo has felt the difficulty of distinguishing clearly between important spiritual influences which become so much a part of the borrower that they are rarely discernible, and textual borrowings, which are often merely incidental and factual. He has collected his material carefully and has properly evaluated Bayle's sway over the skeptical, epicurean, rationalistic society in which the young Voltaire developed; and he has shown admirable restraint in presenting similarities in thought and phrase without drawing definite conclusions of direct borrowing.

He shows that Bayle might well have been the source for the anti-Catholic tenor of Voltaire's *Henriade,* and for the deism of that poem and of the *Epître à Uranie,* to cite only the most pertinent works. Finding in the former only one direct reference to Bayle as a source, he suggests that Voltaire avoided the obvious name and used the names of the authors cited by Bayle. For the deism of the *Epître* he has made a collection of deistic passages from Bayle, and at the same time has not failed to note the very probable influence (among others) of Voltaire's friend, the Abbé Chaulieu (pp. 463-66).

The reviewer notes but one error: Voltaire did not adopt Newton's system of gravitation in 1730 (p. 465, n. 20), but was converted by Maupertuis in 1732 (see Lanson, *Lettres philosophiques,* II, 8); he regrets that the author did not consult E. Sonet, *Voltaire et l'influence anglaise,* to balance his judgment on Locke (pp. 462-63); he believes it unnecessary to attribute Voltaire's early intrepidity and aggressiveness to an admiration for Bayle (pp. 490-91); and finds unconvincing the argument that Bayle influenced to any appreciable degree Voltaire's literary judgments and political opinions (pp. 492-96).

For the most part negative in its conclusions from the point of view of definite source-finding, this study reveals clearly the relations in thought and method between the two writers and is an estimable contribution to the literary history of that seething period of transition between the seventeenth and eighteenth centuries to which Gustave Lanson some twenty years ago invited the attention of his students.—NORMAN L. TORREY.

Hazard, Paul. *Don Quichotte de Cervantes: étude et analyse.* Paris: Librairie Mellottée, [1931]. Pp. 378.

Pp. 329-43 deal with the fortunes of the work during the eighteenth century.

Hazard, Paul. "La pensée de Vico." *RCC,* XXXII[2] (1931), 707-18; XXXIII[1] (1931), 42-53, 127-42.

Jan, Eduard von. "Voltaire und die Gegenwart." *GRM,* XIX (1931), 285-303.

Tendencies in recent scholarship and interpretation.

Baron de Lahontan. Dialogues curieux entre l'auteur et un sauvage de bon sens qui a voyagé et Mémoires de l'Amérique septentrionale. Publiés par Gilbert Chinard. Baltimore: Johns Hopkins press; Paris: A. Margraff; London: Humphrey Milford, Oxford University press, 1931. Pp. 268.

The work from which Chinard here reprints the essential portion in the text of the edition of 1703 is a document of capital importance for the history of ideas at the opening of the eighteenth century. It is, as the *Mémoires de Trévoux* complained on its first appearance, "le précis de ce que les Déistes et les Sociniens disent de plus fort contre la soumission que nous devons à la foy.'' It is also—and this is the aspect which particularly interests Chinard—one of the most complete and forthright expressions in its period of the old tradition of primitivism turned to the uses of a radical and to a large extent communistic attack on Western European society. In short, it is an essential text for whoever would understand the movement of thought in France and England around 1700, and we cannot be too grateful to Chinard for making it accessible to us in so convenient and scholarly a form. His own contribution consists of an Introduction of seventy pages in which, after a brief sketch of Lahontan's career, he studies in some detail the history and content of the edition of 1703 and the relation to this of the revision undertaken by Gueudeville in 1705, and concludes with an extended discussion of the fortunes of Lahontan's work during the eighteenth century and of its influence on various writers in France, Germany, and England, from Leibnitz to Lord Monboddo and Chateaubriand. Among the most interesting of his points in this last chapter is the suggestion, which if not entirely convincing is at least highly plausible, that various traits in Swift's picture of the Houyhnhnms were derived from a reading of the *Mémoires* and the *Dialogues*.—R. S. C.

Laignel-Lavastine, Maxine, and Jean Vinchon. *Les maladies de l'esprit et leurs médecins du XVI*[e] *au XIX*[e] *siècle.* Paris: Norbert Maloine, 1930. Pp. 379.

Rev. by Aldo Mieli in *Archeion,* XIII (1931), 275-76.

Lovejoy, Arthur O. [Review of Albert Schinz, *La pensée de Jean-Jacques Rousseau,* Northampton, Mass., 1929.] *MLN,* XLVI (1931), 41-46.

Lovering, S. *L'activité intellectuelle de l'Angleterre d'après l'ancien "Mercure de France" (1672-1778).* Paris: E. de Boccard, 1930. Pp. 324.

Rev. by Pierre Brunet in *Archeion,* XIII (1931), 133-34; by A. Digeon in *RAA,* IX (1931), 153-54; by A. Koszul in *RC,* LXV (1931), 264-66 (severe criticism).

In length of years and variety of interests the *Mercure* offers a rich field for the student of "Anglomania" in eighteenth-century France. The present volume attempts to trace the growth of French interest in English science, philosophy, and letters as seen first in the *Mercure galant* and its successors (1672-1724); then in the *Mercure de France,* from its founding in 1724 to 1756, when the Seven Years' War broke out; and finally from 1756 to 1778, when the *Mercure* was merged with the *Journal politique.* Such a division, as the author admits, is somewhat arbitrary; it forms a convenient framework for collecting material, but as a plan of exposition it has serious defects, particularly since the material in each section is organized in the same way, beginning with "La médecine" and continuing with "L'histoire naturelle," "La physique" and so on to "La littérature." The evidence thus gathered to show early French interest in English science and philosophy constitutes the chief contribution of the book. One regrets that the author does not attempt to relate this material and the conclusions drawn from it to the general subject of the infiltration of English ideas. Equally disappointing is the author's failure to verify the English originals quoted, so that we have Forgubar for Farquhar (p. 25), Jacques Greggs for James Craggs (p. 112), etc. And it is hard to see what class of readers can be aided by three-line footnotes explaining who Chaucer was, or Spenser, or Milton. In these we are told that Spenser died in 1598 (p. 120), that Gilbert Burnet's chief work was his *History of the Reformation* (p. 15); and to explain John Moore (author of *Columbarium, or the pigeon-house* [1735]) the author gives us a condensed biography of the author of *Utopia* (p. 41)! Finally, one wonders if the material gathered is complete: the earliest allusion to the *Spectator* cited is an incidental one in 1719; yet the *Mercure* in December, 1717 printed two entire papers from the *Spectator*—Addison's famous essays on the dissection of a beau's head and a coquette's heart (Nos. 275, 281).—DONALD F. BOND.

Menzel, Walter. *Der Kampf gegen den Epikureismus in der französischen Literatur des 18. Jahrhunderts.* Breslau: Priebatsch's Buchhandlung, 1931. Pp. 168.

Metzger, Hélène. *Newton, Stahl, Boerhave et la doctrine chimique.* Paris: Alcan, 1930. Pp. 332.

Montgomery, Francis K. *La vie et l'œuvre du P. Buffier.* Paris: Association du doctorat, 1930. Pp. 230.

Rev. by D. Mornet in *RHL,* XXXVIII (1931), 322-23.

Moras, Joachim. *Ursprung und Entwickelung des Begriffs der Zivilisation in Frankreich (1756-1830).* Hamburg: Seminar für romanische Sprachen und Kultur, 1930. Pp. xvi+87.

Rev. by R. Durand in *RC,* LXV (1931), 416-18.

Peoples, Margaret Hill. "La querelle Rousseau-Hume." *Annales de la société Jean-Jacques Rousseau,* XVIII (1927-28), 1-331.

Reesink, H. J. *L'Angleterre et la littérature anglaise dans les trois plus anciens périodiques français de Hollande de 1684 à 1709.* Paris: Champion, 1931. Pp. viii+433.

Robinson, Howard. *Bayle the sceptic.* New York: Columbia University press, 1931. Pp. x+334.

A useful popular account. In thirteen moderately long chapters we are given a sympathetic narrative of the events of Bayle's not very eventful career, studies of the genesis and analyses of the content of his principal writings, and a valuable sketch of the vicissitudes of his fame and influence during the eighteenth century. So far as it goes the book is easily the best introduction to the study of Bayle and Bayleism that has appeared in English. One could wish, however, that it had gone a little farther in at least two directions. The writings of Bayle are not only voluminous but highly complex; even the most superficial analysis of his ideas reveals a number of distinct and not easily reconcilable strains: the man who could expound the purest deism in the *Commentaire philosophique* could also in the *Pensées diverses* and in the *Dictionnaire* give expression to the most thoroughgoing skepticism concerning human reason in its practical and moral aspects. Robinson does not, I think, either in his exposition of Bayle's writings or in his analysis of his influence, recognize clearly enough that he has to do with an author whose thought was far from being all of a piece; preoccupied for the most part with one general aspect of Bayle—his rôle in the liberation of European thought from intolerance and the weight of traditional superstition and error—he is insufficiently aware of the numerous conflicts of assumption and point of view that persist throughout his hero's work. These conflicts were not, of course, peculiar to Bayle, and in part at least Robinson's failure to bring them into proper relief is due to an inadequate acquaintance with the history of ideas, in other than its most general and frequently noted aspects, during the seventeenth century. At any rate, he seldom attempts to exhibit Bayle's doctrines in their historical setting, and he seems not to be familiar with one of the best of the few earlier studies in which the author of the *Dictionnaire* is treated in relation to the movement of thought in contemporary France—Lanson's lectures in *RCC* for

1908-10 on the "Origines et premières manifestations de l'esprit philosophique en France avant 1750."—R. S. C.

Rovillain, Eugène E. "Sur le 'Zadig' de Voltaire; quelques autres influences." *PMLA,* XLVI (1931), 533-39.

Sternberg, Kurt. "Aufklärung, Klassizismus und Romantik bei Kant." *Kant-Studien,* XXXVI (1931), 27-50.

Torrey, Norman L. *Voltaire and the English deists.* New Haven: Yale University press; London: Humphrey Milford, Oxford University press, 1930. Cf. *PQ,* X, 215.

Rev. by F. Baldensperger in *RLC,* XI (1931), 568-72 (valuable suggestions of method in studies of this type); by Louis I. Bredvold in *MLN,* XLVI (1931), 419-20; by E. P. Dargan in *MP,* XXIX (1931), 120-25; by A. Digeon in *RAA,* VIII (1931), 357-58; by R. E. Fitch in *Journal of philosophy,* XXVIII (1931), 103-06; by Henri Sée in *RH,* CLXVI (1931), 151-52.

Wade, Ira O. "Destouches in England." *MP,* XXIX (1931), 27-47.

Welzel, Hans. "Die kulturphilosophischen Grundlagen der Naturrechtslehre Samuel Pufendorfs und ihre kulturhistorische Bedeutung." *DVLG,* IX (1931), 585-606.

Weulersse, Georges. "Le mouvement préphysiocratique en France." *Revue d'histoire économique et sociale,* XIX (1931), 244-72.

Weulersse, Georges. *Les physiocrates.* Paris: Gaston Doin, 1931. Pp. xvi+332.

Wheatley, Katherine E. *Molière and Terence, a study in Molière's realism.* Austin [Texas]: University of Texas, 1931. Pp. 124.

Wilson, Arthur M., Jr. "Sensibility in France in the eighteenth century: a study in word history." *French quarterly,* XIII (1931), 35-46.

The second part of the article, "The growth and change of meaning of 'sensibilité' in the French language," brings together some interesting texts.

1933

ENGLISH LITERATURE, 1660-1800: A CURRENT BIBLIOGRAPHY

By Louis I. Bredvold
University of Michigan

This bibliography attempts to list the more significant books, articles, and reviews published during the year 1932, together with some bearing the date 1931 that were inadvertently omitted from the bibliography for that year (*PQ*, XI, 167-215). I am indebted to Professor Ronald S. Crane for his continued interest in the bibliography and for a considerable number of the titles here given. Those who have become accustomed to consulting this bibliography will hope, with the new editor, that Professor Crane will continue to contribute his notes and criticisms to it.

LIST OF ABBREVIATIONS

AHR=*American historical review.*
Archiv=*Archiv für das Studium der neueren Spra hen und Literaturen.*
Beiblatt=*Beiblatt zur Anglia.*
DVLG=*Deutsche Vierteljahrschrift für Literaturwissenschaft u. Geistesgeschichte.*
EHR=*English historical review.*
ES=*Englische Studien.*
GRM=*Germanisch-romanische Monatschrift.*
JEGP=*Journal of English and Germanic philology.*
JMH=*Journal of modern history.*
LM=*London mercury.*
MLN=*Modern language notes.*
MLR=*Modern language review.*
MP=*Modern philology.*
N & Q=*Notes and queries.*
PMLA=*Publications of the Modern Language Association of America.*
PQ=*Philological quarterly.*
RAA=*Revue anglo-américaine.*
RC=*Revue critique.*
RCC=*Revue des cours et conférences.*
RELV=*Revue de l'enseignement des langues vivantes.*
RES=*Review of English studies.*
RH=*Revue historique.*
RHL=*Revue d'histoire littéraire de la France.*

RHP=*Revue d'histoire de la philosophie.*
RLC=*Revue de littérature comparée.*
RSH=*Revue de synthèse historique.*
SP=*Studies in philology.*
SRL=*Saturday review of literature.*
TLS=*Times literary supplement* (London).

I. BIBLIOGRAPHIES AND BIBLIOGRAPHICAL STUDIES

Addington, Marion H. "Dodsley's *Museum*." *N&Q*, CLXII (1932), 47-48.

Annual bibliography of English language and literature. Volume XII, 1931. Edited for the Modern Humanities Research Association, by Mary S. Serjeantson, assisted by Leslie N. Broughton. Cambridge: Bowes & Bowes, 1932. Pp. 272.

Baugh, Albert C. "American bibliography for 1931: English language and literature." *PMLA*, XLVI (1931).

See especially pp. 1358-66.

Bernbaum, Ernest. "Recent works on prose fiction before 1800." *MLN*, XLVII (1932), 104-13.

Block, Andrew. *The book collector's vade mecum.* London: Denis Archer, 1932.

"Bookseller's binding." *TLS*, March 10, 1932, p. 176.

Also corr. by D. E. Yates, *ibid.*, June 9, 1932, p. 427.

Bond, Richmon P., and MacMillan, Dougald. "Recent publications: Studies in the seventeenth and eighteenth centuries." *SP*, XXIX (1932), 505-14.

Catalogue of an exhibition illustrating the history of the English newspaper through three centuries. From the library of the Press Club, London. May 25 to June 18. London: J. and E. Bumpus, 1932. Pp. 58.

A Catalogue of XVIIIth century verse. Part III, "Scots-Young. Anonymous, Academic-Brooke." London: P.J. & A.E. Dobell, [1932]. Catalogue 122.

Clapp, Sarah L. C. "Subscription publishers prior to Jacob Tonson." *Library*, 4th series, XIII (1932), 158-83.

Crane, Ronald S., and Prior, M. E. "English literature, 1660-1800: a current bibliography." *PQ*, XI (1932), 167-215.

Crawford and Balcarres, Earl of. "Gabriel Naudé and John Evelyn: with some notes on the Mazarinades." *Library*, 4th series, XII (1932), 382-408.

Dowling, Margaret. "Public Record Office research: the Equity side of Chancery, 1558-1714." *RES*, VIII (1932), 185-200.

Fussell, G. E., and Atwater, V. G. B. "Travel and topography in seventeenth-century England: a bibliography of sources for social and economic history." *Library,* XIII (1932), 292-311.

Gillett, Charles Ripley. *Burned books: Neglected chapters in British history and literature.* New York: Columbia University press, 1932. 2 vols.

Rev. in *TLS,* July 7, 1932, p. 498.

Gottschalk, Louis. "Studies since 1920 of French thought in the period of the Enlightenment." *JMH,* IV (1932), 242-60.

Graham, Walter. "The authorship of the *Flapper,* 1796." *N & Q,* CLXII (1932), 25.

See also corr., *ibid.,* pp. 122, 246, 340.

Graham, Walter. "The authorship of the Norwich *Cabinet,* 1794-5." *N & Q,* CLXII (1932), 294-95.

Halkett, Samuel, and Laing, John. *Dictionary of anonymous and pseudonymous English literature.* New and enlarged edition by Dr. James Kennedy, W. A. Smith, and A. F. Johnson. Volume six. Edinburgh and London: Oliver and Boyd, 1932. Pp. 449.

Havens, Raymond Dexter. "A cancel in the *Political Miscellanies.*" *RES,* VIII (1932), 211-12.

Hobhouse, Edmund. "The library of a physician *circa* 1700." *Library,* 4th series, XIII (1932), 89-96.

Jackson, Holbrook. *The anatomy of bibliomania.* New and revised edition. London: The Soncino Press, 1932.

A reprint at a more moderate price.

Jaggard, W. "Robert Tutchin, a bookseller of the seventeenth century." *N & Q,* CLXII (1932), 224.

Laprade, W. T., "The present state of the history of England in the eighteenth century." *JMH,* IV (1932), 581-603.

"London booksellers and publishers 1700-1750." *N & Q,* CLXII (1932), 46-47, 116-20.

McKerrow, R. B. "A publishing agreement of the late seventeenth century." *Library,* 4th series, XIII (1932), 184-87.

Milford, R. T. "The *Female Tatler.*" *MP,* XXIX (1932), 350-51.

Morison, Stanley. *The English newspaper: some account of the physical development of journals printed in London between 1622 and the present day.* Cambridge: University press, 1932. Pp. xii+335.

Rev. by B. H. Newdigate in *LM,* XXVI (1932), 168; in *N & Q,* CLXII (1932), 431.

Prendeville, P. L. "A select bibliography of Irish economic history.

Part two: the seventeenth and eighteenth centuries." *Economic history review,* III (1932), 402-16.

Sparrow, John. "The earlier owners of books in John Selden's library." *Bodleian quarterly record,* VI (1931), 263-71.

"Thirty-third critical bibliography of the history and philosophy of science and of the history of civilization (to December 1931)." *Isis,* XVIII (1932), 334-429.

See especially pp. 349-58.

Van Tieghem, Paul. "Histoire littéraire générale et comparée: Quinzième compte rendu annuel." *RSH,* L (1931), 377-99.

The Year's work in English studies. Volume XI, 1930. Edited for the English Association by F. S. Boas. Oxford: University press; London: Humphrey Milford, 1932. Pp. 400.

II. THE SOCIAL AND POLITICAL ENVIRONMENT

Bolingbroke's defence of the Treaty of Utrecht. Being letters VI-VIII of the *Study and use of history.* With an introduction by G. M. Trevelyan. Cambridge: University press, 1932.

Briggs, Martin S. *The homes of the Pilgrim Fathers in England and America (1620-1688).* Oxford: University press, 1932. Pp. xvi +211.

Points out that New England architecture was derived from the building practice of the county of Essex.

Buchan, Mrs. John. *Lady Louise Stuart.* London: Hodder & Stoughton, 1932. Pp. 275.

Rev. in *TLS,* Oct. 20, 1932, p. 745.

Campbell, Kathleen. *Sarah, Duchess of Marlborough.* London: Thornton Butterworth; New York: Little Brown, 1932. Pp. 319.

Rev. in *TLS,* Sept. 22, 1932, p. 653; by Bonamy Dobrée in *Spectator,* Oct. 1, 1932, p. 408.

Bryant, Arthur. *King Charles II.* London: Longmans, 1931.

Rev. by E. H. in *English historical review,* Oct., 1932, p. 708-09; by Clennell Wilkinson in *LM,* XXV (1932), 312-13; by W. C. Abbott in *Yale Review,* XXI (1931), 410-13; by F. G. Marcham in *AHR,* XXXVII (1932), 592-93.

Chambers, J. D. *Nottinghamshire in the eighteenth century: a study of life and labour under the squirearchy.* London: P. S. King, 1932. Pp. 377.

Chancellor, Frank. *Sarah Churchill.* London: Philip Allan, 1932.

Rev. in *TLS,* Sept. 22, 1932, p. 653.

Corson, James C. "Resistance no rebellion." *Juridical review,* XLII (1930), 245-56.

A discussion of the juridical aspects of the Whig interpretation of the Revolution of 1688.

Davis, E. Jeffries. "Whitehall in the seventeenth century." *TLS,* Sept. 15, 1932, p. 643.

On the difficulties and technical nature of London cartography, and suggestion to students to "avail themselves of the cooperative labours of three societies": the London and Middlesex Archæological Society, the London Topographical Society, and the London Survey Committee.

Dimond, Sydney G. *The psychology of Methodism.* London: Epworth press, 1932. Pp. 154.

Dobrée, Bonamy. *William Penn, Quaker and pioneer.* London: Constable; New York: Houghton Mifflin, 1932. Pp. xi+428.

Rev. in *TLS,* Oct. 6, 1932, p. 701; by H. G. Wood in *Spectator,* Oct. 22, 1932, 546-48; by Hugh Kingsmill in *Bookman* (London), LXXXIII (1932), 126-27.

Dowdell, E. G. *A hundred years of quarter sessions: the government of Middlesex from 1660 to 1760.* Cambridge: University press, 1932. Pp. lxxv+215.

Faÿ, Bernard. "Learned societies in Europe and America in the eighteenth century." *AHR,* XXXVII (1932), 255-66.

Firth, Sir Charles. "Macaulay's third chapter." *History,* XVII (1932), 201-19.

Fortescue, Sir John. *Marlborough.* London: Peter Davies; New York: Appleton, 1932. Pp. 175.

Friedell, Egon. *A cultural history of the modern age.* Volume II. Book two: Baroque and Rococo: from the Thirty Years' War to the Seven Years' War; Book three: Enlightenment and Revolution: from the Seven Years' War to the Congress of Vienna. Translated from the German by Charles Francis Atkinson. New York: Alfred A. Knopf, 1931.

Rev. by Walton H. Hamilton in *Yale Review,* XXI (1932), 416-19.

"A Georgian ladies' club." Leading article, *TLS,* August 11, 1932, pp. 561-62.

Gilboy, Elizabeth Waterman. "Demand as a factor in the Industrial Revolution." *Facts and factors in economic history: articles by former students of Edwin Francis Gay.* Cambridge, Mass.: Harvard University press, 1932, pp. 620-39.

Grey, Charles. *The merchant venturers of London.* London; H. F. & G. Witherby, 1932.

Hervey, John Lord. *Some materials towards memoirs of the reign of King George II.* Edited by Romney Sedgwick. London: Eyre and Spottiswoode, 1931. 3 vols. Cf. *PQ,* XI, 170.

Rev. by Basis Williams in *EHR*, July, 1932, 502-03.

Hunt, R. N. Carew. "Letters from an autograph collection." *Cornhill,* LXXIII (1932), 471-80, 513-20.

Unpublished letters from the collection formed by John Wild, from which a volume was published in 1931.

Innes, Arthur D. *The maritime and colonial expansion of England under the Stuarts (1603-1714).* London: Sampson Low, 1932.

Rev. in *TLS,* April 14, 1932, p. 263.

Johnson, E. A. J. *American economic thought in the seventeenth century.* London: P. S. King, 1932. Pp. xi+292.

Rev. by H. E. Batson in *Economica,* No. 38, 506-09; by O. M. Dickerson in *Mississippi Valley historical review,* XIX (1932), 413; by Broadus Mitchell in *American economic review,* XXII (1932), 698-99.

Johnson, E. A. J. "British mercantilist doctrines concerning the 'exploitation of work' and 'foreign-paid incomes'." *Journal of political economy,* XL (1932), 750-70.

Lee, Umphrey. *The historical backgrounds of early Methodist enthusiasm.* New York: Columbia University press, 1931. Cf. *PQ,* XI, 171.

Rev. by John T. McNeill in *JMH,* IV (1932), 292-93.

Lipson, E. *The economic history of England.* Volumes II and III. *The age of mercantilism.* London: A. and C. Black; New York: Macmillan, 1931. Pp. viii+464 and v+542. Cf. *PQ,* XI, 171.

Rev. by N. S. B. Gras in *American economic review,* XXII (1932), 486-88; by Henri Sée in *Economic history review,* III (1932), 423-25; by T. S. Ashton in *Economica,* No. 35 (1932), 116-19.

Lipson, E. "England in the age of mercantilism," *Journal of economic and business history,* IV (1932), 691-707.

Maxwell, Constantia. *The English travellers in France, 1698-1815.* London: Routledge, 1932. Pp. 310.

Rev. by Henri Sée in *RH,* CLXX (1932), 537-38.

Mowat, R. B. *England in the eighteenth century.* London: Harrap, 1932. Pp. 281.

Rev. in *History,* Oct., 1932, 269-70; by D. C. Somerville in *English review,* LIV (1932), 690-91.

Muddiman, J. H. "Benjamin Harris, the first American journalist." *N & Q,* CLXIII (1932), 129-33, 147-50, 166-70, 223, 273-74.

Petrie, Sir Charles. *The Jacobite movement.* London: Eyre and Spottiswoode, 1932. Pp. 315.

Rev. in *TLS,* May 5, 1932, p. 318.

Pound, Arthur. *The Penns of Pennsylvania and England.* London and New York: Macmillan, 1932. Pp. xx+349.

Rev. in *TLS,* Nov. 10, 1932, p .823.

Realey, Charles Bechdolt. *The early opposition to Sir Robert Walpole.* University of Kansas Humanistic Studies, Vol. IV, nos. ii and iii. Lawrence, Kansas, 1931. Pp. 280.

Rev. by W. T. Laprade in *South Atlantic quarterly,* XXXI (1932), 252.

Richards, R. D. "Mr. Pepys and the goldsmith bankers." *Economic history,* II (1932), 501-20.

Sitwell, Edith. *Bath.* London: Faber & Faber, 1932. Pp. 288.

Rev. in *TLS,* May 12, 1932, p. 343.

Smith, R. W. Innes. *English-speaking students of medicine at the University of Leyden.* London: Oliver and Boyd, 1932. Pp. xxii+258.

Rev. in *TLS,* April 14, 1932.
Contains notes on Sir Thomas Browne, Goldsmith, Boswell's uncle, and others.

Sykes, Norman. "Episcopal administration in England in the eighteenth century." *EHR,* XLVII (1932), 414-46.

Thomson, Mark A. *The secretaries of state, 1681-1782.* Oxford: Clarendon press, 1932. Pp. 206.

Rev. in *TLS,* April 28, 1932, p. 299; by G. H. Guttridge in *JMH,* IV (1932), p. 470.

Trevelyan, G. M. *England under Queen Anne: Ramillies and the union with Scotland.* London: Longmans, 1932. Pp. xv+468.

Rev. in *TLS,* Oct. 6, 1932, p. 699; by Sir John Marriott in *Fortnightly review,* DCCXCII (1932), 793-94.

Whiting, C. E. *Studies in English Puritanism from the Restoration to the Revolution, 1660-1688.* London: S. P. C. K., 1931. Cf. *PQ,* XI, 172.

Rev. by G. D. in *EHR,* April, 1932, pp. 337-38, who calls it "a very important contribution to ecclesiastical literature."

Wienbeck, Dorothea. *Die Stellung der Frau der oberen und mittleren Gesellschaftsklassen Englands in der ersten Hälfte des 18. Jahrh. unter Ausschluss der Vers- und Prosadichtung nach zeitgenöss. Zeugnissen dargestellt.* Halle, 1931. Pp. 98.

Wilkinson, Clennell. *Bonnie Prince Charlie.* London: Harrap, 1932.

Rev. in *TLS,* Nov. 3, 1932, p. 805.

Williams, Basil. *Stanhope: a study in eighteenth century war and diplomacy.* Oxford: Clarendon press, 1932. Pp. xvi+478.

Rev. in *TLS,* May 26, 1932, p. 373.

The life and times of Anthony à Wood (1632-95). Edited by Llewelyn Powys. London: Wishart, 1932. Pp. xix+319.

Rev. in *TLS,* Oct. 6, 1932, pp. 697-98; by Graham Greene in *Spectator,* Nov. 4, 1932, 636-38.
An abridgment from Clark's edition in the publications of the Oxford Historical Society. Intended for popular consumption.

Wright, Luella M. *The literary life of the early Friends, 1650-1725.* With an introduction by Rufus M. Jones. New York: Columbia University press, 1932. Pp. xiv+309.

Wright, Luella M. *Literature and education in early Quakerism.* University of Iowa studies, humanistic series, Vol. V, no. 2. Iowa City: University of Iowa, 1933.

Young, R. Fitzgibbon. "Premonitions of the Industrial Revolution." *TLS,* Jan. 14, 1932, p. 28.

Early opposition by laborers to new inventions indicated by a passage in Shadwell's *Virtuoso.*

III. CURRENTS OF IDEAS AND LITERARY FORMS

Baker, John Tull. *An historical and critical examination of English space and time theories from More to Berkeley.* New York: Columbia University dissertation, 1930. Pp. 90.

Rev. by Rudolph Kagey in *Journal of Philosophy,* Dec. 8, 1932, p. 697.

Baker, John Tull. "Space, time, and God. A chapter in eighteenth-century philosophy." *Philosophical review,* XLI (1932), 577-93.

Becker, Carl L. *The heavenly city of the eighteenth-century philosophers.* (The Storrs lectures.) New Haven: Yale University press, 1932. Pp. [x]+168.

Bond, Richmond P. *English burlesque poetry, 1700-1750.* Cambridge: Harvard University press, 1932. Pp. xiv+483. (Harvard Studies in English, VI.)

Bosker, A. *Literary criticism in the age of Johnson.* Groningen: J. B. Wolters, 1930. Cf. *PQ,* X, 177-78, and XI, 173.

Rev. by Norman Foerster in *PQ,* XI (1932), 216-17; by Percy H. Houston in *JEGP,* XXXI (1932), 159-62; by J. R. Sutherland in *RES,* VIII (1932), 111-12; by Eduard Eckhardt in *Beiblatt,* XLIII (1932), 44-47.

Boswell, Eleanore. *The Restoration court stage.* Cambridge: Harvard University press, 1932. Pp. xviii+370.

Rev. in *TLS,* August 25, 1932.

Brinkley, Roberta Florence. *Arthurian Legend in the seventeenth century.* Baltimore: The Johns Hopkins press, 1932. Pp. xi+228. (Johns Hopkins Monographs in Literary History, Vol. III.)

Buck, Gerhard. *Die Vorgeschichte des historischen Romans in der modernen englischen Literatur.* Hamburg: Friedrichsen de Gruyter and co., 1931. Pp. 115. Cf. *PQ,* XI, 173.

Rev. by S. B. Liljegren in *Beiblatt,* XLIII (1932), 169-72.

Cassirer, Ernst. *Die Platonische Renaissance in England und die Schule von Cambridge.* Leipzig: B. G. Teubner, 1932. Pp. 143.

Rev. in *TLS,* Oct. 13, 1932, p. 735; by J. H. Muirhead in *Mind,* XLI (1932), 516-18.

Clark, W. S. "The definition of the 'Heroic Play' in the Restoration period." *RES,* VIII (1932), 437-44.

A valuable collection of contemporary comments on this *genre.*

Craig, Mary Elizabeth. *The Scottish periodical press, 1750-1789.* Edinburgh and London: Oliver and Boyd, 1931. Cf. *PQ,* XI, 174.

Rev. by Walter Graham in *MP,* XXX (1932), 113-14.

Deane, Cecil V. *Dramatic theory and the rhymed heroic play.* Oxford: University press, 1931. Cf. *PQ,* XI, 175.

Rev. by William S. Clark in *RES,* VIII (1932), 359-62.

De Boer, John. *The theory of knowledge of the Cambridge Platonists.* Madras: Methodist Publishing House, 1931. Pp. 160.

Déprez, E. "Les grands voyages et les grandes découvertes jusqu'à la fin du XVIIIe siècle: origines, développement, conséquences." Bulletin of the international committee of historical sciences, June, 1930.

Dobrée, Bonamy. *Variety of ways.* Oxford: University press, 1932.

Rev. in *TLS,* April 28, 1932, p. 306.
Essays on literary figures of the eighteenth century.

Dodds, M. H. "English provincial theatres, XVIIIth century." *N & Q,* CLXIII (1932), 115.

von Erhardt-Siebold, Erika. "Harmony of the senses in English, German, and French Romanticism." *PMLA,* XLVII (1932), 577-92.

von Erhardt-Siebold, Erika. "Some inventions of the Pre-Romantic period and their influence upon literature." *ES,* LXVI (1932), 347-63.

A study of the influence of the *Camera Obscura,* the Colour-Organ, and the Aeolian Harp, in providing new sense-stimuli and quickening the imagination of the eighteenth century. An interesting collection of curious information.

Draper, J. W. "Poetry and music in eighteenth century æsthetics." *ES,* LXVII (1932), 70-85.

Fairchild, Hoxie Neale. *The romantic quest.* New York: Columbia University press, 1931. Cf. *PQ,* XI, 177.

Rev. in *TLS,* Sept. 29, 1932, p. 694; by Herbert G. Wright in *MLR,* XXVII (1932), 487-88.

Frank, Kath. *Anschauung von Wesen und Beruf des Dichters in Zeitalter des engl. Klassizismus.* Dissertation. Freiburg in Br., 1930. Pp. 73.

Friederich, Werner P. *Spiritualismus und Sensualismus in der Englischen Barocklyrik.* (Wiener Beiträge, vol. LVII.) Vienna and Leipzig: Wilhelm Braumüller, 1932. Pp. 304.

This work is a product of the German school which finds in the conception of "Baroque" the single adequate explanation of the seventeenth century. This school seems ready to take any characteristic of a Baroque painting or work of sculpture and apply it quite literally either to an individual poem, to the personality of a writer, or to a whole century. Friederich studies the peculiar *polarität* which gives such an effect of strain and restlessness in Baroque art; and he finds this polarity in the extremes of sensualism and spiritualism of English lyric poetry of the seventeenth century. Like other writers of his school, he has no misgivings about his theory. But his discussion is stimulating, and abundantly illustrated with quotation.

Correspondence and Papers of Edmond Halley. Edited by Eugene Fairfield MacPike. Oxford: Clarendon press, 1932. Pp. xiv+300.

Rev. in *TLS*, July 28, 1932, p. 543.

Harvey, Sir Paul. *The Oxford companion to English literature*. Oxford: Clarendon press, 1932. Pp. 875.

Holland, A. K. *Henry Purcell: the English musical tradition*. London: Bell, 1932.

Jackson, Alfred. "London playhouses, 1700-1705." *RES*, VIII (1932), 291-302.

A collection of newspaper references to the theatres.

Jaeger, Muriel. *Experimental lives*. London: Bell, 1932.

Includes essays on "Lord Chesterfield: the man of the world," and "Thomas Day: the child of Nature."

Johnson, Charles. *English painting*. London: G. Bell, 1932. Pp. xvi+350. 48 plates.

Rev. in *TLS*, April 7, 1932, p. 245.

Jones, Richard F. "Science and language in England of the mid-seventeenth century." *JEGP*, XXXI (1932), 315-31.

Kitchin, George. *A survey of burlesque and parody in English*. Edinburgh and London: Oliver and Boyd, 1931. Cf. *PQ*, XI, 180.

Rev. by L. Cazamian in *MLN*, XLVII (1932), 469-72.

Lin, Chi-Kai. *L'origine et la développement de la méthode expérimentale*. Paris: F. Loviton et cie, 1931. Pp. 422.

Rev. by P. P. Wiener in *Journal of philosophy*, XXIX (1932), 49-50.

Longaker, Mark. *English biography in the eighteenth century*. Philadelphia: University of Pennsylvania press, 1931. Cf. *PQ*, XI, 181.

Rev. by G. C. Moore Smith in *RES*, VIII (1932), 491-93; by H. W. Taylor in *MP*, XXIX (1932), 381-82; by W. T. Laprade in *South Atlantic quarterly*, XXXI (1932), 421-23; by George R. Stewart, Jr., in *University of California Chronicle*, XXXIV (1932), 488-90; by G. Kitchin in *MLR*, XXVII (1932), 484-86; by Donald A. Stauffer in *MLN*, XLVII (1932), 466-69.

Lovejoy, Arthur O., "The parallel of Deism and Classicism." *MP*, XXIX (1932), 281-99.

A systematic statement of the rationalistic *preconceptions* which, when applied in matters of religion terminated in Deism, when applied in æsthetics produced Classicism. An illuminating synthesis, done throughout with characteristic finesse and discrimination.

Lovejoy, Arthur O. "The first Gothic revival and the return to Nature." *MLN*, XLVII (1932), 419-46.

Marshall, L. Birkett. "Five minor poets." *TLS*, Sept. 29, 1932, p. 687.

Meissner, Paul. "Die Stellung des Menschen im englischen Geistesleben des 17. Jahrhunderts." *ES,* LXVII (1932), 27-69.

Mitchell, W. Fraser. *English pulpit oratory from Andrewes to Tillotson: a study of its literary aspects.* London: S. P. C. K., 1932. Pp. xii+516.

As the title of the book somewhat vaguely indicates, Mitchell has taken as his subject one aspect of the evolution of English prose style in the seventeenth century. His work originated in an interest in the "metaphysical" style of Donne's sermons, and soon extended to the reaction against that style and the introduction of a plain and direct prose after the Restoration. The selection of the sermon style for concentrated study was a happy one, for several reasons: sermons bulk largely in the prose of the century, and exercised a far greater influence on the thought and taste of the nation than at any time since; the sermon was such a traditional *genre* that its inheritance of form and style from earlier ages can be stated with great definiteness; and it was moreover so closely allied with hermeneutics, that the various practices in preaching in the seventeenth century can be related with precision to the theological views of the various parties and sects of that time; and as the sermon was a distinctly learned form, many of its characteristics can be referred to the current practices of education, particularly in rhetoric. All these aspects of his subject Mr. Mitchell has studied with care and discussed with mature judgment; and his book is indispensable to the student of seventeenth-century literature.

A special interest attaches to the work because of the previous studies in the same field by Professors Morris W. Croll and Richard F. Jones. Mitchell has studied Croll's contributions with care, and his many comments on the Senecan style—which can easily be found by means of the admirably full index—in the main corroborate and illustrate the conclusions of Croll. Professor Jones' article on *The Attack on Pulpit Eloquence in the Restoration* (*JEGP,* XXX, 188-217) appeared too late for Mitchell to use it; and, extensive as Mitchell's bibliography is, Jones discusses at least four treatises bearing on pulpit oratory which appear to have been unknown to Mitchell: John Prideaux, *Sacred Eloquence* (1659), Simon Patrick, *A Friendly Debate,* 3rd ed. (1669), James Ardene, *Directions Concerning the Matter and Stile of Sermons* (1671), and Robert Ferguson, *The Interest of Reason* (1675). Mitchell has frequently noted in his volume that there was an influence on sermon style from the "Royal Society divines," but he does not include in that group either South (p. 312) or Barrow (p. 322). He gives, horeover, so many explanations of the trend towards simplicity in style after the Restoration, that the influence of the Royal Society appears from his account less pervasive and less crucial than we might suppose from Professor Jones' article.

In one instance Mitchell has failed to pursue his subject to its original sources. On page 36 he discusses two editions (1591), one authentic and one pirated, of a sermon by Henry Smith, referring to Evelyn Simpson's *Study of the Prose Works of John Donne,* pp. 268-69. But he fails to record, either in his notes or in his bibliography, that both forms of this sermon were edited with an important introduction on shorthand, by H. T. Price (Halle, 1922).

Moreau, Pierre. *Le Classicisme des Romantiques.* Paris: Plon, 1932. Pp. iii+409.

Rev. by Pierre Martino in *RC,* LXVI (1932), 298-300.
A counterblast to Pierre Lassere.

Mornet, Daniel. "Le conflit des méthodes dans l'étude critique de la littérature." *Books Abroad,* VI (1932), 141-42.

Neve, J. L. "Arminianism in its influence upon England: rational theology; Latitudinarianism." *Bibliotheca sacra*, LXXXVIII (1931), 145-65.

Elementary. The author, who is a professor in an American theological seminary, is unable to distinguish clearly between James I and James II. See pp. 148, 150.

Nicoll, Allardyce. "The first Baconian." *TLS*, Feb. 25, 1932, p. 128.

Compatriots of Delia Bacon will be pleased to learn from Nicoll's article that Bacon's authorship of Shakespeare's plays was first suggested by an Englishman of the eighteenth century, the Rev. James Wilmott, D.D., Rector of Barton on the Heath, near Stratford.

Pfitzner, Käthe. *Die Ausländertypen im engl. Drama der Restorationszeit*. Breslau, 1931. Pp. 99.

Ralli, Augustus. *A history of Shakespearian criticism*. Oxford: University press, 1932. 2 vols.

Rev. in *TLS*, June 30, 1932, p. 469.

Rohde, Eleanour Sinclair. "Eighteenth century gardening books." *Bookman* (London), LXXXIII (1932), 34-35.

Shorr, Philip. *Science and superstition in the eighteenth century*. New York: Columbia University press, 1932. Pp. vii+82.

Sickels, Eleanor M. *The gloomy egoist: moods and themes of melancholy from Gray to Keats*. New York: Columbia University press, 1932. Pp. x+456.

de Soet, F. D. *Puritan and Royalist literature in the seventeenth century*. (Amsterdam diss.) Delft, 1932.

Stauffer, Donald A. *English biography before 1700*. Cambridge: Harvard University press, 1930. Cf. *PQ*, X, 191.

Rev. by E. C. Batho in *RES*, VIII (1932), 108-10; by H. W. Taylor in *MP*, XXIX (1932), 380-81.

Stewart, Powell. *An eighteenth-century adaptation of Shakespeare*. University of Texas, *Studies in English*, no. 12, pp. 98-117. Austin: University of Texas, 1932.

The Universal Passion, by the Rev. James Miller, was performed at Drury Lane, Feb. 28, 1737; based on *Much Ado*.

Thomas, P. G. *Aspects of literary theory and practice, 1550-1870*. London: Heath Cranton, 1931. Pp. 210.

Tompkins, J. M. S. *The popular novel in England, 1770-1800*. London: Constable, 1932.

Rev. in *TLS*, August 11, 1932, p. 567; by Graham Greene in *Spectator*, Aug. 20, 1932, p. 238-39.

Troeltsch, Ernst. *The social teaching of the Christian churches*. Translated by Olive Wyon. Halley Stewart Publications, I. London: George Allen and Unwin; New York: Macmillan, 1932. 2 vols. Pp. 1019.

Rev. by Felix Hope in *Hibbert Journal*, XXXI (1932), 309-15.

The English translation of a work which has long been recognized as of the first importance.

Ustick, W. Lee. "Advice to a son: a type of seventeenth-century conduct book." *SP,* XXIX (1932), 409-41.

Ustick, W. Lee. "Changing ideals of aristocratic character and conduct in seventeenth-century England." *MP,* XXX (1932), 147-66.

Ustick's article is not so comprehensive as his title; he studies the subject only as reflected in handbooks for the gentleman. He finds in these two traditions continuing from the Renaissance: "the tradition of the Magnanimous Man as set forth by Aristotle" and the Stoic tradition. In the seventeenth century there is observable an increasing note of piety and emphasis on Christian virtue, and towards the end of the century the virtues of sensibility begin to be stressed: natural goodness of heart and general benevolence towards the species. Ustick's study is therefore an illuminating commentary on the rise of sentimentalism in drama and fiction.

One reads this essay with some mental reservations, however. Do not these handbooks represent only one phase of the ideals of aristocratic character and conduct of the time? There is always a divergence between literature, especially edifying literature, and life. Ustick has so limited his subject as to escape this sociological problem, but it seems unavoidable if we are to judge of the real historical importance or significance of the handbooks he has studied.

Wellek, René. *Immanuel Kant in England, 1793-1838.* Princeton: Princeton University press, 1931. Pp. vii+317.

Rev. by T. E. Jessop in *Mind,* XLI (1932), 518-21.

Wiley, Autrey Nell. "The English vogue of prologues and epilogues." *MLN,* XLVII (1932), 255-57.

Williamson, G. C. *English conversation pictures of the eighteenth and early nineteenth centuries.* With a Foreword by Sir Philip Sassoon. London: Batsford, 1932. Pp. xii+27 and 87 plates.

Rev. in *TLS,* June 30, 1932, p. 475.

Wölfflin, Heinrich. *Principles of art history. The problem of the development of style in later art.* Translated by M. D. Hottinger. London: Bell; New York: Henry Holt, 1932. Pp. xvi -237.

Rev. in *TLS,* June 16, 1932, p. 441.

This work, which deals with the differences between High Renaissance and Baroque art, has long exercised a revolutionary influence on the study of art history, and in Germany has dominated also much of the recent work on the literary history of the seventeenth century. Whatever one may think of Wölfflin's imitators, his own book is a masterly essay.

Wood, Frederick T. "Some aspects of provincial drama in the eighteenth century." *ES,* XIV (1932), 65-74.

Woolf, Virginia. *The common reader:* Second series. London: Hogarth press, 1932. Pp. 270.

Rev. in *TLS,* Oct. 20, 1932, p. 755.

Wright, Benjamin Fletcher. *American interpretations of natural law; a study in the history of political thought.* Cambridge: Harvard University press, 1931. Pp. x+360.

IV. INDIVIDUAL AUTHORS

Joseph Addison

Anderson, Paul Bunyan. "Addison's *Letter from Italy*." *MLN*, XLVII (1932), 318.

Gustafson, Walter W. "The influence of the *Tatler* and *Spectator* in Sweden." *Scandinavian studies and notes* [Menasha, Wis.], XII (1932), 65-72.

More particularly on Olaf von Dalin (1708-1763) and *Den Svänska Argus*, a weekly published from December, 1732, to December, 1734. "Through the intuition of genius it seems, Dalin caught the spirit of the style of Addison and Steele and thus became the founder of modern Swedish prose" (p. 69). The author lists ten other Swedish periodicals of the Tatler-Spectator type between 1730 and 1768.

Jane Austen

Apperson, G. L. *A Jane Austen dictionary*. [London]: C. Palmer [1932]. Pp. 151.

Jane Austen's letters. Collected and edited by R. W. Chapman. Oxford: Clarendon press, 1932. 2 vols. Pp. xlviii+266; xxxii+267-510.

Rev. in *TLS*, Nov. 10, 1932, p. 821.

Rhydderch, David. *Jane Austen: her life and art*. London: Jonathan Cape, 1932. Pp. 252.

Rev. in *TLS*, April 14, 1932, p. 274; by Osbert Burdett in *English review*, LIV (1932), 686-89.

Rhydderch, David. "Darcy and Mr. Blackall." *TLS*, Oct. 20, 1932, p. 762.

Proposes an original for Jane Austen's hero. Cf. comment by R. W. Chapman, *ibid.*, Nov. 3, p. 815.

Tallmadge, Abby L. "Lady Catherine de Bourgh." *TLS*, July 14, 1932, p. 517.

"Jane Austen may have gotten the name of her super-snob . . . directly or indirectly from Sir Egerton Brydges."

William Beckford

Oliver, J. W. *The life of William Beckford*. Oxford: University press, 1932. Pp. x+343.

Rev. in *TLS*, Nov. 3, 1932, p. 797.

Jeremy Bentham

Hirst, W. A. "Jeremy Bentham: a hundred years after." *Contemporary review*, CXLII (1932), 213-19.

George Berkeley

Aaron, R. I. "A catalogue of Berkeley's library." *Mind*, XLI (1932), 465-75.

Hicks, G. Dawes. *Berkeley.* London: Ernest Benn, 1932. Pp. 352.

Rand, Benjamin. *Berkeley's American sojourn.* Cambridge: Harvard University press, 1932. Pp. xi+79.

William Blake

Larrabee, Stephen A. "An interpretation of Blake's *A Divine Image.*" *MLN,* XLVII (1932), 305-08.

Morse, B. J. "Dante Gabriel Rosetti and William Blake." *ES,* LXVI (1932), 364-72.

Poems of Blake. Chosen and edited by Laurence Binyon. New York: Macmillan, 1931. Pp. xi+371.

Rev. by E. M. Forster in *Books* (N. Y.), August 31, 1932, p. 1.

Visions of the Daughters of Albion. Reproduced in facsimile from an original copy of the work printed and illuminated by the author in 1793, now in the British Museum. With a note by J. Middleton Murry. London: Dent, 1932.

Wicksteed, Joseph H. "Blake's Songs of Innocence." *TLS,* Feb. 18, 1932, p. 112.

Nurse's Song and *The Little Boy Lost* were possibly suggested by Salzmann's *Elements of Morality,* translated from the German by Mary Wollstonecraft and illustrated by Blake.

Wilson, Mona. *The life of William Blake.* London: Peter Davies, 1932. Pp. 324.

Rev. by Osbert Burdett in *Criterion,* XI (1932), 714-16.

A new edition of a biography which first appeared in a limited edition in 1927. Unfortunately, the original notes, illustrations and appendices have been omitted.

James Boswell

Private papers of James Boswell from Malahide Castle in the collection of Lt-Colonel Ralph Heyward Isham. Prepared for the press by Geoffrey Scott and Frederick A. Pottle. New York: Privately printed, 1932. Volumes XIII-XVI.

Boswell's Journal for the years 1778-1786.

Chapman, R. W. "Boswell's archives." In *Essays and studies by members of the English Association, vol.* XVII. Oxford: Clarendon press, 1932.

Elovson, Harold. "'Mr. Kristrom' in Boswell's *Life of Dr. Johnson.*" *MLR,* XXVII (1932), 210-12.

Pearson, Hesketh. "Boswell as artist." *Cornhill,* LXXIII (1932), 704-11.

Pottle, Frederick A. "Boswell's shorthand." *TLS,* July 28, 1932, p. 545.

Comment by W. R. Batty, *ibid.,* August 4, p. 557.

Pottle, Frederick A., and Marion S. Pottle. *The private papers of James Boswell from Malahide Castle . . .: a catalogue.* London and New York: Oxford University press, 1931.

Rev. by L. F. Powell in *RES,* VIII (1932), 490-92.

Vulliamy, C. E. *James Boswell.* London: Geoffrey Bles, 1932. Pp. 272.

Rev. by Peter Fleming in *Spectator,* Dec. 2, 1932, p. 796-98.

Robert Boyle

Fulton, J. F. "A bibliography of the Honourable Robert Boyle." *Proceedings and papers of the Oxford Bibliographical Society,* Vol. III, Part II. Oxford: Clarendon press, 1932. Pp. 172.

Rev. in *TLS,* May 12, 1932, p. 356; by G. L. Keynes in *Bodleian quarterly record,* VII (1932), 149-50. Cf. corr. by G. L. Keynes in *TLS,* August 25, 1932, p. 596.

Fulton, J. F. "Robert Boyle and his influence on thought in the seventeenth century." *Isis,* XVIII (1932), 77-102.

Wiener, Philip Paul. "The experimental philosophy of Robert Boyle (1626-91)." *Philosophical review,* XLI (1932), 594-609.

Sir Thomas Browne

Leroy, Olivier. *Le chevalier Thomas Browne (1605-1682), médecin, styliste et métaphysicien.* Paris: Gamber, 1931. Pp. xi+422.

Rev. by Mario Praz in *English Studies,* XIV (1932), 168-71.

Leroy, Olivier. *A French bibliography of Sir Thomas Browne.* London: Harrap, 1932. Pp. 97.

Rev. in *TLS,* Feb. 25, 1932, p. 132.

John Bunyan

Harrison, Frank Mott. *A bibliography of the works of John Bunyan.* Supplement to the Bibliographical Society's Transactions, No. 6. London, 1932. Pp. xviii+83.

Edmund Burke

Murray, Robert H. *Edmund Burke, a biography.* Oxford: University Press, 1931. Cf. *PQ,* XI, 187.

Rev. by F. J. C. Hearnshaw in *History,* April, 1932, 76-77; by W. T. Laprade in *JMH,* IV (1932), 121-22.

Somerset, H. V. F. "Burke and the Cavendishes." *EHR,* XLVII (1932), 280-86.

Sutherland, L. Stuart. "Edmund Burke and the first Rockingham ministry." *EHR,* XLVII (1932), 46-72.

Fanny Burney

Roberts, W. Wright. "Charles and Fanny Burney in the light of the new Thrale correspondence in the John Rylands Library." *The Bulletin of the John Rylands Library,* XVI (1932), 115-36.

Also issued separately by Manchester University press.

Robert Burns

The Letters of Robert Burns. Edited from the original manuscripts by J. DeLancey Ferguson. Oxford: Clarendon press, 1931. Cf. *PQ,* XI, 187-88.

Rev. by Duncan C. Macgregor in *RES,* VIII (1932), 349-52; by George L. Marsh in *MP,* XXX (1932), 118-21; by Franklyn B. Snyder in *MLN,* XLVII (1932), 336-37; by W. A. Neilson in *Yale review,* XXI (1932), 610-12.

Averill, Esther C. "The authenticity of Burns' *When First I Saw Fair Jeanie's Face.*" *MLN,* XLVII (1932), 303-05.

Ferguson, J. DeLancey. "The supressed poems of Burns." *MP,* XXX (1932), 53-60.

Ferguson, J. DeLancey. "Some aspects of the Burns legend." *PQ,* XI (1932), 263-73.

Painter, Anna M. "American editions of the *Poems* of Burns before 1800." *Library,* 4th series, XII (1932), 434-56.

Snyder, Franklyn B. *The Life of Robert Burns.* New York: Macmillan, 1932. Pp. xiv+524.

Rev. in *TLS,* August 4, 1932, p. 554. See also corr., *ibid.,* August 11, p. 569, and Oct. 20, pp. 761-62.

Joseph Butler

Garin, Eugenio. "L'etica di Giuseppe Butler." *Giornale critico della filosofia italiana,* XIII (1932), 281-303.

Thomas Chatterton

Mabbot, Thomas Ollive. "Notes on Chatterton: Letter to William Smith." *N & Q,* CLXII (1932), 242-43.

Meyerstein, E. H. W. *A life of Thomas Chatterton.* London: Ingpen and Grant, 1930. Cf. *PQ,* X, 196 and XI, 188.

Rev. by Esther Parker Ellinger in *MLN,* XLVII (1932), 122-25.

Meyerstein, E. H. W. "Chatterton's spelling of *Ælla.*" *TLS,* Feb. 4, 1932, p. 76.

Chesterfield

The Letters of Philip Dormer Stanhope, Fourth Earl of Chesterfield. Edited by Bonamy Dobrée. London: Eyre and Spottiswoode; New York: The Viking press, 1932. 6 vols.

Rev. in *TLS,* March 10, 1932, p. 161; by F. W. Bain in *Spectator,* March 12, p. 374; by Henry Hazlitt in *The Nation* (N. Y.), CXXXIV (1932), 547-48; by Joseph Wood Krutch in *Books* (N. Y.), June 19, p. 1; by Keith Feiling in *Criterion,* XII (1932), 118-21.

William Congreve

de Beer, E. S. "Congreve's *Incognita:* the source of its setting, with a note on Wilson's *Belphegor.*" *RES,* VIII (1932), 74-77.

Taylor, D. Crane. *William Congreve.* Oxford: University press, 1931. Cf. *PQ,* XI, 190.

Rev. by V. de S. Pinto in *RES,* VIII (1932), 480-83; by Hazelton Spencer in *MLN,* XLVII (1932), 197-99; by Paul Meissner in *Beiblatt,* XLIII (1932), 141-43.

William Cowper

Carmichael, Montgomery. "Cowper and the Throckmortons." *Dublin review,* CXC (1932), 195-210.

Carver, P. L. "A continuation of *John Gilpin.*" *RES,* VIII (1932), 205-10.

Povey, Kenneth. "Further notes for a bibliography of Cowper's letters." *RES,* VIII (1932), 316-19.

George Crabbe

"George Crabbe." Leading article, *TLS,* Feb. 4, 1932, 65-66.

Ottley, May. "George Crabbe." *LM,* XXVI (1932), 153-62.

Selections from the poems of George Crabbe. Edited by Anthony C. Deane. London: Methuen, 1932. Pp. 284.

Rev. by P. L. Carver in *Spectator,* Oct. 15, 1932, p. 486-88.

Thomas Day

Gignilliat, George Warren. *The author of 'Sandford and Merton': a life of Thomas Day, Esq.* New York: Columbia University press, 1932. Pp. 361.

Daniel Defoe

Beeck, Paula van. *Der psychologische Gehalt in de Romanen Defoes.* (Diss.) Münster, 1931. Pp. viii+69.

"Defoe, Ward, Brown and Tutchin, 1700-1703." *N & Q,* CLXII (193), 418-23.

A collection of newspaper references.

Maxfield, Ezra Kempton. "Daniel Defoe and the Quakers." *PMLA,* XLVII (1932), 179-90.

Potter, George Reuben. "Henry Baker, F. R. S. (1698-1774)." *MP,* XXIX (1932), 301-21.

Important new information on Defoe's son-in-law.

John Dryden

Dryden. The dramatic works. Edited by Montague Summers. Volumes III-VI. London: Nonesuch press, 1932. Cf. *PQ,* XI, 192.

Rev. by Bonamy Dobrée in *Spectator,* Sept. 24, 1932, 376-77; by John Hayward in *Criterion,* XI (1932), 519-23; and cf. corr. by William S. Clark in *TLS,* May 12, 1932, p. 351.

Epilogue. Spoken to the King, March Nineteenth, 1681. (Type facsimile reprints.) Oxford: Clarendon press, 1932.

The songs of John Dryden. Edited by Cyrus Lawrence Day. Cambridge: Harvard University press, 1932. Pp. xvi+199.

de Beer, E. S. "Mr. Montague Summers and Dryden's *Essay of Dramatic Poesy.*" *RES,* VIII (1932), 453-56.

Further exposure of the methods of Mr. Summers.

Bredvold, Louis I. "Political aspects of Dryden's *Amboyna* and *The Spanish Fryar.*" University of Michigan *Studies in Language and Literature,* VIII (1932), 119-32.

Eliot, T. S. *John Dryden: the poet, the dramatist, the critic.* New York: Terence & Elsa Holliday, 1932. Pp. 68.

Hiscock, W. G. "Oxford history." *TLS,* Oct. 13, 1932, p. 734.

Dryden's epilogue spoken at Oxford March 19, 1681, was for the performance of *Tamerlane the Great,* by C. Saunders.

Jünemann, Wolfgang. *Drydens Fabeln und ihre quellen.* (*Brittanica,* no. 5.) Hamburg: Friederichsen, de Gruyter & co., 1932. Pp. 103.

Dryden's modifications of his sources are studied as illustrations of Baroque art. A suggestive, but rather too thorough-going application of the theory.

McKeithan, Daniel Morley. "The occasion of *MacFlecknoe.*" *PMLA,* XLVII (1932), 766-71.

Legouis, P. "La religion dans l'œuvre de Dryden avant 1682." *RAA,* IX (1932), 383-92, 525-36.

Ward, Charles E. "A biographical note on John Dryden." *MLR,* XXVII (1932), 206-10.

Ward, Charles E. "Was John Dryden collector of customs?" *MLN,* XLVII (1932), 246-49.

Ward argued ingeniously that the John Dryden who was collector of customs was of a different parish from that of the poet, and cast doubt on the traditional identification. The correctness of his argument is proved by the later volume of the *Calendar of Treasury Books* (1931) which records that on Nov. 2, 1692, royal letters patent were ordered "to constitute Richard Miller, gent., collector of the Customs and subsidies of cloth and petty Customs, London port, *loco* John Dryden, gent., deceased." (p. 1886.)

Whiting, G. W. "The Ellesmere MS. of *The State of Innocence.*" *TLS,* Jan. 14, 1932, p. 28.

Wolf, J. Q. "A note on Dryden's Zimri." *MLN,* XLVII (1932), 97-99.

George Farquhar

Whiting, G. W. "The date of the second edition of *The Constant Couple*." *MLN*, XLVII (1932), 147-48.

Henry Fielding

Jonathan Wild. With engravings by Denis Tegetmeier. London: Golden Cockerel press, 1932.

Glenn, Sidney Erwin. *Some French influences on Henry Fielding*. Abstract of thesis. Urbana: University of Illinois, 1932. Pp. 21.

Graham, Walter. "The date of the *Champion*." *TLS*, Feb. 4, 1932, p. 76; *N & Q*, CLXIII (1932), 150-51.

Joesten, Maria. *Die philosophie Fieldings*. (Kölner Anglistische Arbeiten, vol. XV.) Leipzig: Bernard Tauchnitz, 1932. Pp. 107.

The author begins her study with a section entitled *Der Unbekannte Fielding*, and she proposes a new interpretation of his whole work in terms of Stoicism. Some of her illustrations are very much to the point, but many are not. And her knowledge of the history of English thought in the eighteenth century is far from adequate to the task of unraveling the tangle before her.

Thomas Flatman

Fotheringham, J. K. "Thomas Flatman's horoscope." *Bodleian quarterly record*, VII (1932), 8-10.

John Gay

Whiting, George W. "To Miss Polly Peachum." *TLS*, June 16, 1932, p. 447.

An unnoticed verse commendation.

John Dunton

Howell, A. C. "John Dunton and an imitation of the *Religio Medici*." *SP*, XXIX (1932), 442-62.

Sir George Etherege

Foster, Dorothy. "Sir George Etherege." *RES*, VIII (1932), 458-59.

Edward Gibbon

Helming, Vernon Parker. "Edward Gibbon and Georges Deyverdun, collaborators in the *Memoires littéraires de la Grande Bretagne*." *PMLA*, XLVII (1932), 1028-49.

Hutton, Edward. "The conversion of Edward Gibbon." *Nineteenth Century*, CXI (1932), 362-75.

Joseph Glanvill

Prior, Moody E. "Joseph Glanvill, witchcraft, and seventeenth-century science." *MP*, XXX (1932), 167-93.

Shows that Glanvill's belief in witchcraft was not inconsistent with his interest in science. A valuable study of seventeenth-century thought.

Stimson, Dorothy. *"Ballad of Gresham Colledge." Isis*, XVIII (1932), 103-17.

A ballad, probably composed in 1663, published from manuscripts in the British Museum; Miss Stimson attributes it to Joseph Glanvill.

William Godwin

Storr, M. S. "L'amour et le marriage chez Godwin." *RAA,* X (1932), 31-45.

Thomas Gray

Brown, H. H. "Gray and Shenstone." *TLS,* Jan. 14, 1932, p. 28.

Comment by Leonard Whibley, Jan. 21, p. 44, and by Marjorie Williams, Jan. 28, p. 60.

Toynbee, Paget. "Gray on the origin and date of *Amadis de Gaul.*" *MLR,* XXVII (1932), 60-61.

Toynbee, Paget. "Horace Walpole's Memoir of the poet Gray." *MLR,* XXVII (1932), 58-60.

Thomas Hobbes

Lubiensky, Z. *Die Grundlagen des ethisch-politischen Systems von Hobbes.* Munich: Ernst Reinhardt. Pp. 302.

David Hume

The Letters of David Hume. Edited by J. Y. T. Greig. Oxford: Clarendon press, 1932. 2 vols. Pp. xxxii+552; 498.

Dickson, W. K. "David Hume and the Advocates' Library." *Juridical review,* XLIV (1932), 1-14.

Greig, J. Y. T. "Some unpublished letters to David Hume." *RLC,* XII (1932), 826-56.

Laing, Bertram Mitchell. *David Hume.* London: Ernest Benn, 1932. Pp. 288.

Laird, John. *Hume's philosophy of human nature.* London: Methuen, 1932. Pp. ix+310.

Rev. in *TLS,* April 7, 1932, p. 229; by A. Boyce Gibson in *Philosophy,* VII (1932), 357-60; by C. E. M. Joad in *Spectator,* March 19, 1932, p. 419.

Leroy, André. *La critique et la religion chez David Hume.* Paris: Félix Alcan, 1931. Pp. xvi+376.

Rev. by Mary Shaw Kuypers in *Journal of philosophy,* XXIX (1932), 243-47.

Volpe, Galvano della. *La teoria delle passioni di David Hume.* Bologna: L. Cappelli, 1931. Pp. 44.

Richard Hurd

The Correspondence of Richard Hurd and William Mason and letters of Richard Hurd to Thomas Gray. With introduction and notes by the late Ernest Harold Pearce. Edited with additional notes by Leonard Whibley. Cambridge: University press, 1932. Pp. xxxi+179.

Samuel Johnson

(See also *Hester Lynch Thrale*)

The French Journals of Mrs. Thrale and Doctor Johnson. Edited by Moses Tyson and Henry Guppy. Manchester: University press, 1932. Pp. 274.

Rev. by Bonamy Dobrée in *Spectator,* Jan. 6, 1932, p. 20-21.

Johnson and Queeney: Letters from Dr. Johnson to Queeney Thrale, from the Bowood papers. Edited with an introduction by the Marquis of Lansdowne. London: Cassell & co.; New York: Random house, 1932. Pp. xxxv+64.

Perhaps the most important of recent Johnson discoveries. The letters fall between July 29, 1771, and Sept. 2, 1784.

Some unpublished letters to and from Dr. Johnson; from the originals now in the possession of the John Rylands Library. Edited by J. D. Wright. Manchester: University press, 1932. Pp. 55.

Reprinted from the *Bulletin of the John Rylands Library,* XVI (1932), 32-76. Other Johnsoniana from the Thrale collection described in "Library notes and news" of the same *Bulletin,* pp .9-15. See also corr. by J. D. Wright in *TLS,* Jan. 21, 1932, p. 44, and by L. F. Powell, *ibid.,* June 2, 1932, p. 408.

Sir, Said Dr. Johnson. An anthology compiled by Sir Chartres Biron. London: Jonathan Cape, 1932.

Chapman, R. W. "Johnson's *Journey,* 1775." *RES,* VIII (1932), 315-16.

Distinguishes a third edition of that year.

Laithwaite, P. "Anna Seward and Dr. Johnson." *TLS,* Jan. 7, 1932, p. 12.

Powell, L. F. "Petty and Graunt." *TLS,* Oct. 20, 1932, p. 761.

Dr. Johnson's allusion to Petty explained.

Wright, Herbert. "Iolo Morganwg, Dr. Johnson and others." *RES,* VIII (1932), 129-38.

"Junius"

Monaghan, Frank. "A new document on the identity of *Junius.*" *JMH,* IV (1932), 68-71.

A secret report, in the archives of the French Foreign office, submitted in 1774 to the Comte du Muy by Grant de Blairfindy, states that a Thomas Mante, a secret agent, wrote the famous letters, and that the correspondent himself has seen Mante write the famous letter to the king. See also Helen B. Bates, "Some notes on Thomas Mante (Alias 'Junius')," *ibid.*, IV, 232-34.

John Locke

"A Locke exhibition." *TLS,* May 5, 1932, p. 336.

Books and papers from Locke's library exhibited on the occasion of the tercentenary of his birth; mainly from the library of the present Lord Lovelace.

"John Locke." Leading article, *TLS,* August 25, 1932, pp. 585-86.

Corson, James C. "John Locke." *Juridical review,* XLIV (1932), 315-28.

Matthews, W. "Locke's shorthand diaries." *TLS,* Sept. 29, 1932, p. 691.

William Mason: see *Richard Hurd*

Thomas Otway

The Works of Thomas Otway. Plays, poems and love-letters. Edited by J. C. Ghosh. 2 vols. Oxford: Clarendon press, 1932. Pp. xii+520, 542.

Rev. in *TLS,* March 17, 1932, p. 193; by Levin L. Schücking in *Beiblatt,* XLIII (1932), 166-67; by John Hayward in *Criterion,* XI (1932), 731-33.

Ham, Roswell Gray. *Otway and Lee: biography from a baroque age.* New Haven: Yale University press. Cf. *PQ,* XI, 199.

Rev. by G. W. Whiting in *MP,* XXIX (1932), 111-12; by Hazelton Spencer in *MLN,* XLVII (1932), 267-69; by Paul Meissner in *Beiblatt,* XLIII (1932), 204-07; by James R. Sutherland in *MLR,* XXVII (1932), 342-43.

Thomas Paine

Clark, H. H. "Thomas Paine's relation to Voltaire and Rousseau." *RAA,* IX (1932), 305-18, 393-405.

John Partridge

Eddy, W. A. "The wits *vs.* John Partridge, astrologer." *SP,* XXIX (1932), 29-40.

Samuel Pepys

Letters and the Second Diary of Samuel Pepys. Edited by R. G. Howarth. London: Dent, 1932. Pp. xxiv+456.

Rev. in *TLS,* Nov. 10, 1932, p. 833. Comment by F. McD. C. Turner, *ibid.,* Nov. 17, p. 859.

Borjane, Henry. "Samuel Pepys, Secrétaire de l'Amirauté britannique, et le Désarmament naval." *Revue Bleue,* LXX (1932), 53-56.

"Pepysiana." Corr. in *TLS* by R. G. Howart, April 7, 1932, p. 250; by E. S. de Beer, April 21, p. 291; by G. C. Probert, May 19, p. 368.

Matthews, W. "The text of Pepy's *Diary.*" *TLS,* August 25, 1932, p. 593.

Thomas Percy

Ancient songs chiefly on Moorish subjects. Translated from the Spanish by Thomas Percy. With a preface by David Nichol Smith. Oxford: University press, 1932. Pp. xviii+56.

Watkin-Jones, A. "While Dr. Johnson toured Scotland." *Cornhill,* LXXIII (1932), 193-98.

Thomas Percy was touring Scotland at the same time as Boswell and Johnson. His diary and letters, preserved in the British Museum, are drawn on for this article.

Willinsky, Margarete. *Bischof Percy's Bearbeitung der Volksballaden und Kunstgedichte seines Folio-Manuskriptes (Beiträge zur englischen Philologie,* XXII.) Leipzig: Tauchnitz, 1932. Pp. 227.

Ambrose Phillips

Griffith, R. H. *A variorum text of four pastorals by Ambrose Phillips.* In University of Texas *Studies in English,* no. 12, pp. 118-57. Austin: University press, 1932.

Griffith prints the texts of the 1708 and 1748 versions of four of the pastorals, with variants from the 1709 version. The 1748 version, which is reprinted in the standard collections, is much changed and expanded from the one which Addison praised to the irritation of Pope. It is therefore very desirable to have the original text available. The revisions are an interesting study. One may note, for instance, that "Namby-Pamby" Phillips discarded

and Sleep
With soft Embrace has seiz'd my weary Sheep

for

and sleep
Hath clos'd the eyelids of my weary sheep.

It would be difficult to argue that this line is not improved.

John Pomfret

Baumann, George. *Leben und Dichtungen des Rev. John Pomfret.* Erlangen diss. Pp. 88.

Alexander Pope

Audra, E. *L'influence française dans l'œuvre de Pope.* Paris: Champion, 1931. Cf. *PQ,* XI, 200.

Rev. by A. F. B. Clark in *RLC,* XII (1932), 903-17; by John Butt in *MLR,* XXVII (1932), 481-83.

Chandler, W. K. "Pope's self-plagiarism." *MP,* XXIX (1932), 98-100.

Segar, Mary. "Some notes on Pope's religion." *Dublin review,* CXC (1932), 237-53.

Contends that Pope's adherence to the Roman Catholic faith was not merely nominal, and that the *Essay on Man* is perfectly reconcilable with Roman Catholic theology, though not of course a complete statement of it.

Warren, Austin. "Henry Layng, assistant in Pope's *Odyssey.*" *RES,* VIII (1932), 77-82.

W., S. G. "Ruffhead's Life of Pope." *Bodleian quarterly record,* VII (1932), 12.

Notes on a set of proofs with corrections by Warburton.

Matthew Prior

Barrett, W. P. "Matthew Prior's *Alma.*" *MLR,* XXVII (1932), 454-58.

Points out indebtedness of Prior to Montaigne.

Anne Radcliffe

McKillop, Alan D. "Mrs. Radcliffe on the supernatural in poetry." *JEGP,* XXXI (1932), 352-59.

Allan Ramsay

Martin, Burns. *Bibliography of Allan Ramsay.* Glasgow: Jackson, Wylie, 1932. Pp. 114. (Reprinted from the *Records of the Glasgow Bibliographical Society,* Vol. X.)

Rev. in *TLS,* June 2, 1932.

Sir Joshua Reynolds

Darnall, F. M. "Sir Joshua Reynolds on the picturesque." *MLN,* XLVII (1932), 446-51.

Samuel Richardson

Gwynn, Stephen. "Samuel Richardson." *Quarterly review,* CCLIX (1932), 315-30.

Mrs. Sarah Scott

Crittenden, Walter Marion. *The life and writings of Mrs. Sarah Scott—novelist (1723-1795).* Philadelphia, 1932. (University of Pennsylvania thesis.)

Thomas Shadwell

McKeithan, D. M. "The authorship of *The Medal of John Bayes.*" University of Texas *Studies in English,* no. 12, pp. 92-97. Austin: University of Texas, 1932.

Points out parallel passages from Shadwell's other works.

William Shenstone

(See also *Thomas Gray*)

letters." *MP,* XXIX (1932), 323-34.

Fullington, James F. "Some early versions of William Shenstone's

"A group of his letters in a volume published by Thomas Hull [1778] are in reality earlier versions of letters occurring in the *Works* and in two manuscript collections in the British Museum."

Richard Brinsley Sheridan

Fijn van Draat, P. "Sheridan's *Rivals* and Ben Jonson's *Every Man in his Humour*." *Neuphilologus* (1932), 44-50.

Bob Acres "is a compound of Stephen and Bobadil, with a grain of Brainworm, Cob and Matthew thrown in."

Adam Smith

A catalogue of the library of Adam Smith. Second edition. Prepared for the Royal Economic Society by James Bonar. London: Macmillan, 1932. Pp. xxxiv+218.

Rev. in *TLS,* Nov. 17, 1932, p. 860; by Henry Higgs in *Economic journal,* XLII (1932), 625-27.

A revised and enlarged edition of a catalogue first printed in 1894.

Joseph Spence

Wright, Austin. "*The Charliad,* an unpublished mock-epic by Joseph Spence." *PMLA,* XLVII (1932), 554-58.

Tobias Smollett

Buck, Howard. "A new Smollett anecdote." *MLN,* XLVII (1932), 90-91.

Buck, Howard. "Smollett and Akenside." *JEGP,* XXXI (1932), 10-26.

Knapp, Lewis M. "A sequel to Smollett's *Humphry Clinker.*" *TLS,* Oct. 6, 1932, p. 716.

Knapp, Lewis Mansfield. "Elizabeth Smollett, daughter of Tobias Smollett." *RES,* VIII (1932), 312-15.

Knapp, Lewis Mansfield. "Smollett and Le Sage's *The Devil upon Crutches.*" *MLN,* XLVII (1932), 91-93.

Knapp, Lewis Mansfield. "Smollett's early years in London." *JEGP,* XXXI (1932), 220-27.

Knapp, Lewis Mansfield. "Smollett's works as printed by William Strahan, with an unpublished letter of Smollett to Strahan." *Library,* 4th series, XIII (1932), 282-91.

Lawrence, Alexandre. "L'influence de Lesage sur Smollett." *RLC,* XII (1932), 533-45.

Purcell, J. M. "A note on Smollett's language." *MLN,* XLVII (1932), 93-94.

Cf. also *TLS,* April 14, 1932, p. 271; and comment by Edwin Chappell, *ibid.,* April 21, p. 291 and by R. Stewart-Brown, April 28, p. 311.

Richard Steele

The Christian Hero. Edited by Rae Blanchard. Oxford: University press, 1932. Pp. xxxii+101.

Rev. in *TLS,* Oct. 13, 1932, p. 729.

Blanchard, Rae. "A prologue and epilogue for Nicholas Rowe's *Tamerlane* by Richard Steele." *PMLA,* XLVII (1932), 772-76.

Laurence Sterne

Curtis, Lewis P. "Sterne in Bond Street." *TLS,* March 24, 1932, p. 217.

Curtis, Lewis P. "The first printer of *Tristram Shandy.*" *PMLA,* XLVII (1932), 777-89.

The first edition of the first two volumes of *Tristram Shandy* were printed at York, by Ann Ward.

Jonathan Swift

(See also *John Partridge*)

Satires and personal writings. Edited with an introduction and notes by William Alfred Eddy. Oxford: University press, 1932. Pp. xxxii+499.

Babcock, R. W. "Swift's conversion to the Tory Party." University of Michigan *Studies in Language and Literature,* VIII (1932), 133-49. Ann Arbor: University of Michigan press.

Darnall, F. M. "Swift's belief in immortality." *MLN,* XLVII (1932), 448-51.

Glaser, Hans. *Jonathan Swifts Kritik an der englischen Irland-politik.* Breslau, 1932. Pp. vii+109.

Rossi, M. Manlio. "Essay on the character of Swift." Translated by J. M. Hone. *Life and letters,* VIII (1932), 342-57.

Webster, C. M. "*Hudibras* and Swift." *MLN,* XLVII (1932), 245-46.

Webster, C. M. "Notes on the Yahoos." *MLN,* XLVII (1932), 451-54.

Webster, C. M. "The Puritan's ears in *A Tale of a Tub.*" *MLN,* XLVII (1932), 96-97.

Webster, C. M. "Swift and the English and Irish theatre." *N & Q,* CLXIII (1932), 452-54.

Webster, C. M. "Swift's *Tale of a Tub* compared with earlier satires of the Puritans." *PMLA,* XLVII (1932), 171-78.

Webster, C. M. "Tom Brown and *The Tale of a Tub.*" *TLS,* Feb. 18, 1932, p. 112.

Comment by E. Knox Linton, *ibid.,* Feb. 25, p. 134.

Williams, Harold. *Dean Swift's library.* With a facsimile of the original sale catalogue and some account of two manuscript lists of his books. Cambridge: University press; New York: Macmillan, 1932. Pp. viii+94.

Rev. in *TLS,* August 4, 1932, p. 555; note by J. H. Birss in *N & Q,* CLXIII (1932), 404.

Sir William Temple

Marburg, Clara. *Sir William Temple: a seventeenth century "Libertin."* New Haven: Yale University press; London: Humphrey Milford, 1932. Pp. viii+128.

Rev. in *TLS,* May 12, 1932, p. 347; by Elbert N. S. Thompson in *PQ,* XI (1932), 318-19; by G. C. Moore Smith in *MLN,* XLVII (1932), 484-85.

Miss Marburg has attempted to define the temperament and thought of a man who had no very incisive mind; she devotes her study very largely to Temple's background, the seventeenth century traditions of the *libertin* or *honnête homme,* terms which she uses interchangeably. The word *libertin* on her title-page will arouse surprise in many readers, but she makes out a good case for her contention that Temple represents this tradition in a mild form. Her last chapter, on Temple as a critic, shows that he was much too eclectic to be described simply as a champion of the "Ancients."

Perhaps it is because the traditions of seventeenth-century thought are presented to us in this volume primarily as they were absorbed by the eclectic mind of Temple, that they appear to the reader a little blurred. But occasionally Miss Marburg adds to this blur by indiscriminate classification. She speaks, for instance, of "this mistrust of the ultimate power of the mind, a mistrust expressed, indeed, by the classical philosophers, by the *honnête homme,* by the Cambridge Platonists, as well as by the brotherhood of *libertins,*" (p. 18); but as she is referring to Pyrrhonism in ethics, it is confusing to introduce the "classical philosophers" as a group, and the Cambridge Platonists without qualification, into such a summary statement. On page 55 we are told that Temple was looking for "what Lord Herbert of Cherbury, Hobbes, the Cambridge Platonists, and many others who were under the influence of rationalism, were attempting to discover—the law of nature which underlies all differences in customs and manners." But Hobbes was certainly not looking for the same basic principle of ethics as the Cambridge Platonists; and so far as Temple was looking for the same principle as they, he was not a *libertin,* and he could hardly for the same reason be listed as a "free-thinker." Anthony Collins' list of freethinkers referred to on the same page was evidently inspired by a desire to list as many patrons as possible for the cause; but it is no model for the modern historian.

James Thomson

Havens, Ramond D. "Primitivism and the idea of progress in Thomson." *SP,* XXIX (1932), 41-52.

Krappe, Alexander Haggerty. "The origin of *Rule Britannia* once more." *Beiblatt,* XLIII (1932), 256-60.

Hester Lynch Thrale

(See also *Samuel Johnson*)

Three dialogues by Hester Lynch Thrale. From the hitherto unpublished original manuscript now in the possession of the John

Rylands Library. Edited, with an introduction, by M. Zannick. Manchester: University press, 1932. Pp. 40.

Reprinted from the Bulletin of the John Rylands Library, XVI (1932), 77-114.

Bromhead, H. W. *The heritage of St. Leonard's Parish Church, Streatham.* London: Hatchards, 1932. Pp. xii+83.

Information about the connection of the Thrales with Streatham. See *TLS,* August 11, 1932, p. 572.

Edmund Waller

de Beer, E. S. "An uncollected poem by Waller." *RES,* VIII (1932), 203-05.

Riske, Ella Theodora. "Waller in exile." *TLS,* Oct. 13, 1932, P. 734.

Roeckerath, Netty. *Der Nachruhm Herricks und Wallers.* (Kölner Anglistische Arbeiten, XIII.) Leipzig: Bernhard Tauchnitz; London: Williams and Norgate, 1931. Pp. 116.

Rev. by G. C. Moore Smith in *RES,* VIII (1932), 339-40; by P. Meissner in *Literaturblatt für germ. u. rom. Phil.,* LIII (1932), 322-24; by Edward Niles Hooker in *MLN,* XLVII (1932), 138.

Horace Walpole
(See also *Thomas Gray*)

Anecdotes told me by Lady Denbigh. Edited by W. S. Lewis. Farmington, Conn.: Privately printed, 1932. Pp. iii+10. ("Miscellaneous antiquities," No. 7.)

Gwynn, Stephen. *The life of Horace Walpole.* London: Thornton Butterworth; New York: Houghton Mifflin, 1932. Pp. 286.

Rev. in *TLS,* March 3, 1932, p. 151; by W. S. Lewis in *Yale review,* XXII (1932), 210-11. Cf. corr. in *TLS,* April 14, 1932, p. 271.

Toynbee, Paget. "Horace Walpole and Robert." *TLS,* April 14, 1932, p. 271.

William Warburton
(See also *Alexander Pope*)

Evans, A. W. *Warburton and the Warburtonians: a study in some eighteenth-century controversies.* Oxford: University press, 1932. Pp. viii+315.

Rev. in *TLS,* June 23, 1932, p. 453; by B. D. in *Criterion,* XII (1932), 163-64. The imposing figure of Warburton touches on literary history at so many points that all students of the eighteenth century will be grateful for this extensive study, based on published and unpublished materials. It is judicious and unbiased in tone, and its conclusions are no doubt in the main correct. But a checking of the account of the relations between Richardson and Warburton seems to indicate that the volume can not be absolutely relied on in minor statements of matters of fact. Thus we read (page 125) that "Warburton wrote the preface to the first edition of *Clarissa.*" The preface in question appeared in the fourth volume of the first edition, but was omitted from all later editions. Warburton, however, used it in a revised form as a note to line 146 of the

Epistle to Augustus in his edition of Pope's *Works*, 1751; Fielding's name supplanted Richardson's as representative of the new species of fiction writing in England. All this was pointed out by Ronald S. Crane in *Modern Philology*, XVI (1919), 495-99 and in *Modern Language Review*, XVII (1922), 17-23, two articles which appear to be unknown to Evans. We further read that Richardson was snubbed by Warburton and therefore "tried to revenge himself by endeavoring to persuade Thomas Edwards to undertake an edition of Pope's works which should rival Warburton's, but without success." Edwards refused to edit such a rival edition in a letter of March 20, 1752 (see *Correspondence*, ed. Barbauld, III, 43), and Richardson relates the incident of the snubbing in a letter of April 21, 1753 (*ibid.*, III, 60-62). Evans has therefore reversed the incidents without any explanation for so doing. He might have consulted with profit the discussion of the whole matter by Helen Sard Hughes, *Modern Philology*, XVII (1919), 45-50.

The *Wartons*

Martin, Burns. "Some unpublished *Wartoniana*." *SP*, XXIX (1932), 53-67.

John Wilkes

Bonno, Gabriel. "Lettres inédites de Chastellux à Wilkes." *RLC*, XII (1932), 619-23.

Bonno, Gabriel. "Lettres inédites de Suard à Wilkes." *University of California publications in modern philology*, XV (1932), 161-280.

McCracken, George. "John Wilkes, Humanist." *PQ*, XI (1932), 109-34.

Mary Wollstonecraft

James, H. R. *Mary Wollstonecraft: a sketch.* Oxford: University press, 1932. Pp. xiv+180.

Rev. in *TLS*, August 4, 1932, p. 552; by Richard Church in *Spectator*, Aug. 20, 1932, p. 236-37; by Mary M. Colum in *Nation* (N. Y.) CXXXVI (1932), 183-85.

Sir Christopher Wren

Whitaker-Wilson, C. *Sir Christopher Wren.* London: Methuen, 1932.

Rev. in *TLS*, March 17, 1932, p. 191.

The Parochial Churches of Sir Christopher Wren, 1666-1718. (The Ninth Volume of the Wren Society.) Oxford: Printed for the Wren Society at the University press, 1932. Pp. 29+70, with 43 plates.

Rev. in *TLS*, July 28, 1932, p. 542.

William Wycherley

The Country Wife. By William Wycherley. Edited with a critical introduction, notes, and appendices, by Ursula Todd-Naylor. Northampton, Mass., 1931. Cf. *PQ*, XI, 211.

Rev. by Harold N. Hillebrand in *JEGP*, XXXI (1932), 605-06.

Jones, Howard Mumford. "Wycherley, Montaigne, Tertullian, and Mr. Summers." *MLN,* XLVII (1932), 244-45.

Vincent, Howard P. "The date of Wycherley's birth." *TLS,* March 3, 1932, p. 155.

See corr. by W. G. D. Fletcher, *ibid.,* March 10, p. 172, and by H. Ince Anderton, March 17, p. 202.

Edward Young

Hughes, W. R. "Dr. Young and his curates." *Blackwood's,* CCXXXI (1932), 623-31.

V. THE CONTINENTAL BACKGROUND

Bain, M. *Les Voyageurs français en Ecosse (1770-1830) et leurs curiosités intellectuelles.* Paris: Honoré Champion. 1932.

Bonno, G. *La constitution britannique devant l'opinion française de Montesquieu à Bonaparte.* Paris: Honoré Champion, 1931. Pp. 317.

Bouchard, Marcel. *De l'humanisme à l'Encyclopédie. Essai sur l' évolution des esprits dans la bourgeoisie bourguignonne sous les règnes de Louis XIV et de Louis XV.* Paris: Hachette, 1929. Pp. xiii+178.

Rev. by Daniel Mornet in *RHL,* XXXIX (1932), 303-05 (suggestive notes on method).

Bouchard, Marcel. "Un précurseur de la Bruyère: les 'Refléxions sur l'éloquence' de P. Rapin et le 'Chapitre de la chaire'." *RHL,* XXXVIII (1931), 355-66.

Bray, René. "La dissertation sur 'Joconde': est-elle de Boileau?" *RHL,* XXXVIII (1931), 337-54, 497-517.

Bredvold, Louis I. "A note on Lahontan and the *Encyclopédie.*" *MLN,* XLVII (1932), 508-09.

Brunet, Pierre. *L'introduction des théories de Newton en France au XVIIIe siècle: avant 1738.* Paris: Blanchard, 1931. Pp. vii +355.

Rev. by Pierre Wolff in *RHP,* V (1931), 426-27; by T. E. Jessop in *Mind,* XLI (1932), 259-60.

Cassirer, Ernst. "Das Problem Jean Jacques Rousseau." *Archiv für Geschichte der Philosophie,* XLI (1932), 177-213, 479-513.

Chateaubriand. *Les Natchez;* publiés avec une introduction et des notes par Gilbert Chinard. Paris: E. Droz, 1932. Pp. 557.

Clark, Ruth. *Strangers and sojourners at Port Royal: being an account of the connections between the British Isles and the Jan-*

senists of France and Holland. Cambridge: University press, 1932. Pp. xix+360.

Croce, Benedetto. *Storia della età barocca in Italia.* Laterza: Bari, 1929. Pp. xii+508.

Rev. by Aubrey F. G. Bell in *Litteris*, VII (1930), 50-58; by Friedrich Schürr in *Literaturblatt für germ. u. rom. Phil.*, LIII (1932), 342-49.

Devalle, A. *La critica letteraria nel 700. G. Baretti nei suoi rapporti con Voltaire, Johnson e Parini.* Milan: Hoepli.

A French draft constitution of 1792 modelled on James Harrington's Oceana: Theodore Lesueur, Idées sur l'espèce de gouvernement populaire qui pourroit convenir à un pays de l'étendue et de la population présumée de la France. Edited with an introduction on Harrington's influence in France, and notes by S. B. Liljegren. Lund: C. W. K. Gleerup; London: Oxford University press, 1932. Pp. vi+180.

Rev. by Louis Gottschalk in *MP,* XXX (1932), 232-34; by Alfred Stern in *Beiblatt,* XLIII (1932), 167-68.

Gibson, A. Boyce. *The philosophy of Descartes.* London: Methuen, 1932. Pp. xii+382.

Rev. in *TLS,* April 28, 1932, p. 304; by C. E. M. Joad in *Spectator,* March 19, 1932, p. 419; by B. M. Laing in *Philosophy,* VII (1932), 482-84.

Hatfield, Theodore M. "Some German Picaras of the eighteenth century." *JEGP,* XXXI (1932),509-29.

Havens, George R. "Voltaire's marginal comments on Rousseau." *South Atlantic quarterly,* XXXI (1932), 408-16.

Hazard, Paul. "La fin du dix-septième siècle." *Revue des Deux Mondes,* 8 Période, X (1932), 778-96; XI (1932), 97-112, 407-24.

Hazard, Paul. "Les Rationaux (1670-1700)." *RLC,* XII (1932), 677-711.

Hill, Charles J. "The first English translation of *Werther.*" *MLN,* XLVII (1932), 8-12.

New evidence that Richard Graves was not the translator.

Hunter, Alfred C. "Les opinions du Baron Grimm sur le roman Anglais." *RLC,* XII (1932), 390-400.

Jantzen, H. "Zeugnisse für das Eindringen der englischen Literatur des 18. Jahrhunderts in Deutschland." *ES,* LXVI (1931), 249-53.

Josephson, Matthew. *Jean-Jacques Rousseau.* London: Gollanz; New York: Harcourt Brace, 1932.

Rev. in *TLS,* April 14, 1932, p. 267; by Albert Schinz in *Yale review,* XXI (1932), 623-24.

Kies, Paul Philemon. "Lessing's relation to early English sentimental comedy." *PMLA,* XLVII (1932), 807-26.

Lanson, G. *Le Marquis de Vauvenargues.* Paris: Hachette, [1930]. Pp. x+222.

Las Vergnas, Raymond. *Le chevalier Rutlidge "gentilhomme anglais."* Paris: Honoré Champion, 1932. Pp. 238.

Lynch, Kathleen M. *"Pamela Nubile, L'Écossaise,* and *The English Merchant."* *MLN,* XLVII (1932), 94-96.

Nolte, Fred O. "Lessing and the bourgeois drama." *JEGP,* XXXI (1932), 66-83.

Philips, Edith. "Le Quaker vu par Voltaire." *RHL,* XXXIX (1932), 162-77.

Phillips, Edith. *The good Quaker in French legend.* Philadelphia: University of Pennsylvania press, 1932.

Pinot, Virgile. *La Chine et la formation de l'esprit philosophique en France (1640-1740).* Paris: Librairie orientaliste Paul Geuthner, 1932. Pp. 480.

Price, Lawrence Marsden. *The reception of English literature in Germany.* Berkeley: University of California press, 1932. Pp. vii+596.

Robertson, J. G. "Sophie von La Roche's visit to England in 1786." *MLR,* XXVII (1932), 196-203.

Roscoe, E. S. "An eighteenth-century Abbé in England: Morellet and Shelburne." *Contemporary review,* CXLII (1932), 357-64.

Thomas, Jean. *L'humanisme de Diderot.* Paris: "Les belles lettres," 1932. ("Etudes françaises," No. 29.)

Trahard, Pierre. *Les maîtres de la sensibilité française au XVIIIe siècle (1715-1789).* Vol. II. Paris: Boivin, 1932. Pp. 336.

Rev. by George R. Havens in *MLN,* XLVII (1932), 534-36.

Walzel, Oskar. *Das Prometheussymbol von Shaftesbury zu Goethe.* [Second, revised edition.] Munich: Max Hueber, 1932. Pp. 110.

The influence of Shaftesbury on German theories of poetical creation, through the Swiss school and Lessing.

West, Constance B. "La théorie de la traduction au XVIIIe siècle par rapport surtout aux traductions françaises d'ouvrages anglais." *RLC,* XII (1932), 330-55.

Wood, Kathryn L. "The French theatre in the XVIIIth century according to some contemporary English travellers." *RLC,* XII (1932), 601-18.

1934

ENGLISH LITERATURE, 1660-1800: A CURRENT BIBLIOGRAPHY

By Louis I. Bredvold
University of Michigan

This bibliography attempts to list the more significant books, articles, and reviews published during the year 1933, together with some bearing the date 1932 that were inadvertently omitted from the bibliography for that year (*PQ*, XII, 97-129). I am indebted to Professor Ronald S. Crane for contributing the critical notes signed with his initials.

LIST OF ABBREVIATIONS

AHR=American historical review.
Archiv=Archiv für das Studium der neueren Sprachen und Literaturen.
Beiblatt=Beiblatt zur Anglia.
DVLG=Deutsche Vierteljahrschrift für Literaturwissenschaft u. Geistesgeschichte.
EHR=English historical review.
ES=Englische Studien.
GRM=Germanisch-romanische Monatschrift.
JEGP=Journal of English and Germanic Philology.
JMH=Journal of modern history.
LM=London mercury.
MLN=Modern language notes.
MLR=Modern language review.
MP=Modern philology.
N & Q=Notes and queries.
PMLA=Publications of the Modern Language Association of America.
PQ=Philological quarterly.
RAA=Revue anglo-américaine.
RC=Revue critique.
RCC=Revue des cours et conférences.
RELV=Revue de l'enseignement des langues vivantes.
RES=Review of English studies.
RH=Revue historique.
RHL=Revue d'histoire littéraire de la France.
RHP=Revue d'histoire de la philosophie.
RLC=Revue de littérature comparée.
RSH=Revue de synthèse historique.
SP=Studies in philology.
SRL=Saturday review of literature.
TLS=Times literary supplement (London).

I. BIBLIOGRAPHIES AND BIBLIOGRAPHICAL STUDIES

Annual bulletin of historical literature. No. xxii., dealing with publications of the year 1932. London: G. Bell, for the Historical Association, 1933. Pp. 124.

See especially pp. 54-60.

Annual bibliography of English language and literature. Volume XIII, 1932. Edited for the Modern Humanities Research Association, by Mary S. Serjeantson, assisted by Leslie N. Broughton. Cambridge: Bowes & Bowes, 1933. Pp. 273.

Banks, Theodore H. "Sir John Denham." *TLS,* Feb. 9, 1933, p. 92.

Barnes, G. R. "A Baskerville broadside." *TLS,* Oct. 26, 1933, p. 732.

Barr, Mary-Margaret. "Bibliographical data on Voltaire from 1926 to 1930." *MLN,* XLVIII (1933), 292-307.

Baugh, Albert C. "Annual bibliography for 1932: English language and literature." *PMLA,* XLVII (1932).

See especially pp. 1232-44.

Bernbaum, Ernest. "Recent works on prose fiction before 1800." *MLN,* XLVIII (1933), 370-78.

Block, Andrew. *A short history of the principal London antiquarian booksellers and book-auctioneers.* London: Denis Archer, 1933. Pp. 67.

Reprint of appendix to his *Book Collector's Vade Mecum,* 1932.

Bredvold, Louis I. "English literature, 1660-1800: a current bibliography." *PQ,* XII (1933), 97-129.

The Britwell handlist, or a short-title catalogue of the principal volumes from the time of Caxton to the year 1800, formerly in the library of Britwell Court, Buckinghamshire. London: Bernard Quaritch, 1933. Vol. 1, pp. xiv+554; Vol. II, pp. 555-1067.

Rev. in *TLS,* Nov. 2, 1933, p. 756.

A catalogue of XVIIIth century verse. Part IV, "Anonymous: *Callistia—Yarico;* supplementary alphabet—authors: Addison-Carey." Part V, "Supplementary alphabet—authors: Carlisle-Young; Oratorios; Miscellanies." London: P. J. & A. E. Dobell. [1933.]

Catalogues 128 and 133. Notice in *TLS,* Jan. 25, 1934, p. 64.

Chapman, R. W. "Dodsley's *Collection of poems by several hands." Proceedings and papers of the Oxford Bibliographical Society,* Vol. III, Part III (1933), 269-316.

Chapman, R. W. "Eighteenth-century booksellers." *Book-Collector's quarterly,* no. ix (1933), 25-36.

Notes supplementary to Plomer's *Dictionary,* listed below.

Clapp, Sarah L. C. "The subscription enterprises of John Ogilby and Richard Blome." *MP,* XXX (1933), 365-79.

Collins, Ralph L. "An early edition of B. M. Carew." *MLN,* XLVIII (1933), 249-51.

Fulton, J. F. "Addenda to a bibliography of the Honourable Robert Boyle." *Proceedings and papers of the Oxford Bibliographical Society,* Vol. III, Part III (1933), 339-65.

Gibson, S., and Hindle, C. J. "Philip Bliss (1787-1857)." *Proceedings and papers of the Oxford Bibliographical Society,* Vol. III, Part III (1932).

Hammond, William A. *A bibliography of aesthetics and of the philosophy of the fine arts from 1900 to 1932.* New York: Longmans Green, 1933. Pp. viii+183.

K[eogh], A[ndrew]. "Bishop Berkeley's gift of books in 1733." *Yale university library gazette,* VIII (1933), 1-41.

Macdonald, Duncan B. "A bibliographical and literary study of the first appearance of the *Arabian Nights* in Europe." *Library quarterly,* II (1932), 387-420.

Valuable article by an eminent scholar.

Matthews, W. G. *The works of Richard Baxter: an annotated list.* Farmcote, Oxted, Surrey: Privately printed, 1933. Pp. 52.

Mornet, Daniel. "Bibliographie d'un certain nombre d'ouvrages philosophiques du XVIIIe siècle et particulièrement de D'Holbach [jusqu'en 1789]." *RHL,* XL (1933), 259-81.

Plomer, H. R., Bushnell, G. H., and Dix, E. R. McC. *A dictionary of the printers and booksellers who were at work in England, Scotland and Ireland from 1726 to 1775.* Oxford: At the University press for the Bibliographical Society, 1932.

Rev. by C. J. H[indle], in *Bodleian quarterly record,* VII (1933), 188-89.

Roberts, Donald A. "A speech by Robert South." *TLS,* Nov. 2, 1933, p. 751.

Roberts, W. "Spurius 'English' novels." *TLS,* Jan. 26, 1933, p. 59.

Smith, Alpheus Waldo. "Collections and notes of prose fiction in England, 1660-1714." *Harvard University summaries of theses* (1932), 281-84.

Templeman, William D. "Contributions to the bibliography of eighteenth-century aesthetics." *MP,* XXX (1933), 309-16.

Further contributions supplementary to J. W. Draper's bibliography published in 1931.

"Thirty-fourth critical bibliography of the history and philosophy of science and of the history of civilization (to March 1932)." *Isis,* XVIII (1933), 440-612.

See especially pp. 460-70.

Weber, H. H. "On a file of *Mercurius Politicus* in the Harvard College library." *N & Q,* CLXIV (1933), 364-66.

Whiting, George W. "The authorship of the Ludlow pamphlets." *N & Q,* CLXV (1933), 426-27.

Wood, Frederick T. "Henry Carey and an XVIII. century satire on matrimony." *N & Q,* CLXV (1933), 363-68.

The Year's work in English studies. Volume XII, 1931. Edited for the English Association by Frederick S. Boas and Mary S. Serjeantson. Oxford: University press, 1933. Pp. 342.

II. THE SOCIAL AND POLITICAL ENVIRONMENT.

Abraham, James Johnston. *Lettsom: his life, times, friends and descendants.* London: Heinemann, 1933. Pp. xx+498.

Rev. in leading article, *TLS,* Oct. 26, 1933, pp. 717-18.

Lettsom was a Quaker physician, the "central figure" in the medical history of the late eighteenth century.

Allen, Robert J. *The clubs of Augustan London.* (Harvard Studies in English, VII.) Cambridge, Mass.: Harvard University press, 1933. Pp. 305.

de Beer, E. S. "Members of the Court party in the House of Commons, 1670-1678." *Bulletin of the Institute of Historical Research,* XI (1933), 1-23.

Brayshaw, A. N. *The personality of George Fox.* London: Allenson, 1933. Pp. xx+187.

Brown, Harcourt. "Un cosmopolite du Grand Siècle: Henri Justel." *Bulletin de la Société de l'histoire du Protestantisme français,* LXXXII (1933), 187-201.

Justel was a French Huguenot, librarian to Louis XIV, who made his escape to England before the Revocation of the Edict of Nantes, and who became keeper of the manuscripts in the Royal Library under Charles II and Royal librarian under William III. In this article Brown adds considerable information to the article by Dally in the same publication in 1930; but he has neglected some obvious sources of information, such as the *Calendar of Treasury Papers;* he has nothing to say about the question, as yet unanswered, whether Justel was continued in his post at the Royal library under James II; and he does not know anything about the curious fact that when Justel died his whole salary as librarian to William III was in arrears—an interesting side-light on the administration of the government under the monarch who "neither loved literature nor rewarded it."

Calendar of State Papers, Domestic series, of the reign of William III., 1 January to December 31, 1698, preserved in the Record Office. Edited by Edward Bateson. London: H. M. Stationery office, 1933. Pp. xxx+602.

Calendar of Treasury Books. Edited by William A. Shaw. London: H. M. Stationery office, 1933. Vol. XI, April, 1696, to March, 1696/7, pp. 565. Vol. XII, April to September, 1697, pp. 458. Vol. XIII, October, 1697, to August, 1698, pp. 600. Vol. XV, August, 1699, to September, 1700, pp. 600.

Campbell, Sybil. "The economic and social effect of the usury laws in the eighteenth century." *Transactions of the Royal Historical Society,* Fourth series, XVI (1933), 197-210.

Churchill, Winston S. *Marlborough, his life and times.* Vol. I. London: Harrap, 1933. Pp. 612.

Rev. in *TLS,* Oct. 12, 1933, p. 679, and corr. by G. M. Trevelyan, M. V. Hay, and Henry Ince Anderton, Oct. 19, p. 711; rev. by G. R. Stirling Taylor in *Fortnightly review,* Nov., 1933, pp. 621-22; by Clennell Wilkinson in *LM,* XXIX (1933), 45-49; by Arthur Lyon Cross in *SRL,* X (1933), 319-23; by Bonamy Dobrée in *Spectator,* Oct. 6, 1933, p. 448.

Dawson, Warren R. "The London coffee-houses and the beginnings of Lloyd's." *Essays by divers hands, being the transactions of the Royal Society of Literature of the United Kingdom,* XI (1932), 69-111.

Eardley-Simpson, L. *Derby and the Forty-five.* With an introduction by John Buchan. London: Philip Allan, 1933. Pp. xvi+303.

Rev. in *TLS,* Nov. 16, 1933, p. 788.

Einstein, Louis. *Divided loyalties: Americans in England during the War of Independence.* London: Cobden Sanderson, 1933. Pp. xvi+469.

Goodman, Florence Remington. *The Pretenders from the pulpit.* Sermons, &c., from tracts scarce and curious in the Winchester Chapter library illumined by the tale of the last Stewarts. Cambridge: Heffer, 1933. Pp. xi+140.

Notice in *TLS,* August 24, 1933, p. 563.

Gore, Francis C. "A seventeenth-century barrister." *Quarterly review,* CCLX (1933), 94-108.

On Roger North.

Handasyde, Elizabeth. *Granville the Polite: the life of George Granville Lord Lansdowne.* Oxford: University press, 1933 Pp. 287.

Rev. in *TLS,* March 30, 1933, p. 221.

Huizinga, J. *Holländische Kultur des Siebzehnten Jahrhunderts.* Jena: Eugen Diederichs Verlag, 1933.

Johnson's England. An account of the life and manners of his age. Edited by A. S. Turberville. Oxford: Clarendon press, 1933. 2 vols. Pp. xxiii+405; ix+404.

Rev. in *TLS,* Dec. 28, 1933, pp. 913-14.

MacMunn, Lieut. General Sir George. "The romance and tragedy of Sussex smuggling." *Cornhill,* Oct., 1933, pp. 465-75.

Michael, Wolfgang. "Who is John Bull?" *Contemporary review,* CXLIV (1933), 314-19.

Michael maintains that John Bull in Arbuthnot's satire is Bolingbroke. This article is a popular presentation of the arguments first advanced by Michael long ago in *Historische Zeitschrift,* C (1907-08), 237-62.

Levy, Max. *Der Sabbath in England. Wesen und Entwicklung des englischen Sonntags.* (Kölner Anglistische Arbeiten, XVIII.) Leipzig: Tauchnitz, 1933. Pp. 297.

Memoirs of the life and gallant exploits of the old Highlander, Serjeant Donald Macleod. With introduction and notes by J. G. Fyfe. London: Blackie, 1933. Pp. viii+102.

Rev. in *TLS,* August 24, 1933, p. 555.

The *Memoirs* are reprinted from the original edition of 1791. Macleod served as a soldier under five monarchs.

Munroe, David. "Whigs—old and new." *Dalhousie review,* XIII (1933), 349-58.

Petrie, Sir Charles. *The Stuart Pretenders: a history of the Jacobite movement, 1688-1807.* London: Eyre Spottiswoode; Boston: Houghton Mifflin, 1933. Pp. vi+313.

Rev. by Harold B. Newman in *AHR,* XXXIX (1933), 164-65.

Petrie, Sir Charles. "James the Second: a revaluation." *Nineteenth century,* CXIV (1933), 475-84.

Price, S. J. "Dissenting academies, 1662-1820." *Baptist quarterly,* VI (1933).

The Register of the Privy Council of Scotland. Edited and abridged by Henry Paton. With an introduction by Robert Kerr Hannay. Third series, Vol. XIII, 1686-89. Edinburgh: H. M. General Register House, 1933. Pp. lxxvi+735.

Robertson, H. M. *Aspects of the rise of economic individualism: a criticism of Max Weber and his school.* Cambridge: University press, 1933. Pp. 223.

Rev. in *TLS,* Feb. 8, 1934, p. 82.

A valuable criticism of the celebrated and influential theory of Weber that the spirit of capitalism arose as part of the ethics of Protestantism.

Sophie in London, 1786. Being the diary of Sophie V. La Roche, translated from the German by Clare Williams, with a foreword by G. M. Trevelyan. London: Jonathan Cape, 1933. Pp. 307.

Rev. in *TLS,* July 20, 1933, p. 491; by Clennell Wilkinson in *LM,* XXVIII (1933), 475-77; by Lyn Ll. Irvine in *Spectator,* August 11, 1933, p. 196.

A Frenchman in England, 1784. Being the *Mélanges sur l'Angleterre* of François de la Rochefoucauld. Edited by J. Marchand and translated by S. C. Roberts. Cambridge: University press, 1933. Pp. xxviii+256.

Rev. in *TLS,* Feb. 23, 1933, p. 121.

The memoirs of Sir Robert Sibbald (1641-1722). Edited with an introduction and a refutation of the charge against Sir Robert Sibbald of forging Ben Jonson's *Conversations.* By Francis Paget Hett. Oxford: University press, 1932. Pp. vi+107.

Rev. by A. W. P[ollard], in *Library,* 4th series, XIII (1933), 455-56.

Shafer, Robert. "Hervey's memoirs." *American review,* II (1933), 199-230.

Sigerist, Henry E. *Great doctors: a biographical history of medicine.* Translated by Eden and Cedar Paul. London: Allen and Unwin; New York: Norton, 1933. Pp. 436.

Rev. in *TLS,* Oct. 5, 1933, p. 663.
This interesting and authoritative volume contains chapters on eminent English physicians of the seventeenth and eighteenth centuries.

Sitwell, Edith. *The English eccentrics.* London: Faber and Faber, 1933. Pp. 332.

Rev. in *TLS,* May 18, 1933, p. 343.

Stirk, S. D. *Die Aristokratie und die industrielle Entwicklung in England vom 16. bis zum 18. Jahrhundert.* (Sprache und Kultur der Germanisch-Romanischen Völker. A. Anglistische Reihe, XV.) Breslau: Priebatsch, 1933. Pp. 107.

Sutherland, Lucy Stuart. *A London merchant, 1695-1774.* Oxford: University press, 1933. Pp. viii+164.

Rev. in *TLS,* May 4, 1933, p. 306.
The life and activities of William Braund, merchant, ship-owner and shipping insurer.

Turner, Edward Raymond. *The cabinet council of England in the seventeenth and eighteenth centuries, 1622-1784.* Edited by Gaudence Megaro, Ph.D. With an introduction by E. R. Adair, M.A. Volume two. Baltimore: The Johns Hopkins press, 1932. Pp. xix+480.

Rev. in *TLS,* Feb. 23, 1933, p. 118; by Godfrey Davies in *JMH,* V (1933), 523-24; by Robert L. Schuyler in *Political science quarterly,* XLVIII (1933), 107-12.

Vulliamy, C. E. *William Penn.* London: Geoffrey Bles, 1933. Pp. xii+303.

Rev. in *TLS,* Oct. 19, 1933, p. 703.

Walker, J. "Secret service under Charles II and James II." *Transactions of the Royal Historical Society,* Fourth series, XV (1932), 211-42.

Waters, S. H. *Wakefield in the seventeenth century.* Wakefield: Sanderson and Clayton, 1933.

Rev. in *TLS,* Sept. 28, 1933, p. 643.
The reviewer states that this book "illustrates from the history of a single town of moderate importance the transition from the feudal to the modern system of local government and of local administration of justice."

Woodforde papers and diaries. Edited with an introduction by Dorothy Heighes Woodforde. London: Peter Davies, 1933. Pp. xvi+259.

Rev. in *TLS,* Jan. 12, 1933, p. 21.

Zamick, M. "Edmund Castell." *TLS,* Nov. 2, 1933, p. 751.

On a short hand note-book belonging to Dr. Edmund Castell (1608-1685), the Orientalist, in the Cambridge University library. The book includes copies of letters to persons of eminence.

III. CURRENTS OF IDEAS AND LITERARY FORMS.

Allen, B. Sprague. "The dates of *sentimental* and its derivatives." *PMLA,* XLVIII (1933), 303-7.

Askew, H. "Private theatricals in the eighteenth century." *N. & Q,* CLXIV (1933), 430.

Corr. by M. H. Dodds, H. Southam, and P. McPharlin, *ibid.,* CLXV (1933), 15; and by C. Brooking, p. 32.

Baker, C. H. Collins. *British painting.* London: Medici Society, 1933. Pp. xxxvi+319 and 140 Plates.

Rev. in *TLS,* Jan. 4, 1934, p. 9, and in leading article, Jan. 11, 1934, pp. 17-18.

Becker, Carl L. *The heavenly city of the eighteenth century philosophers.* New Haven: Yale University press, 1932. Cf. *PQ,* XII, 104.

Rev. by Marjorie S. Harris in *Journal of Philosophy,* XXX (1933), 190-93; by Adrian Coates in *Philosophy,* VIII (1933), 495-96; by Ira O. Wade in *JMH,* V (1933), 233-35; by J. Salwyn Schapiro in *Nation,* CXXXVI (1933), 23.
The unifying theme of the four lectures contained in this skillfully written and witty little book is that in the transition from the "world pattern" of the thirteenth century to that of the twentieth, the eighteenth-century *philosophes,* in spite of their revolt against revealed religion, are in reality much closer in general outlook to Dante and Thomas Aquinas than they are to Einstein and H. G. Wells. If the more advanced among them by "following reason" were led to the verge of atheism, it is possible to say of the majority that they "demolished the Heavenly City of St. Augustine only to rebuild it with more up-to-date materials." "They had put off the fear of God, but maintained a respectful attitude

toward the Deity. They ridiculed the idea that the universe had been created in six days, but still believed it to be a beautifully articulated machine designed by the Supreme Being according to a rational plan as an abiding place for mankind. . . . They renounced the authority of church and Bible, but exhibited a naive faith in the authority of nature and reason. . . . They denied that miracles ever happened, but believed in the perfectibility of the human race" (pp. 30-31).

From Becker's thesis as thus stated it is not likely that any one will seriously dissent; the difficulty is with his treatment of the details. And here he is handicapped to begin with by an inadequate command of the general intellectual tradition which the eighteenth century inherited from antiquity and the Middle Ages. Otherwise he would scarcely have allowed himself to imply, as he appears to do in one place (pp. 55-57), that the *a posteriori* argument for the existence of God from the evidences of design in nature—Aquinas' "quinta via"—was a novelty in the Enlightenment, "the result, as everyone knows, of the scientific discoveries of the seventeenth century." Nor would he have said of the *Summa theologica* (p. 67) that St. Thomas "had written twenty volumes . . . to say that it was really right that things should be wrong, God only knows why"! Nor would it have occurred to him to comment on Rousseau's certainly not un-Aristotelian insistence on the necessity of distinguishing between "the variety in human nature and that which is essential to it" by saying (p. 87): "Thus, the innate ideas which Locke had so politely dismissed by way of the hall door had to be surreptitiously brought back again through the kitchen window: the soul that Cartesian logic had eliminated from the individual had to be discovered in humanity" (what Rousseau's statement has to do with "innate ideas" I do not see; as to Descartes' alleged elimination of the soul, cf., *inter alia*, the *Discours de la méthode*, ed. Gilson, pp. 33, 59-60, 165-67, 307-12, 430-38).

Unfortunately he is equally reckless in dealing with some of the writers whom his special purpose in his lectures should have induced him to read with more than ordinary care. Galileo and Locke are instances in point. It is difficult to understand how one familiar with the *Dialogues concerning two new sciences* could have written of Galileo's theory and practice of "the scientific method" in the crudely Baconian terms that Becker uses on pages 20-21. And it is no less hard to conceive how any one with the text of the *Essay concerning human understanding* before him could have asserted, as Becker does on pages 64-65, that what Locks aimed at in his attack on innate ideas was no doubt "the Christian doctrine of total depravity, a black, spreading cloud which for centuries had depressed the human spirit"; or how he could have imputed to that philosopher without qualification the belief (see pp. 64-66) that man's mind owes "nothing to inheritance" but "everything to environment, to the sensations that flowed in upon it from the outer world," so that "all that man does and thinks, all that he has ever done or thought, must be . . . in accord with the laws of nature and of nature's God" (on the other hand, see *Essay,* I, iii, 3, 13; II, i, 3-5; and the correspondence with the Bishop of Worcester).

This occasional distortion of the meaning of individual writers is less distressing, however, than the obscurity and confusion in which Becker frequently involves his exposition when he is characterizing movements of thought. These traits are especially evident in his second and third lectures (on "The laws of nature and of nature's God" and "The new history: philosophy teaching by example," respectively), and they are attributable, in great part, to a failure to recognize how dangerously multivocal were many of the crucial terms in which the "philosophers" were accustomed to express their ideas. To take over into one's own writing such systematically ambiguous words as "reason," or "nature" ("natural law," "law of nature," "harmony with nature"), or "goodness" ("nature is good"), without first having explored analytically the whole range of their possible and actual connotations, is to court inevitable disaster when one attempts to deal with conflicts or transitions of thought in which their meanings are involved. It is not apparent that Becker has seen the necessity of any such preliminary discrimination of terms, and the result is that the pages in which he treats of the appeal to nature (pp. 51-69, 86), of the attempts to solve the problem of evil (pp. 66-69), and of what he calls the "strategic retreat from the advanced position occupied by abstract reason" (pp. 77-88, 108) must certainly appear at times, to readers familiar with any considerable number of the relevant texts, little short of unintelligible.

There are, fortunately, many passages in the book to which none of these strictures apply. The description of the general temper of the "philosophers" (pp. 33-46), the characterization of the principal eighteenth-century historians (pp. 88-118), much at least of the final chapter on the idea of progress—these can be read with general approval for their content and with a satisfaction in Becker's prose style that is unalloyed by considerations of exegesis or terminology.—R. S. C.

Black, F. G. "The technique of letter fiction from 1740 to 1800." *Harvard studies and notes in philology and literature,* XV (1933), 291-312.

Blake, Ralph M. "Sir Isaac Newton's theory of scientific method." *Philosophical review,* XLII (1933), 453-86.

Of value to students interested in the *scepsis scientifica* of the seventeenth century and later. Blake thinks that the only other man of the period who frankly abandoned "the possibility for natural science of any absolute certitude and finality" was Christian Huygens (p. 454). But Newton was not so isolated in his thought as this statement implies, and it is somewhat strange that Blake should overlook such men as Glanvill, Boyle, and others of the Royal Society.

Bond, Richmond P. *English burlesque poetry, 1700-1750.* Cambridge: Harvard University press, 1932. Cf. *PQ,* XII, 104.

Rev. in *TLS,* Feb. 9, 1933, p. 89; by George Kitchin in *MLR,* XXVIII (1933), 527-28; by B. V. Crawford in *PQ,* XII (1933), 316-17.

Boswell, Eleanore. *The Restoration court stage.* Cambridge: Harvard University press, 1932. Cf. *PQ,* XII, 104.

Rev. by Harold N. Hillebrand in *JEGP,* XXXII (1933), 241-43; by Allardyce Nicoll in *MLN,* XLVIII (1933), 193-95; by W. J. Lawrence in *MLR,* XXVIII (133), 101-04.

Boulton, Sir Harold. *Prince Charlie in song.* London: Geoffrey Bles, 1933.

A collection of Jacobite songs.

Brinkley, Roberta Florence. *Arthurian legend in the seventeenth century.* Baltimore: The Johns Hopkins press, 1932. Cf. *PQ,* XII, 104.

Rev. by J. J. Parry in *MLN,* XLVIII (1933), 267-68; by A. G. van Kranendonk in *English studies,* XV (1933), 69-71.

Budd, F. E. "Four unrecorded plays." *TLS,* June 22, 1933, p. 428.

Cassirer, Ernst. *Die Platonische Renaissance in England und die Schule von Cambridge.* Leipzig: B. G. Teubner, 1932. Cf. *PQ,* XII, 104.

Rev. by P. Meissner in *ES,* LXVII (1933), 438-41.

Cassirer, Ernst. "Shaftesbury und die Renaissance des Platonismus in England." *Vorträge, Bibliothek Warburg, 1930-1931,* pp. 136-55. Leipzig: B. G. Teubner, 1932.

Crean, P. J. "Footlights." *N & Q,* CLXIV (1933), 61-62.

Footlights were introduced into theatres in 1765-66.

Cundall, H. M. "Drawings at Windsor Castle." *Connoisseur,* XCI (1933), 353-60; XCII (1933), 3-12, 75-84, 145-50.

Dobrée, Bonamy. *As their friends saw them: biographical conversations.* London: Jonathan Cape, 1933. Pp. 154.

Draper, J. W. "The rise of English neo-classicism." *RAA,* X (1933), 399-409.

Edmunds, J. M. "An example of early sentimentalism." *MLN,* XLVIII (1933), 94-97.

Sentimental touches in *The Spanish Wives* (1696), by Mary Griffith Pix.

Ellehauge, Martin. *English Restoration drama. Its relation to past English and past and contemporary French drama; from Jonson* via *Molière to Congreve.* Copenhagen: Levin og Munksgaard; London: Williams and Norgate, 1933. Pp. 322.

Rev. in *TLS,* June 22, 429.

Emsley, Bert. "James Buchanan and the eighteenth century regulation of English usage." *PMLA,* XLVIII (1933), 1154-66.

Engel, C. E. "Echo de la Révocation dans les Théâtres anglais." *Bulletin de la Société de l'histoire du Protestantisme français,* LXXXI (1932), 278-85.

Gregory, Joshua C. "Cudworth and Descartes." *Philosophy,* VIII (1933), 454-67.

Hamm, Victor Michael. "The imagination in English neo-classical thought and literature (c. 1650-1780)." *Harvard University summaries of theses, 1932,* pp. 251-54.

Harder, J. H. *Observations on some tendencies of sentiment and ethics in minor poetry and essay in the eighteenth century until the execution of Dr. W. Dodd in 1777.* Amsterdam: Drukkerij Portielje, 1933. Pp. 320.

Harris, Robert Brice. "The beast in English satire from Spenser to John Gay." *Harvard University summaries of theses, 1932,* pp. 254-57.

Harrison, Charles Trawick. "The ancient atomists and English humanism of the seventeenth century." *Harvard University summaries of theses, 1932,* pp. 257-59.

Harrison, Charles T. "Bacon, Hobbes, Boyle, and the ancient atomists." *Harvard studies and notes in philology and literature*, XV (1933), 191-218.

In this carefully prepared article Harrison arrives at conclusions somewhat different from those of the standard histories of philosophy regarding the relations of Bacon, Hobbes, and Boyle to ancient atomic thought. In spite of Bacon's repudiation of atomism in *Novum Organum* (II, viii), Harrison maintains that in other passages he accepts it, and that Bacon's whole conception of matter suggests the influence of Lucretius. As for Hobbes, "a cursory examination will show that those who denounced Hobbes's great triology as Epicurean were hardly less right in their interpretation of significance than wrong in their scholarship" (p. 200). "Hobbes is completely un-Epicurean in his conception of matter" (p. 202). On the other hand, in a "limited sense" it is "proper to refer to Boyle as an Epicurean: the whole basis of his description of matter, its properties, and its functions is Epicurean atomism" (p. 214).

Although these challenging conclusions are presented with an abundance of documentation, they suffer from a certain distortion in the author's treatment of them. In its phrasing the article goes far beyond the atomism which the title announces, and throughout there is a tendency to confuse atomism with Epicureanism in general—whereby Boyle becomes an Epicurean—and to assume that the atomic theory is *the* essential doctrine of Epicureanism—whereby Hobbes, due to his lack of interest in atoms, is excluded from the fold . But it is too late now to give such a limited meaning to "Epicurean." Moreover, there are atomisms and atomisms. Harrison seems to set up the Lucretian atomism as the standard and to treat the scientific speculations of the seventeenth century as if they were merely the literary echo of Democritus and Lucretius. Any account of the atomism of Bacon, Hobbes, Gassendi, Boyle, Descartes and Newton must take into consideration the rapid advances in mathematics and physics in the seventeenth century and the inevitable effects of these on any theory of the constitution of matter. The Epicureanism of a learned scientist of the seventeenth century must therefore be Epicureanism with a difference, and this difference is of even greater significance to the historian of thought than any similarity of literary pattern with Lucretius.

Particularly in the case of Boyle, Harrison obscures these vital differences. Not that he entirely ignores them, but he refuses to treat them as important. "Boyle," he says, "finds only one fault with the equipment of Epicurus and Lucretius in their study of nature, and that is the ignorance of mathematics . . ." (p. 214). But it was the application of mathematics to physics and astronomy that had sent the idea of the accidental dance of the atoms to scientific limbo. Of course Boyle was out of sympathy with the whole materialistic tendency of Epicurean thought; and consequently his whole conception of matter and motion was profoundly influenced by problems utterly foreign to the philosophy of Epicurus and Lucretius. Boyle, for instance, found it much more difficult than Harrison would have us believe (p. 215) to accept the Epicurean doctrine of the "congenite motion of atoms," which would tend to eliminate God from the cosmic process (see *Works*, 5 vols., 1744, II, 460-61 and III, 450).

The atomism of the seventeenth century can be explained and described satisfactorily only when related to the complex currents and cross-currents of scientific discovery and speculation in the seventeenth century. Among the authorities in this field, not the least is E. A. Burtt, who remarks, in his *Metaphysical Foundations of Modern Physical Science* (p. 167), that the atoms are "portrayed by Boyle, in spite of Gassendi's revival of Epicureanism, in essentially Cartesian terms." Whether or not Burtt is correct, his contention is one which Harrison should have investigated; and the problem which thus presents itself illustrates very well that the student of Boyle can not be sure of his conclusions unless he has surveyed the scientific thought of Boyle's contemporaries.

Harvey-Jellie, W. *Le théâtre classique en Angleterre.* Montreal: Librairie Beauchemin, 1933.

Hecht, H. *T. Percy, R. Wood und J. D. Michaelis. Ein Beitrag zur Literaturgeschichte der Genieperiode.* Stuttgart: Kohlhammer, 1933. Pp. 94.

Hecht, J. *Der heroische Frauentyp im Restaurationsdrama.* Leipzig dissertation, 1932. Pp. 141.

Hind, A. M. "Studies in English engraving." *Connoisseur,* XCI (1933), 74-80, 223-33, 363-74; XCII (1933), 92-105, 215-27, 382-91.

Valuable studies, with many reproductions, of English art in the seventeenth and eighteenth centuries.

Historic occasions in Westminster Abbey. Memorable sermons from 1662 onwards, selected by Archdeacon Vernon F. Storr and Dr. Jocelyn Perkins. London: Skeffington, 1933.

Hooker, E. N. "Herrick and the song-books." *TLS,* March 2, 1933, p. 147. Cf. corr. by Norman Ault, April 20, p. 276; by E. N. Hooker, June 1, p. 380; and by Norman Ault, June 22, p. 428.

Jackson, Alfred. "Play notices from the Burney newspapers, 1700-1703." *PMLA,* XLVIII (1933), 815-49.

King, C. Harold. "George Whitefield: dramatic evangelist." *Quarterly journal of speech,* XIX (1933), 165-75.

Lieser, P. *Die englische Ode im Zeitalter des Klassizismus.* Bonn dissertation, 1932. Pp. 102.

Lovejoy, Arthur O. "Monboddo and Rousseau." *MP,* XXX (1933), 275-96.

Monboddo's so-called "primitivism," is only a part of a larger group of ideas which issue in a conception of biological and sociological evolution.

Lovejoy, Arthur O. "The Chinese origin of a Romanticism." *JEGP,* XXXII (1933), 1-20.

The influence of Chinese art on irregularity and informality in the eighteenth century, particularly in gardening. Lovejoy emphasizes the importance of Temple's essay *Upon the Gardens of Epicurus.*

Mackenzie, Agnes Mure. *An historical survey of Scottish literature to 1714.* London: MacLehose, 1933. Pp. viii+253.

Rev. in *TLS,* May 25, 1933, p. 360.

McKillop, Alan Dugald. "A critic of 1741 on early poetry." *SP,* XXX (1933), 504-21.

In a volume entitled *The Polite Correspondence* McKillop has found some extended discussion of such topics as Saxon, Welsh, and Danish poetry, with, of course, some reference to primitive poetry in general.

McLachlan, H. *The Unitarian movement in the religious life of England: its contribution to thought and learning, 1700-1900.* London: Allen and Unwin, 1933. Vol. I.

McPeek, James Andrew Scarborough. "The influence of Catullus on English literature to 1700." *Harvard University summaries of theses, 1932,* pp. 264-67.

Matthews, W. "Two notes upon seventeenth century pronunciation." *JEGP,* XXXII (1933), 296-300.

Praz, M. "Il dramma inglese delle Restaurazione e i suoi aspetti preromantici." *La Cultura,* XII (1933).

Praz, M. "Restoration drama." *English studies,* XV (1933), 1-14.

Read, Allen Walker, "British recognition of American speech in the eighteenth century." *Dialect notes,* VI (1933), 313-34.

Read, Allen Walker. "The comment of British travelers on early American terms relating to agriculture." *Agricultural history,* VII (1933), 99-109.

Rose, Ruth O. "Poetic hero-worship in the late eighteenth century. *PMLA,* XLVIII (1933), 1182-1202.

Ross, Julian L. "Dramatist versus audience in the early eighteenth century." *PQ,* XII (1933), 73-81.

Rothenstein, John. *An introduction to English painting.* London: Cassell, 1933. Pp. xii+217.

Rev. in *TLS,* Dec. 14, 1933, p. 893.

Santayana, George. *Some turns of thought in modern philosophy.* Cambridge: University press, 1933.

Contains an essay on "Locke and the frontiers of common sense."

Sharp, Robert Lathrop. "The revolt against Metaphysical poetry: a study in the development of neo-classicism in England." *Harvard University summaries of theses, 1932,* pp. 278-81.

Sickels, Eleanor M. *The gloomy egoist: moods and themes of melancholy from Gray to Keats.* New York: Columbia University press, 1932. Pp. x+456.

Rev. by Paul Van Tieghem in *MP,* XXXI (1933), 213-17.

Singer, Godfrey Frank. *The epistolary novel.* Philadelphia: University of Pennsylvania press; London: Milford, 1933. Pp. ix+266.

Stearns, Bertha Monica. "Early English periodicals for ladies." *PMLA,* XLVIII (1933),38-60.

Strachey, Lytton. *Characters and commentaries.* London: Chatto and Windus, 1933. Pp. xi+320.

Rev. in *TLS,* Nov. 2, 1933, p. 746.

Stroup, T. B. "Philosophy and drama." *TLS,* Jan. 19, 1933, p. 40.

Philosophical ideas in plays by Southerne and Howard.

Sutherland, J. R. "Shakespeare's imitators in the eighteenth century." *MLR,* XXVIII (1933), 21-36.

Underwood, Eric G. *A short history of English painting.* London: Faber and Faber, 1933. Pp. xiii+264.

Rev. in *TLS,* Dec. 14, 1933, p. 893.

Underwood, Eric G. *A short history of English sculpture.* London: Faber and Faber, 1933. Pp. xiv+192.

Rev. in *TLS,* Jan. 18, 1934, p. 43.

Warner, James H. "The reaction in eighteenth century England to Rousseau's two *Discours.*" *PMLA,* XLVIII (1933), 471-87.

An informing and illuminating article on an important subject which has been greatly in need of scholarly investigation.

Weisbach, Werner. "Die klassische Ideologie: Ihre Entstehung und ihre Ausbreitung in den künstlerischen Vorstellungen der Neuzeit." *DVLG* XI (1933), 559-91.

An important study of the esthetics of the Classical age by an eminent historian of the art of the period. It deals primarily with the arts, but for that very reason provides the student of literature with a valuable perspective for viewing his own subject.

Wilenski, R. H. *English painting.* London: Faber and Faber, 1933. Pp. 303 and 160 plates.

Rev. in *TLS,* Dec. 14, 1933, p. 893.

Williamson, George. "The Restoration revolt against enthusiasm." *SP,* XXX (1933), 571-603.

The main theme of this article, as Williamson himself points out, is not new, but it is worked out with a somewhat new emphasis and with much interesting documentation. I remain sceptical regarding Williamson's large claims for the influence of Hobbes on the theories of literary style and language in the seventeenth century (pp. 591-96); something more than resemblances in general ideas is needed to demonstrate that Samuel Parker and Sprat ever championed ideas which at that time could be identified as peculiarly Hobbesian.

Wind, Edgar. "Humanitätsidee und heroisiertes Porträt in der englischen Kultur des 18. Jahrhunderts." *Vorträge Bibliothek Warburg, 1930-1931.* Pp. 156-229. Leipzig: Teubner, 1932.

Wood, Frederick T. "*The Merchant of Venice* in the eighteenth century." *English studies,* XV (1933), 209-18.

Wood, Frederick T. "Sentimental comedy in the eighteenth century, II." *Neophilologus,* XVIII (1933), 281-89.

Woods, Charles B. "*Captain B———'s play.*" *Harvard studies and notes in philology and literature,* XV (1933), 243-55.

On *The Modish Couple* (1732), attributed at the time to Charles Boden. Woods presents reasons for thinking it was written by Lord Hervey. The article throws some interesting light on political and social life of the time.

The parochial churches of Sir Christopher Wren, 1666-1718, Part II. Oxford: Printed for the Wren Society at the University press, 1933.

Wright, Herbert G. "An unpublished manuscript by Lord Herbert of Cherbury entitled *Religio Laici.*" *MLR,* XXVIII (1933), 295-307.

Wright, Reginald W. M. "The city of Bath and its prints." *Print collector's quarterly,* XX (1933), 187-210.

The Wits, or Sport upon Sport. Edited by John James Elson. Ithaca: Cornell University press; London: Milford, 1932. Pp. viii+440.

Rev. by W. J. Lawrence in *MLR,* XXVIII (1933), 254-58.

Wyld, Henry Cecil. *Some aspects of the diction of English poetry.* Oxford: Blackwell, 1933. Pp. 72.

Zeller, Hildegard. *Die Ich-erzählung im englischen Roman.* (Sprache und Kultur der Germanisch-Romanischen Völker. A. Anglistische Reihe, XIV.) Breslau: Priebatsch, 1933. Pp. 99.

IV. INDIVIDUAL AUTHORS.

Joseph Addison

Scott, R. McNair. "An aspect of Addison and Steele." *LM,* XXVII (1933), 524-29.

Taylor, Louise B. "Notes on an unpublished letter of Addison." *N & Q,* CLXIV (1933), 128-30.

Jane Austen

Jane Austen's letters. Collected and edited by R. W. Chapman. Oxford: Clarendon press, 1932. 2 vols. Cf. *PQ,* XII, 110.

Rev. by Ethel Sidgwick in *RES,* IX (1933), 238-40.

"Letters of Jane Austen." Corr. by Abby L. Tallmadge in *TLS,* Jan. 19, 1933, p. 40 and Apr. 13, p. 261; by Ruth C. Koch, John Howard Birss and Thomas Ollive Mabbott, July 13, p. 480; by R. W. Chapman, July 20, p. 496.

Volume the first. Oxford: Clarendon press, 1933. Pp. ix+140.

Rev. in *TLS,* June 22, 1933, p. 425, by John Sparrow in *Bodleian quarterly record,* VII (1933), 298-99; by Helen MacAfee in *Yale review,* XXIII (1933), 192-94.

Juvenilia from a manuscript in the Bodleian.

Butler, E. M. "*Mansfield Park* and Kotzebue's *Lovers' Vows.*" *MLR,* XXVIII (1933), 326-37.

The author contends that "*Mansfield Park* is nothing more nor less than *Lovers' Vows* translated into terms of real life with the moral standard subverted by Kotzebue neatly re-inverted." The article would have been more convincing if the author had pursued the argument a little less relentlessly, with less cleverness and more tact. Cf. Reitzel's article below.

Chapman, R. W. "Jane Austen's library." *Book-collector's quarterly,* no. xi (1933), 28-32.

Reitzel, William. "*Mansfield Park* and *Lovers' Vows.*" *RES,* IX (1933), 451-56.

Kotzebue's play, adapted by Mrs. Inchbald, was regarded as dangerously revolutionary; hence the reactions to it as presented in Jane Austen's novel.

William Beckford

Brulé, A. "Une visite à Fonthill en 1792." *RAA,* X (1933), 33-42.

Aphra Behn

Harris, Brice. "Aphra Behn's *Bajazet to Gloriana.*" *TLS,* Feb. 9, 1933, p. 92.

Jeremy Bentham

Stocks, J. L. *Jeremy Bentham (1748-1832).* The Samuel Hall oration for 1933. Manchester: University press, 1933. Pp. 27.

George Berkeley

Hicks, G. Dawes. *Berkeley.* London: Ernest Benn, 1932. Cf. *PQ,* XII, 111.

Rev. in *TLS,* Jan. 12, 1933, p. 16, by N. Kemp Smith in *Mind,* XLII (1933), 358-64.

William Blake

Seconds livres prophétiques. Traduits de l'Anglais avec une introduction par Pierre Berger. Paris: Rieder, 1933.

Rev. in *TLS,* June 1, 1933, p. 376.

Clutton-Brock, Alan. *Blake.* (Great Lives series.) London: Duckworth, 1933. Pp. 140.

Rev. in *TLS,* August 24, 1933, p. 558.

M[abbott], T[homas] O[llive]. "The text of Blake's *A Fairy stepd upon my knee.*" *N & Q,* CLXIV (1933), 388-89.

Comment by Geoffrey Keynes, *ibid.,* CLXV (1933), 302.

Mabbott, Thomas Ollive. "Blake's American fame." *TLS,* Feb. 23, 1933, p. 127.

Mabbott, Thomas Ollive. "More American references to Blake before 1863." *MLN,* XLVII (1932), 87-88.

Mabbott, Thomas Ollive. "More early American publications of Blake." *N & Q*, CLXV (1933), 279.

Murry, J. Middleton. *William Blake*. London: Jonathan Cape, 1933. Pp. 380.

Rev. in *TLS*, Oct. 26, 1933, p. 727, by R. A. Scott-James in *Spectator*, Sept. 29, 1933, p. 412.

Rhodes, S. A. "William Blake and Pierre Jean Jouve." *Romanic review*, XXIV (1933), 147-49.

Smith, J. C. "A Blake head-piece." *TLS*, Apr. 20, 1933, p. 276.

James Boswell

Private papers of James Boswell from Malahide Castle in the collection of Lt-Colonel Ralph Heyward Isham. Prepared for the press by Geoffrey Scott and Frederick A. Pottle. New York: Privately printed, 1933. Volumes XVII-XVIII.

These volumes contain Boswell's Journal for the years 1786-1794 and a considerable number of letters to Mrs. Boswell and others. They bring to a conclusion the publication of the Boswell papers owned by Colonel Isham.

Life of Johnson. With an introduction by Chauncey Brewster Tinker. New York: Oxford University press, 1933. Pp. xviii+1384.

Foster, Finley. "Piozzian rhymes." *TLS*, March 30, 1933 p, 230.

Cf. comment by E. K. Willing-Denton, *ibid.*, Apr. 20, p. 276.

Kirwan, H. N. "The Boswell supplement." *LM*, XXVII (1933), 331-40.

Vulliamy, C. E. *James Boswell*. London: Geoffrey Bles; New York: Scribners, 1932. Cf. *PQ*, XII, 112.

Rev. by Hugh Kingsmill in *English review*, LVI (1933), 340-43; by Yvonne Ffrench in *LM*, XXVII (1933), 276-78; by Joseph Wood Krutch in *Nation* (New York), CXXXVI (1933), 377; by Matthew Josephson in *New Republic*, LXXVI (1933), 80-81.

Willing-Denton, E. K. "Boswell and the copyright of the *Life*." *TLS*, Dec. 1, 1932, p. 923.

Samuel Boyse

Griffith, R. H. "Boyse's *Albion's Triumph*." *University of Texas studies in English*, no. xiii (1933), 84-94.

Discussion of authorship and reprint of the poem.

Edmund Burke

Bryant, Donald G. "Edmund Burke on oratory." *Quarterly journal of speech*, XIX (1933), 1-18.

Charles and Fanny Burney

The Trial of Midas the Second. An account of Burney's unpublished satire on Hawkins's *History of Music* in the John Rylands Library. Manchester: University press, 1933. Pp. 11.

Reprinted from the *Bulletin of the John Rylands Library.*

Overman, Dr. A. A. *An investigation into the character of Fanny Burney.* Amsterdam: H. T. Paris, 1933. Pp. 221.

Notice in *TLS,* Sept. 28, 1933, p. 656; rev. by F. T. Wood in *English studies,* XV (1933), 200-202.

Robert Burns

Carswell, Catherine. *Robert Burns.* (Great Lives series.) London: Duckworth, 1933. Pp. 142.

Ferguson, J. DeL. "Burns and Jenny Clow." *MLN,* XLVIII (1933), 168-72.

Ross, John D. *The story of the Kilmarnock Burns.* Stirling: Eneas MacKay, 1933. Pp. 96.

Samuel Butler

Gibson, Dan. "Samuel Butler." *Seventeenth century studies by members of the Graduate School, University of Cincinnati.* Edited by Robert Shafer. Pp. 279-335. Princeton: Princeton University press, for the University of Cincinnati, 1933.

An essay on Butler's ideas on society and morals, the state, the church, science, and literary criticism.

Quintana, R. "The Butler-Oxenden correspondence." *MLN,* XLVIII (1933), 1-11.

Publication of a hitherto-unknown letter from Butler, dated 1662, dealing specifically with the composition of *Hudibras.* An important article. Cf. correction by author in same journal, p. 486.

Henry Carey

Wood, Frederick T. "Henry Carey's *Betty.*" *RES,* IX (1933), 64-66

The lost play, *Betty, or the Country Bumpkins,* Wood thinks, was a reworked version of the earlier *Hanging and Marriage.*

Charles Churchill

The Poems of Charles Churchill. Edited by James Laver. London: Eyre and Spottiswoode, 1933. 2 vols. Pp. 1-210 and 211-466.

Rev. in *TLS,* Nov. 9, 1933, p. 769; by G[raham] G[reene] in *Spectator,* Nov. 17, 1933, p. 711.

These expensive volumes are evidently aimed primarily to appeal to the book-collector. Their claim upon the attention of the scholar lies only in their extensive annotations, many of which, however, seem quite unnecessary. One wonders what reader of Churchill would need to have James Quin (p. 41) or David Garrick (p. 45) identified by half-page biographies. Such familiar classical allusions as Dodona's oaks and the three-legged stool of the oracle at Delphi are carefully explained (p. 75). The introduction gives a brief biography based partially on unpublished letters in the British Museum, but is neither critical in method nor final in treatment. Laver has ignored, to the detriment of his own work, the easily accessible articles on Churchill by the American scholar, Joseph M. Beatty. It seems impossible, for instance, to reconcile Laver's account of Churchill's movements in the late summer and autumn of 1763 with that of Beatty, especially with the notices quoted by Beatty from contemporary newspapers (see *PMLA,* XXXV, 1920, 239-42). One wonders why Laver did not consult the newspapers on his own initiative instead of being content to compile from the obvious sources.

Butterfield, L. H. "Charles Churchill and *A Fragment of an Epic Poem.*" *Harvard Studies and notes in philology and literature,* XV (1933), 313-27.

A convincing argument for the inclusion of this "fragment" in the Churchill canon. It is not printed by Laver in the edition noticed above.

Colley Cibber

Griffith, R. H. "A 'Wildfrau story' in a Cibber play." *PQ,* XII (1933), 298-302.

William Collins

Wilmshurst, W. L. "Signatures of Collins." *TLS,* Feb. 9, 1933, p. 92.

William Congreve

The Way of the World. Edited with an introduction and explanatory notes by W. P. Barrett. London: Dent, 1933. Pp. xii+145. (Temple dramatists.)

Hodges, John C. "The ballad in Congreve's *Love for Love.*" *PMLA,* XLVIII (1933), 953-54.

Abraham Cowley

Wallerstein, R. "Cowley as a man of letters." *Transactions of the Wisconsin Academy of Science, Arts and Letters,* XXVII (1932), 127-40.

William Cowper

Selections from Cowper. Edited with an introduction by Lord David Cecil. London: Methuen, 1933. Pp. viii+180.

George Crabbe

George Crabbe, an anthology. Edited by F. L. Lucas. Cambridge: University press, 1933. Pp. xxxii+228.

The life of George Crabbe by his son. Edited with an introduction by E. M. Forster. (World's classics.) Oxford: University press; London: Milford, 1933. Pp. xxiv+324.

Evans, J. H. *The poems of George Crabbe: a literary and historical study.* London: Sheldon press, 1933. Pp. xv+208.

Rev. in *TLS,* Jan. 18, 1934, p. 41.

Richards, Frank. "George Crabbe." *London quarterly and Holborn review,* 1933, pp. 38-47.

Daniel Defoe

Burch, C. E. "British criticism of Defoe as a novelist, 1719-1860." *ES,* LXVII (1932), 178-98.

Fletcher, Edward G. "Some University of Texas copies of *Robinson Crusoe.*" *N & Q,* CLXIV (1933), 4-5.

Hatfield, Theodore M. "*Moll Flanders* in Germany." *JEGP,* XXXII (1933), 51-65.

Moore, J. R. "Defoe, Robin and Crusoe." *N & Q,* CLXIV (1933), 26.

Sutherland, James R. "Some early troubles of Daniel Defoe." *RES,* IX (1933), 275-90.

Important biographical information derived from the Chancery Records in the Public Record Office.

Wright, Thomas. *The life of Daniel Defoe.* London: C. J. Farncombe, 1931. Cf. *PQ,* XI, 192.

Rev. by A. W. Secord in *JEGP* XXXII (1933), 416-17.

John Dryden

The Best of Dryden. Edited with an introduction and notes by Louis I. Bredvold. New York: Thomas Nelson, 1933. Pp. xliv+572.

Bredvold, Louis I. "Notes on John Dryden's pension." *MP,* XXX (1933), 267-74.

Burrows, D. *Relation of Dryden's serious plays and dramatic criticism to contemporary French literature.* Urbana: University of Illinois abstract of thesis, 1933. Pp. 19.

Fletcher, C. R. L. "A Dryden allusion." *TLS,* Feb. 9, 1933, p. 92.

Cf. corr. by Hibernicus and L. R. M. Strachan, *ibid.,* Feb. 16, p. 108, and by Edwin Nungezer, Nov. 2, p. 751.

Hollis, Christopher. *Dryden.* London: Duckworth, 1933. Pp. 224.

Rev. in *TLS,* May 11, 1933, p. 326.

As the publishers state on the jacket of this volume, there is need for a new biography of Dryden; but Hollis's book is not the kind that is needed. Its abundance of errors in even the most elementary matters can only be explained as due to a fertile combination of haste and ignorance. C. Montague Summers appears in the bibliography as "Somers." On page 95 Hollis opines that Dryden was "about the age of forty" in 1682. On pp. 23-24 he speaks of some "occasional political pieces" by Dryden in the years up to 1665, rather to the mystification of the reader; when he ventures to mention two of these pieces the mystery is at least partially cleared up: "one on the victory gained by the Duke of York over the Dutch fleet in June, 1665, another to the Duchess of York." Unless I am much mistaken, Hollis has here simply mis-construed his table of contents and made two poems out of the title *Verses to Her Highness the Dutchess on the Memorable Victory gained by the Duke against the Hollanders, June the 3rd, 1665,* printed in the prefatory letter to *Annus Mirabilis.* This discovery gives us a clue as to how Hollis went about his work. He has not been aware of Professor Allardyce Nicoll's volume on the drama of the period of Dryden; had he consulted it he could have saved himself from much loose statement. He rarely gives the correct date for Dryden's plays, though sometimes the excuse may be made that Hollis is not sure whether he is speaking of the first performance or of the first printing of the play. The burning of the Theatre Royal on January 25, 1672, is advanced by Hollis to somewhere in 1670 (p. 57). In the management of the two theatres Davenant and Killigrew are made to exchange places (p. 25). Hollis is charming on the subject of Dryden's marriage: "Success in *The Indian Emperor* was followed, as literary people's first success so frequently is, by matrimony" (p. 29); and "Dryden did not venture to ask Lady Elizabeth's hand until he had already written the most popular play of the day and until he was on the threshold of the laureateship" (p. 33). Now Dryden was married on December 1, 1663; *The Indian Emperor,* as Hollis himself remarks, was performed in 1665; and Dryden could hardly be described as standing in 1663 on the threshold of the laureateship, inasmuch as Davenant did not die until 1668. On page 58 the *Session of the Poets* is assigned—of all things!—to Dryden, and on page 76 to Rochester; Hollis of course knows nothing about the arguments of Professor Roswell G. Ham for assigning this effusion to Settle (*Otway and Lee,* pp. 109-11). But the depth of Hollis's erudition and the acuteness of his critical faculties can perhaps best be seen in his note on page 100, on the dating of *MacFlecknoe.* He does not believe that the allusion to the poem in *The Loyal Protestant* of Thursday, February 9, 1682, is any evidence of the circulation of the poem previous to that date. Those who argue thus, he says, pointing particularly at the late Thorn-Drury, "have forgotten that the year then began in March." By simply recollecting this fact, of which he assumes that Thorn-Drury was ignorant, he obviates the whole difficulty: "the letter in *The Loyal Protestant* was clearly written in what we should call February, 1683." Unfortunately, Hollis seems not to have thought of verifying this brilliant theory by looking at the periodical in question; Thorn-Drury, who first called attention to the letter in *The Loyal Protestant,* definitely stated in his article that it appears in the issue of February 9, 1681/2. To close our account of this comedy of errors we may note that Hollis gives us an extended quotation from Dryden's letter to the Earl of Rochester, the most famous of his letters, in which he asked for more than his quarterly allowance or some small post in the customs; and Hollis thinks the whole passage is from the dedication to *The Duke of Guise* (p. 124). The book is an hilarious performance .

Mann, W. *Drydens heroische Tragödien als Ausdruck höfischer Barockkultur in England.* Württemberg: Gatzer and Hahre, 1932. Pp. iv+72.

M[undy], P. D. "Portraits of John Dryden." *N & Q,* CLXIV (1933), 423 and CLXV (1933), 194. Corr. by Alfred Sydney Lewis and others, *ibid.,* CLXV (1933), 33, 160, 377.

The songs of John Dryden. Edited by Cyrus Lawrence Day. Cambridge: Harvard University press, 1932. Cf. *PQ,* XII, 115.

Rev. by Harold Williams in *MLR,* XXVIII (1933), 523-25; in *Criterion,* XII (1933), 536-37.

Thorp, Willard. "A new manuscript version of Dryden's epilogue to *Sir Fopling Flutter.*" *RES,* IX (1933), 198-99.

John Evelyn

Ponsonby, Arthur. *John Evelyn.* London: Heinemann, 1933. Pp. xiii+350.

Rev. in *TLS,* Jan. 18, 1934, pp. 33-34.

Henry Fielding

Bissell, Frederick Olds. *Fielding's theory of the novel.* (Cornell studies in English, XXII.) Ithaca: Cornell University press; London: Milford, 1933. Pp. xii+90.

Notice in *TLS,* August 3, 1933, p. 526.

Jones, B. Maelor. *Henry Fielding, novelist and magistrate.* London: Allen & Unwin, 1933. Pp. 256.

Rev. in *TLS,* July 20, 1933, p. 493; corr. by A. R. Leslie-Melville, *ibid.,* July 27, p. 512, and by J. Paul de Castro, August 10, p. 537.

Thornbury, Ethel Margaret. *Henry Fielding's theory of the comic prose epic.* Madison: University of Wisconsin, 1931. Cf. *PQ,* XI, 194.

Rev. by A. W. Secord in *JEGP,* XXXII (1933), 417-18; by J. R. Sutherland in *RES,* IX (1933), 342-43; by G. Kitchin in *MLR,* XXVIII (1933), 110-11.

Edward Gibbon

McCloy, Shelby T. *Gibbon's antagonism to Christianity.* Chapel Hill: University of North Carolina press; London: Williams and Norgate, 1933. Pp. 400.

Rev. in *TLS,* April 13, 1933, p. 259; by Preserved Smith in *AHR,* XXXIX (1933), 167-68.

van de Put, A. "Gibboniana." *TLS,* June 15, 1933, p. 412.

Young, G. M. *Gibbon.* London: Davies, 1932. Pp. 182.

Oliver Goldsmith

Crane, Ronald S. "'Oliver Goldsmith, M.B.'" *MLN,* XLVIII (1933), 462-65.

Points out that he was known as "Dr. Goldsmith" at least as early as 1759; the supposition that he assumed the title of "Doctor" for the purposes of his literary career seems therefore erroneous.

Crane, R. S., and Friedman, Arthur. "Goldsmith and the *Encyclopédie.*" *TLS,* May 11, 1933, p. 331.

Goldsmith's borrowings.

Friedman, Arthur. "An essay by Goldsmith in the *Lady's Magazine.*" *MP,* XXX (1933), 320-22.

Gallaway, W. F. "The sentimentalism of Goldsmith." *PMLA,* XLVIII (1933), 1167-81.

Kent, Elizabeth Eaton. *Goldsmith and his booksellers.* (Cornell studies in English, XX.) Ithaca: Cornell University press; London: Milford, 1933. Pp. xiv+122.

Notice in *TLS,* Oct. 5, 1933, p. 674; rev. by Caroline F. Tupper in *JEGP,* XXXIII (1934), 152-53.

Roberts, W. "Goldsmith in France." *TLS,* Nov. 30, 1933, p. 855, and Dec. 28, p. 921.

The vogue of Goldsmith's writings in France.

Schorer, Mark. *"She Stoops to Conquer:* a parallel." *MLN,* XLVIII (1933), 91-94. Cf. corr. by Schorer in same journal, p. 486.

The parallel is Mrs. Centlivre's *The Man's Bewitched;* the author advances this parallel as only a "remarkable coincidence."

Seitz, R. W. "Goldsmith and the *Annual Register." MP,* XXXI (1933), 183-94.

Tillotson, Arthur. "Dr. Johnson and the *Life of Goldsmith." MLR,* XXVIII (1933), 439-43.

Thomas Gray

An Elegy written in a country churchyard. The three manuscripts, edited by R. Fukuhara and H. Bergen. London: E. Walters and G. Miller, 1933. Pp. xiii+39.

Rev. in *TLS,* leading article, July 27, 1933, pp. 501-02; corr. by E. E. Kellett, August 10, p. 537.

Hall, Edward B. *"The Temple of Tragedy." TLS,* May 18, 1933, p. 348.

Jones, W. Powell. "Books owned by Gray." *TLS,* June 1, 1933, p. 380.

Charles Montague, Earl of Halifax

Kern, John D. "An unpublished MS. of Charles Montague, Earl of Halifax (1661-1715)." *JEGP,* XXXII (1933), 66-69.

A British Museum manuscript of 102 folios, a photostat copy of which is in the library of the University of Pennsylvania.

George Savile, Marquis of Halifax

"George Savile, Marquis of Halifax." Leading article, *TLS,* Nov. 9, 1933, pp. 757-58.

Phare, E. E. "Note on George Savile, first marquess of Halifax." *RES,* IX (1933), 62-63.

Thomas Hobbes

Buddeberg, Else. "Hobbes und das Naturrecht." *Revue internationale de la théorie du droit,* VII (1932), 22-52.

David Hume

The Letters of David Hume. Edited by J. Y. T. Greig. Oxford: Clarendon press, 1932. 2 vols. Cf. *PQ,* XII, 117.

Rev. by N. Kemp Smith in *Mind,* XLII (1933), 523-28; by Frederick A. Pottle in *Yale review,* XXIII (1933), 188-90.

Laird, John. *Hume's philosophy of human nature.* London: Methuen, 1932. Cf. *PQ,* XII, 117.

Rev. by Sterling P. Lamprecht in *Journal of Philosophy,* XXX (1933), 128-36; by C. R. Morris in *Mind,* XLII (1933), 67-75.

Laporte, Jean. "Le scepticisme de Hume." *Revue philosophique,* CXV (1933), 61-127.

de Michelis, E. "D. Hume e il problema critico della conoscenza nella filosofia moderna." *Rivista di filosofia,* XXIV (1933), 285-309.

Elizabeth Inchbald

(See also *Jane Austen*)

Joughlin, George Louis. "The life and works of Elizabeth Inchbald." *Harvard University summaries of theses, 1932.* Pp. 263-64.

Samuel Johnson

(See also *James Boswell* and *Thomas Gray*)

Chapman, R. W. "Johnson's letters." *TLS,* Apr. 13, 1933, p. 261.

Evans, Bergen Baldwin. "Dr. Johnson as a biographer." *Harvard University summaries of theses, 1932,* pp. 248-51.

Hooker, E. N. "Johnson's understanding of Chaucer's metrics." *MLN,* XLVIII (1933), 150-51.

Ketton-Cremer, R. W. "Doctor Messenger Monsey." *LM,* XXVIII (1933), 240-48.

New light on the physician of Chelsea Hospital whom Johnson accused of talking bawdy.

Kingsmill, Hugh. *Samuel Johnson.* London: Barker, 1933. Pp. 291.

Rev. in *TLS,* Jan. 18, 1934, p. 41.

Reade, A. Lyell. *Johnsonian gleanings.* Part VI, the Doctor's life, 1735-1740. London: Privately printed, 1933. Pp. xi+224.

Rev. in *TLS,* May 25, 1933, p. 361; by Paul Meissner in *Beiblatt,* XLIV (1933), 308-10.

Reade, Aleyn Lyell. "Gilbert Walmesley." *TLS,* July 13, 1933, p. 480.

Rendall, Vernon. "Johnson and the unlearned." *LM,* XXVIII (1933), 249-55.

A paper read to the Johnson Club.

Reynolds, W. V. "Johnson's opinions on prose style." *RES,* IX (1933), 433-46.

A useful collection of Johnson's scattered *obiter dicta* on the qualities to be cultivated and the faults to be avoided in prose. The article is somewhat loose in organization; the author might perhaps have done better had he developed his study as a commentary on the passage from the *Adventurer,* No. 115, quoted on page 445; in that case he would doubtless have brought a little more clearly into relief the importance which Johnson attached to "harmony of cadence," "the musick of modulated periods." There is a rather perfunctory introduction on some of the other discussions of prose style which appeared between 1698 and Johnson's death. Among these John Constable's *Reflections upon accuracy of style* (1734) deserves, I think, somewhat more respectful attention than Reynolds gives it if only for the clear insight it affords into the relation between the stylistic movement of the early eighteenth century and the "baroque" tendencies of the preceding period.—R. S. C.

Reynolds, W. V. "A note on Johnson's use of the triplet." *N & Q,* CLXV (1933), 23-24.

Struble, Mildred C. *A Johnson handbook.* New York: Crofts, 1933. Pp. xii+354.

Hugh Kelly

Schorer, Mark. "Hugh Kelly: his place in the sentimental school." *PQ,* XII (1933), 389-401.

Nathaniel Lee

Constantine the Great. Kritisch herausgegeben und mit einer Einleitung versehen, von Walter Häfele. (Englische Textbibliothek, XX.) Heidelberg: Winter, 1933. Pp. 166.

John Locke

Broad, C. D. "John Locke." *Hibbert journal,* XXXI (1933), 249-67.

Gibson, J. *John Locke (1632-1704).* London: Milford, 1933. Pp. 25.

Lamprecht, Sterling P. "John Locke and his *Essay.*" *Columbia University quarterly,* XXV (1933), 204-19.

Stocks, J. L., and Ryle, G. *John Locke.* Oxford: University press, 1933. Pp. 38.

Bernard de Mandeville

Harder, J. H. "The authorship of *A modest defence of public stews,* etc." *Neophilologus,* XVIII (1933), 200-03.

An attempt to show that the late F. B. Kaye was in error when he included *A modest defence* (1724) among the "Authentic works" of Mandeville (*Fable of the bees* [Oxford, 1924], I, xxxi). The main premises of the argument are two:

(1) that although Mandeville acknowledged the authorship of a number of his writings, he did not acknowledge the authorship of this; and (2) that the pamphlet is entered in the registers of the Stationers' Company, not to Mandeville, but to one Lawrence Lafevre (or Le Fever). The article ends rather inconclusviely, but Harder is clearly of the opinion that he has proved *A modest defence* to be the work of Lafevre.

What he has proved is of course merely that Lafevre (concerning whom, unfortunately, no further information appears to be obtainable) was the person who on July 16, 1724—a week before the book was published—took out the copyright of *A modest defence* and supplied the nine copies required under the Act of 1710. That he was also the writer of the piece cannot be deduced from the evidence in hand except on the assumption, for which there is no warrant whatever, that it was the normal practice in the early eighteenth century to enter books at Stationers' Hall to authors as such. It is true, as Harder notes, that in 1711 *A treatise of the hypochondriack and hysterick passions* was entered to Mandeville under the hand of Dryden Leach; but a glance at the title page of this book will show that it was "Printed for and . . . to be had of the Author . . . and D. Leach," etc.; in a word, Mandeville was the publisher of his own work, and it was clearly in this capacity rather than in that of author that he appeared at Stationers' Hall (in the person of the bookseller Leach) and had his "Copy" registered. There is a possibility, of course, that Lafevre stood in a similarly double relationship to *A modest defence;* but strictly speaking all that can be inferred from the testimony of the Stationers' registers is that he was concerned in some way financially with its publication. (The title page of the first edition bears only the name of the printer, A. Moore.)

My belief, in spite of Harder, is that *A modest defence* is in all probability the work of Mandeville. The evidence is almost entirely internal, but as set forth by Kaye in an article which Harder completely ignores, although he must have seen a reference to it in the *Fable* (see *JEGP,* XX [1921], 451-56), it is of a character not to be easily dismissed.—R. S. C.

Deckelmann, Wilhelm. *Untersuchungen zur Bienenfabel Mandevilles und zu ihrer Entstehungsgeschichte im Hinblick auf die Bienenfabelthese.* (Britannica, VII.) Hamburg: Friederichsen, de Gruyter & Co., 1933. Pp. 136.

James Macpherson

Gillies, Alexander. *Herder und Ossian.* Berlin: Junker und Dünnhaupt, 1933. Pp. 189.

Hannah More

Aikin-Sneath, Betsy. "Hannah More." *LM,* XXVIII (1933), 528-35.

Child, Philip. "Portrait of a woman of affairs—old style." *University of Toronto quarterly,* III (1933), 87-102.

Malim, M. C. "Hannah More: 1745-1833." *Contemporary review,* CXLIV (1933), 329-36.

Snodgrass, A. E. "Dr. Johnson's petted lady." *Cornhill,* LXXIV (1933), 336-42.

Peter Anthony Motteux

Cunningham, R. N. "A bibliography of the writings of Peter Anthony Motteux." *Proceedings and papers of the Oxford Bibliographical Society,* Vol. III, Part III (1933), 317-37.

Cunningham, R. N. *Peter Anthony Motteux, 1663-1718.* Oxford: Blackwell, 1933. Pp. x+217.

Rev. in *TLS,* Dec. 7, 1933, p. 872.

Amelia Opie

Macgregor, Margaret Eliot. *Amelia Alderson Opie: worldling and friend.* (Smith College studies in Modern Languages, XIV.) Northampton, Mass.: Smith College, 1933. Pp. 146.

Thomas Otway

Babcock, R. W. "The Reverend Montague Summers as editor of Otway." *PMLA,* XLVIII (1933), 948-52.

Thomas Paine

Clark, Harry Hayden. "Toward a reinterpretation of Thomas Paine." *American literature,* V (1933), 133-45.

Clark, Harry Hayden. "Thomas Paine's theories of rhetoric." *Transactions of the Wisconsin Academy of Science, Arts, and Letters,* XXVIII (1933), 307-40.

Samuel Pepys

Shorthand letters. From a volume entitled "S. Pepys' Official Correspondence 1662-1679," transcribed and edited by Edwin Chappell. Cambridge: University press; New York: Macmillan, 1933. Pp. xvi+104.

Bryant, Arthur. *Samuel Pepys: the man in the making.* Cambridge: University press, 1933. Pp. xiv+436.

Rev. in *TLS,* Nov. 2, 1933, p. 745; by Graham Greene in *Spectator,* Nov. 24, 1933, pp. 777-78; by W. C. Abbot in *SRL,* Dec. 23, p. 367.

The first volume of a definitive biography, bringing the story down to the end of the *Diary.*

Carlton, W. J. "Samuel Pepys, his shorthand books." *Library,* 4th series, XIV (1933), 73-84.

Chappell, Edwin. *Bibliographia Pepysiana.* London: Privately printed, 1933. Pp. 18.

Chappell, Edwin. "Pepys' wedding day." *N & Q,* CLXIV (1933). 452-54.

Cf. corr. by F. W. Read, *ibid.,* CLXV (1933), 30.

Chappell, Edwin. "A Pepys exhibition." *TLS,* Dec. 7, 1933, p. 878.

Chappell, Edwin. "Notes on some relations of Samuel Pepys." *N & Q,* CLXIV (1933), 326-27.

Cf. corr. by H. C. Drury, *ibid.,* June 3, p. 394, and by E. Chappell, June 17, p. 431.

Chappell, Edwin. *The secrecy of the diary.* A paper read before the Samuel Pepys Club, November 24th, 1933. London: Privately printed, 1933. Pp. 8.

Heal, Sir Ambrose. "Samuel Pepys: his trade-cards." *Connoisseur,* XCII (1933), 165-71.

Matthews, W. "The text of Pepys." *TLS,* Feb. 2, 1933, p. 76.

"Pepys' Diary." *TLS,* Feb. 23, 1933, p. 127.

Corr. from G. Bell and Sons, announcing that a new and reliable edition of the *Diary* is under way, edited by F. McD. C. Turner, Fellow and Pepysian Librarian of Magdalene College. Further corr. Jan. 18, 1934, p. 44, announcing that difficulties will delay the publication for another two years.

"Samuel Pepys." Leading article, *TLS,* Feb. 23, 1933, pp. 113-14.

Stewart, Herbert L. "The Pepys tercentenary." *Dalhousie review,* XIII (1933), 273-92.

Thomas Percy

Churchill, Irving L. "The Percy-Warton letters—additions and corrections." *PMLA,* XLVIII (1933), 301-03.

Ogburn, Vincent H. "The Wilkinson MSS. and Percy's Chinese books." *RES,* IX (1933), 30-36.

New information from the Percy MSS. in the Harvard College library.

Ruff, William, "Sir Walter Scott and Bishop Percy." *N & Q,* CLXV (1933), 308-09.

Watkins-Jones, A. "Bishop Percy and the Scottish ballads." *Essays and studies by members of the English Association,* XVIII (1933), 110-21. Oxford: Clarendon press.

Ambrose Philips

Segar, Mary. "Ambrose Philips." *TLS,* Dec. 7, 1933, p. 875.

Correction of numerous errors in the standard accounts of the life of Philips. Cf. corr. by W. G. D. Fletcher, Dec. 21, 1933, p. 909, and by Mary Segar, Jan. 4, 1934, p. 12.

Alexander Pope

Babcock, R. W. "The text of Pope's *To Mrs. M. B. on her birth-day.*" *MLN,* XLVIII (1933), 452-57.

Beck, Richard. "Jón Þorláksson—Icelandic translator of Pope and Milton." *JEGP,* XXXII (1933), 572-85.

"The Essay on Man." Leading article, *TLS,* August 10, 1933, pp. 529-30.

de la Harpe, Jacqueline. "Le Journal des Savants et la renommée de Pope en France au XVIIIe siècle." *University of California publications in modern philology,* XVI (1933), 173-216.

Sherburn, George. "Two notes on the *Essay on Man.*" *PQ,* XII (1933), 402-03.

Important note on *The Universal Prayer.*

Warren, Austin. "To Mr. Pope: epistle from America." *PMLA,* XLVIII (1933), 61-73.

Matthew Prior

Barrett, W. P. "A note on manuscript variants not collated in A. R. Waller's edition of Prior." *RES,* IX (1933), 63-64.

Thomas Purney

The Works of Thomas Purney. Edited by H. O. White. Oxford: Blackwell, 1933. Pp. xxxiv+111.

Rev. in *TLS,* July 13, 1933, p. 477.

Sir Joshua Reynolds

Steegmann, John. *Reynolds.* (Great Lives series.) London: Duckworth, 1933. Pp. 136.

Rev. in *TLS,* March 9, 1933, p. 159.

Samuel Richardson

Broadus, E. K. "Mr. Richardson arrives." *LM,* XXVIII (1933), 425-35.

Lefever, Charlotte. "Richardson's paradoxical success." *PMLA,* XLVIII (1933), 856-60.

McKillop, Alan D. "Richardson's early years as a printer." *RES,* IX (1933), 67-70.

Sale, William M. "*Sir Charles Grandison* and the Dublin pirates." *Yale University Library gazette,* VII (1933), 80-86.

Wentworth Dillon, Earl of Roscommon

Niemeyer, Carl. "The birth date of the Earl of Roscommon." *RES,* IX (1933), 449-51.

George Rust

A letter of resolution concerning Origen and the chief of his opinions. Reproduced from the edition of 1661, with a bibliographical note by Marjorie Hope Nicolson. New York: Columbia University press, for the Facsimile Text Society, 1933. Pp. 136.

Sarah Scott

Crittenden, Walter Marion. *The life and writings of Mrs. Sarah Scott, novelist (1723-1795).* Philadelphia: University of Pennsylvania press, 1932. Pp. 99.

Rev. by Joseph Warren Beach in *JEGP,* XXXII (1933), 111-12.

Elkanah Settle

Fletcher, E. G. "Bibliography of Elkanah Settle." *N & Q,* CLXIV (1933), 114.

Bibliographical notes.

Ham, Roswell G. "The authorship of *A Session of the Poets* (1677)." *RES,* IX (1933), 319-22.

A re-statement of the case for attributing this piece to Settle, with the addition of new evidence.

Anthony Ashley Cooper, third earl of Shaftesbury

Alderman, William E. "Shaftesbury and the doctrine of optimism in the eighteenth century." *Transactions of the Wisconsin Academy of Science, Arts, and Letters.* XXVIII (1933), 297-306.

William Shenstone

Hill, Charles J. "Graves's urn in memory of Shenstone." *N & Q,* CLXV (1933), 165.

Williams, Marjorie. "William Shenstone, letter-writer." *RES,* IX (1933), 291-305.

Williams, Marjorie. *William Shenstone and his friends.* (English Association pamphlet no. 84.) Oxford: University press, 1933. Pp. 19.

Richard Brinsley Sheridan

Darlington, W. A. *Sheridan.* (Great Lives series.) London: Duckworth, 1933. Pp. 144.

Rev. in *TLS,* Oct. 12, 1933, p. 687.

Rhodes, R. Crompton. *Harlequin Sheridan, the man and the legends.* With a bibliography and appendices. Oxford: Blackwell, 1933. Pp. xvii+305.

Rev. in *TLS,* Oct. 12, 1933, p. 687; by W. J. Lawrence in *Spectator,* Nov. 10, 1933, pp. 673-74.

Tobias Smollett

Birss, J. H. "A letter to Tobias Smollett." *N & Q,* CLXIV (1933), 315-16.

Birss, J. H. "Note on Smollett letter no. 37." *N & Q,* CLXV (1933), p. 189.

Knapp, L. M. "More Smollett letters." *MLN,* XLVIII (1933), 246-49.

Parsons, Coleman O. "Smollett's influence on *The Rivals.*" *N & Q,* CLXIV (1933), 39-41.

Thomas Southerne

Dodds, J. W. *Thomas Southerne, dramatist.* (Yale studies in English, LXXXI.) New Haven: Yale University press, 1933. Pp. viii+237.

Rev. in *TLS,* Apr. 27, 1933, p. 290; by Allardyce Nicoll in *MLR,* XXVIII (1933), 525-26.

Leech, Clifford. "A cancel in Southerne's *The Disappointment,* 1684." *Library,* 4th series, XIII (1933), 395-98.

Leech, Clifford. "The political 'disloyalty' of Thomas Southerne." *MLR,* XXVIII (1933), 421-30.

Leech, Clifford. "Thomas Southerne and *On the Poets and Actors in King Charles II's Reign.*" *N & Q,* CLXIV (1933), 401-03.

Mallery, R. D. "Thomas Southerne." *TLS,* Dec. 1, 1932, p. 923; cf. corr. by Clifford Leech, *ibid.,* Dec. 8, p. 943.

Sir Richard Steele

(See also *Joseph Addison*)

Blanchard, Rae. "Some unpublished letters of Richard Steele to the Duke of Newcastle." *MLN,* XLVIII (1933), 232-46.

Cf. corr. by same author, pp. 485-86.

Laurence Sterne

Ollard, S. L. "Sterne as a parish priest." *TLS,* May 25, 1933, p. 364, and June 1, p. 380.

Jonathan Swift

Beattie, Lester M. "The authorship of *The Quidnunckis's.*" *MP,* XXX (1933), 317-20.

Birss, J. H. "A volume from Swift's library." *N & Q,* CLXIII (1932), 404, and CLXIV (1933), 334.

Gregory, Alyse. "Stella, Vanessa, and Swift." *Nineteenth century,* CXIII (1933), 755-64.

Gulick, Sidney L. "Jonathan Swift's *The Day of Judgement.*" *PMLA,* XLVIII (1933), 850-55.

Gwynn, Stephen. *The life and friendships of Dean Swift.* London: Thornton Butterworth; New York: Henry Holt, 1933. Pp. 320.

Rev. in *TLS,* Oct. 19, 1933, p. 707; by Eric Partridge in *Fortnightly,* Dec., 1933, pp. 755-56; by Temple Scott in *SRL,* X (1933), 321.

Rossi, Mario M., and Hone, J. M. *Swift, or the egoist.* London: Gollanz, 1933. Pp. 418.

Rev. in *TLS,* Jan. 25, 1934, p. 56.

Taylor, W. D. *Jonathan Swift, a critical essay.* London: Peter Davies, 1933. Pp. vii+312.

Webster, C. M. "A possible source for *A Tale of a Tub.*" *MLN,* XLVIII (1933), 251-53.

Webster, Clarence M. "Swift and some earlier satirists of Puritan enthusiasm." *PMLA,* XLVIII (1933), 1141-53.

Williams, Harold. *Dean Swift's library.* Cambridge: University press, 1932. Cf. *PQ,* XII, 124.

Rev. by Henry Clinton Hutchins in *RES,* IX (1933), 488-94.

Sir William Temple

Marburg, Clara. *Sir William Temple: a seventeenth century "Libertine."* New Haven: Yale University press, 1932. Cf. *PQ,* XII, 124.

Rev. by Homer E. Woodbridge in *JEGP,* XXXII (1933), 109-11; by Sterling P. Lamprecht in *Journal of philosophy,* XXX (1933), 51-52.

James Thomson

Johnson, Walter G. "A Swedish imitator of Thomson." *Scandinavian studies and notes,* XII (1933), 113-27.

The poem, *Svenska Friheten,* by Olof von Dalin (1708-1763), was influenced by Thomson's *Liberty.*

Whiting, G. W. "James Thomson, editor of *Areopagitica.*" *N & Q,* CLXIV (1933), 457.

Horace Walpole

Whitley, William T. "A letter of Horace Walpole." *TLS,* March 23, 1933, p. 200.

Edward Ward

Five travel scripts commonly attributed to Edward Ward. Reproduced from the earliest editions extant, with a bibliographical note by Howard William Troyer. New York: Columbia University press, for the Facsimile Text Society, 1933.

Joseph Warton

MacClintock, William Darnall. *Joseph Warton's "Essay on Pope."* A history of the five editions. Chapel Hill: University of North Carolina press; London: Milford, 1933. Pp. xii+74.

Notice in *TLS,* Oct. 5, 1933, p. 674; rev. by John Sparrow in *LM,* XXVIII (1933), 565-66.

John and Charles Wesley

Dobrée, Bonamy. *Wesley.* (Great Lives series.) London: Duckworth, 1933. Pp. 139.

Rev. in *TLS,* Jan. 26, 1933, p. 51.

Edwards, Maldwyn. *John Wesley and the eighteenth century.* A study of his social and political influence. London: Allen and Unwin, 1933.

Rev. in *TLS,* July 13, 1933, p. 479; by Bonamy Dobrée in *Spectator,* Aug. 18, 1933, p. 229.

Wiseman, F. Luke. *Charles Wesley, evangelist and poet.* London: Epworth press, 1933.

Rev. in *TLS,* July 13, 1933, p. 479.

William Whitehead

Bitter, August. *William Whitehead—Poeta Laureatus.* Eine Studie zu den literarischen Strömungen um die Mitte des 18 Jahrhunderts. (Studien zur Englischen Philologie, LXXVII.) Halle: Niemeyer, 1933. Pp. vi+106.

William Wycherley

Vincent, Howard P. "The death of William Wycherley." *Harvard studies and notes in philology and literature,* XV (1933), 219-42.

The first correct account of his marriage and death, based on newly-discovered documents in the Record Office.

V. THE CONTINENTAL BACKGROUND

Boas, George. *The happy beast in French thought of the seventeenth century.* Baltimore: The Johns Hopkins press; London: Milford, 1933. Pp. vii+159.

Rev. by Harold A. Larrabee in *Journal of philosophy,* XXX (1933), 610-11. An important and illuminating study, a by-product of the work being done at The Johns Hopkins University on the history of Primitivism.

Brown, Huntington. *Rabelais in English literature.* Cambridge: Harvard University press, 1933. Pp. xvi+254.

Busson, Henri. *La pensée religieuse française de Charron à Pascal.* Paris: J. Vrin, 1933. Pp. 666.

Rev. by F. Mentré in *Revue de philosophie,* IV (1933), 219-26.

Cassirer, E. *Die Philosophie der Aufklärung.* Tübingen: J. C. B. Mohr, 1932. Pp. xviii+491.

Rev. in *Revue philosophique,* CXVI (1933), 134-38; by J. H. Muirhead in *Mind,* XLII (1933), 250-52.

Cousin, Jean. "Rhétorique latine et classicisme française." *RCC,* XXXIV[1] (1933), 502-18, 589-605; XXXIV[2] (1933), 159-68, 234-43, 461-69, 659-72, 737-50.

Facteau, Bernard A. "Note in Chateaubriand's *Atala.*" *MLN,* XLVIII (1933), 492-97.

A Frenchman in America in 1816 wrote to *L'Abeille Américaine,* published in Philadelphia, criticizing Chateaubriand's pretensions to a first-hand knowledge of the country he was describing.

Harvey, F. Brompton. "An English source of La Rochefoucauld's *Maximes.*" *Nineteenth century,* CXIV (1933), 612-18.

A popular presentation of the theory that the Frenchman was re-working thought derived from Daniel Dyke. The author of the article accepts this theory without reservation. The whole matter is discussed critically by H. A. Grubbs in *RHL,* XXXVI (1929), 22-29.

Havens, G. R. *Voltaire's marginalia on the pages of Rousseau: a comparative study of ideas.* Columbus: Ohio State University, 1933. Pp. viii+199.

Based on a study of Voltaire's library, preserved in the Public Library at Leningrad. Voltaire's comments on the *Discours sur l'inégalité, Contrat Social, Émile,* and other works.

Lancaster, Henry Carrington. *A history of French dramatic literature in the seventeenth century.* Part II, the period of Corneille, 1635-51. Baltimore: The Johns Hopkins press; London: Oxford University press; Paris: Belles-Lettres, 1932. 2 vols. Pp. 804.

Rev. by Louis Cons in *MLN,* XLVIII (1933), 338-41; by René Bray in *RHL,* XL (1933), 124-27.

Lützeler, Heinrich. "Der Wandel der Barockauffassung." *DVLG,* XI (1933), 618-36.

Mornet, Daniel. *Les origines intellectuelles de la Révolution française, 1715-1787.* Paris: Armand Colin, 1933. Pp. 556.

de Muralt, B. L. *Lettres sur les Anglois et les François et sur les Voiages.* Edited by Charles Gould. Paris: Champion, 1933.

Rev. in *TLS,* July 6, 1933, p. 459.

Pinot, Virgile. *La Chine et la formation de l'esprit philosophique en France (1640-1740).* Paris: Paul Geuthner, 1932. Pp. 480.

Rev. by Arnold H. Rowbotham in *MP,* XXXI (1933), 210-13.

Schinz, Albert. "Documents sur Rousseau et Voltaire." *Revue de Paris,* CCXXXVI (1933), 299-325, 630-67.

Based on the recently published Boswell papers.

Van Roosbroeck, G. L. *Persian Letters before Montesquieu.* New York: Institute of French Studies, 1933. Pp. 147.

Las Vergnas, Raymond. *Le chevalier Rutlidge "gentilhomme anglois."* Paris: Champion, 1932. Pp. 238.

Rev. by R. W. Babcock in *MLN,* XLIX (1934), 196-200.

Weisbach, Werner. *Französische Malerei des 17. Jahrhunderts im Rahmen von Kultur und Gesellschaft.* Berlin: Heinrich Keller, 1932.

Rev. in *TLS,* Feb. 2, 1933, p. 70; by Karl Vossler in *Historische Zeitschrift,* CXLIX (1933), 125-27.

Williams, David. "The influence of Rousseau on political opinion, 1760-95." *EHR,* XLVIII (1933), 414-30.

A valuable article, but the author of it discusses the question of Rousseau's influence on Jefferson without mentioning Chinard, whose work he apparently does not know.

Woodbridge, B. M. "The *Discours de la Méthode* and the spirit of the Renaissance." *Romanic review,* XXIV (1933), 136-42.

1935

ENGLISH LITERATURE, 1660-1800: A CURRENT BIBLIOGRAPHY

By Louis I. Bredvold
University of Michigan

This bibliography attempts to list the more significant books, articles, and reviews published during the year 1934, together with some bearing earlier dates that were inadvertantly omitted from previous bibliographies in this series. I am indebted to Professor Ronald S. Crane, Professor Everett S. Brown, and Mr. Henry V. S. Ogden for contributing the critical notes signed with their initials. Miss Kathleen Murphy has rendered invaluable assistance in the task of collecting material.

LIST OF ABBREVIATIONS

AHR=*American historical review.*
Archiv=*Archiv für das Studium der neueren Sprachen und Literaturen.*
Beiblatt=*Beiblatt zur Anglia.*
DVLG=*Deutsche Vierteljahrschrift für Literaturwissenschaft und Geistesgeschichte.*
EHR=*English historical review.*
ELH=*ELH, A journal of English literary history.*
ES=*Englische Studien.*
GRM=*Germanisch-romanische Monatschrift.*
JEGP=*Journal of English and Germanic philology.*
JMH=*Journal of modern history.*
LM=*London mercury.*
MLN=*Modern language notes.*
MLR=*Modern language review.*
MP=*Modern philology.*
N & Q=*Notes and queries.*
PMLA=*Publications of the Modern Language Association of America.*
PQ=*Philological quarterly.*
RAA=*Revue anglo-américaine.*
RC=*Revue critique.*
RCC=*Revue des cours et conférences.*
RELV=*Revue de l'enseignement des langues vivantes.*
RES=*Review of English studies.*
RH=*Revue historique.*
RHL=*Revue d'histoire littéraire de la France.*
RHP=*Revue d'histoire de la philosophie.*
RLC=*Revue de littérature comparée.*
RSH—*Revue de synthèse historique.*
SP=*Studies in philology.*
SRL=*Saturday review of literature.*
TLS=*Times literary supplement* (London).

I. BIBLIOGRAPHIES AND BIBLIOGRAPHICAL STUDIES.

Annual bibliography of English language and literature. Volume XIV, 1933. Edited for the Modern Humanities Research Association, by Mary S. Serjeantson, assisted by Leslie N. Broughton. Cambridge: Bowes & Bowes, 1934. Pp. 265.

Annual bulletin of historical literature. No. xxiii, dealing with the publications of the year 1933. London: G. Bell, for the Historical Association, 1934. Pp. 94.

See especially pp. 48-53.

Baugh, Albert C. "Annual bibliography for 1933: English language and literature." *PMLA,* XLVIII (1933).

See especially pp. 1323-33.

Bernbaum, Ernest. "Recent works on prose fiction before 1800." *MLN,* XLIX (1934), 529-34.

Berry, W. Turner. "A note on the Caslon type sheets bearing the date 1734." *Book-Collector's quarterly,* XVI (1934), 58-63.

"A Bibliography of philosophy for 1933." *Journal of Philosophy,* XXXI (1934), 451-503.

Bonner, Willard H. "Moll, Knapton, and Defoe: a note on early serial publication." *RES,* X (1934), 320-23.

Bredvold, Louis I. "English literature, 1660-1800: a current bibliography." *PQ,* XIII (1934), 97-132.

A catalogue of a collection of academies, anthologies, miscellanies, poems on affairs of state, and books of composite authorship. (The Oldenburgh House Bulletin, No. 2.) Tunbridge Wells: Dobell's Antiquarian Bookstore, [1934].

A catalogue of eighteenth-century verse, and a catalogue of books by Dr. Jonathan Swift. Compiled by Percy J. Dobell. London: P. J. and A. E. Dobell, [1934].

Notice in *TLS,* Jan. 25, 1934, p. 64.

Coffman, Bertha Reed. "Bibliographical material for the study of Haller's literary work." *PQ,* XIII (1934), 333-49.

Dolson, G. B., and Houghton, W. E. "A note on the 1674 translation of Boethius *De Consolatione Philosophiae.*" *RES,* X (1934), 71-76.

"Francis Douce, 1757-1834." *TLS,* April 5, 1934, p. 248.

Fletcher, Ifan Kyrle. "What Thicknesse read." *Book-Collector's quarterly,* XVI (1934), 49-57.

On Philip Thicknesse, 1719-1792.

Hindle, C. J. "School-books used at Eton College in the early eighteenth century." *N & Q,* CLXVI (1934), 182-83. Corr. by Rhodon, *ibid.,* p. 232, and by W. Sterry, p. 284.

Hindle, C. J. "Unlocated British newspapers and periodicals." *N & Q,* CLXVII (1934), 100.

Kellett, E. E. "A bookseller of two hundred years ago." *TLS,* July 26, 1934, p. 528. Corr. by C. R. Cheney, August 2, p. 541, and by W. C. Dickinson, August 9, p. 553.

On the ledger of a bookseller, Robert Gosling. Attention is also called to a collection of material dealing with the book trade, recently presented to the British Library of Political and Economic Science.

L., J. R. "Francis Douce, 1757-1834." *Bodleian quarterly record,* VII (1934), 359-82.

McKerrow, R. B. "Rowe's Shakespeare, '1709'." *TLS,* March 8, 1934, p. 168.

McKillop, Alan D. "English circulating libraries, 1725-1750." *Library,* XIV (1934), 477-85.

Morgan, William Thomas. *A bibliography of British history (1700-1715), with special reference to the reign of Queen Anne.* Volume I, 1700-1707. Bloomington, Indiana, 1934. Pp. xvii+524.

This bibliography, when completed, will comprise a chronologically ordered list of contemporary "pamphlets and memoirs" published between 1700 and 1716 inclusive, a list of source materials published in 1717 and later, a chapter on correspondence, autobiographies, diaries, and journals, sections on periodical materials, plays and other dramatic writings, secondary works, and unpublished manuscripts, and finally a comprehensive index to authors and titles. The volume just issued contains, besides a statement of the general design, a useful list of "Some bibliographical aids for British history in the eighteenth century," a chapter in which "the author has attempted to go back [in some instances as far as 1688] and gather up some of the more significant items bearing upon the early years of the eighteenth century," and eight chapters dealing with the pamphlet literature of the period 1700-1707.

Although Morgan's work is the result of many years of research in the principal libraries and pamphlet collections of Europe and America, it makes no pretensions to being a complete inventory of sources for all aspects of the portion of British history with which it deals. "The present bibliography," we are told in the introduction, "is confessedly weak in a number of particulars. Ireland, Scotland, and Wales are little worlds of their own, and have been dealt with somewhat incidentally, although a considerable number of items deal with these areas. No attempt has been made to provide a bibliography for the British Empire of the period, as that would take us too far afield. . . . The enormously significant religious history, which is so intertwined with the political developments of the period, has been somewhat neglected, but by no means ignored. It would have been manifestly impossible, on account of space alone, to list all the sermons published during a decade and a half when religious controversy was so bitter. [The history of science] has received less space than its importance would warrant. Students of English literature will find that great attention has been paid to the literary phases of British history in these years when England was flooded with pamphlets written by the foremost politicians and literary figures of this great era. Lack of space has dictated that poems should be for the most part omitted, except when they may have some political bearing, or shed some light upon the social or economic life of the time. . . . Local history, genealogy, and heraldry have been almost entirely neglected, as belonging in fields rather peculiarly their own" (pp. xi-xii). The bibliography, in a word, is selective and it must be supplemented, for the study of many questions, by other more specialized guides or by direct research in libraries. Nevertheless—and within the limits so candidly set forth by the compiler—it is bound to be of immense and permanent value not merely to political historians but to all students concerned with the social and cultural changes which were taking place in England during the first decade and a half of the eighteenth century.

I have one minor regret, that Morgan did not add to the titles of the pamphlets he has listed—many of them exceedingly rare—indications of the libraries in which copies may be found.—R. S. C.

Munby, A. N. L. "Anstey's *Election Ball* and the *Epistle to Bampfylde.*" *Book-Collector's quarterly,* XVI (1934), 19-23.

Nangle, B. C. *The Monthly Review: First Series, 1749-1789: Indexes of contributors and articles.* Oxford: Clarendon Press, 1934. Pp. xvi+255.

Notice in *TLS,* April 5, 1934, p. 248.

Newsletters and early newspapers. (Catalogue No. 44.) London: Birrell and Garnett, [1934].

Notice in *TLS,* Jan. 11, 1934, p. 32.

Noyes, Robert G. "Contemporary musical settings of the songs in Restoration drama." *ELH,* I (1934), 325-44.

Paul, Henry N. "Mr. Hughs' edition of *Hamlet.*" *MLN,* XLIX (1934), 438-43.

Paul, Henry N. "Players' quartos and duodecimos of *Hamlet.*" *MLN,* XLIX (1934), 369-75.

"Peregrinus." "A year's drama and music." *N & Q,* CLXVII (1934), 219-22; 237-38.

Based on the diary of the first earl of Egmont for the year 1734.

Perkinson, Richard H. "A Restoration 'improvement' of *Doctor Faustus.*" *ELH,* I (1934), 305-24.

Pottle, Frederick A. "Printer's copy in the eighteenth century." *Papers of the Bibliographical Society of America,* XXVII (1933), 65-73.

Roberts, W. "A shelf of eighteenth-century novels." *Book-Collector's quarterly,* XV (1934), 17-33.

"Rhodon." *"The Extraordinary North Briton."* *N & Q,* CLXVI (1934), 187-189, and 225. Corr. by R. T. Milford and others, pp. 230-31, and by Rhodon, pp. 264-65.

Seaton, Ethel. "Two Restoration plays." *TLS,* Oct. 18, 1934, p. 715.

James Howard's *The English Monsieur* was played as early as July 30, 1663, before Dryden's *Rival Ladies,* to which it has hitherto been supposed it was indebted.

"Summary report on the Hastings' manuscripts." *The Huntington Library bulletin,* No. 5 (1934), 2-65.

Sutherland, James R. "The circulation of newspapers and literary periodicals, 1700-1730." *Library,* xv (1934), 110-24.

"Thirty-eighth critical bibliography of the history and philosophy of science and of the history of civilization (to March 1933,—with special reference to the seventeenth and eighteenth centuries)." *Isis,* xx (1934), 506-626.

Also the "Thirty-ninth critical bibliography," to September 1933, *ibid.,* xxi (1934), 338-486; and "Fortieth critical bibliography," to January 1934, *ibid.,* xxii (1934), 322-431.

Thorpe, Clarence D. "Thomas Hanmer and the anonymous essay on *Hamlet.*" *MLN* xlix (1934), 493-98.

Evidence that Hanmer could not have been the author.

Tillotson, Arthur. "Spence's *Anecdotes.*" *TLS,* April 5, 1934, p. 244.

A manuscript copy in four volumes is among the Clumber manuscripts on loan in the British Museum.

Wagner, Bernard M. "Manuscript plays of the seventeenth century." *TLS,* October 4, 1934, p. 675. Corr. by Alfred Harbage, Nov. 8, p. 775, and by A. Watkin-Jones, Nov. 15, p. 795.

Warner, James H. "A bibliography of eighteenth-century English editions of J. J. Rousseau; with notes on the early diffusion of his writings." *PQ,* xiii (1934), 225-47.

Williams, Iolo A. *Points in eighteenth-century verse. A bibliographer's and collector's scrapbook.* With four plates in collotype and nine facsimiles. London: Constable, 1934. Pp. x+144.

Rev. in *TLS,* Jan. 25, 1934, p. 64; by Harold Williams in *Book-Collector's quarterly,* xv (1934), 79-85.

The Year's work in English studies. Vol. xiii, 1932. Edited for the English Association by Frederick Boas and Mary S. Serjeantson. Oxford: University press, 1934. Pp. 348.

II. THE SOCIAL AND POLITICAL ENVIRONMENT.

Allen, Robert J. *The Clubs of Augustan London.* Cambridge, Mass.: Harvard University press, 1933. Cf. *PQ,* xiii, 100.

Rev. in *TLS,* March 8, 1934, p. 166; by Richmond P. Bond in *Virginia quarterly review,* x (1934), 302-307; by Ross D. Waller in *MLR,* xxix (1934),

351-52; by Rae Blanchard in *PQ,* XIII (1934), 314-16; by W. A. Eddy in *SP,* XXXI (1934), 493-94.

"The city of Bath." *TLS,* Sept. 27, 1934, p. 660.

Note on the history of the city in English literature.

Blundell, Margaret, ed. *Cavalier letters of William Blundell to his friends, 1620-1698.* London: Longmans, 1934.

Rev. by David Mathew in *Dublin review,* January, 1934, pp. 161-165; by Osbert Burdett in *Fortnightly review,* January, 1934, pp. 117-18.

Brinton, Crane. *A decade of revolution, 1789-1799.* London: Harper, 1934. Pp. 332.

Rev. in *TLS,* Nov. 22, 1934, p. 808; by Walter Littlefield in *New York Times book review,* Dec. 2, 1934, p. 12.

Brown, Louise Fargo. *The first earl of Shaftesbury.* New York: Appleton-Century Company, 1934. Pp. xi+350.

Rev. in *TLS,* Feb. 15, 1934, pp. 97-98; by W. T. Laprade in *South Atlantic quarterly,* April, 1934, pp. 185-90; by W. C. Abbott in *AHR,* XL (1934), 119-21; by William Macdonald in *Books,* July 8, 1934, p. 13.

Bryant, Arthur. *The England of Charles II.* London: Longmans, 1934. Pp. ix+199.

Rev. in *TLS,* October 11, 1934, pp. 681-82; cf. corr., *ibid.,* Oct. 18, p. 715.

Churchill, Winston S. *Marlborough: his life and times.* Vol. II. London: Harrap; New York: Scribners, 1934. Pp. 651.

Rev. in *TLS,* Oct. 25, 1934, p. 723; by Richard Lodge in *EHR,* XLIX (1934), 715-28.

Clark, G. N. *The later Stuarts, 1660-1714.* Oxford: Clarendon press, 1934. Pp. xx+461.

Rev. in *TLS,* Nov. 29, 1934, p. 849; by Avery Craven in *Books,* Dec. 9, 1934, p. 24.

Dumont-Wilden, L. *The wandering prince: Charles Edward, last of the Stuarts.* Translated from the French by W. B. Wells. London: G. Bell, 1934. Pp. viii+286.

Rev. in *TLS,* Dec. 13, 1934, p. 882.

Gilboy, Elizabeth. *Wages in eighteenth century England.* Cambridge, Mass.: Harvard University press, 1934. Pp. xxix+297.

Rev. in *TLS,* Sept. 13, 1934, p. 610.
An important contribution to economic history.

Guttridge, G. H. "The Whig opposition in England during the American Revolution." *JMH,* VI (1934), 1-13.

Harris, Brice. *"Letters to C------W." MLN,* XLIX (1934), 46-47.

On Judge Edmund Warcup of Popish-Plot fame.

Hartmann, Cyril Hughes. *Charles II and Madame.* London: Heinemann, 1934. Pp. xxii+414.

Rev. in *TLS,* Nov. 1, 1934, p. 745.
Edition of the correspondence between Charles II and his sister.

Hay, Malcolm V. *The Jesuits and the Popish Plot.* London: Kegan Paul, 1934. Pp. xii+220.

Rev. in *TLS,* March 22, 1934, p. 209; by E. S. de Beer in *History,* XIX (1934), 282-83.

Hay, Malcolm V. *Winston-Churchill and James II of England.* London: Harding and More, 1934. Pp. 66.

Notice in *TLS,* April 19, 1934, p. 285.

Hill, Robert H. "Adventures in Old London." *Blackwood's,* CCXXXVI (1934), 325-42.

Calls attention to a neglected account of England by a German, J. W. von Archenholz, *England und Italien,* published in three volumes in Leipzig, 1787.

Hopkinson, M. R. *Anne of England: the biography of a great queen.* London: Constable, 1934. Pp. xvi+383.

Rev. in *TLS,* April 26, 1934, p. 293.

Humphreys, R. A. "British colonial policy and the American Revolution, 1763-1776." *History,* XIX (1934), 42-48.

A critical survey of recent scholarship on the subject.

Maycock, A. L. "The amazing story of George Psalmanasar." *Blackwood's,* CCXXXV (1934), 797-808.

Morris, Dr. Claver. *The diary of a West Country physician.* Edited by Edmund Hobhouse. London: Simpkin Marshall, 1934. Pp. 200.

Rev. in *TLS,* May 3, 1934, p. 318.
Dr. Morris lived at Wells, and his diary was kept from 1718 to 1726.

Mowat, R. B. *The age of reason—the continent of Europe in the eighteenth century.* London: Harrap, 1934. Pp. 336.

Rev. in *TLS,* July 19, 1934, p. 499.

Ogg, David. *England in the reign of Charles II.* Oxford: Clarendon press, 1934. Vol. I, pp. xiv+388; vol. II, pp. vii+389-771.

Rev. in *TLS,* Oct. 11, 1934, pp. 681-82.

Oldham, C. E. A. W. "The Scattergood papers." *TLS,* Nov. 29, 1934, p. 856.

These papers, copies of which are now available in the British Museum and the Record Office, are valuable for the history of commerce and trade in the early eighteenth century.

Oliver, F. S. *The endless adventure.* Vol. III. London: Macmillan, 1934. Pp. vii+241.

Rev. in *TLS,* Jan. 17, 1935, pp. 25-26.
The concluding volume of a brilliant study of the politics of Walpole.

Paget, John. *The new Examen.* With a critical introduction by Winston C. Churchill. Halifax: Haworth press, 1934. Pp. xv+236.

Rev. in *TLS,* March 8, 1934, p. 157.

A reprint of a critical examination of Macaulay's *History* which first appeared in volume form in 1861.

Selley, W. T. *England in the eighteenth century.* London: Black, 1934. Pp. viii+406.

Rev. in *TLS,* July 19, 1934, p. 499.

Stirk, S. D. *Die Aristokratie und die industrielle Entwicklung in England vom 16. bis zum 18. Jahrhundert.* (Sprache und Kultur der germanischen und romanischen Völker, Reihe A, Band 15.) Breslau: Priebatsch, 1934. Pp. 109.

The Torrington diaries, containing the tours through England and Wales of the Hon. John Byng (later Fifth Viscount Torrington) between the years 1781 and 1794. Edited with an introduction by C. Bruyn Andrews, and with a general introduction by John Beresford. London: Eyre and Spottiswoode, 1934. Vol. I. Pp. liii+382.

Rev. in *TLS,* August 30, 1934, pp. 581-82.

Trevelyan, George Macaulay. *England under Queen Anne.* Vol. III. *The peace and the Protestant succession.* London: Longmans, 1934. Pp. xx+383.

Rev. in *TLS,* March 15, 1934, pp. 169-70; by Violet Barbour in *AHR,* XL (1934), 123-25; by William Thomas Morgann in *JMH,* VI (1934), 192-94; by N. Sykes in *EHR,* L (1934), 149-53.

Uffenbach, Z. C. von. *London in 1710: from the travels of Z. C. von Uffenbach.* Edited by W. H. Quarrell and M. Mare. London: Faber and Faber, 1934. Pp. 194.

Rev. in *TLS,* March 29, 1934, pp. 221-22.

Werth, Fritz. "Volksbildungsarbeit der englischen Kirche im Zeitalter der Aufklärung." *Herrig's Archiv,* LXIV (1933), 200-209.

III. CURRENTS OF IDEAS AND LITERARY FORMS.

Aubin, Robert A. "Materials for a study of the influence of *Cooper's Hill.*" *ELH,* I (1934), 197-204.

Aubin, Robert A. "Grottoes, Geology, and the Gothic revival." *SP,* XXXI (1934), 408-16.

Aubin, Robert A. "A note on the eighteenth-century Progress pieces." *MLN,* XLIX (1934), 405-07.

Aubin, Robert A. "Some eighteenth-century sonnets." *MLN,* XLIX (1934), 507-09.

Avery, Emmett L. "Dancing and pantomime on the English stage, 1700-1737." *SP,* XXXI (1934), 417-52.

Avery, Emmett L. "Two French children on the English stage, 1716-1719." *PQ,* XIII (1934), 78-82.

Baker, Ernest A. *The history of the English novel.* Vol. V. The novel of sentiment and the Gothic romance. London: Witherby, 1934. Pp. 300.

Rev. in *TLS,* July 26, 1934, p. 525.

Birnbaum, Johanna. *Die "Memoirs" um 1700: Eine Studie zur Entwicklung der realistischen Romankunst vor Richardson.* (Studien zur englischen Philologie, herausgeg. von L. Morsbach und H. Hecht. Band LXXIX.) Halle: Niemeyer, 1934. Pp. 117.

Bond, Richmond P. *English burlesque poetry, 1700-1750.* Cambridge, Mass.: Harvard University press, 1932. Cf. *PQ,* XII, 104.

Rev. by Brice Harris in *MLN,* XLIX (1934), 340-42; by Louis I. Bredvold in *JEGP,* XXXIII (1934), 308-10; by W. A. Eddy in *SP,* XXXI (1934), 494-95.

Borgman, Albert S. "The Killigrews and Mrs. Corey." *TLS,* Dec. 27, 1934, p. 921.

A document in the Record Office bearing on Restoration theatrical history.

Bredvold, Louis I. "The tendency toward Platonism in Neo-classical esthetics." *ELH,* I (1934), 91-120.

"Christmas pantomime." Leading article in *TLS,* Nov. 22, 1934, pp. 803-04.

Collier, Katharine Brownell. *Cosmogonies of our fathers: some theories of the seventeenth and the eighteenth centuries.* New York: Columbia University press, 1934. Pp. 500.

Crane, Ronald S. "Anglican apologetics and the idea of progress, 1699-1745." *MP,* XXXI (1934), 273-306; 349-82.

It has been customary to assume that the idea of progress was the peculiar property of the "philosophers" of the Enlightenment. In this extremely interesting and illuminating article, Crane shows how it was appropriated by a school of orthodox Anglican apologetics.

Crane, Ronald S. "Suggestions toward a genealogy of the 'Man of Feeling'." *ELH,* I (1934), 205-30.

In this study, which is as valuable for its full documentation as for its general ideas, Crane shows that the essential ideas of the cult of the "man of feeling" were propagated before Shaftesbury by the Anti-Puritan, anti-Stoic, and anti-Hobbesian divines of the Latitudinarian school. The article is a major contribution to the history of sentimentalism.

Creed, J. M., and Smith, J. S. B. *Religious thought in the eighteenth century, illustrated from writers of the period.* Cambridge: University press, 1934. Pp. xl+301.

Rev. in *TLS,* Jan. 3, 1935, p. 4. Cf. corr., Jan. 24, p. 48, and Jan. 31, p. 62.

Edgar, Pelham. *The art of the novel: from 1700 to the present time.* London: Macmillan, 1934. Pp. x+493.

Notice in *TLS,* Nov. 29, 1934, p. 859.

"English epigrams." Leading article in *TLS,* March 8, 1934, pp. 149-50. Corr. by George R. Hamilton and G. L. Apperson, *ibid.,* March 15, p. 194.

"The English poets." Leading article in *TLS,* Dec. 6, 1934, pp. 861-62.

Fay, C. R. *Imperial economy and its place in the formation of economic doctrine.* Oxford: Clarendon press, 1934. Pp. 151.

Rev. in *TLS,* August 23, 1934, p. 572.

"French epigrams." Leading article in *TLS,* August 2, 1934, pp. 533-34. Corr. by Kenneth B. Schofield, *ibid.,* August 16, p. 565.

Fry, Roger. *Reflections on British painting.* London: Faber and Faber, 1934. Pp. 148 and xl plates.

Rev. in *TLS,* April 12, 1934, p. 263.

Funke, Otto. *Englische Sprachphilosophie im späteren 18. Jahrhundert.* (Neu jahrsblatt der literarischen Gesellschaft Bern, Band XI.) Bern: Francke, 1934. Pp. 162.

Gatenby, E. V. "Sharawadgi." *TLS,* Feb. 15, 1934, p. 108.

An important note on the possible Japanese explanation of this word, which Sir William Temple introduced into the vocabulary of European gardening. Attention should be called to a previous explanation of it by Y. Z. Chang in *MLN,* XLV (1930), 221-24.

Gierke, Otto. *Natural law and the theory of society, 1500-1800.* Translated with an introduction by Ernest Barker. Cambridge: University press; New York: Macmillan, 1934. 2 vols. Pp. xci+423.

Rev. in *TLS,* May 17, 1934, p. 352; by Robert H. Murray in *Contemporary review,* CXLVI (1934), 500-02.

Goodman, Paul. "Neo-classicism, Platonism, and Romanticism." *Journal of philosophy,* XXXI (1934), 148-63.

Grundy, C. Reginald. *English art in the XVIIIth century.* London: The Studio, 1934. Pp. xii+82, with plates.

Notice in *TLS,* Jan. 11, 1934, p. 29.

Harvey, F. Brompton. "Methodism and the Romantic movement." *London quarterly and Holborn review,* July 1934, pp. 289-302.

Henn, T. R. *Longinus and English criticism.* Cambridge: University press, 1934. Pp. 163.

Rev. in *TLS,* Jan. 17, 1935, p. 30.

Hooker, Edward Niles. "The discussion of taste from 1750 to 1770 and the new trends in literary criticism." *PMLA,* XLIX (1934), 577-92.

Hooker, Edward Niles. "The reviewers and the new criticism, 1754-1770." *PQ,* XIII (1934), 189-202.

In these articles Hooker has studied two phases of literary criticism in two decades which are usually regarded as of crucial importance in the change from classical to romantic taste. He has attempted to discover how contemporaries reacted to the new ideas. In general, the reviewers seem already to have accepted them very placidly. The writers on "taste" were arguing on behalf of the validity of standards of literary judgment, but by their variety of explanations they became mutually destructive and their net result was really to undermine standards. Both articles tend to discountenance the notion that there was any abrupt turning towards romantic ideas at this time.

Hornbeak, Katherine Gee. *The complete letter-writer in English, 1568-1800.* (Smith College studies in modern languages, Vol. XV, nos. 3-4.) Northampton: Smith College, 1934. Pp. xii+150.

Hughes, Merritt Y. "Zeitgeist and style: an apology for Heinrich Wölfflin against Martin Schütze." *Sewanee review,* XLII (1934), 482-91.

Interesting discussion of the applicability of Wölfflin's theories of art history to the province of poetry.

Jones, Howard Mumford. "American prose style: 1700-1770." *The Huntington Library bulletin,* no. vi (1934), 115-51.

Ordination sermons prove a surprisingly fertile source for the history of changing taste in prose style.

Koch, G. Adolf. *Republican religion: the American Revolution and the cult of reason.* New York: Henry Holt, 1933. Pp. xvi+334.

Rev. by H. H. Clark in *Journal of philosophy,* XXXI (1934), 135-38; by Gilbert Chinard in *AHR,* XL (1934), 143-45.

Leech, Clifford. "A Restoration touring company." *TLS,* May 31, 1934, p. 392.

McManaway, James G. "Philip Massinger and the Restoration drama." *ELH,* I (1934), 276-304.

Meissner, Paul. *Die geistesgeschichtlichen Grundlagen des englischen Literaturbarocks.* Munich: Max Hueber, 1934. Pp. x+292.

Meissner's book is interesting chiefly as the most elaborate attempt that has yet been made to interpret the seventeenth century in England according to the historical method known familiarly in Germany as "Geistesgeschichte."

As the name suggests, what distinguishes this type of history is primarily the fact that it is concerned, not with tracing causal sequences in human affairs, but rather with delimiting ages and characterizing the peculiar "Geist"—the Platonic idea—of each. Its aim, in Spengler's language, is the morphology of epochs, not the explanatory narrative of what has taken place; the facts obtained by research are significant for it rather as examples of the prevailing "spirit" than as happenings to be understood in terms of their antecedents and consequences. Its method is essentially the method of analogy: negative analogy in so far as it tends to emphasize the differences between a given age and other ages and to forget the likenesses; positive analogy in so far as it tends to emphasize the likenesses among the happenings or productions of a particular period and to forget the differences. Starting with the assumption that, as Meissner puts it, "jede Epoche hat ihre besondere Struktur" (p. 281), the "Geisteswissenschaftler" seeks first to discover a formula which will express the peculiar structure of the age he is dealing with and then proceeds, by means of the kind of insight which detects similarities in the midst of apparent differences, to apply this constant term in the interpretation of all the diverse and changing activities which fall within the years in question. His success is obviously in proportion to the number of particular events or productions which his formula enables him to unify; but since that formula, before it can be applied, must be made explicit in words, it follows that its use in illuminating the various manifestations of any given epoch must inevitably involve a degree of ambiguity in statement that will vary directly with the range of phenomena the formula is made to cover.

The specific task which Meissner has set himself is to differentiate the English seventeenth century from the centuries which preceded and followed it by diagnosing all the noteworthy happenings in its social, political, religious, intellectual, and literary life as so many symptoms of a profound inner conflict of antithetical tendencies. "Auf allen Gebieten," he remarks, "macht sich ein dualistischer Zeitgeist, ein 'antithetisches Lebensgefühl' . . . bemerkbar" (p. 8). It is this dualism, so strikingly in contrast (as he imagines) with the unity of the Renaissance on the one hand and of the Enlightenment on the other, that constitutes for him the essential meaning of the expression "Barock" which, in common with nearly all contemporary German students of the seventeenth century, he finds it necessary to use in characterizing the period. The dualism, as he expounds it through the six long chapters into which his book is divided, appears, at first glance, to take on several not very clearly related forms: "Expansion und Konzentration," "Makrokosmos und Mikrokosmos," "Sünde und Erlösung," "Glaube und Vernunft," "Absolutismus und Demokratie," "Atektonischer und Tektonischer Stil." Meissner, however, is too adept in the methods of the historical school to which he belongs not to have succeeded in reducing this seeming pluralism of antitheses to the unity so greatly prized by all true practitioners of "Geistesgeschichte"; and it turns out, on closer examination, that the fundamental terms of his "Barockdualismus" are those suggested in the title of his opening chapter: what characterizes the seventeenth century for him is in the final analysis the constancy through all the forms of its culture of the opposition "Expansionsgeist-Konzentrationswille."

Of his success in finding examples of these conflicting qualities in the speculative and practical activities of the period there can be little question. He has been fortunate in being able to draw freely upon a wide knowledge both of the original sources and of the writings of modern scholars; but it is not so much at Meissner's learning that one marvels in perusing these pages as at his extraordinary ingenuity—worthy of a countryman of Spengler—in discovering the analogies without which "Geistesgeschichte" is impossible. He is never at a loss, even when the exhibition of a likeness between different orders of facts within the period can be accomplished only at the expense of what would appear to an ordinary mind to be downright equivocation. It is doubtful, indeed, whether the analogizing type of history has ever been more richly exemplified—Spengler, of course, apart—than in the pages in which Meissner enumerates the symptoms of what he calls the seventeenth-century "will to concentration." The list is one of which any "Geisteswissenschaftler" might well be proud: Hobbes's theory of the absolutist state; the Covenanting movement in Scotland; the various coalitions against France; the emergence of the custom of dressing soldiers in uniform; the rise of mercantilist economics; the development of joint-stock companies; the popularity of books giving rules for the use of one's time; the flourishing of studies "concentrated" on man's body and mind (in contrast to those "expanded" to a contemplation of the solar system and the fixed stars); the plain style of prose recommended by the leaders of the Royal Society; etc., etc. Nor is he any less happy in finding examples of the complementary "spirit of expansion." Was it not an age of increasing travel, of the founding of overseas colonies, of the multiplication of journals; an age which held knowledge in honor and looked forward to its indefinite enlargement; an age in which Milton and others wrote sentences which by their length suggest inevitably the comment that "der Expansionsgeist der Zeit sei hier stilschöpferisch geworden" (p. 261)?

All this is of course illuminating in the extreme. And the effect of reading Meissner's book would certainly be to shake one's belief in any other conception of history than the new German "Geistesgeschichte" were it not for two disturbing reflections that persist in recurring to one's mind. Would it not be possible, by using the same analogizing devices, to write the history of any other century—the fourteenth, the sixteenth, the eighteenth, the nineteenth, for example—in terms of the identical structure of antithetical qualities which Meissner has revealed so successfully in the seventeenth? And—an even more sobering thought—would there be any insuperable difficulty in composing a book on the seventeenth century which, while making use of all the "facts" here stated, would discover their "meaning" in an entirely different pattern of ideas?

—R. S. C.

Miller, Frances Schouler. "Cherry-Pit." *TLS,* Dec. 27, 1934, p. 921.

An eighteenth century borrowing from Herrick.

Newton, Theodore F. M. "The mask of Heraclitus: a problem in Restoration journalism." *Harvard studies and notes in philology and literature,* XVI (1934), 145-60.

In this study of *Heraclitus Ridens,* the Tory paper of 1681-82, Newton advances Edward Rawlins as the editor, with Flatman and others as contributors.

Nicoll, Allardyce. "In search of the theatre: material for the Yale collection." *Theatre arts monthly,* XVIII (1934), 860-69.

The importance of engravings as a source of information regarding the history of the art of the theatre.

Nicoll, Allardyce. "Mr. T. S. Eliot and the revival of Classicism." *English journal,* XXIII (1934), 269-78.

Peardon, Thomas Preston. *The transition in English historical writing, 1760-1830.* New York: Columbia University press, 1933. Pp. 340.

Rev. by Shelby T. McCloy in *JMH,* VI (1934), 332-33; by Fr. Meinecke in *Historische Zeitschrift,* Dec., 1934, pp. 118-20.

Rhodes, R. Crompton. *"The Mummer's Play."* *TLS,* Jan. 25, 1934, p. 60.

Richter, Walter. *Der Hiatus im englischen Klassizismus* (*Milton, Dryden, Pope*). (Freiburg diss.) Schramberg: Gatzer & Hahn, 1934. Pp. 139.

Rogers, Winfield H. "The reaction against melodramatic sentimentality in the English novel, 1796-1830." *PMLA,* XLIX (1934), 98-122.

Rolfe, Franklin P. "Seventeenth century prose fiction." *PMLA,* XLIX (1934), 1071-86.

Sharp, Robert Lathrop. "Some light on Metaphysical obscurity and roughness." *SP,* XXXI (1934), 497-518.

Sharp, Robert Lathrop. "The pejorative use of *Metaphysical.*" *MLN,* XLIX (1934), 503-05.

Smith, Preserved. *A history of modern culture.* Vol. II. *The Enlightenment, 1687-1776.* London: Routledge; New York: Henry Holt, 1934. Pp. vii+703.

Rev. in *TLS,* Dec, 27. 1934, p. 914; by James Harvey Robinson in *AHR,* XL (1934), 126-28; by John Herman Randall, Jr., in *JMH,* VI (1934), 458-59.

Stoll, Elmer Edgar. "The Beau Monde at the Restoration." *MLN,* XLIX (1934), 425-32.

Summers, Montague. "Betterton and Mrs. Barry in *Hamlet.*" *TLS,* March 29, 1934, p. 229; corr. by C. K. Adams, April 5, p. 244.

Summers, Montague. *The Restoration theatre.* London: Kegan Paul, 1934. Pp. xxi+352.

Rev. in *TLS,* March 29, 1934, p. 227.

Thorp, Willard (ed.). *Songs from the Restoration theatre.* Princeton: University press, 1934. Pp. 138.

Turberville, A. S. (ed.). *Johnson's England.* An account of the life and manners of his age. Oxford: Clarendon press, 1933. Cf. *PQ,* XIII (1934), 102.

Rev. by Samuel C. Chew in *Books,* Jan. 28, 1934, p. 8; by Richmond P. Bond in *Virginia quarterly review,* X (1934), 302-07; by W. T. Laprade in *AHR,* XL (1934), 128-29; by Ronald S. Crane in *New Republic,* LXXIX (1934), 216; by Frederick A. Pottle in *Yale review,* XXIII (1934), 609-11.

Vines, Sherard. *Georgian satirists.* London: Wishart, 1934. Pp. 217.

Rev. in *TLS,* May 10, 1934, p. 339.

The twentieth volume of the Walpole Society, 1932. Pp. xv+160 and viii plates. *The twenty-first volume of the Walpole Society, 1933.* Pp. xi+109 and xlviii plates. Oxford: Printed for the Walpole Society at the University press.

These volumes continue the publication of the manuscript note-books of George Vertue, one of the main sources for the history of British art.

Warren, Austin. "The reputation of Crashaw in the seventeenth and eighteenth centuries." *SP,* XXXI (1934), 385-407.

Whiting, George W. "A Whig reference to *Paradise Lost.*" *TLS,* June 7, 1934, p. 408.

Whiting, George W. "A late seventeenth century Milton plagarism." *SP,* XXXI (1934), 37-50.

Whiting, George W. "*The Temple of Dullness* and other interludes." *RES,* X (1934), 206-11.

Whitney, Lois. *Primitivism and the idea of progress in English popular literature of the eighteenth century.* Baltimore: The Johns Hopkins press, 1934. Pp. xx+343.

Rev. by Louis I. Bredvold in *JMH,* VI (1934), 498-99; by C[harner] M[arquis] P[erry] in *International journal of ethics* XLV (1934), 122-23; by H[arold] A. L[arrabee] in *Journal of philosophy,* XXXI (1934), 579-80.

Willey, Basil. *The seventeenth century background.* Studies in the thought of the age in relation to poetry and religion. London: Chatto and Windus, 1934. Pp. viii+315.

Rev. in *TLS,* April 19, 1934, pp. 269-70; by M. H. Arré in *Mind,* XLIII (1934), 405-06.

Williamson, George. "The Libertine Donne." *PQ,* XIII (1934), 276-91.

Some very interesting discussion of the relation of Donne to later thought in the seventeenth century.

Wright, Louis B. "The reading of plays during the Puritan revolution." *The Huntington Library bulletin,* no. 6 (1934), 73-108.

IV. INDIVIDUAL AUTHORS

Joseph Addison

Boddy, Margaret P. "Burton in the eighteenth century." *N & Q,* CLVII (1934), 206-08.

Borrowings in the *Tatler* and *Spectator.*

Garrison, Fielding H. "Medicine in the *Tatler, Spectator, and Guardian.*" *Bulletin of the Institute of the History of Medicine,* II (1934), 477-512.

Legouis, Pierre. "Marvell and Addison." *RES,* X (1934), 447-50.

Parsons, C. O. "Mr. Addison's official style." *N & Q,* CLVI (1934), 80.

Jane Austen

Hogan, Charles Beecher. "Pride and Prejudice." *TLS,* Nov. 1, 1934, p. 755.

Husbands, H. Winifred. "*Mansfield Park* and *Lovers' Vows*: a reply." *MLR,* XXIX (1934), 176-79.

Criticism of article by E. M. Butler in *MLR,* XXVIII (1934), 326-37; cf. *PQ,* XIII, 113.

Lascelles, Mary. "Miss Austen and some books." *LM,* XXIX (1934), 527-39.

On Jane Austen's reading.

Rawlence, Guy. *Jane Austen.* London: Duckworth, 1934. Pp. 144.

Notice in *TLS,* April 19, 1934, p. 285.

Rhydderch, David. "The first person singular in Jane Austen." *TLS,* Nov. 15, 1934, p. 795.

Roberts, W. "*Jane Austen and Mrs. Sherwood.*" *TLS,* Nov. 8, 1934, p. 780.

Steuart, A. Francis. "Jane Austen's men." *TLS,* August 16, 1934, p. 565.

Tallmadge, Abby L. "Jane Austen: resemblances." *TLS,* Jan. 4, 1934, p. 12.

Joseph Beaumont

Memoirs of Joseph Beaumont, Master of Peterhouse, 1663-1699, Regius Professor of Divinity in the University of Cambridge, 1674. Annotated by Thomas Alfred Walker. Cambridge: University press, 1934. Pp. viii+12.

Notice in *TLS,* Sept. 20, 1934, p. 639.

Aphra Behn

Platt, Harrison Gray. "Astrea and Celadon: an untouched portrait." *PMLA,* XLIX (1934), 544-59.

A new theory regarding Mrs. Behn's visit to Surinam.

George Berkeley

Datta, D. M. "The objective idealism of Berkeley." *Monist,* XLIII (1933), 220-35.

Jessop, T. E. *A bibliography of George Berkeley.* With an inventory of Berkeley's manuscript remains by A. A. Luce. New York: Oxford University press, 1934. Pp. xvi+100.

Rev. by R. J. Aaron in *Mind,* XLIV (1935), 105-07.

Kantonen, T. A. "The influence of Descartes on Berkeley." *Philosophical review,* XLIII (1934), 483-500.

Luce, A. A. *Berkeley and Malebranche.* A study in the origins of Berkeley's thought. Oxford: University press, 1934. Pp. xii+214.

Rev. in *TLS,* Nov. 29, 1934, p. 850.

Oertel, Hans Joachim. *George Berkeley und die englische Literatur.* (Studien zur englischen Philologie, herausgeg. von L. Morsbach und H. Hecht. LXXX.) Halle-Saale: Niemeyer, 1934. Pp. 146.

William Blake

Poetical sketches. By W. B. London, Printed in the year, 1783. New York: Published for the Facsimile Text Society by Columbia University press, 1934. Pp. 70.

Birss, J. H. "Herman Melville and Blake." *N & Q,* CLXVI (1934), 311.

Rasmussen, E. "Blakes rævolusjonäre forkynnerperiode." *Edda,* 1933.

On Swedenborg and Blake's revolutionary prophetic books.

James Boswell

(See also *Samuel Johnson*)

Boswell's Life of Johnson. Together with Boswell's Journal of a Tour to the Hebrides and Johnson's Diary of a Journey into North Wales. Edited by George Birkbeck Hill. Revised and enlarged edition by L. F. Powell. Vol. I, The Life, 1709-1765. Pp. xlv+556. Vol. II, The Life, 1766-1776. Pp. 543. Vol. III, The Life, 1776-1780. Pp. 541. Vol. IV, The Life, 1780-1784. Pp. 557. Oxford: Clarendon press, 1934.

Rev. in *TLS,* June 28, 1934, pp. 449-50.

This standard work, which has long been out of print, is now again available in a much improved form, due to the years of labor bestowed upon it by the Librarian of the Taylor Institution. Two more volumes will be published to complete the set.

Esdaille, Arundell. "Boswell in his diaries." *Library association record,* Feb. 1934, pp. 34-40.

Roberts, W. "Hoppner and Porteus." *TLS,* July 5, 1934, p. 476.

Thomas Brown

Boyce, Benjamin. "The life and works of Thomas Brown, 1663-1704." *Harvard University summaries of theses, 1933,* pp. 278-81.

Sir Thomas Browne

Chalmers, Gordon Keith. "Sir Thomas Browne's thought and its relation to contemporary ideas." *Harvard University summaries of theses, 1933,* pp. 281-84.

John Bunyan

The pilgrim's progress . . . London . . . 1678. New York: Published for the Fascimile Text Society by Columbia University press, 1934. Pp. 242.

Quarder, Edeltraut. *Das Steigerungsphänomen im Stil John Bunyans.* Breslau, diss. (Teildruck). Pp. 54.

Scholes, Percy A. "Bunyan's flute." *TLS,* Jan. 11, 1934, p. 28.

Tindall, William York. *John Bunyan, mechanick preacher.* New York: Columbia University press, 1934. Pp. xii+309.

Wehrsig, George. *John Bunyans Pilgrims Progress als Erziehungsbuch.* Breslau, diss. Pp. 77.

Edmund Burke

Bryant, Donald C. "Edmund Burke's opinions of some orators of his day." *Quarterly journal of speech,* XX (1934), 241-54.

Einandi, Mario. "The British background of Burke's political philosophy." *Political science quarterly,* Dec. 1934, pp. 576-98.

Jensen, Harro de Wet. "Das konservative Welt- und Staatsbild Edmund Burkes." *Anglia,* LVIII (1934), 155-224; 225-91.

Jensen presents "eine sprachwissenschaftliche und geisteswissenschaftliche Untersuchung" (p. 160), in which the semantic study serves as the basis for the treatment of Burke's thought. In blending these two aims, the latter suffers somewhat in the handling of the former. For example, in his discussion of the word *nature,* he includes all the meanings he finds, some of which have no special significance (e. g., p. 203). Furthermore he handicaps himself by considering Burke's language and thought *in vacuo*: "Die vorliegende Untersuchung hat im wesentlichen versucht, Burke aus sich selbst heraus zu verstehen,, ohne grosse Rücksichtnahme auf Vorgänger und Zeitgenossen" (p. 286). Instead of a description of Burke's intellectual *milieu,* he offers analyses and definitions of such words as *nature* from the *OED.* But a dictionary spanning 700 years can not furnish adequate patterns for an exposition of the ideas conveyed by Burke's use of abstract terms. It is partly his lack of historical perspective which underlies the following generalization: "Mit dem Konservativen ist das Organische unlösbar verknüpft. Das organische Denken eignet—um nur einige wenige Beispiele zu geben—Goethe, Moeller van den Bruck und Hitler, Shakespeare, Burke und Galsworthy, eignet den Deutschen und den Engländern in besonderem Masse, es ist eine Eigentümlichkeit germanischen Wesens" (p. 161).

While the student of Burke will be grateful to Jensen for making readily accessible many references to *nature, natural,* and *law of nature,* his treatment exaggerates the rôle of these terms in Burke's thought. The sense of *nature* which is most important for Burke is that of empirical reality, i. e. the whole range of man's actual or potential sensory experience. Jensen includes this meaning (pp. 186-8), but he perceives neither its historical antecedents nor its implications. To follow *nature* for Burke means to act in accordance with the facts, i. e. in accordance with human experience (e. g., *Reflections on the Revolution in France* in *Works* (Boston, 1871), III, 274-6). *Natural* means in accordance with the facts of experience or of human nature (e. g., *ibid.*, p. 337). And for Burke the laws of nature are not, as Jensen supposes, laws imposed on nature or on man by nature, but laws descriptive of constant action, of invariable cause and effect sequence, observable in nature (see Jensen, pp. 183-4). Burke was of course preoccupied with the facts, i. e. truth gained through experience, and *nature* for him was not a particularly fundamental or necessary abstraction, in spite of his frequent lip service to the shibboleth of the Enlightenment. In missing this, Jensen has failed to grasp one of the most significant aspects of Burke's thought, namely his desertion of nature in favor of utility and of art, i. e. the man-made as a means of attaining utilitarian ends (see *Reflections,* p. 276 and p. 310, and *Appeal from the New to the Old Whigs* in *Works,* IV, 176).

Another assumption Jensen makes he states by way of a conclusion: "Die vorliegende Untersuchung zeigt—und das ist das Neue, was sie Bringen will—die *organische Einheit* des Burkeschen Welt- und Staatsbildes . . . " (p. 162). Although he admits that Burke does not present a systematic scheme of political and moral philosophy, he assumes that the fragments of such a system lie scattered through Burke's writings. The inference (which he follows in practice) is that Burke's every phrase was consciously tested before utterance for logical consistency. Yet this would be too much to claim of the most systematic philosopher. To arrange Burke's thought into an "organische Einheit" is to obscure rather than clarify it.—H. V. S. O.

Charles and Fanny Burney

(See *Samuel Johnson* and *Hester Lynch Thrale*)

Robert Burns

Brown, Everett S. "The political ideas of Robert Burns." *Papers of the Michigan Academy of Science, Arts and Letters,* XIX (1934), 477-91.

Burns chronicle and club directory. Second series, Vol. IX. Kilmarnock: The Burns Federation, 1934. Pp. vi+202.

Because of its publication of original materials and reprints of outstanding articles, the *Burns Chronicle* is indispensable to students of the life and writings of Robert Burns. There are several noteworthy articles in the current volume. "A guide to Burns literature," by J. C. Ewing, gives the locations of eight collections of the writings of Burns and describes the new catalogue of the Burns Collection in the Mitchell Library at Glasgow. "Burns and the capture of the Rosamond," by Henry L. Meikle, throws new light on the part Burns played in the capture of the smuggling vessel, a much controverted event in the life of the poet. This article is based on manuscripts found in the Abbotsford Collection, now being catalogued in the National Library of Scotland. "Correspondence of John Syme and Alexander Cunningham, 1789-1811," is the first installment of a correspondence which forms a notable addition to our knowledge of Burns's life.—E. S. B.

Ferguson, J. DeLancey. "Maria Riddell's sketch of Burns." *PQ,* XIII (1934), 261-66.

A study of the text, of which four versions are extant, including the proof-sheets.

Ferguson, J. DeLancey. "Burns's journal of his Border-tour." *PMLA,* XLIX (1934), 1107-15.

Gray, W. Forbes. "The 'discoverer' of Burns." *Cornhill,* CXLIX (1934), 26-35.

Fraser-Harris, D. F. "Burns as a writer of prose." *Dalhousie review,* XIV (1934), 203-13.

Hill, Rev. John C. *The life and work of Robert Burns in Irvine.* London: Lincoln Williams, 1934. Pp. 91.

Notice in *TLS,* Feb. 8, 1934, p. 94.

Murdoch, M. M. (ed.). *Familiar links with Robert Burns.* A selection of Burnsiana from the writings of the late John Mitchell Murdoch. Ayr: Stephen and Pollock, 1934.

Thomas Chatterton

Meyerstein, E. H. W. "A satirical eclogue by Chatterton." *TLS,* July 12, 1934, p. 488.

Meyerstein, E. H. W. "An elegy on Chatterton." *TLS,* Feb. 8, 1934, p. 92.

George Colman

Vincent, Howard Paton. "The life and writings of George Colman the Younger." *Harvard University summaries of theses, 1933,* 302-04.

William Congreve

The way of the world. Edited, with an introduction and explanatory notes, by W. P. Barret. (Temple Dramatists.) London: Dent, 1934.

Norris, Edward T. "A possible source of Congreve's Sailor Ben." *MLN,* XLIX (1934), 334-35.

Abraham Cowley

Sparrow, J. H. A. "The text of Cowley's satire *The Puritan and the Papist.*" *Anglia,* LVIII (1934), 78-102.

Wiley, Autrey N. "The prologue and epilogue to *The Guardian.*" *RES,* X (1934), 443-47.

William Cowper

Povey, Kenneth. "Notes on Cowper's letters. III." *RES,* X (1934), 76-78.

Povey, Kenneth. "Cowper and Lady Austen." *RES,* X (1934), 417-27.

Richard Cumberland

Fletcher, Ifan Kyrle. "Cumberland's *The Princess of Parma.*" *TLS,* March 15, 1934, p. 187.

Sir William Davenant

Laig, Friederich. *Englische und französische Elemente in Sir William Davenants dramatischer Kunst.* Emsdetten: H. und J. Lechte, 1934. Pp. 133.

Richardson, W. R. "Sir William Davenant as American colonizer." *ELH,* I (1934), 61-62.

Daniel Defoe

Burch, Charles Eaton. "Defoe's British reputation, 1869-1894." *ES,* LXVIII (1934), 410-23.

Fletcher, E. G. "Some notes on Defoe's *Review.*" *N & Q,* CLXVI (1934), 218-21.

Fletcher, E. G. "Defoe and the theatre." *PQ,* XIII (1934), 382-89.

Graham, Walter. "Defoe's *Review* and Steele's *Tatler*—the question of influence." *JEGP,* XXXIII (1934), 250-54.

M., A. R. L. "Daniel Defoe's descendants." *N & Q,* CLXVI (1934), 350-51.

Röhnsch, Martha. *Defoes Stellung zu den religiösen Strömungen seiner Zeit.* Breslau diss., 1933. Pp. 108.
Rev. by Paul Dottin in *ES,* LXIX (1934), 264-66.

Sutherland, James R. "A note on the last years of Defoe." *MLR,* XXIX (1934), 137-41.

Important biographical information from Chancery bills in the Record Office.

John Dennis

Hooker, Edward N. "An unpublished autograph manuscript of John Dennis." *ELH,* I (1934), 156-62.

A manuscript in the Folger Library, from which an extract was printed in the *Monthly Magazine* for June, 1817, but which since then had apparently disappeared. Hooker traces its history and gives some account of its contents.

John Dryden

Bredvold, Louis I. *The intellectual milieu of John Dryden.* Studies in some aspects of seventeenth-century thought. Ann Arbor: University of Michigan press, 1934. Pp. viii+189.

Notice in *TLS,* Jan. 24, 1935, p. 50.

Brennecke, Ernest. "Dryden's odes to Draghi's music." *PMLA,* XLIX (1934), 1-36.

Chester, Allan Griffith. "Dryden and Thomas May." *TLS,* July 19, 1934, p. 511.

"Dryden a hymnodist?" *TLS,* April 12, 1934, p. 258.

Ham, Roswell G. "Dryden and the colleges." *MLN,* XLIX (1934), 324-32.

Hooker, Edward Niles. "The Dryden almanac story." *PQ,* XIII (1934), 295.

Thomas D'Urfey

Day, Cyrus Lawrence. *The songs of Thomas D'Urfey.* Cambridge, Mass.: Harvard University press, 1934. Pp. x+168.

Rev. in *TLS,* March 1, 1934, p. 141; by H. J. Byrom in *RES,* X (1934), 470-71.

John Evelyn

Engel, Claire-Eliane. "John Evelyn et le Protestantisme français." *Bulletin de la Société du Protestantisme français,* LXXXIII (1934), 29-48.

Sir George Etherege

Rosenfeld, Sybil. "Sir George Etherege in Ratisbon." *RES,* X (1934), 177-89.

Based on papers newly acquired by the British Museum among the papers of the Earl of Middleton, Secretary of State under James II.

Sir Adam Ferguson

Letters of George Dempster to Sir Adam Ferguson, 1756-1813. With some account of his life. Edited by James Ferguson. London: Macmillan, 1934. Pp. xxviii+364.

Rev. in *TLS,* Sept. 27, 1934, p. 647.

Henry Fielding

Avery, Emmett L. "An early performance of Fielding's *Historical Register.*" *MLN,* XLIX (1934), 407.

Beatty, Richard Croom. "Criticism in Fielding's narratives and his estimate of critics." *PMLA,* XLIX (1934), 1087-1100.

Fischer, Hildegard. *Das subjektive Element in den Romanen Fieldings.* Ohlau: Eschenhagen, 1933. Pp. 84.

David Garrick

Babler, Otto F. "Two letters of David Garrick." *N & Q,* CLXVI (1934), 367.

MacMillan, Dugald. "David Garrick as critic." *SP,* XXXI (1934), 69-83.

Stone, George Winchester. "Garrick's long lost alteration of *Hamlet.*" *PMLA,* XLIX (1934), 890-921.

John Gay

Loiseau, J. "John Gay et le *Beggar's Opera.*" *RAA,* XII (1934), 3-19.

Edward Gibbon

"Remnant of Gibbon's library." *TLS,* Dec. 27, 1934, p. 924.

Oliver Goldsmith

The deserted village, a poem. By Dr. Goldsmith. London, W. Griffin, 1770. New York: Published for the Facsimile Text Society by Columbia University press, 1934. Pp. vii+22.

The citizen of the world and The Bee. Introduction by Richard Church. London: Dent, 1934. Pp. xx+452.

Rev. in *TLS,* March 1, 1934, pp. 133-34; by Frederick T. Wood in *ES,* LXIX (1934), 125.

de Blacam, Hugh. "The Madan family and Goldsmith." *TLS,* Feb. 1, 1934, p. 76.

Crane, R. S. "Goldsmith and Justus Van Effen." *TLS,* March 1, 1934, p. 144.

Crane, R. S. "A neglected mid-eighteenth-century plea for originality and its author." *PQ,* XIII (1934), 21-29.

Goldsmith is identified as the author of the discussion in the *Critical review* for January, 1760, of R. Kedington's *Critical dissertations upon the Iliad of Homer.*

"Oliver Goldsmith." Corr. by "Templar" and by S. C. Roberts in *TLS,* March 8, 1934, p. 162, and by G. S. Ritchie, *ibid.,* March 15, p. 194.

Reding, Katherine. "A study of the influence of Oliver Goldsmith's *Citizen of the World* upon the *Cartas Marruecas* of José Cadalso." *Hispanic review,* II (1934), 226-34.

Stein, Harold. "Goldsmith's translation of the *Roman Comique.*" *MLN,* XLIX (1934), 171-78.

Richard Graves

(See also *Thomas Percy* and *William Shenstone*)

Hecht, Hans. "Kleine Studien zu Graves, Shenstone und Percy." *Anglia,* LVIII (1934), 103-112, 131-154.

Thomas Gray

Micale, O. *Thomas Gray e la sua influenza sulla letteratura italiana.* Catania: Studio Editoriale moderno, 1934.

Martin, Roger. *Chronologie de la vie et de l'œuvre de Thomas Gray.* Thèse présentée à la Faculté des Lettres de l'Université de Paris, 1934. London: Humphrey Milford, Oxford University press. Pp. 199.

Martin, Roger. *Essai sur Thomas Gray.* Thèse pour le Doctorat ès Lettres présentée à la Faculté des Lettres de l'Université de Paris, 1934. London: Humphrey Milford, Oxford University press. Pp. x+458.

"En donnant à ce livre le titre d'*Essai*," we read in the preface to the second of these volumes, "j'entends m'excuser auprès du lecteur de ne pas lui apporter la monographie complète et définitive que, devant l'existence sans histoire de Gray, et devant ses cinquante pages of vers, j'avais d'abord cru pouvoir écrire." The apology seems hardly necessary: it is one of the many virtues of Martin's work that he has solved the problem of organizing the results of his researches on Gray in a manner that is at once novel among French theses for the doctorate in English literature and highly appropriate to the character of his subject. For those who may be interested in the events of Gray's very uneventful career he has established with great care, in the shorter of his two volumes, a minute and precisely documented chronology of the poet's personal life and of the writing and publication of his works (adding to this a useful analysis of the *Commonplace books* and transcriptions of several of their more significant articles); and having thus freed himself from the obligations of biography in the ordinary sense of the word, he has been able to devote the whole of his major thesis to an elaborate portrait of Gray as man and poet under four heads: "Le solitaire de Pembroke," "Les sentiments," "L'activité intellectuelle," and "Le poète."

The *Essai* is on the whole the most informing and penetrating study of its subject that has yet been written. The best parts, to my taste, are the chapters on Gray's relations with his friends, particularly Walpole, West, Mason, and Bonstetten; the long section on his feeling for nature (from the bibliography of which, however, one misses Miss Manwaring's important book on the vogue of Italian landscape painting); the two substantial chapters in Part III which deal with Gray's habits of study and the principal directions of his antiquarian tastes; and lastly the discussions, in Part IV, of Gray's Latin poems, of his somewhat rhetorical theory of poetry, and of the historical settings and technical characteristics of the lyrics by which he is best known. The difficulty in a book so long as this on an author who has been the object of so extensive a body of comment is to avoid saying the often-said and repeating the accepted evaluations. It is the great merit of Martin's study that for the most part he has brought a fresh mind to his task and has succeeded in maintaining, even on points where opinion in the past has been most nearly agreed, an unusual critical independence. He is not deceived by the extravagant things that have been written about Gray's scholarship, knowing well that there were many more learned men in Europe than the fastidious note-taker of Pembroke and many who knew how to direct their reading to more significant ends. His estimate of the poems is a sane one, less severe than Johnson's—less severe, indeed, than I for one could wish—yet quite free from the exaggerated praise of the *Elegy* and the two Pindaric odes that we have inherited from the criticism of the nineteenth century; on the old problem of the poet's "sterility" he has, it seems to me, left very little more to be said (see pp. 341 ff.). It is much to his credit, finally, that he carefully refrains from going into the tiresome and futile question—still a living issue in many academic quarters in America—of Gray's relation to those twin abstractions "classicism" and "romanticism." "Je veux indiquer seulement," he writes in his preface, "qu'à mon avis Gray ne fut jamais beaucoup plus romantique que dans son ode latine *Ad C. Favonium Aristium* écrite en 1738, et rappeler qu'en 1765 il conseillait encore aux jeunes poètes de prendre Dryden comme modèle. On comprendra aussitôt ce que je veux dire." In short, an uncommonly refreshing and intelligent treatment of a hackneyed theme.—R. S. C.

James Harrington

Koebner, Richard. *"Oceana."* *ES,* LXVIII (1934), 358-96.

"I. Harringtons Staatsidee in ihren wissenschaftlichen und politischen Motiven. II. Harrington und die Verfassungsprobleme der Französischen Revolution."

Eliza Haywood

Fletcher, E. G. "The date of Eliza Haywood's death." *N & Q,* CLXVI (1934), 385.

William Herschel

The Herschel Chronicle: the life story of William Herschel and his sister Caroline. Edited by Constance Lubbock. London and New York: Macmillan, 1934. Pp. 400.

Rev. by Gerald Wendt in *Books,* Jan. 21, 1934, p. 14, and by Harold Ward in *New Republic,* March 14, 1934, p. 138. Corr. by Constance Lubbock in *TLS,* June 28, 1934, p. 460.

Thomas Hobbes

Laird, John. *Hobbes.* London: Ernest Benn, 1934. Pp. xii+324.

Rev. in *TLS,* May 10, 1934, p. 332; by A. T. Shillinglaw in *Mind,* XLIV (1935), 75-84.

Samuel Johnson

(See also *James Boswell* and *Hester Lynch Thrale*)

Balderston, Katherine C. "Dr. Johnson and Burney's *History of music.*" *PMLA,* XLIX (1934), 966-68.

Bennett, William. *Doctor Samuel Johnson and the ladies of the Lichfield Amicable Society, 1775.* Birmingham: City of Birmingham School of Printing, 1934. Pp. 7.

Notice in *TLS,* August 16, 1934, p. 567.

Boddey, Margaret P. "Johnson and Burton." *TLS,* June 21, 1934, p. 443; also corr. by Donald C. Dorian, Sept. 13, p. 620.

Chapman, R. W. "Johnson's letters to Taylor." *TLS,* August 16, 1934, p. 565.

Chapman R. W. "Johnsonian bibliography, 1750-1765." *The Colophon,* No. xvi, 1934.

Comment by I. A. Williams in *LM,* XXX (1934), 160-62.

Chapman, R. W. "Johnson's letters." *TLS,* Dec. 6, 1934, p. 875.

Chapman, R. W. "Johnson and Burney." *RES,* X (1934), pp. 329-31.

Johnson's authorship of the dedication to Burney's *History of music.* Cf. Miss Balderston's article above.

Evans, Bergen. "Dr. Johnson's theory of biography." *RES,* x (1934), 301-10.

Hazen, A. T. "A Johnson preface." *TLS,* June 28, 1934, p. 460.

Hornberger, Theodore. "A note on the probable source of Provost Smith's famous curriculum for the College of Philadelphia." *Pennsylvania magazine of history and biography,* LVIII (1934), 370-77.

Johnson's preface to Robert Dodsley's *The Preceptor,* published in 1748.

"A Johnson exhibition." *Bodleian quarterly record,* VII (1934), 466-71.

M., R. B. "Johnson on aviation." *TLS,* March 15, 1934, p. 194.

MacKinnon, Sir Frank. "Address by Sir Frank MacKinnon, president of the Johnson Society of Lichfield, September 30, 1933." Lichfield: Reprinted from the Lichfield Times.

Notice in *TLS,* Jan. 18, 1934, p. 41.

Read, Allen Walker. "The history of Dr. Johnson's definition of *oats.*" *Agricultural History,* VIII (1934), 81-94.

A chapter in the history of lexicography that is both illuminating and amusing. The cream of the jest will be found in Murray's definition of "buck-wheat" in the New English Dictionary.

Reade, Aleyn Lyell. "Francis Barber." *TLS,* April 12, 1934, p. 262; corr. by A. Werner, April 19, p. 282.

Scott, S. H. "Dr. Johnson and Mrs. Thrale." *Nineteenth century,* CXVI (1934), 308-18.

Swanzy, T. Erskine. "Gibbon and Johnson." *TLS,* July 12, 1934, p. 492.

Nathaniel Lee

Wülker, Anton. *Shakespeares Einfluss auf die dramatische Kunst von Nathaniel Lee.* Münster diss., 1934. Pp. 64.

George, Lord Lyttelton

Rao, Amanda Vittal. *A minor Augustan: being the life and works of George, Lord Lyttelton, 1709-1773.* Calcutta: The Book Company, 1934. Pp. viii+387.

Rev. in *TLS,* Sept. 20, 1934, p. 632.

Charles Macklin

Matthews, W. "The piracies of Macklin's *Love à-la-Mode.*" *RES,* x (1934), 311-18.

Bernard Mandeville

Deckelmann, Wilhelm. *Untersuchungen zur Bienenfabel Mandevilles und zu ihrer Entstehungsgeschichte im Hinblick auf die Bienenfabelthese.* Hamburg: Friederichsen, de Gruyter & Co., 1933. Pp. 136.

Rev. by Hans Marcus in *Beiblatt,* XLIV (1934), 59-60.

Mrs. Manley

Anderson, Paul Bunyan. "Dalarivière Manley's prose fiction." *PQ,* XIII (1934), 168-88.

William Julius Mickle

West, S. George. "The work of W. J. Mickle, the first Anglo-Portuguese scholar." *RES,* X (1934), 385-400.

Arthur Murphy

Caskey, J. Homer. "The first edition of Arthur Murphy's *Sallust.*" *PQ,* XIII (1934), 404-08.

It was first published in 1795 under the pseudonym of "George Frederic Sydney."

Sir Isaac Newton

(See also *James Thomson*)

Drennon, Herbert. "Newtonianism: its method, theology, and metaphysics." *ES,* LXVIII (1934), 397-409.

More, Louis Trenchard. *Isaac Newton.* New York: Scribners, 1934. Pp. xii+675.

Rev. in *TLS,* Oct. 11, 1934, p. 684; by Chas. F. Ronayne in *American review,* IV (1934), 121-27.

John Oldham

Brooks, H. "The family of John Oldham." *N & Q,* CLXVI (1934), 30-31.

Brooks, Harold F. "John Oldham." *TLS,* July 12, 1934, p. 492.

Thomas Paine

Clark, Harry H. "An historical interpretation of T. Paine's religion." *University of California chronicle,* XXXV (1933), 56-87.

Samuel Pepys

Birss, J. H. "Books from Pepys' library." *N & Q,* CLXVI (1934), 370. Corr. by H. S. Gladstone and S. Gaselee, *ibid.*, pp. 410-11.

Bryant, Arthur. "Pepys in France." *TLS,* April 26, 1934, p. 303.

Chappell, Edwin. *Samuel Pepys as a naval administrator.* A lecture delivered to the Hull Historical Assŏciation on September 29, 1933. Cambridge: University press, 1934. Pp. 23.

Kirk, Rudolf. "Pepys and Camden's *Brittania.*" *TLS,* May 3, 1934, p. 322.

Matthews, W. "Samuel Pepys, tachygraphist." *MLR,* XXIX (1934), 397-404.

"Pronunciation of *Pepys.*" Corr. by Rupert T. Gould and others in *TLS,* Feb. 1, 1934, p. 76; Feb. 15, p. 108; Feb. 22, p. 126; March 1, p. 144; March 8, p. 162; March 15, p. 194; and May 31, p. 392.

Thomas Percy

(See also *Richard Graves*)

Brooks, Cleanth. "The history of Percy's edition of Surrey's poems." *ES,* LXVIII (1934), 424-30.

Dennis, Leah. "Percy's essay *On the Ancient Metrical Romances.*" *PMLA,* XLIX (1934), 81-97.

Hecht, H. "Th. Percy als Bearbeiter spanischer Romanzen." *Anglia,* LVIII (1934), 146-54.

Leslie, Shane. "The Percy library." *Book-Collector's quarterly,* XIV (1934), 11-24.

Marwell, Heinz. "Percy und die Ossian-Kontroverse." *Anglia,* LVIII (1934), 392-401.

Marwell, Heinz. *Thomas Percy. Studien zur Entstehungsgeschichte seiner Werke.* Göttingen, diss., 1934. Pp. 130.

Shearer, Thomas, and Tillotson, Arthur. "Percy's relations with Cadell and Davies." *Library,* XV (1934), 224-36.

Watkin-Jones, A. "Percy MSS." *TLS,* March 8, 1934, p. 162.

Alexander Pope

Ault, Norman. "Pope and the miscellanies." *Nineteenth century,* CXVI (1934), 566-80.

Beckwith, F. "Audra: 'Les traductions françaises de Pope,' 1717-1825." *MLR,* XXIX (1934), 70-72.

Additions to Audra's list.

Davies, Charles. "*The Rape of the Lock* and Evelyn's *Mundus Muliebris*—a parallel." *RES,* X (1934), 324-29.

Durham, Willard H. "Pope as poet." *Essays in criticism: second series.* By members of the Department of English, University of California. Berkeley: University of California press, 1934. Pp. 91-110.

Kroker, Joh. *Alexander Pope in der Beurteilung des 18. Jahrhunderts.* Ein Beitrag zur Geschichte der Auseinandersetzung zwischen Klassizismus und Romantik in England. Breslau, diss., 1934. Pp. 166.

Sherburn, George. *The early career of Alexander Pope, 1688-1727.* Oxford: Clarendon press, 1934. Pp. 326.

Rev. in *TLS,* Oct. 25, 1934, pp. 721-22.

A long-awaited and definitive work which will henceforth be indispensable to students of Pope.

Stevenson, Samuel W. "'Romantic' tendencies in Pope." *ELH,* I (1934), 126-55.

This essay sets out to show that Pope's classicism "was due to his remarkable adaptability rather than to his natural conformity. One cannot deny that the earlier romantic growth was natural, unforced, pursuant of its own natural bent, whereas nearly all manifestations of the neo-classic ideal may be definitely attributed to the forcing process, or at least encouragement, of outward circumstance" (p. 128). Such a statement, however, is more than likely to be denied by many competent readers of Pope. Stevenson has many interesting things to say about Pope, and his documentation is extensive. But he seems to assume throughout that the esthetic ideal of Neo-classicism is narrow, arid, and unnatural; consequently many of his judgments as to whether a tendency is "Romantic" or "Classic" do not convince us. He has, moreover, been led by his argument into some very doubtful generalizations, such as that it was due to the influence of Bolingbroke after 1725 that "Pope's poetry was henceforth confined to the satiric, the moral, and the philosophic" (p. 149).

Wright, Lawrence S. "Eighteenth-century replies to Pope's Eloisa." *SP,* XXXI (1934), 519-33.

Matthew Prior

Parsons, C. O. "Matthew Prior's extraordinaries." *N & Q,* CLXVI (1934), 148-50.

Edward Ravenscroft

Norris, Edward T. "The Italian source for Ravenscroft's *Italian Husband.*" *RES,* X (1934), 202-05.

James Robertson

Bronson, Bertrand H. "James Robertson, poet and playwright." *MLN*, XLIX (1934), 509-11.

John Wilmot, Earl of Rochester

Poetical works. Edited by Quilter Johns. London: Haworth press, 1933. Pp. xxxii+239.

Pinto, Vivian de Sola. "An unpublished poem attributed to Rochester." *TLS*, Nov. 22, 1934, p. 824.

Pinto, Vivian de S. "A poem attributed to Rochester." *TLS*, Dec. 6, 1934, p. 875.

Pinto, Vivian de S. "Rochester and the Deists." *TLS*, Dec. 13, 1934, p. 895.

"Rochester on Charles II." Corr. by George G. Loane and others in *TLS*, Oct. 4, 1934, p. 675; Oct. 18, p. 715; Oct. 25, p. 735; Nov. 1, p. 755.

Earl of Roscommon

Niemeyer, Carl. "The Earl of Roscommon's Academy." *MLN*, XLIX (1934), 432-37.

Niemeyer, Carl A. "The life and works of the Earl of Roscommon." *Harvard University summaries of theses, 1933*, pp. 290-93.

Elkanah Settle

Moss, W. E. "Elkanah Settle: the armorial binding expert." *Book-Collector's quarterly*, XIII (1934), 7-22.

Cf. "postscript," *ibid.*, pp. 91-96.

Thomas Shadwell

Epsom Wells and *The Volunteers or the Stockjobbers*. Edited by D. M. Walmsley. Boston: D. C. Heath, 1933. Pp. lxvi+387.

Rev. by J. C. Ghosh in *RES*, x (1934), 473-74.

Whitehall, H. "Thomas Shadwell and the Lancashire dialect." *Essays and studies in English and comparative literature*. Ann Arbor, University of Michigan press, 1933. Pp. 261-78.

Earl of Shaftesbury

Meinecke, F. *Shaftesbury und die Wurzeln des Historismus.* Sitzungs ber. der Preuss. Akademie des Wissenschaften. Phil.-Hist. Klasse, 1934, vii.

William Shenstone

(See also *Richard Graves* and *Thomas Percy*)

Hill, Charles J. "Shenstone and Richard Graves's *Columella.*" *PMLA,* XLIX (1934), 566-76.

Richard Brinsley Sheridan

Legouis, Pierre. "Buckingham et Sheridan: ce que le *Critique* doit à la *Répetition.*" *RAA,* XI (1934), 423-34.

Nettleton, George H. "The first edition of *The School for Scandal.*" *TLS,* Oct. 17, 1934, p. 695; corr. by M. J. Ryan, *ibid.,* Oct. 25, p. 735.

Thomas Southerne

Richardson, William R. "The life and works of Thomas Southerne." *Harvard University summaries of theses, 1933,* pp. 299-302.

Tobias Smollett

Birss, J. H. "A letter of Tobias G. Smollett." *N & Q,* CLXVI (1934), 189.

Knapp, Lewis Mansfield. "The naval scenes in *Roderick Random.*" *PMLA,* XLIX (1934), 593-98.

Sir Richard Steele

(See also *Joseph Addison*)

Connely, Willard. *Sir Richard Steele.* London: Jonathan Cape, 1934. Pp. 448.

Rev. in *TLS,* Oct. 4, 1934, p. 671; by Carl Van Doren in *Books,* Sept. 9, 1934, p. 5.

Sharp, Robert L. "Lines in *The Guardian.*" *TLS,* March 8, 1934, p. 162.

Peter Sterry

Pinto, Vivian de Sola. *Peter Sterry, Platonist and Puritan, 1613-1672.* A biographical and critical study with passages selected from his writings. Cambridge: University press, 1934. Pp. xiii+242.
Rev in *TLS,* May 17, 1934, p. 352.

Jonathan Swift

Birss, J. H. "A volume from Swift's library." *N & Q,* CLXVI (1934), 295.

Gold, Maxwell B. "Swift's admission to Mrs. Whiteway confirmed." *PMLA,* XLIX (1934), 964-65.

Gold, Maxwell B. "The Brennan affidavit." *TLS,* May 17, 1934, p. 360; corr. by Harold Williams, *ibid.,* May 24, p. 376.

Heidenhain, Adolf. *Über den Menschenhass. Eine pathographische Untersuchung über Jonathan Swift.* (Tübinger Naturwissenschaftl. Abhandlungen, Heft. 14.) Stuttgart: Ferdinand Enke, 1934.
Rev. in *TLS,* Sept. 13, 1934, p. 620; by M. A. Korn in *ES,* LXIX (1934), 120-24.

Higgins, F. T. "Swiftiana." *TLS,* August 30, 1934, p. 589, and *ibid.,* Dec. 13, p. 895.

Kirkpatrick, T. Percy C. "Faulkner's edition of Swift." *TLS,* April 12, 1934, p. 262.

Martini, Esther. *Jonathan Swift.* Rimini: tip. Garattoni, 1934. Pp. 64.

Morrison, Felix. "A note on *The Battle of the Books.*" *PQ,* XIII (1934), 16-20.

Reimers, Hans. *Jonathan Swift. Gedanken und Schriften über Religion und Kirche.* (Britannica, 9.) Hamburg: Friedrichsen, de Gruyter & Co., 1934. Pp. 194.

Webster, C. M. "Washington Irving as imitator of Swift." *N & Q,* CLXVI (1934), 295.

Nahum Tate

Scott-Thomas, H. F. "Nahum Tate and the seventeenth century." *ELH,* I (1934), 250-75.

James Thomson

Davis, Rose M. "Thomson and Voltaire's *Socrate.*" *PMLA,* XLIX (1934), 560-65.

Drennon, Herbert. "The source of James Thomson's *The Works and Wonders of Almighty Power.*" *MP,* XXXII (1934), 33-36.

Drennon, Herbert. "James Thomson's contact with Newtonianism and his interest in natural philosophy." *PMLA,* XLIX (1934), 71-80.

Drennon, Herbert. "Scientific rationalism and James Thomson's poetic art." *SP,* XXXI (1934), 453-71.

Drennon is publishing an important series of articles, begun in 1931, with one on Henry Needler and Shaftesbury (*PMLA,* XLVI, 1095-1106), on the general subject of the influence of Newtonianism on English literature and religious thought in the early eighteenth century. Under Newtonianism he includes not only the scientific discoveries of Newton, but also the efforts on the part of Newton himself as well as of his theological friends to harmonize these scientific ideas with orthodox religious thought and to deepen a religious sense of the wonders of the created world. Drennon has established beyond doubt the importance of this physico-theological influence on Thomson's interpretation of physical nature and on his art. He has shown the great probability that Thomson came under the influence of the new science while still a student at Edinburgh. And the poem *To the Memory of Sir Isaac Newton,* written in 1727, indicates the interest of Thomson in this direction at the time when he was engaged on *The Seasons.* Altogether, Drennon has made an important contribution to the history of nature poetry in the eighteenth century.

Inevitably, some of the passages in Thomson in which we have heretofore seen the influence of Shaftesbury, must now be explained as Newtonian theology; so far we may agree with Drennon. But he has in places pushed his argument too far, especially in his attempt to minimize other influences on Thomson than the Newtonian. There is no real antinomy between the philosophy of Shaftesbury and the physico-theology of the time; the celebration of nature in *The Moralists* (Part III, section I) may easily be reconciled with the arguments of the Newtonians that the existence of a Creator is deducible from the marvellous order of the universe; for that matter, these arguments were not entirely new, and were the property of others besides Newtonians. It seems unwise to assume that Thomson had to choose one set of ideas to the exclusion of the other.

In his article on Thomson's poetic art, also, Drennon pushes his argument too far He says, for instance (p. 454), that Henry Pemberton, in his introduction to *A View of Sir Isaac Newton's Philosophy* (1728), "summed up in a long passage the views of those who believe that man's desire to penetrate the mysteries of nature lies at the basis of man's taste for 'poetry, oratory, and every branch of literature and science'." Pemberton, in the passage quoted by Drennon, does not say that; he says that "our desire after knowledge is an *effect* [my italics] of that taste for the sublime and the beautiful in things, which chiefly constitutes the difference between human life, and the life of brutes." On the next page Drennon says that Addison saw clearly "the value that a study of natural philosophy had for creating in man a 'taste' for the beautiful and sublime." But in the passage quoted Addison merely says that it "quickens" and "heightens" our esthetic pleasure. In the spirit of his argument Drennon repeatedly asserts that Thomson derived his whole poetic experience of nature from his scientific interest; "Thomson observes the 'facts' with the eye of a 'philosopher' but he seldom if ever tries to catch the mood of nature" (p. 461); "Thomson's response to nature was primarily rationalistic" (p. 463); "when he seeks to get behind the veil, it is to discover the mechanical laws in operation there" (p. 466). Drennon has here put his finger on a very important aspect of

Thomson's poetry, but he has erred in trying to ascribe Thomson's ***whole*** poetic experience to science. In his Preface to the second edition of *Winter* Thomson himself declares that he is following, in his choice of subject, the traditions of the best poets, both ancient and modern, and he says not a word about modern science. All nature poets have tried in some way or other to "catch the mood of nature," and Thomson is no exception; in the opening of *Winter,* for instance, this attempt is more than evident, it is successful; there is mood in "kindred glooms, cogenial horrors"; "trod the pure virgin-snows, myself as pure," is almost Wordsworthian. Or we may take a brilliant example from *The Castle of Indolence*:

> A pleasing land of drowsyhed it was:
> Of dreams that wave before the half-shut eye;
> And of gay castles in the clouds that pass,
> For ever flushing round a summer sky.

Thomson's poetic gifts are obviously not to be derived exclusively from his scientific thought; it would be better to state that his immediate poetic enjoyment of nature was *modified,* or perhaps *overlaid,* by his Newtonianism.

As to the question of Needler's interest in Shaftesbury, attention might be called to a letter by Needler which has not hitherto figured in the discussion. C. A. Moore and Drennon have both discussed the letter from Needler to W. Duncombe, dated December 3, 1711, in which Needler acknowledges the gift of "the fine *Philosophical Meditation* of my Lord Shaftesbury." Does this language imply more than a casual acquaintance with a fragment from *The Moralists,* perhaps copied, as Drennon suggests, into the letter? However, on December 8, Duncombe wrote from London another letter on the question as to whether the manifestations of instinct in animals is to be regarded as evidence that the souls of brutes "are nothing but an efflux, or emanation, from the Deity." He notes that Ralphson had attacked certain philosophers who held such doctrines. He gives, as one reason for transcribing the passage from Ralphson, "that I might not be thought too severe in saying, that if lord Shaftesbury be one of those enthusiasts, of whom Mr. R. here speaks, and if his 'universal genius' is the same as is here called the 'universal intellect,' I do not see how he can believe the immortality of the soul, considered as one distinct individual being; since it is plain, according to these notions, that the mind will, at the dissolution of the body, be swallowed up in the infinite abyss of being." To this Needler replied from Portsmouth, December 20, 1711; he discusses in general the error and absurdity of these notions, devoting one paragraph to Shaftesbury:

"I must confess there are some passages in lord Shaftesbury's 'meditations,' which seem to favour this notion; but, however, I believe there are none (allowance being made for the warmth and freedom of his style) which there is any necessity of understanding in that ill sense. It would be great pity that so pious and elevated a strain of devotion should be tainted with such poisonous notions. I find, though his lordship is reported not to frequent the church, he does not altogether neglect religion. He seems to be of the opinion of the *Quietists,* who believe that the most acceptable worship of the Deity, and that which suits best with his spiritual nature, consists in silent contemplation and inward adoration of his infinite perfections." See *Letters by several eminent persons deceased, including the correspondence of John Hughes,* edited by John Duncombe, Second edition (London, 1773), I, 75-93.

Although this letter shows considerable interest in Shaftesbury and his thought, it, of course, leaves the question as to any *influence* on Needler just where it was.

Hester Lynch Thrale
(See also *Samuel Johnson*)

Mrs. Piozzi and Isaac Watts. Being annotations in the autograph of Mrs. Piozzi on a copy of the first edition of the *Philosophical Essays* of Watts. With an introduction and notes by James P. R. Lyell. London: Grafton, 1934. Pp. 48.

Notice in *TLS,* Nov. 8, 1934, p. 778.

The Queeney letters. Being letters addressed to Hester Maria Thrale by Dr. Johnson, Fanny Burney and Mrs. Thrale-Piozzi. Edited by the Marquis of Lansdowne. London: Cassell, 1934. Pp. xxx+275.

Rev. in *TLS,* March 22, 1934, p. 211; by Joseph Wood Krutch in *The Nation* (N. Y.), Oct. 10, 1934, p. 415; by Fredrick A. Pottle in *Yale review,* XXIV (1934), 211-14.

The first 52 pages of this volume are a reprint of Dr. Johnson's letters to "Queeney" Thrale, published first in a limited edition in 1932. The other letters, from Fanny Burney and Mrs. Thrale, are now published for the first time from manuscripts in the possession of the editor, with some additions for the sake of completeness from manuscripts in the John Rylands Library and the Huntington Library. The importance of these letters lies chiefly in the new light they throw on Mrs. Thrale's marriage to Piozzi and the way in which her friends reacted to this complication. The editor thinks that the letters exonerate Fanny Burney and Queeney, and, by implication, Dr. Johnson, and that Mrs. Thrale's state of mind was almost pathological. With this judgment the reviewer is inclined to agree. It is clear that Mrs. Thrale's friends were not so much concerned about outward respectabilities as about her own happiness and that of her children. Fanny Burney, with a shrewdness and common sense which we are too apt to think of as exclusively modern, interpreted her friend's infatuation for Piozzi as the price she paid for marrying Thrale when young without consulting her inclinations; had she not then "*scorned* and *derided* all personal preference, she would now look *forward* with prudence, and *back* with affection" (p. 70). Even Dr. Johnson's admiration and affection for "little Burney" would have been increased could he have known with what firmness, sagacity, and sympathy she acted as advisor to Queeney throughout this unhappy situation.

Sir John Vanbrugh

Mueschke, Paul, and Fleisher, Jeanette. "A re-evaluation of Vanbrugh." *PMLA,* XLIX (1934), 848-89.

This article is an attempt to break through the critical categories which have been generally accepted in criticism of the comedy of manners since the appearance of John Palmer's brilliant volume in 1913. Palmer established in our minds a factitious norm for this genre, with the consequence that we have either ignored or depreciated some excellent comedy which departed from this norm. Mueschke's richly suggestive article indicates the need for a re-study of both the critical and the historical aspects of the comedy of this period.

Horace Walpole

Mehrota, K. K. *Horace Walpole and the English novel*: a study of the influence of *The Castle of Otranto,* 1764-1820. Oxford: Blackwell, 1934. Pp. xiii+197.

Rev. in *TLS,* May 17, 1934, p. 356.

Stein, Jess M. "Horace Walpole and Shakespeare." *SP,* xxxi (1934), 51-68.

Thomas Warton

Martin, L. C. *Thomas Warton and the early poems of Milton.* (Warton Lecture, British Academy.) London: H. Milford, 1934.

John Wesley

Lofthouse, W. F. "Wesley's doctrine of Christian perfection." *London quarterly and Holborn review,* April, 1934, pp. 178-88.

Simon, John S. *John Wesley: the last phase.* London: Epworth press, 1934. Pp. 355.

Rev. in *TLS,* Nov. 8, 1934, p. 764; by John Telford in *London quarterly review,* Oct., 1934, pp. 461-68.

Simpson, E. J. Sparrow. *John Wesley and the Church of England.* London: S. P. C. K., 1934. Pp. xii+100.

Notice in *TLS,* Nov. 8, 1934, p. 779.

Edward Young

Bliss, Isabel St. John. "Young's *Night Thoughts* in relation to contemporary Christian apologetics." *PMLA,* xlix (1934), 37-70.

Establishes the orthodoxy of Young's poem, the sternness of which sets it apart from the sentimental type of grave-yard meditation.

V. THE CONTINENTAL BACKGROUND.

Aikin-Sneath, Betsy. "An early example of the Bürgerliches Trauerspiel." *MLR,* xxix (1934), 330-32.

Der Zügel-lose, Frankfurt and Leipzig, 1745, represented all the features of this type ten years before *Miss Sara Sampson.*

Allen, Don Cameron. "Early eighteenth-century literary relations between England and Germany." *MLN,* xlix (1934), 99-101.

Anderson, Paul Bunyan. "English drama transferred to Prévost's fiction." *MLN,* xlix (1934), 178-80.

Baldensperger, F. "Intellectuels français hors de France. I. De Descartes à Voltaire." *RCC,* xxx[1] (1934), 193-212; 316-24; 421-34; 548-61; 607-19; 723-38. xxxv[2] (1934), 49-58; 215-31; 329-40; 435-49; 519-34; 613-29.

Beck, T. J. *Northern antiquities in French learning and literature (1755-1855).* New York: Institute of French Studies, 1934. Vol. I., pp. 195.

Blassneck, Marce. *Frankreich als Vermittler englisch-deutscher Einflüsse im 17. und 18. Jahrhundert.*" (Kölner anglistische Arbeiten, 20.) Leipzig: Tauchnitz, 1934. Pp. 181.

Brown, Harcourt. *Scientific organization in seventeenth century France (1620-1680).* Baltimore: Williams and Wilkins, 1934. Pp. xxii +306.

Notice in *TLS,* July 19, 1934, p. 515.

Brown, Harcourt. " Pierre Bayle and natural science: an unpublished letter to Robert Boyle." *Romanic review,* xxv (1934), 361-67.

Carrière, J. M. "Berquin's adaptations from English periodical literature." *PQ,* xiii (1934), 248-60.

Chinard, Gilbert. *L'Amérique et le rêve exotique dans la littérature française au XVIIe et au XVIIIe siècle.* Nouvelle édition. Paris: Droz, 1934. Pp. 454.

Clark, Robert T. "The noble savage and the idea of tolerance in Herder's *Briefe zu Beförderung der Humanität.*" *JEGP,* xxxiii (1934), 46-56.

Engel, Claire Eliane. "L'abbé Prévost et le Protestantisme français." *Bulletin de la Société de l'Histoire du Protestantisme français,* lxxxiii (1934), 593-612.

Fletcher, F. T. H. "Influence of Montesquieu on English political economists." *Economic history,* iii (1934), 77-92.

Fletcher, Frank T. H. "*L'Esprit des Lois* before early English opinion." *RLC,* xiv (1934), 527-41.

Hendel, Charles William. *Jean-Jacques Rousseau: moralist.* Oxford: University press, 1934. 2 vols. Pp. xii+316 and vi+348.

Rev. in *TLS,* Sept. 20, 1934, pp. 625-26; by G[eorge] B[oas] in *Journal of philosophy,* xxxi (1934), 610; by Harold A. Larrabee in *International journal of ethics,* xlv (1934), 110-12.

Michéa, R. "Le Président de Brosses en Italie." *RLC,* xiv (1934), 425-53.

Influence of Addison and Misson on the *Lettres fdmilieres* of the Président de Brosses.

Price, Mary Bell, and Price, Lawrence Marsden. *The publication of English literature in Germany in the eighteenth century.* Berkeley: University of California press, 1934. Pp. 288.

Quigley, H. "Italian criticism in the 18th century. The influence of English philosophy and the development of aesthetics based on imagination: Antonio Conti." In *Mélanges offerts à Henri Hauvette.* Paris: Les presses françaises, 1934.

Seeber, Edward D. "*Humanisme, humanitisme,* and *humanitarisme.*" *MLN,* XLIX (1934), 521-23.

Treske, E. *Der Rosenkreuzerroman 'Le Comte de Gabalis' und die geistigen Strömungen des 17. und 18. Jahrhunderts.* Griefswald, diss., 1933. Pp. 66.

Wesly, Margot. *Das junge Mädchen im deutschen Roman des 18. Jahrhundert bis zum Beginn des Sturm und Dranges.* (Unter bes. Berücksichtung des gleichzeitigen französischen und englischen Romans.) Leipzig: diss., 1933. Pp. 96.

Wolfe, Don M. "Milton and Mirabeau." *PMLA,* XLIX (1934), 1116-28.

1936

ENGLISH LITERATURE, 1660-1800: A CURRENT BIBLIOGRAPHY

By Louis I. Bredvold
University of Michigan

This bibliography attempts to list the more significant books, articles, and reviews published during the year 1935, together with some bearing earlier dates that were inadvertently omitted from previous bibliographies in this series. I am indebted to Professor Ronald S. Crane and Mr. Donald F. Bond for contributing the critical notes signed with their initials, and to Mr. George S. Wykoff for calling my attention to some earlier Berkeley items.

LIST OF ABBREVIATIONS

AHR=American historical review.
Archiv=Archiv für das Studium der neueren Sprachen und Literaturen.
Beiblatt=Beiblatt zur Anglia.
DVLG=Deutsche Vierteljahrschrift für Literaturwissenschaft und Geistesgeschichte.
EHR=English historical review.
ELH=ELH, A journal of English literary history.
ES=Englische Studien.
GRM=Germanisch-romanische Monatschrift.
JEGP=Journal of English and Germanic philology.
JMH=Journal of modern history.
LM=London mercury.
MLN=Modern language notes.
MLR=Modern language review.
MP=Modern philology.
N & Q=Notes and queries.
PMLA=Publications of the Modern Language Association of America.
PQ=Philological quarterly.
RAA=Revue anglo-américaine.
RC=Revue critique.
RCC=Revue des cours et conférences.
RES=Review of English studies.
RH=Revue historique.
RHL=Revue d'histoire littéraire de la France.
RHP=Revue d'histoire de la philosophie.
RLC=Revue de littérature comparée.
RSH=Revue de synthèse historique.
SP=Studies in philology.
SRL=Saturday review of literature.
TLS=Times literary supplement (London).

I. BIBLIOGRAPHIES AND BIBLIOGRAPHICAL STUDIES

(Some special bibliographies will also be found listed under individual authors.)

Annual bibliography of English language and literature. Volume XV, 1934. Edited for the Modern Humanities Research Association, by Mary S. Serjeantson, assisted by Leslie N. Broughton. Cambridge: Bowes & Bowes, 1935.

Annual bulletin of historical literature. No. XXIV, dealing with publications for the year 1934. London: G. Bell, for the Historical Association, 1935.

See especially pp. 33-37.

Baugh, Albert C. "Annual bibliography for 1934: English language and literature." *PMLA,* XLIX (1934).

See especially pp. 1226-36.

Beckwith, Frank. "Desmaizeaux's *Lethe.*" *TLS,* April 18, 1935, p. 257.

A "ghost" book, included in Sir Leslie Stephen's list of the publications of Desmaizeaux in the *D. N. B.* The title originated in the elder Disraeli's misreading of his own notes.

"A bibliography of philosophy, 1934." *Journal of philosophy,* XXXII (1935), 450-504.

An annual bibliography of philosophy.

Black, Frank Gees. "A lady novelist of Colchester." *Essex review,* XLIV (1935), 180-85.

The author of *The Brothers, Stage-Coach,* and *Lucy Wellers* was, according to tradition, a Miss Smythies of Colchester. Cf. also corr. by F. G. Black in *TLS,* Sept. 26, 1935, p. 596.

Boyce, Benjamin. "A Restoration 'improvement' of Thomas Dekker." *MLN,* L (1935), 460-61.

Poor Robin's visions (1677) based on *News from hell.*

Bredvold, Louis I. "English literature, 1660-1800: a current bibliography." *PQ,* XIV (1935), 142-80.

Carlson, C. Lennart. "*The Free Briton; or The Opinion of the People,* and F. Walsingham's *Free Briton.*" *N & Q,* CLXIX (1935), 166-68.

Case, Arthur E. *A bibliography of English poetical miscellanies, 1521-1750.* Oxford: Printed for the Bibliographical Society at the University press, 1935. Pp. 397.

Rev. in *TLS,* Oct. 10, 1935, p. 626.

Catalogue of specimens of printing types by English and Scottish printers and founders, 1665-1830. Compiled by W. Turner Berry and A. F. Johnson. With an introduction by Stanley Morison. Oxford: University press, 1935.

Rev. in *TLS,* Aug. 22, 1935, p. 522, and in *N & Q,* CLXIX (1935), 125-26.

Chalk, E. S. "Circulation of XVIII-century newspapers." *N & Q,* CLXIX (1935), 336.

Dale, Cragsley. "The Glasgow periodical press in the eighteenth century." *Scottish notes and queries,* XIII (1935), 165-68.

"Forty-second critical bibliography of the history and philosophy of science and of the history of civilization (to the end of November 1934)." *Isis,* XXIII[2] (1935).

See especially pp. 504-25.

Galbraith, V. H. *An introduction to the use of the Public Records.* Oxford: Clarendon press, 1934. Pp. 112.

An introductory guide, which explains, by historical treatment, the present arrangement of the public records.

George, Mary Dorothy. *Catalogue of political and personal satires preserved in the department of prints and drawings in the British Museum.* Vol. V, 1771-1783. London: Printed by order of the Trustees, 1935. Pp. xxxix+851.

Rev. in *TLS,* March 14, 1935, p. 151, and by Leonard W. Labaree in *AHR,* XLI (1935), 336-38.

Griffith, R. H. "Early editions of Lillo's *London merchant.*" *University of Texas studies in English,* No. 15 (1935), 23-27.

Harbage, Alfred. "Elizabethan and seventeenth-century play manuscripts." *PMLA,* L (1935), 687-99.

A valuable list, giving location of each manuscript.

Harris, Brice. "Dorset's poem *On the young statesmen.*" *TLS,* April 4, 1935, pp. 227-28.

Argument for Dorset's authorship.

Harvey, F. Brompton. "An unknown translator of Erasmus." *TLS,* June 20, 1935, p. 416.

A translation of *The Colloquies* by "H. M., Gent." in 1671.

Higgs, Henry. *A bibliography of economics, 1751-1775.* (Prepared for the British Academy.) Cambridge: University press; New York: Macmillan, 1935. Pp. xxii+742.

Rev. by J. Bonar in *Economic journal,* XLV (1935), 720-23.

Howarth, R. G. "Some additions to the poems of Lord Dorset." *MLN,* L (1935), 457-59.

Joughin, G. L. "An Inchbald bibliography." *University of Texas studies in English,* No. 14 (1934), 59-74.

Lang, W. J. "Lancashire periodicals printed before 1801." *N & Q,* CLXVIII (1935), 116-17. Corr. by R. S. B., *ibid.,* p. 159.

Lawrence, W. J. "The plates in Settle's *The Empress of Morocco.*" *TLS,* July 11, 1935, p. 448.

Peck, Lewis F. "Lewis's *Monk.*" *TLS,* March 7, 1935, p. 148. Corr. by W. Roberts, *ibid.,* March 14, p. 164; by E. G. Bayford, March 28, p. 216; by Frederick Coykendall, April 25, p. 276.

Ripley, Charles. *Catalogue of the McAlpin collection of British history and theology (1501-1700) in the Union Theological Seminary in the City of New York.* 5 volumes. New York, 1927-30.

Makes more easily available to American scholars the resources of a very rich collection, which has been in process of formation for more than fifty years.

Roberts, W. *"L'Orphelin Anglois,* 1769." *N & Q,* CLXIX (1935), 368.

Roberts, W. "A publisher's stock-book, 1732." *TLS,* Jan. 4, 1936, p. 20.

"Schriftenverzeichnis für 1934." *Zeitschrift für Aesthetik und Allgemeine Kunstwissenschaft,* XXIX (1935), 350-400.

An annual international bibliography on esthetics; for literature see pp. 366-79.

Simpson, Percy. *Proof-reading in the 16th, 17th, and 18th centuries.* Oxford: Clarendon press, 1935. Pp. xii+251, with 20 facsimiles.

Rev. by Geoffrey Tillotson in *History,* XX (1935), 168-69; by Hans Marcus in *Deutsche Literaturzeitung* ser. iii, VI (1935), 1821-26.

Summers, Montague. *A bibliography of the Restoration drama.* London: Fortune press, 1935. Pp. 143.

Cf. corr. by M. Summers in *TLS,* April 25, 1935, p. 272.

Van Tieghem, Paul. "Histoire littéraire générale et comparée: dix-huitième compte rendu annuel." *RSH,* VIII (1934), 217-47.

See especially pp. 224-42.

Van Tieghem, Paul. "Un congrès international d'histoire littéraire." *Revue bleue,* LXXIII (1935), 551-53.

On the meeting in Amsterdam, September, 1935.

The Year's work in English studies. Vol. XIV, 1933. Edited for the English Association by Frederick S. Boas and Mary S. Serjeantson. Oxford: University press, 1935. Pp. 387.

Chapter IX, on the Restoration, by F. E. Budd, and chapter X, on the eighteenth century, by Edith J. Morley.

II. THE SOCIAL AND POLITICAL ENVIRONMENT

Bayne-Powell, Rosamund. *English country life in the eighteenth century.* London: Murray, 1935. Pp. 319.

Rev. in *TLS,* March 28, 1935, p. 215; and by Paul Yvon in *RAA,* XIII (1935), 55-56.

Bebb, E. D. *Nonconformity and social and economic life, 1660-1800.* Some problems of the present as they appeared in the past. London: Epworth press, 1935. Pp. 198.

Rev. in *TLS,* Aug. 29, 1935, p. 532; by P. C. Gordon-Walker in *Economic history review,* VI (1935), 123-24.

Biddulph, Violet. *Kitty, Duchess of Queensbury.* London: Nicholson and Watson, 1935.

Rev. in *TLS,* Dec. 7, 1935, p. 826.

Brown, Beatrice Curtis. *The letters and diplomatic instructions of Queen Anne.* London: Cassell, 1935. Pp. 452.

Rev. in *TLS,* May 23, 1935, p. 319.

Bryant, Arthur. *The letters, speeches, and declarations of Charles II.* London: Cassell, 1935. Pp. 368.

Rev. in *TLS,* March 21, 1935, p. 167.

Calendar of treasury books preserved in the Public Record Office. Introduction to volumes XI-XVII concerning the years 1695-1702. Prepared by William A. Shaw. London: H. M. Stationery Office, 1934. Pp. dciv.

Rev. by Cyrus H. Karraker in *JMH,* VII (1935), 75-76; by F. C. Dietz in *AHR,* XLI (1935), 131-32.

Calendar of treasury books, January, 1693, to March, 1696. Vol. x, parts I, II, III, IV. Prepared by William A. Shaw. London: H. M. Stationery Office, 1935.

Calendar of treasury books, September 1, 1698, to July 31, 1699. Vol. xiv. Prepared by William A. Shaw. London: H. M. Stationery Office, 1935.

Catholic Record Society. London sessions records, 1605-1685. Edited by Dom Hugh Bowles. London: The Society, 1935.

Churchill, Winston S. *Marlborough: his life and times.* Vols. III and IV. London: Harrap; New York: Scribners, 1935. Pp. 364, 296.

Rev. by Robert M. Lovett in *New Republic,* 83 (1935), 369; by Arthur Lyon Cross in *SRL,* March 16, 1935, pp. 545-47; by Violet Barbour in *AHR,* XLI (1935), 332-34.

Davies, A. Mervyn. *Warren Hastings, maker of British India.* London: Nicholson and Watson, 1935. Pp. 582.

Rev. in *TLS,* April 11, 1935, p. 234.

The diary and visits of John Yeoman to London in the years 1774-and 1777. Edited, with an introduction, by Macleod Yearsley. London: Watts, 1935.

Notice in *TLS,* Feb. 7, 1935, p. 78.

Dobrée, Bonamy. *The letters of George III.* London: Cassell, 1935.

Rev. in *TLS,* Nov. 2, 1935, p. 685.

Griffiths, O. M. *Religion and learning*: a study in English Presbyterian thought from the Bartholomew ejections (1662) to the foundation of the Unitarian movement. Cambridge: University press, 1935.

Rev. in *TLS,* Dec. 14, 1935, p. 848.

Hauser, Henri. "Crises de crédit et de spéculation en France et Angleterre au lendemain de la paix d'Utrecht." *Revue d'histoire moderne,* Nov. 1935, pp. 435-39.

Heckscher, Eli F. *Mercantilism* (first published in Swedish in 1931, translated from the German edition by Mendel Shapiro and revised by the author). 2 vols. London: Allen and Unwin; New York: Macmillan, 1935. Pp. 472, 424.

Rev. in *TLS,* Jan. 4, 1936, p. 7; by Jacob Viner in *Economic history review,* VI (1935), 99-101; by T. H. Marshall in *Economic Journal,* XLV (1935), 716-19.

Already accepted as a classic treatise on the subject, and important as a contribution to social history as well as to economic theory.

Hertfordshire county records. Volume VIII. Sessions books, 1752-1799. Hertford: Clerk of the peace, 1935.

Rev. in *TLS,* Aug. 1, 1935, pp. 481-82.

Higham, F. M. G. *King James the second.* London: Hamish Hamilton, 1935. Pp. 366.

The diary of Robert Hooke, F. R. S., 1672-1680. Edited by Henry W. Robinson and Walter Adams. London: Taylor and Francis, 1935. Pp. 552.

Rev. in *TLS,* July 18, 1935, pp. 453-54; by G. N. Clark in *History,* XX (1935), 273-75.

Hoskins, W. G. *Industry, trade, and people in Exeter, 1688-1800.* Manchester: University press, 1935.

Rev. in *TLS,* Oct. 24, 1935, p. 662.

A monograph of specialized nature, but dealing with a development which "reflected in a remarkable manner the transformations in the national economic life."

Joly, A. *James Drummond, Duc de Perth (1648-1716).* Paris: Économat des Facultés catholiques, 1935. Pp. 514.

Jones, P. E., and Judges, A. V. "London population in the late seventeenth century." *Economic history review,* VI (1935), 41-63.

Kirby, Ethyn Williams. "The Quakers' efforts to secure civil and religious liberty, 1660-96." *JMH,* VII (1935), 401-21.

Kloeren, Maria. *Sport und Rekord.* (Kultursoziologische Untersuchungen zum England des 16. bis 18. Jahrhunderts.) (Kölner Anglistische Arbeiten, 23.) Leipzig: Tauchnitz, 1935. Pp. iv+294.

Leslie-Melville, R. *The life and work of Sir John Fielding.* London: Lincoln Williams, 1935. Pp. xv+323.

Rev. by F. E. B. in *MLR,* XXX (1935), 553.

McIlwain, Charles H. "Whig sovereignty and real sovereignty." *Annual report of the Michigan Academy of Science, Arts, and Letters,* 1935, pp. 37-54.

An illuminating examination of Whig theory of the seventeenth and eighteenth centuries by an eminent scholar.

MacInnes, C. M. *England and slavery.* London: Arrowsmith, 1935.

Notice in *TLS,* March 7, 1935, p. 145; rev. by A. T. M. in *History,* XX (1935), 191-92.

Mackenzie, W. C. *Andrew Fletcher of Saltoun.* London: Faber and Faber, 1935. Pp. 372.

Rev. by George Scott Moncrieff in *Criterion,* XIV (1935), 142-44.

Martin, Martin. *A description of the Western Islands of Scotland.* With *A late voyage to St. Kilda.* Edited by D. J. Macleod. Stirling: Eneas Mackay, 1935.

Rev. in *TLS,* March 28, 1935, p. 194.

The *Description* was first published in 1703, and the *Voyage* in 1718.

Mason, John E. *Gentlefolk in the making.* Studies in the history of English courtesy literature and related topics from 1531 to 1774. Philadelphia: University of Pennsylvania press; London: Milford, 1935. Pp. xiv+393.

Rev. in *TLS,* Sept. 19, 1935, p. 577.

Michael, Wolfgang. *Englische Geschichte im 18ten Jahrhundert.* III Band. Das Zeitalter Walpoles. Berlin: Grunewald Verlag.

Rev. in *TLS,* Jan. 31, 1935, p. 57. Corr. by Romney Sedgwick, Feb. 14, p. 92. A long-awaited installment of an important history.

Newton, Theodore F. M. "William Pittis and Queen Anne journalism." *MP,* XXXII (1935), 169-86.

Petrie, Sir Charles. *The four Georges.* London: Eyre and Spottiswode; New York: Houghton Mifflin, 1935.

Rev. in *TLS,* Oct. 17, 1935, p. 650.

Phillips, P. A. S. *Paul de Lamerie, citizen and goldsmith of London: a study of his life and work, A. D. 1688-1751.* London: Batsford, 1935.

The subject of this work was the son of a Huguenot who had fled from France upon the Revocation of the Edict of Nantes.

Radice, F. R. "The reign of Queen Anne." *History,* xx (1935), 29-39.

Survey of recent publications in this period.

Roth, Cecil. "Charles II and the Jews." *Contemporary review,* CXLVII (1935), 721-28.

Schöffler, Herbert. *England das Land des Sportes.* Eine Kultursoziologische Erklärung. (Hefte zur Englandkunde, 9.) Leipzig: Tauchnitz, 1935. Pp. 86.

Sitwell, Osbert, and Barton, Margaret. *Brighton.* London: Faber and Faber, 1935. Pp. 373.

Rev. in *TLS,* March 14, 1935. p. 155.

Surrey Quarter Session records. Volume VII. Order Book and Sessions Rolls, 1661-1663. Edited by Dorothy L. Powell and Hilary Jenkinson. County Hall, Kingston-upon-Thames, 1935.

Rev. in *TLS,* Aug. 1, 1935, pp. 481-82.

Sykes, N. *Church and state in the eighteenth century.* Cambridge: University press, 1934. Pp. xi+455.

Rev. by A. S. Turberville in *History,* XX (1935), 178-79; by W. T. Laprade in *AHR,* XLI (1935), 335-36; by J. M. Creed in *EHR,* L (1935), 720-22.

Sykes, N. "Queen Anne and the Episcopate." *EHR,* L (1935), 433-64.

Thomson, Mark A. "The age of Johnson." *History,* xx (1935), 221-32.

A survey of recent literature on the period.

The Torrington diaries. Containing the tours through England and Wales of the Hon. John Byng (later fifth Viscount Torrington) between the years 1781 and 1794. Edited by C. Bruyn Andrews. Vol. II. London: Eyre and Spottiswode, 1935. Pp. 430.

Rev. in *TLS,* June 20, 1935, p. 387.

Williams, Clare. "As others saw us, 1764." *Contemporary review,* CXLVII (1935), 337-44.

Winstanley, D. A. *Unreformed Cambridge*: a study of certain aspects of the university in the eighteenth century. Cambridge: University press, 1935.

Rev. in *TLS,* Oct. 17, 1935, p. 643; in *N & Q,* CLXIX (1935), 322-23.

Wright, Louis B. *Middle-class culture in Elizabethan England.* Chapel Hill: University of North Carolina press, 1935. Pp. xiv+733.

Although this volume deals with the preceding period, its theme makes it of importance to students of the eighteenth century.

The Wynne diaries. Edited by Anne Fremantle. Vol. I, 1789-1794. Oxford: University press, 1935.

Rev. in *TLS,* Nov. 9, 1935, p. 711.

III. CURRENTS OF IDEAS AND LITERARY FORMS

Allen, Robert Joseph. "Ned Ward and *The Weekly comedy.*" *Harvard studies and notes in philology and literature,* XVII (1935), 1-14.

Aubin, Robert Arnold. "Some Augustan Gothicists." *Harvard studies and notes in philology and literature,* XVII (1935), 15-26.

Aubin, Robert A. "Three notes on 'Graveyard' poetry." *SP,* XXXII (1935), 103-09.

Austin, E. M. *The ethics of the Cambridge Platonists.* Philadelphia: University of Pennsylvania dissertation, 1935. Pp. 86.

Aykroyd, W. R. *Three philosophers.* London: Heinemann, 1935. Pp. xi+227.

Rev. in *TLS,* March 7, 1935, p. 136; by A. F. Titley in *History,* XX (1935), 272-73.

A study of Lavoisier, Joseph Priestley, and Henry Cavendish.

Babcock, R. W. "The idea of taste in the eighteenth century." *PMLA,* L (1935), 922-26.

Comment on E. N. Hooker's article in *PMLA,* June, 1934, with much supplementary information.

Bader, Arno L. "The Modena troupe in England." *MLN,* L (1935), 367-69.

A note on the *commedia dell'arte* players who visited England in 1678.

Blomfield, Sir Reginald. *Six architects.* London: Macmillan, 1935.

Rev. in *TLS,* Oct. 3, 1935, p. 608.

A distinguished architect discusses among others, Wren and Bernini.

Bond, Donald F. "'Distrust' of imagination in English Neo-Classicism." *PQ,* XIV (1935), 54-69.

This "distrust," the author says, was neither so great nor so fundamental as is frequently represented by modern scholars. The article should be a wholesome corrective.

Borgman, Albert S. *The life and death of William Mountfort.* Cambridge: Harvard University press, 1935. Pp. 221.

Professor Borgman, whose volume on Shadwell is well known, has investigated further the famous actor of the period, William Mountfort, and written an account of his life and death which he chooses to call "an extended footnote" to Cibber's account of Mountfort in the *Apology.* The section devoted to the life becomes to a large extent a study in stage history, which Borgman knows intimately, and this feature of the volume will probably constitute its greatest value to many of his readers. The account of Mountfort's death is not substantially new, although Borgman publishes new documents which he thinks may be depositions made by witnesses. The whole narration is fresh and vivid as well as documented and scholarly, and one puts it down with a curious feeling of having been a contemporary witness of the sombre and exciting tragedy enacted so long ago.

Malone, in his *Life of Dryden,* I, 203-04, published a letter from Atterbury to Tonson, dated Nov. 15, 1687, in which Atterbury asked the publisher to speak to Mountfort for a copy of the "Oxford Prologue." This passage has escaped Borgman, and there is nothing in his volume to explain it. As the Act had been omitted at Oxford in 1686 and 1687, the prologue would seem not to have been recent. And the fragmentary records now available do not mention Mountfort's acting at Oxford at all.

Brodrick, J. *The economic morals of the Jesuits: an answer to Dr. H. M. Robertson.* New York: Oxford University press, 1934. Pp. 158.

Rev. by Maurice Freeman in *American economic review,* XXV (1935), 508-10; by F. L. Nussbaum in *AHR,* XL (1935), 328-29.

A refutation of Robertson's "contention that it was the Jesuits rather than the Puritans who made nascent capitalism respectable by giving it religious encouragement."

Davies, Cicely. "Ut pictura poesis." *MLR,* xxx (1935), 159-69.

A study of the parallelism in theories of poetry and painting.

Deane, C. V. *Aspects of eighteenth century nature poetry.* Oxford: Blackwell, 1935. Pp. 145.

Rev. in *TLS,* Jan. 4, 1936, pp. 1-2.

Durling, Dwight L. *Georgic tradition in English poetry.* New York: Columbia University press; London: Milford, 1935. Pp. xii+259.

Rev. in *TLS,* Jan. 4, 1936, pp. 1-2.

Fanfani, Amintore. *Catholicism, Protestantism, and capitalism.* New York: Sheed and Ward, 1935. Pp. 224.

Frantz, R. W. *The English traveller and the movement of ideas, 1660-1732.* Lincoln, Nebraska: University of Nebraska press, 1934. Pp. 176. (University studies, 32-33.)

The subject of the influence of travel literature on ideas in France has been presented in a number of well-known works by Lanson, Chinard, and Atkinson. This study by Frantz is the only extended publication so far to attempt to survey the parallel developments in English thought. Frantz has been judicious in his claims for the influence of the voyage literature, and perhaps most important of all, he has always observed that the voyagers were not originators of ideas, but merely provided illustrative material which served to enhance ideas already circulating.

Funke, Otto. *Englische Sprachphilosophie im späteren 18. Jahrhundert.* Bern: Francke, 1934. Pp. 162.

Rev. by Ants Oras in *MLN,* L (1935), 405-06.

Fynmore, A. H. W. "English provincial playhouses in the eighteenth century." *N & Q.* CLXVII (1934), 356.

Green, C. C. *Neo-classic theory of tragedy in England during the eighteenth century.* (Harvard studies in English, xi.) Cambridge: Harvard University press, 1934. Pp. x+245.

Notice in *TLS,* April 11, 1935, p. 246.

Green, F. C. *Minuet: a critical survey of French and English literary ideas in the eighteenth century.* London: Dent, 1935. Pp. x+489.

Rev. in *TLS,* March 7, 1935, p. 139; by P. Mansell Jones in *LM,* XXXI (1935), 494-95.

van Gunsteren, W. F. *Kalvinismus und Kapitalismus.* Ein Beitrag zur Erkenntnis der Beziehungen zwischen kalvinistischer Sozial-Ethik und kapitalistischem Wirtschaftsgeist. Amsterdam: Nordhollandsche, 1934. Pp. 239.

Rev. by C. Brinkmann in *Vierteljahrschrift für Sozial- und Wirtschaftsgeschichte,* XXVIII (1935), 293-98.

The letters and writings of George Frideric Handel. Edited by Eric H. Müller. London: Cassell, 1935. Pp. viii+98.

Rev. in *TLS,* March 7, 1935, p. 137.

Jansen, Hildegard. *Die soziologische Selbstcharakteristik des Adels in der Restaurationskomödie.* Bonn, 1934. Pp. viii+75.

Lamprecht, Sterling P. "The role of Descartes in seventeenth century England." *Studies in the history of ideas,* Vol. iii. Columbia University press, 1935, pp. 181-240.

Professor Lamprecht has long been known as a student of English thought in the seventeeth century and his essay will be of general interest to the specialist in literature as well as to philosophers, for whom it is primarily intended. He makes a good deal of what he calls the Scepticism of Descartes, which he seems to regard as something distinct from Pyrrhonism, and which he thinks was an important influence on both Glanville and Locke. One hesitates to challenge statements by Professor Lamprecht in this field but his account would have been better balanced if he had recognized explicitly that the seventeenth century was pervaded by a scepticism quite distinct from the Cartesian; Glanville, at least, shows definitely the influence of Sextus Empiricus, Montaigne, and Charron, as well as of Descartes. A curious, and rather unfortunate slip (p. 183) attributes the *Telluris theoria sacra* to Gilbert Burnet, instead of to Thomas.

Lange, Victor. *Die Lyrik und ihr Publikum im England des 18. Jahrhunderts.* Eine geschmacksgeschichtliche Untersuchung über die englischen Anthologien von 1670-1780. Weimar: Böhlau, 1935. Pp. 117.

Lovett, David. "Shakespeare as a poet of realism in the eighteenth century." *ELH,* ii (1935), 267-89.

Lovejoy, Arthur O., and Boas, George. *Primitivism and related ideas in antiquity.* With supplementary essays by W. F. Albright and P. E. Dumont. Baltimore: The Johns Hopkins press, 1935. Pp. xiii+482.

This work, which is the first volume of a *Documentary history of primitivism and related ideas,* to be brought down to modern times in further volumes now in preparation, may safely be called epoch-making in the history of the subject. Even a superficial glance through its pages will bring home the fact that these ideas in the eighteenth century cannot be understood apart from their manifestations in Greek and Latin writings of antiquity.

Macaulay, T. C. "French and English drama in the seventeenth century: some contrasts and parallels." *Essays and studies by members of the English Association,* XX (1935), 45-74.

Matthews, William. "The Lincolnshire dialect in the eighteenth century." *N & Q,* CLXIX (1935), 398-404.

Matthews, William. "London slang at the beginning of the eighteenth century." *N & Q,* CLXVIII (1935), 416-18, 439-41, 454-56.

Matthews, William. "Sailors' pronunciation in the second half of the seventeenth century." *Anglia,* LIX (1935), 193-251.

Mayo, T. F. *Epicurus in England, 1650-1725.* Dallas, Texas: Southwest press, 1934. Pp. xxviii+237.

McKeon, Richard. "Renaissance and method in philosophy." *Studies in the history of ideas,* Vol. III, Columbia University press, 1935, pp. 37-114.

A very interesting and arresting study, not only of the concept of the "Renaissance," but also of the general problems of method in the history of ideas. Our histories, the author contends, have been carrying on essentially a philosophical debate, each historian, however purely descriptive he may conceive his aim and method to be, never succeeding in disentangling his own philosophical ideas from the pattern which he gives to the past. And thus "the interpretation of the Renaissance as a whole, its character and limits, the fact and manner of the intellectual rebirth, its differences from the Middle Ages which it named and criticized, its relation to the Reformation and the events which have followed since the sixteenth century, all betray history as disguised philosophy" (p. 43). The remedy for this situation, according to the author, can not be found in further refinement of scientific techniques in historical study, but only in facing the fact that philosophical questions must be treated philosophically before they can be understood in their historical relations. What he gives us in this study is therefore, in his own words, an illustration of "the assimilation of questions of historical truth into questions of philosophic truth" (p. 49).

The study of the attitudes of Abailard, Erasmus, and Luther toward the methods of grammar, rhetoric, and dialectic, forms the subject of the essay proper. The transition from the Middle Ages to the Renaissance is thus presented as "the transformation which knowledge and action have undergone as a result of the shifting places of grammar, rhetoric, and dialectic" (p. 105). And the study concludes with a return to the problem of methods and a reassertion of the necessity of dialectic in any historical study that raises philosophical problems. The whole essay, so the author concludes by saying, "is itself an illustration once more of Abailard's favorite quotation from Cicero, that all controversies are concerned with writings or reasons, but ultimately the controversies concerning writing are controversies about reasons" (p. 114).

Meinecke, Friedrich. "Die englische Präromantik des 18. Jahrhunderts ald Vorstufe des Historismus." *Historische Zeitschrift,* CLII (1935), 256-85.

Monk, Samuel H. *The sublime: a study of critical theories in XVIII-century England.* New York: Modern Language Association of America, 1935. Pp. 252.

This is a competent and useful book. The writer has explored with great thoroughness the mass of eighteenth-century writings in which the topic of the Sublime is discussed; he has neglected few if any important texts; and he has shown judgment in subordinating merely incidental or unoriginal treatments of the idea to those discussions which because either of their fulness of analysis or of their influence on later writers may be said to constitute the essential events in its history. Except in a too-brief section of his chapter on "The Sublime in painting" he makes no effort to show the effects of the critical theorizing he has studied on the contemporary production of works of art, but he has provided ample materials for any future historian of eighteenth-century verse or fiction who may be interested in tracing the responses of poets or novelists—made all too often at the expense of the integrity of their art—to the new taste for the "great" and the "terrible" in description and incident.

I have only one reservation of any importance: Monk does not, I think, distinguish with sufficient sharpness between two essentially distinct, though related, aspects of the story he tells. The distinction can be made in terms of the major preoccupations of the writers whose successive publications make up the narrative of the book; it forces itself on the attentive reader as he attempts to adjust his understanding of what was being done by critics like Dennis, the Warton brothers, Lowth, Young, Reynolds, Duff (to name only a few) to his understanding of the approach exemplified by writers like Hume, Akenside, Baillie, Burke, Gerard, and Reid. Both groups of writers had in common, to be sure, as the central term of their discussions, the word "Sublime," and there was naturally as we shall see, much interaction between them. Nevertheless, it is indispensable to clear thinking about the whole matter to recognize that the two lists of names represent in general two different lines of development related in different ways to the criticism of both the past and the future.

For the writers in the first list the "Sublime" was in the main the "Sublime" of Longinus, i.e, that quality, difficult to define but easily detectable by sensitive minds familiar with the great masterpieces, which gives distinction to works of literature and plastic art; and their typical procedure, like that of Longinus himself, consisted in viewing works in terms of the mental powers—the genius, imagination, creative energy—of their authors and in determining their value by reference to the quality of the soul that shines through them or through particular passages or parts of them. It was essentially a rhetorical approach, and in that respect it harmonized fundamentally with the approach implicit in most of the criticism which Monk calls "neo-classical"; the difference —and it is an important one—lay in the circumstance that whereas the preoccupation of a critic like Boileau in the *Art poétique* was with the "thought" of the poet's audience, that of the Eighteenth Century Longinians was with the "thought" of the poet himself; the tendency of the first type of criticism was to subject the work to the audience through an insistence on the need of conformity to good taste, rules, traditions as a condition of pleasing; that of the second was to subordinate the audience to the artist as an exalted being whom not to admire is to confess oneself lacking in taste and sensitivity. On the one hand, there is Boileau's declaration, in the preface to the 1701 edition of his works, that the poet achieves greatness by expressing justly the thoughts already possessed by a majority of his readers; on the other hand, there is the conviction stated by an anonymous essayist in Dodsley's *Museum* in 1747 (No. 34, p. 282) that the greatness of the major English poets, Chaucer, Spenser, Shakespeare, and Milton, lies precisely in their immense superiority to the times in which they lived. The history of English literary criticism between 1660 and 1800 can be interpreted, without too much over-simplification, as a gradual shift from the one of these rhetorical poles to the other, with results that were to be reflected in the main course of critical effort in the next century, from Coleridge and Hazlitt through Arnold and Swinburne to Middleton Murry: in spite of the neglect of Longinus after 1800, it was the spirit and method of *Peri Hupsous* that continued to rule.

The distinctive thing about the writers in the second list was that they sought the "Sublime" not primarily in works of literature or plastic art but in natural objects of one kind or another, and more particularly in the states of mind which such objects have the power to induce in human spectators. Though their vocabulary was borrowed in part from Longinus, their essential preoccupations separated them sharply from that ancient rhetorician and his modern disciples; their characteristic subject-matter was not compositions and authors but "the pleasures of the imagination"—the varied responses of men's feelings to stimuli from the outer world; they were psychologists inquiring about the emotions, not critics investigating the sources of high excellence in art. It is therefore somewhat confusing to find them treated, in Monk's account, as if they formed part of the same narrative sequence as the writers of a more purely Longinian sort, distinguished from these mainly in being slightly more modern and progressive in their approach. Nor can one be entirely satisfied with the statement Monk gives of the effect which their speculations had on criticism proper in the eighteenth century. That effect was certainly not, as he supposes (e.g., p. 85), to emancipate criticism from "rules" and the distinction of styles; it was merely to provide a new basis upon which rules for pleasing audiences could be erected, different in substance, to be sure, from the rules of Boileau, but of essentially the same "neo-classical" sort. Of this new *art poétique* the letter of Thomson to Mallet quoted on page 90 is a revealing specimen: "Here if you could insert a sketch of the deluge, what more affecting and noble? Sublimity must be the character of your piece." The argument is clear, and it is the same kind of argument that underlay the prescriptions of the neo-classicists: All readers of poetry feel sublime emotions at the description of sublime objects of nature or history; the deluge is such an object; therefore if you wish to be affecting to your readers, insert a description of it. (Cf. Horace: Old men like moral maxims; hence if you wish your play to please old men insert some moral maxims.) And "Sublimity must be the character of your piece": what is this but the old decorum of literary genres and styles? Only the styles are now the "sublime," the "beautiful," and the "picturesque" rather than (say) the "elevated," the "plain," the "elegant," and the "forcible"; and they are defined more exclusively than before in terms of the kinds of objects in nature the description of which will produce in readers the emotional effects appropriate to each. In spite of the constant recurrence in such discussions of the word "sublime," all this is far enough removed from the proper Longinian approach. But the eighteenth-century Longinians themselves did not escape the contagion of the new pychological aesthetics. Of what sort are the elevated conceptions and emotions in the poet which constitute the most important sources of the sublime in writing? Longinus did not say, and it is one of his merits that he left the matter vague. But many of his modern disciples, from Dennis on, had no such scruples about definition.

The great writer is one who thinks about "great things—"Gods, Daemons, Hell, Spirits and Souls of Men, Miracles, Prodigies, Enchantments, Witchcraft, Thunder, Tempests, raging Seas. Inundations, Torrents, Earthquakes, Volcanoes, Monsters, Serpents, Lions, Tygers, Fire, War, Pestilence, Famine, etc."—, feels the pleasing terror which such objects inspire, and imparts his thoughts and emotions in words. For how much bad criticism—and poetry—this degraded kind of Longinianism was responsible in the eighteenth century and after I need not say.—R. S. C.

More, P. E., and Cross, F. L. *Anglicanism*: the thought and practice of the Church of England, illustrated from the religious literature of the seventeenth century. London: S. P. C. K., 1935. Pp. lxxvi+811.

Rev. in *TLS,* June 20, 1935, p. 390; by Charles Smyth in *Criterion,* XIV (1935), 115-18; by Evelyn Underhill in *LM,* XXXII (1935), 289.

Nicolson, Marjorie. "Milton and the telescope." *ELH,* II (1935), 1-32.

Nicolson, Marjorie. "The 'new astronomy' and English literary imagination." *SP,* XXXII (1935), 428-62.

Nicolson, Marjorie. "The telescope and imagination." *MP,* XXXII (1935), 233-60.

Nicolson, Marjorie. *The microscope and English imagination.* (Smith College studies in Modern Languages, Vol. XVI, No. 4), Northampton, Mass.: Smith College, 1935. Pp. 92.

In these studies Miss Nicolson has begun the publication of the results of her extended investigation of the influence of the telescope and the microscope on the literary and religious imagination of England. The three articles on the telescope, which bring the subject down to Milton, will presumably be followed by others which will deal more specifically with the period covered by this bibliography. The study of the microscope begins, of course, with the late seventeenth century. Miss Nicolson is not primarily concerned with problems in the history of science, but with the effect the experience with the new "optics" had on the English imagination. The material she has gathered is striking for its wide range, its importance, and its pertinence. Her discussion of Milton is a fine commentary on the remark she quotes from David Masson that "Shakespeare lived in a world of time, Milton in a universe of space." *Paradise Lost* was undoubtedly written by a man who retained a vivid sense of looking through a telescope. Even where Milton uses the Ptolemaic scheme in his epic, he adds to the conception an awe-inspiring sense of vastness that we do not feel in the youthful treatment of the spheres in the *Nativity Ode.* As for the microscope, we learn that it was not only a new tool for scientists, but became one of the popular playthings of the eighteenth century, and Swift once pondered buying one for Stella. The marvels revealed by it seemed then to confirm some of the favorite doctrines of the age, such as that the productions of Nature are more perfect than those of Art (the finest lace seen under the microscope appears very imperfect compared with the details of the wings of a butterfly); the completeness of the scale of being appeared a more reasonable conception than ever before; and with a new sense of the mysteriousness and complexity of the minutest object, the idea almost inevitably followed that God is revealed even in the smallest particle of his creation. One may speculate as to whether Blake would ever have written his line about seeing Infinity in a grain of sand had it not been for the revelations of the microscope, which had already made the idea something of a commonplace; Henry Brooke anticipated Blake in his poem *Universal Beauty,* and Miss Nicolson quotes two somewhat similar passages from Traherne (p. 83) and Algarotti (p. 45). The idea suggests itself that the microscope may have stimulated the characteristic modern development of the imagination in the direction of pantheism.

Nitchie, Elizabeth. "Longinus and the theory of poetic imitation in the seventeenth and eighteenth century England." *SP,* XXXII (1935), 580-97.

By a happy circumstance, this essay appears in the same year with Monk's volume on *The Sublime,* and supplements this work by presenting evidence of the influence of Longinus on another aspect of literary theory.

Nolte, Fred O. *Early middle class drama, 1696-1774.* (New York University Ottendorfer Memorial Series of Germanic Monographs, XIX.) Lancaster, Pa.: Lancaster press, 1935. Pp. vi+213.

Noyes, Robert Gale. *Ben Jonson on the English stage, 1660-1776.* (Harvard studies in English, XVII.) Cambridge: Harvard University press, 1935. Pp. 350.

Noyes, Russell. "Drayton's literary vogue since 1631." *Indiana University studies,* XXII (1935), 1-23.

Parsons, Talcott. "H. M. Robertson on Max Weber and his school." *Journal of political economy,* XLIII (1935), 688-96.

On the dispute regarding the relation of religion and the rise of capitalism.

Peyre, Henri. *Qu'est-ce que le classicisme? (Essai de mise au point.)* Paris: E. Droz, 1933. Pp. 229.

Rev. by F. J. Tanquerey in *MLR,* XXX (1935), 251.

This little volume, which was unfortunately not noted here when it first appeared, makes no pretension either to profundity or originality. But in spite of the modesty of its aims, it may prove of great service to many a reader who has lost his sense of direction in this very tangled subject. Peyre presents his survey from a point of view frankly French, and gives a running criticism of the various theories which he summarizes. He is, moreover, familiar with the classical tendencies in the French and English literature of our own day, which in themselves are not easily understood apart from the earlier classical period, and which in turn are rich in stimulus and suggestion to the student of the classicism of the seventeenth century.

Rosenfeld, Sybil. "The Restoration stage in newspapers and Journal, 1660-1700." *MLR,* XXX (1935), 445-59.

A collection of notices and announcements, many of them from *The Gentleman's journal.*

Seaton, Ethel. *Literary relations of England and Scandinavia in the 17th century.* Oxford: Clarendon press, 1935. Pp. xvi+384.

Smith, Dane Farnsworth. "Plays about the theatre in England from *The Rehearsal* in 1671 to the Licensing Act in 1737." *Harvard University summaries of theses, 1934,* pp. 335-37.

Snodgrass, A. E. "The best actor in the world." Cornhill, December, 1935.

On Thomas Betterton.

Stedman, Ralph E. "The ethics of William Wollaston." *Nineteenth century,* August, 1935.

Summers, Montague. *The playhouse of Pepys.* London: Kegan Paul, 1935. Pp. xvi+485, with 24 collotype plates.

Rev. in *TLS,* July 11, 1935, p. 444; by Bonamy Dobrée in *Criterion,* XIV (1935), 152-55.

Thielke, Karl L. F. *Literatur- und Kunstkritik in ihren Wechselbeziehungen.* Ein Beitrag zur englischen Aesthetik des 18. Jahrhunderts. (Studien zur englischen Philologie, LXXXIV.) Halle: Niemeyer, 1935. Pp. 125.

This work is somewhat obvious in both theme and treatment, but it is written with judgment and it assembles a good deal of pertinent illustrative material. It might serve as a useful introduction to some aspects of the esthetics of the century.

Tietje, Hans. "Le style Baroque." *Revue de snythèse,* IX (1935), 116-22.

Ustick, W. Lee, and Hudson, Hoyt H. "Wit, 'mixt wit', and the bee in amber." *Huntington Library bulletin,* No. 8, October, 1935, pp. 103-30.

A study in the varying conceptions of Wit in the seventeenth century.

Van der Veen, H. R. S. *Jewish characters in eighteenth century English fiction and drama.* Groningen, Batavia: J. B. Wolters, 1935. Pp. 308.

Wallerstein, Ruth C. "The development of the rhetoric and metre of the heroic couplet, especially in 1625-1645." *PMLA,* L (1935), 166-209.

An important contribution to a subject which has long been in need of reexamination. It supplements the essay by George Williamson on the related subject of the rhetorical pattern of Neo-classical wit.

The twenty-second volume of the Walpole Society, 1933-1934. Vertue note books. Oxford: Printed for the Walpole Society by John Johnson at the University press, 1935.

Rev. in *TLS,* April 25, 1935, p. 269.

The twenty-third volume of the Walpole Society, 1934-1935. The drawings and sketches of John Robert Cozens. A catalogue with an historical introduction. By C. F. Bell and Thomas Girtin. Oxford: Printed for the Walpole Society, 1935.

Rev. in *TLS,* Nov. 2, 1935, p. 689.

Walter, H. B. "Some English antiquaries." *Transactions of the Royal Society of literature,* XIII (1934), 77-108.

Weber, Carl August. *Bristols Bedeutung für die Englische Romantik und die Deutsch-Englischen Beziehungen.* (Studien zur englischen Philologie, LXXXIX.) Halle: Niemeyer, 1935. Pp. xv+304.

Wells, Mitchell P. "Some notes on the early eighteenth century pantomime." *SP,* XXXII (1935), 598-607.

Whelan, Sister M. Kevin. *Enthusiasm in English poetry of the eighteenth century (1700-1774).* Washington, D. C.: The Catholic University of America, 1935. Pp. viii+169.

Whitney, Lois. *Primitivism and the idea of progress in English popular literature of the eighteenth century.* Baltimore: The Johns Hopkins press, 1934. Cf. *PQ,* XIV, 156.

Rev. by M. E. Prior in *MP,* XXXIII (1935), 99-101; in *Monist,* XLV (1935), 153; by F. E. Budd in *MLR,* XXX (1935), 526-27.

Wild, Friedrich. "Zum Problem des Barocks in der Englischen Dichtung." *Anglia,* LIX (1935), 414-22.

Williamson, George. "Milton and the Mortalist heresy." *SP,* XXXII (1935), 553-79.

Williamson, George. "Mutability, decay, and seventeenth-century melancholy." *ELH,* II (1935), 121-50.

Williamson, George. "The rhetorical pattern of Neo-classical wit." *MP,* XXXIII (1935), 55-81.

An admirable study in the origins of the Neo-classical movement. Cf. the essay by Ruth Wallerstein noticed above.

Wilson, Mona. "The twilight of the Augustans." *Essays and studies by members of the English Association,* XX (1935), 75-85.

Wolf, A. *A history of science, technology, and philosophy in the sixteenth and seventeenth centuries.* With coöperation of F. Dannemann and A. Armitage. London: Allen and Unwin, 1935. Pp. 692.

Rev. in *TLS,* June 13, 1935, p. 374; by G. Sarton in *Isis,* XXIV (1935), 164-67; by W. C. D. Dampier in *Philosophy,* X (1935), 487-90.

Wolff, Lucien. "Thomas Gainsborough: aperçus sur l'homme et l'artiste." *Annales de Bretagne,* XLII (1935), 204-26.

The eleventh volume of the Wren Society, 1934. Oxford: Printed for the Wren Society at the University press, 1934. Pp. 124+lxiv.

Rev. in *TLS,* Jan. 10, 1935, p. 18.

IV. INDIVIDUAL AUTHORS

Joseph Addison
(See also *Alexander Pope*)

Fawcett, J. W. "Addison of Mauds Meaburn." *N & Q,* CLXIX (1935), 194.

On Gulston Addison, Joseph's brother.

Greenough, Chester Noyes. "Did Joseph Addison write *The Playhouse?*" *Harvard studies and notes in philology and literature,* XVII (1935), 55-66.

Thorpe, Clarence DeWitt. "Addison and Hutcheson on the imagination." *ELH,* II (1935), 215-34.

This article undertakes to show that Hutcheson, however close to Shaftesbury he may be in ethical point of view, is in aesthetics more indebted to Addison, particularly with regard to the "pleasures" of the imagination. Professor Thorpe demonstrates that Hutcheson read and admired Addison's *Spectator* essays. He then proceeds to show that instead of Shaftesbury's conception of beauty as "an imagined harmony and excellence, indissolubly connected with pre-established ideas of moral good and truth," Hutcheson follows Addison in recognizing "only a natural response of a nervous organization so constituted by the creator as to experience pleasure upon the perception of certain objects." The article is to be valued not only for its lucid analysis of the aesthetic ideas of Addison and Hutcheson but also for its appraisal of the relative positions of Shaftesbury and the followers of Locke. Two minor points perhaps deserve mention. P. 225: Addison's view of imagination as lying midway between sense and the understanding was not specifically founded on the sensational psychology of Locke; it was a prevalent view, deriving ultimately from Aristotle (*De anima* iii). See e.g., Charron, *Of wisdom,* trans. G. Stanhope (2nd ed., London, 1707). I, 74-75; F. Loryot, *Les secretz moraux* (Paris, 1614), pp. 686-87; J. F. Senault, *The use of passions,* trans. Henry Cary (London, 1649), pp. 12-15; Louis de la Forge, *Traité de l'esprit* (Amsterdam [1669]), p. 284; Walter Charleton, *Natural history of the passions* (London, 1674) pp. 49-67. P. 234: Would not the popularity of the *Spectator* essays alone, guarantee a diffusion of Addison's ideas throughout the eighteenth century, without the aid of Hutcheson?—D. F. B.

Thorpe, Clarence DeWitt. "Two Augustans cross the Alps: Dennis and Addison on mountain scenery." *SP,* XXXII (1935), 463-82.

The older view of Gray as the first eighteenth-century writer to find beauty in mountains has been considerably modified as scholars like R. D. Havens and C. A. Moore have submitted evidence of appreciation for rugged scenery from the earlier part of the century. Professor Thorpe presents the case for two representative neo-classicists: John Dennis and Joseph Addison. The former, in a letter of 21 October 1688, describes in some detail his crossing of the Alps and confesses "a delightful Horrour, a terrible Joy," in the experience. The evidence from Addison is more extensive: the *Letter from Italy* to Halifax (1703), the *Remarks on Italy* (1705), the two well-known letters to Wortley Montague (1701) and to Wood (1703), and finally various passages in the *Spectator* and *Tatler.* From these Thorpe draws a number of passages which show Addison's interest in "huge precipices of naked rocks" and "rude prospects." "Individually and isolated," Thorpe concludes, "perhaps these remarks would be of small importance, but viewed collectively, in connection with all Addison had to say showing appreciation of mountains, they become impressive" (pp. 477-78). This is true; such a collection of evidence should make the future historian pause before dismissing Addison as one who only tolerated wild and rugged scenery. At the same time, a reading of the *Remarks* hardly warrants the conclusion that Addison was very deeply moved by scenery of any kind. Against these passages of two or three sentences we have lengthy paragraphs on Roman statuary or on the character of the Neapolitans. Even Mount Vesuvio ("there is nothing about *Naples,* nor indeed in any part of *Italy,* which deserves our admiration so much as this mountain") arouses Addison's curiosity only over its geological formation, and his lengthy description shows the point of view of the amateur scientist ("The air of this place must be very much impregnated with Salt-petre"). And it is significant that when Addison speaks of ending his chapters with "descriptions" of the Appenines or the Alps, these turn out to be quotations from Ovid, Claudius, and Silius Italicus. Too much should not be made therefore, it seems to me, of his chance—and infrequent—remarks on mountain scenery. The quotations cited from the later periodical essays, particularly the series on imagination, show convincingly that Addison included vast mountain views among the various objects capable of arousing the mind to sublimity.—D. F. B.

John Arbuthnot

(See also *Alexander Pope*)

"John Arbuthnot, M.D. Died February 27, 1735." Leading article in *TLS,* Febr. 28, 1935, pp. 113-14.

Beattie, Lester M. *John Arbuthnot: mathematician and satirist.* Cambridge: Harvard University press, 1935. Pp. 416.

Rev. in *TLS,* Jan. 25, 1936, p. 71.

This volume is not a biographical study, although it fills in details from the publications of the Historical Manuscripts Commission and from other sources not yet available when Aitken published his memoir of Arbuthnot in 1892. Mr. Beattie calls his approach "critical rather than biographical." He takes up the genuine works and the attributions, discussing in each case such questions as arise regarding authorship, editions, sources, parallels, and imitations. In a searching review he shatters pretty well the theory advanced in 1925 by Herman Teerink, that Swift was the author of *The History of John Bull.* Mr. Beattie has been particularly thorough in his investigation of the *Stoffgeschichte* of this satire, and has culled from the journalism of the time a multitude of parallels, which he at times pushes a little too hard as "sources." But whether we regard them as sources or merely as parallels, they reveal the taste of the time for homespun narratives, even though none of them were spun with such skill as Arbuthnot's.

Jane Austen

Cecil, Lord David. *Jane Austen.* The Leslie Stephen lecture. Cambridge: University press, 1935. Pp. 43.

Dudley, O. H. T. "Jane Austen: two conjectures." *TLS,* March 28, 1935, p. 210.

Two problems of text.

Tallmadge, Abby L. "Sense and sensibility." *TLS,* Jan. 18, 1936, p. 55.

The source of the title in Cowper?

Villard, Léonie. "Les *Juvenilia* de Jane Austen." *RAA,* XII (1935), 206-18.

William Beckford

Hunter, A. O. "Le *Vathek* de William Beckford: historique des éditions françaises." *RLC,* XV (1935), 119-26.

Dr. Peter Bellon

Anderson, Paul Bunyan. "Buckingham's chemist." *TLS,* Oct. 3, 1935, p. 612.

New information about Dr. Peter Bellon, who is not in the *D. N. B.*, with some account of his literary career.

Simon Berington

Ellison, Lee Monroe. "*Gaudentio di Lucca*: a forgotten Utopia." *PMLA,* L (1935), 494-509.

George Berkeley

Aldrich, Virgil Charles. "Berkeley's conception of nature." *Rice Institute pamphlet,* XXII (1935), 83-104.

Colum, Padraic. "Berkeley and the modern artist." *SRL,* June 15, 1935, pp. 3-4.

Luce, A. A. "Some unpublished Berkeley letters with some new Berkeleiana." *Proceedings of the Royal Irish academy,* XLI 1932-1934), Section C, 141-161.

Luce, A. A. "Berkeley's Bermuda project and his benefactions to American universities, with unpublished letters and extracts from the Egmont papers." *Proceedings of the Royal Irish academy,* XLII (1934), Section C, 97-120.

Luce, A. A. "Berkeley's *Description of the cave of Dunmore.*" *Hermathena: a series of papers on literature, science, and philosophy, by members of Trinity College, Dublin,* No. XLVI (1931), 149-61.

Luce, A. A. "Two sermons by Bishop Berkeley." *Hermathena*, No. XLVII (1932), 1-42.

Includes comment and a reprint of the two sermons, The Sermon on Religious Zeal (undated, but belonging to Berkeley's first years as a Resident Fellow at Trinity College), and the Sermon on the Will of God, 1751.

Luce, A. A. "Berkeley's *Commonplace Book*—Its date, purpose, structure, and marginal signs." *Hermathena*, No. XLVII (1932), 99-132.

Luce, A. A. "More unpublished Berkeley letters and new Berkeleiana." *Hermathena*, No. XLVIII (1933), 25-54.

Hugh Blair

Jiriczek, Otto L. "Zur Bibliographie und Textgeschichte von Hugh Blair's *Critical dissertation on the Poems of Ossian.*" *ES*, LXX (1935), 181-89.

William Blake

Blake's Note-book. London: Nonesuch press, 1935.

A collotype facsimile of the Rossetti manuscript.

Illustrations of the Book of Job. Introduction by Laurence Binyon and Geoffrey Keynes. New York: Pierpont Morgan Library; London: Quaritch, 1935.

Rev. in *TLS,* June 6, 1935, p. 359; by Frank Jewett Mather in *SRL,* Jan. 18, 1936, p. 16.

Saurat, Denis. *Blake and Milton.* London: Stanley Nott, 1935.

Rev. in *TLS,* Dec. 28, 1935, p. 895. Corr. by Saurat, *ibid.,* Jan. 11, 1936, p. 35.

Schorer, Mark. "William Blake and the cosmic nadir." *Sewanee review,* XLIII (1935), 210-21.

James Boswell

Boswell's Life of Johnson. Edited by George Birkbeck Hill. Revised and enlarged edition by L. F. Powell. 4 vols. Oxford: Clarendon press, 1934. Cf. *PQ,* XIV, 158.

Rev. by J. R. Sutherland in *MLR,* XXX (1935), 375-79; by Charles H. Bennett in *JEGP,* XXXIV (1935), 256-59; by George Sherburn in *PQ,* XIV (1935), 374-75; by Chauncey B. Tinker in *SRL,* Jan. 26, 1935, pp. 446-47.

Tom Brown

Boyce, Benjamin. "Two debits for Tom Brown, with a credit from Joseph Addison." *PQ,* XIV (1935), 263-69.

Wiley, Autrey Nell. "The Poussin doctor." *MLN,* L (1935), 506-08.

Explains an allusion to Charles Davenant in Tom Brown's *The Stage beaux toss'd in a blanket* (1704).

Edmund Burke

Buehler, Reginald Guyon. "Burke and Rousseau." *Harvard University summaries of theses, 1934,* pp. 313-14.

Drew, Helen L. "The date of Burke's *Sublime and beautiful.*" *MLN,* L (1935), 510-21.

Advertised in the *London chronicle* in April, 1757.

Einaudi, Mario. "The British background of Burke's political philosophy." *Political science quarterly,* XLIX (1934), 576-98.

Charles Burney

A general history of music. Edited with critical and historical notes by Frank Mercer. 2 vols. London: Foulis, 1935.

Rev. in *TLS,* Aug. 29, 1935, p. 533.

Robert Burns

Burns chronicle and club directory. Second series, Vol. x. Kilmarnock: The Burns Federation, 1935.

This inexpensive annual publication is the organ of Burns Clubs, and some of its contents are not of a scholarly nature. But it also contains original and reprinted articles of importance to the student, an annual guide to the recent Burns literature, and frequently publishes hitherto unprinted letters and documents.

Cook, Davidson. "Allan Cunningham's literary ghost." *TLS,* March 21, 1935, p. 180, and March 28, p. 216. Corr. by Anthony C. Deane, *ibid.,* April 4, p. 232, and by Davidson Cook, April 11, p. 248.

Fitzhugh, Robert T. "The paradox of Burns' character." *SP,* XXXII (1935), 110-19.

A protest against excessive idealization of the character of Burns.

Heron-Allen, E. "The true story of Burns's poem, *The Deil's awa' wi' th' Exciseman.*" *N & Q,* CLXVII (1934), 417.

The account is in a letter by Burns.

Snyder, Franklin Bliss. "Burns and the smuggler *Rosamond.*" *PMLA,* L (1935), 510-21.

Thomas Chatterton

Staubert, Paul. *Thomas Chatterton und seine Rowley-Dichtung*. (Bonner Studien zur englischen Philologie, xxiv.) Bonn, 1935. Pp. 162.

Watkins-Jones, A. "Bishop Percy, Thomas Warton, and Chatterton's Rowley poems (1773-1790)." *PMLA*, L (1935), 769-84.

Contains unpublished letters.

Philip Dormer Stanhope, fourth Earl of Chesterfield

Letters and other pieces. Selected and edited by Richmond P. Bond. New York: Doubleday Doran, 1935. Pp. lvii+321.

Rev. by Virgil B. Heltzel in *MP*, XXXIII (1935), 216-17.

Gulick, Sidney L. *A Chesterfield bibliography to 1800.* Reprinted from *The papers of the Bibliographical Society of America*, Vol. xxix (1935). University of Chicago press. Pp. 114.

Shellabarger, Samuel. *Lord Chesterfield.* London: Macmillan, 1935. Pp. xiv+422.

Rev. in *TLS*, Nov. 9, 1935, p. 713.

Colley Cibber

Vincent, H. P. "Two letters of Colley Cibber." *N & Q*, CLXVIII (1935), 3-4.

William Cole

Palmer, W. M. *William Cole of Milton.* Cambridge: Galloway and Porter, 1935.

Notice in *TLS*, April 11, 1935, p. 246.

William Collins

Page, Frederick. "An essay by Collins." *TLS*, July 11, 1935, p. 448. Comment by E. H. W. Meyerstein, *ibid.*, July 25, p. 477; by E. Blunden, *ibid.*, August 8, p. 501.

The essay here ascribed to Collins appeared in Dodsley's *Museum* for July 4, 1747, under the title "Of the essential excellencies in poetry." The conclusion that Collins was probably the author rests on the following arguments: that both the essayist and Collins thought of poetry as a kind of divinely inspired power of creating; that both exalted Spenser, Shakespeare, and Milton; that both believed the function of poetry was to transcend rather than merely to copy nature; and that both admired Mallet's description of St. Kilda in *Amyntor and Theodora*, since the essayist praised it in the essay and Collins seems to have borrowed certain details from it two years later in his *Ode on the popular superstitions*. Unfortunately this particular combination of traits is not one of which any well read student of the eighteenth century would be prepared to say that it could have been possessed by one person only among those who may have written for the *Museum* in 1747. It circumscribes, to be sure, a relatively small group of individuals, and Collins belonged to the group, but that is as far as we can legitimately go in the present state of our knowledge. It is possible that Collins wrote the essay, but a plausible case could also be made out for Mark Akenside, who, as is well known, had expressed no less "romantic" views of poetry three years before in his *Pleasures of imagination* and who, on assuming the editorship of the *Museum* in 1746, had agreed with Dodsley to contribute an essay to each of the fortnightly numbers. In view of the fact that "Of the essential excellencies in poetry" is the only essay in the issue for July 4, 1747, the suggestion ought not to be dismissed too easily. And there were also, among known contributors to the *Museum* whose poetic principles, to say the least, did not disqualify them for the task, Joseph Spence, Joseph Warton, Robert Lowth, and John Gilbert Cooper. —R. S. C.

Meyerstein, E. H. W. "Collins's ode on Colonel Ross." *TLS*, July 4, 1935, p. 432.

George Colman

Page, Eugene R. *George Colman the elder, 1732-1794.* New York: Columbia University press, 1935. Pp. xi+334.

Rev. in *TLS*, Dec. 21, 1935, p. 874.

William Congreve

Hodges, John C. "On the date of Congreve's birth." *MP*, XXXIII (1935), 83-85.

William Cowper

Thomas, Gilbert. *William Cowper and the eighteenth century.* London: Nicholson and Watson, 1935. Pp. 396.

Rev. in *TLS*, Sept. 5, 1935, p. 549.

Sir William Davenant

Dowlin, C. M. *Sir William Davenant's 'Gondibert,' its preface, and Hobbes's answer.* Philadelphia: University of Pennsylvania press, 1934. Pp. 127.

Harbage, Alfred. *Sir William Davenant, poet venturer, 1606-1668.* Philadelphia: University of Pennsylvania press, 1935. Pp. 317.

Rev. in *TLS*, May 2, 1935, p. 285; by Arthur H. Nethercot in *MP*, XXXIII (1935), 95-99.

Thomas Day

Carrière, J. M. "A French adaptation of *Sandford and Merton.*" *MLN,* L (1935), 238-42.

Scott, Sir S. H. *The exemplary Mr. Day, 1748-1789.* London: Faber and Faber, 1935. Pp. 178.

Rev. in *TLS,* Feb. 7, 1935, p. 73; by Edith Shackleton. in *LM,* XXXI (1935), 486-87.

Daniel Defoe

'A Journal of the Plague Year' and other pieces. Edited by Arthur W. Secord. New York: Doubleday Doran, 1935. Pp. xxxv+337.

Deneke, O. *Robinson Crusoe in Deutschland: Die Frühdrucke 1720-1780.* (Göttingische Nebenstunden, 11.) Göttingen: Deneke, 1935.

Fletcher, Edward G. "Defoe on Milton." *MLN,* L (1935), 31-32.

Fletcher, Edward G. "The London and Edinburgh printings of Defoe's *Review,* volume VI." *University of Texas studies in English,* No. xiv (1934), 50-58.

Häusermann, H. W. "Aspects of life and thought in *Robinson Crusoe.*" *RES,* XI (1935), 299-312, 439-56.

Moore, John Robert. "Daniel Defoe and modern economic theory." *Indiana University studies,* XXI (1935), 1-28.

Mrs. Delany

Vulliamy, C. E. *Aspasia: the life and letters of Mary Granville, Mrs. Delaney (1700-1788).* London: Geoffrey Bles, 1935.

Rev. in *TLS,* Nov. 2, 1935, p. 681.

John Dryden

Marriage à la Mode. Edited with an introduction, notes, and glossary by J. R. Sutherland. (Temple classics.) London: Dent, 1935. Pp. 153.

Allen, Ned Bliss. *The sources of John Dryden's comedies.* Ann Arbor: University of Michigan press, 1935. Pp. xvii+298.

Bredvold, Louis I. *The intellectual milieu of John Dryden.* Ann Arbor: University of Michigan press, 1934. Cf. *PQ,* XIV, 163.

Rev. by James R. Sutherland in *History,* XIX (1935), 353; in *RLC,* XV (1935), 155; by Alan D. McKillop in *PQ,* XIV (1935), 375-76; by A. W. Secord in *JEGP,* XXXIV (1935), 462-64; by M. E. Prior in *MP,* XXXII (1935), 324-29.

Brooks, Harold. "Some notes on Dryden, Cowley, and Shadwell." *N & Q,* CLXVIII (1935), 94-95.

Brooks, Harold. "When did Dryden write *MacFlecknoe?*—Some additional notes." *RES,* XI (1935), 74-78.

Fletcher, Edward G. "A Dryden anecdote." *MLN,* L (1935), 366.

Ham, R. G. "Dryden as Historiographer-Royal." *RES,* XI (1935), 284-98.

Ham, Roswell G. "Dryden's dedication for *The Music of the Prophetesse,* 1691." *PMLA,* L (1935), 1065-75.

Havens, P. S. "Dryden's 'tagged' version of *Paradise Lost.*" In *Essays in dramatic literature: the Parrott presentation volume.* Princeton: University press, 1935. Pp. 383-98.

Hooker, E. N. "Dryden's allusion to the poet of excessive wit." *N & Q,* CLXVIII (1935), 421.

Nettleton, George H. "Author's changes in Dryden's *Conquest of Granada, Part I.*" *MLN,* L (1935), 360-64.

Parsons, Coleman O. "Dryden's letter of attorney." *MLN,* L (1935), 364-65.

Turnell, G. M. "Dryden and the religious elements in the Classical tradition." *ES,* LXX (1935), 244-61.

Ward, Charles E. "Massinger and Dryden." *ELH,* II (1935), 263-66.

Henry Fielding

Jensen, Gerard E. "A Fielding discovery." *Yale University Library gazette,* X (1935), 23-32.

Ronte, Heinz. *Richardson und Fielding:* Geschichte ihres Ruhms; literarsoziologischer Versuch. (Kölner Anglistische Arbeiten, XXV.) Leipzig: Tauchnitz, 1935. Pp. 217.

Seymour, Mabel. "Fielding's history of the Forty-five." *PQ,* XIV (1935), 105-25.

John Gay

The Beggar's opera. Edited with an introduction, notes, and glossary by F. W. Bateson. (Temple classics.) London: Dent, 1935. Pp. 123.

Bryce, John C. "'Addition' to Gay's Fables." *TLS,* July 4, 1935, p. 432.

Sutherland, James R. "The Beggar's opera." *TLS,* April 25, 1935, p. 272.

Contemporary anecdote regarding its origin.

Tolksdorf, Cäcelie. *John Gays "Beggar's Opera" und Bert Brechts "Dreigroschenoper."* Bonn diss., 1934. Pp. 80.

Oliver Goldsmith

Churchill, Irving L. "Editions of Percy's memoir of Goldsmith." *MLN,* L (1935), 464-65.

Friedman, Arthur. "Goldsmith and the *Weekly magazine.*" *MP,* XXXII (1935), 281-99.

Friedman, Arthur. "Goldsmith's *Life of Bolingbroke* and the *Biographia Britannica.*" *MLN,* L (1935), 25-29.

Gwynn, Stephen. *Oliver Goldsmith.* London: Butterworth; New York: Henry Holt [1935]. Pp. vi+326.

Apart from the account of Goldsmith's early life in Ireland, which reveals some insight into social backgrounds and distinctions usually lacking in English biographers, and apart from some fresh pages on Goldsmith's character, this book contains little or nothing that will be recognized as new by students familiar with the lives by Prior, Forster, or Dobson. The author pays a tribute in his preface to Miss Balderston's edition of the correspondence, but he does not always avail himself of her criticism of the texts; thus, instead of presenting the Fiddleback episode (pp. 47-51) in the words of Mrs. Hodson's narrative—the only clearly authentic source—he prefers to quote in full the literary version in the form of a letter from Goldsmith to his mother which Prior printed in 1837 and which is certainly not above suspicion of being a forgery. In dealing with the date of the poet's birth (p. 4), he takes no account of Miss Balderston's argument in the *TLS* for March 7, 1929, pp. 185-86, that the year was in all probability not 1728 but 1730; and he remains equally unaware of recent studies on Goldsmith's activities as a contributor to periodicals and on the history of the legend that he had a medical degree. —P. 185: an examination of the proof-sheets of *The traveller,* now in the British Museum, makes clear that the lines contributed by Johnson to the text of that poem were all added in proof—R. S. C.

Hawkins, Aubrey. "The 'security' of our odes." *TLS,* Nov. 16, 1935, p. 746.

A serious misprint in Goldsmith's allusion to Gray's odes; the first edition reads "obscurity."

"Olybrius." "Fragment of a letter of Goldsmith." *N & Q,* CLXVII (1935), 358.

Richard Graves

Hill, Charles Jarvis. *The literary career of Richard Graves. Smith College studies in modern languages,* XVI (1935), 1-148.

Hill, Charles Jarvis. "Applause for Dodsley's *Cleone.*" *PQ,* XIV (1935), 181-84.

Unpublished letters by Graves.

Thomas Gray
(See also *William Cole* and *Oliver Goldsmith*)

Correspondence. Edited by the late Paget Toynbee and Leonard Whibley. 3 vols. Oxford: Clarendon press, 1935. Pp. lx, 454; xxxvi, 455-909; xxxiv, 901-1360.

Fisher, J. "James Hammond and the quatrain of Gray's *Elegy.*" *MP,* XXXII (1935), 301-10.

Ketton-Cremer, R. W. *Thomas Gray.* London: Duckworth, 1935.

Rev. in *TLS,* Aug. 15, 1935, p. 511.

Micale, Olga. *Thomas Gray e la sua influenza sulla letteratura Italiana.* Catania: Studio editoriale moderno, 1934.

Rev. by Joseph G. Fucilla in *JEGP,* XXXIV (1935), 277-79.

Thomas Hearne

"Thomas Hearne." Leading article in *TLS,* June 6, 1935, pp. 353-54.

"Thomas Hearne and Richard Gough." *TLS,* Feb. 14, 1935, p. 96.

Bulloch, J. M. "Hearne's first master, the Rev. Patrick Gordon." *N & Q,* CLXIX (1935), 344-46.

David Hume

Dialogues concerning natural religion. Ed. by N. Kemp Smith. Oxford: Clarendon press, 1935. Pp. xii+284.

Rev. in *TLS,* Nov. 2, 1935, p. 686; by S. P. Lamprecht in *Journal of philosophy,* XXXII (1935), 665-66.

Church, Ralph W. *Hume's theory of the understanding.* Ithaca: Cornell University press; London: Allen and Unwin, 1935. Pp. 238.

Rev. in *TLS,* May 23, 1935, p. 329; by J. D. Mabbott in *Philosophy,* X (1935), 370-73; by S. P. Lamprecht in *Journal of philosophy,* XXXII (1935), 691.

Stanley, Philip. "The scepticisms of David Hume." *Journal of philosophy,* XXXII (1935), 421-31.

Samuel Johnson

(See also *James Boswell* and *Alexander Pope*)

Barnouw, A. J. "*Rasselas* in Dutch." *TLS,* April 11, 1935, p. 244.

Hazen, Allen T., and McAdam, Edward L. *A catalogue of an exhibition of first editions of the works of Samuel Johnson.* New Haven, 1935. Pp. 32.

Lists an edition of 1739 of Johnson's translation of Crousaz's *Commentary* on Pope's *Essay on Man.* Cf. also *Yale University Library gazette,* X (1936), 45-51; and *TLS,* Nov. 2, 1935.

Murphy, Mallie J. "*The Rambler,* no. 191." *PMLA,* L (1935), 926-28.

Metzdorf, Robert F. "An unpublished Johnson letter concerning Percy's *Reliques.*" *MLN,* L (1935), 509-13.

Interesting and important letter, dated Oct. 4, 1760, in which Johnson acts as intermediary between Dodsley and Percy.

Osborn, James M. "Johnson on the sanctity of an author's text." *PMLA,* L (1935), 928-29.

Read, Allen Walker. "The contemporary quotations in Johnson's dictionary." *ELH,* II (1935), 246-51.

Reade, Aleyn Lyell. *Johnsonian gleanings, part VII.* The Jervis, Porter, and other allied families. London: For the author, by Percy Lund, Humphries, and Co., 1935. Pp. vi+226.

Rev. in *TLS,* Jan. 11, 1936, p. 37.

Reynolds, W. Vaughan. "The reception of Johnson's prose style." *RES,* XI (1935), 145-62.

Roberts, S. C. *Doctor Johnson.* (Great Lives.) London: Duckworth, 1935. Pp. 142.

Notice in *TLS,* May 23, 1935, p. 332.

Schinz, A. "Samuel Johnson, le Boileau anglais." *Revue des deux mondes,* 1 February, 1935.

Smith, D. Nichol. "The contributors to *The Rambler* and *The Idler.*" *Bodleian quarterly record,* VII (1934), 508-09.

Tillotson, Geoffrey. "*Rasselas* and the *Persian Tales.*" *TLS,* Aug. 29, 1935, p. 534. Corr. by R. H. Griffith, Nov. 16, p. 752.

Wohlers, Heinz. *Der persönliche Gehalt in den Shakespeare-Noten Samuel Johnsons.* Hamburg diss., 1934. Pp. 92.

Edward Kimber

Black, Frank Gees. "Edward Kimber: anonymous novelist of the mid-eighteenth century." *Harvard studies and notes in philology and literature,* XVII (1935), 27-42.

Nathaniel Lee

Stroup, Thos. B. "*The Princess of Cleve* and sentimental comedy." *RES,* XI (1935), 200-03.

Greene, Graham. "Rochester and Lee." *TLS,* Nov. 2, 1935, p. 697. Corr. by W. J. Lawrence, Nov. 9, p. 722.

Charlotte Ramsay Lennox

Small, Miriam Rossiter. *Charlotte Ramsay Lennox: an eighteenth-century lady of letters.* New Haven: Yale University press, 1935. Pp. 264.

Rev. in *TLS,* Jan. 18, 1936, p. 49.

James Macpherson
(See also *Hugh Blair* and *Thomas Chatterton*)

Jiriczek, Otto L. "Loda in Macpherson's *Ossian.*" *Anglia,* LIX (1935), 435-40.

Sir Isaac Newton

de Carvalho, Joaquim. "Jacob de Castro Sarmento et l'introduction des conceptions de Newton en Portugal." *Archeion,* XVI (1934), 319-23.

"Halley, Flamsteed and Newton." *N & Q,* CLXVIII (1935), 434; CLXIX (1935), 122 and 159.

Hiscock, W. G. "The war of the scientists: new light on Newton and Gregory." *TLS,* Jan. 11, 1936, p. 34. Corr. by Joseph Larmor, Jan. 18, p. 55.

MacPike, Eugene F. "Sir Isaac Newton in American libraries." *N & Q,* CLXIX (1935), 391-92.

Northrop, F. S. C. "Newton and the modern age." *SRL,* Feb. 2, 1935, pp. 453-54.

Popp, K. R. *Jakob Böhme und Isaac Newton.* Leipzig: S. Hirzel, 1935. Pp. xii+97.

Russell, A. S. "Sir Isaac Newton." *Quarterly review*, CCLXIV (1935), 126-38.

Samuel Pepys

The Tangier papers of Samuel Pepys. Transcribed, edited, and collated with the transcription of Mr. W. Matthews. By Edwin Chappell. London: Navy Records Society, 1935. Pp. 376.

Rev. in *TLS,* June 6, 1935, p. 356; corr. by Edwin Chappell, *ibid.,* June 13, p. 380; rev. by Wilbur C. Abbott in *SRL,* March 16, 1935, p. 553.

Bryant, Arthur. *Samuel Pepys: the years of peril.* Cambridge: University press, 1935.

Rev. in *TLS,* Nov. 2, 1935, p. 690.

Chappell, Edwin. "Pepys and the Huguenots." *N & Q,* CLXIX (1935), 318.

Chappell, Edwin. "Pepysiana." *TLS,* March 14, 1935, p. 160.

Kirk, Rudolf. *Mr. Pepys upon the state of Christ's Hospital.* Philadelphia: University of Pennsylvania press; London: Milford, 1935.

Rev. in *TLS,* Dec. 7, 1935, p. 833.

Marburg, Clara. *Mr. Pepys and Mr. Evelyn.* Philadelphia: University of Pennsylvania press; London: Milford, 1935.

Rev. in *TLS,* Dec. 7, 1935, p. 833.
Contains thirty-seven unpublished letters.

Matthews, W. "Pepys's transcribers." *JEGP,* XXXIV (1935), 213-24.

Matthews, W. "Samuel Pepys and Spain." *Neophilologus,* XX (1935), 120-29.

Thomas Percy

(See also *Hugh Blair, Thomas Chatterton, Oliver Goldsmith,* and *Samuel Johnson*)

Brooks, Cleanth. "Percy's *History of the Wolf in Great Britain.*" *JEGP,* XXXIV (1935), 101-03.

Ambrose Phillips

Griffith, R .H. "Persian tales." *TLS,* Nov. 16, 1935, p. 752. Corr. by Duncan B. Macdonald, *ibid.,* Dec. 14, p. 864.

Bibliographical notes on Phillips' translation and a competing translation, both of 1714.

de la Torre Bueno, Lillian. "Was Ambrose Phillips a ballad editor?" *Anglia,* LIX (1935), 252-70.

Alexander Pope

Pope's own Miscellany. Being a reprint of *Poems on several occasions,* 1717. Edited by Norman Ault. London: Nonesuch press, 1935. Pp. xcvii+165.

Rev. in *TLS,* May 16, 1935, p. 311; by Geoffrey Tillotson in *Criterion,* XIV (1935), 155-56.

Ault, Norman. "Pope's lost sermon on glass-bottles." *TLS,* June 6, 1935, p. 360. Corr. by W. Fraser Mitchell, E. Heath, and C. W. B., June 13, p. 380; by George Sherburn, June 20, p. 399; by J. R. Sutherland, June 27, p. 416; by Norman Ault, July 4, p. 432; and by George Sherburn, July 11, p. 448.

Concerning the supposed identification of a pamphlet by Pope, published in May 1715, in which his enemies are attacked.

Ault, Norman. "Pope and the miscellanies." *TLS,* Dec. 7, 1935, p. 838.

Beck, Richard. "Jón Þorláksson—Icelandic translator of Pope and Milton." *JEGP,* XXXIV (1935), 74-100.

Case, Arthur. "Pope, Addison, and the *Atticus* lines." *MP,* XXXIII (1935), 187-93.

Fletcher, Edward G. "Belinda's game of ombre." *University of Texas studies in English,* no. 15 (1935), 28-38.

Munby, A. N. L. "A Pope problem." *TLS,* Jan. 10, 1935, p. 21. Cf. corr. by Howard P. Vincent, Feb. 14, p. 92.

Sherburn, George. "'Timon's Villa' and Cannons." *Huntington Library bulletin,* no. 8 (1935), 131-52.

An important article on the relations of Pope with the Earl of Burlington.

Sherburn, George. *The early career of Alexander Pope.* Oxford: Clarendon press, 1934. Cf. *PQ,* XIV, 171.

Rev. by Robert K. Root in *MLN,* L (1935), 547-48; by William King in *Criterion,* XIV (1935), 504-06; by James R. Sutherland in *RES,* XI (1935), 354-56; by Walter F. Schirmer in *Deutsche Literaturzeitung,* Ser. III, VI (1935), 375-78; by R. W. Babcock in *Sewanee review,* XLIII (1935), 362-66; by Joseph Wood Krutch in *The Nation,* 140 (1935), 22; by John Butt in *MLR,* XXX (1935), 524-25; by E. N. S. Thompson in *PQ,* XIV (1935), 92-93.

Sutherland, James R. "Pope or Arbuthnot?" *TLS,* Nov. 22, 1935, p. 770.

On the authorship of the prose pamphlet, *Annus mirabilis* (1722).

Tickell, R. Eustace. "Pope and Tickell." *TLS,* Feb. 28, 1935, p. 124.

Matthew Prior

Dunlop, W. W. C. "A riddle by Prior." *TLS,* April 4, 1935, p. 228. Corr. by John Robert Moore, July 4, 1935, p. 432.

Hills, Alfred. "Matthew Prior in Essex." *Essex review,* XLIV (1935), 236-42.

Samuel Richardson
(See also *Henry Fielding*)

Askew, H. "Samuel Richardson's birthplace." *N & Q,* CLXIX (1935), 263; reply by F. Williamson, *ibid.,* 300-01.

Coe, Ada M. "Richardson in Spain." *Hispanic review,* III (1935), 56-63.

Sale, William M. "The first dramatic version of *Pamela.*" *Yale University Library gazette,* IX (1935), 83-88.

Sale, William M. "Samuel Richardson's house at Fulham." *N & Q,* CLXIX (1935), 133-34.

Sale, William M. "Samuel Richardson and *Sir William Harrington.*" *TLS,* Aug. 29, 1935, p. 537.

Schleck, Florian J. "Richardson on the Index." *TLS,* April 25, 1935, p. 272.

Joseph Ritson

Moreland, Carroll C. "Ritson's life of Robin Hood." *PMLA,* L (1935), 522-36.

An illustration of Ritson's uncritical methods.

John Wilmot, Earl of Rochester
(See also *Nathaniel Lee*)

Brooks, Harold. "Attributions to Rochester." *TLS,* May 9, 1935, p. 301.

Pinto, Vivian de Sola. *Rochester: portrait of a Restoration poet.* London: John Lane, 1935. Pp. 281.

Rev. in *TLS,* July 4, 1935, p. 429; by Bonamy Dobrée in *LM,* XXXII (1935), 392-93.

Pinto, Vivian de Sola. "The poetry of John Wilmot, Earl of Rochester." *Transactions of the Royal Society of Literature,* XIII (1934), 109-33.

Wilkinson, C. H. "Lord Rochester." *TLS,* July 11, 1935, p. 448.

Poems by Rochester in *The Triumph of wit,* 1688.

Williams, Charles. *Rochester.* London: Barker, 1935. Pp. 274.

Rev. in *TLS,* Sept. 5, 1935, p. 549; by John Hayward in *LM,* XXXII (1935), 600-01.

Nicholas Rowe

Whiting, George W. "Rowe's debt to *Paradise lost.*" *MP,* XXXII (1935), 271-79.

Richard Brinsley Sheridan

The Rivals, a comedy. As it was first acted at the Theatre-Royal in Covent-Garden. Edited from the Larpent Manuscript by Richard Little Purdy. Oxford: Clarendon press, 1935. Pp. lii+122.

Rev. in *TLS,* March 28, 1935, p. 199.

Nettleton, George H. "*The School for scandal*: an early edition." *TLS,* March 28, 1935, p. 200.

Nettleton, George H. "*The School for scandal*: first edition of the authentic text." *TLS,* Dec. 21, 1935, p. 876. Cf. corr. by F. W. Bateson, Jan. 4, 1936, p. 15.

Christopher Smart

Binyon, L. *The case of Christopher Smart.* (English Association pamphlet, 90.) Oxford: University press, 1934. Pp. 20.

Adam Smith

Cooke, C. A. "Adam Smith and Jurisprudence." *Law quarterly review,* April, 1935.

Scott, W. R. "An early draft of part of *The wealth of nations.*" *Economic journal,* XLV (1935), 427-38.

Tobias Smollett

An essay on the external use of water. Edited by Claude E. Jones. Baltimore: The Johns Hopkins press, 1935. Pp. 31-82.

Reprinted from the *Bulletin of the Institute of the History of Medicine.*

Grant, A. J. "Smollett and billiards." *TLS,* Nov. 16, 1935, p. 746.

Joliat, Eugène. *Smollett et la France* (Bibliothèque de la Revue de littérature comparée, CV.) Paris: Champion, 1935. Pp. 277.

Jones, Claude. "A Smollett letter." *MLN,* L (1935), 242-43.

Kahrl, George M. "The influence of Shakespeare on Smollett." In *Essays in dramatic literature: the Parrott presentation volume.* Princeton: University press, 1935. Pp. 399-420.

Knapp, Lewis M. "Smollett and the case of James Annesley." *TLS,* Dec. 28, 1935, p. 899.

Laurence Sterne

Letters. Edited by L. P. Curtis. Oxford: Clarendon press, 1935. Pp. xxxiv+495.

Rev. in *TLS,* March 21, 1935, p. 173; corr. by Margaret R. B. Shaw, *ibid.,* June 6, 1935, p. 364.

Curtis, Lewis P. "Forged letters of Laurence Sterne." *PMLA,* L (1935), 1076-1106.

Jonathan Swift

The Drapier's letters to the people of Ireland. Edited by Herbert Davis. Oxford: Clarendon press, 1935. Pp. xcvi+400.

Rev. in *TLS,* May 30, 1935, p. 345; by Alois Brandl in *Deutsche Literaturzeitung,* ser. III, VI (1935), 1785-86; by A. V. Judges in *Economic history review.* VI (1935), 125-26. Corr. by Harold Williams in *TLS,* June 6, 1935, p. 364.

Gulliver's travels and selected writings in prose and verse. Edited by John Hayward. London: Nonesuch press, 1934. Pp. xviii+868.

Rev. in *TLS,* Jan. 10, 1935, pp. 13-14.

Letters of Jonathan Swift to Charles Ford. Edited by D. Nichol Smith. Oxford: Clarendon press, 1935. Pp. xlviii+260.

Rev. in *TLS,* Jan. 10, 1935, pp. 13-14; by Harold Williams in *RES,* XI (1935), 489-94; by Alois Brandl in *Deutsche Literaturzeitung,* ser. III, VI (1935), 1782-84; by Shane Leslie in *SRL,* Feb. 16, 1935, p. 496.

Boyce, Benjamin. "Predecessors of *The Tale of a tub.*" *N & Q,* CLXVIII (1935), 110-11.

Korn, Max Arnim. *Die Weltanschauung Jonathan Swifts.* Jena: Frommann, 1935. Pp. 143.

Notice in *TLS,* Aug. 22, 1935, p. 525.

Leslie, Shane. *The script of Jonathan Swift and other essays.* Philadelphia: University of Pennsylvania press, 1935.

McCain, J. W. "Swift and Heywood." *N & Q,* CLXVIII (1935), 236-38.

Analogue to *The Battle of the books.*

McClue, G. S. "A seventeenth-century Gulliver." *MLN,* L (1935), 32-34.

O'Conor, Charles. "George Faulkner and Jonathan Swift." *Studies, an Irish quarterly,* XXIV (1935), 473-86.

Reimers, Hans. *Jonathan Swift. Gedanken und Schriften über Religion und Kirche.* (Britannica, 9.) Hamburg: Friedrichsen, de Gruyter & Co., 1934. Cf. *PQ* XIV, 174.

Rev. by Walter Graham in *JEGP,* XXXIV (1935), 601-03; by M. A. Korn in *Beiblatt,* XLVI (1935), 149-55.

Rockwell, Frederick S. "A probable source for *Gulliver's travels.*" *N & Q,* CLXIX (1935), 131-33.

Webster, C. M. "The satiric background of the attack on the Puritans in Swift's *A Tale of a tub.*" *PMLA,* L (1935), 210-23.

Williams, Harold. "Jonathan Swift and the *Four last years of the Queen.*" *Library,* XVI (1935), 61-90.

James Thomson

Drennon, Herbert. "James Thomson's ethical theory and scientific rationalism." *PQ,* XIV (1935), 70-82.

Fletcher, E. G. "Notes on two poems by James Thomson." *N & Q,* CLXVIII (1935), 274-75.

Seeber, Edward D. "Anti-slavery opinion in the poems of some early French followers of James Thomson." *MLN,* L (1935), 427-34.

Horace Walpole

Lewis, W. S. *The genesis of Strawberry Hill.* (Metropolitan Museum studies, Vol. V, part I.) New York: Metropolitan Museum of Art, 1934.

Lewis, W. S. "Horace Walpole." *TLS,* Jan. 24, 1935, p. 48.

Walpole's contributions to periodicals, 1747-49.

Lewis, W. S. "Horace Walpole's correspondence." *TLS,* June 20, 1935, p. 399.

Lewis, W. S. "Yale edition of Horace Walpole's correspondence." *N & Q,* CLXIX (1935), 45-46, 63, 84-85, 99, 101, 118, 124, 136, 140, 209.

William Walsh

Freeman, Phyllis. "William Walsh's letters and poems in *Ms. Malone 9.*" *Bodleian quarterly record,* VII (1934), 503-07.

Isaac Watts

Pinto, V. de Sola. "Isaac Watts and the adventurous muse." *Essays and studies by members of the English Association,* xx (1935), 86-107.

John Wesley

Cell, George Croft. *The rediscovery of John Wesley.* New York: Holt, 1935. Pp. 420.

Rev. by Jay Barrett Botsford in *JMH,* VII (1935) 242.

Jackson, George. "John Wesley as a bookman." *London quarterly and Holborn review,* July, 1935, pp. 294-305.

John Wilson

The Cheats. Edited by Milton C. Nahm. Oxford: Blackwell, 1935. Pp. 280.

Rev. in *TLS,* Feb. 14, 1935, p. 89.

William Wycherley

The country wife, a comedy. First played 1672-1673. Decorated by Steven Spurrier. London: Hutchinson, 1935. Pp. 125.

Notice in *TLS,* Jan. 31, 1935, p. 64.

Allen, Robert J. "Two Wycherley letters." *TLS,* April 18, 1935, p. 257.

Unpublished letters to the Earl of Mulgrave from originals in the Harvard College Library.

V. THE CONTINENTAL BACKGROUND

Adams, H. P. "Giambattista Vico." *Contemporary review,* CXLVIII (1935), 79-85.

Adams, H. P. *The life and writings of Giambattista Vico.* London: Allen and Unwin, 1935. Pp. 236.

Notice in *TLS,* April 25, 1935, p. 275; corr. by Angus McBain, *ibid.,* May 2, p. 288.

André, Louis. *Les sources de l'histoire de France au XVIIe siècle (1610-1715).* Tome VII: Histoire économique, histoire administrative. Paris: Picard, 1934. Pp. 452.

Rev. by Henri Sée in *Annales de Bretagne,* XLII (1935), 228-29.

Baldensperger, F. "Intellectuels français hors de France." (See *PQ,* xiv, 178.) *RCC,* xxxvi[1] (1935), 41-52; 227-42; 289-98; 510-21; 630-40. xxxvi[2] (1935), 70-82; 134-44; 249-60; 353-62; 445-57; 553-63; 730-43.

Baldensperger, F. "Louise de Kerouålle et ses quinze ans d'Angleterre." *Revue bleue,* lxxiii (1935), 694-700.

Betteridge, H. T. "The Ossianic poems in Herder's *Volkslieder.*" *MLR.* xxx (1935), 334-38.

Briggs, E. R. "L'incrédulité et la pensée anglaise en France au debut du dix-huitième siècle." *RHL,* xli (1934), 497-538.

Bruford, W. H. *Germany in the 18th century.* The social background of the literary revival. Cambridge: University press, 1935. Pp. 354.

Rev. in *TLS,* March 7, 1935, p. 134; by H. G. Atkins in *History,* XX (1935), 174-75; by Stefan Zweig in *SRL,* July 6, 1935, p. 18; by William Rose in *LM,* XXXI (1935), 602-03.

Brugmans, Henri L. *Le séjour de Christian Huygens à Paris et ses relations avec les milieux scientifiques français, suivi de son Journal de Voyage à Paris et à Londres.* Paris: E. Droz, 1935. Pp. 200.

Rev. by E. J. Dijksterhuis in *De Gids,* 1935, pp. 240-50; by Harcourt Brown in *Romanic review,* XXVI (1935), 260-61, who says: "For the study of ideas and the scientific *milieu* in the period 1660-1685 such a volume as this is indispensable."

Carré, J. R. "Pascal et Voltaire: raison ou sentiment." *Revue de métaphysique et de morale,* xlii (1935), 357-73.

Corsano, A. *Umanesimo e religione in G. B. Vico.* Bari: Laterza, 1935. Pp. 183.

Rev. by G. d. R. in *La Critica,* XXXIII (1935), 134-36.

Fucilla, Joseph G. "*De morte et amore.*" *PQ,* xiv (1935), 97-104.

Influence of Alciati, with some information about English imitations in the eighteenth century.

Hauser, Henri. "L'économie Calvinienne." *Bulletin de la Société de l'histoire du Protestantisme français,* lxxxiv (1935), 227-42.

Hazard, Paul. *La crise de la conscience européenne (1680-1715).* 3 vols. Paris: Boivin, 1934. Pp. viii+326, 316, 160.

Rev. in *TLS,* Dec. 7, 1935, p. 828; by P. A. Muenier in *RCC,* XXXVI[1] (1935), 282-88; by B. Munteano in *RLC,* XV (1935), 364-78; by G. d. R. in *La Critica,* XXXIII (1935), 295-99; by Gaillard de Champris in *Revue bleue,* LXXIII (1935), 318-21; by Victor Giraud in *Revue des deux mondes,* April 15, 1935, pp. 890-912; by Daniel Mornet in *RHL,* XLII (1935), 396-400, who discusses critically the methods of Hazard in writing history.

Hubert, René. "Essai sur l'histoire de l'idée de Progrès." *Revue d'histoire de la philosophie,* October 15, 1934, pp. 289-305, and January 15, 1935, pp. 1-32.

Kies, Paul P. "Lessing and Burnaby." *MLN,* L (1935), 225-30.

The Modish husband (1702) as the source of Lessing's *Die aufgebrachte Tugend,* a projected play of which the fragmentary scenario is extant.

King, George V. "Michel de la Roche et ses *Mémoires littéraires de la Grande-Bretagne.*" *RLC,* XV (1935), 298-300.

Libby, Margaret S. *The attitude of Voltaire to magic and the sciences.* New York: Columbia University press; London: P. S. King, 1935. Pp. ii+300.

Rev. in *TLS,* Sept. 26, 1935, p. 592; by Robert E. Fitch in *Journal of philosophy,* XXXII (1935), 556.

Marshall, R. *Italy in English literature, 1755-1815.* New York: Columbia University press; London: Milford, 1934. Pp. 432.

Rev. in *RLC,* XV (1935), 338-39; by Benedetto Croce in *La Critica,* XXXIII (1935), 376-77.

Mathiez, Albert. "Les philosophes et le pouvoir au milieu du XVIIIe siècle." *Annales historiques de la Révolution française,* XII (1935), 1-12.

Mathiez, Albert. "Les nouveaux courants d'idées dans la littérature française à la fin du XVIIIe siècle." *Annales historiques de la Révolution française,* XII (1935), 193-204.

Mélèze, Pierre. *Répertoire analytique des documents contemporains d'information et de critique concernant le théâtre à Paris sous Louis* XIV (*1659-1715*). Paris: E. Droz, 1934. Pp. 235.

Rev. by Daniel Mornet in *RHL,* XLII (1935), 265-67.

Mélèze, Pierre. *Le théâtre et le public à Paris sous Louis* XIV (*1659-1715*). Paris: E. Droz, 1934. Pp. 466.

Rev. by Daniel Mornet in *RHL,* XLII (1935), 265-67.

Peter, René. *La vie secrète de l'Académie française.* Première période. Paris: Librairie des Champs-Elysées, 1935.

Rev. in *TLS,* March 14, 1935, pp. 149-50.

Robertson, M. E. J. "Quelques notes sur la contrefaçon Hollandaise du *Pour et Contre.*" *RLC,* XV (1935), 111-18.

Sayous, André E. "Calvinisme et capitalisme: l'expérience Genevoise." *Annales d'histoire économique et sociale,* VII (1935), 227-44.

Spalatin, K. *Saint-Evremond.* Paris: Belles Lettres, 1935.

Spörl, Johannes. "Hugo Grotius und der Humanismus des 17. Jahrhunderts." *Historische Jahrbuch,* LV (1935), 350-57.

van Stockum, Th. C. "Der Begriff 'Deutsche Klassik'." *Neophilologus,* xx (1934), 14-25.

Stoll, E. E. "*Œdipus* and *Othello*: Corneille, Rymer and Voltaire." *RAA,* XII (1935), 385-400.

Torrey, Norman. "Voltaire's reaction to Diderot." *PMLA,* L (1935), 1107-43.

Trevelyan, Humphry. *The popular background to Goethe's Hellenism.* London: Longmans, 1934. Pp. xii+108.

Rev. by P. Leon in *Mind,* XLIV (1935), 406-07.

Van Duzer, Charles Hunter. *Contribution of the Ideologues to French revolutionary thought.* (The Johns Hopkins studies in historical and political science, Series LIII, number 4.) Baltimore: The Johns Hopkins press, 1935. Pp. 176.

Wais, Kurt. *Das antiphilosophische Weltbild des französischen Sturm und Drang, 1760-1789.* Berlin: Junker und Dünnhaupt, 1934. Pp. 262.

Waterhouse, G. "Schiller's *Räuber* in England before 1800." *MLR,* XXX (1935), 355-57.

1937

ENGLISH LITERATURE, 1660-1800: A CURRENT BIBLIOGRAPHY

By Louis I. Bredvold
University of Michigan

This bibliography attempts to list the more significant books, articles, and reviews published during the year 1936, together with some bearing earlier dates that were inadvertently omitted from previous bibliographies in this series. I am indebted to Professors Ronald S. Crane and Herbert Davis for contributing the critical notes signed with their initials.

LIST OF ABBREVIATIONS

AHR=American historical review.
Archiv=Archiv fur das Studium der neueren Sprachen und Literaturen.
Beiblatt=Beiblatt zur Anglia.
DVLG=Deutsche Vierteljahrschrift für Literaturwissenschaft und Geistesgeschichte.
EHR=English historical review.
ELH=ELH, A journal of English literary history.
ES=Englische Studien.
GRM=Germanisch-romanische Monatschrift.
JEGP=Journal of English and Germanic philology.
JMH=Journal of modern history.
LM=London mercury.
MLN=Modern language notes.
MLR=Modern language review.
MP=Modern philology.
N & Q=Notes and queries.
PMLA=Publications of the Modern Language Association of America.
PQ=Philological quarterly.
RAA=Revue anglo-américaine.
RC=Revue critique.
RCC=Revue des cours et conférences.
RES=Review of English studies.
RH=Revue historique.
RHL=Revue d'histoire littéraire de la France.
RHP=Revue d'histoire de la philosophie.
RLC=Revue de litérature comparée.
RSH=Revue de synthèse historique.
SP=Studies in philology.
SRL=Saturday review of literature.
TLS=Times literary supplement (London).

I. BIBLIOGRAPHIES AND BIBLIOGRAPHICAL STUDIES

(Some bibliographies of individual authors are listed in Section IV.)

Anderson, Paul Bunyan. "Bernard Mandeville." Corr. in *TLS,* Nov. 28, 1936, p. 996.

On some periodical contributions by "B.M."

Anderson, Paul Bunyan. "Splendor out of scandal: The Lucinda-Artesia papers in *The Female Tatler.*" *PQ,* xv (1936), 286-300.

Internal evidence that these contributions were by Mandeville.

Annual bibliography of English language and literature. Volume XVI, 1935. Edited for the Modern Humanities Research Association, by Mary S. Serjeantson, assisted by Leslie N. Broughton. Cambridge: Bowes & Bowes, 1936.

Annual bibliography of the history of British art. I, 1934. Cambridge: University press, 1936.

Annual bulletin of historical literature. No. xxv, publications for the year 1935. London: Published for the Historical Association by G. Bell & Sons, 1936. Pp. 60.

Section vi, the 17th and 18th centuries edited by Andrew Browning.

Baugh, Albert C. "Annual bibliography for 1935: English language and literature." *PMLA,* L (1935).

See especially pp. 1262-73.

de Beer, E. S. "John Wilmot, earl of Rochester: a conversation and a speech." *N & Q,* CLXX (1936), 420.

Evidence as to authenticity.

Bernbaum, Ernest. "Recent works on prose fiction before 1800." *MLN,* LI (1936), 244-55.

"A bibliography of philosophy, 1935." *Journal of philosophy,* XXXIII (1936), nos. 17 and 18, for August 13 and 27.

Boas, F. S. "Old plays in Columbia University." *TLS,* April 25, 1936, p. 360. Corr. by Montague Summers, May 2, p. 379; by William Van Lennep and Robert Gale Noyes, June 6, p. 480; by F. S. Boas and Montague Summers, June 13, p. 500.

On *Neglected Virtue,* 1696.

Bourne, J. A. "Some English translations of seventeenth-century Spanish novels." *MLR,* XXXI (1936), 555-56.

Bredvold, Louis I. "English literature, 1660-1800: a current bibliography." *PQ,* xv (1936), 153-93.

Brooks, Harold F. "A bibliography of John Oldham, the Restoration satirist." *Proceedings and papers of the Oxford Bibliographical Society,* v (1936), 1-38.

Comment in *TLS,* Nov. 14, 1936, p. 932.

Brown, Huntington. "The Classical tradition in English literature: a bibliography." *Harvard studies and notes in philology and literature,* XVIII (1935), 7-46.

Bryce, John C. *"Anecdotes of polite literature." TLS,* April 18, 1936, p. 340.

Buckler, W. H. "Edward Buckler (1610-1706), poet and preacher." *The Library,* XVII (1936), 349-53.

Catalogue of a collection of works on publishing and bookselling in the British Library of Political and Economic Science. London: London School of Economics and Political Science, 1936. Pp. 194.

Rev. by R. B. McK[errow] in *The Library,* XVII (1936), 368.

Chapman, Guy. "Beckford and *Al Raoui.*" Corr. in *TLS,* Oct. 31, 1936, p. 887.

Arguments against attribution to Beckford.

Chapman, R. W. "Bibliographical notes: Young's *Night Thoughts.*" *TLS,* March 28, 1936, p. 284.

Cox, Edward Godfrey. *A reference guide to the literature of travel.* Vol. I. (University of Washington publications in language and literature, IX.) Seattle: University of Washington, 1936. Pp. 401.

Day, Cyrus L., and Murrie, Eleanore B. "English song-books, 1651-1702, and their publishers." *The Library,* XVI (1936), 356-401.

"Forty-fourth critical bibliography of the history and philosophy of science and of the history of civilization (to the end of May 1935)." *Isis,* XXIV (1936), 468-536.

See especially pp. 484-90. The forty-fifth and forty-sixth bibliographies in this series, *ibid.,* XXV (1936), 176-317 and 522-613; see especially pp. 212-31 and 539-48.

Gilder, Rosamond, and Freedley, George. *Theatre collections in libraries and museums*: an international handbook; published under the auspices of the New York Public Library and the National Theatre Conference, with the cooperation of the American Library Association. New York: Theatre Arts; London: B. F. Stevens and Brown, 1936. Pp. 182.

Rev. in *TLS,* Dec. 19, 1936, p. 1056, points out some important omissions.

Guide to the reports of the Royal Commission on Historical Manuscripts, 1870-1911. Edited by Francis Bickley. Part 2, *Index of persons,* first section: *A-Lever.* London: H. M. Stationery office. 1935. Pp. 448.

Hawke, Edward G. *A brief history of the British newspaper press.* Paris: Les Presses Universitaires de France, 1935.

Reprinted from the *Bulletin du Comité International des Sciences Historiques* for September, 1935.

Hazen, Allen T. "Eighteenth-century quartos with vertical chain-lines." *The Library,* XVI (1935), 337-42.

Hindle, C. J. "A broadside by Samuel Butler." Corr. in *TLS,* March 21, 1936, p. 244.

International bibliography of historical sciences. Edited by the International Committee of Historical Sciences. New York: H. W. Wilson; London: Oxford university press; Berlin: De Gruyter & Co.; Paris: Armand Colin. *Fifth year, 1930* (1935), pp. 514; *sixth year, 1931* (1936), pp. 529; *eighth year 1933* (1936), pp. 509.

Rev. by Lillian M. Penson in *EHR,* LI (1936), 723-25.

James, G. F. "Burchett, Joshia: a newly discovered poem." *N & Q,* CLXXI (1936), 57.

Cf. *N & Q,* CLXX (1936), 28 and 68.

McCabe, William H. *"The Imperial Tragedy." PQ,* XV (1936), 311-14.

Generally ascribed to Sir William Killigrew.

Macmillan, Dugald. "Unrecorded eighteenth century plays." *N & Q,* CLXX (1936), 193-95.

Titles supplementary to Wood's list (see below), from the Larpent Manuscripts.

MacPike, E. F. "Sir Issac Newton in American libraries." *N & Q,* CLXXI (1936), 337.

Milford, R. T., and Sutherland, D. M. *A catalogue of English newspapers and periodicals in the Bodleian Library, 1622-1800.* Oxford: Bibliographical Society, 1936.

Separate issue from the *Proceedings and papers,* vol. IV. Rev. in *TLS,* Jan. 9, 1937, p. 32.

"The Newton papers: notes on sales." *TLS,* July 18, 1936, p. 604.

Nolte, Fred Otto. "German literature and the Classics: a bibliographical guide." *Harvard studies and notes in philology and literature,* XVIII (1935), 125-64.

Noyes, Robert Gale. "Songs from Restoration drama in contemporary and eighteenth-century poetical miscellanies." *ELH,* III (1936), 291-316.

Pochmann, Henry A., and others. "Anglo-German bibliography for 1935." *JEGP,* XXXV (1936), 271-82.

Primrose, J. B. "The first review of *Athenae Oxonienses.*" *Bodleian quarterly record,* VIII (1936), 206-07.

Roberts, W. "M. Le Texier: reader of plays." *TLS,* Sept. 19, 1936, p. 752.

Rosenfeld, Sybil. "Dramatic advertisements in the Burney newspapers, 1660-1700." *PMLA,* LI (1936), 123-52.

"Schriftenverzeichnis für 1935." *Zeitschrift für Aesthetik und Allgemeine Kunstwissenschaft,* XXX (1936), 346-400.

Van Lennep, William. "*The Princess of Parma.*" Corr. in *TLS,* Oct. 24, 1936, p. 863.

Date of Cumberland's play established, etc.

Van Lennep, William. "*The new-made Nobleman.*" Corr. in *TLS,* June 20, 1936, p. 523.

Explanation of a "ghost play."

Wallace, A. Dayle. "A note on *The City Patriots,* a satirical print." *N & Q,* CLXXI (1936), 169.

Watkin-Jones, A. "Langbaine's *Account of the English Dramatick Poets* (1691)." *Essays and studies by members of the English Association,* XXI (1936), 75-85.

Weber, Hilmar H. "The *Mercurius Poeticus* of 1660." *N & Q,* CLXIX (1935), 454-55.

Wood, F. T. "Unrecorded eighteenth-century plays." *N & Q,* CLXX (1936), 56-58 and 319.

From advertisements in provincial newspapers.

The Year's work in English studies. Vol. XV, 1934. Edited for the English Association by Frederick S. Boas and Mary S. Serjeantson. Oxford: University press, 1936. Pp. 372.

Chap. IX, The Restoration, by F. E. Budd, pp. 247-61; Chap. X, The eighteenth century, by Edith J. Morley, pp. 262-98.

The Year's work in modern language studies. Edited for the Modern Humanities Research Association by William J. Entwistle, with the assistance of L. W. Tancock. Vol. VI, year ending June 30, 1935. Cambridge: University press, 1936. Pp. 228.

II. THE SOCIAL AND POLITICAL ENVIRONMENT

Bamford, Francis (ed). *Dear Miss Heber.* An eighteenth century correspondence. With an introduction by Georgia and Sacheverell Sitwell. London: Constable, 1936. Pp. 336.

Rev. in *TLS,* Dec. 5, 1936, p. 1011.

Boehn, Max von. *Modes and manners.* Translated by Joan Joshua. Vol. III. The seventeenth century. Pp. 228. Vol. IV. The eighteenth century. Pp. 316. London: Harrap; New York, Lippincott, 1936.

Rev. in *TLS,* May 9, 1936, p. 392.

Bowen, Marjorie. *William Hogarth: the Cockney's mirror.* London: Methuen, 1936. Pp. xii+340, and 33 plates.

Rev. in *TLS,* Sept. 26, 1936, p. 762.

Burn, W. L. "*In aid of the civil power* in the eighteenth century." *Juridical review,* XLVIII (1936), 328-38.

On the legal aspect of the use of the military to preserve order.

Bryant, Arthur. *Postman's horn.* An anthology of the letters of latter seventeenth century England. London: Longmans, 1936. Pp. 318.

Rev. in *TLS,* Nov. 7, 1936, p. 900.
The letters represent all social classes and supply "the everyday background of our social history."

Cahen, L. "L'évolution de la Grande-Bretagne dans la seconde moitié du XVIIIe siècle d'aprés les travaux récents." *Revue d'histoire moderne,* XI (1936), 60-77.

Deals with economic history, religious problems, the parliamentary problem; survey of recent work.

Carr, John Dickson. *The murder of Sir Edmund Godfrey.* London: Hamish Hamilton; New York: Harper, 1936. Pp. 352.

Rev. in *TLS,* Oct. 10, 1936, p. 803; in *Juridical review,* XLVIII (1936), 401-02.
A study of this famous mystery by an author of detective stories.

Churchill, Winston S. *Marlborough: his life and times.* London: Harrap, 1936. Vol. III. Pp. 608.

Rev. in *TLS,* Oct. 24, 1936, p. 847; by Bonamy Dobrée in *Spectator,* Nov. 27, 1936, p. 953; by Henry W. Nevinson in *LM,* XXXV (1936), 68-69.

Clark, G. N. "Early capitalism and invention." *Economic history review,* VI (1936), 143-56.

Cole, Major D. H., and Priestley, Major E. C. *An outline of British military history, 1660-1936.* London: Sifton Praed, 1936. Pp. 448.

Rev. in *TLS,* Aug. 1, 1936, p. 626.

County of Buckingham. Calendar of the sessions records. Vol. II, 1694-1705. Edited by William le Hardy and Geoffrey Ll. Reckitt. Aylesbury: Guy R. Crouch, 1936.

Cremer, John. *Ramblin' Jack*: the journal of Captain John Cremer (1700-1774). Transcribed and edited by R. Reynell Bellamy. London: Jonathan Cape, 1936. Pp. 250.

Rev. in *TLS,* May 16, 1936, p. 410.

Darby, H. C. (ed.) *An historical geography of England before 1800.* Fourteen studies by eleven contributors. Cambridge: University press; New York: Macmillan, 1936. Pp. xii+568, and 87 maps.

Rev. in *TLS,* July 25, 1936, p. 614; by R. H. Tawney in *Economica,* III (1936), 478-80.

Davis, Godfrey, and Tinling, Marion. "Letters from James Brydges, created Duke of Chandos, to Henry St. John, created Viscount Bolingbroke." *Huntington Library bulletin,* no. 9 (1936), 119-66.

Davis, J. D. Griffith. *George the third.* A record of a king's reign. London: Nicholson & Watson, 1936. Pp. xii+348.

A defence of the king.

Fifoot, C. H. S. *Lord Mansfield.* Oxford: Clarendon press, 1936. Pp. 268.

Rev. in *TLS,* Oct. 17, 1936, p. 827; in *Juridical review,* XLVIII (1936), 404-05.

Fussell, G. E. "English agriculture: from Arthur Young to William Cobbett." *Economic history review,* VI (1936), 214-22.

A study of works on agriculture and rural life in the late eighteenth century.

Hanson, Laurence. *Government and the press, 1695-1763.* (Oxford books on bibliography.) Oxford: University press, 1936. Pp. ix+149.

Rev. in *N & Q,* CLXXI (1936), 34-35; by J. L. Hammond in *Spectator,* Sept. 11, 1936, pp. 423-24.

A study "based throughout on unpublished sources." Cf. the related studies, listed below, by W. T. Laprade and Charles B. Realey.

Hopkinson, M. R. *Married to Mercury.* A sketch of Lord Bolingbroke and his wives. London: Constable, 1936. Pp. 275.

Rev. in *TLS,* Oct. 24, 1936, p. 851.

More valuable and better documented than the title would suggest.

Imbert-Terry, Sir Henry. "An unwanted prince." *Essays by divers hands, being the transaction of the Royal Society of Literature,* XV (1936), 135-60.

On Prince Frederick, son of George II.

Jones, P. E., and Judges, A. V. "London population in the late seventeenth century." *Economic history review,* VI (1936), 45-63.

A valuable statistical study.

Kulsrud, Carl J. *Maritime neutrality to 1780.* The main principles governing neutrality and belligerency in maritime warfare to 1780. Boston: Little, Brown, 1936. Pp. x+351.

L., J. R. "Lady Carnarvon." *Bodleian quarterly record,* VIII (1936), 165-69.

Calls attention to manuscript letters by Lady Caroline Brydges in the Bodleian.

Lascelles, Edward. *The life of Charles James Fox.* Oxford: University press, 1936. Pp. 345.

Rev. in *TLS,* June 20, 1936, pp. 505-06.

Laprade, William Thomas. *Public opinion and politics in eighteenth century England.* New York: Macmillan, 1936. Pp. viii+463.

Deals with the period from William III to the fall of Walpole in 1742. Cf. related studies by Laurence Hanson and Charles B. Realey.

Laski, H. J. *The rise of European liberalism.* London: Allen & Unwin, 1936. Pp. 287.

Rev. by G. C. Field in *Mind,* XLV (1936), 525-29; by J. L. Hammond in *Spectator,* CLVI (1936), 939; by Max Ascoli in *New Republic,* Oct. 7, 1936, p. 259; by B. C[roce] in *La Critica,* XXXIV (1936), 458-60.

Le Branchu, J. Y. *Les origines du capitalisme en Angleterre.* Paris: Recueil Sirey, 1935. Pp. 95.

Lee, Grace Lawless. *The Huguenot settlements in Ireland.* London: Longmans, 1936. Pp. 281.

Rev. in *TLS,* Feb. 29, 1936, p. 174.

Lloyd, Roger B. "A Stuart squire." *Spectator,* July 31, 1936, pp. 194-95.

The author found in an obscure eighteenth century collection a portrait of a country gentleman, a Mr. Hastings, which he justifiably felt should be rescued from oblivion. But he was not aware that the portrait is already famous; it is from the pen of the first Earl of Shaftesbury; it can be read in Christie's life of the Earl, in Mark Van Doren's study of Dryden, and in Miss Murphy's anthology of character writings.

Longdon, Rev. Henry Isham. *The visitation of the County of Northampton in the year 1681.* Harleian Society, vol. LXXXVII.

Rev. in *TLS,* March 14, 1936, p. 220.

Lyons, Frederick J. *Jonathan Wild: prince of robbers.* London: Michael Joseph, 1936. Pp. 320.

Notice in *TLS,* Oct. 31, 1936, p. 889.

Matthews, David. *Catholicism in England, 1535-1935.* London: Longmans, 1936. Pp. 304.

Rev. in *TLS,* April 4, 1936, p. 291.

Maxwell, Constantia. *Dublin under the Georges, 1714-1830.* London: Harrap, 1936. Pp. 301.

Rev. in *TLS,* July 4, 1936, p. 553; by Seán O'Faloáin in *LM,* XXXIV (1936), 360-61.

Menary, George. *The life and letters of Duncan Forbes of Culloden,* Lord President of the Court of Session, 1685-1747. London: MacLehose, 1936. Pp. xii+419.

Rev. in *TLS,* Dec. 5, 1936, p. 1005.

Michael, Wolfgang. *England under George I: the beginnings of the Hanoverian dynasty.* Translated under the supervision of L. B. Namier. London: Macmillan, 1936. Pp. 414.

Rev. in *TLS,* March 21, 1936, p. 231.

The five sons of "Bare Betty." By her descendant, Colonel Hon. Arthur C. Murray. Preface by Lord Tweedsmuir. London: Murray, 1936. Pp. 211.

The sons of the wife of the fourth Lord Elibank were all prominent in the eighteenth century.

Newton, T. F. M. "William Pittis and Queen Anne journalism, II." *MP,* XXXIII (1936), 279-302.

Oman, Carola. *Henrietta Maria.* London: Hodder and Stoughton, 1936. Pp. 366.

Rev. in *TLS,* Sept. 5, 1936, p. 706.

Pemberton, W. Baring. *Carteret: the brilliant failure of the eighteenth century.* London: Longmans, 1936. Pp. xv-353.

Rev. in *TLS,* April 25, 1936, p. 347; by W. T. Laprade in *AHR,* XLII (1937), 387; by Sir Richard Lodge in *EHR,* LII (1937), 132-33.

Realey, Charles B. *The London Journal and its authors, 1720-1723. University of Kansas Humanistic studies,* Vol. v., no. 3 (1935). Pp. 38.

A valuable study of Thomas Gordon's contributions to *The London Journal,* later frequently reprinted as *Cato's Letters.* Realey is known for his monograph on *The early opposition to Sir Robert Walpole,* 1720-1727, published in 1931.

Reddaway, W. F. *A history of Europe from 1715 to 1814.* London: Methuen, 1936. Pp. xiii+573.

Rev. in *TLS,* July 4, 1936, p. 556.

Reed, Irma Hoyt. "The European hard-paste porcelain manufacture of the eighteenth century." *JMH,* VIII (1936), 273-96.

A study in economic and art history.

Memoirs of Sir John Reresby. The complete text and a selection from his letters. Edited, with an introduction and notes, by Andrew Browning. Glasgow: Jackson; London: Simpkin Marshall, 1936. Pp. xlv+626.

Rev. in *TLS,* Aug. 22, 1936, p. 673; by E. E. Kellett in *Spectator,* July 10, 1936, p. 66; by Caroline Robbins in *History,* XXI (1936), 272-72, who says: "Previous editors mangled the style and very greatly curtailed the content of Reresby's work. Students of literature can now for the first time study Reresby's rough but engaging language, and find reflected in it the character of what the editor calls 'a typical member of the class which in the seventeenth century formed the backbone of English society'."

Roberts, B. Dew. *Mr. Bulkeley and the pirate.* A Welsh diarist of the eighteenth century. Oxford: University press, 1936. Pp. viii+194.

Rev. *in TLS,* Oct. 3, 1936, p. 781; in *N & Q,* CLXXI (1936), 413-14.
Of some special interest as a picture of life among Welsh country squires.

Sergeant, Philip W. *Witches and warlocks.* With an introduction by Arthur MacLen. London: Hutchinson, 1936. Pp. 290.

Rev. in *TLS,* Oct. 10, 1936, p. 810.

Simms, V. H. "The organization of the Whig party during the Exclusion crisis." (Summary of thesis.) *Bulletin of the Institute of Historical Research,* XIII (1936), 176-77.

Stuart, Dorothy M. *Molly Lepell, Lady Hervey.* London: Harrap, 1936. Pp. 376.

Rev. in *TLS,* April 11, 1936, p. 314; corr. by Dorothy M. Stuart, *ibid.,* April 18, p. 336; rev. by Paul Yvon in *RAA,* XIII (1936), 519.

Thompson, C. J. S. *Love, marriage, and romance in old London.* London: Heath, Cranton, 1936. Pp. 260.

Notice in *TLS,* Oct. 31, 1936, p. 890.
A sociological study, dealing mainly with the seventeenth and eighteenth centuries.

The Torrington diaries. Containing the tours through England and Wales of the Hon. John Byng (later fifth Viscount Torrington) between the years 1781 and 1794. Edited by C. Bruyn Andrews. Vol. III. London: Eyre and Spottiswoode; New York: Holt, 1936. Pp. xii+326.

Rev. in *TLS,* Sept. 26, 1936, p. 761.

Willan, T. S. *River navigation in England, 1600-1750.* Oxford: University press, 1936. Pp. 163.

Rev. by Arthur P. Newton in *History,* XXI (1936), 267-68.

The Wynne diaries. Edited by Anne Fremantle. Vol. I, 1789-1794. Oxford: University press, 1936. Pp. 376.

Notice by Eugene N. Curtis in *JMH,* VIII (1936), 384-85.

Woodforde. Edited by John Beresford. Oxford: University press, 1936. Pp. 534.

A volume of selections from the complete diary.

III. CURRENTS OF IDEAS AND LITERARY FORMS

Abers, Jacob Hanna. "Scientific rationalism in the seventeenth century: a study of Bacon and his successors." *Abstracts of dissertations, Stanford University, 1933-1934,* pp. 45-48.

Antal, Friedrich. "Reflections on Classicism and Romanticism, II." *Burlington magazine,* March, 1936, pp. 130-39.

Social and political background of tendencies in French painting in the late eighteenth and early nineteenth centuries.

Anstermann, Maria. *Die grosse englische Revolution im Spiegel der zeitgenössischen Lyrik.* Münster (diss.), 1935. Pp. 72.

Ashcroft, T. *English art and English society.* London: Peter Davies, 1936. Pp. 251.

Rev. in *TLS,* March 28, 1936, p. 265.

Aubin, Robert Arnold. "Some Augustan Gothicists." *Harvard studies and notes in philology and literature,* XVII (1935), 15-26.

Aubin, Robert Arnold. *Topographical poetry in eighteenth-century England.* New York: The Modern Language Association of America; London: Milford, 1936. Pp. xii+419.

Rev. in *TLS,* June 27, 1936, p. 538; by John W. Draper in *JEGP,* XXXV (1936), 610-11.

Avery, Emmett L., and Deupree, Mildred Avery. "The new theatre in the Haymarket, 1734 and 1737." *N & Q,* CLXXI (1936), 41-42.

Information from the *Daily Advertiser.*

Beyer, Jos. *Ralph Cudworth als Ethiker, Staatsphilosoph und Aesthetiker auf Grund der gedruckten Schriften.* Bonn (diss.), 1935. Pp. 91.

Bond, Richmond P. "Eighteenth century correspondence: a survey." *SP,* XXXIII (1936), 572-86.

Boys, R. C. "Rural setting in the drama: an early example." *N & Q,* CLXX (1936), 207.

Charles Johnson's *Country Lasses,* 1714.

Brinkley, Roberta Florence (ed.). *English poetry of the seventeenth century.* New York: Norton, 1936. Pp. xiv+584.

An attractive anthology, with excellent introductions and bibliographies, reflecting the most recent scholarship.

Brown, Wallace Cable. "The popularity of English travel books about the Near East, 1775-1825." *PQ,* XV (1936), 70-80.

Brugmans, Hk. "Défense de la dialectique." *Neophilologus,* XXI (1935), 1-16.

On the methods of literary study.

Clark, W. S. "Restoration prompt notes and stage practices." *MLN,* LI (1936), 226-30.

Dale, Antony. *James Wyatt, architect, 1746-1813.* Oxford: Blackwell, 1936. Pp. 139.

Rev. in *TLS,* Sept. 19, 1936, p. 739.

Dorow, Kurt-Günter. *Die Beobachtungen des Sprachmeisters James Elphinston über die schottische Mundart (1787).* Berlin (diss.), 1936. Pp. 79.

Fehr, Bernhard. "The antagonism of forms in the eighteenth century." *English studies,* XVIII (1936), 115-21, 193-205.

The starting-point of this series of essays (the last of which has unfortunately not yet appeared) is a twofold assumption: (1) that the end of the study of any art in any period is the discovery of the character or spirit of the age, and (2) that such a discovery, if it is to be complete, necessitates the consideration of whatever art may be selected in terms not of its own proper evolution but rather of analogies set up between it and the other arts that flourished at the same time. The art which chiefly interests Fehr is literature, or, more particularly, poetry; and his main problem is to illuminate the "antagonism of forms" which he discerns in the eighteenth century between the classic school of Pope and the obviously very different school of Thomson, Mallet, Akenside, and others—an antagonism which, if it can be fully understood, will, he implies (see p. 115), furnish a clue to the "attitudes and forces" representative of the age as a whole. Since his method requires the choice of a basic analogy, he begins by sketching rapidly the history of styles in architecture from about 1625 to 1800. "England is in a unique position. What was an undercurrent in Germany was here the main current. . . . . In other words: there runs in England a straight uninterrupted line of *classicism in architecture* beginning with Inigo Jones . . . . and going right through the 17th and the 18th century. About, let us say, 1770 this English classicism passed through a process of over-classicalisation which coincided with the classical phase on the Continent. . . . But this is not all. There runs parallel to that two-centuries-long main line a much shorter but distinct side line: the *Baroque,* manifesting itself in the 17th century in erratic outbursts and then, at the beginning of the 18th century [in Vanbrugh, 1664-1726], in full display. During the super-Palladian phase (1714-1760) we find it hiding itself in interior decoration and, between 1740 and 1760, showing its smiling head as *English Rococo*. . . . Then it vanishes. In the meanwhile a new style had been preparing, dynamic like the Baroque, the *Neo-Gothic,* which we now find running along by the side of the pedantic English classicism of the late 18th century" (pp. 116-17). It is thus from the development of architecture, outlined in terms which are for the most part literally descriptive of the medium proper to the art of building, that Fehr derives the ratio which he is to expand into the central metaphor of his history: as classical architecture is to baroque architecture, so. . . . The process of expansion begins when various other non-literary arts are introduced as equivalent terms on either side of this basic opposition. The formal rectilinear garden of the seventeenth and early eighteenth centuries is "classical"; the later irregular garden with its "free and easy paths" is obviously "baroque"; "baroque" also are the aesthetics of Burke's *Sublime and beautiful,* the vogue of seventeenth-century Italian landscape painting, and—in one context at least (see pp. 196-97)—music. In the light of this pattern of analogies, the nature of the fundamental opposition of forms in the spirit of the age becomes more clear and with it the rythmical sequence of their manifestations from the later seventeenth century to the end of the eighteenth. It is a simple matter now to extend the metaphor, thus enriched, to poetry, and to reveal in the succession of its styles, too, the same alternation of attitudes and forces. We need for the purpose no systematic poetical or prosodical analysis. We are required merely to recognize, in the poetry of Pope and his school, that the structure of the heroic couplets, in their strict "rectilinearity," "make up a body of equidistant parallels like the string courses and cornices of a Palladian building," that the succession of rimes "breaks up the parallels into a flight of couples to be compared to the colonnades of the pavilions so fashionable in Pope's day," that the experience of reading poems in this style is equivalent to the experience of walking along the straight and right-angled paths of a formal garden, that the personifications in the verse of Pope's followers are like "the ever recurring statues in the centre of grassplots or on the tops of houses" (pp. 193-96). And similarly it is enough to observe, in the later poetry of Mallet, Thomson, Akenside, and the rest, that "convolutions" have now taken the place of straight lines, that the verses of these poets "move to the *grammar of music,* like a tune continuing itself indefinitely," that the flow of their lines is "like going up the stairs in the interior of a *Baroque palace,*" that their syntax suggests "the broken frontage of a Baroque building and the recesses of its groundplan, such as may be noted in Blenheim Castle," that their rhythms are those which would inevitably direct the steps of one traversing the serpentines and S's of an English garden, "with his eyes alternately gliding along the outlines of scroll-work and losing themselves in the far-off background" (pp. 196-99).

If all this seems to any one illuminating with respect to eighteenth-century poetry or the spirit of the age, well and good: I know of no critical devices for discussing either the truth or the relevance of metaphors such as constitute the essential pattern of histories conceived in this neo-platonic mode. Here are no propositions to be verified from the documents, no narrative sequences to be judged in the light of their causal adequacy; analogy is all. There are two questions, however, which may be legitimately put to Fehr. First, why should the process of analogizing invariably run, as it does in the historical school of which he belongs, from architecture to poetry rather than (say) from poetry to architecture? Surely, if buildings can illuminate poems, poems can illuminate buildings! And second, why should he limit himself, in his quest for understanding of the age, to analogies merely from within the domain of the arts? Surely, as Paul Meissner has recently shown, in a book which Fehr cites with approval (p. 115, n. 2, and cf. *PQ,* XIV, 152-54), the structure of an age is universal enough to coordinate more than its artistic manifestations alone.—R. S. C.

Frantz, R. W. *The English traveller and the movement of ideas, 1660-1732.* Lincoln, Nebraska: University of Nebraska press, 1934. Cf. *PQ,* xv, 162.

Rev. by George B. Parks in *MLN,* LI (1936), 555-56; by J. M. S. Tompkins in *RES,* XII (1936), 473-75.

Gayley, Charles M., and Thaler, Alwin (eds.). *Representative English comedies.* Vol. IV. Dryden and his contemporaries: Cowley to Farquhar. New York: Macmillan, 1936. Pp. xii+777.

Guttmacher, Manfred S. "Catherine Macauley and Patience Wright: patronesses of the American Revolution." *Johns Hopkins alumni magazine,* XXIV (1936), 308-26.

Hadzits, George Depue. *Lucretius and his influence.* (Our debt to Greece and Rome series.) New York: Longmans, 1935. Pp. viii+372.

Heil, Liselotte. *Die Darstellung der englischen Tragödie zur Zeit Bettertons.* Berlin (diss.), 1936. Pp. 131.

Henriot, Emile. "La méthode de Gustave Lanson." *Revue internationale de l'enseignement,* LV (1935), 77-83.

Herbert, T. Walter. *"Sentimental."* Corr. in *TLS,* May 16, 1936, p. 420. Further corr. by Ernest A. Baker and W. M. Parker, *ibid.,* May 23, p. 440.

Calling attention to Wesley's well-known objection to the word.

Hobhouse, Stephen. "*Fides et Ratio,* the book which introduced Jacob Boehme to William Law." *Journal of theological studies,* XXXVII (1936), 350-68.

Important contribution to history of English religious thought.

Hooker, E. N. "The reviewers and the new trends in poetry, 1754-1770." *MLN,* LI (1936), 207-14.

Horace: three phases of his influence. Lectures given at Mount Holyoke College in celebration of the Bimillennium Horatianum 1935, by Paul Frédéric Saintonge, Leslie Gale Burgevin, and Helen Griffith. Chicago: University of Chicago Press, [1936]. Pp. vi+120.

The three lectures deal with "The influence of Horace on Ronsard and Montaigne," "A little farm" (echoes of Horace's conception of rural felicity in English poetry from the sixteenth to the nineteenth centuries), and "The Horatian strain in literary criticism." All three, being addressed to a general audience on a ceremonial occasion, are relatively slight in substance, without pretensions to freshness of thought or erudition; only the third calls for brief comment since it raises a question of general interest to students of the seventeenth and eighteenth centuries: the question, namely, of the terms in which the influence of Horace on the criticism of that period can be best understood.

The answer given by Miss Griffith is one for which much support could be found in the scholarly literature mentioned in her notes and bibliography. The Horatian strain in Renaissance and neo-classical criticism is to be noted chiefly, she holds, in the persistence of three themes contained in the *Ars poetica*—the theme of the poet's function in the state (*Aut prodesse volunt aut delectare poetae*), the theme of the imitation of models, and the theme of the importance of art or craftsmanship. It would not be difficult, certainly, to adduce many seventeenth- and eighteenth-century references to the authority of Horace on each of these points. But neither, I suspect, would such a collection of quotations be particularly significant, since, on the one hand, the three doctrines in question were not peculiar in antiquity to Horace, and since, on the other hand, their meaning, importance, and interrelations for any critic, ancient or modern, can be stated only when the total structure of his analysis has been determined. The problem, then, for the student interested in tracing Horace's influence in early modern criticism is first of all to establish the character of the general approach to poetry contained in the *Ars poetica*—the major terms it employs and their ordering with respect to one another, its method and its criteria—and then, with this as guide, to read the later texts. Of one of the two most important elements in the critical method of Horace Miss Griffith is indeed aware, but she dismisses it as not distinctive of the "Horatian strain." "Many matters that he stresses," she writes, "such as the principles of unity, harmony, and proportion, we now associate rather with Aristotle, who after all had enunciated them nearly three hundred years before Horace. His discussion of decorum belongs in this group too, although Horace developed the idea more fully than Aristotle and was directly responsible for the Renaissance dependence on it" (p. 91). I venture to suggest that her assimilation of Horace to the *Poetics* in the matters of unity and decorum is itself a result of that Renaissance misinterpretation of Aristotle in the light of Horace to which she elsewhere refers (p. 87). This is not the place to argue the point, but there seem to me excellent reasons for believing that whereas in Aristotle the criteria for unity and appropriateness of character are both intrinsic, the criteria for Horace involve always a reference to something outside the poem—to things as they are or as we know them, to nature, in short (cf. e.g., *Ars poetica* 1-13, 105-11). At all events, it is to "nature" that he bids the young poet look for guidance in unifying his poem, in selecting his meters and his diction, in constructing his characters; but—and this is the second major term in his analysis, of which

Miss Griffith makes no mention—he posits an equivalence between what is "natural" or according to decorum in the poem and what will give pleasure to the highly selected Roman audience, the applause of which is to measure the poet's success. There is, he says, a relation established by nature between thoughts and the words we use to express them—a relation which he supposes known to the audience, so that

> Si dicentis erunt fortunis absona dicta,
> Romani tollent equites peditesque cachinnum [112-13].

Similarly with characters—if you wish to please, follow nature:

> Tu, quid ego et populus mecum desideret, audi.
> Si plausoris eges aulaea manentis et usque
> Sessuri donec cantor 'Vos plaudite' dicat,
> Aetatis cujusque notandi sunt tibi mores,
> Mobilibusque decor naturis dandus et annis [153-57].

It is, I suggest, in the interplay of these two criteria—natural decorum and the pleasure of the properly selected audience, the two being exact equivalents the one of the other—that the distinctive character of the Horatian approach to the criticism of poetry is to be found; and if this is the case, the appropriate history of the "Horatian strain" in Renaissance and neo-classical criticism would be a history, not of particular Horatian maxims or doctrines, but of the acceptance, development, and modification in the context of other ancient approaches (Platonic, Aristotelian, Longinian, etc.) of the twofold appeal to the audience and to "nature" which gave form to the *Ars poetica.* When this history has been written, we shall better understand, I suspect, some of the things that have proved puzzling in the critical systems of men like Dryden and Johnson.—R. S. C.

Huse, W. A. "A noble savage on the stage." *MP,* XXXIII (1936), 303-16.

The pantomime, *Omai,* at the Covent Garden in 1785.

Jones, Joseph Jay. "British literary men's opinions about America, 1750-1832." *Abstracts of dissertations, Stanford University, 1933-1934,* pp. 49-50.

Jones, Richard Foster. *Ancients and moderns*: a study of the background of the *Battle of the Books.* St. Louis: *Washington University studies, Language and literature,* no. 6, 1936. Pp. x+358.

An expansion of the first part of an important work first published in 1921. The present volume embodies the results of Professor Jones's study during this interval of the history of the idea of science and of the conception of progress through scientific advancement in the seventeenth century.

Kain, Richard M. "The problem of civilization in English Abolition literature, 1772-1808." *PQ,* XV (1936), 103-25.

Kapp, Rudolf. "Können wir aus der englischen Predigt volkstypologische Rückschlüsse ziehen?" *Anglia,* LX (1936), 211-33.

Kökeritz, H. "English pronunciation as described in shorthand systems of the 17th and 18th centuries." *Studia neophilologica,* VII (1935), 73-146.

Lawrence, W. J. "The French opera in London: a riddle of 1686." *TLS,* March 28, 1936, p. 268.

Leavis, F. R. *Revaluations.* London: Chatto & Windus, 1936.

Rev. by Bonamy Dobrée in *Spectator,* Oct. 23, 1936, p. 694.
Includes essays on Pope, the Augustan tradition, etc.

Lehnert, Martin. *Die Grammatik des englischen Sprachmeisters John Wallis (1616-1703)*. (*Sprache und Kultur der germanischen und romanischen Völker*. A. Anglistische Reihe, Bd. XXI.) Breslau: Priebatsch, 1936. Pp. ix+156.

Leisering, Walter. *Das Motiv des Einsiedlers in der englischen Literatur des 18. Jahrhunderts und der Hochromantik*. (Diss.) Halle: R. Mayr, 1935. Pp. 78.

Lovejoy, Arthur O. *The great Chain of Being*: a study of the history of an idea. (The William James lectures delivered at Harvard University, 1933.) Cambridge: Harvard University press, 1936. Pp. ix+382.

Rev. by H. T. C[ostello] in *Journal of philosophy*, XXXIII (1936), 580-81; by Marjorie Nicolson in *The Johns Hopkins alumni magazine*, XXV (1937), 190-94.

Indispensable for the student of eighteenth century thought.

Lovejoy, Arthur O., and Boas, George. *Primitivism and related ideas in antiquity*. Baltimore: The Johns Hopkins press, 1935. Cf. *PQ*, XV, 164.

Rev. by G. S[arton] in *Isis* XXV (1936), 169-72; by George Depue Hadzits in *Classical weekly*, XXX (1936), 73-74; by A. W. Gomme in *Classical review*, L (1936), 77-78; by R. K. Hack in *AHR*, XLI (1936), 728-30; by H. T. C[ostello] in *Journal of philosophy*, XXXIII (1936), 192-93; by A. Pigamiol in *RH*, CLXXVII (1936), 148-49.

McClelland, John. "The course of realism in the English novel from Addison and Steele through Sir Walter Scott." *Abstracts of dissertations, Stanford University, 1933-1934*, pp. 52-54.

Marshall, L. Birkett. *Rare poems of the seventeenth century*. Selected and edited, with brief biographies. Cambridge: University press, 1936. Pp. viii+234.

Rev. in *TLS*, Dec. 12, 1936, p. 1031; corr. by L. Birkett Marshall and by reviewer, *ibid.*, Dec. 26, p. 1068.

Matthews, William. "The character-writings of Edward Ward." *Neophilologus*, XXI (1936), 116-34.

Matthews, William, "Some eighteenth century phonetic spellings." *RES*, XII (1936), 42-60, 177-88.

Correspondence used as guide to the pronunciation current among the upper and middle classes during the first half of the century.

Matthews, William. "William Tiffin, an eighteenth century phonetician." *English studies*, XVIII (1936), 97-114.

Cf. the work by Kökeritz, listed above.

Mendels, Judica I. H. "Een phoneticus uit de 17de eeuw." *Neophilologus*, XXI (1936), 219-25.

Francis Lodwick's *Essay towards an Universal Alphabet* in *Philosophical transactions* of the Royal Society, XVI, 1686-87.

Mews, Hazel. "Middle class conduct books in the seventeenth century." (Summary of thesis.) *Bulletin of the Institute of Historical Research,* XIII (1936), 168.

Monk, Samuel H. *The sublime: a study of critical theories in XVIII-century England.* New York: Modern Language Association of America, 1935. Cf. *PQ,* XV, 165.

Rev. by Mario Praz in *English studies,* XVIII (1936), 226-30; by P. Meissner in *Beiblatt,* XLVII (1936), 305-07.

Nicoll, Allardyce. "Scenery between Shakespeare and Dryden." *TLS,* Aug. 15, 1936, p. 658.

Nicolson, Marjorie. *A world in the moon*: a study of the changing attitude toward the moon in the seventeenth and eighteenth centuries. (Smith College studies in Modern Languages, Vol. XVII, no. 2) Northampton, Mass.: Smith College, 1936. Pp. 72.

Another installment of a series dealing with the influence of science on the English poetic imagination in these two centuries.

Noyes, Robert Gale. "Ben Jonson's masques in the eighteenth century." *SP,* XXXIII (1936), 427-36.

Pagel, Walter. "Religious motives in the medical biology of the XVIIth century." *Bulletin of the Institute of the History of Medicine,* 1935. Pp. 88.

Rev. by E. Unger in *Revue philosophique,* LXI (1936), 103-04, who calls it an important contribution to the history of modern scientific ideas.

Perkinson, Richard H. "Topographical comedy in the seventeenth century." *ELH,* III (1936), 270-90.

These comedies, the author contends, were not given their special locales in order to present realistic pictures of these places; the tendency was rather to "use topography for technical ends, to secure plausibility, to carry on or solve a plot, or to demonstrate a theme." However, it might also be fairly argued on the other side that the dramatists did not overlook the opportunity for a little local color.

Philosophy and history. Essays presented to Ernst Cassirer. Edited by Raymond Klibansky and H. J. Paton. Oxford: Clarendon press, 1936. Pp. xii+355.

Rev. by W. G. de Burgh in *Mind,* XLV (1936), 514-25; by R. G. Collingwood in *EHR, LII* (1936), 141-46.

Ramsey, Robert W. "Some English letter writers of the seventeenth century." *Essays by divers hands,* being the transactions of the Royal Society of Literature, XIV (1935), 1-28.

Rosenberg, Ben B. "The new German *Geisteswissenschaft.*" *PQ,* XV (1936), 301-06.

A defense of this school of German literary research against the strictures by Professor R. S. Crane in *PQ,* XIV (1935), 153.

Rosenfeld, Sybil. "Actors in Bristol, 1741-1748." *TLS,* Aug. 29, 1936, p. 700.

Rosenfeld, Sybil. "The players in Norwich, 1669-1709." *RES,* XII (1936), 129-38.

An account of strolling companies playing in Norwich, based mainly on the Court Books of the city of Norwich.

Rosenfeld, Sybil. "The players in Norwich, 1710-1750." *RES,* XII (1936), 285-304.

Based largely on newspaper advertisements and notices. Valuable information on the provincial theatre.

Schirmer, Walter F. "Das Problem des religiösen Epos im 17. Jahrhundert in England." *DVLG,* XIV (1936), 60-74.

Schütze, Martin. "Toward a modern humanism." *PMLA,* LI (1936), 284-99.

On the theory of literary study.

Sitwell, Sacheverell. *Conversation pieces.* A survey of English domestic portraits and their painters. With notes on the illustrations by Michael Sevier. London: Batsford, 1936.

Rev. in *TLS,* Nov. 28, 1936, p. 990.

Smith, Dane F. *Plays about the theatre in England from 'The Rehearsal' in 1671 to the Licensing Act in 1737,* or, the selfconscious stage in its burlesque and satirical reflections in the age of criticism. New York and London: Oxford University press, 1936. Pp. xxiv+287.

Sparrow, Walter Shaw. "Our earliest sporting artist: Francis Barlow, 1626-1704." *Connoisseur,* XCVIII (1936), 36-40.

Steegman, John. *The rule of taste: from George I. to George IV.* London: Macmillan, 1936. Pp. xviii+203.

Rev. in *TLS,* May 9, 1936, pp. 385-86; by E. L. Woodward in *Spectator,* CLVI (1936), 944-46.

This volume seems to have been written for a popular audience. It is a bright and pleasant account of the changes in taste in England during the Georges, with special emphasis on the influence exercised by the patrons of the polite world upon the fine arts. The author has evidently read a number of good books in preparation for his task, he has looked at pictures and buildings, and he has scattered through his own pages some good comments which every reader will enjoy. For all that, however, the book is not so important as it seems to be regarded in some quarters, and there are passages in it which shake the reader's confidence in the learning of the author. We are presented, for instance, from the very beginning with a curious notion that a revolution was accomplished in the arts in the "reign of George I;" compared with the ages of Elizabeth or Charles II, this reign may seem without imagination and without character, but "examined by itself, it will be seen to be, so to speak, trying to make a fresh start. The only way to avoid the mistakes and stupidities of adolescence was, it was felt, to make rigid rules for its own guidance and never depart from the canon thus established. . . . It was time to stop being young and romantic; the dying fires of the Renaissance had no longer any warmth, " etc. (p. 4). Such, we are asked to believe, is the profound significance of the year 1714. Not only were the "Augustan rules" established after this date, but the idea of art as an ideal treatment of nature was also new. When Jonathan Richardson, in the reign of George I, wrote that "the business of painting is not only to represent nature and to make the best choice of it, but to raise and improve it," we are assured that "here the early eighteenth century speaks in its own particular voice" and does not repeat something that might "equally have been said at any time after 1660" (p. 13). Such pretentious absurdities are a little exasperating. Some explanation of all this to-do about the reign of George I may perhaps be derived from a sentence in the Introduction: "The victory of Pope, and through him of Dryden and Waller, may be dated from the appearance of *The Dunciad* in 1712; three years earlier Shaftesbury had published his *Letter concerning Design*, and three years later the Georgian age was successfully inaugurated with the collapse of the Jacobite Rising" (p. xvi). Now it has been agreed for some time that *The Dunciad* was published in 1728; and, although Shaftesbury had published *A Letter concerning Enthusiasm* in 1708, his *Letter concerning Design* was first printed in the fifth edition of *The Characteristics* in 1732. Dates and titles are, perhaps, minor matters on which one should not insist too acrimoniously. But anyone with an elementary knowledge of the history of English poetry could controvert the statement that the victory of Dryden and Waller, as well as of Pope himself, had to await the appearance of *The Dunciad.* However, as our author is especially interested in the history of art, it is only fair to give a specimen of his learning in that field. Winckelmann is twice referred to as the author of the "famous treatise" on the sculpture called the Laocoön (pp. 149-50), apparently a confusion with Lessing. Aside from this treatise, Winckelmann seems to be known only for his "industrious excavations," from the "published results" of which "it may be presumed that the youthful David, while Louis XV was still reigning, derived his first incitement to the Classic." And as we observe that republican France after the Revolution found fitting expression in the imitation of the art of republican Rome, we may accordingly conclude that "it is posssble to hear, through all the noise and tumult of 1789, the pickaxe of Winckelmann helping to demolish the Bastille" (p. 135). In the whole chapter on the revival of Greek and Roman artistic ideals in the late eighteenth century, there is no mention of Winckelmann's *History of Ancient Art;* he appears only with his pickaxe and the fictitious treatise on the Laocoön. Such scholarship is neither patient nor mature nor critical.

Summers, Montague. "The illustrations of the 'Gothick' novels." *Connoisseur,* XCII (1936), 266-71.

Swayne, Mattie. "The progress piece in the seventeenth century." *University of Texas studies in English,* no. 16 (1936), 84-92.

Weir, John L. "A Claverhouse garland: lesser-known poems on Viscount Dundee." *N & Q,* CLXXI (1936), 38-41.

Wellek, Albert. "Das Doppelempfinden im 18. Jahrhundert." *DVLG,* XIV (1936), 75-102.

White, Helen C. *The Metaphysical poets: a study in religious experience.* New York: Macmillan, 1936. Pp. 444.

Rev. by Alfred Kazin in *Books,* Dec. 6, 1936, p. 18.

Whitney, Lois. *Primitivism and the idea of progress in English popular literature in the eighteenth century.* Baltimore: The Johns Hopkins press, 1934. Cf. *PQ,* XIV, 156, and XV, 170.

Rev. by F. Krog in *Beiblatt,* XLVII (1936), 70-74; by Ernest Hunter Wright in *JEGP,* XXXV (1936), 430-33; by Marjorie Nicolson in *MLN* LI (1936), 398-400; by Robert Shafer in *American review,* V (1935), 361-68.

Wiley, Margaret Lee. "Genius: a problem in definiton." *University of Texas studies in English,* no. 16 (1936), 77-83.

Williams, Iolo A. "English book-illustration, 1700-1775." *The Library,* XVII (1936), 1-21.

Williamson, George. "*The Ephesian Matron* versus the *Platonic Lady.*" *RES,* XII (1936), 445-49.

Williamson, George, "Richard Whitlock, learning's apologist." *PQ,* XV (1936), 254-72.

Williamson, George. "Senecan style in the seventeenth century." *PQ,* XV (1936), 321-51.

An important article on a subject which has been much discussed since Professor Croll published his studies on seventeenth century style. It is richly documented with contemporary passages on the Senecan style.

Williamson, George. " 'Strong lines'." *English studies,* XVIII (1936), 152-59.

A very interesting and well-documented interpretation of a critical phrase much used in the seventeenth century.

Woesler, R. "Ueber englisches Literaturbarock." *Literaturwiss. Jahrbuch der Görres-Gesellschaft,* 1936, pp. 139-50.

The thirteenth volume of the Wren Society. Designs and drawings by Sir Christopher Wren for St. Paul's Cathedral, the Residentiaries' Houses, and the Deanery. Oxford: Printed for the Wren Society at the University press, 1936.

Rev. in *TLS,* Oct. 17, 1936, p. 831.

Wurtsbaugh, Jewel. *Two centuries of Spenserian scholarship, 1609-1805.* Baltimore: The Johns Hopkins press, 1936. Pp. ix+174.

Young, R. FitzGibbon. "The invisible college (1645-1660)." Corr. in *TLS,* Dec. 12, 1936, p. 1035.

IV. INDIVIDUAL AUTHORS

Joseph Addison

(See also *Samuel Johnson*)

Gelobter, Hanna. *'Le Spectateur' von Pierre Marivaux und die englischen Wochenschriften.* Frankfurt a. M. (diss.), 1936. Pp. 94.

Graham, Walter. "Addison and Sir Henry Newton." *N & Q,* CLXX (1936), 110-11.

Graham, Walter, "Addison's travel letters in the *Tatler* and *Guardian.*" *PQ,* XV (1936), 97-102.

Peterson, H. "Notes on the influence of Addison's *Spectator* and Marivaux's *Spectateur Français* upon *El Pensador.*" *Hispanic review,* IV (1936), 256-63.

Thorpe, Clarence DeWitt. "Addison's theory of the imagination as 'perceptive response'." *Papers of the Michigan Academy of Science, Arts and Letters,* XXI (1936), 509-30.

Jane Austen

Bowen, Elizabeth. "Jane Austen." In *The English novelists: a survey of the novel by twenty contemporary novelists.* Ed. Derek Verschoyle. London: Chatto & Windus; New York: Harcourt, Brace, 1936. Pp. 97-110.

Also printed in *SRL,* August 15, 1936, pp. 3-4, 13-14.

"Cantab." "Verrall on Jane Austen." *N & Q,* CLXXI (1936), 20-22.

Textual notes in the *Cambridge Observer,* Nov. 15, 1892. These notes were, however, used by Chapman in his edition of Jane Austen. Cf. corr. by M. H. Dodds, p. 69.

Chapman, R. W. "Jane Austen." Corr. in *TLS,* Sept. 19, 1936, p. 748.

George Berkeley

Hedenius, Angemar. *Sensationalism and theology in Berkeley's philosophy.* Upsala: Almquist & Wiksella; Oxford: Blackwell, 1936. Pp. iv+238.

Stocks, J. L. "What did Berkeley mean by '*Esse* is *Percipi*'?" *Mind,* XLV (1936), 310-23.

Wild, John. *George Berkeley: a study of his life and philosophy.* Cambridge: Harvard University press; London: Milford, 1936. Pp. 552.

Rev. in *TLS,* Aug. 22, 1936, p. 678; by Paul Weiss in *New Republic,* August 19, 1936, pp. 52-53; by R. L. Calhoun in *Yale review,* XXVI (1936), 214-16.

Thomas Betterton

Summers, Montague. "The comedies of Thomas Betterton." *N & Q,* CLXX (1936), 454-56.

Sir Richard Blackmore

Newton, Theodore F. M. "Blackmore's *Eliza.*" *Harvard studies and notes in philology and literature,* XVIII (1935), 114-24.

William Blake

Bagdasarianz, Waldemar. *William Blake.* Versuch einer Entwicklungsgeschichte des Mystikers. (Swiss studies in English, Vol. II.) Zürich: Niehau, 1936. Pp. vii+171.

Baker, C. H. Collins. "William Blake, painter." *Huntington Library bulletin,* no. 10 (1936), 135-48.

Lowery, Margaret Ruth. "A census of copies of William Blake's *Poetical Sketches,* 1783." *The Library,* XVII (1936), 354-60.

James Boswell

Boswell's Journal of a tour to the Hebrides with Samuel Johnson, LL. D. Now first published from the original manuscript. Prepared for the press, with preface and notes, by Frederick A. Pottle and Charles H. Bennett. New York: Viking press; London: Heinemann, 1936. Pp. xviii+435.

Rev. in *TLS,* Nov. 7, 1936, p. 903; cf. corr. by A. S. Frere Reeves, *ibid.,* Nov. 14, p. 928; rev. by Peter Monro Jack in *New York Times book review,* Nov. 8, 1936, p. 1; by Charles G. Osgood in *SRL,* Nov. 7, 1936, pp. 5-6; by Dixon Wector in *Yale review,* XXVI (1936), 401-04.

Boswell's Life of Johnson. Edited by George Birkbeck Hill. Revised and enlarged edition by L. F. Powell. 4 vols. Oxford: Clarendon press, 1934. Cf. *PQ,* XIV, 158 and XV, 174.

Rev. by James R. Sutherland in *RES,* XII (1936), 78-80; by Robert Kilbourne in *MLN,* LI (1936), 552-54.

Abbott, Claude Colleer. *A catalogue of papers relating to Boswell, Johnson, and Sir William Forbes, found at Fettercairn House.* Oxford: Clarendon press, 1936. Pp. xxvii+257.

A catalogue of the documents discovered in 1930-1931, including over a thousand letters to Boswell, more than a hundred of them from Johnson, and other manuscripts, with three of Boswell's journals.

Cowie, Alexander. "A Boswell misquotation." Corr. in *TLS,* April 25, 1936, p. 356.

Warnock, Robert. "Boswell and Wilkes in Italy." *ELH,* III (1936), 257-69.

An article without references, giving no indication to the reader as to whether any of the material is new.

Wecter, Dixon. "The soul of James Boswell." *Virginia quarterly review,* XII (1936), 195-206.

Sir Thomas Browne

Chalmers, Gordon Keith. "Sir Thomas Browne, true scientist." *Osiris,* II (1936), 28-79.

A very careful and thorough study, maintaining that Browne was a genuine scientist and that his knowledge was substantial.

Chalmers, Gordon Keith. "Three terms of the Corpuscularian philosophy." *MP,* XXXIII (1936), 243-60.

An investigation of the history of the words *effluvium, efflexion,* and *emission,* used by Browne and others, which throws light on the modern revival of atomism.

Thomas Brown

Boyce, Benjamin. "Milton and Thomas Brown's translation of Gelli." *N & Q,* CLXXI (1936), 328-29.

John Bunyan

Harrison, Frank Mott. "Some illustrators of *The Pilgrim's Progress* (part one)." *The Library,* XVII (1936), 241-63.

Sachs, W. *Der typisch puritanische Ideengehalt in Bunyans "Life and Death of Mr. Badman."* Leipzig (diss.), 1936. Pp. 95.

Edmund Burke

Buehler, Reginald Guyon. "Burke and Rousseau." *Harvard University summaries of thesis, 1934,* pp. 313-14.

Fanny Burney

Bracey, Robert. "Hawkins in Madame D'Arblay's *Diary.*" *N & Q,* CLXXI (1936), p. 43.

Delachaux, E. "Fanny Burney, intermédiaire manquée entre l'Angleterre et la France." *RLC,* XV (1935), 381-86.

Lloyd, Christopher. *Fanny Burney.* London: Longmans, 1936. Pp. 328.

Rev. in *TLS,* Oct. 17, 1936, p. 873; by Edith Shackelton in *LM,* XXXV (1936), 81.

Wauchope, A. J. "The D'Arblays in July, 1815." *Cornhill,* CLIV (1936), 25-32.

Robert Burns

Besterman, Theodore. "Burns documents." *TLS,* March 7, 1936, p. 208.

The National Library of Scotland has acquired the documents of the firm Cadell and Davies relative to the publication of the first and some subsequent collected editions of the poet's works.

Burns chronicle and club directory. Second series, Vol. XI. Kilmarnock: The Burns Federation, 1936.

A three shilling annual which should be found more generally than it is in college libraries. It frequently prints new documents and articles of importance.

Hecht, Hans. *Robert Burns: the man and his work.* Translated by Jane Lymburn. London: Hodge, 1936. Pp. 375.

This translation is of a revised and expanded form of Hecht's work, in which the results of more recent research have been incorporated.

Snyder, Franklin Bliss. *Robert Burns: his personality, his reputation, and his art.* (The Alexander lectures in English at the University of Toronto, 1936) Toronto: University of Toronto press, 1936. Pp. 119.

Joseph Butler

"The analogy of religion: Joseph Butler's achievement." Leading article in *TLS,* April 11, 1936, pp. 305-06.

Mossner, Ernest Campbell. *Bishop Butler and the age of reason.* A study in the history of thought. New York: Macmillan, 1936. Pp. xv+271.

As the title indicates, Dr. Mossner has undertaken to study the relation of Butler's thought to the intellectual climate of his age. His volume seems to fall into four main divisions. The first two chapters set forth the developments in Deism which stimulated Butler to his task; two chapters are devoted to *The Analogy* and the sermons; two chapters deal with the developments in thought immediately after Butler, which Mossner says had inevitably to take two directions, the scepticism of Hume and the religious enthusiasm of Wesley; the last three chapters present a survey of Butler's reputation down to the present time.

On the whole, the author has achieved his purpose, and has given us a more complete documentation of Butler's relation to his age than we have had. He has shown how closely the main arguments of Butler articulate with the current debates of the first half of the century. In the course of this exposition Mossner emphasizes that *The Analogy* is limited in value to succeeding generations precisely because it was so exactly fitted to the peculiar preconceptions of its own day. A more sympathetic discussion of this work may be found in the *Times Literary Supplement* (see above). Mossner is, however, generous enough, as even Leslie Stephen was before him, in his estimate of the permanent value of the sermons, which still retain their interest as a treatise on the psychological aspects of the moral life.

Some reservations must be made regarding Mossner's account of the rise and spread of Deism. For instance, although he quotes (page 46) the passage in which Viret in 1564 referred to the existence of the new "band" of Deists, he does not give any impression of how widely such Deism as Lord Herbert's was diffused in Europe before 1624; his discussion seems to confuse Deism with Montaigne's scepticism, which was quite another matter. An unqualified statement, referring in a general way to English religious thought in the latter part of the seventeenth century, affirms that "in the field of religion, reason was considered capable of finding in itself and by itself the essential truths touching the nature of God and the duties of man; as a guiding principle it was sufficient in itself" (p. 14). But anyone who had sought ordination on that creed, would certainly have been refused. One of the constant dangers of modern students of the eighteenth century is that they do not distinguish carefully between rational Anglicans, who insisted that reason must be supplemented by Revelation, and Deists, who regarded reason as self-sufficient. The age was truly an age of reason—although even this statement needs some important qualifications—but we must not conclude from this fact that Deism was universally accepted.

The manuscript should have been submitted to a more careful scrutiny before publication. Glanvill's *Scepsis scientifica* is dated 1675 (pp. 30 and 246), instead of 1664; on the next page it is said to have appeared "shortly" before 1718. Matthew Clifford's *Treatise of Human Reason* was published in 1674, but possibly Dr. Mossner has seen a copy dated 1675 (p. 49). Burke's *Reflections on the Revolution in France* was not published in 1789 (p. 175). The "historico-critical examination of the Testaments" did not "begin" with Charles Blount (p. 51). I do not find much point in the statement that "it was mere chance but yet prophetical that two such famous Deists as Voltaire and Franklin were in London in 1726" (pp. 69-70); were they "famous Deists" in 1726? There is a reference to Bishop Burnet turning over the hour-glass and preaching a second hour "with a low hum of approval from the congregation" (p. 106). Did the author's memory play him false here? In Burnet's day not many congregations cared to listen beyond an hour, and the good Bishop told his own clergy in his *Pastoral Care* that "the shorter sermons are, they are generally both better heard, and better remembered. . . . In half an hour a man may lay open his matter in its full extent, and cut off those superfluities which come in only to lengthen the discourse." (Third ed., 1713, p. 198). Fielding is misquoted (p. 182) and made to say that Butler's principle of conscience is "familiar to the present age"; what the passage in *Tom Jones* really does say is that a comparison of the idea of conscience with "the lord high-chancellor of this kingdom in his court" gives "a higher idea of the principle I mean, as well as one more familiar to the present age" than his reference in the preceding paragraph to "the famous trunk-maker in the playhouse." Such faults in finish are the more regrettable in a work so essentially valuable.

Tristram, Rev. Henry. "Bishop Butler's *Analogy*." *Dublin review,* c (1936), 122-33.

Stedman, R. E. "Bishop Butler and his *Analogy of Religion*." *Nineteenth century,* CXIX (1936), 612-23.

Henry Carey

Ewens, J. Baird. "Henry Carey, John Wesley, and 'namby-pamby'." *London quarterly and Holborn review,* January, 1936, pp. 40-51.

Noyes, Robert Gale. "The contemporary reception of *Sally in Our Alley*." *Harvard studies and notes in philology and literature,* XVIII (1935), 165-76.

Thomas Chatterton

Meyerstein, E. H. W. "Chatterton's Birtha." *TLS,* July 18, 1936, p. 600.

Wright, G. W. "Chatterton set to music." *N & Q,* CLXXI (1936), 228-29.

Philip Dormer Stanhope, fourth Earl of Chesterfield

Cock, F. William. "Chesterfield and Dowdeswell: letters." *N & Q,* CLXXI (1936), 219-21.

Gulick, Sidney L. "The publication of Chesterfield's *Letters to his Son*." *PMLA,* LI (1936), 165-77.

Shellabarger, Samuel. *Lord Chesterfield.* London: Macmillan, 1935. Cf. *PQ,* XV, 176.

Rev. by Bonamy Dobrée in *Criterion,* XV (1936), 561-63; by Frederick T. Wood in *ES,* LXXI (1936), 123-25.

William Collins

McKillop, Alan D. "Collins's *Ode to the Passions*." *TLS,* March 7, 1936, p. 204.

George Colman

Knochen, Helmut. *Der Dramatiker George Colman.* Göttingen (diss.), 1935. Pp. 83.

Vincent, Howard P. "George Colman the Younger: 'adopted son'." *PQ,* xv (1936), 219-20.

William Congreve

Hodges, John C. "The dating of Congreve's letters." *PMLA,* LI (1936), 153-64.

Hodges, John C. "William Congreve: confused signatures." Corr. in *TLS,* August 15, 1936, p. 664.

Swaen, A. E. H. "The authorship of *A Soldier and a Sailor.*" *Archiv,* CLXVIII (1935), 237-40.

Ben's song in *Love for Love.*

Abraham Cowley

Krempien, Hans-Helmut. *Der Stil der "Davideis" von Abraham Cowley im Kreise ihrer Vorläufer.* Ein Beitrag zur Untersuchung des "metaphysical wit" und des Epos vor Milton. (*Britannica,* no. 11.) Hamburg: Friedrichsen, de Gruyter & Co., 1936. Pp. 147.

Walton, Geoffrey. "A poem by Cowley." Corr. in *TLS,* Dec. 5, 1936, p. 1016.

William Cowper

Church, Leslie F. "The madness of William Cowper." *London quarterly and Holborn review,* January, 1936, pp. 102-04.

Povey, K. "Notes on Cowper's letters. IV." *RES,* XII (1936), 333-35.

Erasmus Darwin

Logan, James V. *The poetry and aesthetics of Erasmus Darwin.* (*Princeton studies in English,* no. 15.) Princeton: University press, 1936. Pp. 162.

Daniel Defoe

Klingender, F. D. "Coleridge on *Robinson Crusoe.*" *TLS,* Feb. 1, 1936, p. 96.

Meyerstein, E. H. W. "Daniel, the Pope and the Devil: a caricaturist's portrait of the true Defoe." *TLS,* Feb. 15, 1936, p. 134.

Pritchett, V. S. "Daniel Defoe." In *The English novelists: a survey of the novel by twenty contemporary novelists.* Ed. by Derek Verschoyle. London: Chatto & Windus, 1936. Pp. 49-66.

Stamm, Rudolf G. "Daniel Defoe: an artist in the Puritan tradition." *PQ,* xv (1936), 225-46.

Stamm, Rudolf G. *Der aufgeklärte Puritanismus Daniel Defoes.* (*Swiss studies in English,* I.) Zürich: M. Niehau, 1936. Pp. 343.

John Dryden

Allen, Ned Bliss. *The sources of John Dryden's comedies.* Ann Arbor: University of Michigan press, 1935. Cf. *PQ,* xv, 178.

Rev. by V. de Sola Pinto in *MLR,* XXXI (1936), 572; by Pierre Legouis in *RAA,* XIII (1936), 517-18.

Bredvold, Louis I. *The intellectual milieu of John Dryden.* Ann Arbor: University of Michigan press, 1934. Cf. *PQ,* xiv, 163, and xv, 179.

Rev. by R. G. Ham in *RES,* XII (1936), 353-55; by Robert Shafer in *American review,* V (1935), 361-68; by G. M. Turnell in *ES,* LXXI (1936), 115-18; by V. de Sola Pinto in *MLR,* XXXI (1936), 429-31; by G. Williamson in *MLN,* LI (1936), 195-96.

Dobrée, Bonamy. "Milton and Dryden: a comparison and contrast in poetic ideas and poetic method." *ELH,* III (1936), 83-100.

Eidson, John Olin. "Dryden's criticism of Shakespeare." *SP,* XXXIII (1936), 273-80.

Hiscock, W. G. "A poem attributed to Dryden." *TLS,* April 18, 1936, p. 340. Corr. by W. G. Hiscock, April 25, p. 360; by E. S. de Beer, May 16, p. 420; by W. G. Hiscock, May 23, p. 440; By E. S. de Beer, May 30, p. 461; by W. G. Hiscock, Oct. 10, p. 815.

Macdonald, Hugh. "The attacks on Dryden." *Essays and studies by members of the English Association,* XXI (1936), 41-74.

Based on the author's forthcoming bibliography of Dryden. It offers as complete an account of these pamphlet attacks as is now possible.

Macdonald, Hugh. "*A journal from Parnassus*: an unpublished satire on Dryden." *TLS,* Oct. 17, 1936, p. 844.

A manuscript recently acquired by the Bodleian.

Mundy, P. D. "Portraits of John Dryden." *N & Q,* CLXX (1936), 318-19.

Walcott, Fred G. "John Dryden's answer to Thomas Rymer's *The Tragedies of the Last Age.*" *PQ,* XV (1936), 194-214.

Ward, Charles E. "The dates of two Dryden plays." *PMLA,* LI (1936), 786-92.

Jonathan Edwards

Jonathan Edwards: representative selections, with introduction, bibliography, and notes, by Clarence H. Faust and Thomas H. Johnson. New York: American Book Company, 1935. Pp. cxlii+434.

The excellent introduction and biblography will prove of great value also to students of English literature of the same period.

John Evelyn

Bowman, Francis Ezra. "Studies in the life of John Evelyn (1620-1706)." *Harvard University summaries of theses, 1934,* pp. 308-11.

A devotionarie book of John Evelyn of Wotton, 1620-1706. Now first published with an introduction by Walter Frere. London: Murray, 1936.

Rev. in *TLS,* Jan. 2, 1937, p. 4.

Thomas Ellwood

Thomas Ellwood's "Davideis." A reprint of the first edition of 1712 with various readings of later editions. Edited with an introduction and notes by Walther Fischer. (*Englische Textbibliothke,* ed. by Dr. Johannes Hoops, Vol. 21). Pp. xxviii+248.

Rev. by Frederick T. Wood in *English studies,* XVIII (1936), 230-32; by W. Fischer in *Beiblatt,* XLVII (1936), 248-49.

Henry Fielding
(See also *Charles Macklin*)

Avery, Emmett L. "Some notes on Fielding's plays." *Research studies of the State College of Washington* (Pullman, Washington), III (1935), 48-50.

Coolidge, Archibald. "A Fielding pamphlet?" Corr. in *TLS,* May 9, 1936, p. 400.

Gill, W. W. "Early Fielding documents." *N & Q,* CLXXI (1936), 242.

Lind, Levi Robert. "Lucian and Fielding." *Classical weekly,* xxix (1936), 84-86.

Mundy, P. D. "Fielding's *Tom Jones.*" *N & Q,* clxix (1935), 456.

A contemporary letter regarding its publication.

Sherburn, George. "Fielding's *Amelia*: an interpretation." *ELH,* iii (1936), 1-14.

Against the current conception that this novel marks a decline in the power of Fielding.

John Gay

Berger, A. V. "The Beggar's Opera, the burlesque, and Italian opera." *Music and Letters,* xvii (1936), 93-105.

Swaen, A. E. H. "The airs and tunes of John Gay's *Polly.*" *Anglia,* lx (1936), 403-22.

Edward Gibbon

Dawson, Christopher. "Edward Gibbon." In *Proceedings of the British Academy, 1934* (1936).

Mowat, R. B. *Gibbon.* London: Barker, 1936. Pp. 275.

Rev. by John Garrett in *Criterion,* XV (1936), 722-24; by Paul Yvon in *RAA,* XIII (1936), 437.

William Godwin

"William Godwin: apostle of universal benevolence." Leading article in *TLS,* April 4, 1936, pp. 285-86.

Oliver Goldsmith

Seitz, R. W. "Goldsmith to Sir William Chambers: bibliographical notes." *TLS,* Sept. 26, 1936, p. 772.

Thomas Gray

Von Hook, La Rue. "New light on the Classical scholarship of Thomas Gray." *American journal of philology,* lvii (1936), 1-9.

Matthew Green

The Spleen. Edited, with an introduction, notes, and appendices by W. H. Williams. London: Methuen, 1936. Pp. 88.

Notice in *TLS,* July 25, 1936, p. 618.

Thomas Hobbes

Shillinglaw, Arthur T. "Hobbes and Ben Jonson." Corr. in *TLS,* April 18, 1936, p. 336.

Tribute to Bacon in Ben Jonson's *Discoveries* borrowed from Hobbes?

Soulhié, J., and others. *La pensée et l'influence de Th. Hobbes.* Paris Blanchesne, 1936.

Strauss, Leo. *The political philosophy of Hobbes: its basis and its genesis.* Translated from the German manuscript by Elsa M. Sinclair. Oxford: Clarendon press, 1936. Pp. xviii+172.

Teeter, Louis. "The dramatic use of Hobbes's political ideas." *ELH,* III (1936), 140-69.

Vialatoux, J. *La cité de Hobbes, théorie de l'État totalitaire.* Essai sur la conception naturaliste de la civilisation. Paris: Gabalda, 1935. P. 224.

Rev. by Maxime Joos in *Revue de philosophie,* LVI (1936), 462-67.

Thomas Holcroft

Stallbaumer, Virgil R. "Thomas Holcroft: a satirist in the stream of sentimentalism." *ELH,* III (1936), 31-62.

Stallbaumer, Virgil R. "Holcroft's German." *TLS,* Jan. 23, 1937, p. 60. Cf. Corr. by Oskar Teichman, Feb. 6, p. 92.

David Hume

Boys Smith, J. S. "Hume's Dialogues concerning natural religion." *Journal of theological studies,* XXXVII (1936), 337-49.

Holmberg, O. *David Hume in Carlyle's "Sartor Resartus."* Lund: Gleerup, 1934. Pp. 19.

Mossner, Ernest C. "The enigma of Hume." *Mind,* XLV (1936), 334-49.

Samuel Johnson
(See also *James Boswell* and *Mrs. Thrale*)

Boyle, Sir Edward. *Biographical essays, 1790-1890.* Oxford: University press, 1936. Pp. 273.

Contains essays on Johnson, Sir John Hawkins, and Pasquale Paoli.

Brunskill, F. R. "The ancestry of Dr. Johnson's wife." *London quarterly and Holborn review,* April, 1936, pp. 228-30.

Clifford, James Lowry. "Further letters of the Johnson circle." *Bulletin of the John Rylands Library,* XX (1936), 268-85.

Some account of letters and family papers once belonging to Mrs. Piozzi, now in the John Rylands Library.

"Dr. Johnson and nature: English poets in the Highlands." Leading article in *TLS,* August 15, 1936, pp. 653-54.

Hazen, Allen T. "Samuel Johnson and Dr. Robert James." *Bulletin of the Institute of the History of Medicine,* IV (1936), 455-65.

Hazen, A. T., and McAdam, E. L. "First editions of Samuel Johnson: an important exhibiton and a discovery." *Yale University Library gazette,* X (1936), 45-51.

McAdam, E. L. "A Johnson pamphlet." *TLS,* March 14, 1936, p. 228.

There was a pamphlet publication of Johnson's *Life of Admiral Blake* in 1740.

Moody, Dorothy. "Johnson's translation of Addison's *Battle of the Cranes and Pygmies.*" *MLR,* XXXI (1936), 60-65.

Smith, Florence A. "The light reading of Dr. Johnson." *University of Toronto quarterly,* V (1936), 118-27.

Watkins, W. B. C. *Johnson and English poetry before 1660.* (*Princeton studies in English,* no. XIII.) Princeton: University press; London: Milford, 1936. Pp. 120.

Notice in *TLS,* Aug. 22, 1936, p. 682; rev. by P. Meissner in *Beiblatt,* XLVII (1936), 333-34.

The author uses as evidence the quotations in Johnson's dictionary and shows that Johnson was, for his time, quite well read in this early period.

Wright, Herbert G. "Robert Potter as a critic of Johnson." *RES,* XII (1936), 305-21.

A judicious account of an interesting clash of personalities and tastes; Potter is treated as representative of certain general tendencies of the time.

Henry Killigrew

Niemeyer, Carl. "Henry Killigrew and the Duke of Buckingham." *RES,* XII (1936), 326-28.

The Countess Dowager of Roscommon, in a letter, gives an account of their quarrel.

Nathaniel Lee

Van Lennep, William Bird. "Nathaniel Lee: a study of his life and works." *Harvard University summaries of theses, 1934,* pp. 337-41.

Martin Lluelyn

Wallerstein, Ruth. "Martin Lluelyn, Cavalier and 'Metaphysical'." *JEGP,* xxxv (1936), 94-111.

John Locke

Aaron, R. I., and Gibb, Jocelyn. *An early draft of Locke's "Essay."* Together with excerpts from his Journals. Oxford: Clarendon press, 1936. Pp. xxviii+132.

Rev. in *TLS,* Sept. 26, 1936, p. 764.

MacLean, Kenneth. *John Locke and English literature of the eighteenth century.* New Haven: Yale University Press, 1936. Pp. viii+176.

It is difficult to know what the author means by the second term of his title. Although his inquiry seems to be restricted to England, he devotes some space in his introduction to listing translations of the *Essay* published on the Continent, and in the main body of his treatise there are occasional discussions of Voltaire and briefer allusions (by way of John Morley) to Helvétius and Diderot; Condillac and Rousseau, on the other hand, do not appear. Moreover, even within the domain of English literature properly speaking, the principle which has led him to select certain writers and to omit others is never made entirely plain. It is true that he gives no connected or systematic account of Locke's influence on the eighteenth-century English philosophers from Berkeley and Hume to Hartley, Bentham, and Priestley; and this would be an understandable omission in a book by a professional student of literature were it not that some philosophers—especially Watts, Bolingbroke, and Hume—do appear, and in contexts which involve fragments of their philosophical systems. So, too, it would be no grave fault to have left out entirely the question of Locke's significance for the theology of the period, whether orthodox or deistic, and for all practical purposes this is what MacLean has done; yet Bishop Butler is one of his heroes, and there are several brief discussions (which miss the more important points) of Thomas Paine. On the other hand, one might reasonably expect that a book concerned with the influence of Locke on eighteenth-century English "literature" would have taken serious account of what the *Essay* contributed to the ideas or vocabulary of literary criticism; yet apart from a superficial analysis of Addison's papers on the pleasures of the imagination, the question is not taken up. We are forced, in short, to conclude that what "English literature of the eighteenth century" means to the author is merely those well known writers—few in number but highly miscellaneous in character since the list includes essayists, poets, novelists, satirists, theologians, and philosophers—whom he has selected, quite arbitrarily so far as one can see, for special (but never exhaustive) study—these, and a certain number of others, French and English, whom for one reason or another—not always because they were less influenced by Locke—he has thought worthy of merely incidental mention.

The Locke whose influence he has attempted to trace is a Locke who appears, in the restatement here given of the *Essay concerning human understanding,* as a singularly unsystematic and fragmentary writer. This is no doubt a result in part of the device of exposition which MacLean has adopted: a series of four chapters, corresponding to the four books of the *Essay,* in which summaries of Locke's conclusions and quotations from him are interspersed with passages from later writers criticising or dapting what he said. But the selection of this device is in itself symptomatic: it would have been impossible except to one whose conception of what is significant and important in a great philosopher was confined to the mere matter of his work—his solutions of particular problems, his dicta on this or that disputed point—to the neglect of its form and method. Of this latter aspect of the *Essay*—its properly philosophical aspect—MacLean tells us nothing; Locke, as he presents him, becomes in large part a mere announcer of conclusions—some of them announced by others before him—, at times simply a writer of passages of "engaging human interest" (e. g., pp. 21, 22, 106, 144-45). It is not that MacLean neglects the more famous doctrines of the *Essay*—the rejection of innate ideas, the reduction of all ideas to sensation and reflection, the distinction between knowledge and probability; as a matter of fact, he treats of all these matters at considerable length: what is missing is any attempt to coordinate them with one another or to discover the precise character of the philosophical approach which gives the rationale of the inquiry in which they appear. It is possible that a more adequate training in the history of philosophy before Locke might have furnished him with the apparatus necessary to such an interpretation. That he has been seriously handicapped in this regard is suggested by one of the statements in his introductory chapter (p. 13): "The examination of the mind conducted in the *Essay* not only disclosed the constitution and workings of the intellect, but also revealed the fact, ***never before stressed in philosophy,*** that human knowledge is limited. About this ***astounding*** conclusion all Eighteenth-Century thought was to revolve" (italics mine).

It is thus largely in terms of an *Essay* separated from its historical antecedents, atomized into fragments of ideas and arguments, and reduced all too frequently to a level of commonplace opinion that MacLean has undertaken to trace Locke's influence on a few writers of the eighteenth century. He has been most successful perhaps with Sterne: readers of *Tristram Shandy* will be glad to have recalled to them the many passages in that work which mention Locke or reflect the novelist's familiarity with one or another of his doctrines. On the other hand, many of the parallels he adduces elsewhere, even when they can be taken as fairly clear signs of an influence, turn on purely trivial details; e. g., the story of the blind man who identified scarlet with the sound of a trumpet (pp. 106-07), or the remarks on the place of the oyster in the chain of being (pp. 144-45). Of the others, not a few are frankly unconvincing: it is difficult to believe, for example, that it was Locke's "interpretation of the human mind" that impelled Lord Chesterfield to devote so much care and attention to his son's education (pp. 38-39) or to keep urging on the boy the importance of not wasting time (p. 45), or that the "first stage in the evolution of the theory of ruling passions" is to be found in Locke's assertion that man has an innate "desire of happiness and an aversion to misery" (pp. 45-46), or that the influence of Locke's distinction between primary and secondary qualities is reflected in the (supposedly new) habit of eighteenth-century writers of thinking about all sorts of other matters "in terms of primary and secondary" (pp. 95-96), or that when Square exclaimed, after Tom Jones had broken his arm, that "it was a mere abuse of words to call those things evil, in which there was no moral unfitness," his creator was recalling the chapters in Locke's *Essay* which deal with the "abuse of words" (p. 112).—R. S. C.

Lord Lyttelton

Blunt, Reginald. *Thomas Lord Lyttelton.* The portrait of a rake with a brief memoir of his sister, Lucy Lady Valentia. With an introduction by Maud Wyndham. London: Hutchinson, 1936. Pp. 288.

Rev. in *TLS,* March 7, 1936, p. 193.

Davis, Rose M. *"The Correspondents." PMLA,* LI (1936), 207-20.

Questions the authenticity of letters purporting to have passed between George, the first Lord Lyttleton and Mrs. Apphia Peach, who married the second, or "wicked," Lord Lyttelton. The work is in reality a fiction in the current mode of sensibility.

James Macpherson

Hanson, W. G. "James Macpherson (1736-1796)." *London quarterly and Holborn review,* October, 1936, pp. 510-15.

Charles Macklin

Macmillan, Dougald. "The censorship in the case of Macklin's *The Man of the World.*" *Huntington Library bulletin,* no. 10 (1936), 79-102.

Raushenbush, Esther M. "Charles Macklin's lost play about Henry Fielding." *MLN,* LI (1936), 505-14.

Mary de la Rivière Manley

Anderson, Paul B. "Mistress Delarivière Manley's biography." *MP,* XXXIII (1936), 261-78.

Andrew Marvell

Robbins, Caroline. "A note on a hitherto unprinted speech by Andrew Marvell." *MLR,* XXXI (1936), 549-50.

Wattie, Margaret. "The death of Marvell." *TLS,* May 2, 1936, p. 379. Corr. by Caroline Robbins, *ibid.,* May 9, p. 400.

William Mason

Chase, Isabel W. "William Mason and Sir William Chambers' *Dissertation on Oriental Gardening.*" *JEGP,* XXXV (1936), 517-29.

Henry More

Jentsch, Heisiz Günther. *Henry More in Cambridge.* Göttingen (diss.), 1935. Pp. 96.

Thomas Otway

Riva, S. "Otway, Saint-Réal, e la Venezia salvata." *Dante,* June, 1936.

Richardson Pack

Cain, R. D. "Richardson Pack (1682-1728)." *N & Q,* CLXX (1936), 344-46.

Information supplementary to the *D. N. B.*

Thomas Paine

Blunck, R. *Thomas Paine, Ein Leben für Amerika.* Berlin: Holle, 1936. Pp. 318.

Nicolson, Marjorie. "Thomas Paine, Edward Nares, and Mrs. Piozzi's marginalia." *Huntington Library bulletin,* no. 10 (1936), 103-33.

Samuel Pepys

Chappell, Edwin. *Eight generations of the Pepys family, 1500-1800.* Published by the author at 41, Westcombe Park Road, Blackheath, London, 1936.

Manchée, W. H. *Samuel Pepys and his link with the Huguenots.* (From *Proceedings of the Huguenot Society of London,* Vol. xv, no. 2.) London: Spottiswoode, 1936.

Pendleton, Louis. "Pepys as a dramatic critic." *South Atlantic quarterly,* xxxv (1936), 411-19.

Samuel, Wilfred S. "Carvajal and Pepys." (Reprinted from the *Miscellanies,* Part II., *Jewish Historical Society of England.*) London: Printed for the Society by Purnell & Sons, 1935. Pp. 6.

Talbot, Lieut.-Commander Melvin, U. S. Navy. "Samuel Pepys, naval administrator." *Nineteenth century,* CXIX (1936), 624-39.

Woodbridge, Homer. "Pepys after the diary." *Yale review,* XXV (1936), 638-40.

John Phillips

Swaen, A. E. H. "The songs in John Phillips' *Patient Grisell.*" *Archiv,* CLXVIII (1935), 77-79.

Thomas Percy

Churchill, Irving L. "William Shenstone's share in the preparation of Percy's *Reliques.*" *PMLA,* LI (1936), 960-74.

Munby, A. N. L. "Cancels in Percy's *Reliques.*" *TLS,* Oct. 31, 1936, p. 892. Corr. by L. F. Powell, Nov. 7, p. 908.

Ogburn, Vincent H. "Thomas Percy's unfinished collection, *Ancient English and Scottish Poems.*" *ELH,* III (1936), 183-89.

Ogburn, Vincent H. "Further notes on Thomas Percy." *PMLA,* LI (1936), 449-58.

Ogburn, Vincent H. "A forgotten chapter in the life of Bishop Thomas Percy." *RES,* XII (1936), 202-08.

Alexander Pope

The prose works of Alexander Pope. Newly collected and edited by Norman Ault. Vol. I., the earlier works, 1711-1720. Oxford: Shakespeare Head press, 1936. Pp. cxxvii+326.

Ault, Norman. "Pope's lost prologue." *TLS,* Sept. 19, 1936, p. 742.

Butt, John. *Pope's taste in Shakespeare.* Oxford: University press for the Shakespeare Association, 1936. Pp. 21.

"Hibernicus." "Pope's bit of bathos." *N & Q,* CLXXI (1936), 388-89.

Hodges, J. C. "Pope's debt to one of his dunces." *MLN,* LI (1936), 154-58.

Sherburn, George. *The early career of Alexander Pope.* Oxford: Clarendon press, 1934. Cf. *PQ,* XIV, 171, and XV, 185.

Rev. by E. Audra in *RAA,* XIII (1936), 345-46; by H. Papajewski in *Beiblatt,* XLVII (1936), 303-05.

Sutherland, James R. "The *Dunciad* of 1729." *MLR,* XXXI (1936), 347-53.

Tillotson, Geoffrey. "Lady Mary Wortley Montague and Pope's *Elegy to the Memory of an Unfortunate Lady.*" *RES,* XII (1936), 401-12.

Matthew Prior

Wright, H. B. "William Jackson on Prior's use of Montaigne." *MLR,* XXXI (1936), 203-05.

Edward Ravenscroft

Lancaster, H. C. "Calderon, Boursault, and Ravenscroft." *MLN,* LI (1936), 523-28.

Parshall, Raymond E. "The source of Ravenscroft's *The Anatomist.*" *RES,* XII (1936), 328-33.

Sir Joshua Reynolds

Hillis, Frederick Whiley. *The literary career of Sir Joshua Reynolds.* Cambridge: University press, 1936. Pp. xx+318.

Rev. in *TLS,* May 9, 1936, pp. 385-86; in *N & Q,* CLXXI (1936), 161-62.

An admirable study with much new information, based to a considerable extent on manuscript sources in the possession of the author and elsewhere.

Samuel Richardson

Black, Frank Gees. "The continuations of *Pamela*." *RAA*, XIII (1936), 499-507.

Boas, F. S. *From Richardson to Pinero*. Some innovators and idealists. London: John Murray, 1936.

Includes an essay on Richardson already published by the English Association.

Dottin, Paul. "Samuel Richardson et le roman épistolaire." *RAA*, XIII (1936), 481-99.

McKillop, Alan Dugald. *Samuel Richardson, printer and novelist*. Chapel Hill: University of North Carolina press, 1936. Pp. xii+357.

Sale, William M. "A bibliographical note on Richardson's *Clarissa*." *The Library*, XVI (1936), 448-51.

Sale, William M. *Samuel Richardson, a bibliographical record of his literary career with historical notes*. New Haven: Yale University press, 1936. Pp. xxiv+141.

Wentworth Dillon, fourth Earl of Roscommon

Stuart, D. M. "Roscommon of the 'Unspotted Bays'." *English: the magazine of the English Association*, I (1936).

Anna Seward

The Swan of Lichfield. Being a selection from the correspondence of Anna Seward. Edited, with a short biography and preface, by Hesketh Pearson. London: Hamish Hamilton, 1936. Pp. 316.

Rev. in *TLS*, Sept. 26, 1936, p. 760.

Pearson, Hesketh. "The Swan of Lichfield." *Life and letters to-day*, XV (1936).

Thomas Shadwell

Harris, Brice. "The date of Thomas Shadwell's birth." Corr. in *TLS*, Oct. 10, 1936, p. 815; by D. M. Walmsley, Oct. 17, p. 839.

William Shenstone

(See also *Thomas Percy*)

Ward, M. M. "Shenstone's birthplace." *MLN*, LI (1936), 440-41.

Christopher Smart

Brittain, Robert E. "Christopher Smart and Dr. Delany." *TLS,* March 7, 1936, p. 204.

Edmund Smith

Geffen, Elizabeth M. "The expulsion from Oxford of Edmund ('Rag') Smith." *N & Q,* CLXX (1936), 398-401.

Adam Smith

Scott, W. R. "New light on Adam Smith." *Economic journal,* XLVI (1936), 401-11.

Scott, W. R. "Adam Smith at Downing Street, 1766-67." *Economic history review,* VI (1935), 79-89.

Tobias Smollett

Knapp, Lewis M. "An important Smollett letter." *RES,* XII (1936), 75-77.

Knapp, Lewis M. "The publication of Smollett's *Complete History . . . and Continuation.*" *The Library,* XVI (1935), 295-308.

Sir Richard Steele

Allen, R. J. "Steele and the Molesworth family." *RES,* XII (1936), 449-54.

The identity of the characters described in *Tatler,* No. 189.

Laurence Sterne

Calder-Marshall, A. "Laurence Sterne." In *The English novelists, a survey of the novel by twenty contemporary novelists.* London: Chatto & Windus, 1936. Pp. 81-96.

Fluchère, Henri. "Sterne épistolier." *RAA,* XIII (1936), 297-310.

Hallamore, Gertrude Joyce. *Das Bild Laurence Sternes in Deutschland von der Aufklärung bis zur Romantik.* (*Germanische Studien,* 172.) Berlin: Emil Ebering, 1936. Pp. 86.

Maack, R. *Laurence Sterne im Lichte seiner Zeit.* (*Britannica,* no. x.) Hamburg: Friederichsen, 1936. Pp. 182.

Pope-Hennesy, Dame Una. "Lawrence Sterne." *Quarterly review,* CCLXVI (1936), 87-101.

Jonathan Swift

The Drapier's letters to the people of Ireland. Edited by Herbert Davis. Oxford: Clarendon press, 1935. Cf. *PQ,* xv, 188.

Rev. by Harold Williams in *RES,* XII (1936), 355-59; by M. A. Korn in *Beiblatt,* XLVII (1936), 75-78; by W. R. S. in *EHR,* LI (1936), 739; by Louis A. Landa in *University of Toronto quarterly,* V (1936), 295-99.

Goodwin, A. "Wood's halfpence." *EHR,* LI (1936), 647-74.

Handro, Lilli. *Swift: "Gulliver's Travels."* Eine Interpretation im Zusammenhang mit den geistesgeschichtlichen Beziehungen. (*Britannica,* no. 12.) Hamburg: Friederichsen, 1936. Pp. 168.

Looten, C. *La pensée religieuse de Swift et ses antinomies.* Paris: Desclée et Brouwer, 1936.

Rev. in *TLS,* March 21, 1936, p. 248.

Quintana, Ricardo. *The mind and art of Jonathan Swift.* London and New York: Oxford University press, 1936. Pp. xii+398.

Rev. in *TLS,* Jan. 2, 1937, p. 9; by Howard Mumford Jones in *SRL,* Dec. 26, 1936, p. 10; by Harold Strauss in *New York Times book review,* Nov. 29, 1936, p. 2.

This is an admirable piece of work, even if it does not altogether justify the title. The general plan indeed shows that Mr. Quintana has been content in the first place to perform the modest and useful task of providing us with a reliable study of the life and writings of Swift, founded upon a thorough investigation of all that recent scholarship has contributed to increase our knowledge both of Swift himself and of the age in which he lived. The completeness of the investigation is shown by the excellence of the well-chosen bibliography. It is a book to be recommended to all students of Swift as the best available introduction to the subject. Mr. Quintana is most scrupulous throughout both the text and the notes in giving the sources of all his material; his use of it in drawing his own conclusions indicates the carefulness of his judgment and his caution. Sometimes indeed there is almost an excessive balancing of evidence as, for example, in his discussion of the influence upon Swift of his life with Sir William Temple at Moor Park, which may be due perhaps to a natural hesitation to challenge outright the traditional view that there was too much difference between their characters for the relationship to have been really fruitful. We shall not always agree with the conclusions given here, but before we differ with them we are bound to recognize that they are always made with full knowledge and after careful consideration. Mr. Quintana, for instance, is inclined to include Swift 'among the most relentless enemies of the new science' and to emphasize the fact that he was irrevocably committed to this point of view from as early as 1693 though it was not until he wrote the third book of *Gulliver's Travels* that he was to give full satirical expression to his contempt. It must not be forgotten however that the satirist can only deal with subjects in which he is interested. As a close friend of Dr. Arbuthnot, as a member of the Scriblerus Club, and as one to whom even projectors applied for patronage, Swift may rather be regarded as no more the enemy of science than of learning. Even though he was misguided enough to attack for personal reasons both Bentley and Newton, his general satire was at least aimed at those whom he regarded as virtuosoes and pedants, the abusers of learning and science, and shows that he was not contemptuous either of science or of learning insofar as they seemed to him to serve their real purpose of enriching man's life. It may be significant in this connection that as an artist, in his prose, Swift achieved more perfectly than any other writer the kind of prose that the scientists were demanding as ideal for their purpose.

In view of his special interest in the mind and art of Swift Mr. Quintana has very justifiedly devoted less attention to the enigma of Swift's personality and the unsolved problems of his relationship to Stella and Vanessa which have always attracted the attention of the biographers. But in trying to make his study as complete as possible, he has inevitably been compelled to sacrifice the unity of effect which might have been obtained by ruthlessly excluding all other considerations and concentrating only upon the development of Swift's mind and art. He has divided his work into six books, covering the divisions into which Swift's life naturally falls; and within each book there is a constant shift of position, as we are given first a biographical sketch, then an examination of the background of ideas at the time, or of Swift's own attitude to church and state, and then a section of purely literary criticism or history, dealing with the sources or the form of a particular book or a commentary upon it. All these parts are well done, but the constant change of view is disturbing; there is no unity, no organic development in the study of the changing phases of the mind and art of the writer.

This may be in part due to the theory that Mr. Quintana puts forward that there was no gradual development in the mind and art of Swift, but that he arrived suddenly at full growth in the *Tale of a Tub,* and that there is a remarkable sameness in his attitude and in his ideas throughout the rest of his life. Without altogether questioning this very high place given to the *Tale of a Tub*—for it may be said to contain examples of almost all the varying modes of Swift's satire—it must also be admitted that they were to be more fully developed separately in his later works, as the occasion for their particular use arose. And at least there is an extraordinary richness and variety in the changing roles that Swift assumes, and a delightful play and adaptability of mind as he turns from one to the other—*Dean, Drapier, Bickerstaff* or *Gulliver*—and above all a most significant development in his art, from the sheer inventiveness and ingenuity of the Partridge papers to the plain driving force of the political pamphlets, and so on to the cunning of the Drapier and the final full mastery of the special weapon, irony, which he was born to introduce, shown in the best of *Gulliver's Travels* and in *The Modest Proposal.* In a book with this title it is perhaps permissible to ask that there should emerge a clearer impression of the extraordinary versatility of Swift, the consummate play of his intelligence, and the increasing mastery that he displays in his experiments with so many forms of satiric art.—H. D.

Secord, A. W. "Gulliver and Dampier." *MLN,* LI (1936), 159.

Smith, D. Nichol. "Jonathan Swift: some observations." *Essays by divers hands*: being the transactions of the Royal Society of Literature, XIV (1935), 29-48.

Thompson, Paul V. "*Verses on Blenheim.*" *TLS,* Aug. 22, 1936, p. 680.

Van Lennep, William. "Three unnoticed writings of Swift." *PMLA,* LI (1936), 793-802.

Webster, C. M. "A source for Swift's *A Meditation upon a Broomstick.*" *MLN,* LI (1936), 160.

Webster, C. M. "Two Swift imitations." *MLN,* LI (1936), 441.

Williams, Harold. "Stella's friends." *TLS,* May 9, 1936, p. 400.

Williams, Harold, and Davis, Herbert. "Jonathan Swift and the *Four Last Years of the Queen.*" *The Library,* XVI (1935), 343-46.

Wilson, M. "Swift's *Polite Conversation.*" *English*: *the magazine of the English Association,* I (1936).

William Taylor

Tronchon, Henri. "William Taylor de Norwich et Herder, le 'Platon du monde chrétien'." *Revue germanique,* XXVII (1936), 1-22.

Lewis Theobald

Castle, E. "Theobalds *Double Falsehood* und *The history of Cardenio* von Fletcher und Shakespeare." *Archiv,* CLXIX (1936), 182-99.

James Thomson

Drennon, Herbert. "Newtonianism in James Thomson's poetry." *ES,* LXX (1936), 358-72.

Johnson, Walter Gilbert. *James Thomson's influence on Swedish literature in the eighteenth century. University of Illinois studies in language and literature,* Vol. XIX (1936). Pp. 202.

Wells, John Edwin. "Manuscripts of Thomson's poems to Amanda and elegy on Aikman." *PQ,* XV (1936), 405-08.

Wells, John Edwin. "James Thomson and *To Dr. De la Cour.*" *TLS,* April 4, 1936, p. 300.

Wells, John Edwin. "Variants in the 1746 edition of Thomson's *Seasons.*" *The Library,* XVII (1936), 214-20.

Wells, John Edwin. "Thomson's [?] *A poem to the memory of Mr. Congreve.*" *TLS,* Oct. 3, 1936, p. 791.

Hester Lynch Thrale
(See also *Thomas Paine*)

Clifford, James Lowry. "The printing of Mrs. Piozzi's anecdotes of Dr. Johnson." *Bulletin of the John Rylands Library,* XX (1936), 157-72.

Vulliamy, C. E. *Mrs. Thrale of Streatham.* London: Jonathan Cape, 1936. Pp. 334.

Rev. in *TLS,* April 25, 1936, p. 350; by E. H. W. Meyerstein in *LM,* XXXIV (1936), 74-75; in *Bulletin of the John Rylands Library,* XX (1936), 183-84, where errors and mis-statements are pointed out.

Horace Walpole

Perkinson, Richard H. "Walpole and a Dublin pirate." *PQ,* XV (1936), 391-400.

Smith, Warren Hunting. "Strawberry Hill and Otranto." *TLS,* May 23, 1936, p. 440.

Joseph and *Thomas Warton*

Martin, L. C. "Thomas Warton and the early poems of Milton." *Proceedings of the British Academy, 1934,* xx (1936).

Miller, F. S. "Did Thomas Warton borrow from himself " *MLN,* LI (1936), 151-54.

Trowbridge, Hoyt. "Joseph Warton's classification of English poets." *MLN,* LI (1936), 515-18.

John Wesley
(See also *Henry Carey*)

Hutchinson, F. E. "John Wesley and George Herbert." *London quarterly and Holborn review,* October, 1936, pp. 439-55.

V. THE CONTINENTAL BACKGROUND

Abercrombie, Nigel. "Cartesianism and Classicism." *MLR,* XXXI (1936), 358-76.

A superfluous attack on Krantz's *Essai sur l'esthétique de Descartes.* The definitive discussion of Krantz's thesis is by Gastav Lanson in the *Revue de métaphysique et de morale* in 1896, to which no reference is made in this article.

Abercrombie, Nigel. *The origins of Jansenism.* (Oxford studies in modern languages and literature.) Oxford: Clarendon press, 1935. Pp. xii+341.

Rev. by H. C. Lancaster in *MLN,* LII (1937), 137-38; by H. F. Stewart in *MLR,* XXXI (1936), 586-87.

Aikin-Sneath, Betsy. *Comedy in Gemany in the first half of the eighteenth century.* (Oxford studies in modern languages and literature.) Oxford: Clarendon press, 1936. Pp. 122.

Epistolario di Giuseppe Baretti. Edited by Luigi Piccioni. 2 vols. Bari: Laterza, 1936. Pp. 443 and 387.

Cassirer, Ernst. "Schiller und Shaftesbury." *Publications of the English Goethe Society,* XI (1935), 37-59.

Courtines, Léo Pierre. "Bayle and his English correspondents: four unpublished letters." *Romanic review,* XXVII (1936), 104-09.

Diderot, Denis. *Supplément au voyage de Bougainville.* Publiée d'après le manuscrit de Léningrad, avec une introduction et des notes par Gilbert Chinard. Baltimore: The Johns Hopkins press, 1935. Pp. 213.

Rev. in *TLS,* March 7, 1936, p. 199; by Daniel Mornet in *RHL,* XLIII (1936), 304; by N. L. Torrey in *MLN,* LI (1936), 469-71.

Ewen, Frederic. "Criticism of English literature in Grimm's *Correspondance Littéraire.*" *SP,* XXXIII (1936), 397-404.

Green, F. C. (ed.). *Diderot's writings on the theatre.* Cambridge: University press, 1936. Pp. vi+317.

Kelly, John A. *German visitors to English theaters in the eighteenth century.* Princeton: University press, 1936. Pp. 178.

Kies, Paul P. "The authorship of *Die Englische Schaubühne.*" *Research studies of the State College of Washington* (Pullman, Washington), III (1935), 51-71.

Lancaster, Henry Carrington. *A history of French dramatic literature in the seventeenth century.* Part III, The Period of Moliere, 1652-1672. 2 Vols. Baltimore: The Johns Hopkins press; London: Milford, 1936.

Rev. in *TLS,* Jan. 9, 1937, pp. 17-18.

Lowenstein, Robert. *Voltaire as an historian of seventeenth-century French drama.* Baltimore: The Johns Hopkins press, 1935. Pp. 195.

Rev. by N. L. Torrey in *MLN,* LI (1936), 477-78.

Mayoux, J. J. "Diderot and the technique of modern literature." *MLR,* XXXI (1936), 518-31.

Merian-Genast, Ernst. "Goethe und Racine." *Archiv,* CLXVIII (1935), 197-224.

Paxeco, Fran. "The literary relations between Portugal and Great Britain." *Modern languages,* XVIII (1936), 6-20, 56-63.

Pintard, R. "L'influence de la pensée philosophique de la Renaissance italienne sur la pensée française (XVIIe siècle)." *Revue des études italiennes,* I (1936), 194-227.

Critical survey of scholarly literature on the subject.

Schaller, Heinrich. *Die Welt des Barock.* Munich: Reinhardt, 1936. Pp. 77.

Rev. by T. M. G[reene] in *Journal of philosophy,* XXXIII (1936), 249-50.

Schultz, Franz. *Klassik und Romantik der Deutschen.* I. Teil. Die Grundlagen der klassisch-romantischen Literatur. Stuttgart: Metzler, 1935. Pp. 309.

Rev. by Kurt May in *Historische Zeitschrift,* CLIV (1936), 617-20.

Seeber, Edward D. "*Oroonoko* in France in the eighteenth century." *PMLA,* LI (1936), 953-59.

Vail, Curtis C. D. *Lessing's relation to the English language and literature.* New York: Columbia University press, 1936. Pp. vi+220.

1938

ENGLISH LITERATURE, 1660-1800: A CURRENT BIBLIOGRAPHY

By Richmond P. Bond

The University of North Carolina

This bibliography attempts to list the more significant books, articles, and reviews[1] published during the year 1937, together with some bearing earlier dates that were omitted from previous bibliographies in this series. I am indebted to Dean Robert K. Root and Professors Ronald S. Crane and Austin Warren for contributing the critical notes signed with their initials, to Mr. Carl L. Cannon and Mrs. Alice K. Lewis and other members of the staff of the Yale University Library for numerous courtesies, and to Dr. H. T. Swedenberg, Jr., of the University of California at Los Angeles for assistance in the collection of material.[2]

A survey of the year's work will show the major tendencies in classical studies. Again Jonathan Swift among individual authors has in a combination of quantity and quality led the field. During 1937 he has inspired, aside from the usual miscellaneous articles, a superlatively good edition of his verse, a large bibliography, a biography, two important source studies, a book on his marriage, a psychoanalysis, and a novel.[3] Dr. Johnson has regained the ascendency over his biographer, the only important Boswell contribution being an index to the *Private Papers.* Books of a critical or biographical nature have appeared on Bunyan, Defoe, Wesley, Shenstone, Gray, Collins, Beckford, Jane Austen, Mary Wollstonecraft, Gibbon, and Paine; it is the bicentenary of the birth of the last two, and the approaching Celebration of 1938 probably accounts for the Wesleyan activity. Also, Dryden, Chesterfield, Burns, and Blake have received their due in pages, and the philosophers Hobbes, Locke, Berkeley, and Hume have fared very well. But little or no significant research has been published in 1937 on the poets Prior, Gay, Pope, Thomson, Young, and Cowper. Of editions, the work by Harold Williams on Swift's poetry is the outstanding complete collection, and Boyle's

---

[1]The year of a review is to be understood as 1937 unless otherwise specified; a few reviews of 1936 and 1938 have been included.

[2]The editor of this bibliography will be aided in his collection and analysis if students of the period will notify him as to very obscure publications and will have copies of their studies sent to him. Address: 1803 Yale Station, New Haven, Connecticut, until September, and thereafter Chapel Hill, North Carolina.

[3]Moreover, in February, 1938, *Shadow and Substance* is being well received on Broadway, with one of its chief characters (according to the playwright) a resurrection of the Dean in contemporary Ireland.

plays may now be read in entirety; the *Yale Edition of Horace Walpole's Correspondence,* initiated with two volumes of the letters between Walpole and Cole, is in all likelihood the most ambitious eighteenth century project of this generation.

Biographies—the lives of princes, kings, queens, king's ladies, uncrowned queens, lords and judges, Jacobites and United Irishmen—enlist "human interest" and even exploit new materials; tales of ships and charlatans, accounts of manors and merchants, and records of trade and diplomacy seek to give a broad view of English activity two hundred years ago. Indeed, studies historical, political, and economic, studies in the widest sense "social," have gained an extremely prominent place in the eyes of scholars and the semi-popular audience. Whatever may be the proper reasons (the War, depression, "progress," the decline of the humanities, or a cycle of interest) the advance of the social sciences is apparent in the number of books and articles on the England of 1660-1800. The literary scholar who (like the Bee and Swift himself) would venture as freebooter over the fields and gardens of human life may use these social studies, and he may range through other corners of nature in the abundant research which students now give to the history of art, ideas, and science. On this last subject several new serials contain articles concerning the men and manner of seventeenth and eighteenth century science.

It is a common observation that the Restoration and eighteenth century, the end of one age and the beginning of another, continue to grow in general interest, an observation amply justified by the large number of current publications—"private vices, publick benefits."

LIST OF ABBREVIATIONS

AHR	*American historical review*
EA	*Études anglaises*
EHR	*English historical review*
ELH	*ELH, A journal of English literary history*
ES	*Englische Studien*
HTB	New York *Herald tribune books*
JEGP	*Journal of English and Germanic philology*
JMH	*Journal of modern history*
LM	*London mercury*
MLN	*Modern language notes*
MLR	*Modern language review*
MP	*Modern philology*
N & Q	*Notes and queries*
PMLA	*Publications of the Modern Language Association of America*
PQ	*Philological quarterly*
QR	*Quarterly review*
RES	*Review of English studies*
RLC	*Revue de litérature comparée*
SAQ	*South Atlantic quarterly*
SP	*Studies in philology*
SRL	*Saturday review of literature*
TBR	New York *Times book review*
TLS	London *Times literary supplement*

I. BIBLIOGRAPHIES AND BIBLIOGRAPHICAL STUDIES

(Bibliographies of individual authors are listed in Section IV)

Albrecht, Otto E. "18th century music in the university library." *University of Pennsylvania Library chronicle,* v (1937), 13-24.

Allen, Don Cameron. "A short-title catalogue of English books prior to 1700 in the library of the State College of Washington." *Research studies of the State College of Washington,* Vol. v (1937), no. 2, supp., pp. 109-26.

Annual bibliography of English language & literature. Vol. XVII, 1936. Edited for the Modern Humanities Research Association by Mary S. Serjeantson, assisted by Leslie N. Broughton. Cambridge: University press, 1938. Pp. xi + 279.

Annual bibliography of the history of British art. Vol. II, 1935. Courtauld Institute of Art, London University. Cambridge: University press, 1937. Pp. xx + 159.

Annual bulletin of historical literature. No. XXVI. Publications of the year 1936. London: Published for the Historical Association by G. Bell & Sons, 1937. Pp. 1-71.

Chap. VI on the seventeenth and eighteenth centuries by Andrew Browning.

Austen-Leigh, R. A. "Joseph Pote of Eton and Bartlet's *Farriery.*" *Library,* XVII (1936), 131-54.

Babcock, R. W. "Eighteenth-century comic opera manuscripts." *PMLA,* LII (1937), 907-08.

Baugh, Albert C.; Chester, Allan G.; and Harbage, Alfred B. "American bibliography for 1936: English language and literature." *PMLA,* LI (1936).

See especially pp. 1234-44.

de Beer, E. S. "The earliest Fellows of the Royal Society." *Bulletin of the Institute of Historical Research,* XV (1937), 79-93.

Bennett, William. *John Baskerville, the Birmingham printer: his press, relations, and friends.* Vol. I. Birmingham: City of Birmingham School of Printing, Central School of Arts and Crafts, 1937. Pp. 172.

Rev. in *TLS,* May 8, p. 368; by B. H. Newdigate in *LM,* XXXVI, 191.

Bernbaum, Ernest. "Recent works on prose fiction before 1800." *MLN,* LII (1937), 580-93.

"A bibliography of philosophy, 1936." *Journal of philosophy,* XXXIV (1937), 422-76.

Bibliography of the collection of books and tracts on commerce, currency, and poor law (1557-1763) formed by Joseph Massie. Transcribed from Lansdowne manuscript MXLIX with historical and bibliographical introduction by William A. Shaw. London: George Harding's Bookshop, 1937. Pp. xlii + 173.

Black, George F. "A calendar of cases of witchcraft in Scotland, 1510-1727." *Bulletin of the New York Public Library,* XLI (1937), 811-47, 917-36; XLII (1938), 34-74.

Bond, D. F. "Two chap-book versions of 'The Seven Sages of Rome.'" *MLN,* LII (1937), 494-98.

"Books and articles on the economic history of Great Britain and Ireland." Compiled by J. de L. Mann. *Economic history review,* VIII (1937), 111-15.

This annual list contains a number of references to detailed studies of the seventeenth and eighteenth centuries.

Bredvold, Louis I. "English literature, 1660-1800: a current bibliography." *PQ,* XVI (1937), 149-91.

Bronson, Bertrand Harris. "Ritson's *Bibliographia Scotica.*" *PMLA,* LII (1937), 122-59.

Carlson, C. Lennart. "A further note on Thomas Godfrey in England." *American literature,* IX (1937), 73-76.

Ralph Griffiths reprinted in the *Grand magazine of universal intelligence* (1759) four poems by Godfrey from the *American magazine* (1758).

Carr, Charles T. "Early German grammars in England." *JEGP,* XXXVI (1937), 455-74.

"Check list of the John Baskerville collection of Perry Williams Harvey, including some specimens of the work of contemporary Continental printers." *Yale University Library gazette,* XI (1937), 63-80.

Cheney, C. R. "Early Banbury chap-books and broadsides." *Library,* XVII (1936), 98-108.

Crossley, E. W. "The MSS. of Nathaniel Johnston, M.D., of Pontefract." *Yorkshire archæological journal,* XXXII (1936), 429-41.

Day, Cyrus Lawrence, and Murrie, Eleanore Boswell. "Playford *versus* Pearson." *Library,* XVII (1937), 427-47.

"Edward Buckler." *Notes and queries for Somerset and Dorset,* XXII (1937), 121-24. Cf. *PQ,* XVI, 151.

Ewing, J. C. "Brash and Reid, booksellers in Glasgow, and their collection of *Poetry Original and Selected.*" *Records of the Glasgow Bibliographical Society,* XII (1936), 1-20.

"Fiftieth critical bibliography of the history and philosophy of science and of the history of civilization." *Isis,* XXVII (1937), 364-410.

See especially pp. 372-79. The forty-seventh, forty-eighth, and forty-ninth bibliographies in this series appeared *ibid.,* XXVI (1936), 244-98, XXVI (1937), 490-604, XXVII (1937), 117-200; see especially pp. 255-61; 513-26, 133-41.

Fulton, John F. "A bibliography of two Oxford physiologists, Richard Lower, 1631-1691, and John Mayow, 1643-1679." *Proceedings and papers of the Oxford Bibliographical Society, 1934-35,* IV (1936), 1-62.

Graham, Walter. "Thomas Baker, Mrs. Manley, and the *Female Tatler.*" *MP,* XXXIV (1937), 267-72.

Combats P. B. Anderson's attribution of the Bragge-Baldwin *Female tatler* to Mrs. Manley; favors traditional acceptance of Baker as author.

Harbage, Alfred. "Elizabethan and seventeenth-century play manuscripts: addenda." *PMLA*, LII (1937), 905-07.
Supplements author's own catalogue; cf. *PQ*, xv, 155.

Hazen, A. T. "Baskerville's Virgil." *Yale University Library gazette*, XI (1937), 90-93.

Heym, Gerald. "An introduction to the bibliography of alchemy. Part I." *Ambix*, I (1937), 48-60.
Contains a few entries of books published in England.

Holmes, Maurice. *An introduction to the bibliography of Captain James Cook, R.N.* London: Francis Edwards, 1936. Pp. 59.
Rev. in *TLS*, Jan. 23, p. 64.

Hughes, Philip. "The 'Westminster Archives.'" *Dublin review*, CI (1937), 300-10.
A survey of the archives in the MSS. of the Archbishop of Westminster, important for the study of the English Catholics during the seventeenth and eighteenth centuries.

International bibliography of historical sciences. Ninth year, 1934. Edited for the International Committee of Historical Sciences. New York: H. W. Wilson; London: Oxford University Press; Paris: Armand Colin; Berlin: Walter de Gruyter, 1936. Pp. xliii + 489.

Jaggard, William. "Imitations of Shakespeare." *N & Q*, CLXXIII (1937), 370-73.

Jillson, Willard Rouse. "The first English poem on Kentucky." *Register of the Kentucky State Historical Society*, XXXV (1937), 198-201.
"An ode to Kentucky" appeared in the *Philanthropist*, London, 1795, No. 24.

Johnson, A. F. "An unrecorded specimen sheet of a Scottish printing house." *Edinburgh Bibliographical Society transactions*, I, pt. i (1936), 63-64.

Jones, Claude. "Christopher Smart, Richard Rolt, and *The Universal Visiter*." *Library*, XVIII (1937), 212-14.

LeFanu, W. R. "British periodicals of medicine: a chronological list. Part I: 1684-1899." *Bulletin of the Institute of the history of medicine*, V (1937), 735-61, 827-55.

Lloyd, Llewelyn C. "The book-trade in Shropshire. Some account of the stationers, booksellers and printers at work in the county to about 1800." *Transactions of the Shropshire Archæological Society*, XLVIII (1935-36), 65-142, 145-200.

Longman, Charles James. *The house of Longman, 1724-1800.* A bibliographical history with a list of signs used by booksellers of that period. Edited by John E. Chandler. London, New York, Toronto: Longmans, Green, 1936. Pp. xv + 488.

McCabe, William H. "The play-list of the English College of St. Omers, 1592-1762." *RLC*, XVII (1937), 355-75.

McColley, Grant. "The third edition of Francis Godwin's *The Man in the Moone*." *Library*, XVII (1937), 472-75.

Transfers date of this edition from 1768 to 1686, and shows popularity of the work.

Madan, Falconer; Craster, H. H. E.; and Denholm-Young, N. *A summary catalogue of western manuscripts in the Bodleian Library at Oxford* which have not hitherto been catalogued in the quarto series with references to the Oriental and other manuscripts. Vol. II, Part ii. Collections and miscellaneous MSS. acquired during the second half of the 17th century. Oxford: Clarendon press, 1937. Pp. x + 655-1216.

Includes antiquarian collections of Dodsworth, Dugdale, Junius, and Marshall.

Martin, Edward A. *A bibliography of Gilbert White the naturalist & antiquarian of Selborne.* With a biography and a descriptive account of the village of Selborne. London: Halton, 1934. Pp. viii + 195.

Milne, Alexander Taylor. *Writings on British history, 1934.* A bibliography of books and articles on the history of Great Britain from about 450 A.D. to 1914, published during the year 1934. (Royal Historical Society) London: Jonathan Cape, 1937. Pp. 427.

Rev. in *TLS,* Feb. 19, 1938, p. 121. § The first annual volume in a new series. Stuart period, 1603-1714, pp. 192-223; eighteenth century, 1714-1815, pp. 224-65.

Morgan, William Thomas, assisted by Chloe Siner Morgan. *A bibliography of British history (1700-1715), with special reference to the reign of Queen Anne.* Vol. II, 1708-1715. Bloomington, Indiana: 1937. Pp. vi + 684.

This volume, listing some 5,700 pamphlets and memoirs published in the years 1708-1716, with numerous cross references, will prove of great value to students of English history and literature. The entries for each year are prefaced by a useful summary statement. Errors and omissions may be the more easily condoned when one considers the magnitude of the project and the complexities of the Queen Anne pamphlet wars. It is unfortunate that Morgan did not include references to the libraries containing copies of the rarest tracts.

Murray, Edward Croft. "Sketch-books of Samuel Ireland." *British Museum quarterly,* XI (1937), 135-39.

Noyes, Gertrude E. *Bibliography of courtesy and conduct books in seventeenth-century England.* New Haven: 1937. Pp. 111.

Noyes, Robert Gale. "A manuscript Restoration prologue for *Volpone.*" *MLN,* LII (1937), 198-200.

Noyes, Robert Gale, and Lamson, Roy, Jr. "Broadside-ballad versions of the songs in Restoration drama." *Harvard studies and notes in philology and literature,* XIX (1937), 199-218.

Perkinson, Richard H. "The Anti-Jacobin." *N & Q,* CLXXII (1937), 164.

Pochmann, Henry A. "Anglo-German bibliography for 1936." *JEGP,* XXXVI (1937), 246-62.

Pomfret, J. E. "Some further letters of William Strahan, printer." *Pennsylvania magazine of history and biography,* LX (1936), 455-89.

Ransom, Harry. "From a gentleman in Edinburgh: 1769. An early sidelight on literary property." *Sewanee review,* XLIV (1936), 366-71.

Répertoire d'art et d'archéologie. Dépouillement des périodiques, bibliographie des ouvrages d'art français et étrangers. Année 1935, fascicule 40. Publié sous la direction de Marcel Aubert. Par Mme. Lucien-Herr et M. H. Stein. (Bibliothèque d'art et d'archéologie de l'Université de Paris) Paris: Albert Morance, 1936. Pp. 340.

See especially pp. 155-89.

Rollins, Carl Purington. "John Baskerville." *Yale University Library gazette,* XI (1937), 55-61.

"Schriftenverzeichnis für 1936." *Zeitschrift für Ästhetik und allgemeine Kunstwissenschaft,* XXXI (1937), 363-414.

Sims, E. R. "Four seventeenth century translations of *Lazarillo de Tormes.*" *Hispanic review,* V (1937), 316-32.

One of these is an English translation published in London, 1688.

Stockwell, La Tourette. "The Dublin pirates and the English laws of copyright, 1710-1801." *Dublin magazine,* XII (1937), iv, 30-40.

Terry, Charles Sanford. "John Forbes's 'Songs and Fancies.'" *Musical quarterly,* XXII (1936), 402-19.

Union catalogue of the periodical publications in the university libraries of the British Isles with their respective holdings. Excluding titles in the *World list of scientific periodicals,* 1934. Compiled on behalf of the Joint Standing Committee on Library Co-operation by Marion G. Roupell. London: Joint Standing Committee on Library Co-operation, National Central Library, 1937. Pp. xii + 712.

Rev. by W. Kerr in *Lib. quar.,* XIII (1938), 142-43. § 23,115 different periodicals are included, with cross references to make the total entries more than double that number. There is no chronological index.

Upton, Eleanor S. "The location of seventeenth-century documents described in the first nine reports of the Historical Manuscripts Commission." *Bulletin of the Institute of Historical Research,* XV (1937), 73-78.

Williams, Robert H. "A manuscript document on the translations from Spanish by Captain John Stevens." *RLC,* XVI (1936), 144-66.

Wood, Frederick T. "The attack on the stage in the eighteenth century." *N & Q,* CLXXIII (1937), 218-22.

Wood, Frederick T. "Unrecorded eighteenth-century plays." *N & Q,* CLXXII (1937), 43.

Wormald, F. "Poetical manuscripts of William Hammond." *British Museum quarterly,* XI (1936), 24-26.

William Hammond (1719-1783), the Moravian hymn-writer.

Wright, Lyle H. "Sporting books in the Huntington Library." *Huntington Library lists,* no. 2, 1937. Pp. vii + 132.

Rev. by V. B. Heltzel in *JEGP,* xxxvii (1938), 123-24. § A bibliography of 1,344 items, including many editions of *The compleat angler.*

The year's work in English studies. Vol. xvi, 1935. Edited for the English Association by Frederick S. Boas and Mary S. Serjeantson. Oxford: University press, 1937. Pp. 380.

Chap. x, the Restoration, by F. E. Budd, pp. 265-81; chap. xi, the eighteenth century, by Edith J. Morley, pp. 282-317.

The year's work in modern language studies. Vol. vii, year ending 30 June 1936. Edited for the Modern Humanities Research Association by William J. Entwistle, L. W. Tancock, and A. Gillies. Cambridge: University press, 1937. Pp. 281.

II. THE SOCIAL AND POLITICAL ENVIRONMENT

Arneke, Heinrich. *Kirchengeschichte und Rechtsgeschichte in England* (von der Reformation bis zum frühen 18. Jahrhundert). (Studien zur englischen Philologie, Heft xci) Halle: Niemeyer, 1937. Pp. vi + 355.

Arnold-Forster, Rear-Admiral D. *At war with the smugglers.* Career of Doctor Arnold's father. London: Ward, Lock, 1936. Pp. 256.

Rev. by G.P.B.N. in *Mariner's mirror,* xxiii, 115-16.

Arthur, Sir George. *Seven heirs apparent.* London: Thornton Butterworth, 1937. Pp. 292.

Includes history of the apprenticeships of George II, Prince Frederick, and George III.

Athill, Lawrence. "Eccentric Englishwomen: v. Hannah Snell." *Spectator,* May 14, 1937, pp. 899-900.

Austen-Leigh, R. A. "The commission for the relief of poor proselytes, 1717-1730." *Proceedings of the Huguenot Society of London,* xv, iii (1936), 376-94.

Austen-Leigh, R. A. "Dr. Michel Malard, the proselyte." *Proceedings of the Huguenot Society of London,* xv, iv (1937), 555-65.

d'Auvers, Marquis. "Le couronnement de Jacques II (3 May 1685)." *France-Grands Bretagne,* xx (1937), 127-36.

Baily, F. E. *Sophia of Hanover and her times.* London: Hutchinson, 1936. Pp. 288.

Barton, Margaret, *Tunbridge Wells.* London: Faber & Faber, 1937. Pp. 363.

Rev. in *TLS,* May 29, p. 406; by C. Hobhouse in *Spectator,* June 18, p. 1152.

Baumgartner, Leona. "John Howard and the public health movement." *Bulletin of the Institute of the History of Medicine,* v (1937), 489-508.

Bayne-Powell, Rosamond. *Eighteenth-century London life.* London: Murray, 1937. Pp. vii + 385.

Rev. in *TLS,* May 29, p. 404; by A. R. Humphreys in *Cambridge rev.,* lviii,

441; by J. Bélanger in *EA,* II (1938), 49; by M. D. George in *History,* XXII, 273-74. § A superficial and frequently inaccurate survey.

Beresford, John. "An undergraduate's account book, 1789-93." *Oxford,* III (1937), 43-50.

Bilainkin, George. *Front page news — once.* Events, important, comic and startling, exactly as read by our forebears. London: Methuen, 1937. Pp. xvii + 288.

Not. in *TLS,* Dec. 11, p. 948. § Extracts from news stories, 1642-1815.

Bowden, Witt; Karpovich, Michael; and Usher, Abbott Payson. *An economic history of Europe since 1750.* New York: American Book Co., 1937. Pp. viii + 948.

Brett-James, Norman G. *The growth of Stuart London.* With a foreword by Alderman Sir Charles H. Collett. London: George Allen & Unwin, 1935. Pp. 556.

Rev. by G. Parsloe in *History,* XXII, 77-78.

Bruce, George. " 'The Bishop's Gillie.' " *Blackwood's magazine,* CCXLI (1937), 667-94.

On General Sir Robert Rollo Gillespie.

Bruce, Maurice. "The Duke of Mar in exile, 1716-32." *Transactions of the Royal Historical Society,* XX (1937), 61-82.

Bruford, W. H. "Germany and the Germans — eighteenth-century English travellers' tales." *German life and letters,* I (1937), 81-95.

Burn, W. L. "Church and state in Scotland under George I." *Church quarterly review,* CXXII (1936), 283-91.

Butterfield, H. "Lord North and Mr. Robinson, 1779." *Cambridge historical review,* V (1937), 255-79.

Calendar of state papers and manuscripts relating to English affairs existing in the archives and collections of Venice and in other libraries of northern Italy. Vol. XXXVI, 1669-1670. Edited by Allen B. Hinds. London: H. M. Stationery Office, 1937. Pp. lv + 421.

Calendar of state papers, colonial series, America and West Indies, 1724-1725, preserved in the Public Record Office. Edited by Cecil Headlam. With an introduction by Arthur Percival Newton. London: H. M. Stationery Office, 1936. Pp. l + 570. *Calendar . . . 1726-27,* 1936. Pp. xl + 507. *Calendar . . . 1728-29,* 1937. Pp. xlv + 632.

Rev. by C. P. Gould in *Miss. valley hist. rev.,* XXIV, 376-78.

Calendar of state papers, domestic series, of the reign of William III. 1 January, 1699 — 31 March, 1700, preserved in the Public Record Office. Edited by Edward Bateson. London: H. M. Stationery Office, 1937. Pp. lxi + 545. *Calendar . . . 1 April, 1700 — 8 March, 1702,* 1937. Pp. iv + 859.

Calendar of the Inner Temple Records. Vol. V, 25 George II, 1751 — 41 George III, 1800. Edited by R. A. Roberts. London: George Barber, 1937. Pp. 738.

Rev. in *TLS,* June 5, p. 420.

Calendar of treasury books, 1703, preserved in the Public Record Office. Vol. xviii. Prepared by William A. Shaw. London: H. M. Stationery Office, 1936. Pp. cxcii + 664.

The Cambridge history of India. Vol. iv. The Mughul period. Planned by Lt. Colonel Sir Wolseley Haig. Edited by Sir Richard Burn. Cambridge: University press, 1937. Pp. xxvi + 670.
A study of the sixteenth, seventeenth, and eighteenth centuries.

Cammell, Charles Richard. "Rupert, Prince Palatine: portraits of a royal artist." *Connoisseur,* c (1937), 59-64.
See also *ibid.*, pp. 322-23.

Carpenter, Edward. *Thomas Sherlock, 1678-1761.* Bishop of Bangor 1728; of Salisbury 1734; of London 1748. London: S.P.C.K.; New York: Macmillan, 1936. Pp. xii + 335.
Rev. by H. B. Washburn in *Anglican theol. rev.*, xix, 326-28; by R. H. Murray in *Contemp. rev.*, cli, 378-79; by M. A. Thomson in *History,* xxii, 78-79; by R.P. in *Oxford mag.*, lv, 712; by W. R. Matthews in *Spectator,* Feb. 19, pp. 321-22.

Carter, E. H. *The Norwich subscription books.* A study of the subscription books of the diocese of Norwich, 1637-1800. London: Thomas Nelson & Sons, 1937. Pp. xxii + 201.
Rev. in *TLS,* Nov. 6, p. 825. § Contains considerable source material for the history of education.

Churchill, Winston S. *Marlborough: his life and times.* Vol. v, 1705-1708. New York: Scribner's, 1937. Pp. 608.
Rev. by V. Barbour in *AHR,* xliii (1938), 376-77; by W. MacDonald in *HTB,* April 18, p. 4; by W. T. Morgan in *JMH,* ix, 511-14; by P. W. Wilson in *TBR,* March 28, p. 10.

Clark, Dora Mae. "The office of secretary to the treasury in the eighteenth century." *American historical review,* xlii (1936), 22-45.

Clark, G. N. "Social and economic aspects of science in the age of Newton." *Economic history,* iii (1937), 362-79.

Colson, Percy. *The strange history of Lord George Gordon.* London: Robert Hale, 1937. Pp. xix + 286.
Rev. in *TLS,* May 22, p. 397.

Connell, Neville. *Anne: the last Stuart monarch.* London: Thornton Butterworth, 1937. Pp. 338.
Rev. in *TLS,* May 22, p. 388; by C. Petrie in *Eng. rev.*, lxiv, 624-25; by J. Hayward in *Spectator,* April 16, pp. 722-24.

Cook, D. "The representative history of the county, town, and university of Cambridge, 1689-1832." University of London thesis abstract, *Bulletin of the Institute of Historical Research,* xv (1937), 42-44.

Cundall, Frank. *The governors of Jamaica in the first half of the eighteenth century.* London: West India committee, 1937. Pp. xxxi + 229.

D'Auvergne, Edmund B. *Envoys extraordinary.* The romantic careers of some remarkable British representatives abroad. London: Harrap, 1937. Pp. 318.

Not. in *Queen's quar.*, XLIV, 433; rev. by W. R. Copp in *Dalhousie rev.*, XVII, 390. § Contains studies of James Harris, first Earl of Malmesbury, and of Hugh Elliot.

Davies, Godfrey. *The early Stuarts, 1603-1660.* (Oxford History of England) Oxford: Clarendon press, 1937. Pp. xxi + 452.

Rev. in *TLS*, June 5, p. 422; by M. W. Baldwin in *Cath. hist. rev.*, XXIII, 489-90; by R. P. Stearns in *Church hist.*, VI, 279-80; in *Contemp. rev.*, CLII, 117-19; by K. B. Murdock in *New England quar.*, X, 603-04; by J.E.C.H. in *Oxford mag.*, LVI, 232; in *QR*, CCLXIX, 178-79; by W. T. Laprade in *SAQ*, XXXVI, 478-79. § Useful as a one-volume survey of the era preceding the classical period.

Davies, J. D. Griffith. *Honest George Monck.* London: John Lane, 1936. Pp. xiii + 365.

Not. by B.H.G.W. in *Cambridge rev.*, LVIII, 320.

Daviot, Gordon. *Claverhouse.* London: Collins, 1937. Pp. 398.

Rev. in *TLS*, Dec. 11, p. 938.

The diary of a surgeon in the years 1751-1752. By John Knyveton. Edited & transcribed by Ernest Gray. New York: D. Appleton-Century, 1937. Pp. xiv + 322.

Rev. in *TLS*, Feb. 12, 1938, p. 103. § A reconstruction of gruesome medical conditions in London and at sea. For anachronisms see the review by Dr. Saul Jarcho in *TBR*, Dec. 12, p. 2. The entry for Dec. 11, 1751, is a description of a tavern dinner given by Johnson (already "a famous novelist known to his friends as the Doctor") probably based on Hawkins; on March 24, 1752, Knyveton receives a letter from his uncle, who "quotes from an article in the Spectator written by Doctor Johnson."

Dickinson, H. W. *Matthew Boulton.* Cambridge: University press, 1937. Pp. xiv + 218.

Rev. in *TLS*, Feb. 20, p. 121; by A.G. in *Oxford mag.*, LVI, 171-72; by M. in *Queen's quar.*, XLIV, 270. § The first separate biography of the Birmingham industrialist, engineer, and partner of James Watt.

Dilks, T. Bruce. *Charles James Fox and the borough of Bridgwater.* (Bridgwater booklets, no. 6) Bridgwater: East Gate press, 1937. Pp. 50.

Rev. in *TLS*, Aug. 21, p. 609.

Dobrée, Bonamy, ed. *From Anne to Victoria.* Essays by various hands. New York: Scribner's, 1937. Pp. x + 630.

Rev. in *TLS*, Feb. 27, p. 143; by R.E. in *Burlington mag.*, LXXI, 57; by A. Digeon in *EA*, I, 345-46; by F. T. Wood in *ES*, LXXII, 152-54; by A. M. Davies in *HTB*, July 25, p. 5; by H. Levin in *Nation*, Aug. 7, 154-56; by J. Cournos in *TBR*, Aug. 1, p. 9; by C. D. Abbott in *SRL*, July 24 p. 10.

The essays on eighteenth century figures, averaging about fifteen pages, deal with Marlborough, Addison and Steele, Swift, the Duchess of Marlborough, Defoe, Berkeley, Pope, Robert Walpole, Handel, Clive, Mrs. Montagu, the elder Pitt, Wesley, Johnson, Wilkes, Chesterfield, Mansfield, Horace Walpole, Fielding and Sterne, Captain Cook, Hogarth, Rodney, Coke of Norfolk, Garrick, Hastings, Priestley, Sheridan, Burke and Fox, Burns, Adam Smith, Robert Adam and his brothers, the younger Pitt, Blake, John Hunter, James Wyatt, Paine, and Nelson. The essays illustrate the abundant variety of personality and achievement which accompanies any century of English life. Most of the pieces employ the biographical-critical method, though the one on Swift is entirely a psychological analysis, that on Pope is mainly an essay on Augustan verse, and that on Horace Walpole is a discourse on his memoirs and the evils of memoir-editing. No amount of supervision can dispose of stylistic unevenness in a symposium, but Dobrée (himself the author of an excellent chapter on Chesterfield) has wisely selected the figures and has generally chosen essayists who can attractively present them. These two score men and women are sympathetically treated — but without benefit of tinsel. Occasional unfounded statements appear, but they are balanced by provocative ideas. Such a semi-popular volume needs no apology for existence.

Edwards, William. *Crown, people and parliament, 1760-1935.* London: Arrowsmith, 1937. Pp. 256.

Rev. in *TLS,* Dec. 18, p. 956.

Ettinger, Amos Aschbach. *James Edward Oglethorpe, imperial idealist.* Oxford: Clarendon press, 1936. Pp. xi + 348.

Not. by G.H.G. in *EHR,* LII, 748; rev. by A. S. Turberville in *History,* XXII, 79-80.

European civilization: its origin and development. By various contributors. Under the direction of Edward Eyre. Vol. v. Economic history of Europe since the Reformation. London: Oxford University press, 1937. Pp. vi + 1,328.

Rev. by F. L. Nussbaum in *JMH,* IX, 502-03; by G. O'B. in *Studies: an Irish quar. rev.,* XXVI, 163-64.

Evans, G. Nesta. *Social life in mid-eighteenth century Anglesey.* Cardiff: 1936. Pp. 216.

Rev. in *TLS,* June 19, p. 467; by M.D.G. in *History,* XXII, 93.

Fawcett, Sir Charles. *The English factories in India.* Vol. I (new series) (The Western Presidency) 1670-1677. Oxford: Clarendon press, 1936. Pp. xxviii + 389.

Rev. in *TLS,* March 20, p. 220; by P.E.R. in *EHR,* LIII (1938), 172-73.

Fergusson, James. "The laird's books: an eighteenth-century library." *Cornhill magazine,* CLVI (1937), 90-96.

The unnamed laird is Sir Adam Fergusson, Boswell's rival for a seat in Parliament and opponent in the Douglas Cause.

Fieldhouse, H. N. "Bolingbroke and the d'Iberville correspondence, August 1714 — June 1715." *EHR,* LII (1937), 673-82.

Fieldhouse, H. N. "Bolingbroke's share in the Jacobite intrigue of 1710-14." *EHR,* LII (1937), 443-59.

Fieldhouse, H. N. "Oxford, Bolingbroke, and the Pretender's place of residence, 1711-14." *EHR,* LII (1937), 289-96.

Fletcher, F. T. H. "Montesquieu and penal law reform in England." *University of Toronto quarterly,* VI (1937), 497-515.

Forster, E. M. "Eccentric Englishwomen: vii. Luckie Buchan." *Spectator,* May 28, 1937, pp. 986-87.

On the founder of the Scottish sect of Buchanites.

Fussell, G. E. "Animal husbandry in eighteenth century England." *Agricultural history,* XI (1937), 96-116, 189-214.

Fussell, G. E. "Country life 150 years ago: Thomas Bewick, the Northumbrian Cobbett." *English review,* LXIV (1937), 568-76.

Fussell, G. E. "English countryside and population in the eighteenth century." *Economic geography,* XII (1936), 294-310, 411-30.

Gary, A. T. "The political and economic relations of English and American Quakers (1750-85)." *University of Oxford abstracts of dissertations, 1935,* VIII (1936), 23-28.

George, R. H. "Parliamentary elections and electioneering in 1685." *Transactions of the Royal Historical Society,* XIX (1936), 167-95.

George, Robert H. "A note on the Bill of Rights." *AHR,* XLII (1937), 670-79.

"A Georgian prelate: Jonathan Shipley and his friends." Leading article in *TLS,* July 24, 1937, pp. 533-34. Cf. corr. by Gilbert H. Doane, *ibid.,* Aug. 21, p. 608.

Gibbon, Reginald. "The order book of the dean and chapter of Ely, 1729-1769." *Church quarterly review,* CXXIV (1937), 250-65.

Shows the use of church revenues for personal advantage of dean and prebendaries.

Gipson, Lawrence Henry. *The British Empire before the American Revolution.* Provincial characteristics and sectional tendencies in the era preceding the American crisis. Vol. I. Great Britain and Ireland. Vol. II. The southern plantations. Vol. III. The northern plantations. Caldwell, Idaho: Caxton Printers, 1936. Pp. xxix + 301, xxx + 383, xxxvi + 347.

Rev. in *Nineteenth century,* CXXIII (1938), 114-15.

Hartmann, Cyril Hughes. *Clifford of the cabal.* A life of Thomas, first Lord Clifford of Chudleigh, Lord High Treasurer of England (1630-1673). London: William Heinemann, 1937. Pp. xix + 350.

Rev. in *TLS,* May 15, p. 373; by C. Petrie in *Eng. rev.,* LXIV, 742-43; by P. Legouis in *EA,* I, 534-36; by B. Dobreé in *Spectator,* July 9, p. 67.

Hayes, Richard. *The last invasion of Ireland: when Connacht rose.* Dublin: M. H. Gill and Son, 1937. Pp. xxvi + 341.

On the Insurrection of 1798.

Heape, R. Grundy. *Georgian York.* A sketch of life in Hanoverian England. London: Methuen, 1937. Pp. xii + 120.

Rev. in *TLS,* June 5, p. 423; by C.R.B. in *Connoisseur,* C, 163.

Henderson, G. D. *Religious life in seventeenth-century Scotland.* Cambridge: University press, 1937. Pp. vii + 311.

Rev. by M. M. Knappen in *AHR,* XLIII (1938), 371-72; by J. A. Smith in *Criterion,* XVII, 162-64; by Ruaraidh Erskine of Marr in *Dublin rev.,* CI, 174-76; by J. T. McNeill in *Jour. of religion,* XVII, 328-29; by C. J. Wright in *London quar. and Holborn rev.,* July, pp. 411-12.

Heriot, Duncan B. "Anabaptism in England during the 17th century." *Congregational Historical Society transactions,* XIII (1937), 22-40.

Higginson, A. Henry. *Peter Beckford, Esquire, sportsman, traveller, man of letters.* A biography. London: Collins, 1937. Pp. 307.

Rev. in *TLS,* Nov. 6, p. 821; by J. Hayward in *Spectator,* Nov. 19, p. 30.

Hindle, Wilfrid. *The Morning Post, 1772-1937.* Portrait of a newspaper. London: George Routledge & Sons, 1937. Pp. xi + 260.

Rev. in *TLS,* Dec. 4, p. 919.

Hoff, Ebbe C. and Phebe M. "The life and times of Richard Lower, physiologist and physician (1631-1691)." *Bulletin of the Institute of the History of Medicine,* IV (1936), 517-35.

Holdsworth, W. S. "Lord Mansfield." *Law quarterly review,* LIII (1937), 221-34.

Review-article on Fifoot's *Lord Mansfield,* 1936.

Hull, William I. *Eight first biographies of William Penn in seven languages and seven lands.* (Swarthmore College monographs on Quaker history, no. 3) 1936. Pp. xviii + 136.

Rev. by R. E. E. Harkness in *Church hist.,* VI, 90; by J. M. Morse in *Miss. valley hist. rev.,* XXIV, 379-80.

Hull, William I. *William Penn.* A topical biography. New York: Oxford University press, 1937. Pp. xvi + 362.

Rev. in *SRL,* July 24, p. 19; in *TLS,* Oct. 30, p. 804; by C. G. Stillman in *HTB,* July 4, p. 6; by E. C. O. Beatty in *JMH,* IX, 509-10; by C. E. Vulliamy in *Spectator,* July 16, pp. 115-16; by N. G. Goodman in *TBR,* June 20, p. 4.

Ilchester, the Earl of. *The home of the Hollands, 1605-1820.* London: Murray, 1937. Pp. xviii + 410.

Rev. in *Contemp. rev.,* CLII, 113-15; in *TLS,* April 24, p. 302; by Ralph Edwards in *Burlington mag.,* LXXI, 195-96; by C.R.C. in *Connoisseur,* C, 161-62; by C. Hobhouse in *Spectator,* July 9, pp. 68-69.

Irwin, Margaret. *The stranger prince.* The story of Rupert of the Rhine. New York: Harcourt, Brace, 1937. Pp. viii + 527.

Rev. in *TLS,* Jan. 9, p. 26; by I. Barry in *HTB,* March 7, p. 2; by W. R. Benét in *SRL,* March 6, p. 5; by J. S. Southron in *TBR,* March 21, p. 6. § Fictional biography.

Jacob, Rosamond. *The rise of the United Irishmen, 1791-94.* London: George G. Harrap, 1937. Pp. 266.

James, G. F. "Josiah Burchett, Secretary to the Lords Commissioners of the Admiralty, 1695-1742." *Mariner's mirror,* XXIII (1937), 477-98.

James, G. F., and Shaw, J. J. Sutherland. "Admiralty administration and personnel, 1619-1714." *Bulletin of the Institute of Historical Research,* XIV (1936-37), 10-24, 166-83.

Johnson, E. A. J. *Predecessors of Adam Smith.* The growth of British economic thought. New York: Prentice-Hall, 1937. Pp. xii + 426.

Rev. in *TLS,* Aug. 21, p. 598; by E.R.A. Seligman in *AHR,* XLIII (1938), 375-76. § Includes essays on William Petty, Nehemiah Grew, Charles King, David Hume, Malachy Postlethwayt, Sir James Steuart. Appendix A is a checklist of the more important articles devoted to proposals for economic improvement contained in the *Philosophical transactions* of the Royal society, 1665-1776.

Jones, Joseph. "The 'distress'd' negro in English magazine verse." *University of Texas studies in English,* no. 17, 1937, pp. 88-106.

Nearly half of the poems cited appeared in the eighteenth century.

Jones, Maurice Bethell. *Restoration carnival: Catherine of Braganza at the court of Charles II.* A romantic biography. New York: Julian Messner, 1937. Pp. 307.

Rev. by M. Chatain in *HTB,* May 2, p. 13; by C. Wright in *TBR,* May 16, p. 18.

Joshi, K. L. "Augustan age." Corr. in *TLS,* July 10, 1937, p. 512.

Journal of the commissioners for trade and plantations from January 1764 to December 1767 preserved in the Public Record Office. London: H. M. Stationery Office, 1936. Pp. viii + 484.

Knittle, Walter Allen. *Early eighteenth century Palatine emigration.* A British government redemptioner project to manufacture naval stores. Philadelphia: Dorrance, 1937. Pp. xix + 320.

Rev. by C. P. Gould in *Miss. valley hist. rev.*, XXIV, 72-73; by W. F. Dunaway in *Pa. mag. of hist. and biog.*, LXI, 101-02. § A careful study of the large Palatine migration from the Rhine Valley through England to America and Ireland in Anne's reign, written from the point of view of the British government.

Konkle, Burton Alva. "A new view of William Penn." *Pennsylvania history,* IV (1937), 103-05.

Kraus, Michael. "Eighteenth century humanitarianism: collaboration between Europe and America." *Pennsylvania magazine of history and biography,* LX (1936), 270-86.

Kraus, Michael. "Slavery reform in the eighteenth century: an aspect of transatlantic intellectual cooperation." *Pennsylvania magazine of history and biography,* LX (1936), 53-66.

Lambert, R. S., ed. *Grand Tour.* A journey in the tracks of the age of aristocracy. Conducted by Mona Wilson, Douglas Woodruff, Edmund Blunden, Janet Adam Smith, Richard Pyke, Sacheverell Sitwell, Malcolm Letts. London: Faber and Faber, 1935. Pp. 167.

Rev. in *HTB,* Feb. 28, p. 3; in *TBR,* Feb. 7, p. 12; by R. R. Palmer in *JMH,* IX, 256; by H. Davis in *SRL,* Jan. 30, pp. 6-7. § Much of the material is drawn from the Restoration and eighteenth century.

Lansdowne, Marquis of. *Glanerought and the Petty-Fitzmaurices.* London: Oxford University press, 1937. Pp. xxviii + 226.

Contains a note by R. W. Chapman on Lansdowne's Johnsonian studies.

Lathrope, George H. "Count Cagliostro: an excursion into eighteenth century charlatanism." *Bulletin of the New York Academy of Medicine,* XIII (1937), 466-88.

Lawson-Tancred, Sir Thomas. *Records of a Yorkshire manor.* London: Edward Arnold, 1937. Pp. xii + 384.

Rev. in *N & Q,* CLXXII, 431-32.

Lindsey, John, *pseud.* [John St. Clair Muriel] *Charles II and Madame Carwell.* London: Andrew Melrose, 1937. Pp. 288.

Rev. in *TLS,* Sept. 11, p. 657.

The Liverpool Tractate. An eighteenth century manual on the procedure of the House of Commons. Edited with an introduction by Catherine Strateman. (Studies in history, economics, and public law edited by the faculty of political science of Columbia University, No. 430) New York: Columbia University press, 1937. Pp. xcii + 105.

Rev. in *TLS,* Jan. 1, 1938, p. 4.

Longfield, Ada K. "History of the Irish linen and cotton printing industry in the 18th century." *Journal of the Royal Society of Antiquaries of Ireland,* LXVII (1937), 26-56.

Lynch, Kathleen M. "Henrietta, Duchess of Marlborough." *PMLA*, LII (1937), 1072-93.

McCabe, Leo. *Wolfe Tone and the United Irishmen.* For or against Christ? (1791-1798) Vol. I. London: Heath Cranton, 1937. Pp. 258.

MacDonald, D. F. *Scotland's shifting population, 1770-1850.* Glasgow: Jackson, Son and Co., 1937. Pp. vii + 172.

McHugh, Roger J. *Henry Grattan.* New York: Sheed & Ward, 1937. Pp. 222.

Rev. by S. O'Sheel in *HTB*, Jan. 16, 1938, p. 10. § First published in 1935.

Mackay, Janet. *Catherine of Braganza.* London: John Long, 1937. Pp. 320. Cf. corr. by S. George West, *TLS*, Nov. 27, p. 911.

Rev. in *TLS*, Nov. 20, p. 883.

Mackenzie, Agnes Mure. *The passing of the Stewarts.* London: Alexander Maclehose, 1937. Pp. xvi + 461.

Rev. in *Juridical rev.*, XLIX, 447; in *TLS*, Oct. 9, pp. 721-22; by C. Smyth in *Criterion*, XVII (1938), 329-30; by G. E. A. Coley in *Fortnightly*, CXLVIII, 626-27; by A. M. Davies in *HTB*, Dec. 26, p. 4; by C. Wright in *TBR*, Dec. 5, p. 38.

MacKinnon, Sir Frank Douglas. *Grand larceny.* Being the trial of Jane Leigh Perrot, aunt of Jane Austen. London: Oxford University press, 1937. Pp. 131.

Rev. in *TBR*, June 27, p. 8; by E. Tinkham in *HTB*, June 27, p. 4.

McLachlan, Jean Olivia. "Anglo-Spanish diplomatic and commercial relations, 1731-59." *Abstracts of dissertations, University of Cambridge, 1936-1937*, 1937, pp. 85-86.

Malcolm-Smith, E. *British diplomacy in the eighteenth century, 1700-1789.* London: Williams and Norgate, 1937. Pp. 256.

Rev. in *TLS*, April 10, p. 277; by A. M. Wilson in *JMH*, IX, 555-56.

Manchée, W. H. "Some Huguenot smugglers. The impeachment of London silk merchants, 1698." *Proceedings of the Huguenot Society of London*, xv, iii (1936), 406-27.

The Marlay Letters, 1778-1820. Edited by R. Warwick Bond. London: Constable, 1937. Pp. xxiii + 476.

Rev. in *TLS*, June 5, p. 423; by F. S. Boas in *MLR*, XXXIII (1938), 79-80; by C. Hobhouse in *Spectator*, June 11, pp. 1106-08.

Marshall, Dorothy. "The old poor law (1662-1795)." *Economic history review*, VIII (1937), 38-47.

Menzies-Wilson, Jacobine, and Lloyd, Helen. *Amelia: the tale of a Plain Friend.* London: Oxford University press, 1937. Pp. xii + 299.

Rev. in *TBR*, Jan. 30, 1938, p. 27; in *TLS*, Nov. 27, p. 907. § Biography of the wife of John Opie, the painter, and friend of Elizabeth Fry.

Merton, Robert K. "Some economic factors in seventeenth century English science." *Scientia*, LXII (1937), 142-52.

Metzger, Charles. "An appraisal of Shelburne's western policy." *Mid-America*, XIX (1937), 169-81.

Michael, Wolfgang. *Englische Geschichte im achtzehnten Jahrhun-*

dert. Vierter Band. Das Zeitalter Walpoles. Dritter Teil. Berlin: Verlag für Staatswissenschaften und Geschichte, 1937. Pp. xvi + 608.

Rev. in *TLS,* Aug. 28, p. 615; by R. H. Murray in *Contemp. rev.,* CLII, 379-80.

Miscellanies of the Jewish Historical Society of England. Part III. Paulton (Somerset) and London: Purnell & Sons, 1937. Pp. viii + 120.

This volume contains well-documented articles and notes of interest on Anglo-Jewish history, such as "The lesser London synagogues of the eighteenth century," "The Jews and the great plague," and "Jew brokers of the City of London."

Mitchiner, Margaret. *No crown for the queen.* Louise de Stolberg, Countess of Albany and wife of the Young Pretender. London: Jonathan Cape, 1937. Pp. 317.

Rev. in *TLS,* Nov. 6, p. 820.

Montgomerie, H. S. *William Bligh of the "Bounty" in fact and in fable.* London: Williams and Norgate, 1937. Pp. xiv + 309.

Mood, Fulmer. "William Penn and English politics in 1680-81. New light on the granting of the Pennsylvania charter.". *Journal of the Friends' Historical Society,* XXXII (1935), 3-21.

Mullett, Charles F. "The English plague scare of 1720-23." *Osiris,* II (1936), 484-516.

A study of the preventive legislation and of the publications by Edmund Gibson, Blackmore, Richard Mead, Joseph Browne, Richard Boulton, John Quincy, Richard Bradley, and Defoe stimulated by the plague threat from Marseilles.

Mullett, Charles F. "The legal position of English Protestant Dissenters, 1689-1767." *Virginia law review,* XXIII (1937), 389-418.

Mullett, Charles F. "Some aspects of religion and politics in England, 1660-1767." *Southwestern social science quarterly,* XVIII (1937), 44-53.

Mundy, P. D. "Peter Mundy, traveller, 1596-?1667." *N & Q,* CLXXII (1937), 170-71.

The travels of Peter Mundy in Europe and Asia, 1608-1667. Vol. v. Travels in south-west England and western India, with a diary of events in London, 1658-1663, and in Penryn, 1664-1667. Edited by Sir Richard Carnac Temple and Lavinia Mary Austey. (Hakluyt Society, Vol. LXXVIII) London: Hakluyt Society, 1936. Pp. xxvii + 226.

Rev. by G.N.C. in *EHR,* LIII (1938), 171.

Murray, Sir Oswyn A. R. "The admiralty, iii." *Mariner's mirror,* XXIII (1937), 316-31.

A study of naval administration during the Restoration.

Namier, L. B. *Additions and corrections to Sir John Fortescue's edition of the correspondence of King George the Third.* (*Volume* I). Manchester: University press, 1937.

Not. in *TLS,* Dec. 25, p. 981.

Newton, A. Edward. "Newton on Blackstone," *Atlantic monthly*, CLIX (1937), 1-9.

The life and adventures of John Nicol, mariner. With a foreword and afterword by Alexander Laing. New York: Farrer & Rinehart, 1936. Pp. vi + 214.

Rev. in *TLS*, Dec. 11, p. 944; by O. La Farge in *SRL*, Jan. 9, p. 15. § A reissue of the edition of 1822 edited by John Howell.

Nobbs, D. "Philip Nye on church and state." *Cambridge historical journal*, v (1935), 41-59.

John Norton & Sons, merchants of London and Virginia. Being the papers from their counting house for the years 1750 to 1795. Edited by Frances Norton Mason. Richmond: Dietz press, 1937. Pp. 573.

Rev. by H. I. Brock in *TBR*, Aug. 29, p. 24.

Nulle, Stebelton H. "The Duke of Newcastle and the election of 1727." *JMH*, IX (1937), 1-22.

O'Brien, Eris. *The foundation of Australia (1786-1800).* A study in penal colonisation. London: Sheed and Ward, 1936. Pp. xiii + 432.

Rev. in *TLS*, June 26, p. 470; by N.W.P. in *Downside rev.*, LV, 400-01; by T.C. in *Studies: an Irish quar. rev.*, XXVI, 336. § Contains considerable discussion of political, social, and economic conditions in Great Britain and Ireland.

Oldham, J. B. *Headmasters of Shrewsbury School, 1552-1908.* Shrewsbury: Wilding and Son, 1937. Pp. 85.

Rev. in *TLS*, April 24, p. 310.

The Oxinden and Peyton letters, 1642-1670. Being the correspondence of Henry Oxinden of Barham, Sir Thomas Peyton of Knowlton and their circle. Edited with notes and introduction by Dorothy Gardiner. London: Sheldon press; New York: Macmillan, 1937. Pp. xliv + 371.

Rev. in *N & Q* CLXXII, 179-80; in *TLS*, Feb. 13, p. 103; by B. Willey in *Cambridge rev.*, LVIII, 295; by E.S. deB. in *History*, XXII, 276.

Palm, Franklin Charles. *The middle classes then and now.* New York: Macmillan, 1936. Pp. xiv + 421.

Rev. by S. Neumann in *Amer. soc. rev.*, II, 550-51; by E. P. Lilly in *Mid-America*, XIX, 231-32; by S. B. Clough in *Polit. science quar.*, LII, 610-11.

Pares, R. "The manning of the navy in the West Indies, 1702-63." *Transactions of the Royal Historical Society*, XX (1937), 31-60.

Pares, Richard. *War and trade in the West Indies, 1739-1763.* Oxford: Clarendon press, 1936. Pp. xii + 631.

Rev. by J. F. Rees in *Econ. hist. rev.*, VIII, 91-93; by A. P. Newton in *EHR*, LIII (1938), 143-44; by M.A.L. in *Mariner's mirror*, XXIII, 113-14; by W.L.B. in *Oxford mag.*, LV, 577-78.

Parkinson, C. Northcote. *Trade in the eastern seas, 1793-1813.* Cambridge: University press, 1937. Pp. xiii + 435.

Rev. in *TLS*, Oct. 9, p. 726; by Admiral Sir Herbert Richmond in *Fortnightly*, CXLVIII, 749-50.

Petrie, Sir Charles. *Bolingbroke.* London: Collins, 1937. Pp. 368.

Rev. in *TLS*, Feb. 27, p. 143; by D. Walker-Smith in *Eng. rev.*, LXIV, 489-92;

by Sir John Marriott in *Fortnightly,* CXLVII, 623-24; by A. L. Rowse in *Spectator,* March 5, p. 418.

Petrie, Sir Charles. *The Stuarts.* London: Eyre and Spottiswoode, 1937. Pp. xii + 359.

Rev. in *TLS,* Oct. 9, pp. 721-22; by A. M. Davies in *HTB,* Dec. 26, p. 4; by D. A. Roberts in *TBR,* Jan. 16, 1938, p. 4. § An effort to "show how the subjects of the Stuarts were affected by, and how they regarded, the chief events of their day."

Philips, C. H. "The East India Company 'interest' and the English government, 1783-4." *Transactions of the Royal Historical Society,* XX (1937), 83-101.

Plumb, J. H. "The elections to the Convention Parliament of 1689." *Cambridge historical journal,* V (1937), 235-54.

Plumb, John Harold. "Elections to the House of Commons in the reign of William III." *Abstracts of dissertations, University of Cambridge, 1935-1936,* 1936, pp. 70-71.

Pritchard, Earl H. *The crucial years of early Anglo-Chinese relations, 1750-1800. Research studies of the State College of Washington,* Vol. IV (1936), nos. 3-4, pp. 91-442.

Ramsey, Robert W. *Richard Cromwell, Protector of England.* London, New York, Toronto: Longmans, Green, 1935. Pp. xv + 239.

Rev. by M.C. in *Oxford mag.,* LV, 325-26.

Ransom, John E. "John Howard on communicable diseases." *Bulletin of the Institute of the History of Medicine,* V (1937), 131-47.

Riches, Naomi. *The agricultural revolution in Norfolk.* Chapel Hill: University of North Carolina press, 1937. Pp. ix + 194.

A study of the leadership of Norfolk in the agricultural revolution of eighteenth century England, based on contemporary accounts, including those of Defoe, Cobbett, Woodforde, and Arthur Young.

Robson-Scott, W. D. "Baron Pöllnitz and the English." *German life and letters,* I (1937), 284-92.

Ronalds, Francis S. *The attempted Whig revolution of 1678-1681.* (Illinois studies in the social sciences, Vol. XXI, nos. 1-2) Urbana: University of Illinois, 1937. Pp. 202.

Rosenberg, Charles. "Samuel Bowden of Frome, Somersetshire." *N & Q,* CLXXIII (1937), 344-45.

New facts on a physician-poet.

Rowntree, C. Brightwen. "Benjamin Lay (1681-1759) of Colchester, London, Barbadoes, Philadelphia." *Journal of the Friends' Historical Society,* XXXIII (1936), 3-19.

Russell, Phillips. *The glittering century.* New York: Scribner's, 1936. Pp. 326.

Rev. in *TLS,* Jan. 2, p. 3; by E.W.N. in *Dalhousie rev.,* XVI, 537; by C. G. Stillman in *HTB,* Dec. 20, 1936, p. 12; by L. Kronenberger in *TBR,* Dec. 13, 1936, p. 26.

The private papers of John, Earl of Sandwich, first Lord of the Admiralty, 1771-1792. Vol. III, May 1779 — December 1780. Edited by G. R. Barnes and J. H. Owen. (Publications of the Navy Records Society, Vol. LXXV) London: Navy Records Society, 1936. Pp. 333.

Rev. by C. T. Atkinson in *EHR*, LII, 133-35.

Schofield, Seymour. *Jeffreys of "the bloody assizes."* London: Thornton Butterworth, 1937. Pp. 320.

Rev. in *TLS*, Oct. 9, p. 729, cf. reply by author, *ibid.*, Oct. 30, p. 803; in *Juridical rev.*, XLIX, 446; by C. Hobhouse in *Spectator*, Oct. 22, p. 694.

Scott, W.F. "The naval chaplain in Stuart times." *University of Oxford abstracts of dissertations, 1935,* VIII (1936), 57-64.

Senior, Dorothy. *The king's ladies.* Charles II and his ladies of pleasure. London: Hale, 1936. Pp. xix + 287.

Seton-Watson, R. W. *Britain in Europe, 1789-1914.* A survey of foreign policy. New York: Macmillan; Cambridge: University press, 1937. Pp. ix + 716.

Rev. in *TLS*, July 17, p. 519; by J. H. Rose in *Cambridge rev.*, LIX, 133-34; by G.P.G. in *Contemp. rev.*, CLII, 497-501; by G. R. S. Taylor in *Fortnightly*, CXLVIII, 371-72; by W. L. Langer in *HTB*, Nov. 28, p. 18; by H. A. Stephenson in *LM*, XXXVI, 390-91; by R. J. Sontag in *SRL*, Sept. 18, p. 18; by V. Valentin in *Slavonic rev.*, XVI (1938), 477-81.

Siebert, Fred S. "Regulation of the press in the seventeenth century. Excerpts from the records of the Court of the Stationers' Company." *Journalism quarterly,* XIII (1936), 381-93.

Simpson, Alan. "Notes of a noble lord, 22 January to 12 February 1688/9." *EHR,* LII (1937), 87-98.

On a MS. by second Earl of Clarendon in Pepys Library, Cambridge.

Smith, D. Bonner. "More light on Bligh and the *Bounty.*" *Mariner's mirror,* XXIII (1937), 210-28.

Southam, Herbert. "A Herefordshire man's diary, 1727/8." *N & Q,* CLXXIII (1937), 417-20.

Straus, Ralph. *Lloyd's: a historical sketch.* London: Hutchinson, 1937. Pp. 292.

Rev. in *TLS*, Nov. 13, p. 860; by R. Doughton in *HTB*, Jan. 30, 1938, p. 2; by R. Van Gelder in *TBR*, Jan. 30, 1938, p. 9.

Stuart, Marie W. "Countess charming." *Cornhill magazine,* CLVI (1937), 64-73.

On Susannah, Countess of Eglintown, the Jacobite beauty whom Johnson and Boswell visited.

Symonds, R. W. "The craft of furniture making in the XVIth and XVIIth centuries with examples from the collection of Mr. Geoffrey Hart." *Connoisseur,* XCIX (1937), 130-36.

Symonds, R. W. "English furniture making in the eighteenth century: examples in Mr. Armand Gobiet's collection." *Connoisseur,* XCVIII (1936), 253-61.

Tayler, Alistair and Henrietta. *A Jacobite exile.* London: Alexander Maclehose, 1937. Pp. vii + 219.

Not. in *TLS*, Jan. 1, 1938, p. 13. § On Andrew Hay of Rannes.

Tayler, Alistair and Henrietta. *1715: the story of the rising.* London: Nelson, 1936. Pp. xiv + 345.

Rev. in *TLS*, June 20, 1936, p. 511; by J.D.M. in *History*, XXII, 184-85.

Taylor, Rear-Admiral A. H. "William Bligh at Camperdown." *Mariner's mirror*, XXIII (1937), 417-33.

Thomas, John. "The pottery industry and the Industrial Revolution." *Economic history*, III (1937), 399-414.

Thomson, Gladys Scott. *Life in a noble household, 1641-1700*. London: Jonathan Cape, 1937. Pp. 407.

Rev. in *TLS*, Jan. 30, p. 68; by R. Edwards in *Burlington mag.*, LXX, 200-01; by B. Willey in *Cambridge rev.*, LVIII, 295; by R. H. Tawney in *Econ. hist. rev.*, VIII, 87-91; by H. R. Williamson in *Fortnightly*, CXLVII, 379-80; by S. C. Chew in *HTB*, Aug. 8, p. 4; by C. Robbins in *History*, XXII, 171-73; by M. Crosbie in *LM*, XXXV, 435; by M.C. in *Oxford mag.*, LVI (1938), 425-27; by W. E. C. Harrison in *Queen's quar.*, XLIV, 268-69; by G. Eland in *RES*, XIV (1938), 99-101; by C. D. Abbott in *SRL*, Aug. 7, p. 17; by G. Greene in *Spectator*, Jan. 29, pp. 178-80; by K. Woods in *TBR*, Aug. 15, p. 8. § A readable account of seventeenth century life from the financial point of view, based on the household papers of the fifth Earl and first Duke of Bedford. The chapter on the library is especially interesting.

The autobiography of Theobald Wolfe Tone. Abridged and edited by Sean O'Faolain. London: Nelson, 1937. Pp. xxxi + 307.

Rev. in *TLS*, May 22, pp. 398-99.

Trappes-Lomax, Michael. *Bishop Challoner*. A biographical study derived from Dr. Edwin Burton's *The Life and Times of Bishop Challoner*. London: Longmans, Green, 1936. Pp. ix + 285.

Rev. in *TLS*, June 6, 1936, p. 470; by G.R.H. in *Downside rev.*, CIV, (1936), 584-86; by M. A. Thomson in *History*, XXII, 79.

Turberville, A. S. "The episcopal bench in the House of Lords in the Revolutionary period, 1783-1837." *Church quarterly review*, CXXIII (1937), 261-85.

Turberville, A. S. "The younger Pitt and the House of Lords." *History*, XXI (1937), 350-58.

The visitation of Sussex Anno Domini 1662 made by Sir Edward Bysshe, Knt. Edited and annotated by A. W. Hughes Clarke. (Publications of the Harleian Society, Vol. LXXXIX) London: 1937. Pp. vi + 141.

Vulliamy, C. E. *Royal George*. A study of George III, his experiment in monarchy, his decline and retirement; with a view of society, politics and historic events during his reign. New York, London: D. Appleton-Century, 1937. Pp. 318.

Rev. in *TLS*, Jan. 9, p. 21; by N.W.P. in *Downside rev.*, LV, 264-66; by L. P. Curtis in *HTB*, May 23, p. 7; by L.H.B. in *SRL*, July 24, p. 20; by K. Feiling in *Spectator*, Jan. 8, p. 53; by J. S. Southron in *TBR*, May 16, p. 9.

Waddell, Helen. "Eccentric Englishwomen: viii. Mrs. Charke." *Spectator*, June 4, 1937, pp. 1047-48.

On the adventuresome actress-daughter of Colley Cibber.

Wakeham, Eric. *The bravest soldier: Sir Rollo Gillespie, 1766-1814*. A historical military sketch. Edinburgh and London: William Blackwood & Sons, 1937. Pp. xvi + 292.

Rev. in *TLS*, Sept. 25, p. 685.

Walcott, R. R. "Division-lists in the House of Commons, 1689-1715." *Bulletin of the Institute of Historical Research,* XIV (1936), 25-36.

Walcutt, Charles Child. "The ghost of Jemmy Twitcher," *N & Q,* CLXXIII (1937), 56-62.
Examination of the history of Sandwich's nickname.

Walker, J. "Dissent and republicanism after the Restoration." *Baptist quarterly,* VIII (1937), 263-80.

Walker, Kenneth. "William Henry, Earl of Rochford. An Essex diplomat." *Essex review,* XLVI (1937), 65-72.

Wall, Cecil. *The history of the Surgeons' Company, 1745-1800.* London: Hutchinson, 1937. Pp. 256.
Rev. in *TLS,* Sept. 25, p. 692.

Walters, H. B. "Two eighteenth century travellers in Worcestershire." *Transactions of the Worcestershire Archæological Society for 1935,* XII (1936), 30-41; *for 1936,* XIII (1937), 65-74.
Extracts from British Museum MSS. of William Cole's account of a visit to Worcestershire in 1746 and Arthur Whaley's diary of a tour in 1733.

Warner, Oliver. *Hero of the Restoration.* A life of General George Monck, 1st Duke of Albemarle, K.G. London: Jarrolds, 1936. Pp. 288.
Not. by B.H.G.W. in *Cambridge rev.,* LVIII, 320; rev. by C.R. in *Devon and Cornwall notes and queries,* XIV, 281-83.

Warrender letters. Correspondence of Sir George Warrender Bt., Lord Provost of Edinburgh, and Member of Parliament for the city, with relative papers 1715. Transcribed by Marguerite Wood. Edited with an introduction and notes by William Kirk Dickson. (Publications of the Scottish History Society, Vol. XXV) Edinburgh: University press, 1935. Pp. lxviii + 119.

Wead, Eunice. "A packet of news from eighteenth century England." *Colophon,* I (1936), 441-42.

Wedlake, H. J. "Eighteenth-century love letters." *N & Q,* CLXXII (1937), 182-86.

Weir, J. L. "Thoughts on the Jacobite movement." *N & Q,* CLXXIII (1937), 385-87.

Whitton, F. E. "The great siege of Gibraltar, 1779-1783." *Blackwood's magazine,* CCXLII (1937), 35-55.

Wilding, Peter. *Adventurers in the eighteenth century.* New York: Putnam's, 1937. Pp. 350.
Rev. in *TBR,* Dec. 26, p. 8; in *TLS,* Feb. 20, p. 124; by C. J. Finger in *HTB,* Oct. 31, p. 18; by C. E. Vulliamy in *Spectator,* Feb. 26, pp. 370-72. § Essays on John Law, Casanova, Cagliostro, James Keith, Alexandre de Bonneval, and Theodore von Neuhoff.

Williams, Trevor. "The cabinet in the eighteenth century." *History,* XXII (1937), 240-52.

Wilson, Arthur McCandless. *French foreign policy during the administration of Cardinal Fleury, 1726-1743.* A study in diplomacy and commercial development. (Harvard historical studies, Vol. XL) Cambridge: Harvard University press, 1936. Pp. ix + 433.

The Wynne diaries. Vol. II, 1794-1798. Edited by Anne Fremantle. London: Oxford University press, 1937. Pp. xx + 274.

Rev. in *TBR,* March 7, p. 12; in *TLS,* Jan. 30, p. 70; by C. B. in *English,* I, 569; by A.F.F. in *History,* XXII, 282; by E. N. Curtis in *JMH,* IX, 396; in *Queen's quar.,* XLIV, 280.

Yeaman, William. "Edinburgh before the 'Fifteen." *Juridical review,* XLIX (1937), 152-73.

Based on the letters of Charles Cockburn, Advocate, Keeper of the Signet, 1714-15.

Young, Sir George. *Poor Fred: the people's prince.* London: Oxford University press, 1937. Pp. xxxi + 232.

Rev. in *Contemp. rev.,* CLI, 762; in *TBR,* April 25, p. 3; in *TLS,* April 10, p. 264; by D. M. Clark in *AHR,* XLIII (1938), 378-79; by R. Levin in *Spectator,* May 7, p. 870. § A biography of the father of George III.

III. CURRENTS OF IDEAS AND LITERARY FORMS

Allen, B. Sprague. *Tides in English taste (1619-1800).* A background for the study of literature. 2 vols. Cambridge: Harvard University press, 1937. Pp. xvii + 269, viii + 282.

Rev. in *TLS,* July 17, pp. 517-18; by J. Evans in *Burlington mag.* LXXI, 244; by S. C. Chew in *HTB,* July 11, p. 6; by A. Nicoll in *JEGP,* XXXVI, 574-75; by M. R. Rogers in *SRL,* July 10, p. 17; by A. Kazin in *TBR* Nov. 28, p. 18.

"This book," says the author, "has grown out of my gradual realization of the extent to which the history of art constitutes a most vivid, enlightening commentary on the history of literature. . . . As the forces, intellectual and emotional, that mold art also influence literature, they have in each period of culture imparted a common, characteristic quality to such apparently divergent manifestations of the sense of beauty as poetry, textile design, ceramic decoration, and garden and house planning" (I, vii). In the light of this introductory statement we might naturally expect to find in Allen's two volumes another essay in that species of analogical history of which we have recently had a number of striking examples in the very field to which his book is devoted (cf. *PQ,* XIV, 152-54; XVI, 160-61). It is true that he has not altogether escaped the temptation to exploit the ambiguity of words like "classic," "formal," "proportion," "ornamentation," "order," "discipline," "symmetry," "imaginative exuberance," "surprise," in order to bring the evolution of the arts with which he is specially concerned into dialectical relation with the contemporary changes in literary styles (see, e.g., I, 17-18, 19, 21, 78-79; II, 107-8, 128-29, 180, 188-90, 231). But for the most part the task of formulating the analogies is left to the reader, and Allen's main attention is concentrated on a narrative of the transformations that took place in England, between the early seventeenth century and the end of the eighteenth, in popular conceptions of what is the desirable mode in architecture, gardening, and the minor arts related to them.

The story he tells exhibits three chief phases, which succeed one another in time though not without a good deal of overlapping: (1) the tradition in architecture which stemmed from Palladio and which owed its prestige in England principally to Inigo Jones, Wren, and their followers, and, parallel with this, the model of garden design afforded by Le Nôtre; (2) the vogue of Oriental styles, Gothic, rococo, and the "natural" garden; and (3) the new popularity of the antique following the excavations at Herculaneum and Pompeii. On all these topics Allen writes with the modesty of one who professes only an amateur's familiarity with the technical aspects of his subject; but, thanks to his first-hand examination of many surviving monuments of the arts he has selected for study and to his wide reading in the literary sources, he has been able to supplement the works of the specialists (duly listed in his notes) with many fresh details. Particularly instructive are the pages in which he exhibits the antecedents in the middle and later seventeenth century of the taste for Oriental designs and for Gothic architecture which flourished so widely toward 1750.

As a compendium of information his book thus has many virtues; its most notable weakness appears when he touches, as he frequently does, on the theoretical issues involved in the interpretation of his facts. His guiding formula is one with which we have been long familiar in writings on the eighteenth century: variously expressed, it can be resolved into an opposition of convention or tradition to experiment and individuality, with a negative value assigned to the terms on the first side of the antithesis (see, e.g., II, 128, 189). As applied to the productions of the schools dominant in the early part of the period treated in his study, this somewhat one-sided aesthetic leads to critical judgments like the following, the unsympathetic tone of which is more suggestive of the scholarship of the last generation than of that of our day: "The experimental spirit rarely stirred through neo-classical art. Standardized diction, deference for decorum and tradition, solemn fussiness about inconsequential matters of form, inexplicable patience with platitude repressed those effervescences of personality that are creative of surprise" (II, 128). Given a bias such as this, it is not strange that Allen should be occasionally embarrassed in dealing with the theoretical statements of critics in the seventeenth and eighteenth centuries whose doctrines of art turn on a more balanced manipulation of contrary terms. The result at times is the reduction of one of the terms to a merely negative status; thus in the summary of Addison's discussion of gardens (II, 123), in place of the paradox that "If the Products of Nature rise in Value, according as they more or less resemble those of Art, ... artificial Works receive a greater Advantage from their Resemblance of such as are natural" (*Spectator*, No. 414), we are told simply that when Addison played "on the obvious antithesis between nature and art, the latter always emerged from the comparison with her credit damaged." In another connection (cf. I, 85), although both of the contrary terms which constitute the critics' basic principles are recognized, at least implicitly, the dialectical links between them are neglected in favor of a relegation of one of the terms and its equivalents to the influence of current prejudices or education and of the other to the liberalizing effect of "natural taste." Or again (see II, 128-32), the problem of explaining how certain critics who exalt variety or surprise as artistic virtues can at the same time produce or recommend works which to modern sensibility seem highly stylized and regular is solved, not by making explicit the full context of the discussions, but merely by positing a curious and disappointing discrepancy between practice and principle (but cf. II, 143, where Allen cautions his readers against this very error). R. S. C.

Anderson, Paul Bunyan. "La Bruyère and Mrs. Crackenthorpe's *Female Tatler*." *PMLA*, LII (1937), 100-03.

Andrade, E. N. da C. "The real character of Bishop Wilkins." *Annals of science*, I (1936), 4-12.

On John Wilkins' *Essay towards a real character and a philosophical language* (1668).

Avery, Emmett L. "Ben Jonson in the provinces." *N & Q*, CLXXIII (1937), 238.

Avery, Emmett L. "Foreign performers in the London theaters in the early eighteenth century." *PQ*, XVI (1937), 105-23.

Avery, Emmett L. "The summer theatrical seasons at Richmond and Twickenham, 1746-1753." *N & Q*, CLXXIII (1937), 290-94, 312-15, 328-32.

Avery, Emmett L. "Vaudeville on the London stage, 1700-1737."

Research studies of the State College of Washington, Vol. v (1937), no. 2, pp. 65-77.

Babb, Lawrence. "The cave of spleen." *RES,* XII (1936), 165-76.

Babcock, R. W. "An early eighteenth century note on Falstaff." *PQ,* XVI (1937), 84-85.

Baldensperger, Fernand. "'Romantique,' ses analogues et ses équivalents: tableau synoptique de 1650 à 1810." *Harvard studies and notes in philology and literature,* XIX (1937), 13-105.

A very valuable table of uses of "romantic" and related terms in English, French, German and other languages, with from one to a dozen references for each year.

Barnes, Harry Elmer. *A history of historical writing.* Norman: University of Oklahoma press, 1937. Pp. x + 434.

Rev. by B. E. Josephson in *Miss. valley hist. rev.,* XXIV, 428-30; by L. Huberman in *New republic,* Jan. 12, 1938, pp. 288-89; by D. C. McKay in *SRL,* Dec. 25, p. 18. § See Chap. vii, "The rise of social and cultural history: the era of discovery and the growth of rationalism."

Barnes, Sherman B. "The editing of early learned journals." *Osiris,* I (1936), 155-72.

Batten, M. I. "The architecture of Dr. Robert Hooke, F.R.S." *The twenty-fifth volume of the Walpole Society, 1936-1937.* Oxford: Walpole Society, 1937. Pp. 83-113, with plates xxxv-xl.

Beekman, Fenwick. "The rise of British surgery in the eighteenth century." *Annals of medical history,* IX (1937), 549-66.

Bell, E. T. *Men of mathematics.* New York: Simon and Schuster, 1937. Pp. xxi + 592.

Rev. in *TLS,* July 10, p. 506; by J. O. Wisdom in *Life and letters to-day,* XVII, 169-70; by E. Nagel in *New republic,* June 2, pp. 106-08; by J. Riordan in *SRL,* March 13, p. 10; by A. J. Ayer in *Spectator,* Aug. 6, p. 249; by W. M. Malisoff in *TBR,* Apr. 11, p. 3. § Includes essays on Descartes, Fermat, Pascal, Newton, Leibniz, the Bernoullis, Euler, Lagrange, Laplace, Monge, Fourier.

Bett, Henry. *The spirit of Methodism.* London: Epworth press, 1937. Pp. 254.

Rev. by F. B. Harvey in *London quar. and Holborn rev.,* Oct., p. 539.

Betz, Siegmund A. E. "Francis Osborn's 'Advice to a Son.'" *Seventeenth century studies, second series.* By members of the Graduate School, University of Cincinnati. Edited by Robert Shafer. Princeton: Princeton University press for the University of Cincinnati, 1937. Pp. 3-67.

Black, Matthew W. "Shakespeare's seventeenth century editors." *Proceedings of the American Phiolosophical Society,* LXXVI (1936), 707-17.

Bogenschneider, Hans-Joachim. *Die englische Lautentwicklung im 17. Jahrhundert nach den Briefen der Familie Verney.* Berlin diss. 1936. Pp. xiii + 108.

Bond, Donald F. "The neo-classical psychology of the imagination." *ELH*, IV (1937), 245-64.

A well-executed article showing that because of the rise of the empiricist psychology "the prestige of the imagination was enhanced" and "a more intensive, and unbiassed, study was made of its operations."

Bonner, Carey. "Some Baptist hymnists." *Baptist quarterly*, VIII (1937), 256-62, 302-11.

Boys, Richard C. "An eighteenth-century essay on spelling." *MLN*, LII (1937), 209-10.

On John LaFond's preface to his *New system of music* (1725).

Brede, Alexander. "The idea of an English language academy." *English journal*, college edition, XXVI (1937), 560-68.

Summary of the work by Hermann Flasdieck.

Brown, Wallace Cable. "English travel books and minor poetry about the Near East, 1775-1825." *PQ*, XVI (1937), 249-71.

Bush, Douglas. *Mythology and the romantic tradition in English poetry.* (Harvard studies in English, XVIII) Cambridge: Harvard University press, 1937. Pp. xvi + 647.

Rev. in *TLS*, June 19, p. 461; by J. Stinchcomb in *Classical weekly*, XXX, 276-77; by L. Wolff in *EA*, II (1938), 53-54; by W. C. DeVane in *MP*, XXXV, 211-13; by L. Bacon in *SRL*, July 10, p. 7; by S. A. Coblentz in *TBR*, Aug. 1, p. 2; by G. Norwood in *Univ. of Toronto quar.*, VI, 593-97. § The first chapter of this pleasantly instructive book is on the eighteenth century. See also pp. 539-47 for list of mythological poems 1680-1800.

Carlson, C. Lennart. "Richard Lewis and the reception of his work in England." *American literature*, IX (1937), 301-16.

Carruthers, S. W. "Bartholomew Day, 1662, in the contemporary news-sheets." *Journal of the Presbyterian Historical Society of England*, VI (1937), 116-22.

Caw, Sir James L. "Allan Ramsay, portrait painter, 1713-1784." *The twenty-fifth volume of the Walpole Society, 1936-1937.* Oxford: Walpole Society, 1937. Pp. 33-81, with plates xviii-xxxiv.

Chalmers, Gordon Keith. "The lodestone and the understanding of matter in seventeenth century England." *Philosophy of science*, IV (1937), 75-95.

With emphasis on William Gilbert and Sir Thomas Browne.

Clark, G. N. *Science and social welfare in the age of Newton.* Oxford: Clarendon press, 1937. Pp. 159.

Clark, Kenneth. "On the painting of English landscape." *Proceedings of the British Academy, 1935*, XXI, 185-200.

Contains comment on Richard Wilson, Gainsborough, Alexander Cozens, J. R. Cozens, Girtin, Turner, Crome, Constable. Clark gives "the search for poetry and the search for style" as the reasons for the fact that English "painters have seldom been content to draw their inspiration directly from the English landscape."

Clark, William S. "Corpses, concealments, and curtains on the Restoration stage." *RES*, XIII (1937), 438-48.

Clarke, Archibald L. "Three writers connected with Woodford, Essex." *Essex review*, XLVI (1937), 47-51.

On William Master, theologian, James Greenwood, grammarian, and Thomas Maurice, keeper of antiquities.

Clarke, M. L. *Richard Porson*. A biographical essay. Cambridge: University press, 1937. Pp. viii + 133.

Rev. in *TLS*, Nov. 20, p. 887; by S. C. Chew in *HTB*, Dec. 26, p. 10.

Coffin, Charles Monroe. *John Donne and the new philosophy*. (Columbia University studies in English and comparative literature, no. 126) New York: Columbia University press, 1937. Pp. viii + 311.

Rev. in *TLS*, Aug. 21, p. 604; by G. McColley in *Annals of science*, II, 475-76; by P. Legouis in *EA*, II (1938), 46-48; by J. T. McNeill in *Jour. of religion*, XVIII, 306-09; by M. Van Doren in *Nation*, Apr. 17, pp. 442-43; by P. Hutchison in *TBR*, Sept. 26, p. 9. § An excellent study of the intellectual background of the classical period.

Cook, Thomas I. *History of political philosophy from Plato to Burke*. New York: Prentice-Hall, 1936. Pp. xviii + 725.

Rev. by H.W.S. in *Jour. of phil.*, XXXIV, 110; by O. E. Norton in *Southwestern social science quar.*, XVIII, 111-12.

Crundell, H. W. " 'The Taming of the Shrew' on the xvii. century stage." *N & Q*, CLXXIII (1937), 207.

Dent, Edward. *Händel in England*. (Hallische Universitätsreden, 68) Halle: Niemeyer, 1936. Pp. 17.

Rev. by E.B. in *Music and letters*, XVIII, 90-91.

Draper, John W. "The metrical tale in XVIII-century England." *PMLA*, LII (1937), 390-97.

Duggan, G. C. *The stage Irishman*. A history of the Irish play and stage characters from the earliest time. Dublin & Cork: Talbot press, 1937. Pp. 331.

Rev. in *Theatre arts monthly*, XXI, 824; by S. O'Faoláin in *Spectator*, June 4, p. 1062. § Largely devoted to the Restoration and the eighteenth century.

Easson, D. E. "Robert Monteith, an Edinburgh graduate." *University of Edinburgh journal*, VIII (1936), 24-29.

An essay on the author of *A theater of mortality*, with two unpublished poems.

Egilsrud, Johan S. *Le 'Dialogue des Morts' dans les littératures française, allemande et anglaise (1644-1789)*. Paris: Éditions Véga, 1934. Pp. 223.

European civilization: its origin and development. By various contributors. Under the direction of Edward Eyre. Vol. VI. Political and cultural history of Europe since the Reformation. London: Oxford University press, 1937. Pp. 1624.

Rev. by C. W. Cole in *AHR*, XLIII (1938), 368-70.

Fâche, E. Charles. "Huguenots and the stage." *Proceedings of the Huguenot Society of London*, XV, iv (1937), 597-611.

Fehr, Bernard. "The antagonism of forms in the eighteenth century." *English studies*, XIX (1937), 1-13, 49-57. Cf. *PQ*, XVI, 160-61.

Fell, H. Granvill. "Two portraits by Gainsborough with some unpublished letters." *Connoisseur,* XCVIII (1936), 209-11.

Fifoot, C. H. S. "Blackstone — outside the Commentaries." *Fortnightly,* CXLVII (1937), 716-23.

Gaertner, Adelheid. *Die englische Epithalamienliteratur im siebzehnten Jahrhundert und ihre Vorbilder.* Erlangen diss. 1936. Pp. 100.

Gagey, Edmond McAdoo. *Ballad opera.* (Columbia University studies in English and comparative literature, no. 130) New York: Columbia University press, 1937. Pp. ix + 259.

Rev. in *TLS,* Nov. 27, p. 907; by P. Bowdoin in *HTB,* Oct. 31, p. 12.

Gardiner, H. M.; Metcalf, Ruth Clark; and Beebe-Center, John G. *Feeling and emotion.* A history of theories. (American psychology series) New York: American Book Company, 1937. Pp. xiii + 445.

See chapters vi-ix for the psychological theories in England, France, and Germany in the seventeenth and eighteenth centuries.

Gaselee, Stephen. "Job's daughters: an XVIII cent. epigram." *N & Q,* CLXXIII (1937), 170-71.

Gibson, Strickland. "Francis Wise, B.D., Oxford anitquary, librarian, and archivist." *Oxoniensia,* I (1936), 173-95.

Gill, Frederick C. *The Romantic movement and Methodism.* A study of English Romanticism and the Evangelical revival. London: Epworth press, 1937. Pp. 189.

Deals with the eighteenth century more than the nineteenth.

Gough, J. W. *The social contract.* A critical study of its development. Oxford: Clarendon press, 1936. Pp. vi + 234.

Rev. in *TLS,* Feb. 6, p. 83; by O. Jászi in *Amer. polit. science rev.,* XXXI, 324-26; by P. L. Léon in *Archives de philosophie du droit et de sociologie juridique,* VII, 235-36; by R. H. Murray in *Contemp. rev.,* CLI, 508-09; by D. Nobbs in *EHR,* LII, 704-06; by C. Brinkmann in *Historische Zeitschrift,* CLVI, 386-87; by S.P.L. in *Jour. of phil.,* XXXIV, 416-17; by A. H. Campbell in *Law quar. rev.,* LIII, 416-18. § Chapters on "Hobbes, Spinoza, and Pufendorf" and "Locke and the English revolution."

Gray, Basil. *The English print.* London: Adam & Charles Black, 1937. Pp. xv + 225.

Rev. in *TLS,* Jan. 1, 1938, p. 8. § Chapters on the eighteenth century, "The folk print and Bewick," and Blake.

Grose, Clyde L. "The religion of Restoration England." *Church history,* VI (1937), 223-32.

Gunther, R. T. *Early science in Cambridge.* Oxford: Printed for the author at the University press, 1937. Pp. xii + 513.

Rev. in *TLS,* Feb. 6, p. 95; by H. H. Thomas in *Cambridge rev.,* LVIII, 434-36.

Gunther, R. T. *Early science in Oxford.* Vol. XI. Oxford colleges and their men of science. Oxford: Printed for the author, 1937. Pp. xvi + 429.

Rev. in *TLS,* Dec. 25, p. 973.

Harbage, Alfred. *Cavalier drama.* An historical and critical supplement to the study of the Elizabethan and Restoration stage.

New York: Modern Language Association of America; London: Oxford University press, 1936. Pp. ix + 302.

Rev. in *HTB*, May 23, p. 22; in *N & Q*, CLXXIII, 413-14; in *TLS*, Jan. 8, 1938, p. 25; by A. Nicoll in *JEGP*, XXXVI, 586-88; by R. Kirk in *PQ*, XVII (1938), 92-94.

Harlow, Henry. "William Jackson, musician, artist and author." *Devon and Cornwall notes and queries*, XIX (1937), 206-10.

Hearnshaw, F. J. C. *Some great political idealists of the Christian era.* London: Harrap, 1937. Pp. 274.

Contains chapters on "Bolingbroke and progressive conservatism," "Rousseau and the secular plan of salvation," and "Burke and sublimated common sense," all reprinted.

Heilman, Robert Bechtold. *America in English fiction, 1760-1800.* The influences of the American Revolution. (Louisiana State University studies, no. 33) Baton Rouge: Louisiana State University press, 1937. Pp. ix + 480.

Rev. in *QR*, CCLXX (1938), 176; by C. Arnavon in *EA*, II (1938), 82; by J. Jones in *SAQ*, XXXVII (1938), 89-90.

Heilman, Robert Bechtold. "The English novel, 1760-1800, and the American Revolution." *Harvard University summaries of theses, 1935,* 1937, pp. 271-74.

Heinrich, Theodore Allen. "Payne Knight, Price, and the picturesque." *Abstracts of dissertations, University of Cambridge, 1936-1937,* 1937, pp. 76-77.

Heltzel, Virgil B. (ed.) "Richard Earl of Carbery's *Advice to His Son.*" *Huntington Library bulletin,* no. 11, April, 1937, pp. 59-105.

A courtesy book written in 1651, well edited from a MS. in the Huntington Library.

Hilckman, Anton. "Der Psychologismus als Wurzel des englischen Empirismus." *Philosophisches Jahrbuch des Görres-Gesellschaft,* L (1937), 478-90.

Hindle, Wilfred. *The Morning Post, 1772-1937.* Portrait of a newspaper. London: Routledge, 1937. Pp. xi + 260.

Rev. in *TLS*, Dec. 4, p. 919.

Honey, W. B. "Royal portraits in pottery and porcelain." *Burlington magazine,* LXX (1937), 218-29.

Jansen, B. "Die scholastische Philosophie des 17. Jahrhunderts." *Philosophisches Jahrbuch des Görres-Gesellschaft,* L (1937), 401-44.

Johnson, Francis R. *Astronomical thought in Renaissance England.* A study of the English scientific writings from 1500 to 1645. Baltimore: Johns Hopkins press, 1937. Pp. xv + 357.

Useful as background for students of later history of science. Contains list of books printed in England dealing with astronomy to 1640.

Jolliffe, Harold R. "Bentley versus Horace." *PQ,* XVI (1937), 278-86.

Jones, Richard Foster. *Ancients and moderns.* A study of the background of the *Battle of the Books* (Washington University studies, new series. Language and literature, no. 6) St. Louis: 1936. Pp. xi + 358. Cf. *PQ*, XVI, 163.

Rev. by H. Brown in *Annals of science*, II, 130-33; by C. S. Northup in *JEGP*, XXXVI, 278-81; by R. S. Crane in *JMH*, IX, 416-17; by R. W. Frantz in *MLN*, LII, 447-49; by M. E. Prior in *MP*, XXXIV, 322-26.

Jones, W. P. "The vogue of natural history in England, 1750-1770." *Annals of science*, II (1937), 345-52.

A journal from Parnassus. Now printed from a manuscript circa 1688. With an introduction by Hugh Macdonald. London: P. J. Dobell, 1937. Pp. xiv + 67.

Rev. in *TLS*, Sept. 4, p. 642; by V. de Sola Pinto in *English*, I, 567-69. § A prose attack, mainly on Dryden, in the "Sessions of the poets" mode.

Knights, L. C. "Restoration comedy: the reality & the myth." *Scrutiny*, VI (1937), 122-43.

Kruuse, Jens. *Det følsomme drama.* Copenhagen: Leven & Munksgaard, 1934. Pp. 383.

Lawler, D. "The influence of Descartes on modern science." *Thought*, XII (1937), 637-52.

Lightwood, James T. *Samuel Wesley, musician.* The story of his life. London: Epworth press, 1937. Pp. 238.

Rev. in *TLS*, Feb. 27, p. 147.

Lovejoy, Arthur O. *The great chain of being.* A study of the history of an idea. Cambridge: Harvard University press, 1936. Pp. ix + 382. Cf. *PQ*, XVI, 164.

Rev. by S. Buchanan in *International jour. of ethics*, XLVII, 486-90; by H. T. Davis in *Isis*, XXVII, 111-14; by A. S. P. Woodhouse in *JEGP*, XXXVII (1938), 109-14; by B. W. Brotherston in *Jour. of religion*, XVII, 204-06; by H. C. L. Heywood in *Jour. of theol. studies*, XXXVIII, 212-15; by J. Laird in *Mind*, XLVI, 400-05; by R. Demos in *MLN*, LII, 518-20; by B. M. Laing in *Philosophy*, XII, 113-14; by E. Nagel in *Science and society*, I, 252-56 (cf. corr. *ibid.*, I, 410-16); by E. C. Knowlton in *SAQ*, XXXVII (1938), 93-94; by C. Barrett in *TBR*, May 9, p. 11.

McColley, Grant. "The seventeenth-century doctrine of a plurality of worlds." *Annals of science*, I (1936), 385-430.

McKeon, Richard. "Literary criticism and the concept of imitation in antiquity." *MP*, XXXIV (1936), 1-35.

Important study for students of neo-classic literary theory.

MacPike, Eugene Fairfield. *Hevelius, Flamsteed and Halley.* Three contemporary astronomers and their mutual relations. London: Taylor and Francis, 1937. Pp. ix + 140.

Mansfield, Orlando A. "Rippon's tunes." *Baptist quarterly*, VIII (1936), 36-43.

Matthews, William. "Polite speech in the eighteenth century." *English*, I (1937), 493-511.

Matthews, William. "Sailors' pronunciation, 1770-1783." *Anglia*, LXI (1937), 72-80.

Matthews, William. "Some eighteenth-century vulgarisms." *RES*, XIII (1937), 307-25.

Miller, Frances Schouler. "Notes on some eighteenth-century dramas." *MLN*, LII (1937), 203-06.

Miller, Thomas. "Judge-Admiral James Graham of Airth (1702-1746) with special reference to his civil law library." *Juridical review*, XLIX (1937), 390-413.

Minkowski, Helmut. "Die geistesgeschichtliche und die literarische Nachfolge der Neu-Atlantis des Francis Bacon." *Neophilologus*, XXII (1937), 120-39, 185-200.

Mitford, W. Slade. "John Keyse Sherwin, engraver." *Connoisseur*, XCVIII (1936), 99-101.

Morley, Edith J. "Eighteenth century ideals in life and in literature." *Essays by divers hands.* Being the transactions of the Royal Society of Literature of the United Kingdom. XVI (1937), 117-35.

Motzo Dentice di Accadia, C. "La supremazia dello stato. I. Tindal. II. Bolingbroke." *Giornale critico della filosofia italiana*, XVII (1936), 225-55.

Mozley, Geraldine. "Joseph Ames, F.S.A., and the Blake portrait." *N & Q*, CLXXII (1937), 308-10.

Mullett, Charles F. "Lord Mansfield and English Dissenters." *Missouri law review*, II (1937), 46-62.

Packard, Francis R. "William Cheselden, some of his contemporaries, and their American pupils." *Annals of medical history*, IX (1937), 533-48.

Pavière, Sydney H. "Biographical notes on the Devis family of painters." *The twenty-fifth volume of the Walpole Society, 1936-1937.* Oxford: Walpole Society, 1937. Pp. 115-66, with plates xli-xlviii.

Piggott, Stuart. "Prehistory and the Romantic movement." *Antiquity*, XI (1937), 31-38.

Suggests a close relation between the study of British archaeology by such antiquaries as Stukeley, Rowlands, Wise, Borlase, Grose, Hoare, and Higgins and the literary fashions of the eighteenth and the early nineteenth century.

Poppers, Hirsch Leib. *Die Entstehung des Kongregationalismus aus der puritanischen Bewegung und seine Bedeutung als Independentismus für die englische Staatsgeschichte des 17. Jahrhunderts.* Berlin diss. 1936. Pp. x + 127.

Read, Allen Walker. "Projected English dictionaries, 1755-1828." *JEGP*, XXXVI (1937), 188-205, 347-66.

Philosophical orations of Thomas Reid. Delivered at graduation ceremonies in King's College, Aberdeen, 1753, 1756, 1759, 1762. Edited, with an introduction, from the Birkwood MS. by Walter Robson Humphries. (Aberdeen University studies, no. 113) Aberdeen: University press, 1937. Pp. 47.

Richard, Gaston. "La critique de l'hypothèse du contrat social avant Jean-Jacques Rousseau." *Archives de philosophie du droit et de sociologie juridique,* VII (1937), 45-80.

Richards, Edward Ames. *Hudibras in the burlesque tradition.* (Columbia University studies in English and comparative literature, no. 127) New York: Columbia University press, 1937. Pp. x + 184.

Rev. by C. G. Stillman in *HTB,* July 11, p. 2. § An analysis of Butler's temperament, opinions, and work, and a discussion of the political, intellectual, and narrative followers of *Hudibras,* with a list of poems in Hudibrastic verse, 1662-1830.

Richardson, A. E. "The Gothic revival in the early 18th century." *Journal of the Royal Institute of British Architects,* XLV (1937), 140-41.

On Browne Willis, author of *A survey of the cathedrals* (1727-30).

Roberts, Michael. *The modern mind.* London: Faber & Faber, 1937. Pp. 284.

Rev. by G. Every in *Criterion,* XVII, 129-33; by E.-M. Reynaud in *EA,* I, 453-54; by M. Oakeshott in *Scrutiny,* VI, 208-10; by W. R. Matthews in *Spectator,* June 4, p. 1,058. § Chapters on "The seventeenth century: materialism and scientific language," "The seventeenth century: metaphysical poets and the Cambridge Platonists," and "Reason and imagination in the eighteenth century."

Roberts, W. "George Allen." Corr. in *TLS,* June 26, 1937, p. 480.

Rosenfield, Léonora Cohen. "Un chapitre de l'histoire de l'animal-machine (1645-1749)." *RLC,* XVII (1937), 461-87.

Sabine, George H. *A history of political theory.* (American political science series) New York: Holt, 1937. Pp. xvi + 797.

Rev. by H. Janzen in *Amer. polit. science rev.,* XXXI, 959-60; by H.W.S. in *Jour. of phil.,* XXXIV, 527-29. § See especially Chaps. xxiii-xxix.

Scheffer, John D. "The idea of decline in literature and the fine arts in eighteenth-century England." *MP,* XXXIV (1936), 155-78.

A good article on an interesting and significant topic.

Scott, Hugh Arthur. "London's earliest public concerts." *Musical quarterly,* XXII (1936), 446-57.

Scott, Hugh Arthur. "London's first concert room." *Music and letters,* XVIII (1937), 379-90.

Scott, J. F. "John Wallis as a historian of mathematics." *Annals of science,* I (1936), 335-57.

Sesmat, Augustin. *Le système absolu classique et les mouvements réels.* Étude historique et critique. Paris: Hermann, 1936. Pp. 691.

Chapter v is on "Principes de la mécanique newtonienne." This thesis appeared also as *Actualités scientifiques et industrielles,* nos. 479-485, 1937.

Sewall, Richard B. "Rousseau's first *Discourse* in England." *PMLA,* LII (1937), 908-11.

Supplements Warner's article; cf. *PQ,* XIII, 111.

Shepperson, Archibald Bolling. *The novel in motley.* A history of the burlesque novel in English. Cambridge: Harvard University press, 1936. Pp. viii + 301.

Rev. by J. W. Beach in *JEGP,* XXXVI, 440-42; by M. Van Doren in *Nation,* Jan. 30, p. 136; by G. B. Newman in *SRL,* Jan. 23, p. 10; by W. L. Myers in *Virginia quar. rev.,* XIII, 296-97.

As a history of burlesque fiction from Fielding to Thackeray this volume elaborates the extremes which satirists sought to correct with extremities. The author uses two terms, "burlesque" and "parody-burlesque," and differentiates on the basis of particularity; his main purpose, however, is not one of subtle distinctions so much as the illustration of such vogues as those enjoyed by the Pamelan and Shandyan novels, the mock romances fathered by *Don Quixote,* the sentimental fictions and the doctrinaire, the Gothic and the historical tales. By means of liberal quotations and summaries and his own rather entertaining style Shepperson presents an interesting account of the numerous burlesques he has found. The chapter on Jane Austen stresses her artistic development from burlesque beginnings. The appendix, a list of burlesque stories from 1830 to 1900, is a bibliographical contribution, but a list including all the burlesque fiction discussed in the book would have proved more convenient.

Shirley, the Hon. Ralph. "'Cruden's Concordance' (1737-1937)." *Cornhill magazine,* CLVI (1937), 741-47.

Shorr, Philip. "Sir John Freind (1675-1728) M.D., pioneer historian of medicine." *Isis,* XXVII (1937), 453-74.

Silvette, Herbert. "The doctor on the stage: medicine and medical men in seventeenth century English drama." *Annals of medical history,* VIII (1936), 520-40; IX (1937), 62-87, 174-88, 264-79, 371-94, 482-507.

Sitwell, Sacheverell. *Narrative pictures.* A survey of English genre and its painters. With notes on the illustrations by Michael Sevier. London: B. T. Batsford, 1937. Pp. vi + 122.

Chapters on Hogarth and eighteenth century painters.

Sloane, William. "A XVII-century Chaucer allusion." *N & Q,* CLXXIII (1937), 226.

Smith, Alexander Brent. "Henry Purcell." *Music and letters,* XVIII (1937), 162-68.

Smith, David Nichol. *Some observations on eighteenth century poetry.* (Alexander lectures in English at the University of Toronto, 1937) London, New York: Oxford University press, 1937. Pp. 81.

Rev. in *TLS,* Jan. 15, 1938, pp. 33-34; by A. Humphries in *Cambridge rev.,* LIX (1938), 256-57. § Three pleasant and thoughtful essays on "Pope — poetic diction," "The heroic couplet — Johnson," and "Thomson — Burns."

Starnes, D. T. "English dictionaries of the seventeenth century." *University of Texas studies in English,* no. 17, 1937, p. 15-51.

An important and penetrating study of early lexicography, including analysis of the "purposes of the dictionary makers, the audience for whom they work, the sources of information, the interrelationships of the English dictionaries, their debt to bilingual dictionaries, the development of a technique."

Stearns, Raymond Phineas. "Correspondence of John Woodbridge, Jr., and Richard Baxter." *New England quarterly,* X (1937), 557-83.

Stearns, Raymond Phineas. "The course of Capt. Edmond Halley in the year 1700." *Annals of science,* I (1936), 294-301.

Stroup, Thomas B. "Supernatural beings in Restoration drama." *Anglia,* LXI (1937), 186-92.

Struck, Wilhelm. *Der Einfluss Jakob Bœhmes auf die englische Literatur des 17. Jahrhunderts* (Neue deutsche Forschungen, Bd. 69, Abteilung englische Philologie, Bd. 6) Berlin: Junker und Dünnhaupt, 1936. Pp. 262.

Rev. by F. L. Taft in *JEGP,* XXXVI, 287-88; by S. Hobhouse in *Jour. of Friends' hist. soc.,* XXXIII (1936), 52-54.

Tapp, Major W. H. "The art of James Banford, painter of Derby ceramics." *Connoisseur,* XCIX (1937), 76-80, 206-09.

Taube, Mortimer. *Causation, freedom and determinism.* An attempt to solve the causal problem through a study of its origins in seventeenth-century philosophy. London: George Allen & Unwin, 1936. Pp. 262.

Rev. by J. S. in *Studies: an Irish quar. rev.,* XXVI, 692-93. § Contains analysis of the ideas of Descartes, Spinoza, Malebranche, Leibniz, Hobbes, Locke, and Hume.

Tucker, William John. "Irish masters of prose." *Catholic World,* CXLIV (1937), 712-17.

On Swift, Goldsmith, and Burke.

Utter, Robert Palfrey, and Needham, Gwendolyn Bridges. *Pamela's daughters.* New York: Macmillan, 1936. Pp. xiii + 512.

Rev. by I. Paterson in *HTB,* Nov. 29, 1936, p. 10. § A study of eighteenth and nineteenth century heroines as exemplars of fashionable delicacy and virtue. The sources are dramas, novels, and works on morals and manners. The style is often coy.

Venturi, Lionello. *History of art criticism.* Translated from the the Italian by Charles Marriott. New York: Dutton, 1936. Pp. xv + 345.

Rev. by G. Price-Jones in *Burlington mag.,* LXXI, 102-03. § See chapters 5-7, "The baroque period," "Illuminism and neoclassicism," "Romanticism and the Middle Ages."

Vertue note books, Vol. IV. *The twenty-fourth volume of the Walpole Society, 1935-1936.* Oxford: Walpole Society, 1936. Pp. xii + 197.

Von Erdberg, Eleanor. *Chinese influence in European garden structures.* Edited by Bremer Whidden Pond. (Harvard landscape architecture monographs, I) Cambridge: Harvard University press, 1936. Pp. 221.

Rev. by R.W.S. in *Connoisseur,* C, 162-63.

Warner, James H. "Eighteenth-century English reactions to the *Nouvelle Héloïse.*" *PMLA,* LII (1937), 803-19.

Wasserman, Earl Reeves. "The scholarly origin of the Elizabethan revival." *ELH,* IV (1937), 213-43.

Wattie, Margaret. "Robert Hooke on his literary contemporaries." *RES,* XIII (1937), 212-16.

Westrup, J. A. *Purcell.* (The master musicians) London: J. M. Dent; New York: E. P. Dutton, 1937. Pp. xi + 323.

Rev. by A.G.M. in *Downside rev.*, LV, 283-84; by W. A. Chislett in *Eng. rev.*, LXIV, 629-30; by E. Audra in *EA*, I, 467-68; by C. H. Warren in *Fortnightly*, CXLVII, 629; by P. Bowdoin in *HTB*, May 9, p. 25; by E.W. in *Music and letters*, XVIII, 287-88; by B. Pattison in *Scrutiny*, VI, 106-09; by R. Aldrich in *TBR*, June 13, p. 4; by D. Hussey in *Spectator*, April 30, p. 814.

Whitehorn, R. D. "Richard Baxter, Catholick." *Journal of the Presbyterian Historical Society of England*, VI (1937), 99-109.

Wiles, Roy McKeen. "Prose fiction in English periodical publications before 1750." *Harvard University summaries of theses, 1935*, 1937, pp. 289-92.

Early letters of Robert Wodrow, 1698-1709. Edited from the manuscript in Edinburgh University Library, with notes and extracts from the answers to these letters in the National Library of Scotland, by L. W. Sharp. (Publications of the Scottish History Society, Vol. XXIV) Edinburgh: University press, 1937. Pp. lvi + 332.

Wright, Walter Francis. *Sensibility in English prose fiction, 1760-1814: a reinterpretation.* (Illinois studies in language and literature, Vol. XXII, nos. 3-4) Urbana: 1937. Pp. 158.

Yamagiwa, Joseph K. "A Shakespeare allusion." *MLN*, LII (1937), 201-02.

From *A great historical, geographical and poetical dictionary* (1694).

Yost, Calvin Daniel, jr. *The poetry of the Gentleman's Magazine.* A study in eighteenth century literary taste. University of Pennsylvania dissertation. Philadelphia: 1936. Pp. 147.

Rev. by W. Graham in *JEGP*, XXXVI, 613-14; by C. L. Carlson in *MP*, XXXV, 204-05.

Yvon, Paul. *Les crises de la morale et de la moralité dans l'histoire de la civilisation et de la littérature des pays anglo-saxons.* Paris: Boivin, 1937. Pp. 126.

Rev. in *TLS*, Jan. 8, 1938, p. 25. § Originally appeared serially in *Revue des cours et conférences*, 1936-37.

IV. INDIVIDUAL AUTHORS

Joseph Addison

Carritt, E. F. "Addison, Kant, and Wordsworth." *Essays and studies by members of the English Association.* Vol. XXII, collected by Helen Darbishire, 1937. Pp. 26-36.

Graham, Walter. "Joseph Addison's letters to Joshua Dawson." *PQ*, XVI (1937), 97-104.

Hamm, Victor M. "Addison and the pleasures of the imagination." *MLN*, LII (1937), 498-500.

Thorpe, Clarence DeWitt. "Addison and some of his predecessors on 'novelty.'" *PMLA*, LII (1937), 1114-29.

Zeitvogel, Albert. *Addisons Cato.* Eine geschichtl. u. dramat. Quellenuntersuchung. Münster diss. 1936. Pp. 65.

Jane Austen

Austen-Leigh, Emma. *Jane Austen and Steventon.* London: Spottiswoode, Ballantyne, 1937. Pp. ix + 54.
Rev. in *TLS,* June 19, p. 467.

Bühler, Willi. *Die "Erlebte Rede" im englischen Roman.* Ihre Vorstufen und ihre Ausbildung im Werke Jane Austens. (Swiss studies in English, Band 4) Zürich and Leipzig: Max Niehan, [1937]. Pp. 183.
Rev. by L. Villard in *EA,* I, 540-41.

Chapman, R. W. "Jane Austen's text: authoritative manuscript corrections." *TLS,* Feb. 13, 1937, p. 116.
Notes, perhaps by Cassandra Austen, on *Pride and prejudice* and *Persuasion.*

Haferkorn, Reinhard. "Zum Begriff des Sentimentalen: Bemerkungen zu Jane Austen's Sense and Sensibility." *Englische Kultur in sprachwissenschaftlicher Deutung.* Max Deutschbein zum 60. Geburtstage. Leipzig: Verlag von Quelle & Meyer, 1936. Pp. 109-20.

Seymour, Beatrice Kean. *Jane Austen: study for a portrait.* London: Michael Joseph, 1937. Pp. 256.
Rev. in *TLS,* Nov. 13, p. 873.

Turpin, A. R. "Jane Austen: limitations or defects?" *English review,* LXIV (1937), 53-68.

John Banks

Tupper, Fred Salisbury. "John Banks: a study in the origins of the pathetic tragedy." *Harvard University summaries of theses, 1935,* 1937, pp. 282-86.

William Beckford

Armour, Richard W. "The caliph of Fonthill." *Reading and collecting,* I (1937), 9-10.

Carter, John. "The Lausanne edition of Beckford's *Vathek.*" *Library,* XVII (1937), 369-94.

Chapman, Guy. *Beckford.* London: Jonathan Cape, 1937. Pp. 365.
Rev. in *TLS,* March 13, p. 185; by W. King in *Criterion,* XVII (1938), 367-69; by C. G. Stillman in *HTB,* May 9, p. 32; by R. Church in *LM,* XXXVI, 86; by M. Geismar in *Nation,* May 15, p. 568; by E. Johnson in *New republic,* Aug. 18, p. 55; by A. Cowie in *SRL,* May 29, p. 6; by J. Hayward in *Spectator,* March 12, p. 478; by L. Kronenberger in *TBR,* July 25, p. 2.

Aphra Behn

Mizener, Arthur. "Poems by Mrs. Behn." Corr. in *TLS,* May 8, 1937, p. 364.

Edward Benlowes

Jenkins, Harold. "A poet in chancery: Edward Benlowes." *MLR,* XXXII (1937), 382-93.

Jenkins, Harold. "Towards a biography of Edward Benlowes." *RES,* XII (1936), 273-84.

Niemeyer, Carl. "New light on Edward Benlowes." *RES,* XII (1936), 31-41.

George Berkeley

Frondizi, Risieri. "Influencia de Descartes sobre el idealismo de Berkeley." *Descartes.* Homenaje en el tercer centenario del "Discurso del Metodo." Buenos Aires: Universidad de Buenos Aires, 1937. I, 329-40.

Jessop, T. E. "Great thinkers: (xi) Bishop Berkeley." *Philosophy,* XII (1937), 276-90.

Leyburn, Ellen Douglass. "Bishop Berkeley: *The Querist.*" *Proceedings of the Royal Irish Academy,* Vol. XLIV (1937), sec. C, no. 3, pp. 75-98.

Luce, A. A."Is there a Berkeleian philosophy?" *Hermathena: a series of papers on literature, science, and philosophy by members of Trinity College, Dublin,* No. L (1937), 184-210.
Review-article on books by Wild and Hedenius.

Luce, A. A. "Two sermons by Bishop Berkeley." *Proceedings of the Royal Irish Academy,* Vol. XLIII (1936), sec. C, no. 8, pp. 271-90.

Luce, A. A. "The unity of the Berkeleian philosophy." *Mind,* XLVI (1937), 44-52, 180-90.

Moorman, Mary C. "A dream of Bermuda, 1724-1732." *East and west review,* II (1936), 306-15.

Nikander, Viljo Kustaa. "Berkeley's *Seris.*" *Harvard University summaries of theses, 1935,* 1937, pp. 346-49.

The querist. Edited with an introduction by J. M. Hone. Dublin: Talbot press, 1935. Pp. 122.

Stäbler, Eugen. *George Berkeley's Auffassung und Wirkung in der deutschen Philosophie bis Hegel.* Tübingen diss. 1935. Pp. 102.

Wild, John. "The unity of the Berkeleian philosophy. A reply to Mr. Luce." *Mind,* XLVI (1937), 454-64.

William Blake

Alfassa, Paul. "L'Exposition Blake et Turner." *Revue de Paris,* XLIV (1937), iii, 665-78.

Gillet, Louis. "Un mystique anglais: William Blake." *Revue des deux mondes,* XXXVIII (1937), 190-206.

Illustrations of the Book of Job. By William Blake. Reproduced in facsimile from the original "New Zealand" set made about 1823-4, in the possession of Philip Hofer. With a note by Philip Hofer. New York: Dutton, 1937. Plates 21 + pp. 9.
Rev. in *TLS,* Dec. 25, p. 976; by H. R. Wackrill in *LM,* XXXVII (1938), 346.

The illustrations of William Blake for Thornton's Virgil with the First Eclogue and the Imitation by Ambrose Philips. Introduction by Geoffrey Keynes. London: Nonesuch press, 1937. Pp. 38.

Rev. in *TLS,* Dec. 25, p. 976.

Larrabee, Stephen A. "John Gibson visits William Blake." Corr. in *TLS,* April 3, 1937, p. 256.

Lindsay, Jack. "Donne and Blake." Corr. in *TLS,* July 24, 1937, p. 544.

Nanavutty, Piloo. "'Puzzling names' in Blake." Corr. in *TLS,* July 3, 1937, p. 496. Cf. Mark E. Perugini, *ibid.,* July 10, p. 512.

Quinn, Kerker. "Blake and the new age." *Virginia quarterly review,* XIII (1937), 271-85.

Schorer, Mark. "How the eighteenth century died to music." *Reading and collecting,* II (1937), 7-8.

Wackrill, H. R. *The inscription over the gate.* London: Peter Davies, 1937. Pp. 125.

Rev. in *TLS,* Dec. 25, p. 976; by R. A. Scott-James in *LM,* XXXVII (1938), 357.

Wahl, Jean. "Magie et romantisme: notes sur Novalis et Blake." *Hermes,* Brussels, deuxième série, June, 1936, pp. 7-13.

James Boswell

Bennett, Charles H. "The Auchinleck entail." Corr. in *TLS,* Feb. 27, 1937, p. 151.

Esdaile, K. A. "A footnote to Boswell." Corr. in *TLS,* Oct. 23, 1937, p. 783.

Pearson, Hesketh, and Kingsmill, Hugh. *Skye high.* The record of a tour through Scotland in the wake of Samuel Johnson and James Boswell. London: Hamish Hamilton, 1937. Pp. 312.

Rev. in *TLS,* Dec. 18, p. 958.

Pottle, Frederick A. *Boswell and the girl from Botany Bay.* New York: Viking press, 1937. Pp. 56.

Rev. by W. L. C. Carlton in *HTB,* Jan. 2, 1938, p. 3. § A beautifully printed and well-presented essay on Mary Bryant, who was befriended by Boswell after her remarkable escape from Australia.

Pottle, Frederick A., with the assistance of Joseph Foladare, John P. Kirby and others. *Index to the private papers of James Boswell from Malahide Castle in the collection of Lt. Colonel Ralph Heyward Isham.* London and New York: Oxford University press, 1937. Pp. xx + 359.

Rev. in *HTB,* August 1, p. 13. § A very useful aid to students of eighteenth century biography and literary history.

Smith-Dampier, J. L. *Who's who in Boswell?* Oxford: Shakespeare Head press, 1935. Pp. xx + 366.

Watts, Henry. "Boswell: was he a Catholic?" *America,* LVI, (1936), 186-87.

Roger Boyle, Earl of Orrery

The dramatic works of Roger Boyle, Earl of Orrery. Edited by William Smith Clark, II. 2 vols. Cambridge: Harvard University press, 1937. Pp. xv + 965.

Rev. in *TLS,* July 17, p. 525; by S. C. Chew in *HTB,* May 9, p. 24; by G. Greene in *Spectator,* Aug. 27, p. 356. § This elaborate edition, the first complete collection of Boyle's dramatic works, includes ten plays, with one (*Zoroastres*) hitherto unpublished, another (*The generall*) printed from a new manuscript, a third (*King Saul*) now first assigned to Orrery, and the remaining seven re-edited and collated. These two large and well-printed volumes contain also a long historical preface, a critical preface, an editor's preface to each play, explanatory and textual notes (at the end of the second volume), bibliography of Orrery's dramatic works, and a list of manuscripts. The noble playwright now has his monument.

Tom Brown

Boyce, Benjamin. "Tom Brown and Elia." *ELH,* IV (1937), 147-50.

Sir Thomas Browne

Buchinger, Hans. *Beiträge zur Erkenntnis des individuellen Moments im Wortschatz der Religio Medici des Sir Thomas Browne.* Könisberg diss. 1936. Pp. xi + 64.

Finch, Jeremiah S. "'Musaeum Clausum.'" Corr. in *TLS,* Nov. 13, 1937, p. 871.

Iseman, Joseph Seeman. *A perfect sympathy: Charles Lamb and Sir Thomas Browne.* (Harvard honors theses in English, no. 10) Cambridge: Harvard University press, 1937. Pp. 90.

John Bunyan

Harrison, Frank Mott. "The Pilgrim's Progress." Corr. in *TLS,* Jan. 23, 1937, p. 60. Cf. corr. by W. Kent, *ibid.,* Jan. 30, p. 76.

Lindsay, Jack. *John Bunyan, maker of myths.* London: Methuen, 1937. Pp. xiii + 271. Cf. corr., *TLS,* Nov. 13, p. 871.

Rev. in *TLS,* Oct. 23, p. 784; by F. A. Lea in *Adelphi,* XIV, 81-85; by R. Church in *LM,* XXXVII, 86-87; by B. Dobrée, in *Spectator,* Nov. 5, pp. 812-14.

Edmund Burke

Wecter, Dixon. "Burke's birthday." *N & Q,* CLXXII (1937), 441.

Robert Burns

"Alexander Wood, surgeon and friend of Robert Burns." *Annals of medical history,* IX (1937), 193-94.

Burns chronicle and club directory. Second series, Vol. XII. Kilmarnock: Burns Federation, 1937. Pp. 219.

The current issue of this inexpensive annual contains facsimiles of the manuscript of "The Lass o' Ballochmyle" and of a letter regarding its composition, an article by B. R. Leftwich on "Burns's colleagues in the Excise, 1789-1796," and a critical examination by J. C. Ewing into the Burns tradition in an article on "Burns's tour of Galloway in 1783 and the fable of the composition of *Scots wha hae.*"

Crichton-Browne, Sir James. *Burns from a new point of view.* London, Edinburgh, Glasgow: William Hodge, 1937. Pp. xv + 130.

Reprint of the title essay from 1926, with three new short articles on "Burns and the drama," "Burns annotations," and "Jean Armour."

Ewing, J. C. "Illustrated bindings." *TLS,* July 24, 1937, p. 548.
On the 1831 edition of the *Works.*

Ferguson, De Lancey. "'The immortal memory.'" *American scholar,* v (1936), 441-50.

Ferguson, De Lancey. "Some new Burns letters." *PMLA,* LI (1936), 975-84.

Fitzhugh, Robert T. "Burns' Highland Mary." *PMLA,* LII (1937), 829-34.

Fitzhugh, Robert T. "The composition of 'Scots wha hae.'" *MLN,* LI (1936), 423-26.

Heindel, R. H. "A letter of Robert Burns." *N & Q,* CLXXIII (1937), 152.

Jeffery, Sydney. "W. Roscoe and Burns." Corr. in *TLS,* Oct. 2, 1937, p. 715.

Joseph Butler

Beck, Lewis White. "A neglected aspect of Butler's ethics." *Sophia,* v (1937), 11-15.

Leslie, A. H. "Butler's *Analogy*: a chapter in the history of apologetics." *London quarterly and Holborn review,* April, 1937, pp. 236-41.

Sykes, N. "Bishop Butler and the primacy. Did he decline the see of Canterbury in 1747?" *Journal of historic Christianity,* XXXIII (1936), 129-37.

Susannah Centlivre

Anderson, Paul Bunyan. "Innocence and artifice: or, Mrs. Centlivre and *The Female Tatler.*" *PQ,* XVI (1937), 358-75.
Regards *Female tatler, written by a society of ladies,* as product of the collaboration of Mrs. Centlivre and Mandeville, writing on alternate days.

Thomas Chatterton

Meyerstein, E. H. W. "Chatterton, Coleridge and Bristol: 'the sacred river.'" *TLS,* Aug. 21, 1937, p. 606. Cf. corr. by F. Wylie Sypher and Meyerstein, *ibid.,* Aug. 28, p. 624.

Meyerstein, E. H. W. "Chatterton: his significance to-day." *Essays by divers hands.* Being the transactions of the Royal Society of Literature of the United Kingdom. XVI (1937), 61-91.

Philip Dormer Stanhope, Earl of Chesterfield

Gardner, Juliet. "Chesterfield and Voltaire." *Cornhill magazine,* CLV (1937), 107-19.

Holsapple, Cortell. "Some early verses by Chesterfield." *MLN,* LII (1937), 411.

Radice, Sheila. "Lord Chesterfield. I. Mademoiselle du Bouchet. II. James Hammond and others." Corr. in *TLS,* July 24, 31, 1937, pp. 544, 560.

Some unpublished letters of Lord Chesterfield. With an introduction by Sidney L. Gulick, jr. Berkeley: University of California press, 1937. Pp. 84.

Rev. in *TLS,* Dec. 11, p. 943. § Twenty-five letters to the godson and a letter to Dayverdun, the godson's tutor, containing a plan "which I wish you to follow in order to put the last touch to his education." Sixteen of the letters belong to the last year of the Earl's life.

William Cobbett

Letters from William Cobbett to Edward Thornton written in the years 1797 to 1800. Edited with an introduction and notes by G. D. H. Cole. London, New York, Toronto: Oxford University press, 1937. Pp. xlvi + 127.

Rev. by M. C. Burkett in *Cambridge rev.,* LIX, 156. § Twenty-three new letters to the secretary of the British Embassy in the United States.

Jeremy Collier

Anthony, Sister Rose. *The Jeremy Collier stage controversy, 1698-1726.* Milwaukee: Marquette University press, 1937. Pp. xv + 328.

Not. in *TLS,* Nov. 13, p. 873.

Ressler, Kathleen. "Jeremy Collier's essays." *Seventeenth century studies, second series.* By members of the Graduate School, University of Cincinnati. Edited by Robert Shafer. Princeton: Princeton University press for the University of Cincinnati, 1937. Pp. 179-285.

A welcome corrective to the conventional estimate of the author of the *Short view.*

William Collins

(See also *Thomas Gray*)

Ainsworth, Edward Gay, jr. *Poor Collins.* His life, his art, and his influence. Ithaca: Cornell University press; London: Milford, 1937. Pp. x + 340.

Rev. in *TLS,* April 3, p. 252; by G. Tillotson in *MLR,* XXXII, 616-17; by R.S.C. in *MP,* XXXV, 106-07; by S. A. Coblentz in *TBR,* July 25, p. 10.

After a preface which, with its limited critical vocabulary and its interminable acknowledgments, is almost a parody of the scholar's preface, and a title which, on the first page of the text, is properly repudiated as calumny, so that the reader wonders why the author should elect to perpetuate it, Ainsworth sets competently if pedestrianly to work. The style is throughout inept; all the trite metaphors and faded purples reappear: "cull," "wealth of material," ''gleaner in the field,'' ''life's tumult''; one ''senses'' too much and too often. In organization, the book is simple and solid; after a chapter narrating Collins' life, the remaining chapters of Section I consider the topics treated or referred to in the poems — nature, the arts, contemporary events—and survey his theory of poetry and his practice of the art; Section II, misleadingly entitled ''Sources and Influences,'' assembles parallel passages indicating Collins' obligations to the classics, the Elizabethans, Milton, Pope, and the poet's contemporaries (chiefly Thomson and Warton); and Section III is a study of Collins' reputation to the end of the Romantic Age, a useful survey which might, with profit, have been prolonged to the present. An appendix collects ''verbal echoes from Milton in the poetry of Collins,'' that poet not having found place in the appendices to Raymond Havens' *Influence of Milton.* The list contains much that is dubiously Miltonic; indeed, at its conclusion the compiler admits that ''many words included . . . . are also the common property of Shakespeare and the Elizabethans.'' Like many works of exemplary scholarship, *Poor Collins* might be described as an anthology of annotated quotations and lends itself more aptly to consultation than to consecutive reading. Indeed, the materials would better have been disposed had Ainsworth brought out an edition of the poems including a prefixed *Vita* and introduction and a suffixed commentary of the poems, some of which have their undeniable obscurities. The parallel passages might, to advantage, be printed at the bottom of the poetic page, after the fashion employed by Pope, and other 18th century writers of ''imitations.'' The study of Collins' reputation, which would form the appendix to such an edition, should be printed as a catena of citations with prefatory interpretation entirely in the compiler's words.

These strictures past, I have chiefly praise for the book. The misprints are commendably few; the facts, wherever I have checked them, are accurate; the index is elaborate. I miss a bibliography; but the notes show the author's acquaintance with the researches of such contemporary Collinsians as McKillop, Woodhouse, and H. O. White, as well as with the critical observations of Langhorne, Mrs. Barbauld, and Swinburne. In short, as a work of scholarship the book is reliable. It contains all the *information* the teacher or the critic needs, and forms the necessary companion to Bronson's or Blunden's or Lane Poole's edition of the poems and to Garrod's critical essay.

The most significant part of the book concerns Collins' ''sources,'' to which Ainsworth has given exhaustive attention; and, because Collins is an eminently *livresque* poet, the approach to him through his reading is the approach most profitable. The surprises in this analysis of sources are the paucity of Collins' obligations to Spenser and the comparatively frequent borrowings from Pope, — borrowings not limited to Collins' eclogues or the epistle to Hanmer. The chapter on Milton is at once the fullest and most valuable, and abundantly demonstrates that Collins' devotion to Milton was as intense and central as one might infer from the ecstatic tribute in the finale to ''The Poetical Character.'' It is a distinction to be able to make a stronger case for the influence of Milton than does Havens; but Ainsworth succeeds. The influence was pervasive, and it assumed many forms, — now structural, now thematic, now stylistic. It seems to me altogether likely that it was ''Lycidas'' which first aroused Collins' interest in the Druids and the Hebrides, an interest later quickened by Thomson and, for the islands, satisfied by the books of Martin Martin. In the ''Passions,'' the poet intended, I have no doubt, to recall ''Il Penseroso'' through the figure of Melancholy and ''L'Allegro'' through the figure of Cheerfulness. What marks Collins as an artist is the sensitive way in which he avoids the bald imitations employed by the younger Thomas Warton (e.g., in ''Ode on the Approach of Summer''): Collins always combines, adapts. ''The phrases 'upland Fallows gray' and 'Hamlets brown' represent a transposition of two phrases in *L'Allegro,* 'russet lawns and fallows gray' and 'upland hamlets'.'' I am not convinced that the ''Ode on the Poetical Character'' is ''fully and thoroughly Miltonic in substance, in imagery, and in diction''; but the pages (141-4) which Ainsworth give to parallels repay analysis. In Collins' painted backdrop for Milton, he undoubtedly had in recollection Milton's description of Eden (*Paradise Lost,* IV, 133); but, unlike Milton, Collins subordinates Eden to the steep wilderness leading up to it, making the wilderness more wild till it becomes a landscape limned by the savage "pencil" of Salvator Rosa. Nor is the scene thus romantically heightened a typical setting for its figure: Collins has his own Milton, a creature of melancholy, solitude, and ecstasy. A.W.

William Combe

Montgomery, Franz. "Alexander Mackenzie's literary assistant." *Canadian historical review,* XVIII (1937), 301-04.

William Congreve

"Congreve's comedies: speed, stillness and meaning." Leading article in *TLS,* Sept. 25, 1937, pp. 681-82.

Snider, Rose. *Satire in the comedies of Congreve, Sheridan, Wilde, and Coward. University of Maine studies, second series,* no. 42, 1937. Pp. x + 135.

Wilson, J. Dover. "Shakespeare, Milton, and Congreve." Corr. in *TLS,* Jan. 16, 1937, p. 44.

Abraham Cowley

Bald, R. C. "Three metaphysical epigrams." *PQ,* XVI (1937), 402-05.

The third epigram is a new poem by Cowley.

Walton, Geoffrey. "Abraham Cowley and the decline of metaphysical poetry." *Scrutiny,* VI (1937), 176-94.

William Cowper

Mabbott, T. O. "The Miltonic epitaph on Mazarin: Cowper's opinion." *N & Q,* CLXXII (1937), 188.

Weiss, Harry B. "William Cowper's frolic in rhyme: *The Diverting History of John Gilpin.*" *Bulletin of the New York Public Library,* XLI (1937), 675-80.

Daniel Defoe

A., T. P. "German translations of Defoe." *N & Q,* CLXXII (1937), 11.

Burch, Charles Eaton. "The moral elements in Defoe's fiction." *London quarterly and Holborn review,* April, 1937, pp. 207-13.

Burch, Charles Eaton. "Notes on the contemporary popularity of Defoe's *Review.*" *PQ,* XVI (1937), 210-13.

Greenough, Chester N. "Defoe in Boston." *Publications of the Colonial Society of Massachusetts.* Transactions, 1930-1933. XXVIII (1935), 461-93.

Hutchins, Henry Clinton. "Robinson Crusoe at Yale." *Yale University Library gazette,* XI (1936), 17-37.

Newton, Theodore F. M. "The civet-cats of Newington Green: new light on Defoe." *RES,* XIII (1937), 10-19.

Sutherland, James. *Defoe.* London: Methuen, 1937. Pp. xiii + 300.

Rev. in *QR,* CCLXIX, 367; in *TLS,* June 26, p. 476; by S. Potter in *Fortnightly,* CXLVIII, 247-48; by S. C. Chew in *HTB,* Feb. 20, 1938, p. 5; by T. Good in *Life and letters to-day,* XVII, 181; by H. M. Jones in *SRL,* Feb. 26, 1938, p. 10; by V. S. Pritchett in *Spectator,* July 16, p. 113; by P. Geyl in *Tijdschrift voor geschiedenis,* LII, 419-20; by L. Kronenberger in *TBR,* Feb. 13, 1938, p. 5.

John Dryden

Bennett, J. A. W. "Dryden and All Souls." *MLN,* LII (1937), 115-16.

"Dryden's conversion: the struggle for faith." Leading article in *TLS,* April 17, 1937, pp. 281-82.

Ham, Roswell G. "Dryden's epilogue to *The Rival Ladies,* 1664." *RES,* XIII (1937), 76-80.

Hartsock, Mildred E. "Dryden's plays: a study in ideas." *Seventeenth century studies, second series.* By members of the Graduate School, University of Cincinnati. Edited by Robert Shafer. Princeton: Princeton University press for the University of Cincinnati, 1937. Pp. 71-176.

An extension and a criticism of Bredvold's investigations through an examination of Dryden's plays, which show the effect of the materialism of Hobbes and the Pyrrhonism of Montaigne.

"Hibernicus." "Dryden's epigram on Milton." *N & Q,* CLXXIII (1937), 149-50.

Hymns attributed to John Dryden. Edited with an introduction and notes by George Rapall Noyes and George Reuben Potter. Berkeley: University of California press, 1937. Pp. ix + 221.

Rev. in *TLS,* Nov. 27, p. 906. § Attempts refutation of argument that Dryden was translator of the hymns, except the *Veni, creator spiritus,* in the 1706 *Primer, or, office of the B. Virgin Mary.*

Leavis, F. R. "'Antony and Cleopatra' and 'All for Love.'" *Scrutiny,* V (1936), 158-69.

Legouis, Pierre. "Dryden and Eton." *MLN,* LII (1937), 111-15.

Mundy, P. D. "The baptism of John Dryden." *N & Q,* CLXXIII (1937), 225.

Osborn, James M. "Edmond Malone and the Dryden almanac story." *PQ,* XVI (1937), 412-14.

Stroup, Thomas B. "Scenery for *The Indian Queen.*" *MLN,* LII (1937), 408-09.

Ward, C. E. "Some notes on Dryden." *RES,* XIII (1937), 297-306.

Wasserman, Earl R. "Pre-Restoration poetry in Dryden's Miscellany." *MLN,* LII (1937), 545-55.

John Evelyn

(See also *Sir George Mackenzie*)

Acetaria. A discourse of sallets. By John Evelyn, Esq. Brooklyn: Women's Auxiliary, Brooklyn Botanic Garden, 1937. Pp. 148.

Keynes, Geoffrey. *John Evelyn: a study in bibliophily.* A bibliography of his writings. Cambridge: University press, 1937. Pp. xvii + 308.

Rev. in *TLS,* Sept. 18, p. 610; by I. A. Williams in *LM,* XXXVI, 565.

George Farquhar

Sutherland, James R. "New light on George Farquhar." Corr. in *TLS,* March 6, 1937, p. 171.

Elijah Fenton

Harlan, Earl. *Elijah Fenton, 1683-1730.* University of Pennsylvania diss. Philadelphia: 1937. Pp. 205.

Henry Fielding

Chandler, Knox. "Two 'Fielding' pamphlets." *PQ,* XVI (1937), 410-12.

Esdaile, Mrs. "Fielding's Danish translator: Simon Charles Stanley the sculptor." *TLS,* April 3, 1937, p. 252. Cf. corr. by Bernard Rackham, *ibid.,* April 17, p. 292.

Jensen, Gerard E. "Proposals for a definitive edition of Fielding's *Tom Jones.*" *Library,* XVIII (1937), 314-30.

Woods, Charles B. "Notes on three of Fielding's plays." *PMLA,* LII (1937), 359-73.

On *The letter-writers* (1731), *The modern husband* (1732), and *Eurydice hiss'd* (1737).

Woods, Charles Burton. "Studies in the dramatic works of Henry Fielding." *Harvard University summaries of theses, 1935,* 1937, pp. 292-94.

George Fox

"A. R. Barclay MSS." *Journal of the Friends' Historical Society,* XXXIII (1936), 55-64.

Extracts from letters to Fox. Continued from previous volumes.

Cadbury, Henry J. "Richardson MSS. Further unpublished writings of George Fox." *Journal of the Friends' Historical Society,* XXXII (1935), 34-37.

A day-book of counsel & comfort from the epistles of George Fox. Compiled by L. V. Hodgkin (Mrs. John Holdsworth). London: Macmillan, 1937. Pp. xxiii + 314.

Rev. in *TLS,* Sept. 25, p. 684.

David Garrick

Stone, George Winchester, jr. "Garrick's presentation of *Antony and Cleopatra.*" *RES,* XIII (1937), 20-38.

Edward Gibbon

"The historian and 'the Gibbon.'" Leading article in *TLS,* April 24, 1937, pp. 297-98.

J., W.H. "Gibbon and Johnson." *N & Q,* CLXXIII (1937), 97.

Lloyd, Roger. "Gibbon and the Christians." *London quarterly and Holborn review,* Jan., 1937, pp. 41-50.

Low, D. M. *Edward Gibbon, 1737-1794.* London: Chatto & Windus, 1937. Pp. xiv + 370.

Rev. in *TLS,* March 20, p. 211; by P. Yvon in *EA,* I, 332-33; by F. T. Wood in *ES,* LXXII, 119-20; by C. G. Salter in *HTB,* Aug. 8, p. 5; by R. Lewin in *LM,* XXXVI, 94; by J. W. Krutch in *Nation,* Aug. 7, 153-54; by M. D. Zabel in *New republic,* Sept. 15, p. 164; by J. Heyward in *Spectator,* March 19, p. 534; by C. D. Abbott in *SRL,* Aug. 14, p. 12; by L. Kronenberger in *TBR,* Aug. 15, p. 2.

Thompson, James Westfall. "The library of Gibbon the historian." *Library quarterly,* VII (1937), 343-53.

Thomson, David. "Edward Gibbon: the master builder." *Contemporary review,* CLI (1937), 583-91.

Joseph Glanvill

Habicht, Hartwig. *Joseph Glanvill, ein spekulativer Denker im England des XVII. Jahrhunderts.* Eine Studie über das frühwissenschaftliche Weltbild. Zürich diss. 1936. Pp. 183.

Oliver Goldsmith

(See also *James Ralph*)

Fraser-Harris, D. F. "Goldsmith on his teachers." *Dalhousie review,* XVI (1936), 362-70.

Magnus, Philip. "Goldsmith and the Burkes." Corr. in *TLS,* Dec. 11, 1937, p. 947. Cf. corr. by Anthony C. Deane, *ibid.,* Dec. 18, p. 964.

Schulze, Ivan L. "An inconsistency in the thought of Goldsmith." *MLN,* LII (1937), 206-07.

Seitz, Robert W. "The Irish background of Goldsmith's social and political thought." *PMLA,* LII (1937), 405-11.

Thomas Gray

(See also *William Shenstone*)

"Hibernicus." "Gray's Elegy: 'await' or 'awaits'?" *N & Q,* CLXXII (1937), 320-21.

Jones, William Powell. *Thomas Gray, scholar.* The true tragedy of an eighteenth-century gentleman. With two youthful notebooks now published for the first time from the original manuscripts in the Morgan Library, New York City. Cambridge: Harvard University press, 1937. Pp. xi + 191.

Rev. in *TLS,* Feb. 5, 1938, p. 88.

By far the fullest and most intelligent account we have had hitherto of Gray's activities as a scholar is that contained in Roger Martin's recent *Essai sur Thomas Gray* (see *PQ,* XIV, 166). What Martin has to say about Gray's methods of study, about the relation of his investigations to those of contemporary and earlier scholars, and about the content and value of his notebooks is still well worth considering; there is a sophistication in his judgments which is not always apparent in Jones's more detailed discussion. Nevertheless, Jones has done an excellent and useful piece of work. He has examined independently all the sources at the disposal of Martin and in addition has made use of the manuscript notebooks in the Morgan library and of similar materials in other widely scattered collections; his appendixes contain not only heretofore unpublished extracts from the Morgan notebooks, including Gray's early catalogue of his library (now supplemented by an important article in *MP* for February, 1938), but also a systematic register of those autograph manuscripts of Gray that concern the theme of the volume. His narrative of Gray's studies, from about 1744, in ancient literature, history, and geography, in English poetry and history, and in natural history (he rightly omits, as irrelevant to his subject, the earlier academic concern with the classics which is reflected in the Latin poems) does not materially differ, in its main lines, from that given by Martin, but it is richer in details on a number of points and somewhat clearer in its chronology. Except in a few places (e.g., pp. 21, 129-32), Jones is content to tell the story of Gray's scholarly occupations almost exclusively in personal terms, without attempting to indicate how far his interests and methods were shaped by contemporary fashions in erudition. He is well aware that Gray was far from being "the most learned man in Europe," but he is not altogether free from the exaggerated estimate of his subject's intellectual powers which has become traditional since Temple's eulogy. A somewhat wider acquaintance with the history of scholarship in Gray's century and a somewhat more adequate conception of historical and philosophical method would perhaps have made him less sure of what he calls "the tremendous sweep" of Gray's mind (p. 147) or of the promise exhibited in the very amateurish notes on Plato (p. 145). R. S. C.

The poems of Gray and Collins. Edited by Austin Lane Poole. Third edition, revised. (Oxford standard authors) London: Oxford University press, 1937. Pp. 328.

Stokes, Francis Griffin. "Gray's 'Elegy.'" Corr. in *TLS,* Feb. 6, 1937, p. 92.

Whibley, Leonard. "A new letter by Gray." *TLS,* Oct. 23, 1937, p. 776.

Wolf, Edwin, 2nd. "Wolfe's copy of Gray's Elegy." *Colophon,* II (1937), 381-91.

Ralph Griffiths

Gilbert, Mizpah. "Griffiths of the *Monthly Review* and a Brentford church." *N & Q,* CLXXIII (1937), 206-07.

George Savile, Marquis of Halifax

Glessner, J. J., II. "Sir George Savile." Corr. in *TLS,* Sept. 25, p. 695.W

Klose, Kurt. *George Savile, Marquis von Halifax, als Politiker und Staatsdenker (1633-1695).* (Historische Untersuchung, Heft 18) Breslau: M. & H. Marcus, 1936. Pp. viii + 187.

Thomas Hobbes

Capitant, René. "Hobbes et l'état totalitaire: à propos d'un livre récent [*La cité de Hobbes,* by J. Vialatoux, 1935]." *Archives de philosophie du droit et de sociologie juridique,* VI (1936), 46-75.

Francis Bacon: Thomas Hobbes: John Locke. Edited by Gail Kennedy. (Doubleday-Doran series in philosophy) Garden City: Doubleday, Doran, 1937. Pp. xliii + 393.

Rev. by H.W.S. in *Jour. of phil.* XXXIV, 334. § Contains long selections from the *Leviathan* and the *Essay concerning human understanding* with summaries of omitted portions.

Ledig, Gerhard. "Philosophie der Strafe bei Thomas Hobbes." *Revue internationale de la théorie du droit,* x (1936), 293-99.

Oakeshott, M. "Dr. Leo Strauss on Hobbes." *Politica,* II (1937), 364-79.

Thomas Holcroft

Stallbaumer, Virgil R. "Holcroft's German." Corr. in *TLS,* Jan. 23, 1937, p. 60. Cf. corr. by Oskar Teichman, *ibid.,* Feb. 6, p. 92, and Stallbaumer, March 20, p. 222.

Stallbaumer, Virgil R. "Translations by Holcroft." *N & Q,* CLXXIII (1937), 402-05.

Sir Robert Howard

Scott, Florence R. "Sir Robert Howard as a financier." *PMLA,* LII (1937), 1094-1100.

David Hume

Bayley, Francis Chilton. *The causes and evidence of beliefs.* An examination of Hume's procedure. Mt. Hermon, Mass.: Printed for the author, 1936. Pp. v + 80.

Doering, J. Frederick. "Hume and the theory of tragedy." *PMLA,* LII (1937), 1130-34.

Ebert, Hermann. *Jean-Jacques Rousseau und David Hume.* Versuch einer psychologischen Darstellung ihrer persönlichen Beziehungen. Würzburg diss. 1936. Pp. 74.

Giorgiantonio, Michele. "Hume e Descartes." *Sophia,* v (1937), 30-40.

Hedenius, Ingemar. "Studies in Hume's ethics." Reprinted from *Adolf Phalén in Memoriam.* Uppsala & Stockholm: Almqvist & Wiksell, 1937. Pp. 388-485.

Laing, B. M. "Hume's *Dialogues concerning Natural Religion.*" *Philosophy,* XII (1937), 175-90.

Magnino, Bianca. *Il pensiero filosofico di David Hume.* (Collezione di studi filosofici. Serie storica monografie, no. 23) Naples: Casa editrice Rondinella Alfredo, 1935. Pp. 217.

Maund, Constance. *Hume's theory of knowledge.* A critical examination. London: Macmillan, 1937. Pp. xxi + 310.

Rev. in *TLS,* July 17, p. 526; by E. Barrett in *London quar. and Holborn rev.,* Oct., pp. 551-53; by J. D. Mabbott in *Philosophy,* XII, 488-89.

Richard Hurd

Hamm, Victor M. "A seventeenth-century French source for

Hurd's *Letters on Chivalry and Romance.*" *PMLA,* LII (1937), 820-28.

Charles Johnson

Hooker, Edward Niles. "Charles Johnson's *The Force of Friendship* and *Love in a Chest*: a note on tragi-comedy and licensing in 1710." *SP,* XXXIV (1937), 407-11.

Samuel Johnson

(See also *James Boswell* and *Edward Gibbon*)

Alexander, Henry. "Jonson and Johnson." *Queen's quarterly,* XLIV (1937), 13-21.

Babcock, R. W. "Dr. Thomas Birch as transcriber of Johnson." *PQ,* XVI (1937), 220-21.

Boas, Guy. "Dr. Johnson on schools and schoolmasters." *English,* I (1937), 537-49.

Brown, Stuart Gerry. "Dr. Johnson and the old order." *Marxist quarterly,* I (1937), 418-30.

Chapman, R. W. "Johnson's letters." *RES,* XIII (1937), 139-76.
An exploratory checklist of Johnson's extant letters, which total more than one thousand.

Clifford, James Lowry. "Lucy Porter to Dr. Johnson: her only known letter." *TLS,* Aug. 28, 1937, p. 620.

Cooper, Lane. "Dr. Johnson on oats and other grains." *PMLA,* LII (1937), 785-802.

Gray, W. Forbes. "Dr. Johnson in Edinburgh." *QR,* CCLXIX (1937), 281-97.

Hazen, Allen T. *Samuel Johnson's prefaces & dedications.* New Haven: Yale University press; London: Oxford University press, 1937. Pp. xxiii + 257.
Rev. in *N & Q,* CLXXIII, 215-16; by I. A. Williams in *LM,* XXXVI, 384. § Hazen reprints the prefaces and dedications which Johnson wrote for books by other persons, gives his reasons for attribution, and furnishes careful bibliographical descriptions and notes. Because of their scarcity the text of many of these pieces will be welcome to Johnsonians, and the technique of the volume can serve as a model for similar works.

Macdonald, Angus. "Johnson as lexicographer." *University of Edinburgh journal,* VIII (1936), 17-23.

Martin, R. G.; Matthews, A. G.; and Nuttall, G. F. "Dr. Johnson and the nonconformists." *Transactions of the Congregational Historical Society,* XII (1936), 330-36.

Powys, Llewelyn. "Dr. Johnson — Idler, Rambler, and straggler." *Dublin magazine,* XII (1937), ii, 9-15.

R., V. Johnson and Scotland: early prejudice?" *N & Q,* CLXXIII (1937), 315-16.

R., V. "Johnson: two sayings." *N & Q,* CLXXII (1937), 116-17.

Reade, Aleyn Lyell. *Johnsonian gleanings.* Part VIII. A miscellany. London: Privately printed for the author by Percy Lund, Humphries & Co., 1937. Pp. v + 216.

Rev. in *N & Q*, CLXXIII, 467-68; in *QR*, CCLXX (1938), 184. § Twenty-seven further notes on topics more or less connected with Johnson's life before 1740.

Reading, J. "Poems by Johnson." Corr. in *TLS*, Sept. 11, 1937, p. 656.

Smith, Neil G. "The piety of Doctor Johnson." *Queen's quarterly*, XLIV (1937), 477-82.

Warburg, Frede. *Samuel Johnson als Biograph.* Hamburg diss. 1937. Pp. 61.

John Locke

(See also *Thomas Hobbes*)

Aaron, R. I. "Great thinkers: (x) John Locke." *Philosophy*, XII (1937), 19-32.

Aaron, R. I. *John Locke.* (Leaders of philosophy series) London, New York, Toronto: Oxford University press, 1937. Pp. ix + 328.

Rev. in S.P.L. in *Jour. of phil.*, XXXIV, 635-38; by A. C. Ewing in *Philosophy*, XII, 478-79; by J. Buchler in *TBR*, Dec. 12, p. 26.

Buchler, Justus. "Act and object in Locke." *Philosophical review*, XLVI (1937), 528-35.

Clapp, James Gordon. *Locke's conception of the mind.* Columbia University diss. 1937. Pp. ix + 122.

Rev. by S.P.L. in *Jour. of phil.*, XXXIV, 638-39.

Curti, Merle. "The great Mr. Locke: America's philosopher, 1783-1861." *Huntington Library bulletin*, no. 11, April, 1937, pp. 107-51.

Ewing, A. C. "Some points in the philosophy of Locke." *Philosophy*, XII (1937), 33-46.

Halpin, Anthony John. "The location of qualitative essence. II. Locke and Meyerson." *New scholasticism*, X (1936), 226-44.

Hazard, Paul. "Note sur la connaissance de Locke en France." *RLC*, XVII (1937), 705-06.

Hofstadter, Albert. *Locke and scepticism.* Columbia University diss. New York: Albee press, 1935. Pp. ii + 134.

Massey, D. "Locke on education." Corr. in *TLS*, Feb. 27, 1937, p. 156.

Petzäll, Aake. *Ethics and epistemology in John Locke's Essay concerning Human Understanding.* Göteborg: Wettergren & Kerber, 1937. Pp. 83.

Rev. by S.P.L. in *Jour. of phil.*, XXXIV, 666-67.

Powys, Llewelyn. "John Locke." *SRL*, June 19, 1937, pp. 3-4.

Reprinted in Powys' *Somerset essays*, 1937.

Sir George Mackenzie

de Beer, E. S. "The letters of Sir George Mackenzie to Evelyn." *N & Q*, CLXXII (1937), 402-03.

Ferguson, F. S. "A bibliography of the works of Sir George Mackenzie, Lord Advocate, founder of the Advocates' Library." *Edinburgh Bibliographical Society transactions,* Vol. I, pt. i (1936), pp. 1-60.
Rev. in *TLS,* Feb. 13, p. 116.

James Macpherson

Jiriczek, Otto L., "Brumo in Macpherson's Ossian." *Beiblatt zur Anglia,* XLVIII (1937), 154-59.

David Mallet

Little, David Mason. "The letters of David Mallett." *Harvard University summaries of theses, 1935,* 1937, pp. 278-81.

Bernard Mandeville

(See also *Susannah Centlivre*)

Anderson, Paul Bunyan. "Cato's obscure counterpart in *The British Journal,* 1722-25." *SP,* XXXIV (1937), 412-28.

Lecler, Joseph. "Libéralisme économique et libre pensée au XVIIIe siècle: Mandeville et la *Fable des Abeilles.*" *Études,* CCXXX (1937), 624-45.

Lady Mary Wortley Montagu

Baker, C. H. Collins. "Lady Mary Wortley Montagu's fiancé." Corr. in *TLS,* Sept. 4, 1937, p. 640.

Henry More

Baker, John Tull. "Henry More and Kant: a note to the second argument on space in the *Transcendental Aesthetic.*" *Philosophical review,* XLVI (1937), 298-306.

Cohen, Leonora D. "Descartes and Henry More on the beast-machine—a translation of their correspondence pertaining to animal automatism." *Annals of science,* I (1936), 48-61.

John Sheffield, Earl of Mulgrave

Irvine, Maurice. "Identification of characters in Mulgrave's 'Essay upon Satyr.'" *SP,* XXXIV (1937), 533-51.

Sir Isaac Newton

Burke, Henry R. "Sir Isaac Newton's formal conception of scientific method." *New scholasticism,* X (1936), 93-115.

David Gregory, Isaac Newton and their circle. Extracts from David Gregory's memoranda, 1677-1708. Edited by W. G. Hiscock. Oxford: Printed for the editor, 1937. Pp. ix + 48.
Not. in *TLS,* June 5, p. 431.

Fay, C. R. "Newton and the gold standard." *Cambridge historical journal,* V (1935), 109-17.

Memoirs of Sir Isaac Newton's life by William Stukeley, M.D., F.R.S. 1752. Being some account of his family and chiefly of the junior part of his life. Edited by A. Hastings White. London: Taylor and Francis, 1936. Pp. xv + 86.

Rev. by E. N. daC. Andrade in *Annals of science,* I (1936), 468.

Osieka, Herbert. *Der Raum und Zeitbegriff bei Newton.* Breslau diss. 1934. Pp. 90.

Pelseneer, J. "Une lettre inédite de Newton à Pepys (23 décembre 1693)." *Osiris,* I (1936), 497-99.

Thomas Otway

Eich, Louis M. "A previous adaptation of *Romeo and Juliet.*" *Quarterly journal of speech,* XXIII (1937), 589-94.

Thomas Paine

Connell, J. M. "Thomas Paine — the man as he was. A bicentenary notice." *Hibbert journal,* XXXV (1937), 213-26.

"The English Voltaire. Tom Paine: citizen of the world." Leading article in *TLS,* Jan. 30, 1937, pp. 65-66.

Ensor, R. C. K. "Tom Paine's bicentenary." *Spectator,* Jan. 29, 1937, pp. 163-64.

Laski, Harold J. "A valiant pamphleteer: the Thomas Paine bicentenary." *Manchester guardian weekly,* Feb. 5, 1937, p. 116.

Pearson, Hesketh. *Tom Paine: friend of mankind.* New York and London: Harper, 1937. Pp. 293.

Rev. in *TLS,* Jan. 30, p. 77; by A. Delagoutte in *EA,* I, 452-53; by C. Van Doren in *HTB,* Jan. 31, p. 5; by J. W. Krutch in *Nation,* Feb. 6, pp. 157-58; by J. H. Preston in *New republic,* July 7, pp. 258-59; by C. Brinton in *SRL,* Feb. 6, p. 7; by F. Winwar in *TBR,* Feb. 7, p. 7. § Despite the subtitle, this is a study of Paine "primarily as a man, not as the founder of a faith or the formulator of a political philosophy" on the basis that "Creeds die; humanity endures; and human beings are much more interesting than their causes or their beliefs."

Serveau, Paul. "Thomas Paine." *Flambeau,* XX (1937), 585-94.

Samuel Pepys

(See also *Sir Isaac Newton*)

Chappell, Edwin. *Leviora Pepysiana.* London: Printed for the author, 1936. Pp. xvi.

Manchée, W. H. "Samuel Pepys and his link with the Huguenots." *Proceedings of the Huguenot Society of London,* xv, iii (1936), 539-41.

Addenda to author's article in *Proceedings,* xv, ii (1935), 317-37.

Murray, Howard. "A new Pepys letter." *Dalhousie review,* XVI (1936), 212-15.

Thomas Percy

(See also *William Shenstone*)

Watkin-Jones, A. "A pioneer Hispanist: Thomas Percy." *Bulletin of Spanish studies,* XIV (1937), 3-9.

Ambrose Philips

The poems of Ambrose Philips. Edited by M. G. Segar. (Percy reprints, no. xiv) Oxford: Blackwell, 1937. Pp. lvi + 192.
Rev. in *TLS,* Dec. 11, p. 943.

Katherine Philips

Alspach, R. K. "The Matchless Orinda." *MLN,* LII (1937), 116-17.
Gives passage from Newcomb's *Bibliotheca* (1712).

Letitia Pilkington

Ponsonby, Lord. "Letitia Pilkington (1712-50) — a curiosity of literature." *English,* I (1937), 297-306.

Alexander Pope

Baker, H. Kendra. *Pope and Bacon: the meaning of "meanest."* A new light on an old belief. London: Bacon Society, 1937. Pp. 24.

Bishop, Carter R. "Alexander Pope and *The Battle of the Poets.*" *West Virginia University studies,* I (1936), 19-27.

Case, Arthur E. "New attributions to Pope." *MP,* XXXIV (1937), 305-13.
This review-article is an able answer to the claims of Norman Ault in *Pope's own miscellany* (1935). See Ault's reply, *MP,* XXXV (1937), 179-87, and Case's counter-reply, pp. 187-91.

Haraszti, Zoltán. "First editions of Alexander Pope." *More books,* XII (1937), 437-50.

Meyerstein, E. H. W. "Concealed verse in Pope's prose." Corr. in *TLS,* July 17, 1937, p. 528.

The prose works of Alexander Pope. Vol. I. The earlier works, 1711-1720. Newly collected and edited by Norman Ault. Oxford: Shakespeare Head press, 1936. Pp. cxxvii + 326. Cf. *PQ,* XVI, 184.
Rev. in *TLS,* Feb. 6, p. 89; by G. Rylands in *Cambridge rev.,* LVIII, 209; by H. Williams in *RES,* XIII, 488-93; by J. Hayward in *Spectator,* Feb. 19, p. 322. § Scholarly reviews of this book should be studied before Ault's attributions are accepted in entirety.

W[ind], E[dgar]. "An emendation of Pope by Lessing." *Journal of Warburg Institute,* I (1937), 78-79.
On a passage in the *Essay on man.*

James Ralph

Kenny, Robert W. "Ralph's *Case of Authors*: its influence on Goldsmith and Isaac D'Israeli." *PMLA,* LII (1937), 104-13.

Allan Ramsay

Weir, J. L. "Allan Ramsay and the Scottish Archers." *N & Q*, CLXXII (1937), 435-38.

Sir Joshua Reynolds

Davies, Martin. "Reynolds in Park Lane: exhibition at Sir Philip Sassoon's." *Connoisseur*, XCIX (1937), 123-29.

Tinker, Chauncey Brewster. "A new portrait of Omai." *Bulletin of the Associates in Fine Arts at Yale University*, VII (1937), 45-47.

Waterhouse, Ellis K. "A review of Reynolds." *Burlington magazine*, LXX (1937), 105-11.

W[ind], E[dgar]. "The mænad under the cross. I. Comments on an observation by Reynolds." *Journal of the Warburg Institute*, I (1937), 70-71.

Samuel Richardson

Liljegren, S. B. *The English sources of Goethe's Gretchen tragedy.* A study on the life and taste of literary motives. (Skrifter utgivna av Kungl. Humanistiska Vetenskapssamfundet i Lund, XXIV) Lund: C. W. K. Gleerup; London: Oxford University press, 1937. Pp. 278.

McKillop, Alan Dugald. *Samuel Richardson, printer and novelist.* Chapel Hill: University of North Carolina press, 1936. Pp. xi + 357. Cf. *PQ*, XVI, 185.

Rev. in *TLS*, April 10, p. 270; by F. T. Wood in *ES*, LXXII, 115-17; by C. G. Stillman in *HTB*, Jan. 10, p. 17; by J. W. Beach in *JEGP*, XXXVI, 438-40; by G. Kitchin in *MLR*, XXXIII (1938), 77-79; by H. Williams in *RES*, XIV (1938), 106-07; by L. Kronenberger in *TBR*, Dec. 27, 1936, p. 5.

Mitrani, Charles. "Richardson and Mme. de Souza." *West Virginia University studies*, I (1936), 28-35.

Mary Robinson

Steen, Marguerite. *The lost one.* A biography of Mary (Perdita) Robinson. London: Methuen, 1937. Pp. xiii + 239.

Rev. by P. Penarth in *Life and letters to-day*, XVII, 182-84; by R. Levin in *Spectator*, May 7, p. 870.

John Wilmot, Earl of Rochester

Crocker, S. F. "Rochester's *Satire against Mankind*: a study of certain aspects of the background." *West Virginia University studies*, III (1937), 57-73.

Legouis, Pierre. "Rochester et sa réputation." *EA*, I (1937), 53-69.

Whitfield, Francis. *Beast in view.* A study of the Earl of Rochester's poetry. (Harvard honors theses in English, no. 9) Cambridge: Harvard University press, 1936. Pp. 75.

Rev. in *TLS*, Feb. 13, p. 113.

Wilson, J. Harold. "The dating of Rochester's 'Scaen.'" *RES,* XIII (1937), 455-58.

Wilson, J. Harold. "Rochester's *Valentinian* and heroic sentiment." *ELH,* IV (1937), 265-73.

Wilson, J. Harold. "Satiric elements in Rochester's *Valentinian.*" *PQ,* XVI (1937), 41-48.

Anna Seward

Addleshaw, S. "The swan of Lichfield: Anna Seward and her circle." *Church quarterly review,* CXXIV (1937), 1-34.

Thomas Shadwell

Iacuzzi, Alfred. "The naïve theme in *The Tempest* as a link between Thomas Shadwell and Ramón de la Cruz." *MLN,* LII (1937), 252-56.

Ward, Charles E. "Shadwell 1658-68." Corr. in *TLS,* April 3, 1937, p. 256.

Anthony Ashley Cooper, Earl of Shaftesbury

Casati, E. "Un carnet de Shaftesbury pendant son voyage en France et en Italie (1711-1713)." *RLC,* XVI (1936), 530-37.

William Shenstone

Churchill, Irving L. "Shenstone's billets." *PMLA,* LII (1937), 114-21.

Lists of songs and ballads, with some comment, which Shenstone sent to Percy during the preparation of the *Reliques.* From the Percy MSS. in the Harvard College Library.

Fisher, J. "Shenstone, Gray, and the 'Moral Elegy.'" *MP,* XXXIV (1937), 273-94.

Humphreys, A. R. *William Shenstone.* An eighteenth-century portrait. Cambridge: University press, 1937. Pp. 136.

Rev. in *N & Q,* CLXXIII, 358; in *TBR,* Jan. 16, 1938, p. 23; in *TLS,* Nov. 13, p. 867; by J. A. E. Smart in *Cambridge rev.,* LIX (1938), 217.

Williams, Marjorie. *William Shenstone.* A chapter in eighteenth century taste. Birmingham: Cornish Brothers, 1935. Pp. 152.

Not. by G. Tillotson in *MLR,* XXXII, 661-62.

Adam Smith

Goetz-Girey, Robert. "Réflexions sur la théorie du capital d'Adam Smith." *Revue d'histoire économique et sociale,* XXIII (1936-37), 311-32.

Scott, W. R. "New MSS. relating to Adam Smith." *Economic history review,* VII (1937), 229-30.

Scott, William Robert. *Adam Smith as student and professor.* With unpublished documents, including parts of the "Edinburgh Lectures," a draft of *The Wealth of Nations,* extracts from the muniments of the University of Glasgow and cor-

respondence. (Glasgow University publications, XLVI) Glasgow: Jackson, Son & Co., 1937. Pp. xxiv + 445.
Rev. in *TLS,* Dec. 4, p. 922.

Vanderblue, Homer B. "An incident in the life of Adam Smith, Commissioner of His Majesty's Customs." *American economic review,* XXVII (1937), 305-08.

Tobias Smollett

Brown, Samuel H. "Tobias George Smollett, physician." University of Pennsylvania *General magazine and historical chronicle,* XXXIX (1937), 252-55.

Powell, L. F. "William Huggins and Tobias Smollett." *MP,* XXXIV (1936), 179-92.

Roberts, W. "Gainsborough and Smollett." Corr. in *TLS,* Sept. 18, 1937, p. 675. Cf. corr., *ibid.,* by Roberts, Sept. 25, p. 695, by L. Rice-Oxley, Oct. 2, p. 715, by M. H. Grant, Oct. 9, p. 735, by L. F. Powell, Oct. 16, p. 759.
On the identification of a landscape painter in *Humphrey Clinker* as Gainesborough or John Taylor.

Sir Richard Steele

Inkle and Yarico album. Selected and arranged by Lawrence Marsden Price. Berkeley: University of California press, 1937. Pp. 171.
Rev. in *TLS,* Jan. 1, 1938, p. 8. § By reprinting, quoting, summarizing, and commenting Price has given a thorough history of the story which Steele wrote for *Spectator* No. 11 and of its great vogue in various forms in England and on the Continent. Rarely can the vicissitudes of one short narrative so well illustrate a century of mode and taste.

McCoy, Raymond F. "Hygienic recommendations of *The Ladies Library.*" *Bulletin of the Institute of the History of Medicine,* IV (1936), 367-72.

Laurence Sterne

Baird, Theodore. "The time-scheme of *Tristram Shandy* and a source." *PMLA,* LI (1936), 803-20.

Behrmann, Friedrich. *Laurence Sterne und sein Einfluss auf die englische Prosa des achtzehnten Jahrhunderts.* Zürich diss. 1936. Pp. 141.

Mander, Gerald P. "The shorn lamb." Corr. in *TLS,* July 17, 1937, p. 528.

Work, James A. "Tristram Shandy." Corr. in *TLS,* Sept. 4, 1937, p. 640.

Jonathan Swift

Allen, Robert Joseph. "Swift's earliest political tract and Sir William Temple's essays." *Harvard studies and notes in philology and literature,* XIX (1937), 3-12.

Duff, I. F. Grant. "A one-sided sketch of Swift." *Psychoanalytic quarterly,* VI (1937), 238-59.

Abstract in *Journal of mental and nervous disease,* LXXXVI (1937), 729. § Duff uses various works of Swift, especially the "terror-ridden" *Gulliver's travels,* to explain by symbols supposed obscure traits of Swift.

Gold, Maxwell B. *Swift's marriage to Stella.* Together with unprinted and misprinted letters. Cambridge: Harvard University press, 1937. Pp. x + 189.

Rev. in *N & Q,* CLXXII, 359-60; in *TLS*, April 24, p. 304; by G. L. Rose in *Dalhousie rev.*, XVII, 121-22; by E. Pons in *EA*, I, 537-40; by C. Van Doren in *HTB*, March 21, p. 2; by H. Davis in *MP,* XXXIV, 434-35; by H. Williams in *RES*, XIV (1938), 108-10; by S. Leslie in *Spectator,* May 14, pp. 913-14.

Dr. Gold has devoted the greater part of this interesting study to a systematic presentation and evaluation of the evidence *pro* and *contra* as to Swift's supposed marriage to Stella. To the evidence already available he has added new evidence from manuscript notes in an interleaved copy of Lord Orrery's *Remarks* (1751) now in the Harvard College Library. These notes are partly in Orrery's own hand, partly in that of an amanuensis who wrote under his direction. The entries which assert the marriage avowedly depend on information derived from Mrs. Whiteway. They constitute additional proof that Mrs. Whiteway, like many other persons who had been close to Swift, believed that a marriage had taken place, and that shortly before Stella's death Swift had offered to acknowledge it.

In his weighing of the evidence, Mr. Gold stresses the fact that from about 1750 there are many assertions of the marriage, and only one recorded denial. But this is only what one would expect. Most gossip is positive rather than negative; and in 1750 none of the principals was alive to issue an authoritative denial.

Mr. Gold arrays the evidence (which seems to him conclusive) and discusses the credibility of the witnesses; but he never examines the inherent credibility of the supposed facts. One will look in vain for any treatment of so fundamental a matter as the laws, civil and ecclesiastical, applicable to marriage in the Ireland of 1716, and the strictness or laxity with which these laws were observed. (See the communication from T. Percy C. Kirkpatrick in *TLS*, June 19, 1937, p. 464.)

A definite discussion of this much-vexed (and probably insoluble) problem should at least take into account the following obstinate questions:

(1) Does what we know of Stella make it reasonable to suppose that she should have asked for an unacknowledged and empty ceremony of marriage? Or does what we know of Swift make it seem likely that he should have consented to such a sham? As Mr. Quintana has put the matter: "Both Swift and Stella lived with superb pride by the code of rational conduct. If they broke this code to participate in a secret ceremony that had no significance, the explanation must be sought not in the realm of reason but of nonsense." (p. 233)

(2) Was Dr. Ashe, Bishop of Clogher, the sort of man who would consent to perform a marriage under conditions that were highly irregular, and perhaps illegal—a marriage performed in his garden rather than in his church, apparently without witnesses, and certainly never recorded? Or, if out of friendship for Swift he did consent, is it likely that within eighteen months (Ashe died 27 February 1718) he should have betrayed the confidence of one of his close friends by blabbing the secret to his son's tutor?

(3) Was Dr. Sheridan so unworthy a priest, and so disloyal a friend, that, while Swift was still alive (Sheridan died in 1738), he should have revealed in gossip to Mrs. Whiteway a secret entrusted to him by Stella on her death-bed "before he gave her the Sacrament for the last time"?

Mr. Gold might better have devoted to the discussion of such matters as these the pages (126-46) in which, on the authority of Krafft-Ebing, he seeks to show that Swift was the viction of "sexual anaesthesia." *Post mortem* diagnosis two centuries after the fact is not a very profitable form of speculation.

One may add that the "unprinted and misprinted letters" referred to in the title, which fill pp. 147-80, are from originals in the Pierpont Morgan Library. They are a valuable supplement to Ball's edition of the *Correspondence,* but have no bearing on the subject of Mr. Gold's essay. R. K. R.

Kirkpatrick, T. Percy C. "Swift and Stella." *TLS,* June 19, 1937, p. 464.

Kruuse, Jens. "Holberg og Swift." *Fem danske Studier* tilegnet Vilh. Andersen den 16. Oktober 1934. (Fililogisk-historiske Samfund. Studier fra Sprog-og Oldtids Forskning. Nr. 167) Copenhagen: P. Branner, 1934. Pp. 48-67.

Linn, Irving. "Dean Swift, Pope Innocent, and Oliver Wendell Holmes." *PQ,* XVI (1937), 317-20.

Suggests source for Swift's figure of man as an inverted tree.

Newman, Bertram. *Jonathan Swift.* London: George Allen & Unwin, 1937. Pp. 432.

Rev. in *QR,* CCLXIX, 184; in *TLS,* June, 5, p. 425; by R. H. Murray in *Contemp. rev.,* CLII, pp. 250-51; by E. Blunden in *Fortnightly,* CXLVII, 755-56; by G. F. Whicher in *HTB,* Aug. 29, p. 6; by P. O'Connor in *Life and letters today,* XVII, 181-82; by F. A. Barrett in *LM,* XXXVI, 303-04; by L. Bogan in *Nation,* Aug. 28, pp. 223-24; by H. M. Jones in *SRL,* Sept. 18, p. 16; by L. Kronenberger in *TBR,* Sept. 5, p. 5.

Nicolson, Marjorie, and Mohler, Nora M. "The scientific background of Swift's *Voyage to Laputa.*" *Annals of science,* II (1937), 299-334.

Nicolson, Marjorie, and Mohler, Nora M. "Swift's 'Flying Island' in the *Voyage to Laputa.*" *Annals of Science,* II (1937), 405-30.

These two articles present abundant evidence that Swift for the objects and instruments of his satire in Part III of *Gulliver* drew upon the works of seventeenth and eighteenth century scientists, especially the *Philosophical transactions* of the Royal Society. Such source studies add considerably to our knowledge of Swift's mind and art.

Petitjean, A. M. "Swift et Stella." *Cahiers du Sud,* XXIV (1937), 720-33.

The poems of Jonathan Swift. Edited by Harold Williams. 3 vols. Oxford: Clarendon press, 1937. Pp. lxii, vii, vii + 1242.

Rev. in *HTB,* Aug. 29, p. 17; in *TLS,* Aug. 21, pp. 597-98; by Rothschild in *Cambridge rev.,* LIX, 147-48; by A. L. Rowse in *Criterion,* XVII (1938), 305-11; by M. J. MacManus in *Dublin mag.,* XII, iv, 52-54; by S. Potter in *LM,* XXXVI, 477-78; by H. Davis in *MP,* XXXV (1938), 335-38; by E. Wilson in *New republic,* Dec. 8, pp. 138-39; by S. Leslie in *Nineteenth century,* CXXII, 495-96; by H. M. Jones in *SRL,* Sept. 18, p. 16; by W. A. Eddy in *TBR,* Dec. 26, p. 2.

Mr. Williams has edited Swift's poems with such thoroughness and scholarly competence that his edition may be regarded as certainly definitive. In the three handsome volumes before us Swift, the poet, at last has his garland and singing robes about him in proper form. Now that the canon of his verse has been purged of the apocrypha, and the poems printed in chronological order with adequate commentary, one can much better appraise Swift's qualities as poet. The orderly reading of the poems, many of which are now for the first time properly dated, does much to illuminate the character of the man.

Each poem is preceded by a headnote which cites and evaluates the various authorities for the text, discusses the date and, in all doubtful cases, the evidence for and against Swift's authorship, and concisely states the occasion which called for the poem. The text is printed from a single manuscript, first edition, or other early text, with due entry of variant readings from the other authorities. Often, however, one is left in doubt as to the reasons which governed the editor's choice of one authority rather than another to serve as basis for his text. It may well be that in many cases there were no adequate grounds for determining precedence, and that the choice as between a manuscript copy (in Stella's hand, for example) and a first edition was of necessity an arbitrary one. In spelling, punctuation, and the use of italics and capitals, each text conforms scrupulously to the chosen original. Many readers will doubtless be annoyed because they must look to the commentary at the bottom of the page to interpret the names which appear cryptically abbreviated with first and last letters and intervening dashes; but the principle of rigorous fidelity could hardly have permitted a different procedure. A tangle of square brackets would very seriously have marred the beauty of the page.

Mr. Williams has done with excellent competence a task that very much needed to be done. Students of Swift, and of eighteenth-century England, are greatly in his debt. R. K. R.

Pons, E. "Du nouveau sur le 'Journal à Stella.'" *EA,* I (1937), 210-29.

A study of the fragmentary MS. of the *Journal* leads Pons to believe that the defacement of the MS. is Swift's own playful work and was done before the letters were ever sent to Stella. Reasons and methods in this play are specified, and the "little language" comes in for some new interpretations.

Pons, E. "Rabelais et Swift à propos du Lilliputien." *Mélanges offerts à M. Abel Lefranc.* Paris: E. Droz, 1936. Pp. 219-28.

Quintana, Ricardo. *The mind and art of Jonathan Swift.* London, New York: Oxford University press, 1936. Pp. xii + 398. Cf. *PQ,* XVI, 187.

Rev. by A. L. Rowse in *Criterion,* XVII, 164-68; by C. Van Doren in *HTB,* Jan. 24, p. 4; by F. A. Barrett in *LM,* XXXV, 528; by G. Kitchin in *MLR,* XXXIII (1938), 73-74; by L. A. Landa in *MP,* XXXV, 202-04; by H. Williams in *RES,* XIII, 235-38; by W. T. Laprade in *SAQ,* XXXVI, 241-42; by J. Hayward in *Spectator,* Jan. 15, p. 91.

Sitwell, Edith. *I live under a black sun.* A novel. London: Victor Gollancz, 1937. Pp. 400.

Rev. in *TLS,* Oct. 2, p. 713; by C. Row in *Life and letters to-day,* XVII, 182-83; by P. M. Jack in *TBR,* Feb. 27, 1938, p. 21. § A novel about the Jonathan-Stella-Vanessa triangle, with changes in framework and detail and with the characters brought into the twentieth century.

Teerink, H. *A bibliography of the writings in prose and verse of Jonathan Swift, D.D.* The Hague: Martinus Nijhoff, 1937. Pp. xi + 434.

Rev. in *TLS,* March 20, p. 228; by M. J. MacManus in *Dublin mag.,* XII, iii, 55-56; by Rothschild (with additions and corrections) in *Library,* XVIII, 224-28; by E. A. Baker in *MLR,* XXXII, 614-15; by H. Williams in *RES,* XIII, 366-72.

A comprehensive and detailed bibliography of Swift has long been one of the major needs of scholars in eighteenth-century literature. It is matter of very deep regret to find that in spite of Dr. Teerink's ponderous and laborious volume this important work still remains to be done. A competently trained bibliographer who may undertake the task will, of course, find that his work has been to some extent lightened by Dr. Teerink's collections; but he will need to reexamine every single volume for himself. In the meantime scholars must be content to use a very inadequate and unbelievably clumsy compilation.

It would have been hard to devise a more inconvenient arrangement of the materials. The 1574 titles are disposed into six "sections." Section I contains "collected works," ranging in date from 1710 to 1935. But the term "collected works'' is interpreted to include any publication which contains more than a single piece (except that the various editions of the volume containing *A Tale of a Tub, The Battle of the Books,* and *The Mechanical Operation of the Spirit* are recorded by themselves in Section II). Thus, a volume containing three of Swift's sermons, or *The Intelligencer* of 1729, or a volume of Swift's letters is entered under ''collected works'' along with the *Miscellanies* and the collected editions of Swift's *Works.* Section III is devoted to *Gulliver's Travels.* Sections IV and V are headed respectively ''Separate Works'' and ''Doubtful.'' But some of the pieces entered in Section IV are very doubtful; and many of those entered in Section V are certainly spurious. Dr. Teerink very rarely discusses the soundness of an attribution; though he continues to insist that *The History of John Bull* is by Swift rather than by Arbuthnot. Section VI is devoted to ''Biography and Criticism''; but it is here that one finds imitations and parodies of *Gulliver's Travels,* which might more reasonably have been included in Section III. The user of the volume soon learns that he cannot hope to master the intricate jumble of entries. Only by constant use of the index can one find one's way at all.

Dr. Teerink disarmingly confesses in his Preface that when he began his work he ''had practically no experience of what a proper description of books means.'' Unfortunately he has never acquired this ''experience.'' A list of the particulars in which his descriptions fall short of what scientific bibliography considers ''proper'' would be a long one. Most serious is the lack of any information as to the physical construction of a volume. The preface warns us that the terms *folio, quarto, octavo,* etc., are to be understood to be merely indications of approximate *size* and do not refer to the folding of the paper! On examination many of the items described as ''8vo'' (e.g., Nos. 764, 875, 970, 1075, 1081) turn out to be small quartos. Collations are by pages only. For eighteenth-century editions of Swift's own writings — or at the very least for editions which appeared during his life-time — one has a right to expect a full collation by gatherings with due notice of cancellations and insets. Only very exceptionally is there any attempt to determine month and day of publication.

It is distressing that so much industry should have been expended with such unsatisfactory results. R. K. R.

James Thomson

Kern, Jean B.''The fate of James Thomson's *Edward and Eleanora.*'' *MLN,* LII (1937), 500-02.

Sir John Vanbrugh

Vincent, Howard P. ''Two unpublished letters of Vanbrugh.'' *N & Q,* CLXXIII (1937), 128-29.

George Walker

MacMullan, Hugh H. ''The satire of Walker's *Vagabond* on Rousseau and Godwin.'' *PMLA,* LII (1937), 215-29.

Horace Walpole

Finberg, Hilda F. ''Radnor House, Twickenham: drawing by Samuel Scott.'' *Burlington magazine,* II (1937), 168-71.

On a drawing (which includes a prospect of Strawberry Hill) once the property of Horace Walpole.

Gray, W. Forbes. ''Horace Walpole: two unpublished letters.'' *TLS,* Sept. 11, 1937, p. 660.

Select observations. Being a compendium of passages and opinions illustrative of men and manners: assembled by the Honourable

Horace Walpole. New Haven: Bibliographical press, 1937. Pp. 7.

Stuart, Dorothy Margaret. "Horace Walpole in Kensington." *English,* I (1937), 389-99.

The Yale edition of Horace Walpole's correspondence. Edited by W. S. Lewis. Horace Walpole's correspondence with the Rev. William Cole. Edited by W. S. Lewis and A. Dayle Wallace. 2 vols. New Haven: Yale University press, 1937. Pp. lxii + 388, 464.

Rev. in *TLS,* Oct. 30, pp. 789-90 (cf. corr., *ibid.,* by S. Gaselee, Nov. 13, p. 871, and reviewer, Nov. 20, p. 891); by H. S. Bennett in *Cambridge rev.,* LIX (1938), 191-92; by S. C. Chew in *HTB,* Oct. 17, pp. 1-2; by J. W. Krutch in *Nation,* Dec. 11, p. 653; by L. Bacon in *SRL,* Nov. 20, p. 7; by J. Hayward in *Spectator,* Dec. 17, pp. 1111-12; by P. W. Wilson in *TBR,* Nov. 7, p. 3.

Though Horace Walpole was playwright, novelist, poet, essayist, historian, iconographer, connoisseur, Member of Parliament, and wit, the ruling passion of this man of taste was his letters. And the quantity and quality of these letters make of him the annalist of his age. He chose his correspondents with care, for he was choosing a subject as well as a person; W. S. Lewis has seen that Walpole used each major correspondence as the channel for a special interest, and has wisely elected to follow chronology within the unit of a single correspondence. This procedure, it must be noted, is also imperative for practical reasons, such as the very large body of letters both to and from Walpole, the fact that new letters continue to come to light, and the special knowledge necessary for the annotation of a single correspondence.

The initiation of a complete edition of Walpole's correspondence becomes a scholarly event of tremendous importance. The editor of the *Yale edition* proposes a total of about fifty volumes to be issued during the next fifteen years. Lewis has spared no pains to collect the manuscripts or photostats of existing letters to and by Walpole: at present his gathering contains in the original or in reproduction about sixty-two hundred of the estimated total of seventy-two hundred letters which have survived in some form, and approximately four hundred letters by Walpole and sixteen hundred to him will be printed in entirety for the first time. The chief advantages which this edition will have over the Cunningham and the Toynbee editions are the organization by correspondence, the inclusion of letters to Walpole, the addition of many unpublished letters, the accurate text, and the detailed annotation. For the encyclopedic documentation (in itself sufficient reason for a new edition) Lewis is able to draw upon the resources of a great university library and of his own exceptional collection. In the latter may be found, among other interesting items, such illustrative material as two-thirds of the located volumes in Walpole's personal library, many of them annotated; hundreds of letters to Sir Joseph Banks, George Selwyn, and Townshend; one quarter of the Grenville correspondence; copies of Lady Mary Coke's unpublished journals; Bentley's designs and preliminary sketches for Strawberry Hill, Gray's poems, and the *Memoirs*; dozens of water colors, family portraits, and Walpoleana — as substance for the comment after the mastery of "learning's crabbed text." Moreover, Lewis has in preparation various supplemental studies which will aid in the reconstruction of Walpole and his England — the iconography of Walpole; his library; his autobiography; the guests at Strawberry Hill; a bibliography of the detached pieces printed at the private press; and even Walpole's greatest enemy, the gout.

Lewis, his coadjutors, and the Yale University Press deserve the best cooperation of students, collectors, and librarians in such a magnificent undertaking. The two volumes just published, the correspondence between Walpole and the antiquary William Cole, give evidence of great editorial diligence. Only one hitherto unpublished letter by Walpole himself appears, but about three-quarters of the Cole letters are new. The notes are a thorough commentary, and the excellent illustrations really illustrate. The next correspondence to appear will be that of Walpole and Mme. du Deffand in six volumes (probably in 1938), to be followed by one volume containing the Walpole-Gray-West-Ashton correspondence and by two volumes of the Walpole-Montagu letters.

Horace Walpole, the patron of fine printing, the master of the epistolary word, the chronicler of large and small, may rest secure of his proper fame.

Izaak Walton

Bennett, R. E. "Walton's use of Donne's letters." *PQ,* XVI (1937), 30-34.

Coon, Arthur M. "The family of Izaak Walton," Corr. in *TLS,* May 15, 1937, p. 380.

Coon, Arthur M. "Izaak Walton's mother." Corr. in *TLS,* Dec. 25, 1937, p. 980.

McElderry, B. R., jr. "Walton's *Lives* and Gillman's *Life of Coleridge.*" *PMLA,* LII (1937), 412-22.

Oliver, Peter. *A new chronicle of the Compleat Angler.* New York: Paisley press; London: Williams & Norgate, 1936. Pp. xv + 301.

Rev. in *TLS,* June 12, p. 452.

Joseph Warton

Trowbridge, Hoyt. "Joseph Warton on the imagination." *MP,* XXXV (1937), 73-87.

John Wesley

Body, Alfred H. *John Wesley and education.* London: Epworth press, 1936. Pp. 168.

Bowen, Marjorie. *Wrestling Jacob.* A study of the life of John Wesley and some members of the family. London: Heinemann, 1937. Pp. x + 395.

Rev. by R. Church in *LM,* XXXVII (1938), 349-50; by C. E. Vulliamy in *Spectator,* Nov. 26, p. 960.

Greeves, Frederic. "John Wesley and divine guidance." *London quarterly and Holborn review,* July, 1937, pp. 379-95.

Harrison, G. Elsie. *Haworth parsonage.* A study of Wesley and the Brontës. London: Epworth press, 1937. Pp. 45.

Rev. in *TLS,* Sept. 4, p. 642.

Harrison, G. Elsie. *Son to Susanna.* The private life of John Wesley. London: Ivor Nicholson and Watson, 1937. Pp. 354.

Rev. in *TLS,* Oct. 16, p. 746; by R. Church in *LM,* XXXVII (1938), 349-50.

Ingram, W. G. "John Wesley's books." Corr. in *TLS,* Aug. 14, 1937, p. 592. Cf. corr., *ibid.,* Sept. 18, p. 675.

Joy, James Richard. *John Wesley's awakening.* New York, Cincinnati, Chicago: Methodist Book Concern, 1937. Pp. 128.

Lee, Umphrey. *John Wesley and modern religion.* Nashville: Cokesbury press, 1936. Pp. xiii + 354.

Rev. by W. W. Sweet in *AHR,* XLII, 590; by A. W. Nagler in *Church hist.,*

VI, 79-80; by J. H. Holmes in *HTB*, Oct. 4, 1936, p. 17; by G. C. Cell in *Jour. of religion*, XVII, 341-43; by A. C. Wyckoff in *SRL*, Aug. 7, p. 18; by R. Goodloe in *Southwest rev.*, XXII, 208-10.

MacArthur, Kathleen Walker. *The economic ethics of John Wesley.* New York, Cincinnati, Chicago: Abingdon press, 1936. Pp. 166.

Rev. by A. W. Nagler in *Church hist.*, VI, 194-95.

Piette, Maximin. *John Wesley in the evolution of Protestantism.* Translated by J. B. Howard. New York: Sheed & Ward, 1937. Pp. xlviii + 569.

Rev. by N.W.P. in *Downside rev.*, LV, 567-71; by C. E. Vulliamy in *Spectator*, Nov. 26, p. 960. § Translation of the work issued twelve years ago.

Shepherd, T. B. "John Wesley and Matthew Prior." *London quarterly and Holborn review*, July, 1937, pp. 368-73.

John Wilkes

Bonno, G. "Lettre inédite d'un correspondant parisien de John Wilkes." *RLC*, XVII (1937), 712-14.

Murray, Edward Croft. "Hogarth's portrait of John Wilkes." *British Museum quarterly*, XI (1937), 132-35.

John Wolcot

Gale, Fred. R. "Peter Pindar and Canning." *N & Q*, CLXXIII (1937), 255-57.

Mabbott, T. O. "A poem by John Wolcot." *N & Q*, CLXXIII (1937), 97-98.

Mary Wollstonecraft

Four new letters of Mary Wollstonecraft and Helen M. Williams. Edited by Benjamin P. Kurtz and Carrie C. Autrey. Berkeley: University of California press, 1937. Pp. 82.

Rev. in *N & Q*, CLXXIII, 198; in *TLS*, Sept. 11, p. 658; by M. R. Adams in *Amer. lit.*, IX, 386-88; by L. Bacon in *SRL*, Jan. 15, 1938, p. 12; by C. Dean in *TBR*, Aug. 8, p. 8.

Preedy, George R. *This shining woman: Mary Wollstonecraft Godwin, 1759-1797.* London: Collins, 1937. Pp. 324.

Rev. in *TLS*, Feb. 20, p. 126; by C. B. Stillman in *HTB*, Sept. 12, p. 20 (Cf. corr., *ibid.*, by D. B. Woolsey, Sept. 26, p. 18); by C. Dean in *TBR*, July 11, p. 6; by A. Cowie in *SRL*, July 10, p. 12.

Sir Christopher Wren

The fourteenth volume of the Wren Society. Engravings of St. Paul's Cathedral and Part II of the building accounts for the years 1685-95. Oxford: Printed for the Wren Society at the University press, 1937. Pp. xxiii + 171, with 54 plates.

Rev. in *Journal of the Royal Institute of British Architects*, XLIV, 696; in *TLS*, April 10, p. 269.

Summerson, John. "The tyranny of intellect: a study of the mind of Sir Christopher Wren, in relation to the thought of his time." *Journal of the Royal Institute of British Architects,* XLIV (1937), 373-90.

Webb, Geoffrey. *Wren.* (Great lives series) London: Duckworth, 1937. Pp. 144.

Rev. in *Journal of the Royal Institute of British Architects,* XLIV, 956; in *TLS,* June 12, p. 441; by C. Hobhouse in *Spectator,* June 4, p. 1060.

William Wycherley

Seely, Frederick F. "The last eighteenth century performance of Wycherley's *The Country Wife.*" *PQ,* XVI (1937), 217-18.

Vincent, Howard P. "William Wycherley's *Miscellany Poems.*" *PQ,* XVI (1937), 145-48.

Edward Young

Mutschmann, H. "Der Schlüssel zu Youngs 'Nachtgedanken.'" *Englische Kultur in sprachwissenschaftlicher Deutung.* Max Deutschbein zum 60. Geburtstage. Leipzig: Verlag von Quelle & Meyer, 1936. Pp. 101-08.

V. THE CONTINENTAL BACKGROUND

Artz, Frederick B. "Les débuts de l'éducation technique en France (1500-1700)." *Revue d'histoire moderne,* XII (1937), 469-519.

Baldensperger, Fernand. "Pour une 'revaluation' littéraire du XVIIe siècle classique." *Revue d'histoire littéraire de la France,* XLIV (1937), 1-15.

Balet, Leo, and Gerhard, E. *Die Verbürgerlichung der deutschen Kunst, Literatur und Musik im 18. Jahrhundert.* (Sammlung Musik-Wissenschaftlicher Abhandlungen, Bd. 18) Leipzig, Strassburg, Zürich: Heitz, 1936. Pp. 508.

Rev. by F. Benoit in *Revue germanique,* XXVIII, 196; by W. Ziegenfuss in *Zeitschrift für Ästhetik und allgemeine Kunstwissenschaft,* XXXI, 74-76.

Bartz, Karl. *Louis XIV.* Translated from the German by L. Marie Sieveking. London: Constable, 1937. Pp. vii + 346.

de Beauvillé, Guillemette. *Gasparo Gozzi, journaliste vénitien du dix-huitième siècle.* Paris: Lipschutz, 1937. Pp. 263.

Rev. by P. Renucci in *Revue des études italiennes,* II, 394-96. § Chap. vi: "Gozzi moraliste et imitateur d'Addison."

Beck, Thor J. *Northern antiquities in French learning and literature (1755-1855).* A study in preromantic ideas. Vol. II. The Odin legend and the Oriental fascination. New York: Institute of French studies, 1935. Pp. 362.

Rev. by E. Haugen in *Germanic rev.,* XII, 139-40; by V. H. in *Neophilologus,* XXIII, 75; by P. Van Tieghem in *RLC,* XVII, 594-97.

Brown, Harcourt. "The utilitarian motive in the age of Descartes." *Annals of science,* I (1936), 182-92.

Clayton, Vista. *The prose poem in French literature of the eigh-*

teenth century. New York: Institute of French studies, 1936. Pp. xi + 248.

Contains chapter on the influence of *Ossian.*

Colleville, Maurice. *La renaissance du lyrisme dans la poésie allemande au XVIIIe siècle (période préclassique).* Paris: Librarie Henri Didier, [1936]. Pp. 671.

With special reference to Günther, Brockes, Haller, Hagedorn, Gleim, and Uz.

Crisafulli, Allesandro S. "Parallels to ideas in the *Lettres Persanes.*" *PMLA,* LII (1937), 773-77.

Suggests possible influence of Malebranche, Leibniz, and Shaftesbury.

Feugère, Anatole. "Le mouvement religieux dans la littérature du XVIIe siècle." *Revue des cours et conférences,* XXXVIII, i (1936), 10-21; iii (1937), 234-43; iv, 299-308; vi, 533-46; viii, 713-25; x, 115-30; xi, 236-48; xiii, 455-67; xv, 645-58; xvi, 721-35.

Fidas-Justiniani, J.-E. "Discours sur la raison classique." *Revue des cours et conférences,* XXXVIII (1937), ix, 81-93; x, 177-89; xi, 277-87; xii, 372-84; xiv, 561-76; xv, 659-69.

Gillies, A. "Herder's essay on Shakespeare: 'Das Herz der Untersuchung.'" *MLR,* XXXII (1937), 262-80.

Gillies, A. "Ludwig Tieck's English studies at the University of Göttingen, 1792-1794." *JEGP,* XXXVI (1937), 206-23.

Giraud, Victor. "Catholicisme et romantisme. I. Les précurseurs." *Revue des deux mondes,* XXXIX (1937), 580-613.

Gradenwitz, Peter. "Mid-eighteenth-century transformations of style." *Music and letters,* XVIII (1937), 265-75.

Hastings, Hester. *Man and beast in French thought of the eighteenth century.* (Johns Hopkins studies in Romance literatures and languages, Vol. XXVII) Baltimore: Johns Hopkins press, 1936. Pp. 297.

Hazard, Paul. "Les origines philosophiques de l'homme de sentiment." *Romanic review,* XXVIII (1937), 318-41.

Kot, Stanislas. "Le mouvement antitrinitaire au XVIe et au XVIIe siècle." *Humanisme et Renaissance,* IV (1937), 16-58, 109-56.

Léon, Paul L. "L'idée de volonté générale chez J.-J. Rousseau et ses antécédents historiques." *Archives de philosophie du droit et de sociologie juridique,* VI (1936), 148-200.

Levin, Lawrence Meyer. *The political doctrine of Montesquieu's Esprit des Lois: its classical background.* New York: Institute of French studies, 1936. Pp. xiii + 359.

Rev. by E. Carcassonne in *Revue d'histoire littéraire de la France,* XLIV, 283-85.

Louis-Jaray, Gabriel. "La maçonnerie française, l'Angleterre et les États-Unis au XVIIIe siècle." *Mercure de France,* CCLXXVI (1937), 316-29.

McClelland, I. L. *The origins of the Romantic movement in Spain.*

(Studies in Hispanic literatures) Liverpool: Institute of Hispanic studies, 1937. Pp. xii + 402.

Rev. in *TLS*, June 5, p. 425; by A. F. G. Bell in *Bulletin of Spanish studies*, XIV, 156-57; by J. T. Reid in *Hispania*, XX, 294-95; by N. B. Adams in *Hispanic rev.*, VI (1938), 80-82; by R. Hilton in *MLR*, XXXII, 643-45; by W. J. E. in *Oxford mag.*, LVI, 100-01; by S. A. Stoudemide in *Romanic rev.*, XXVIII, 360-61.

Marni, Archimede. *Allegory in the French heroic poem of the seventeenth century.* Princeton: University press for the University of Cincinnati, 1936. Pp. 211.

Rev. by F. J. Tanquerey in *MLR*, XXXII, 466-67.

Miller, Minnie M. "The English people as portrayed in certain French journals, 1700-1760." *MP*, XXXIV (1937), 365-76.

"Molière among the heretics. The classic tradition in France." Leading article in *TLS*, Jan. 9, 1937, pp. 17-18.

Morrissey, Robert B. "A Jesuit ahead of his time." *Thought*, XII (1937), 666-76.

On Girolamo Saccheri (1667-1733), whose *Euclides* was the first non-Euclidean geometry.

Pagès, G. "Histoire de France: fin des temps modernes (1660-1789)." *Revue historique: bulletins critiques*, CLXXXI (1937), 384-404.

Palmer, Robert R. "Posterity and the hereafter in eighteenth-century French thought." *JMH*, IX (1937), 145-68.

Parker, Harold T. *The cult of antiquity and the French Revolutionaries.* A study of the development of the Revolutionary spirit. Chicago: University of Chicago press, 1937. Pp. ix + 215.

Rev. by J. H. Stewart in *AHR*, XLIII (1938), 447; by G. B. in *Jour. of phil.*, XXXIV, 270; by C. Becker in *Philosophical rev.*, XLVI, 440-41.

Pascal, R. *Shakespeare in Germany, 1740-1815.* Cambridge: University press, 1937. Pp. x + 199.

Rev. in *TLS*, Oct. 9, p. 730; by N. S. in *Cambridge rev.*, LIX, 155; by A. R. in *Criterion*, XVII (1938), 378. § Collection of texts of Shakespeare criticism and translations, with long introduction.

Patterson, Warner Forrest. *Three centuries of French poetic theory.* A critical history of the chief arts of poetry in France (1328-1630). (University of Michigan publications. Language and literature, Vols. XIV-XV) 2 vols. Ann Arbor: University of Michigan press, 1935. Pp. xx + 978, 523.

Rev. by L. Cons in *MLN*, LII, 122-24; by B. Weinberg in *MP*, XXXIV, 319-22; by W. L. Wiley in *SP*, XXXIV, 252-57. § An important work for the French background of neo-classic literary theory.

Pennink, R. *Nederland en Shakespeare: achttiende eeuw en vroege romantiek.* The Hague: Martinus Nijhoff, 1936. Pp. viii + 304.

Rev. by R. J. Barnouw in *Germanic rev.*, XII, 141-42; by B. W. Downs in *MLR*, XXXII, 610-12.

Rasch, Wolfdietrich. *Freundschaftskult und Freundschaftsdichtung im deutschen Schrifttum des 18. Jahrhunderts vom Ausgang des Barock bis zu Klopstock.* (Deutsche Vierteljahrsschrift für Literaturwissenschaft und Geistesgeschichte, Bd. 21) Halle: Niemeyer, 1936. Pp. x + 266.

Rev. by H. Rüdiger in *Literatur,* XXXIX, 375-76.

Roth, Leon. *Descartes' Discourse on Method.* Oxford: Clarendon press, 1937. Pp. viii + 142.

Rev. in *TLS,* Oct. 23, p. 785; by A.D.W. in *Oxford mag.,* LVI (1938), 400; by A. L. in *Studies: an Irish quar. rev.,* XXVI, 691-92. § A good critical study, not an edition. The tercentenary of the publication of the famous *Discours* has brought forth many articles on Descartes and Cartesianism; see Roth's essay in *Mind,* XLVI (1937), 32-43.

Rumney, J. "Anglo-jewry as seen through foreign eyes (1730-1830)." *Transactions of the Jewish Historical Society of England, 1932-1935,* XIII (1936), 323-40.

Searles, Colbert. "Chapelain and the genesis of the French Academy." *MP,* XXXIV (1937), 355-64.

Simpson, W. J. Sparrow. *A study of Bossuet.* London: S.P.C.K., 1937. Pp. viii + 226.

Rev. in *TLS,* July 31, p. 555; by R. H. M. in *Church quar. rev.,* CXXIV, 353-54. § Chap. x: "Bossuet and the Church of England."

Streeter, Harold Wade. *The eighteenth century English novel in French translation.* A bibliographical study. New York: Institute of French studies, 1936. Pp. viii + 256.

Sylwan, Otto. "'Snille och smak.'" *Edda,* XXXVII (1937), 18-34.

Tisserand, Roger. *Au temps de l'Encyclopédie: l'Académie de Dijon de 1740 à 1793.* Vesoul: Imprimerie Nouvelle, 1936. Pp. 683.

Trahard, Pierre. *La sensibilité révolutionnaire (1789-1794).* Paris: Boivin, 1936. Pp. 283.

Rev. by M. Bardon in *Revue des cours et conférences,* XXXVIII, ix, 94-96; by M. Lhéritier in *Revue des études historiques,* CIV, 318-20.

Wloka, Bruno-Walter. *Die moralpädagogischen und psychologischen Grundlagen der französischen Rhétorique-Bücher des 17. u. 18. Jahrhunderts.* Breslau diss. 1935. Pp. vii + 128.